Blackstone's Statutes on

Criminal Law

32nd edition

edited by

Matthew Dyson

Professor of Civil and Criminal Law at the Faculty of Law, University of Oxford and Tutorial Fellow of Corpus Christi College, Oxford

OXFORD
UNIVERSITY PRESS

OXFORD
UNIVERSITY PRESS

Great Clarendon Street, Oxford, OX2 6DP,
United Kingdom

Oxford University Press is a department of the University of Oxford.
It furthers the University's objective of excellence in research, scholarship,
and education by publishing worldwide. Oxford is a registered trade mark of
Oxford University Press in the UK and in certain other countries

First published by Blackstone Press 1989

Twenty-ninth edition 2019
Thirtieth edition 2020
Thirty-first edition 2021
Thirty-second edition 2022
Impression: 1

Published in the United States of America by Oxford University Press
198 Madison Avenue, New York, NY 10016, United States of America

British Library Cataloguing in Publication Data

Data available

ISBN 978–0–19–285859–7

Printed in the UK by
Bell & Bain Ltd., Glasgow

Editor's preface

A quarter of a century's worth of law students relied on Peter Glazebrook's precision, judgment, and dedication to enrich their study of criminal law and the tradition he created continues with this edition. What became the *Blackstone's Statutes on Criminal Law* had begun as an attempt to provide for the students of Peter's university and rapidly became a valued resource for students around the country. In an unfamiliar world, where a pandemic can change how we study, handle examinations, and simply interact as people, the importance of rules, their purpose, their interpretation, and the strengths of the law-making process continue.

England is one of only a handful of jurisdictions among the developed countries of the world which is still without a Criminal Code. Most economically underdeveloped countries are, in this respect at least, better provided for. For close on forty years, the Law Commission's declared aim was to make good this lack of a single, comprehensive enactment specifying both the conduct which is prohibited under threat of imprisonment and other severe penalties, and the conditions which must be satisfied before a person who has engaged in such conduct may be convicted and punished. But though there was much labouring, little was achieved, and in 2008 the Commission finally abandoned the project. Since then, the Commission has laboured away at long-overdue proposals for replacing the common law offences and updating other offences. However, even when the Government's own legislative programme is a light one, the opportunity is not taken to bring forward any of the Commission's long-standing and widely welcomed reform proposals. Sadly, criminal law—whether substantive or procedural—is, it seems, nowadays too emotive a subject, politically and parliamentarily, for there to be any hope of a Code being enacted in the foreseeable future.

Even after the Law Commission had narrowed its sights and confined its recommendations to specific areas of the law, the Home Office and its successor, the Ministry of Justice, has treated most of them with ill-disguised disdain. Having, for instance, asked the Commission to undertake a comprehensive review of the law of murder and manslaughter, they did not bother to offer any reasons for not proceeding with its carefully worked out proposals for a new Homicide Act (Law Commission Report No. 304), announcing simply that the Government would instead proceed on a 'step-by-step basis'. Its new version of s. 2 of the Homicide Act 1957 and ss. 54 and 55 of the Coroners and Justice Act 2009 revealed what stumbling steps these were. Their effect has been to widen the offence of murder with its mandatory sentence, which is the opposite of what the Commission had intended and, to professional acclaim, recommended. And new offences and heavier penalties continue to be added to the statute book in a manner both reminiscent of the late eighteenth century and reckless of the shape and intelligibility of the law. Our inordinately elaborate patchwork of multiple and overlapping offences encourages plea and charge bargaining, with the consequence that the convictions arrived at, and the sentences passed, in the courts often bear only a distant relationship to what had actually happened—and could be proved to have happened.

To make matters worse, the drafting of all this legislation has become ever more prolix and convoluted. As Professor John Spencer has amply demonstrated ((2008) 67 *Cambridge Law Journal* 585–605), there is no need for criminal legislation to be as impenetrable as nowadays it frequently is. Codes of criminal law and criminal procedure would unquestionably offer, as a succession of distinguished judges have said, the best remedy. But if there is not to be a Criminal Code, there should at least be an Interpretation (Criminal Offences) Act which would both ensure greater consistency in the language employed and reduce prolixity in drafting. In the absence of a Code, students and teachers of criminal law (not to mention police officers, magistrates, jurors, lawyers, and judges) have to confront a great jumble of statutory provisions, having no uniformity of structure and exhibiting many different drafting styles, which are replete with detail, but short on principle.

There are believed to be well over 8,000 different criminal offences on the statute book—tens of hundreds added in the last 15 years most likely—and secondary legislation contains many thousands more. This present selection, which is intended to be no more than a convenient means of reference to the main statutory framework of the substantive criminal law, is inevitably a personal and, to a degree, an arbitrary one. But it is hoped that it is extensive and varied enough to meet the needs both of those students following criminal law courses of a traditional sort, which involve a detailed study of the principal offences of personal violence and fraud (who will learn much about their inadequacies by studying the less familiar legislation designed to supplement them), and of those whose courses place more emphasis on the use of the criminal law to regulate less obvious, yet often equally harmful, forms of objectionable behaviour. As in other books in the Blackstone's series, the statutory provisions are arranged chronologically—according to the year of enactment—rather than, as in earlier editions and as they might be in a Code, according to their subject matter, thus vividly illustrating the disorderly—indeed, chaotic—character of English criminal legislation that is directed against harms that range from the extremely serious to the absurdly trivial. A table of principal subjects is provided to help the user locate provisions relating to similar conduct or harms and those lurking in less obvious places.

This volume focuses on substantive criminal law in primary legislation. It does not engage with sentencing for reasons of space even though that is an important part of understanding the substantive rules (see especially the Sentencing Act 2020 with what is, in effect, a Sentencing Code), nor does it cover every possible offence within substantive areas; similarly, it cannot stay up to date with the rapidly changing but hopefully soon removed Covid Regulations.

In general, the statutory provisions selected are printed in the form in which they were law on 10 April 2022. However, take note that:

1. Where a provision in a statute amends an earlier statute, the amendment is made in that earlier statute and the amending provision is not included. For example, if you seek the effect of the Coroners and Justice Act 2009, s. 52 with respect to the law of provocation, look to the Homicide Act 1957, s. 2, since the 2009 Act amended the 1957 Act. That provision of the 2009 Act does not appear separately in this statute book.

2. Historical accuracy in the statutes is important, but must sometimes give way to other concerns. The most important is the effect of other statutes. The most significant example of this is that 'penal servitude' is the term which appears on the face of a number of, particularly nineteenth-century, statutes which are still in force but it does not appear in this book. The effect of the Criminal Law Act 1948, s. 1(1) is that the sentence of penal servitude no longer exists and all references to it 'shall be construed as . . . a sentence of imprisonment': for that reason, all references to penal servitude in statutes prior to 1948 have been replaced with references to imprisonment without any marking in the text (and as per the first point above, s. 1(1) of the 1948 Act does not appear in this book). By contrast, while under the Criminal Justice Act 1967, s. 1 'All distinctions between felony and misdemeanor are hereby abolished', this provision does not have the practical effect of changing the words of the statute, but only to deprive of meaning the distinction between what were theoretically the more serious offences (felonies) from the less serious ones (misdemeanours). A final slight reduction in historical accuracy is in aid of the accessibility of the text: where amendments are made to earlier statutes, the text of those statutes does not contain any markings to show the fact of amendment save, where appropriate, ellipses.

3. In addition, considerations of space and cost have demanded the excision of most of the procedural, evidentiary, and administrative provisions of these statutes, as also of almost all penalty provisions where these are separate from the offence-creating ones. Where statutory material quoted refers to a 'Part', such as where it limits the meaning of an interpretation to 'in this Part' only, the markers for the Parts in that statute are given.

I am particularly grateful to Christopher Sargeant for his assistance in preparing this volume, and to the team at OUP for their support in producing it.

Matthew Dyson
Oxford
12 April 2022

New to this edition

The 32nd edition of *Blackstone's Statutes on Criminal Law* has been fully revised and updated to include all recent developments through to 10 April 2022. It includes:

New statutes in this edition are:

- Botulinum Toxin and Cosmetic Fillers (Children) Act 2021
- Domestic Abuse Act 2021
- Finance Act 2021
- Overseas Operations (Service Personnel and Veterans) Act 2021

The amendments made are the result of the following Acts and Regulations:

- Public Health (Wales) Act 2017—amending Health Act 2006, s. 8
- Space Industry Act 2018—amending Aviation Security Act 1982, s. 38; Terrorism Act 2006, s. 20
- Offensive Weapons Act 2019—amending Prevention of Crime Act 1953, s. 1A; Restriction of Offensive Weapons Act 1959, s. 1; Criminal Justice Act 1988, ss. 139A, 139AA, 141, 141A, 141B
- Children (Abolition of Defence of Reasonable Punishment) Wales Act 2020—amending Children Act 2004, s. 58
- Sentencing Act 2020—amending Protection from Harassment Act 1997, s. 5
- Domestic Abuse Act 2021—amending Protection from Harassment 1997, s. 4B; Sexual Offences Act 2003, s. 72, Sch. 2 para. 1, Sch. 2 para. 1A, Sch. 3 para. 3; Criminal Justice and Courts Act 2015, ss. 33, 35; Serious Crime Act, s. 76
- Financial Services Act 2021—amending Proceeds of Crime Act 2002, ss. 327, 328, 329, 339A, 340
- Registration of Marriages Regulations 2021/411—amending Perjury Act 1911, s. 3

Blackstone's Statutes
Unsurpassed in authority, reliability, and accuracy

The titles in the Blackstone's Statutes series are a collection of carefully reviewed and selected unannotated legislative material and official documents.

We make every effort to ensure titles in the series meet the needs of their target market. They are reviewed by lecturers to match university courses closely and are expertly edited to be manageable in size, whilst retaining their comprehensive coverage.

The editors only include material that will be valuable to students and lecturers and it is therefore abridged where necessary.

Conventions used in *Blackstone's Statutes on Criminal Law*

An ellipsis symbol . . . indicates text which has not been included in this volume as a result of abridgement by the editor. It is not used where lists of sections, subsections, or paragraphs are truncated, unless the grammatical structure would be broken.

The material in this book is reproduced in its most up-to-date form, incorporating any changes made by statutory amendment. Supplementary notes and details of amending provisions are generally not indicated.

 Visit **www.oup.com/uk/statutes** for accompanying online resources including video guides to reading and interpreting statutes, exam tips, and an interactive sample Act of Parliament.

Contents

UK Secondary Legislation   **438**

Table of principal subjects

Classification of offences

The mode of trial for an offence, when the person charged is an adult, has been indicated by the addition of a letter at the end of the provision creating it—

[I]:   triable only on indictment (i.e. only in the Crown Court)

[E]:   triable either way (i.e. in either Crown or Magistrates' Court)

[S]:   triable only summarily (i.e. only in the Magistrates' Court)

This classification, it should be noted, is different from that of the Schedule to s. 5, Interpretation Act 1978 (pages 83–4, below), which does not distinguish offences triable only on indictment from those triable either way.

Statutes 1824–2022

Vagrancy Act 1824

4 Persons committing certain offences shall be deemed rogues and vagabonds and may be imprisoned for three months

. . . Every person wandering abroad and lodging in any barn or outhouse, or in any deserted or unoccupied building, or in the open air, or under a tent, or in any cart or waggon, and not giving a good account of himself or herself; every person wandering abroad, and endeavouring by the exposure of wounds or deformities to obtain or gather alms; every person going about as a gatherer or collector of alms, or endeavouring to procure charitable contributions of any nature or kind, under any false or fraudulent pretence; every person being found in or upon any dwelling house, warehouse, coach-house, stable, or outhouse, or in any inclosed yard, garden, or area, for any unlawful purpose; . . . and every person apprehended as an idle and disorderly person, and violently resisting any constable, or other peace officer so apprehending him or her, and being subsequently convicted of the offence for which he or she shall have been so apprehended; shall be deemed a rogue and vagabond, within the true intent and meaning of this Act; and, subject to section 70 of the Criminal Justice Act 1982, it shall be lawful for any justice of the peace to commit such offender (being thereof convicted before him by the confession of such offender, or by the evidence on oath of one or more credible witness or witnesses,) to the house of correction, . . . for any time not exceeding three calendar months. [S]

Town Police Clauses Act 1847

28 Penalty on persons committing any of the offences herein named

Every person who in any street, to the obstruction, annoyance, or danger of the residents or passengers, commits any of the following offences, shall be liable to a penalty not exceeding level 3 on the standard scale for each offence, or, in the discretion of the justice before whom he is convicted, may be committed to prison, there to remain for a period not exceeding fourteen days; (that is to say,)

Every person who suffers to be at large any unmuzzled ferocious dog, or sets on or urges any dog or other animal to attack, worry, or put in fear any person or animal:

Every person who rides or drives furiously any horse or carriage, or drives furiously any cattle:

Every person who wantonly discharges any firearm, or throws or discharges any stone or other missile, or makes any bonfire, or throws or sets fire to any firework:

Provided always, that it shall not be deemed an offence to lay sand or other materials in any street in time of frost, to prevent accidents, or litter or other suitable materials to prevent the freezing of water in pipes, or in case of sickness to prevent noise, if the party laying any such things causes them to be removed as soon as the occasion for them ceases . . .

Accessories and Abettors Act 1861

8   Abettors

Whosoever shall aid, abet, counsel, or procure the commission of any indictable offence, whether the same be an offence at common law or by virtue of any Act passed or to be passed, shall be liable to be tried, indicted, and punished as a principal offender.

Forgery Act 1861

36   Destroying, injuring, forging, or falsifying registers of births, baptisms, marriages, deaths, or burials, or certified copies

Whosoever shall unlawfully destroy, deface, or injure, or cause or permit to be destroyed, defaced, or injured, any register of births, baptisms, marriages, deaths, or burials which now is or hereafter shall be by law authorised or required to be kept in England or Ireland, or any part of any such register, or any certified copy of any such register, or any part thereof, or shall knowingly and unlawfully insert or cause or permit to be inserted in any such register, or in any certified copy thereof, any false entry of any matter relating to any birth, baptism, marriage, death, or burial, or shall knowingly and unlawfully give any false certificate relating to any birth, baptism, marriage, death, or burial, or shall certify any writing to be a copy or extract from any such register, knowing such writing, or the part of such register whereof such copy or extract shall be so given, to be false in any material particular or shall offer, utter, dispose of, or put off any such register, entry, certified copy, certificate, knowing the same to be false, or shall offer, utter, dispose of, or put off any copy of any entry in any such register, knowing such entry to be false, shall be guilty of felony, and being convicted thereof, shall be liable to imprisonment for life [I]

37   Making false entries in copies of registers of baptisms, marriages, or burials, directed to be sent to any registrar, or destroying or concealing copies of registers

Whosoever shall knowingly and wilfully insert or cause or permit to be inserted in any copy of any register directed or required by law to be transmitted to any registrar or other officer any false entry of any matter relating to any baptism, marriage, or burial or shall knowingly and wilfully sign or verify any copy of any register so directed or required to be transmitted as aforesaid, which copy shall be false in any part thereof, knowing the same to be false, or shall unlawfully destroy, deface, or injure, or shall for any fraudulent purpose take from its place of deposit, or conceal, any such copy of any register, shall be guilty of felony, and being convicted thereof shall be liable to imprisonment for life. [I]

Malicious Damage Act 1861

35   Placing wood, etc., on railway, taking up rails, etc., turning points, showing or hiding signals, etc., with intent to obstruct or overthrow any engine, etc.

Whosoever shall unlawfully and maliciously put, place, cast, or throw upon or across any railway any wood, stone, or other matter or thing, or shall unlawfully and maliciously take up, remove, or displace any rail, sleeper, or other matter or thing belonging to any railway, or shall unlawfully and maliciously turn, move, or divert any points or other machinery belonging to any railway, or shall unlawfully and maliciously make or show, hide or remove, any signal or light upon or near to any railway, or shall unlawfully and maliciously do or cause to be done any other matter or thing, with intent, in any of the cases aforesaid, to obstruct, upset, overthrow, injure, or destroy any engine, tender, carriage, or truck using such railway, shall be guilty of felony, and being convicted thereof shall be liable, at the discretion of the court, to be imprisoned for life. [I]

36   Obstructing engines or carriages on railways

Whosoever, by any unlawful act, or by any wilful omission or neglect, shall obstruct or cause to be obstructed any engine or carriage using any railway, or shall aid or assist therein, shall be guilty of a misdemeanor, and being convicted thereof shall be liable, at the discretion of the court, to be imprisoned for any term not exceeding two years. [E]

58   Malice against owner of property unnecessary

Every punishment and forfeiture by this Act imposed on any person maliciously committing any offence, whether the same be punishable upon indictment or upon summary conviction, shall equally apply and be enforced, whether the offence shall be committed from malice conceived against the owner of the property in respect of which it shall be committed, or otherwise.

Offences Against the Person Act 1861

4   Soliciting to commit murder

Whosoever shall solicit, encourage, persuade, or endeavour to persuade, or shall propose to any person, to murder any other person, whether he be a subject of Her Majesty or not, and whether he be within the Queen's dominions or not, shall be guilty of a misdemeanor, and being convicted thereof shall be liable to imprisonment for life. [I]

9   Murder or manslaughter abroad

Where any murder or manslaughter shall be committed on land out of the United Kingdom, whether within the Queen's dominions or without, and whether the person killed were a subject of Her Majesty or not, every offence committed by any subject of Her Majesty in respect of any such case, whether the same shall amount to the offence of murder or of manslaughter, may be dealt with, inquired of, tried, determined, and punished in England or Ireland ...

10   Provision for the trial of murder and manslaughter where the death or cause of death only happens in England or Ireland

Where any person being criminally stricken, poisoned, or otherwise hurt upon the sea, or at any place out of England or Ireland, shall die of such stroke, poisoning, or hurt in England or Ireland, or, being criminally stricken, poisoned or otherwise hurt in any place in England or Ireland, shall die of such stroke, poisoning, or hurt upon the sea, or at any place out of England or Ireland, every offence committed in respect of any such case, whether the same shall amount to the offence of murder or of manslaughter, may be dealt with, inquired of, tried, determined, and punished in England or Ireland.

16   Threats to kill

A person who without lawful excuse makes to another a threat, intending that that other would fear it would be carried out, to kill that other or a third person, shall be guilty of an offence and liable on conviction on indictment to imprisonment for a term not exceeding ten years. [E]

17   Impeding a person endeavouring to save himself or another from shipwreck

Whosoever shall unlawfully and maliciously prevent or impede any person, being on board of or having quitted any ship or vessel which shall be in distress, or wrecked, stranded, or cast on shore, in his endeavour to save his life, or shall unlawfully and maliciously prevent or impede any person in his endeavour to save the life of any such person as in this section first aforesaid, shall be guilty of an offence, and being convicted thereof shall be liable to imprisonment for life. [I]

18   Shooting or attempting to shoot, or wounding, with intent to do grievous bodily harm, or to resist apprehension

Whosoever shall unlawfully and maliciously by any means whatsoever wound or cause any grievous bodily harm to any person, with intent to do some grievous bodily harm to any person, or with intent to resist or prevent the lawful apprehension or detainer of any person, shall be guilty of an offence, and being convicted thereof shall be liable, to imprisonment for life. [I]

20   Inflicting bodily injury, with or without weapon

Whosoever shall unlawfully and maliciously wound or inflict any grievous bodily harm upon any other person, either with or without any weapon or instrument, shall be guilty of an offence, and being convicted thereof shall be liable to imprisonment for a term not exceeding five years. [E]

21   Attempting to choke, etc., in order to commit or assist in the committing of any indictable offence

Whosoever shall, by any means whatsoever, attempt to choke, suffocate, or strangle any other person, or shall by any means calculated to choke, suffocate, or strangle, attempt to render any other person insensible, unconscious, or incapable of resistance, with intent in any of such cases thereby to enable himself or any other person to commit, or with intent in any of such cases thereby to assist any other person in committing any indictable offence, shall be guilty of an offence, and being convicted thereof shall be liable to imprisonment for life. [I]

22   Using chloroform, etc., to commit or assist in the committing of any indictable offence

Whosoever shall unlawfully apply or administer to or cause to be taken by, or attempt to apply or administer to or attempt to cause to be administered to or taken by, any person, any chloroform, laudanum, or other stupefying or overpowering drug, matter, or thing, with intent in any of such cases thereby to enable himself or any other person to commit, or with intent in any of such cases thereby to assist any other person in committing any indictable offence, shall be guilty of an offence, and being convicted thereof shall be liable to imprisonment for life. [I]

23   Maliciously administering poison, etc., so as to endanger life or inflict grievous bodily harm

Whosoever shall unlawfully and maliciously administer to or cause to be administered to or taken by any other person any poison or other destructive or noxious thing, so as thereby to endanger the life of such person, or so as thereby to inflict upon such person any grievous bodily harm, shall be guilty of an offence, and being convicted thereof shall be liable to imprisonment for any term not exceeding ten years. [I]

24   Maliciously administering poison, etc., with intent to injure, aggrieve, or annoy any other person

Whosoever shall unlawfully and maliciously administer to or cause to be administered to or taken by any other person any poison or other destructive or noxious thing, with intent to injure, aggrieve, or annoy such person, shall be guilty of an offence, and being convicted thereof shall be liable to imprisonment for a term not exceeding five years. [I]

26   Not providing apprentices or servants with food, etc., or doing bodily harm, whereby life is endangered, or health permanently injured

Whosoever, being legally liable, either as a master or mistress, to provide for any apprentice or servant necessary food, clothing, or lodging, shall wilfully and without lawful excuse refuse or neglect to provide the same, or shall unlawfully and maliciously do or cause to be done any bodily harm to any such apprentice or servant, so that the life of such apprentice or servant shall be endangered, or the health of such apprentice or servant shall be likely to be permanently injured, shall be guilty of an offence, and being convicted thereof shall be liable to imprisonment for a term not exceeding five years. [E]

27   Exposing child, whereby life is endangered, or health permanently injured

Whosoever shall unlawfully abandon or expose any child, being under the age of two years, whereby the life of such child shall be endangered, or the health of such child shall have been or shall be likely to be permanently injured, shall be guilty of an offence, and being convicted thereof shall be liable to imprisonment for a term not exceeding five years. [E]

28   Causing bodily injury by gunpowder

Whosoever shall unlawfully and maliciously, by the explosion of gunpowder or other explosive substance, burn, maim, disfigure, disable, or do any grievous bodily harm to any person, shall be guilty of an offence, and being convicted thereof shall be liable, at the discretion of the court, to imprisonment for life. [I]

29   Causing gunpowder to explode, or sending to any person an explosive substance, or throwing corrosive fluid on a person, with intent to do grievous bodily harm

Whosoever shall unlawfully and maliciously cause any gunpowder or other explosive substance to explode, or send or deliver to or cause to be taken or received by any person any explosive substance or any other dangerous or noxious thing, or put or lay at any place, or cast or throw at or upon or otherwise apply to any person, any corrosive fluid or any destructive or explosive substance, with intent in any of the cases aforesaid to burn, maim, disfigure, or disable any person, or to do some grievous bodily harm to any person, shall, whether any bodily injury be effected or not, be guilty of an offence, and being convicted thereof shall be liable, at the discretion of the court, to imprisonment for life. [I]

30   Placing gunpowder near a building, etc., with intent to do bodily injury to any person

Whosoever shall unlawfully and maliciously place or throw in, into, upon, against, or near any building, ship, or vessel any gunpowder or other explosive substance, with intent to do any bodily injury to any person, shall, whether or not any explosion take place, and whether or not any bodily injury be effected, be guilty of an offence, and being convicted thereof shall be liable, at the discretion of the court, to imprisonment for any term not exceeding fourteen years. [I]

31   Setting or allowing to remain spring guns, etc., with intent to inflict grievous bodily harm

Whosoever shall set or place, or cause to be set or placed, any spring gun, man trap, or other engine calculated to destroy human life or inflict grievous bodily harm, with the intent that the same or whereby the same may destroy or inflict grievous bodily harm upon a trespasser or other person coming in contact therewith, shall be guilty of an offence, and being convicted thereof shall be liable to imprisonment for a term not exceeding five years; and whosoever shall knowingly and wilfully permit any such spring gun, man trap, or other engine which may have been set or placed in any place then being in or afterwards coming into his possession or occupation by some other person to continue so set or placed, shall be deemed to have set and placed such gun, trap, or engine with such intent as aforesaid: Provided, that nothing in this section contained shall extend to make it illegal to set or place any gun or trap such as may have been or may be usually set or placed with the intent of destroying vermin: Provided also, that nothing in this section shall be deemed to make it unlawful to set or place, or cause to be set or placed, or to be continued set or placed, from sunset to sunrise, any spring gun, man trap, or other engine which shall be set or placed, or caused or continued to be set or placed, in a dwelling-house, for the protection thereof. [I]

32   Placing wood, etc., on railway, taking up rails, showing or hiding signals, etc., with intent to endanger passengers

Whosoever shall unlawfully and maliciously put or throw upon or across any railway any wood, stone, or other matter or thing, or shall unlawfully and maliciously take up, remove, or displace any rail, sleeper, or other matter or thing belonging to any railway, or shall unlawfully and maliciously turn, move or divert any points or other machinery belonging to any railway, or shall unlawfully and maliciously make or show, hide or remove, any signal or light upon or near to any railway, or shall unlawfully and maliciously do or cause to be done any other matter or thing, with intent, in any of the cases aforesaid, to endanger the safety of any person travelling or being upon such railway, shall be guilty of an offence, and being convicted thereof shall be liable, at the discretion of the court, to imprisonment for life. [I]

33   Casting stone, etc., upon a railway carriage, with intent to endanger the safety of any person therein, or in any part of the same train

Whosoever shall unlawfully and maliciously throw, or cause to fall or strike, at, against, into, or upon any engine, tender, carriage, or truck used upon any railway, any wood, stone, or other matter or thing, with intent to injure or endanger the safety of any person being in or upon such engine, tender, carriage, or truck, or in or upon any other any other engine, tender, carriage, or truck of any train of which such first-mentioned engine, tender, carriage, or truck shall form part, shall be guilty of an offence, and being convicted thereof shall be liable to imprisonment for life. [I]

34   Doing or omitting anything so as to endanger passengers by railway

Whosoever, by any unlawful act, or by any wilful omission or neglect, shall endanger or cause to be endangered the safety of any person conveyed or being in or upon a railway, or shall aid or assist therein, shall be guilty of an offence, and being convicted thereof shall be liable, at the discretion of the court, to be imprisoned for any term not exceeding two years. [E]

35   Drivers of carriages injuring persons by furious driving

Whosoever, having the charge of any carriage or vehicle, shall by wanton or furious driving or racing, or other wilful misconduct, or by wilful neglect, do or cause to be done any bodily harm to any person whatsoever, shall be guilty of an offence, and being convicted thereof shall be liable, at the discretion of the court, to be imprisoned for any term not exceeding two years. [I]

38   Assault with intent to resist arrest

Whosoever shall assault any person with intent to resist or prevent the lawful apprehension or detainer of himself or of any other person for any offence, shall be guilty of an offence, and being convicted thereof shall be liable, at the discretion of the court, to be imprisoned for any term not exceeding two years. [E]

47   Assault occasioning bodily harm

Whosoever shall be convicted upon an indictment of any assault occasioning actual bodily harm shall be liable to be imprisoned for any term not exceeding five years. [E]

57   Bigamy

Whosoever, being married, shall marry any other person during the life of the former husband or wife, whether the second marriage shall have taken place in England or Ireland or elsewhere, shall be guilty of felony, and being convicted thereof shall be liable to be kept in penal servitude for any term not exceeding seven years. Provided, that nothing in this section contained shall extend to any second marriage contracted elsewhere than in England and Ireland by any other than a subject of Her Majesty, or to any person marrying a second time whose husband or wife shall have been continually absent from such person for the space of seven years then last past, and shall not have been known by such person to be living within that time, or shall extend to any person who, at the time of such second marriage, shall have been divorced from the bond of the first marriage, or to any person whose former marriage shall have been declared void by the sentence of any court of competent jurisdiction. [E]

58 Administering drugs or using instruments to procure abortion

Every woman, being with child, who, with intent to procure her own miscarriage, shall unlawfully administer to herself any poison or other noxious thing, or shall unlawfully use any instrument or other means whatsoever with the like intent, and whosoever, with intent to procure the miscarriage of any woman, whether she be or be not with child, shall unlawfully administer to her or cause to be taken by her any poison or other noxious thing, or shall unlawfully use any instrument or other means whatsoever with the like intent, shall be guilty of felony, and being convicted thereof shall be liable to be imprisoned for life. [I]

59 Procuring drugs, etc., to cause abortion

Whosoever shall unlawfully supply or procure any poison or other noxious thing, or any instrument or thing whatsoever, knowing that the same is intended to be unlawfully used or employed with intent to procure the miscarriage of any woman, whether she be or be not with child, shall be guilty of a misdemeanor, and being convicted thereof shall be liable to imprisonment. [I]

60 Concealing the birth of a child

If any woman shall be delivered of a child, every person who shall, by any secret disposition of the dead body of the said child, whether such child died before, at, or after its birth, endeavour to conceal the birth thereof, shall be guilty of a misdemeanor, and being convicted thereof shall be liable, at the discretion of the court, to be imprisoned for any term not exceeding two years. [E]

64 Making or having gunpowder, etc., with intent to commit or enable any person to commit any felony mentioned in this Act

Whosoever shall knowingly have in his possession, or make or manufacture, any gunpowder, explosive substance, or any dangerous or noxious thing, or any machine, engine, instrument, or thing, with intent by means thereof to commit, or for the purpose of enabling any other person to commit, any of the felonies in this Act mentioned shall be guilty of a misdemeanor, and being convicted thereof shall be liable, at the discretion of the court, to be imprisoned for any term not exceeding two years. [I]

Licensing Act 1872

12 Penalty on persons found drunk

Every person found drunk in any highway or other public place, whether a building or not, or on any licensed premises, shall be liable to a penalty not exceeding level 1 on the standard scale. [S]

Every person who is drunk while in charge on any highway or other public place of any carriage, horse, cattle, or steam engine, or who is drunk when in possession of any loaded firearms, shall be liable to a penalty not exceeding level 1 on the standard scale or in the discretion of the court to imprisonment for any term not exceeding one month. [S]

Territorial Waters Jurisdiction Act 1878

2 Amendment of law as to jurisdiction of the Admiral

An offence committed by a person, whether he is or is not a subject of Her Majesty, on the open sea within the territorial waters of Her Majesty's dominions, is an offence within the jurisdiction of the Admiral, although it may have been committed on board or by means of a foreign ship, and the person who committed such offence may be arrested, tried, and punished accordingly.

Explosive Substances Act 1883

2   Causing explosion likely to endanger life or property
A person who in the United Kingdom or (being a citizen of the United Kingdom and Colonies) in the Republic of Ireland unlawfully and maliciously causes by any explosive substance an explosion of a nature likely to endanger life or to cause serious injury to person or property shall, whether any injury to person or property has been actually caused or not, be guilty of an offence and on conviction on indictment shall be liable to imprisonment for life. [I]

3   Attempt to cause explosion, or making or keeping explosive with intent to endanger life or property
A person who in the United Kingdom or a dependency or (being a citizen of the United Kingdom and Colonies) elsewhere unlawfully and maliciously—
  (a) does any act with intent to cause, or conspires to cause, by an explosive substance an explosion of a nature likely to endanger life, or cause serious injury to property, whether in the United Kingdom or elsewhere, or
  (b) makes or has in his possession or under his control an explosive substance with intent by means thereof to endanger life, or cause serious injury to property, whether in the United Kingdom or elsewhere, or to enable any other person so to do,
shall, whether any explosion does not take place, and whether any injury to person or property has been actually caused or not, be guilty of an offence and on conviction on indictment shall be liable to imprisonment for life, and the explosive substance shall be forfeited. [I]

4   Making or possession of explosive under suspicious circumstances
(1) Any person who makes or knowingly has in his possession or under his control any explosive substance, under such circumstances as to give rise to a reasonable suspicion that he is not making it or does not have it in his possession or under his control for a lawful object, shall, unless he can show that he made it or had it in his possession or under his control for a lawful object, be guilty of an offence.

(1A) A person who is guilty of an offence under subsection (1) is liable, on conviction on indictment, to imprisonment for life.

(1B) Where a person is convicted of an offence under subsection (1) the explosive substance is to be forfeited.

5   Punishment of accessories
Any person who within or (being a subject of Her Majesty) without Her Majesty's dominions by the supply of or solicitation for money, the providing of premises, the supply of materials, or in any manner whatsoever, procures, counsels, aids, abets, or is accessory to, the commission of any crime under this Act, shall be guilty of an offence, and shall be liable to be tried and punished for that crime, as if he had been guilty as a principal.

9   Definitions
(1) In this Act, unless the context otherwise requires—
The expression "explosive substance" shall be deemed to include any materials for making any explosive substance; also any apparatus, machine, implement, or materials used, or intended to be used, or adapted for causing, or aiding in causing, any explosion in or with any explosive substance; also any part of any such apparatus, machine, or implement.

Trial of Lunatics Act 1883

2   Special verdict where accused found guilty, but insane at date of act or omission charged, and orders thereupon

(1) Where in any indictment or information any act or omission is charged against any person as an offence, and it is given in evidence on the trial of such person for that offence that he was insane, so as not to be responsible, according to law, for his actions at the time when the act was done or omission made, then, if it appears to the jury before whom such person is tried that he did the act or made the omission charged, but was insane as aforesaid at the time when he did or made the same, the jury shall return a special verdict that the accused is not guilty by reason of insanity.

Licensing Act 1902

2   Penalty for being drunk while in charge of child

(1) If any person is found drunk in any highway or other public place, whether a building or not, or on any licensed premises, while having the charge of a child apparently under the age of seven years, he shall, if the child is under that age, be liable on summary conviction, to a fine not exceeding level 2 on the standard scale or to imprisonment for any period not exceeding one month. [S]

(2) If the child appears to the court to be under the age of seven the child shall, for the purposes of this section, be deemed to be under that age unless the contrary is proved.

8   Interpretation of "public place"

For the purposes of section twelve of the Licensing Act, 1872, and of sections one and two of this Act, the expression "public place" shall include any place to which the public have access, whether on payment or otherwise.

Official Secrets Act 1911

1   Penalties for spying

(1) If any person for any purpose prejudicial to the safety or interests of the State—

 (a) approaches, inspects, passes over or is in the neighbourhood of, or enters any prohibited place within the meaning of this Act; or

 (b) makes any sketch, plan, model, or note which is calculated to be or might be or is intended to be directly or indirectly useful to an enemy; or

 (c) obtains, collects, records, or publishes, or communicates to any other person any secret official code word or pass word, or any sketch, plan, model, article, or note, or other document or information which is calculated to be or might be or is intended to be directly or indirectly useful to an enemy;

he shall be guilty of felony . . . [I]

(2) On a prosecution under this section, it shall not be necessary to show that the accused person was guilty of any particular act tending to show a purpose prejudicial to the safety or interests of the State, and, notwithstanding that no such act is proved against him, he may be convicted if, from the circumstances of the case, or his conduct, or his known character as proved, it appears that his purpose was a purpose prejudicial to the safety or interests of the State; and if any sketch, plan, model, article,

note, document, or information relating to or used in any prohibited place within the meaning of this Act, or anything in such a place or any secret official code word or pass word, is made, obtained, collected, recorded, published, or communicated by any person other than a person acting under lawful authority, it shall be deemed to have been made, obtained, collected, recorded, published or communicated for a purpose prejudicial to the safety or interests of the State unless the contrary is proved.

3   Definition of prohibited place

For the purposes of this Act, the expression "prohibited place" means—

(a) any work of defence, arsenal, naval or air force establishment or station, factory, dockyard, mine, minefield, camp, ship, or aircraft belonging to or occupied by or on behalf of His Majesty, or any telegraph, telephone, wireless or signal station, or office so belonging or occupied, and any place belonging to or occupied by or on behalf of His Majesty and used for the purpose of building, repairing, making or storing any munitions of war, or any sketches, plans, models or documents relating thereto, or for the purpose of getting any metals, oil or minerals of use in time of war;

(b) any place not belonging to His Majesty where any munitions of war, or any sketches, models, plans or documents relating thereto, are being made, repaired, gotten or stored under contract with, or with any person on behalf of, His Majesty, or otherwise on behalf of His Majesty; and

(c) any place belonging to or used for the purposes of His Majesty which is for the time being declared by order of a Secretary of State to be a prohibited place for the purposes of this section on the ground that information with respect thereto, or damage thereto, would be useful to an enemy; and

(d) any railway, road, way, or channel, or other means of communication by land or water (including any works or structures being part thereof or connected therewith), or any place used for gas, water, or electricity works or other works for purposes of a public character, or any place where any munitions of war, or any sketches, models, plans, or documents relating thereto, are being made, repaired, or stored otherwise than on behalf of His Majesty, which is for the time being declared by order of a Secretary of State to be a prohibited place for the purposes of this section, on the ground that information with respect thereto, or the destruction or obstruction thereof, or interference therewith, would be useful to an enemy.

7   Penalty for harbouring spies

If any person knowingly harbours any person whom he knows, or has reasonable grounds for supposing, to be a person who is about to commit or who has committed an offence under this Act, or knowingly permits to meet or assemble in any premises in his occupation or under his control any such persons, or if any person having harboured any such person, or permitted to meet or assemble in any premises in his occupation or under his control any such person, wilfully omits or refuses to disclose to a superintendent of police any information which it is in his power to give in relation to any such person he shall be guilty of a misdemeanour. [E]

Perjury Act 1911

1   Perjury

(1) If any person lawfully sworn as a witness or as an interpreter in a judicial proceeding wilfully makes a statement material in that proceeding, which he knows to be false or does not believe to be true, he shall be guilty of perjury, and shall, on conviction thereof on indictment, be liable to imprisonment for a term not exceeding seven years, or to a fine or to both such imprisonment and fine. [I]

(2) The expression "judicial proceeding" includes a proceeding before any court, tribunal, or person having by law power to hear, receive, and examine evidence on oath.

(3) Where a statement made for the purposes of a judicial proceeding is not made before the tribunal itself, but is made on oath before a person authorised by law to administer an oath to the person who makes the statement, and to record or authenticate the statement, it shall, for the purposes of this section, be treated as having been made in a judicial proceeding.

(4) A statement made by a person lawfully sworn in England for the purposes of a judicial proceeding—

(a) in another part of Her Majesty's dominions; or

(b) in a British tribunal lawfully constituted in any place by sea or land outside Her Majesty's dominions; or

(c) in a tribunal of any foreign state,

shall, for the purposes of this section, be treated as a statement made in a judicial proceeding in England.

(5) Where for the purposes of a judicial proceeding in England, a person is lawfully sworn under the authority of an Act of Parliament—

(a) in any other part of Her Majesty's dominions; or

(b) before a British tribunal or a British officer in a foreign country, or within the jurisdiction of the Admiralty of England;

a statement made by such person so sworn as aforesaid (unless the Act of Parliament under which it was made otherwise specifically provides) shall be treated for the purposes of this section as having been made in the judicial proceeding in England for the purposes whereof it was made.

(6) The question whether a statement on which perjury is assigned was material is a question of law to be determined by the court of trial.

1A   False unsworn statement under Evidence (Proceedings in other Jurisdictions) Act 1975

If any person in giving any testimony (either orally or in writing) otherwise than on oath, where required to do so by an order under section 2 of the Evidence (Proceedings in other Jurisdictions) Act 1975, makes a statement—

(a) which he knows to be false in a material particular, or

(b) which is false in a material particular and which he does not believe to be true,

he shall be guilty of an offence . . . [E]

2   False statements on oath made otherwise than in a judicial proceeding

If any person—

(1) being required or authorised by law to make any statement or oath for any purpose, and being lawfully sworn (otherwise than in a judicial proceeding) wilfully makes a statement which is material for that purpose and which he knows to be false or does not believe to be true; or

(2) wilfully uses any false affidavit for the purposes of the Bills of Sale Act, 1878, as amended by any subsequent enactment,

he shall be guilty of a misdemeanour, . . . [E]

3   False statements, etc., with reference to marriage

(1) If any person—

(a) for the purpose of procuring a marriage, or a certificate or licence for marriage, or a marriage document or a marriage schedule, knowingly and wilfully makes a false oath, or makes or signs a false declaration, notice or certificate required under any Act of Parliament for the time being in force relating to marriage; or

(b) knowingly and wilfully makes, or knowingly and wilfully causes to be made, for the purpose of being inserted in any register of marriage or register of conversions, a false statement as to any particular required by law to be known and registered relating to any marriage or any civil partnership which is to be converted into a marriage; or

(c) forbids the issue of any certificate or licence for marriage or marriage schedule by falsely representing himself to be a person whose consent to the marriage is required by law knowing such representation to be false, or

(d) with respect to a declaration made under section 16(1A) or 27B(2) of the Marriage Act 1949—

    (i)   enters a caveat under subsection (2) of the said section 16, or

    (ii) makes a statement mentioned in subsection (4) of the said section 27B,

    which he knows to be false in a material particular,

he shall be guilty of a misdemeanour, . . .

4   False statements, etc., as to births or deaths

(1) If any person—

(a) wilfully makes any false answer to any question put to him by any registrar of births or deaths relating to the particulars required to be registered concerning any birth or death, or, wilfully gives to any such registrar any false information concerning any birth or death or the cause of any death; or

(b) wilfully makes any false certificate or declaration under or for the purposes of any Act relating to the registration of births or deaths, or, knowing any such certificate or declaration to be false, uses the same as true or gives or sends the same as true to any person; or

(c) wilfully makes, gives or uses any false statement or declaration as to a child born alive as having been still-born, or as to the body of a deceased person or a still-born child in any coffin, or falsely pretends that any child born alive was still-born; or

(d) makes any false statement with intent to have the same inserted in any register of births or deaths,

he shall be guilty of a misdemeanour . . . [E]

5   False statutory declarations and other false statements without oath

If any person knowingly and wilfully makes (otherwise than on oath) a statement false in a material particular, and the statement is made—

(a) in a statutory declaration; or

(b) in an abstract, account, balance sheet, book, certificate, declaration, entry, estimate, inventory, notice, report, return, or other document which he is authorised or required to make, attest, or verify, by any public general Act of Parliament for the time being in force; or

(c) in any oral declaration or oral answer which he is required to make by, under, or in pursuance of any public general Act of Parliament for the time being in force,

he shall be guilty of a misdemeanour . . . [E]

6   False declarations, etc., to obtain registration, etc., for carrying on a vocation

If any person—

(a) procures or attempts to procure himself to be registered on any register or roll kept under or in pursuance of any public general Act of Parliament for the time being in force of persons qualified by law to practise any vocation or calling; or

(b) procures or attempts to procure a certificate of the registration of any person on any such register or roll as aforesaid,

by wilfully making or producing or causing to be made or produced either verbally or in writing, any declaration, certificate, or representation which he knows to be false or fraudulent, he shall be guilty of misdemeanour . . . [E]

7   Aiders, abettors, suborners, etc.

(1) Every person who aids, abets, counsels, procures, or suborns another person to commit an offence against this Act shall be liable to be proceeded against, indicted, tried and punished as if he were a principal offender.

(2) Every person who incites another person to commit an offence against this Act shall be guilty of a misdemeanour, . . . [E]

15   Interpretation, etc.

(1) For the purposes of this Act, the forms and ceremonies used in administering an oath are immaterial, if the court or person before whom the oath is taken has power to administer an oath for the purpose of verifying the statement in question, and if the oath has been administered in a form and with ceremonies which the person taking the oath has accepted without objection, or has declared to be binding on him.

(a) In this Act—

The expression "oath" includes "affirmation" and "declaration", and the expression "swear" includes "affirm" and "declare"; and

The expression "statutory declaration" means a declaration made by virtue of the Statutory Declarations Act, 1835, or of any Act, Order in Council, rule or regulation applying or extending the provisions thereof.

Official Secrets Act 1920

1   Unauthorised use of uniforms; falsification of reports, personation, and false documents

(1) If any person for the purpose of gaining admission, or of assisting any other person to gain admission, to a prohibited place within the meaning of the Official Secrets Act 1911 (hereinafter referred to as "the principal Act"), or for any other purpose prejudicial to the safety or interests of the State within the meaning of the said Act—

(a) uses or wears, without lawful authority, any naval, military, air-force, police, or other official uniform, or any uniform so nearly resembling the same as to be calculated to deceive, or falsely represents himself to be a person who is or has been entitled to use or wear any such uniform; or

(b) orally, or in writing in any declaration or application, or in any document signed by him or on his behalf, knowingly makes or connives at the making of any false statement or any omission; or

(c) tampers with any passport or naval, military, air-force, police, or official pass, permit, certificate, licence, or other document of a similar character (hereinafter in this section referred to as an official document), or has in his possession any forged, altered, or irregular official document; or

(d) personates, or falsely represents himself to be a person holding, or in the employment of a person holding office under His Majesty, or to be or not to be a person to whom an official document or secret official code word or pass word has been duly issued or communicated, or with intent to obtain an official document, secret official code word or pass word, whether for himself or any other person, knowingly makes any false statement; or

(e) uses, or has in his possession or under his control, without the authority of the Government Department, or the authority concerned, any die, seal, or stamp of or belonging to, or used, made or provided by any Government Department, or by any diplomatic, naval, military, or air-force authority appointed by or acting under the authority of His Majesty, or any die, seal or stamp so nearly resembling any such die, seal or stamp as to be calculated to deceive, or counterfeits any such die, seal or stamp, or uses, or has in his possession, or under his control, any such counterfeited die, seal or stamp;

he shall be guilty of a misdemeanour.

(2) If any person—

(a) retains for any purpose prejudicial to the safety or interests of the State any official document, whether or not completed or issued for use, when he has no right to retain it, or when it is contrary to his duty to retain it, or fails to comply with any directions issued by any Government Department or any person authorised by such department with regard to the return or disposal thereof; or

(b) allows any other person to have possession of any official document issued for his use alone, or communicates any secret official code word or pass word so issued, or, without lawful authority or excuse, has in his possession any official document or secret official code word or pass word issued for the use of some person other than himself, or on obtaining possession of any official document by finding or otherwise, neglects or fails to restore it to the person or authority by whom or for whom or for whose use it was issued, or to a police constable; or

(c) without lawful authority or excuse, manufactures or sells, or has in his possession for sale any such die, seal or stamp as aforesaid;

he shall be guilty of a misdemeanour.

(3) In the case of any prosecution under this section involving the proof of a purpose prejudicial to the safety or interests of the State, subsection (2) of section one of the principal Act shall apply in like manner as it applies to prosecutions under that section.

2 Communications with foreign agents to be evidence of commission of certain offences

(1) In any proceedings against a person for an offence under section one of the principal Act, the fact that he has been in communication with, or attempted to communicate with, a foreign agent, whether within or without the United Kingdom, shall be evidence that he has for a purpose prejudicial to the safety or interests of the State, obtained or attempted to obtain information which is calculated to be or might be or intended to be directly or indirectly useful to an enemy.

(2) For the purpose of this section, but without prejudice to the generality of the foregoing provision—

(a) A person shall, unless he proves the contrary, be deemed to have been in communication with a foreign agent if—

(i) He has, either within or without the United Kingdom, visited the address of a foreign agent or consorted or associated with a foreign agent; or

(ii) Either, within or without the United Kingdom, the name or address of, or any other information regarding a foreign agent has been found in his possession, or has been supplied by him to any other person, or has been obtained by him from any other person;

(b) The expression "foreign agent" includes a person who is or has been or is reasonably suspected of being or having been employed by a foreign power either directly or indirectly for the purpose of committing an act, either within or without the United Kingdom, prejudicial to the safety or interests of the State, or who has or is reasonably suspected of having, either within or without the United Kingdom, committed, or attempted to commit, such an act in the interests of a foreign power;

(c) Any address, whether within or without the United Kingdom, reasonably suspected of being an address used for the receipt of communications intended for a foreign agent, or any address at which a foreign agent resides, or to which he resorts for the purpose of giving or receiving communications, or at which he carries on any business, shall be deemed to be the address of a foreign agent, and communications addressed to such an address to be communications with a foreign agent.

3   Interfering with officers of the police or members of His Majesty's forces

No person in the vicinity of any prohibited place shall obstruct, knowingly mislead or otherwise interfere with or impede the chief officer or a superintendent or other officer of police, or any member of His Majesty's forces engaged on guard, sentry, patrol, or other similar duty in relation to the prohibited place, and, if any person acts in contravention of, or fails to comply with, this provision, he shall be guilty of a misdemeanour. [E]

7   Attempts, incitements, etc.

Any person who attempts to commit any offence under the principal Act or this Act, or solicits or incites or endeavours to persuade another person to commit an offence, or aids or abets and does any act preparatory to the commission of an offence under the principal Act or this Act, shall be guilty of a felony or a misdemeanour or a summary offence according as the offence in question is a felony, a misdemeanour or a summary offence, and on conviction shall be liable to the same punishment, and to be proceeded against in the same manner, as if he had committed the offence.

Infant Life (Preservation) Act 1929

1   Punishment for child destruction

(1) Subject as hereinafter in this subsection provided, any person who, with intent to destroy the life of a child capable of being born alive, by any wilful act causes a child to die before it has an existence independent of its mother, shall be guilty of felony, to wit, of child destruction, and shall be liable on conviction thereof on indictment to penal servitude for life:

Provided that no person shall be found guilty of an offence under this section unless it is proved that the act which caused the death of the child was not done in good faith for the purpose only of preserving the life of the mother. [I]

(2) For the purposes of this Act, evidence that a woman had at any material time been pregnant for a period of twenty-eight weeks or more shall be a prima facie proof that she was at that time pregnant of a child capable of being born alive.

2   Prosecution of offences

(2) Where upon the trial of any person for the murder or manslaughter of any child, or for infanticide, or for an offence under section fifty-eight of the Offences against the Person Act, 1861 (which relates to administering drugs or using instruments to procure abortion), the jury are of opinion that the person charged is not guilty of murder, manslaughter or infanticide, or of an offence under the said section fifty-eight, as the case may be, but that he is shown by the evidence to be guilty of the felony of child destruction, the jury may find him guilty of that felony, and thereupon the person convicted shall be liable to be punished as if he had been convicted upon an indictment for child destruction.

(3) Where upon the trial of any person for the felony of child destruction the jury are of opinion that the person charged is not guilty of any felony, but that he is shown by the evidence to be guilty of an offence under the said section fifty-eight of the Offences against the Person Act, 1861, the jury may find him guilty of that offence, and thereupon the person convicted shall be liable to be punished as if he had been convicted upon an indictment under that section.

Children and Young Persons Act 1933

PART I   PREVENTION OF CRUELTY AND EXPOSURE TO MORAL AND PHYSICAL DANGER

1   Cruelty to persons under sixteen

(1) If any person who has attained the age of sixteen years and has responsibility for any child or young person under that age, wilfully assaults, ill-treats (whether physically or otherwise), neglects, abandons, or exposes him, or causes or procures him to be assaulted, ill-treated (whether physically or otherwise), neglected, abandoned, or exposed, in a manner likely to cause him unnecessary suffering or injury to health (whether the suffering or injury is of a physical or psychological nature) that person shall be guilty of an offence . . . [E]

(2) For the purposes of this section—

    (a) a parent or other person legally liable to maintain a child or young person or the legal guardian of a child or young person shall be deemed to have neglected him in a manner likely to cause injury to his health if he has failed to provide adequate food, clothing, medical aid or lodging for him, or if, having been unable otherwise to provide such food, clothing, medical aid or lodging, he has failed to take steps to procure it to be provided under the enactments applicable in that behalf;

    (b) where it is proved that the death of an infant under three years of age was caused by suffocation (not being suffocation caused by disease or the presence of any foreign body in the throat or air passages of the infant) while the infant was in bed with some other person who has attained the age of sixteen years, that other person shall, if he was, when he went to bed or at any later time before the suffocation, under the influence of drink or a prohibited drug, be deemed to have neglected the infant in a manner likely to cause injury to its health.

(2A) The reference in subsection (2)(b) to the infant being "in bed" with another ("the adult") includes a reference to the infant lying next to the adult in or on any kind of furniture or surface being used by the adult for the purpose of sleeping (and the reference to the time when the adult "went to bed" is to be read accordingly).

(2B) A drug is a prohibited drug for the purposes of subsection (2)(b) in relation to a person if the person's possession of the drug immediately before taking it constituted an offence under section 5(2) of the Misuse of Drugs Act 1971.

(3) A person may be convicted of an offence under this section—

    (a) notwithstanding that actual suffering or injury to health, or the likelihood of actual suffering or injury to health, was obviated by the action of another person;

    (b) notwithstanding the death of the child or young person in question.

3   Allowing persons under sixteen to be in brothels

(1) If any person having responsibility for a child or young person who has attained the age of four years and is under the age of sixteen years, allows that child or young person to reside in or to frequent a brothel, he shall be liable on summary conviction, to a fine not exceeding level 2 on the standard scale, or alternatively . . . or in addition thereto, to imprisonment for any term not exceeding six months. [S]

5   Giving intoxicating liquor to children under five

If any person gives, or causes to be given, to any child under the age of five years any alcohol (within the meaning given by section 191 of the Licensing Act 2003, but disregarding subsection (1)(f) to (i) of that section), except upon the order of a duly qualified medical practitioner, or in case of sickness, apprehended sickness, or other urgent cause, he shall, on summary conviction, be liable to a fine not exceeding level 1 on the standard scale. [S]

7   Sale of tobacco, etc., to persons under eighteen

(1) Any person who sells to a person under the age of eighteen years any tobacco or cigarette papers, whether for his own use or not, shall be liable on summary conviction to a fine not exceeding level 4 on the standard scale. [S]

(1A) It shall be a defence for a person charged with an offence under subsection (1) above to prove that he took all reasonable precautions and exercised all due diligence to avoid the commission of the offence.

(5) For the purposes of this section the expression "tobacco" includes cigarettes, any product containing tobacco and intended for oral or nasal use and smoking mixtures intended as a substitute for tobacco, and the expression "cigarette" includes cut tobacco rolled up in papers, tobacco leaf, or other material in such form as to be capable of immediate use for smoking.

11   Exposing children under twelve to risk of burning

If any person who has attained the age of sixteen years, having responsibility for any child under the age of twelve years, allows the child to be in any room containing an open fire grate or any heating appliance liable to cause injury to a person by contact therewith not sufficiently protected to guard against the risk of his being burnt or scalded without taking reasonable precautions against that risk, and by reason thereof the child is killed or suffers serious injury, he shall on summary conviction be liable to a fine not exceeding level 1 on the standard scale:

  Provided that neither this section, nor any proceedings taken thereunder shall affect any liability of any such person to be proceeded against by indictment for any indictable offence. [S]

17   Interpretation of Part I

(1) For the purposes of this Part of this Act, the following shall be presumed to have responsibility for a child or young person—

  (a) Any person who—
    (i)   has parental responsibility for him (within the meaning of the Children Act 1989); or
    (ii) is otherwise legally liable to maintain him; and
  (b) any person who has care of him.

(2) A person who is presumed to be responsible for a child or young person by virtue of subsection (1)(a) shall not be taken to have ceased to be responsible for him by reason only that he does not have care of him.

PART II   EMPLOYMENT

18   Restrictions on employment of children

(1) Subject to the provisions of this section and of any byelaws made thereunder no child shall be employed—

  (a)   so long as he is under the age of fourteen years; or
  (aa) to do any work other than light work or;
  (b)   before the close of school hours on any day on which he is required to attend school; or
  (c)   before seven o'clock in the morning or after seven o'clock in the evening on any day; or
  (d)   for more than two hours on any day on which he is required to attend school; or
  (da) for more than twelve hours in any week in which he is required to attend school; or
  (e)   for more than two hours on any Sunday; or
  (g)   for more than eight hours or, if he is under the age of fifteen years, for more than five hours in any day—
    (i)   on which he is not required to attend school, and
    (ii) which is not a Sunday; or

(h) for more than thirty-five hours or, if he is under the age of fifteen years, for more than twenty-five hours in any week in which he is not required to attend school; or

(i) for more than four hours in any day without a rest break of one hour; or

(j) at any time in a year unless at that time he has had, or could still have, during a period in the year in which he is not required to attend school, at least two consecutive weeks without employment.

23 Prohibition against persons under sixteen taking part in performances endangering life or limb

No person under the age of sixteen, and no child aged sixteen years shall take part in any performance to which section 37 of the Children and Young Persons Act 1963 applies and in which his life or limbs are endangered and every person who causes or procures such a person or child, or being his parent or guardian allows him, to take part in such a performance, shall be liable on summary conviction to a fine not exceeding level 3 on the standard scale:

Provided that no proceedings shall be taken under this subsection except by or with the authority of a chief officer of police. [S]

24 Restrictions on training for performances of a dangerous nature

(1) No child under the age of twelve years shall be trained to take part in performances of a dangerous nature, and no child who has attained that age shall be trained to take part in such performances except under and in accordance with the terms of a licence granted and in force under this section; and every person who causes or procures a person, or being his parent or guardian allows him, to be trained to take part in performances of a dangerous nature in contravention of this section, shall be liable on summary conviction to a fine not exceeding level 3 on the standard scale. [S]

(2) A local authority may grant a licence for a child who has attained the age of twelve years to be trained to take part in performances of a dangerous nature.

PART III PROTECTION OF CHILDREN AND YOUNG PERSONS IN RELATION TO CRIMINAL AND SUMMARY PROCEEDINGS

50 Age of criminal responsibility

It shall be conclusively presumed that no child under the age of ten years can be guilty of any offence.

Incitement to Disaffection Act 1934

1 Penalty on persons endeavouring to seduce members of His Majesty's forces from their duty or allegiance

If any person maliciously and advisedly endeavours to seduce any member of His Majesty's forces from his duty or allegiance to His Majesty, he shall be guilty of an offence under this Act. [E]

2 Provisions for the prevention and detection of offences under this Act

(1) If any person, with intent to commit or to aid, abet, counsel, or procure the commission of an offence under section one of this Act, has in his possession or under his control any document of such a nature that the dissemination of copies thereof among members of His Majesty's forces would constitute such an offence, he shall be guilty of an offence under this Act. [S]

Public Order Act 1936

1   Prohibition of uniforms in connection with political objects

(1) Subject as hereinafter provided, any person who in any public place or at any public meeting wears uniform signifying his association with any political organisation or with the promotion of any political object shall be guilty of an offence:

Provided that, if the chief officer of police is satisfied that the wearing of any such uniform as aforesaid on any ceremonial, anniversary, or other special occasion will not be likely to involve risk of public disorder, he may, with the consent of a Secretary of State, by order permit the wearing of such uniform on that occasion either absolutely or subject to such conditions as may be specified in the order. [S]

2   Prohibition of quasi-military organisations

(1) If the members or adherents of any association of persons, whether incorporated or not, are—

(a) organised or trained or equipped for the purpose of enabling them to be employed in usurping the functions of the police or of the armed forces of the Crown; or

(b) organised and trained or organised and equipped either for the purpose of enabling them to be employed for the use or display of physical force in promoting any political object, or in such manner as to arouse reasonable apprehension that they are organised and either trained or equipped for that purpose;

then any person who takes part in the control or management of the association, or in so organising or training as aforesaid any members or adherents thereof, shall be guilty of an offence under this section:

Provided that in any proceedings against a person charged with the offence of taking part in the control or management of such an association as aforesaid it shall be a defence to that charge to prove that he neither consented to nor connived at the organisation, training, or equipment of members or adherents of the association in contravention of the provisions of this section. [E]

Infanticide Act 1938

1   Offence of infanticide

(1) Where a woman by any wilful act or omission causes the death of her child being a child under the age of twelve months, but at the time of the act or omission the balance of her mind was disturbed by reason of her not having fully recovered from the effect of giving birth to the child or by reason of the effect of lactation consequent upon the birth of the child, then, if the circumstances were such that but for this Act the offence would have amounted to murder or manslaughter, she shall be guilty of felony, to wit of infanticide, and may for such offence be dealt with and punished as if she had been guilty of the offence of manslaughter of the child. [I]

(2) Where upon the trial of a woman for the murder of her child, being a child under the age of twelve months, the jury are of opinion that she by any wilful act or omission caused its death, but that at the time of the act or omission the balance of her mind was disturbed by reason of her not having fully recovered from the effect of giving birth to the child or by reason of the effect of lactation consequent upon the birth of the child, then the jury may, if the circumstances were such that but for the provisions of this Act they might have returned a verdict of murder or manslaughter, return in lieu thereof a verdict of infanticide.

(3) Nothing in this Act shall affect the power of the jury upon an indictment for the murder of a child to return a verdict of manslaughter, or a verdict of guilty but insane . . .

Statutory Instruments Act 1946

3   Supplementary provisions as to publication

(1) Regulations made for the purposes of this Act shall make provision for the publication by His Majesty's Stationery Office of lists showing the date upon which every statutory instrument printed and sold by or under the authority of the King's printer of Acts of Parliament was first issued by or under the authority of that office; and in any legal proceedings a copy of any list so published purporting to bear the imprint of the King's printer shall be received in evidence as a true copy, and an entry therein shall be conclusive evidence of the date on which any statutory instrument was first issued by or under the authority of His Majesty's Stationery Office.

(2) In any proceedings against any person for an offence consisting of a contravention of any such statutory instrument, it shall be a defence to prove that the instrument had not been issued by or under the authority of His Majesty's Stationery Office at the date of the alleged contravention unless it is proved that at that date reasonable steps had been taken for the purpose of bringing the purport of the instrument to the notice of the public, or of persons likely to be affected by it, or of the person charged.

Criminal Justice Act 1948

31   Jurisdiction and procedure in respect of certain indictable offences committed in foreign countries

(1) Any British subject employed under His Majesty's Government in the United Kingdom in the service of the Crown who commits in a foreign country, when acting or purporting to act in the course of his employment, any offence which, if committed in England, would be punishable on indictment, shall be guilty of an offence and subject to the same punishment, as if the offence had been committed in England.

Hypnotism Act 1952

3   Prohibition on hypnotising persons under eighteen

A person who gives an exhibition, demonstration or performance of hypnotism on a person who has not attained the age of eighteen years at or in connection with an entertainment to which the public are admitted, whether on payment or otherwise, shall, unless he had reasonable cause to believe that that person had attained that age, be liable on summary conviction to a fine not exceeding level 3 on the standard scale. [S]

Prison Act 1952

39   Assisting prisoner to escape

(1) A person who—
    (a) assists a prisoner in escaping or attempting to escape from a prison, or
    (b) intending to facilitate the escape of a prisoner—
        (i)   brings, throws or otherwise conveys anything into a prison,
        (ii)   causes another person to bring, throw or otherwise convey anything into a prison, or
        (iii) gives anything to a prisoner or leaves anything in any place (whether inside or outside a prison),
is guilty of an offence. [I]

40A   Sections 40B and 40C: classification of articles

(1) This section defines the categories of articles which are referred to in sections 40B and 40C.

(2) A List A article is any article or substance in the following list ("List A")—

(a) a controlled drug (as defined for the purposes of the Misuse of Drugs Act 1971);

(b) an explosive;

(c) any firearm or ammunition (as defined in section 57 of the Firearms Act 1968);

(d) any other offensive weapon (as defined in section 1(9) of the Police and Criminal Evidence Act 1984).

(3) A List B article is any article or substance in the following list ("List B")—

(a) alcohol (as defined for the purposes of the Licensing Act 2003);

(b) a mobile telephone;

(c) a camera;

(d) a sound-recording device.

(4) In List B—

"camera" includes any device by means of which a photograph (as defined in section 40E) can be produced;

"sound-recording device" includes any device by means of which a sound-recording (as defined in section 40E) can be made.

(5) The reference in paragraph (b), (c) or (d) of List B to a device of any description includes a reference to—

(a) a component part of a device of that description; or

(b) an article designed or adapted for use with a device of that description (including any disk, film or other separate article on which images, sounds or information may be recorded).

(6) A List C article is any article or substance prescribed for the purposes of this subsection by prison rules.

40B   Conveyance etc. of List A articles into or out of prison

(1) A person who, without authorisation—

(a) brings, throws or otherwise conveys a List A article into or out of a prison,

(b) causes another person to bring, throw or otherwise convey a List A article into or out of a prison,

(c) leaves a List A article in any place (whether inside or outside a prison) intending it to come into the possession of a prisoner, or

(d) knowing a person to be a prisoner, gives a List A article to him,

is guilty of an offence. [I]

(2) In this section "authorisation" means authorisation given for the purposes of this section—

(a) in relation to all prisons or prisons of a specified description, by prison rules or by the Secretary of State; or

(b) in relation to a particular prison, by the Secretary of State or by the governor or director of the prison.

In paragraph (a) "specified" means specified in the authorisation.

(3) Authorisation may be given to specified persons or persons of a specified description—

(a) in relation to specified articles or articles of a specified description;

(b) in relation to specified acts or acts of a specified description; or

(c) on such other terms as may be specified.

In this subsection "specified" means specified in the authorisation.

(4) Authorisation given by the Secretary of State otherwise than in writing shall be recorded in writing as soon as is reasonably practicable after being given.

(5) Authorisation given by the governor or director of a prison shall—

    (a) be given in writing; and

    (b) specify the purpose for which it is given.

40C   Conveyance etc. of List B or C articles into or out of prison

(1) A person who, without authorisation—

    (a) brings, throws or otherwise conveys a List B article into or out of a prison,

    (b) causes another person to bring, throw or otherwise convey a List B article into or out of a prison,

    (c) leaves a List B article in any place (whether inside or outside a prison) intending it to come into the possession of a prisoner, or

    (d) knowing a person to be a prisoner, gives a List B article to him,

is guilty of an offence. [E]

(2) A person who, without authorisation—

    (a) brings, throws or otherwise conveys a List C article into a prison intending it to come into the possession of a prisoner,

    (b) causes another person to bring, throw or otherwise convey a List C article into a prison intending it to come into the possession of a prisoner,

    (c) brings, throws or otherwise conveys a List C article out of a prison on behalf of a prisoner,

    (d) causes another person to bring, throw or otherwise convey a List C article out of a prison on behalf of a prisoner,

    (e) leaves a List C article in any place (whether inside or outside a prison) intending it to come into the possession of a prisoner, or

    (f) while inside a prison, gives a List C article to a prisoner,

is guilty of an offence. [S]

(3) A person who attempts to commit an offence under subsection (2) is guilty of that offence.

(4) In proceedings for an offence under this section it is a defence for the accused to show that—

    (a) he reasonably believed that he had authorisation to do the act in respect of which the proceedings are brought, or

    (b) in all the circumstances there was an overriding public interest which justified the doing of that act.

(7) In this section "authorisation" means authorisation given for the purposes of this section; and subsections (1) to (3) of section 40E apply in relation to authorisations so given as they apply to authorisations given for the purposes of section 40D.

40CA   Unauthorised possession in prison of knife or offensive weapon

(1) A person who, without authorisation, is in possession of an article specified in subsection (2) inside a prison is guilty of an offence. [E]

(2) The articles referred to in subsection (1) are—

    (a) any article that has a blade or is sharply pointed;

    (b) any other offensive weapon (as defined in section 1(9) of the Police and Criminal Evidence Act 1984).

(3) In proceedings for an offence under this section it is a defence for the accused to show that—

    (a) he reasonably believed that he had authorisation to be in possession of the article in question, or

    (b) in all the circumstances there was an overriding public interest which justified his being in possession of the article.

(4) A person guilty of an offence under this section is liable—

    (a) on conviction on indictment, to imprisonment for a term not exceeding four years or to a fine (or both);

    (b) on summary conviction, to imprisonment for a term not exceeding 12 months or to a fine (or both).

(5) In this section "authorisation" means authorisation given for the purposes of this section; and subsections (1) to (3) of section 40E apply in relation to authorisations so given as they apply to authorisations given for the purposes of section 40D.

40CB   Throwing articles into prison

(1) A person who, without authorisation, throws any article or substance into a prison is guilty of an offence. [E]

(2) For the purposes of subsection (1)—

(a) the reference to an article or substance does not include a reference to a List A article, a List B article or a List C article (as defined by section 40A);

(b) the reference to "throwing" an article or substance into a prison includes a reference to doing anything from outside the prison that results in the article or substance being projected or conveyed over or through a boundary of the prison so as to land inside the prison.

(3) In proceedings for an offence under this section it is a defence for the accused to show that—

(a) he reasonably believed that he had authorisation to do the act in respect of which the proceedings are brought, or

(b) in all the circumstances there was an overriding public interest which justified the doing of that act.

(4) A person guilty of an offence under subsection (1) is liable—

(a) on conviction on indictment, to imprisonment for a term not exceeding two years or to a fine (or both);

(b) on summary conviction, to imprisonment for a term not exceeding 12 months or to a fine (or both).

(5) In this section "authorisation" means authorisation given for the purposes of this section; and subsections (1) to (3) of section 40E apply in relation to authorisations so given as they apply to authorisations given for the purposes of section 40D.

40D   Other offences relating to prison security

(1) A person who, without authorisation—

(a) takes a photograph, or makes a sound-recording, inside a prison, or

(b) transmits, or causes to be transmitted, any image, sound or information from inside a prison by electronic communications for simultaneous reception outside the prison,

is guilty of an offence. [E]

(2) It is immaterial for the purposes of subsection (1)(a) where the recording medium is located.

(3) A person who, without authorisation—

(a) brings or otherwise conveys a restricted document out of a prison or causes such a document to be brought or conveyed out of a prison,

is guilty of an offence. [E]

(3A) A person who, without authorisation, is in possession of any of the items specified in subsection (3B) inside a prison is guilty of an offence. [E]

(3B) The items referred to in subsection (3A) are—

(a) a device capable of transmitting or receiving images, sounds or information by electronic communications (including a mobile telephone);

(b) a component part of such a device;

(c) an article designed or adapted for use with such a device (including any disk, film or other separate article on which images, sounds or information may be recorded).

(4) In proceedings for an offence under this section it is a defence for the accused to show that—

(a) he reasonably believed that he had authorisation to do the act in respect of which the proceedings are brought, or

(b) in all the circumstances there was an overriding public interest which justified the doing of that act.

40E   Section 40D: meaning of "authorisation" and other interpretation

(1) In section 40D (and the following provisions of this section) "authorisation" means authorisation given for the purposes of that section—

  (a) in relation to all prisons or prisons of a specified description, by prison rules or by the Secretary of State;

  (b) in relation to a particular prison—

    (i) by the Secretary of State;

    (ii) by the governor or director of the prison;

    (iii) by a person working at the prison who is authorised by the governor or director to grant authorisation on his behalf.

In paragraph (a) "specified" means specified in the authorisation.

(2) Authorisation may be given—

  (a) to persons generally or to specified persons or persons of a specified description; and

  (b) on such terms as may be specified.

In this subsection "specified" means specified in the authorisation.

(3) Authorisation given by or on behalf of the governor or director of a prison must be in writing.

(4) In section 40D "restricted document" means the whole (or any part of)—

  (a) a photograph taken inside the prison;

  (b) a sound-recording made inside the prison;

  (c) a personal record (or a document containing information derived from a personal record);

  (d) any other document which contains—

    (i) information relating to an identified or identifiable relevant individual, if the disclosure of that information would or might prejudicially affect the interests of that individual; or

    (ii) information relating to any matter connected with the prison or its operation, if the disclosure of that information would or might prejudicially affect the security or operation of the prison.

(5) In subsection (4)—

"personal record" means any record which is required by prison rules to be prepared and maintained in relation to any prisoner (and it is immaterial whether or not the individual concerned is still a prisoner at the time of any alleged offence);

"relevant individual" means an individual who is or has at any time been—

  (a) a prisoner or a person working at the prison; or

  (b) a member of such a person's family or household.

(6) In section 40D and this section—

"document" means anything in which information is recorded (by whatever means);

"electronic communications" has the same meaning as in the Electronic Communications Act 2000;

"photograph" means a recording on any medium on which an image is produced or from which an image (including a moving image) may by any means be produced; and

"sound-recording" means a recording of sounds on any medium from which the sounds may by any means be reproduced.

40F   Offences under sections 40B, 40C or 40D: extension of Crown immunity

(1) An individual who—

  (a) works at a prison;

  (b) does not do that work as a servant or agent of the Crown; and

  (c) has been designated by the Secretary of State for the purposes of this section, shall be treated for the purpose of the application of sections 40B, 40C or 40D as if he were doing that work as a servant or agent of the Crown.

(2) A designation for the purposes of this section may be given—

(a) in relation to persons specified in the designation or persons of a description so specified; and

(b) in relation to all work falling within subsection (1)(a) or only in relation to such activities as the designation may provide.

Prevention of Crime Act 1953

1 Prohibition of the carrying of offensive weapons without lawful authority or reasonable excuse

(1) Any person who without lawful authority or reasonable excuse, the proof whereof shall lie on him, has with him in any public place any offensive weapon shall be guilty of an offence. [E]

(2) Where any person is convicted of an offence under subsection (1) of this section the court may make an order for the forfeiture or disposal of any weapon in respect of which the offence was committed.

(4) In this section "public place" includes any highway and any other premises or place to which at the material time the public have or are permitted to have access, whether on payment or otherwise; and "offensive weapon" means any article made or adapted for use for causing injury to the person, or intended by the person having it with him for such use by him or by some other person.

1A Offence of threatening with weapon in public

(1) A person is guilty of an offence if that person—

(a) has an offensive weapon with him or her in a public place,

(b) unlawfully and intentionally threatens another person ("A") with the weapon, and

(c) does so in such a way that a reasonable person ("B") who was exposed to the same threat as A would think that there was an immediate risk of serious physical harm to B. [E]

(3) In the section "public place" and "offensive weapon" have the same meaning as in section 1.

Children and Young Persons (Harmful Publications) Act 1955

1 Works to which this Act applies

This Act applies to any book, magazine or other like work which is of a kind likely to fall into the hands of children or young persons and consists wholly or mainly of stories told in pictures (with or without the addition of written matter), being stories portraying—

(a) the commission of crimes; or

(b) acts of violence or cruelty; or

(c) incidents of a repulsive or horrible nature;

in such a way that the work as a whole would tend to corrupt a child or young person into whose hands it might fall.

2 Penalty for printing, publishing, selling, etc., works to which this Act applies

(1) A person who prints, publishes, sells or lets on hire a work to which this Act applies, or has any such work in his possession for the purpose of selling it or letting it on hire, shall be guilty of an offence and liable, on summary conviction, to imprisonment for a term not exceeding four months or to a fine not exceeding level 3 on the standard scale or to both:

Provided that, in any proceedings taken under this subsection against a person in respect of selling or letting on hire a work or of having it in his possession for the purpose of selling it or letting it on hire, it shall be a defence for him to prove that he had not examined the contents of the work and had no reasonable cause to suspect that it was one to which this Act applies. [S]

(2) A prosecution for an offence under this section shall not, in England or Wales, be instituted except by, or with the consent of, the Attorney-General.

4   Prohibition of importation of works to which this Act applies and articles for printing them
The importation of—
>   (a) any work to which this Act applies; and
>   (b) any plate prepared for the purpose of printing copies of any such work and any photographic film prepared for that purpose;
is hereby prohibited.

Homicide Act 1957

1   Abolition of "constructive malice"
(1) Where a person kills another in the course or furtherance of some other offence, the killing shall not amount to murder unless done with the same malice aforethought (express or implied) as is required for a killing to amount to murder when not done in the course or furtherance of another offence.

(2) For the purposes of the foregoing subsection, a killing done in the course or for the purpose of resisting an officer of justice, or of resisting or avoiding or preventing a lawful arrest, or of effecting or assisting an escape or rescue from legal custody, shall be treated as a killing in the course or furtherance of an offence.

2   Persons suffering from diminished responsibility
(1) A person ("D") who kills or is a party to the killing of another is not to be convicted of murder if D was suffering from an abnormality of mental functioning which—
>   (a) arose from a recognised medical condition,
>   (b) substantially impaired D's ability to do one or more of the things mentioned in subsection (1A), and
>   (c) provides an explanation for D's acts and omissions in doing or being a party to the killing.

(1A) Those things are—
>   (a) to understand the nature of D's conduct;
>   (b) to form a rational judgment;
>   (c) to exercise self-control.

(1B) For the purposes of subsection (1)(c), an abnormality of mental functioning provides an explanation for D's conduct if it causes, or is a significant contributory factor in causing, D to carry out that conduct.

(2) On a charge of murder, it shall be for the defence to prove that the person charged is by virtue of this section not liable to be convicted of murder.

(3) A person who but for this section would be liable, whether as a principal or as accessory, to be convicted of murder shall be liable instead to be convicted of manslaughter.

(4) The fact that one party to a killing is by virtue of this section not liable to be convicted of murder shall not affect the question whether the killing amounted to murder in the case of any other party to it.

4   Suicide pacts

(1) It shall be manslaughter, and shall not be murder, for a person acting in pursuance of a suicide pact between him and another to kill the other or be a party to the other being killed by a third person.

(2) Where it is shown that a person charged with the murder of another killed the other or was a party to his being killed, it shall be for the defence to prove that the person charged was acting in pursuance of a suicide pact between him and the other.

(3) For the purposes of this section "suicide pact" means a common agreement between two or more persons having for its object the death of all of them, whether or not each is to take his own life, but nothing done by a person who enters into a suicide pact shall be treated as done by him in pursuance of the pact unless it is done while he has the settled intention of dying in pursuance of the pact.

Obscene Publications Act 1959

1   Test of obscenity

(1) For the purpose of this Act an article shall be deemed to be obscene if its effect or (where the article comprises two or more distinct items) the effect of any one of its items is, if taken as a whole, such as to tend to deprave and corrupt persons who are likely, having regard to all relevant circumstances, to read, see or hear the matter contained or embodied in it.

(2) In this Act "article" means any description of article containing or embodying matter to be read or looked at or both, and sound record, and any film or other record of a picture or pictures.

(3) For the purposes of this Act a person publishes an article who—

(a) distributes, circulates, sells, lets on hire, gives, or lends it, or who offers it for sale or for letting on hire; or

(b) in the case of an article containing or embodying matter to be looked at or a record, shows, plays or projects it, or, where the matter is data stored electronically, transmits that data.

(4) For the purposes of this Act a person also publishes an article to the extent that any matter recorded on it is included by him in a programme included in a programme service.

(5) Where the inclusion of any matter in a programme so included would, if that matter were recorded matter, constitute the publication of an obscene article for the purposes of this Act by virtue of subsection (4) above, this Act shall have effect in relation to the inclusion of that matter in the programme as if it were recorded matter.

(6) In this section "programme" and "programme service" have the same meaning as in the Broadcasting Act 1990.

2   Prohibition of publication of obscene matter

(1) Subject as hereinafter provided, any person who, whether for gain or not publishes an obscene article or who has an obscene article for publication for gain (whether gain to himself or gain to another) shall be liable—

(a) on summary conviction to a fine not exceeding the prescribed sum or to imprisonment for a term not exceeding six months;

(b) on conviction on indictment to a fine or to imprisonment for a term not exceeding five years or both. [E]

(3) A prosecution for an offence against this section shall not be commenced more than two years after the commission of the offence.

(3A) Proceedings for an offence under this section shall not be instituted except by or with the consent of the Director of Public Prosecutions in any case where the article in question is a moving picture film of a width of not less than sixteen millimetres and the relevant publication or the only other publication which followed or could reasonably have been expected to follow from the relevant publication took place or (as the case may be) was to take place in the course of an exhibition of a film; and in this subsection "the relevant publication" means—

(a) in the case of any proceedings under this section for publishing an obscene article, the publication in respect of which the defendant would be charged if the proceedings were brought; and

(b) in the case of any proceedings under this section for having an obscene article for publication for gain, the publication which, if the proceedings were brought, the defendant would be alleged to have had in contemplation.

(4) A person publishing an article shall not be proceeded against for an offence at common law consisting of the publication of any matter contained or embodied in the article where it is of the essence of the offence that the matter is obscene.

(4A) Without prejudice to subsection (4) above, a person shall not be proceeded against for an offence at common law—

(a) in respect of an exhibition of a film or anything said or done in the course of a film exhibition, where it is of the essence of the common law offence that the exhibition or, as the case may be, what was said or done was obscene, indecent, offensive, disgusting or injurious to morality; or

(b) in respect of an agreement to give an exhibition of a film or to cause anything to be said or done in the course of such an exhibition where the common law offence consists of conspiring to corrupt public morals or to do any act contrary to public morals or decency.

(5) A person shall not be convicted of an offence against this section if he proves that he had not examined the article in respect of which he is charged and had no reasonable cause to suspect that it was such that his publication of it would make him liable to be convicted of an offence against this section.

(6) In any proceedings against a person under this section the question whether an article is obscene shall be determined without regard to any publication by another person unless it could reasonably have been expected that the publication by the other person would follow from publication by the person charged.

(7) In this section "exhibition of a film" has the meaning given in paragraph 15 of Schedule 2 to the Licensing Act 2003.

4 Defence of public good

(1) Subject to subsection (1A) of this section—

A person shall not be convicted of an offence against section two of this Act, and an order for forfeiture shall not be made under the foregoing section, if it is proved that publication of the article in question is justified as being for the public good on the ground that it is in the interests of science, literature, art or learning, or of other objects of general concern.

(1A) Subsection (1) of this section shall not apply where the article in question is a moving picture film or soundtrack, but—

(a) a person shall not be convicted of an offence against section 2 of this Act in relation to any such film or soundtrack, and

(b) an order for forfeiture of any such film or soundtrack shall not be made under section 3 of this Act,

if it is proved that publication of the film or soundtrack is justified as being for the public good on the grounds that it is in the interests of drama, opera, ballet or any other art, or of literature or learning.

(2) It is hereby declared that the opinion of experts as to the literary, artistic, scientific or other merits of an article may be admitted in any proceedings under this Act either to establish or to negative the said ground.

(3) In this section "moving picture soundtrack" means any sound record designed for playing with a moving picture film, whether incorporated with the film or not.

Restriction of Offensive Weapons Act 1959

1 Penalties for offences in connection with dangerous weapons

(1) Any person who manufactures, sells or hires or offers for sale or hire or exposes or has in his possession for the purpose of sale or hire, or lends or gives to any other person—

    (a) any knife which has a blade which opens automatically—

        (i) from the closed position to the fully opened position, or

        (ii) from a partially opened position to the fully opened position,

        by manual pressure applied to a button, spring or other device in or attached to the knife, and which is sometimes known as a "flick knife" or "flick gun"; or

    (b) any knife which has a blade which is released from the handle or sheath thereof by the force of gravity or the application of centrifugal force and which, when released, is locked into place by means of a button, spring, lever, or other device, sometimes known as a "gravity knife";

shall be guilty of an offence. [S]

(1A) Any person who possesses any knife of a kind described in subsection (1) is guilty of an offence.

(2) The importation of any knife of a kind described in subsection (1) is hereby prohibited.

(3) It is a defence for a person charged in respect of any conduct of that person relating to a knife of a kind described in subsection (1)—

    (a) with an offence under subsection (1),

    (b) with an offence under section 50(2) or (3) of the Customs and Excise Management Act 1979,

to show that the conduct was only for the purposes of making the knife available to a museum or gallery to which this subsection applies.

(4) It is a defence for a person charged with an offence under subsection (1A) to show that they possessed the knife only in their capacity as the operator of, or as a person acting on behalf of, a museum or gallery.

(5) If the operator of, or a person acting on behalf of, a museum or gallery to which this subsection applies is charged with hiring or lending a knife of a kind described in subsection (1), it is a defence for them to show that they had reasonable grounds for believing that the person to whom they lent or hired it would use it only for cultural, artistic or educational purposes.

(6) Subsection (3) or (5) applies to a museum or gallery only if it does not distribute profits.

(7) In this section "museum or gallery" includes any institution which has as its purpose, or one of its purposes, the preservation, display and interpretation of material of historical, artistic or scientific interest and gives the public access to it.

(8) A person is to be taken to have shown a matter mentioned in subsection (3), (4) or (5) if—

    (a) sufficient evidence of the matter is adduced to raise an issue with respect to it, and

    (b) the contrary is not proved beyond reasonable doubt.

Street Offences Act 1959

1 Loitering or soliciting for purposes of prostitution

(1) It shall be an offence for a person aged 18 or over (whether male or female) persistently to loiter or solicit in a street or public place for the purpose of prostitution. [S]

(4) For the purposes of this section—

(a) conduct is persistent if it takes place on two or more occasions in any period of three months;

(b) any reference to a person loitering or soliciting for the purposes of prostitution is a reference to a person loitering or soliciting for the purposes of offering services as a prostitute;

(c) "street" includes any bridge, road, lane, footway, subway, square, court, alley or passage, whether a thoroughfare or not, which is for the time being open to the public; and the doorways and entrances of premises abutting on a street (as hereinbefore defined), and any ground adjoining and open to a street, shall be treated as forming part of the street.

Suicide Act 1961

1 Suicide to cease to be a crime

The rule of law whereby it is a crime for a person to commit suicide is hereby abrogated.

2 Criminal liability for complicity in another's suicide

(1) A person ("D") commits an offence if—

(a) D does an act capable of encouraging or assisting the suicide or attempted suicide of another person, and

(b) D's act was intended to encourage or assist suicide or an attempt at suicide. [I]

(1A) The person referred to in subsection (1)(a) need not be a specific person (or class of persons) known to, or identified by, D.

(1B) D may commit an offence under this section whether or not a suicide, or an attempt at suicide, occurs.

(2) If on the trial of an indictment for murder or manslaughter of a person it is proved that the deceased person committed suicide, and the accused committed an offence under subsection (1) in relation to that suicide, the jury may find the accused guilty of the offence under subsection (1).

2A Acts capable of encouraging or assisting

(1) If D arranges for a person ("D2") to do an act that is capable of encouraging or assisting the suicide or attempted suicide of another person and D2 does that act, D is also to be treated for the purposes of this Act as having done it.

(2) Where the facts are such that an act is not capable of encouraging or assisting suicide or attempted suicide, for the purposes of this Act it is to be treated as so capable if the act would have been so capable had the facts been as D believed them to be at the time of the act or had subsequent events happened in the manner D believed they would happen (or both).

(3) A reference in this Act to a person ("P") doing an act that is capable of encouraging the suicide or attempted suicide of another person includes a reference to P doing so by threatening another person or otherwise putting pressure on another person to commit or attempt suicide.

2B Course of conduct

A reference in this Act to an act includes a reference to a course of conduct, and a reference to doing an act is to be read accordingly.

Criminal Procedure (Insanity) Act 1964

4   Finding of unfitness to plead

(1) This section applies where on the trial of a person the question arises (at the instance of the defence or otherwise) whether the accused is under a disability, that is to say, under any disability such that apart from this Act it would constitute a bar to his being tried.

(2) If, having regard to the nature of the supposed disability, the court are of opinion that it is expedient to do so and in the interests of the accused, they may postpone consideration of the question of fitness to be tried until any time up to the opening of the case for the defence.

(3) If, before the question of fitness to be tried falls to be determined, the jury return a verdict of acquittal on the count or each of the counts on which the accused is being tried, that question shall not be determined.

(4) Subject to subsections (2) and (3) above, the question of fitness to be tried shall be determined as soon as it arises.

(5) The question of fitness to be tried shall be determined by the court without a jury.

(6) The court shall not make a determination under subsection (5) above except on the written or oral evidence of two or more registered medical practitioners at least one of whom is duly approved.

4A   Finding that the accused did the act or made the omission charged against him

(1) This section applies where in accordance with section 4(5) above it is determined by a court that the accused is under a disability.

(2) The trial shall not proceed or further proceed but it shall be determined by a jury—

(a) on the evidence (if any) already given in the trial; and

(b) on such evidence as may be adduced or further adduced by the prosecution, or adduced by a person appointed by the court under this section to put the case for the defence,

whether they are satisfied, as respects the count or each of the counts on which the accused was to be or was being tried, that he did the act or made the omission charged against him as the offence.

(3) If as respects that count or any of those counts the jury are satisfied as mentioned in subsection (2) above, they shall make a finding that the accused did the act or made the omission charged against him.

(4) If as respects that count or any of those counts the jury are not so satisfied, they shall return a verdict of acquittal as if on the count in question the trial had proceeded to a conclusion.

(5) Where the question of disability was determined after arraignment of the accused, the determination under subsection (2) is to be made by the jury by whom he was being tried.

5   Powers to deal with persons not guilty by reason of insanity or unfit to plead etc.

(1) This section applies where—

(a) a special verdict is returned that the accused is not guilty by reason of insanity; or

(b) findings have been made that the accused is under a disability and that he did the act or made the omission charged against him.

(2) The court shall make in respect of the accused—

(a) a hospital order (with or without a restriction order);

(b) a supervision order; or

(c) an order for his absolute discharge.

(3) Where—

(a) the offence to which the special verdict or the findings relate is an offence the sentence for which is fixed by law, and

(b) the court have power to make a hospital order,

the court shall make a hospital order with a restriction order (whether or not they would have power to make a restriction order apart from this subsection).

(3A) Where the court have power under subsection (2)(c) to make an order for the absolute discharge of the accused, they may do so where they think, having regard to the circumstances, including the nature of the offence charged and the character of the accused, that such an order would be most suitable in all the circumstances of the case.

(4) In this section—

"hospital order" has the meaning given in section 37 of the Mental Health Act 1983;

"restriction order" has the meaning given to it by section 41 of that Act;

"supervision order" has the meaning given in Part 1 of Schedule 1A to this Act.

6   Evidence by prosecution of insanity or diminished responsibility

Where on a trial for murder the accused contends—

(a) that at the time of the alleged offence he was insane so as not to be responsible according to law for his actions; or

(b) that at that time he was suffering from such abnormality of mental functioning as is specified in subsection (1) of section 2 of the Homicide Act 1957 (diminished responsibility),

the court shall allow the prosecution to adduce or elicit evidence tending to prove the other of those contentions, and may give directions as to the stage of the proceedings at which the prosecution may adduce such evidence.

Abortion Act 1967

1   Medical termination of pregnancy

(1) Subject to the provisions of this section, a person shall not be guilty of any offence under the law relating to abortion when a pregnancy is terminated by a registered medical practitioner if two registered medical practitioners are of the opinion, formed in good faith—

(a) that the pregnancy has not exceeded its twenty-fourth week and that the continuance of the pregnancy would involve risk, greater than if the pregnancy were terminated, of injury to the physical or mental health of the pregnant woman or any existing children of her family; or

(b) that the termination is necessary to prevent grave permanent injury to the physical or mental health of the pregnant woman; or

(c) that the continuance of the pregnancy would involve risk to the life of the pregnant woman, greater than if the pregnancy were terminated; or

(d) that there is a substantial risk that if the child were born it would suffer from such physical or mental abnormalities as to be seriously handicapped.

(2) In determining whether the continuance of a pregnancy would involve such risk of injury to health as is mentioned in paragraph (a) or (b) of subsection (1) of this section, account may be taken of the pregnant woman's actual or reasonably foreseeable environment.

(3) Except as provided by subsection (4) of this section, any treatment for the termination of pregnancy must be carried out in a hospital vested in the Secretary of State for the purpose of his functions under the National Health Service Act 2006 . . . or in a hospital vested in a National Health Service trust or an NHS foundation trust or in a place for the time being approved for the purposes of this section by the Secretary of State.

(3A) The power under subsection (3) of this section to approve a place includes power, in relation to treatment consisting primarily in the use of such medicines as may be specified in the approval and carried out in such manner as may be so specified, to approve a class of places.

(4) Subsection (3) of this section, and so much of subsection (1) as relates to the opinion of two registered medical practitioners, shall not apply to the termination of a pregnancy by a registered practitioner in a case where he is of the opinion, formed in good faith, that the termination is immediately necessary to save the life or to prevent grave permanent injury to the physical or mental health of the pregnant woman.

2   Notification

(1) The Minister of Health in respect of England and Wales, and the Secretary of State in respect of Scotland, shall by statutory instrument make regulations to provide—

    (a) for requiring any such opinion as is referred to in section 1 of this Act to be certified by the practitioners or practitioner concerned in such form and at such time as may be prescribed by the regulations, and for requiring the preservation and disposal of certificates made for the purposes of the regulations;

    (b) for requiring any registered medical practitioner who terminates a pregnancy to give notice of the termination and such other information relating to the termination as may be so prescribed;

    (c) for prohibiting the disclosure, except to such persons or for such purposes as may be so prescribed, of notices given or information furnished pursuant to the regulations.

(3) Any person who wilfully contravenes or wilfully fails to comply with the requirements of regulations under subsection (1) of this section shall be liable on summary conviction to a fine not exceeding level 5 on the standard scale. [S]

4   Conscientious objection to participation in treatment

(1) Subject to subsection (2) of this section, no person shall be under any duty, whether by contract or by any statutory or other legal requirement, to participate in any treatment authorised by this Act to which he has a conscientious objection:

Provided that in any legal proceedings the burden of proof of conscientious objection shall rest on the person claiming to rely on it.

(2) Nothing in subsection (1) of this section shall affect any duty to participate in treatment which is necessary to save the life or to prevent grave permanent injury to the physical or mental health of a pregnant woman.

5   Supplementary provisions

(1) No offence under the Infant Life (Preservation) Act 1929 shall be committed by a registered medical practitioner who terminates a pregnancy in accordance with the provisions of this Act.

(2) For the purposes of the law relating to abortion, anything done with intent to procure a woman's miscarriage (or, in the case of a woman carrying more than one foetus, her miscarriage of any foetus) is unlawfully done unless authorised by section 1 of this Act and, in the case of a woman carrying more than one foetus, anything done with intent to procure her miscarriage of any foetus is authorised by that section if—

    (a) the ground for termination of the pregnancy specified in subsection (1)(d) of that section applies in relation to any foetus and the thing is done for the purpose of procuring the miscarriage of that foetus, or

    (b) any of the other grounds for termination of the pregnancy specified in that section applies.

6   Interpretation

In this Act, the following expressions have meanings hereby assigned to them:—

"the law relating to abortion" means sections 58 and 59 of the Offences against the Person Act 1861, and any rule of law relating to the procurement of abortion.

Criminal Justice Act 1967

8   Proof of criminal intent

A court or jury, in determining whether a person has committed an offence,—

    (a) shall not be bound in law to infer that he intended or foresaw a result of his actions by reason only of its being a natural and probable consequence of those actions; but

(b) shall decide whether he did intend or foresee that result by reference to all the evidence, drawing such inferences from the evidence as appear proper in the circumstances.

89   False written statements tendered in evidence

(1) If any person in a written statement tendered in evidence in criminal proceedings by virtue of section 9 of this Act wilfully makes a statement material in those proceedings which he knows to be false or does not believe to be true, he shall be liable on conviction on indictment to imprisonment for a term not exceeding two years or a fine or both. [I]

(2) The Perjury Act 1911 shall have effect as if this section were contained in that Act.

91   Drunkenness in a public place

(1) Any person who in any public place is guilty, while drunk, of disorderly behaviour shall be liable on summary conviction to a fine not exceeding level 3 on the standard scale. [S]

(4) In this section "public place" includes any highway and any other premises or place to which at the material time the public have or are permitted to have access, whether on payment or otherwise.

Criminal Law Act 1967

1   Abolition of distinction between felony and misdemeanour

(1) All distinctions between felony and misdemeanour are hereby abolished.

(2) Subject to the provisions of this Act, on all matters on which a distinction has previously been made between felony and misdemeanour, including mode of trial, the law and practice in relation to all offences cognisable under the law of England and Wales (including piracy) shall be the law and practice applicable at the commencement of this Act in relation to misdemeanour.

3   Use of force in making arrest, etc.

(1) a person may use such force as is reasonable in the circumstances in the prevention of crime, or in effecting or assisting in the lawful arrest of offenders or suspected offenders or of persons unlawfully at large.

(2) Subsection (1) above shall replace the rules of the common law on the question when force used for a purpose mentioned in the subsection is justified by that purpose.

4   Penalties for assisting offenders

(1) Where a person has committed a relevant offence, any other person who, knowing or believing him to be guilty of the offence or of some other relevant offence, does without lawful authority or reasonable excuse any act with intent to impede his apprehension or prosecution shall be guilty of an offence. [I] and [E]

(1A) In this section and section 5 below, "relevant offence" means—

(a) an offence for which the sentence is fixed by law,

(b) an offence for which a person of 18 years or over (not previously convicted) may be sentenced to imprisonment for a term of five years (or might be so sentenced but for the restrictions imposed by section 33 of the Magistrates' Courts Act 1980).

(2) If on the trial of an indictment for a relevant offence the jury are satisfied that the offence charged (or some other offence of which the accused might on that charge be found guilty) was committed, but find the accused not guilty of it, they may find him guilty of any offence under subsection (1) above of which they are satisfied that he is guilty in relation to the offence charged (or that other offence).

(3) A person committing an offence under subsection (1) above with intent to impede another person's apprehension or prosecution shall on conviction on indictment be liable to imprisonment according to the gravity of the other person's offence, as follows:—

(a) if that offence is one for which the sentence is fixed by law, he shall be liable to imprisonment for not more than ten years; [I]

(b) if it is one for which a person (not previously convicted) may be sentenced to imprisonment for a term of fourteen years, he shall be liable to imprisonment for not more than seven years; [I]

(c) if it is not one included above but is one for which a person (not previously convicted) may be sentenced to imprisonment for a term of ten years, he shall be liable to imprisonment for not more than five years; [E]

(d) in any other case, he shall be liable to imprisonment for not more than three years. [E]

5 Penalties for concealing offences or giving false information

(1) Where a person has committed a relevant offence, any other person who, knowing or believing that the offence or some other relevant offence has been committed, and that he has information which might be of material assistance in securing the prosecution or conviction of an offender for it, accepts or agrees to accept for not disclosing that information any consideration other than the making good of loss or injury caused by the offence, or the making of reasonable compensation for that loss or injury, shall be liable on conviction on indictment to imprisonment for not more than two years. [I] [E]

(2) Where a person causes any wasteful employment of the police by knowingly making to any person a false report tending to show that an offence has been committed, or to give rise to apprehension for the safety of any persons or property, or tending to show that he has information material to any police inquiry, he shall be liable on summary conviction to imprisonment for not more than six months or to a fine of not more than level 4 on the standard scale or to both. [S]

(5) The compounding of an offence other than treason shall not be an offence otherwise than under this section.

6 Trial of offences

(1) Where a person is arraigned on an indictment—

(a) he shall in all cases be entitled to make a plea of not guilty in addition to any demurrer or special plea;

(b) he may plead not guilty of the offence specifically charged in the indictment but guilty of another offence of which he might be found guilty on that indictment;

(c) if he stands mute of malice or will not answer directly to the indictment, the court may order a plea of not guilty to be entered on his behalf, and he shall then be treated as having pleaded not guilty.

(2) On an indictment for murder a person found not guilty of murder may be found guilty—

(a) of manslaughter, or of causing grievous bodily harm with intent to do so; or

(b) of any offence of which he may be found guilty under an enactment specifically so providing, or under section 4(2) of this Act; or

(c) of any attempt to commit murder, or an attempt to commit any other offence of which he might be found guilty;

but may not be found guilty of any offence not included above.

(3) Where, on a person's trial on indictment for any offence except treason or murder, the jury find him not guilty of the offence specifically charged in the indictment, but the allegations in the indictment amount to or include (expressly or by implication) an allegation of another offence falling within the jurisdiction of the court of trial, the jury may find him guilty of that other offence or of an offence of which he could be found guilty on an indictment specifically charging that other offence.

(3A) For the purposes of subsection (3) above an offence falls within the jurisdiction of the court of trial if it is an offence to which section 40 of the Criminal Justice Act 1988 applies (power to join in indictment count for common assault etc.), even if a count charging the offence is not included in the indictment.

(3B) A person convicted of an offence by virtue of subsection (3A) may only be dealt with for it in a manner in which a magistrates' court could have dealt with him.

(4) For purposes of subsection (3) above any allegation of an offence shall be taken as including an allegation of attempting to commit that offence; and where a person is charged on an indictment with attempting to commit an offence or with any assault or other act preliminary to an offence, but not with the completed offence, then (subject to the discretion of the court to discharge the jury or otherwise act with a view to the preferment of an indictment for the completed offence) he may be convicted of the offence charged notwithstanding that he is shown to be guilty of the completed offence.

(5) Where a person arraigned on an indictment pleads not guilty of an offence charged in the indictment but guilty of some other offence of which he might be found guilty on that charge, and he is convicted on that plea of guilty without trial for the offence of which he has pleaded not guilty, then (whether or not the two offences are separately charged in distinct counts) his conviction of the one offence shall be an acquittal of the other.

Criminal Appeal Act 1968

1 Right of appeal

(1) Subject to subsection (3) below a person convicted of an offence on indictment may appeal to the Court of Appeal against his conviction.

(2) An appeal under this section lies only—

(a) with the leave of the Court of Appeal; or

(b) if, within 28 days from the date of the conviction, the judge of the court of trial grants a certificate that the case is fit for appeal.

(3) Where a person is convicted before the Crown Court of a scheduled offence it shall not be open to him to appeal to the Court of Appeal against the conviction on the ground that the decision of the court which sent him to the Crown Court for trial as to the value involved was mistaken.

(4) In subsection (3) above "scheduled offence" and "the value involved" have the same meanings as they have in section 22 of the Magistrates' Courts Act 1980 (certain offences against property to be tried summarily if value of property or damage is small).

2 Grounds for allowing an appeal under s. 1

(1) Subject to the provisions of this Act, the Court of Appeal—

(a) shall allow an appeal against conviction if they think that the conviction is unsafe; and

(b) shall dismiss such an appeal in any other case.

(2) In the case of an appeal against conviction the Court shall, if they allow the appeal, quash the conviction.

(3) An order of the Court of Appeal quashing a conviction shall, except when under section 7 below the appellant is ordered to be retried, operate as a direction to the court of trial to enter, instead of the record of conviction, a judgment and verdict of acquittal.

3 Power to substitute conviction of alternative offence

(1) This section applies on an appeal against conviction, where the appellant has been convicted of an offence to which he did not plead guilty and the jury could on the indictment have found him guilty of some other offence, and on the finding of the jury it appears to the Court of Appeal that the jury must have been satisfied of facts which proved him guilty of the other offence.

(2) The Court may, instead of allowing or dismissing the appeal, substitute for the verdict found by the jury a verdict of guilty of the other offence, and pass such sentence in substitution for the sentence passed at the trial as may be authorised by law for the other offence, not being a sentence of greater severity.

12   Appeal against verdict of not guilty by reason of insanity
A person in whose case there is returned a verdict of not guilty by reason of insanity may appeal to the Court of Appeal against the verdict—
(a) with the leave of the Court of Appeal; or
(b) if, within 28 days from the date of the verdict, the judge of the court of trial grants a certificate that the case is fit for appeal.

Firearms Act 1968

PART I   PROVISIONS AS TO POSSESSION, HANDLING AND DISTRIBUTION OF WEAPONS AND AMMUNITION; PREVENTION OF CRIME AND MEASURES TO PROTECT PUBLIC SAFETY

1   Requirement of firearm certificate
(1) Subject to any exemption under this Act, it is an offence for a person—
(a) to have in his possession, or to purchase or acquire, a firearm to which this section applies without holding a firearm certificate in force at the time, or otherwise than as authorised by such a certificate;
(b) to have in his possession, or to purchase or acquire, any ammunition to which this section applies without holding a firearm certificate in force at the time, or otherwise than as authorised by such a certificate, or in quantities in excess of those so authorised. [E]
(2) It is an offence for a person to fail to comply with a condition subject to which a firearm certificate is held by him. [S]
(3) This section applies to every firearm except—
(a) a shot gun within the meaning of this Act, that is to say a smooth-bore gun (not being an air gun) which—
(i) has a barrel not less than 24 inches in length and does not have any barrel with a bore exceeding 2 inches in diameter;
(ii) either has no magazine or has a non-detachable magazine incapable of holding more than two cartridges; and
(iii) is not a revolver gun; and
(b) an air weapon (that is to say, an air rifle, air gun or air pistol which does not fall within section 5(1) and which is not of a type declared by rules made by the Secretary of State under section 53 of this Act to be specially dangerous).
(3A) A gun which has been adapted to have such a magazine as is mentioned in subsection (3)(a)(ii) above shall not be regarded as falling within that provision unless the magazine bears a mark approved by the Secretary of State for denoting that fact and that mark has been made, and the adaptation has been certified in writing as having been carried out in a manner approved by him, either by one of the two companies mentioned in section 58(1) of this Act or by such other person as may be approved by him for that purpose.
(4) This section applies to any ammunition for a firearm, except the following articles, namely:—
(a) cartridges containing five or more shot, none of which exceeds 0.36 inch in diameter;
(b) ammunition for an air gun, air rifle or air pistol; and
(c) blank cartridges not more than one inch in diameter measured immediately in front of the rim or cannelure of the base of the cartridge.

2   Requirement of certificate for possession of shot guns
(1) Subject to any exemption under this Act, it is an offence for a person to have in his possession, or to purchase or acquire, a shot gun without holding a certificate under this Act authorising him to possess shot guns. [E]

(2) It is an offence for a person to fail to comply with a condition subject to which a shot gun certificate is held by him. [S]

3   Business and other transactions with firearms and ammunition

(1) A person commits an offence if, by way of trade or business, he—

(a) manufactures, sells, transfers, repairs, tests or proves any firearm or ammunition to which section 1 of this Act applies, or a shot gun;

(b) exposes for sale or transfer, or has in his possession for sale, transfer, repair, test or proof any such firearm or ammunition, or a shot gun, or

(c) sells or transfers an air weapon, exposes such a weapon for sale or transfer or has such a weapon in his possession for sale or transfer,

without being registered under this Act as a firearms dealer. [E]

(2) It is an offence for a person to sell or transfer to any other person in the United Kingdom, other than a registered firearms dealer, any firearm or ammunition to which section 1 of this Act applies, or a shot gun, unless that other produces a firearm certificate authorising him to purchase or acquire it or as the case may be, his shot gun certificate, or shows that he is by virtue of this Act entitled to purchase or acquire it without holding a certificate. [E]

(3) It is an offence for a person to undertake the repair, tests or proof of a firearm or ammunition to which section 1 of this Act applies, or of a shot gun, for any other person in the United Kingdom other than a registered firearms dealer as such, unless that other produces or causes to be produced a firearm certificate authorising him to have possession of the firearm or ammunition or, as the case may be, his shot gun certificate, or shows that he is by virtue of this Act entitled to have possession of it without holding a certificate. [E]

(4) Subsections (1) and (3) above have effect subject to any exemption under subsequent provisions of this Part of this Act.

(5) A person commits an offence if, with a view to purchasing or acquiring, or procuring the repair, test or proof of, any firearm or ammunition to which section 1 of this Act applies, or a shot gun, he produces a false certificate or a certificate in which any false entry has been made, or personates a person to whom a certificate has been granted, or knowingly or recklessly makes a statement false in any material particular. [E]

(6) It is an offence for a pawnbroker to take in pawn any firearm or ammunition to which section 1 of this Act applies, or a shot gun. [S]

4   Conversion of weapons

(1) Subject to this section, it is an offence to shorten the barrel of a shot gun to a length less than 24 inches. [E]

(2) It is not an offence under subsection (1) above for a registered firearms dealer to shorten the barrel of a shot gun for the sole purpose of replacing a defective part of the barrel so as to produce a barrel not less than 24 inches in length.

(3) It is an offence for a person other than a registered firearms dealer to convert into a firearm anything which, though having the appearance of being a firearm, is so constructed as to be incapable of discharging any missile through its barrel. [E]

(4) A person who commits an offence under section 1 of this Act by having in his possession, or purchasing or acquiring, a shot gun which has been shortened contrary to subsection (1) above or a firearm which has been converted contrary to subsection (3) above (whether by a registered firearms dealer or not), without holding a firearm certificate authorising him to have it in his possession, or to purchase or acquire it, shall be treated for the purposes of provisions of this Act relating to the punishment of offences as committing that offence in an aggravated form.

4A   Possession of articles for use in connection with conversion

(1) A person, other than a registered firearms dealer, commits an offence if—

(a) the person has in his or her possession or under his or her control an article that is capable of being used (whether by itself or with other articles) to convert an imitation firearm into a firearm, and

(b) the person intends to use the article (whether by itself or with other articles) to convert an imitation firearm into a firearm.

5 Weapons subject to general prohibition

(1) A person commits an offence if, without authority, he has in his possession, or purchases or acquires—

(a) any firearm which is so designed or adapted that two or more missiles can be successively discharged without repeated pressure on the trigger;

(ab) any self-loading or pump-action rifled gun other than one which is chambered for .22 rim-fire cartridges;

(aba) any firearm which either has a barrel less than 30 centimetres in length or is less than 60 centimetres in length overall, other than an air weapon, a muzzle-loading gun or a firearm designed as signalling apparatus;

(ac) any self-loading or pump-action smooth-bore gun which is not an air weapon or chambered for .22 rim-fire cartridges and either has a barrel less than 24 inches in length or is less than 40 inches in length overall;

(ad) any smooth-bore revolver gun other than one which is chambered for 9mm rim-fire cartridges or a muzzle-loading gun;

(ae) any rocket launcher, or any mortar, for projecting a stabilised missile, other than a launcher or mortar designed for line-throwing or pyrotechnic purposes or as signalling apparatus;

(af) any air rifle, air gun or air pistol which uses, or is designed or adapted for use with, a self-contained gas cartridge system;

(ag) any rifle with a chamber from which empty cartridge cases are extracted using—
   (i) energy from propellant gas, or
   (ii) energy imparted to a spring or other energy storage device by propellant gas, other than a rifle which is chambered for .22 rim-fire cartridges;

(b) any weapon of whatever description designed or adapted for the discharge of any noxious liquid, gas or other thing; and

(ba) any device (commonly known as a bump stock) which is designed or adapted so that—
   (i) it is capable of forming part of or being added to a self-loading lethal barrelled weapon (as defined in section 57(1B) and (2A)), and
   (ii) if it forms part of or is added to such a weapon, it increases the rate of fire of the weapon by using the recoil from the weapon to generate repeated pressure on the trigger; and

(c) any cartridge with a bullet designed to explode on or immediately before impact, any ammunition containing or designed or adapted to contain any such noxious thing as is mentioned in paragraph (b) above and, if capable of being used with a firearm of any description, any grenade, bomb (or other like missile), or rocket or shell designed to explode as aforesaid. [I]

(1A) Subject to section 5A of this Act, a person commits an offence if, without authority, he has in his possession, or purchases or acquires,—

(a) any firearm which is disguised as another object [I];

(b) any rocket or ammunition not falling within paragraph (c) of subsection (1) of this section which consists in or incorporates a missile designed to explode on or immediately before impact and is for military use;

(c) any launcher or other projecting apparatus not falling within paragraph (ae) of that subsection which is designed to be used with any rocket or ammunition falling within paragraph (b) above or with ammunition which would fall within that paragraph but for its being ammunition falling within paragraph (c) of this subsection;

(d) any ammunition for military use which consists in or incorporates a missile designed so that a substance contained in the missile will ignite on or immediately before impact;

(e) any ammunition for military use which consists in or incorporates a missile designed, on account of its having a jacket and hard-core, to penetrate armour plating, armour screening or body armour;

    (f) any ammunition which is designed to be used with a pistol and incorporates a missile designed or adapted to expand on impact;

    (g) anything which is designed to be projected as a missile from any weapon and is designed to be, or has been, incorporated in—

        (i) any ammunition falling within any of the preceding paragraphs; or

        (ii) any ammunition which would fall within any of those paragraphs but for its being specified in subsection (1) of this section. [E]

(2) The weapons and ammunition specified in subsections (1) and (1A) of this section (including, in the case of weapons, any devices falling within subsection (1)(ba) of this section and, in the case of ammunition, any missiles falling within subsection (1A)(g) of this section) are referred to in this Act as "prohibited weapons" and "prohibited ammunition" respectively.

(2A) A person commits an offence if without authority—

    (a) he manufactures any weapon, device or ammunition specified in subsection (1) of this section,

    (b) he sells or transfers any prohibited weapon or prohibited ammunition,

    (c) he has in his possession for sale or transfer any prohibited weapon or prohibited ammunition, or

    (d) he purchases or acquires for sale or transfer any prohibited weapon or prohibited ammunition. [I]

(3) In this section "authority" means an authority given in writing by—

    (a) the Secretary of State (in or as regards England and Wales)

(5) It is an offence for a person to whom an authority is given under this section to fail to comply with any condition of the authority. [S]

(7) For the purposes of this section and section 5A of this Act—

    (a) any rocket or ammunition which is designed to be capable of being used with a military weapon shall be taken to be for military use;

    (b) references to a missile designed so that a substance contained in the missile will ignite on or immediately before impact include references to any missile containing a substance that ignites on exposure to air; and

    (c) references to a missile's expanding on impact include references to its deforming in any predictable manner on or immediately after impact.

(8) For the purposes of subsection (1)(aba) and (ac) above, any detachable, folding, retractable or other movable butt-stock shall be disregarded in measuring the length of any firearm.

(9) Any reference in this section to a muzzle-loading gun is a reference to a gun which is designed to be loaded at the muzzle end of the barrel or chamber with a loose charge and a separate ball (or other missile).

5A   Exemptions from requirement of authority under section 5

(1) Subject to subsection (2) below, the authority of the Secretary of State shall not be required by virtue of section 5 of this Act for any person to have in his possession, or to purchase, acquire, sell or transfer, any weapon, ammunition or missile specified in subsection (1A) of that section if he is authorised by a certificate under this Act to possess, purchase or acquire that weapon or ammunition subject to a condition that he does so only for the purpose of its being kept or exhibited as part of a collection.

(2) No sale or transfer may be made under subsection (1) above except to a person who—

    (a) produces the authority of the Secretary of State under section 5 of this Act for his purchase or acquisition; or

    (b) shows that he is, under this section or a licence under the Schedule to the Firearms (Amendment) Act 1988 (museums etc.), entitled to make the purchase or acquisition without the authority of the Secretary of State.

(4) The authority of the Secretary of State shall not be required by virtue of section 5 of this Act for any person to have in his possession, or to purchase or acquire or to sell or transfer, any expanding ammunition or the missile for any such ammunition if—

    (a) he is authorised by a firearm certificate or visitor's firearm permit to possess, or purchase or acquire, any expanding ammunition; and

(b) the certificate or permit is subject to a condition restricting the use of any expanding ammunition to use in connection with any one or more of the following, namely—

(i)   the lawful shooting of deer;

(ii) the shooting of vermin or, in the course of carrying on activities in connection with the management of any estate other wildlife;

(iii) the humane killing of animals;

(iv) the shooting of animals for the protection of other animals or humans.

(5) The authority of the Secretary of State shall not be required by virtue of section 5 of this Act for any person to have in his possession any expanding ammunition or the missile for any such ammunition if—

(a) he is entitled, under section 10 of this Act, to have a slaughtering instrument and the ammunition for it in his possession; and

(b) the ammunition or missile in question is designed to be capable of being used with a slaughtering instrument.

(6) The authority of the Secretary of State shall not be required by virtue of section 5 of this Act for the sale or transfer of any expanding ammunition or the missile for any such ammunition to any person who produces a certificate by virtue of which he is authorised under subsection (4) above to purchase or acquire it without the authority of the Secretary of State.

(7) The authority of the Secretary of State shall not be required by virtue of section 5 of this Act for a person carrying on the business of a firearms dealer, or any servant of his, to have in his possession, or to purchase, acquire, sell or transfer, any expanding ammunition or the missile for any such ammunition in the ordinary course of that business.

(8) In this section—

(a) references to expanding ammunition are references to any ammunition which is designed to be used with a pistol and incorporates a missile which is designed to expand on impact; and

(b) references to the missile for any such ammunition are references to anything which, in relation to any such ammunition, falls within section 5(1A)(g) of this Act.

7   Police permit

(1) A person who has obtained from the chief officer of police for the area in which he resides a permit for the purpose in the prescribed form may, without holding a certificate under this Act, have in his possession a firearm and ammunition in accordance with the terms of the permit.

(2) It is an offence for a person knowingly or recklessly to make a statement false in any material particular for the purpose of procuring, whether for himself or for another person, the grant of a permit under this section. [S]

16   Possession of firearm with intent to injure

It is an offence for a person to have in his possession any firearm or ammunition with intent by means thereof to endanger life, or to enable another person by means thereof to endanger life, whether any injury has been caused or not. [I]

16A   Possession of firearm with intent to cause fear of violence

It is an offence for a person to have in his possession any firearm or imitation firearm with intent—

(a) by means thereof to cause, or

(b) to enable another person by means thereof to cause,

any person to believe that unlawful violence will be used against him or another person. [I]

17   Use of firearm to resist arrest

(1) It is an offence for a person to make or attempt to make any use whatsoever of a firearm or imitation firearm with intent to resist or prevent the lawful arrest or detention of himself or another person. [I]

(2) If a person, at the time of his committing or being arrested for an offence specified in Schedule 1 to this Act, has in his possession a firearm or imitation firearm, he shall be guilty of an offence under this subsection unless he shows that he had it in his possession for a lawful object. [I]

(4) For purposes of this section, the definition of "firearm" in section 57(1) of this Act shall apply without paragraphs (b) and (c) of that subsection, and "imitation firearm" shall be construed accordingly.

18   Carrying firearm with criminal intent

(1) It is an offence for a person to have with him a firearm or imitation firearm with intent to commit an indictable offence, or to resist arrest or prevent the arrest of another, in either case while he has the firearm or imitation firearm with him. [I]

(2) In proceedings for an offence under this section proof that the accused had a firearm or imitation firearm with him and intended to commit an offence, or to resist or prevent arrest, is evidence that he intended to have it with him while doing so.

19   Carrying firearm in a public place

A person commits an offence if, without lawful authority or reasonable excuse (the proof whereof lies on him) he has with him in a public place—

   (a) a loaded shot gun,
   (b) an air weapon (whether loaded or not),
   (c) any other firearm (whether loaded or not) together with ammunition suitable for use in that firearm, or
   (d) an imitation firearm. [E]

20   Trespassing with firearm

(1) A person commits an offence if, while he has a firearm or imitation firearm with him, he enters or is in any building or part of a building as a trespasser and without reasonable excuse (the proof whereof lies on him). [E]

(2) A person commits an offence if, while he has a firearm or imitation firearm with him, he enters or is on any land as a trespasser and without reasonable excuse (the proof whereof lies on him). [S]

(3) In subsection (2) of this section the expression "land" includes land covered with water.

21A   Firing an air weapon beyond premises

(1) A person commits an offence if—

   (a) he has with him an air weapon on any premises; and
   (b) he uses it for firing a missile beyond those premises.

(2) In proceedings against a person for an offence under this section it shall be a defence for him to show that the only premises into or across which the missile was fired were premises the occupier of which had consented to the firing of the missile (whether specifically or by way of a general consent). [S]

22   Acquisition and possession of firearms by minors

(1) It is an offence for a person under the age of eighteen to purchase or hire any firearm or ammunition. [S]

(2) It is an offence for a person under the age of fourteen to have in his possession any firearm or ammunition to which section 1 of this Act or section 15 of the Firearms Amendment Act 1988 applies, except in circumstances where under section 11 (1), (3) or (4) of this Act he is entitled to have possession of it without holding a firearm certificate. [S]

(3) It is an offence for a person under the age of fifteen to have with him an assembled shot gun except while under the supervision of a person of or over the age of twenty-one, or while the shot gun is so covered with a securely fastened gun cover that it cannot be fired. [S]

(4) Subject to section 23 below, it is an offence for a person under the age of eighteen to have with him an air weapon or ammunition for an air weapon. [S]

23   Exceptions from s. 22(4)

(1) It is not an offence under section 22 (4) of this Act for a person to have with him an air weapon or ammunition while he is under the supervision of a person of or over the age of twenty-one; but where a person has with him an air weapon on any premises in circumstances where he would be

prohibited from having it with him but for this subsection, it is an offence for the person under whose supervision he is to allow him so to use it for firing any missile beyond those premises.

(1A) In proceedings against a person for an offence under subsection (1) it shall be a defence for him to show that the only premises into or across which the missile was fired were premises the occupier of which had consented to the firing of the missile (whether specifically or by way of a general consent);

(2) It is not an offence under section 22(4) of this Act for a person to have with him an air weapon or ammunition at a time when—

    (a) being a member of a rifle club or miniature rifle club for the time being approved by the Secretary of State for the purposes of this section or section 15 of the Firearms (Amendment) Act 1988, he is engaged as such a member in connection with target shooting; or

    (b) he is using the weapon or ammunition at a shooting gallery where the only firearms used are either air weapons or miniature rifles not exceeding 0.23 inch calibre.

(3) It is not an offence under section 22(4) of this Act for a person of or over the age of fourteen to have with him an air weapon or ammunition on private premises with the consent of the occupier.

24   Supplying firearms to minors

(1) It is an offence to sell or let on hire any firearm or ammunition to a person under the age of eighteen. [S]

(2) It is an offence—

    (a) to make a gift of or lend any firearm or ammunition to which section 1 of this Act applies to a person under the age of fourteen; or

    (b) to part with the possession of any such firearm or ammunition to a person under that age, except in circumstances where that person is entitled under section 11 (1), (3) or (4) of this Act or section 15 of the Firearms (Amendment) Act 1988 to have possession thereof without holding a firearm certificate. [S]

(3) It is an offence to make a gift of a shot gun or ammunition for a shot gun to a person under the age of fifteen. [S]

(4) It is an offence—

    (a) to make a gift of an air weapon or ammunition for an air weapon to a person under the age of eighteen; or

    (b) to part with the possession of an air weapon or ammunition for an air weapon to a person under that age except where by virtue of section 23 of this Act the person is not prohibited from having it with him. [S]

(5) In proceedings for an offence under any provision of this section it is a defence to prove that the person charged with the offence believed the other person to be of or over the age mentioned in that provision and had reasonable ground for the belief.

24ZA   Failing to prevent minors from having air weapons

(1) It is an offence for a person in possession of an air weapon to fail to take reasonable precautions to prevent any person under the age of eighteen from having the weapon with him. [S]

(2) Subsection (1) does not apply where by virtue of section 23 of this Act the person under the age of eighteen is not prohibited from having the weapon with him.

(3) In proceedings for an offence under subsection (1) it is a defence to show that the person charged with the offence—

    (a) believed the other person to be aged eighteen or over; and

    (b) had reasonable ground for that belief.

(4) For the purposes of this section a person shall be taken to have shown the matters specified in subsection (3) if—

    (a) sufficient evidence of those matters is adduced to raise an issue with respect to them; and

    (b) the contrary is not proved beyond a reasonable doubt.

24A   Supplying imitation firearms to minors

(1) It is an offence for a person under the age of eighteen to purchase an imitation firearm. [S]

(2) It is an offence to sell an imitation firearm to a person under the age of eighteen. [S]

(3) In proceedings for an offence under subsection (2) it is a defence to show that the person charged with the offence—

    (a) believed the other person to be aged eighteen or over; and

    (b) had reasonable ground for that belief.

(4) For the purposes of this section a person shall be taken to have shown the matters specified in subsection (3) if—

    (a) sufficient evidence of those matters is adduced to raise an issue with respect to them; and

    (b) the contrary is not proved beyond a reasonable doubt.

25 Supplying firearm to person drunk or insane

It is an offence for a person to sell or transfer any firearm or ammunition to, or to repair, prove or test any firearm or ammunition for, another person whom he knows or has reasonable cause for believing to be drunk or of unsound mind. [S]

PART IV MISCELLANEOUS AND GENERAL

57 Interpretation

(1) In this Act, the expression "firearm" means—

    (a) a lethal barrelled weapon (see subsection (1B));

    (b) a prohibited weapon;

    (c) a relevant component part in relation to a lethal barrelled weapon or a prohibited weapon (see sub-section (1D));

    (d) an accessory to a lethal barrelled weapon or a prohibited weapon where the accessory is designed or adapted to diminish the noise or flash caused by firing the weapon;

and so much of section 1 of this Act as excludes any description of firearm from the category of firearms to which that section applies shall be construed as also excluding component parts of, and accessories to, firearms of that description.

(1B) In subsection (1)(a), "lethal barrelled weapon" means a barrelled weapon of any description from which a shot, bullet or other missile, with kinetic energy of more than one joule at the muzzle of the weapon, can be discharged.

(1C) Subsection (1) is subject to section 57A (exception for airsoft guns).

(1D) For the purposes of subsection (1)(c), each of the following items is a relevant component part in relation to a lethal barrelled weapon or a prohibited weapon—

    (a) a barrel, chamber or cylinder,

    (b) a frame, body or receiver,

    (c) a breech block, bolt or other mechanism for containing the pressure of discharge at the rear of a chamber,

but only where the item is capable of being used as a part of a lethal barrelled weapon or a prohibited weapon.

(2) In this Act, the expression "ammunition" means ammunition for any firearm and includes grenades, bombs and other like missiles, whether capable of use with a firearm or not, and also includes prohibited ammunition.

(2A) In this Act "self-loading" and "pump-action" in relation to any weapon mean respectively that it is designed or adapted (otherwise that as mentioned in section 5(1)(a)) so that it is automatically re-loaded or that it is so designed or adapted that it is re-loaded by the manual operation of the fore-end or forestock of the weapon.

(2B) In this Act "revolver", in relation to a smooth-bore gun, means a gun containing a series of chambers which revolve when the gun is fired.

(4) In this Act—

"acquire" means hire, accept as a gift or borrow and "acquisition" shall be construed accordingly;

"air weapon" has the meaning assigned to it by section 1 (3)(b) of this Act;

"area" means a police area;

"certificate" (except in a context relating to the registration of firearms dealers) and "certificate under this Act" means a firearm certificate or a shot gun certificate and—

(a) "firearm certificate" means a certificate granted by a chief officer of police under this Act in respect of any firearm or ammunition to which section 1 of this Act applies...; and

(b) "shot gun certificate" means a certificate granted by a chief officer of police under this Act and authorising a person to possess shot guns;

"civilian officer" means—

(a) as respects England and Wales—

   (i) a person employed by a chief constable established under section 2 of the Police Reform and Social Responsibility Act 2011,

   (ii) a person employed by the Commissioner of Police of the Metropolis, or

   (iii) a person employed by the Corporation of the City of London who is under the direction and control of the Commissioner of Police for the City of London;

"European weapons directive" means the directive of the Council of the European Communities No. 91/477/EEC (directive on the control of the acquisition and possession of weapons);

"firearms dealer" means a person who, by way of trade or business,

(a) manufactures, sells, transfers, repairs, tests or proves firearms or ammunition to which section 1 of this Act applies or shot guns; or

(b) sells or transfers air weapons.

"imitation firearm" means any thing which has the appearance of being a firearm (other than such a weapon as is mentioned in section 5 (1)(b) of this Act) whether or not it is capable of discharging any shot, bullet or other missile;

"member of a police force" means—

(a) as respects England and Wales, a constable who is a member of a police force or a special constable appointed under section 27 of the Police Act 1996;

"member of the British Transport Police Force" includes a special constable appointed under section 25 of the Railways and Transport Safety Act 2003;

"premises" includes any land;

"prescribed" means prescribed by rules made by the Secretary of State under section 53 of this Act;

"prohibited weapon" and "prohibited ammunition" have the meanings assigned to them by section 5(2) of this Act;

"public place" includes any highway and any other premises or place to which at the material time the public have or are permitted to have access, whether on payment or otherwise;

"registered", in relation to a firearms dealer, means registered either—

(a) in Great Britain, under section 33 of this Act, or

and references to "the register", "registration" and a "certificate of registration" shall be construed accordingly, except in section 40;

"rifle" includes carbine;

"shot gun" has the meaning assigned to it by section 1(3)(a) of this Act and, in sections 3(1) and 45(2) of this Act and in the definition of "firearms dealer", includes any component part of a shot gun and any accessory to a shot gun designed or adapted to diminish the noise or flash caused by firing the gun;

"slaughtering instrument" means a firearm which is specially designed or adapted for the instantaneous slaughter of animals or for the instantaneous stunning of animals with a view to slaughtering them; and

"transfer" includes let on hire, give, lend and part with possession, and "transferee" and "transferor" shall be construed accordingly.

(5) The definitions in subsections (1) to (3) above apply to the provisions of this Act except where the context otherwise requires.

(6) For the purposes of this Act—

(a) the length of the barrel of a firearm shall be measured from the muzzle to the point at which the charge is exploded on firing; and

(b) a shot gun or an air weapon shall be deemed to be loaded if there is ammunition in the chamber or barrel or in any magazine or other device which is in such a position that the ammunition can be fed into the chamber or barrel by the manual or automatic operation of some part of the gun or weapon.

57A   Exception for airsoft guns

(1) An "airsoft gun" is not to be regarded as a firearm for the purposes of this Act.

(2) An "airsoft gun" is a barrelled weapon of any description which—

(a) is designed to discharge only a small plastic missile (whether or not it is also capable of discharging any other kind of missile), and

(b) is not capable of discharging a missile (of any kind) with kinetic energy at the muzzle of the weapon that exceeds the permitted level.

(3) "Small plastic missile" means a missile that—

(a) is made wholly or partly from plastics,

(b) is spherical, and

(c) does not exceed 8 millimetres in diameter.

(4) The permitted kinetic energy level is—

(a) in the case of a weapon which is capable of discharging two or more missiles successively without repeated pressure on the trigger, 1.3 joules;

(b) in any other case, 2.5 joules.

58   Particular savings

(2) Apart from—

(a) sections 19, 20 and 21 and Schedule 3, and

(b) any other provision of this Act so far as it applies in relation to an offence under sections 19, 20 or 21,

nothing in this Act relating to firearms shall apply to an antique firearm which is sold, transferred, purchased, acquired or possessed as a curiosity or ornament.

(2A) For the purposes of subsection (2), a firearm is an "antique firearm" if—

(a) either the conditions in subsection (2B) are met or the condition in subsection (2C) is met, and

(b) if an additional condition is specified in regulations under subsection (2D), that condition is also met.

(2B) The conditions in this subsection are that—

(a) the firearm's chamber or, if the firearm has more than one chamber, each of its chambers is either—

(i) a chamber that the firearm had when it was manufactured, or

(ii) a replacement for such a chamber that is identical to it in all material respects;

(b) the firearm's chamber or (as the case may be) each of the firearm's chambers is designed for use with a cartridge of a description specified in regulations made by statutory instrument by the Secretary of State (whether or not it is also capable of being used with other cartridges).

(2C) The condition in this subsection is that the firearm's propulsion system is of a description specified in regulations made by statutory instrument by the Secretary of State.

(2D) The Secretary of State may by regulations made by statutory instrument specify either of the following conditions for the purposes of subsection (2A)(b)—

(a) a condition that a number of years specified in the regulations has elapsed since the date on which the firearm was manufactured;

(b) a condition that the firearm was manufactured before a date specified in the regulations.

(3) The provisions of this Act relating to ammunition shall be in addition to and not in derogation of any enactment relating to the keeping and sale of explosives.

SCHEDULE 1   OFFENCES TO WHICH SECTION 17(2) APPLIES

1. Offences under section 1 of the Criminal Damage Act 1971.

2. Offences under any of the following provisions of the Offences against the Person Act 1861—
section 20 to 22 (inflicting bodily injury; garrotting; criminal use of stupefying drugs);
section 30 (laying explosive to building etc.);

section 32 (endangering railway passengers by tampering with track);

section 38 (assault with intent to commit felony or resist arrest);

section 47 (criminal assaults); . . .

2A. Offences under Part 1 of the Child Abduction Act 1984 (abduction of children).

4. Theft, robbery, burglary, blackmail and any offence under section 12(1)(taking of motor vehicle or other conveyance without owner's consent) of the Theft Act 1968.

5. Offences under section 89(1) of the Police Act 1996 (assaulting constable in execution of his duty) . . .

5A. An offence under section 90(1) of the Criminal Justice Act 1991 (assaulting prisoner custody officer).

5B. An offence under section 13(1) of the Criminal Justice and Public Order Act 1994 (assaulting secure training centre custody officer).

6. Offences under any of the following provisions of the Sexual Offences Act 2003—

(a) section 1 (rape);

(b) section 2 (assault by penetration);

(c) section 4 (causing a person to engage in sexual activity without consent), where the activity caused involved penetration within subsection (4)(a) to (d) of that section;

(d) section 5 (rape of a child under 13);

(e) section 6 (assault of a child under 13 by penetration);

(f) section 8 (causing or inciting a child under 13 to engage in sexual activity), where an activity involving penetration within subsection (3)(a) to (d) of that section was caused;

(g) section 30 (sexual activity with a person with a mental disorder impeding choice), where the touching involved penetration within subsection (3)(a) to (d) of that section;

(h) section 31 (causing or inciting a person, with a mental disorder impeding choice, to engage in sexual activity), where an activity involving penetration within subsection (3)(a) to (d) of that section was caused.

6A. An offence under paragraph 14 or 24 of Schedule 10 to the Criminal Justice and Courts Act 2015 (assaulting secure college custody officer).

8. Aiding or abetting the commission of any offence specified in paragraphs 1 to 6A of this Schedule.

9. Attempting to commit any offence so specified.

Theft Act 1968

1   Basic definition of theft

(1) A person is guilty of theft if he dishonestly appropriates property belonging to another with the intention of permanently depriving the other of it; and "theft" and "steal" shall be construed accordingly. [E]

(2) It is immaterial whether the appropriation is made with a view to gain, or is made for the thief's own benefit.

(3) The five following sections of this Act shall have effect as regards the interpretation and operation of this section (and, except as otherwise provided by this Act, shall apply only for purposes of this section).

2   "Dishonestly"

(1) A person's appropriation of property belonging to another is not to be regarded as dishonest—

(a) if he appropriates the property in the belief that he has in law the right to deprive the other of it, on behalf of himself or of a third person; or

(b) if he appropriates the property in the belief that he would have the other's consent if the other knew of the appropriation and the circumstances of it; or

(c) (except where the property came to him as trustee or personal representative) if he appropriates the property in the belief that the person to whom the property belongs cannot be discovered by taking reasonable steps.

(2) A person's appropriation of property belonging to another may be dishonest not withstanding that he is willing to pay for the property.

3 "Appropriates"

(1) Any assumption by a person of the rights of an owner amounts to an appropriation, and this includes, where he has come by the property (innocently or not) without stealing it, any later assumption of a right to it by keeping or dealing with it as owner.

(2) Where property or a right or interest in property is or purports to be transferred for value to a person acting in good faith, no later assumption by him of rights which he believed himself to be acquiring shall, by reason of any defect in the transferor's title, amount to theft of the property.

4 "Property"

(1) "Property" includes money and all other property, real or personal, including things in action and other intangible property.

(2) A person cannot steal land, or things forming part of land and severed from it by him or by his directions, except in the following cases, that is to say—

(a) when he is a trustee or personal representative, or is authorised by power of attorney, or as liquidator of a company, or otherwise, to sell or dispose of land belonging to another, and he appropriates the land or anything forming part of it by dealing with it in breach of the confidence reposed in him; or

(b) when he is not in possession of the land and appropriates anything forming part of the land by severing it or causing it to be severed, or after it has been severed; or

(c) when, being in possession of the land under a tenancy, he appropriates the whole or part of any fixture or structure let to be used with the land.

For purposes of this subsection "land" does not include incorporeal hereditaments; "tenancy" means a tenancy for years or any less period and includes an agreement for such a tenancy, but a person who after the end of a tenancy remains in possession as statutory tenant or otherwise is to be treated as having possession under the tenancy, and "let" shall be construed accordingly.

(3) A person who picks mushrooms growing wild on any land, or who picks flowers, fruit or foliage from a plant growing wild on any land, does not (although not in possession of the land) steal what he picks, unless he does it for reward or for sale or other commercial purpose. For purposes of this subsection "mushroom" includes any fungus, and "plant" includes any shrub or tree.

(4) Wild creatures, tamed or untamed, shall be regarded as property; but a person cannot steal a wild creature not tamed nor ordinarily kept in captivity, or the carcase of any such creature, unless either it has been reduced into possession by or on behalf of another person and possession of it has not since been lost or abandoned, or another person is in course of reducing it into possession.

5 "Belonging to another"

(1) Property shall be regarded as belonging to any person having possession or control of it, or having in it any proprietary right or interest (not being an equitable interest arising only from an agreement to transfer or grant an interest).

(2) Where property is subject to a trust, the persons to whom it belongs shall be regarded as including any person having a right to enforce the trust, and an intention to defeat the trust shall be regarded accordingly as an intention to deprive of the property any person having that right.

(3) Where a person receives property from or on account of another, and is under an obligation to the other to retain and deal with that property or its proceeds in a particular way, the property or proceeds shall be regarded (as against him) as belonging to the other.

(4) Where a person gets property by another's mistake, and is under an obligation to make restoration (in whole or in part) of the property or its proceeds or of the value thereof, then to the extent of that obligation the property or proceeds shall be regarded (as against him) as belonging to the person entitled to restoration, and an intention not to make restoration shall be regarded accordingly as an intention to deprive that person of the property or proceeds.

(5) Property of a corporation sole shall be regarded as belonging to the corporation notwithstanding a vacancy in the corporation.

6 "With the intention of permanently depriving the other of it"

(1) A person appropriating property belonging to another without meaning the other permanently to lose the thing itself is nevertheless to be regarded as having the intention of permanently

depriving the other of it if his intention is to treat the thing as his own to dispose of regardless of the other's rights; and a borrowing or lending of it may amount to so treating it if, but only if, the borrowing or lending is for a period and in circumstances making it equivalent to an outright taking or disposal.

(2) Without prejudice to the generality of subsection (1) above, where a person, having possession or control (lawfully or not) of property belonging to another, parts with the property under a condition as to its return which he may not be able to perform, this (if done for purposes of his own and without the other's authority) amounts to treating the property as his own to dispose of regardless of the other's rights.

7 Theft

A person guilty of theft shall on conviction on indictment be liable to imprisonment for a term not exceeding seven years. [E]

8 Robbery

(1) A person is guilty of robbery if he steals, and immediately before or at the time of doing so, and in order to do so, he uses force on any person or puts or seeks to put any person in fear of being then and there subjected to force.

(2) A person guilty of robbery, or of an assault with intent to rob, shall on conviction on indictment be liable to imprisonment for life. [I]

9 Burglary

(1) A person is guilty of burglary if—
  (a) he enters any building or part of a building as a trespasser and with intent to commit any such offence as is mentioned in subsection (2) below; or
  (b) having entered into any building or part of a building as a trespasser he steals or attempts to steal anything in the building or that part of it or inflicts or attempts to inflict on any person therein any grievous bodily harm. [I] and [E]

(2) The offences referred to in subsection (1)(a) above are offences of stealing anything in the building or part of a building in question, of inflicting on any person therein any grievous bodily harm therein, and of doing unlawful damage to the building or anything therein.

(3) A person guilty of burglary shall on conviction on indictment be liable to imprisonment for a term not exceeding—
  (a) where the offence was committed in respect of a building or part of a building which is a dwelling, fourteen years;
  (b) in any other case, ten years.

(4) References in subsection (1) and (2) above to a building, and the reference in subsection (3) above to a building which is a dwelling, shall apply also to an inhabited vehicle or vessel, and shall apply to any such vehicle or vessel at times when the person having a habitation in it is not there as well as at times when he is.

10 Aggravated burglary

(1) A person is guilty of aggravated burglary if he commits any burglary and at the time has with him any firearm or imitation firearm, any weapon of offence, or any explosive; and for this purpose—
  (a) "firearm" includes an airgun or air pistol, and "imitation firearm" means anything which has the appearance of being a firearm, whether capable of being discharged or not; and
  (b) "weapon of offence" means any article made or adapted for use for causing injury to or incapacitating a person, or intended by the person having it with him for such use; and
  (c) "explosive" means any article manufactured for the purpose of producing a practical effect by explosion, or intended by the person having it with him for that purpose. [I]

11 Removal of articles from places open to the public

(1) Subject to subsections (2) and (3) below, where the public have access to a building in order to view the building or part of it, or a collection or part of a collection housed in it, any person who without lawful authority removes from the building or its grounds the whole or part of any article displayed or kept for display to the public in the building or that part of it or in its grounds shall be guilty of an offence.

For this purpose "collection" includes a collection got together for a temporary purpose, but references in this section to a collection do not apply to a collection made or exhibited for the purpose of effecting sales or other commercial dealings. [E]

(2) It is immaterial for purposes of subsection (1) above, that the public's access to a building is limited to a particular period or particular occasion; but where anything removed from a building or its grounds is there otherwise than as forming part of, or being on loan for exhibition with, a collection intended for permanent exhibition to the public, the person removing it does not thereby commit an offence under this section unless he removes it on a day when the public have access to the building as mentioned in subsection (1) above.

(3) A person does not commit an offence under this section if he believes that he has lawful authority for the removal of the thing in question or that he would have it if the person entitled to give it knew of the removal and the circumstances of it.

12   Taking motor vehicle or other conveyance without authority

(1) Subject to subsections (5) and (6) below, a person shall be guilty of an offence if, without having the consent of the owner or other lawful authority, he takes any conveyance for his own or another's use or, knowing that any conveyance has been taken without such authority, drives it or allows himself to be carried in or on it. [S]

(4) If on the trial of an indictment for theft the jury are not satisfied that the accused committed theft, but it is proved that the accused committed an offence under subsection (1) above, the jury may find him guilty of the offence under subsection (1), and if he is found guilty of it, he shall be liable as he would have been liable under subsection (2) above on summary conviction.

(5) Subsection (1) above shall not apply in relation to pedal cycles; but, subject to subsection (6) below, a person who, without having the consent of the owner or other lawful authority, takes a pedal cycle for his own or another's use, or rides a pedal cycle knowing it to have been taken without such authority, shall on summary conviction be liable to a fine not exceeding level 3 on the standard scale.

(6) A person does not commit an offence under this section by anything done in the belief that he has lawful authority to do it or that he would have the owner's consent if the owner knew of his doing it and the circumstances of it.

(7) For purposes of this section—
  (a) "conveyance" means any conveyance constructed or adapted for the carriage of a person or persons whether by land, water, or air, except that it does not include a conveyance constructed or adapted for use only under the control of a person not carried in or on it, and "drive" shall be construed accordingly; and
  (b) "owner", in relation to conveyance which is the subject of a hiring agreement or hire-purchase agreement, means the person in possession of the conveyance under that agreement.

12A   Aggravated vehicle-taking

(1) Subject to subsection (3) below, a person is guilty of aggravated taking of a vehicle if—
  (a) he commits an offence under section 12(1) above (in this section referred to as a "basic offence") in relation to a mechanically propelled vehicle; and
  (b) it is proved that, at any time after the vehicle was unlawfully taken (whether by him or another) and before it was recovered, the vehicle was driven, or injury or damage was caused, in one or more of the circumstances set out in paragraphs (a) to (d) of subsection (2) below. [I]

(2) The circumstances referred to in subsection (1)(b) above are—
  (a) that the vehicle was driven dangerously on a road or other public place;
  (b) that, owing to the driving of the vehicle, an accident occurred by which injury was caused to any person;
  (c) that, owing to the driving of the vehicle, an accident occurred by which damage was caused to any property, other than the vehicle;
  (d) that damage was caused to the vehicle.

(3) A person is not guilty of an offence under this section if he proves that, as regards any such proven driving, injury or damage as is referred to in subsection (1)(b) above, either—

(a) the driving, accident or damage referred to in subsection (2) above occurred before he committed the basic offence; or

(b) he was neither in nor on nor in the immediate vicinity of the vehicle when that driving, accident or damage occurred.

(4) A person guilty of an offence under this section shall be liable on conviction on indictment to imprisonment for a term not exceeding two years or, if it is proved that, in circumstances falling within subsection (2)(b) above, the accident caused the death of the person concerned, fourteen years.

(5) If a person who is charged with an offence under this section is found not guilty of that offence but it is proved that he committed a basic offence, he may be convicted of the basic offence.

(7) For the purposes of this section a vehicle is driven dangerously if—

(a) it is driven in a way which falls far below what would be expected of a competent and careful driver; and

(b) it would be obvious to a competent and careful driver that driving the vehicle in that way would be dangerous.

(8) For the purposes of this section a vehicle is recovered when it is restored to its owner or to other lawful possession or custody; and in this subsection "owner" has the same meaning as in section 12 above.

13 Abstracting of electricity

A person who dishonestly uses without due authority, or dishonestly causes to be wasted or diverted, any electricity shall on conviction on indictment be liable to imprisonment for a term not exceeding five years. [E]

17 False accounting

(1) Where a person dishonestly, with a view to gain for himself or another or with intent to cause loss to another,—

(a) destroys, defaces, conceals or falsifies any account or any record or document made or required for any accounting purpose; or

(b) in furnishing information for any purpose produces or makes use of any account, or any such record or document as aforesaid, which to his knowledge is or may be misleading, false or deceptive in a material particular;

he shall, on conviction on indictment, be liable to imprisonment for a term not exceeding seven years. [E]

(2) For purposes of this section a person who makes or concurs in making in an account or other document an entry which is or may be misleading, false or deceptive in a material particular, or who omits or concurs in omitting a material particular from an account or other document, is to be treated as falsifying the account or document.

18 Liability of company officers for certain offences by company

(1) Where an offence committed by a body corporate under section 17 of this Act is proved to have been committed with the consent or connivance of any director, manager, secretary or other similar officer of the body corporate or any person who was purporting to act in any such capacity, he as well as the body corporate shall be guilty of that offence, and shall be liable to be proceeded against and punished accordingly.

(2) Where the affairs of a body corporate are managed by its members, this section shall apply in relation to the acts and defaults of a member in connection with his functions of management as if he were a director of the body corporate.

19 False statements by company directors, etc.

(1) Where an officer of a body corporate or unincorporated association (or person purporting to act as such), with intent to deceive members or creditors of the body corporate or association about its affairs, publishes or concurs in publishing a written statement or account which to his knowledge is or may be misleading, false or deceptive in a material particular, he shall on conviction on indictment be liable to imprisonment for a term not exceeding seven years. [E]

(2) For the purposes of this section a person who has entered into a security for the benefit of a body corporate or association is to be treated as a creditor of it.

(3) Where the affairs of a body corporate or association are managed by its members, this section shall apply to any statement which a member publishes or concurs in publishing in connection with his functions or management as if he were an officer of the body corporate or association.

20   Suppression, etc., of documents

(1) A person who dishonestly, with a view to gain for himself or another or with intent to cause loss to another, destroys, defaces or conceals any valuable security, any will or other testamentary document or any original document of or belonging to, or filed or deposited in, any court of justice or any government department shall on conviction on indictment be liable to imprisonment for a term not exceeding seven years. [E]

21   Blackmail

(1) A person is guilty of blackmail if, with a view to gain for himself or another or with intent to cause loss to another, he makes any unwarranted demand with menaces; and for this purpose a demand with menaces is unwarranted unless the person making it does so in the belief—

(a) that he has reasonable grounds for making the demand; and

(b) that the use of the menaces is a proper means of reinforcing the demand. [I]

(2) The nature of the act or omission demanded is immaterial, and it is also immaterial whether the menaces relate to action to be taken by the person making the demand.

22   Handling stolen goods

(1) A person handles stolen goods if (otherwise than in the course of the stealing) knowing or believing them to be stolen goods he dishonestly receives the goods, or dishonestly undertakes or assists in their retention, removal, disposal or realisation by or for the benefit of another person, or if he arranges to do so. [E]

23   Advertising rewards for return of goods stolen or lost

Where any public advertisement of a reward for the return of any goods which have been stolen or lost uses any words to the effect that no questions will be asked, or that the person producing the goods will be safe from apprehension or inquiry, or that any money paid for the purchase of the goods or advances by way of a loan on them will be repaid, the person advertising the reward and any person who prints or publishes the advertisement shall on summary conviction be liable to a fine not exceeding level 3 on the standard scale. [S]

24   Scope of offences relating to stolen goods

(1) The provisions of this Act relating to goods which have been stolen shall apply whether the stealing occurred in England or Wales or elsewhere, and whether it occurred before or after the commencement of this Act, provided that the stealing (if not an offence under this Act) amounted to an offence where and at the time when the goods were stolen; and references to stolen goods shall be construed accordingly.

(2) For purposes of those provisions references to stolen goods shall include, in addition to the goods originally stolen and parts of them (whether in their original state or not),—

(a) any other goods which directly or indirectly represent or have at any time represented the stolen goods in the hands of the thief as being the proceeds of any disposal or realisation of the whole or part of the goods stolen or of goods so representing the stolen goods; and

(b) any other goods which directly or indirectly represent or have at any time represented the stolen goods in the hands of a handler of the stolen goods or any part of them as being the proceeds of any disposal or realisation of the whole or part of the stolen goods handled by him or of goods so representing them.

(3) But no goods shall be regarded as having continued to be stolen goods after they have been restored to the person from whom they were stolen or to other lawful possession or custody, or after

that person and any other person claiming through him have otherwise ceased as regards those goods to have any right to restitution in respect of the theft.

(4) For purposes of the provisions of this Act relating to goods which have been stolen (including subsections (1) to (3) above) goods obtained in England or Wales or elsewhere either by blackmail or, subject to subsection (5) below, by fraud (within the meaning of the Fraud Act 2006), shall be regarded as stolen; and "steal", "theft" and "thief" shall be construed accordingly.

(5) Subsection (1) above applies in relation to goods obtained by fraud as if—

(a) the reference to the commencement of this Act were a reference to the commencement of the Fraud Act 2006, and

(b) the reference to an offence under this Act were a reference to an offence under section 1 of that Act.

24A Dishonestly retaining a wrongful credit

(1) A person is guilty of an offence if—

(a) a wrongful credit has been made to an account kept by him or in respect of which he has any right or interest;

(b) he knows or believes that the credit is wrongful; and

(c) he dishonestly fails to take such steps as are reasonable in the circumstances to secure that the credit is cancelled. [E]

(2) References to a credit are to a credit of an amount of money.

(2A) A credit to an account is wrongful to the extent that it derives from—

(a) theft;

(b) blackmail;

(c) fraud (contrary to section 1 of the Fraud Act 2006); or

(d) stolen goods.

(5) In determining whether a credit to an account is wrongful, it is immaterial (in particular) whether the account is overdrawn before or after the credit is made.

(7) Subsection (8) below applies for purposes of provisions of this Act relating to stolen goods (including subsection (2A) above).

(8) References to stolen goods include money which is dishonestly withdrawn from an account to which a wrongful credit has been made, but only to the extent that the money derives from the credit.

(9) "Account" means an account kept with—

(a) a bank;

(b) a person carrying on a business which falls within subsection (10) below; or

(c) a person falling within any of paragraphs (a) to (j) of the definition of "electronic money issuer" in regulation 2(1) of the Electronic Money Regulations 2011.

(10) A business falls within this subsection if—

(a) in the course of the business money received by way of deposit is lent to others; or

(b) any other activity of the business is financed, wholly or to any material extent, out of the capital of or the interest on money received by way of deposit.

(11) References in subsection (10) above to a deposit must be read with—

(a) section 22 of the Financial Services and Markets Act 2000;

(b) any relevant order under that section; and

(c) Schedule 2 to that Act;

but any restriction on the meaning of deposit which arises from the identity of the person making it is to be disregarded.

(12) For the purposes of subsection (10) above—

(a) all the activities which a person carries on by way of business shall be regarded as a single business carried on by him; and

(b) "money" includes money expressed in a currency other than sterling.

25 Going equipped for stealing, etc.

(1) A person shall be guilty of an offence if, when not at his place of abode, he has with him any article for use in the course of or in connection with any burglary or theft. [E]

(3) Where a person is charged with an offence under this section, proof that he had with him any article made or adapted for use in committing a burglary or theft shall be evidence that he had it with him for such use.

(5) For purposes of this section an offence under section 12 (1) of this Act of taking a conveyance shall be treated as theft.

27 Evidence and procedure on charge of theft or handling stolen goods

(3) Where a person is being proceeded against for handling stolen goods (but not for any offence other than handling stolen goods), then at any stage of the proceedings, if evidence has been given of his having or arranging to have in his possession the goods the subject of the charge, or of his undertaking or assisting in, or arranging to undertake or assist in, their retention, removal, disposal or realisation, the following evidence shall be admissible for the purpose of proving that he knew or believed the goods to be stolen goods:—

    (a) evidence that he has had in his possession, or has undertaken or assisted in the retention, removal, disposal or realisation of, stolen goods from any theft taking place not earlier than twelve months before the offence charged; and

    (b) (provided that seven days' notice in writing has been given to him of the intention to prove the conviction) evidence that he has within the five years preceding the date of the offence charged been convicted of theft or of handling stolen goods.

30 Spouses and civil partners

(2) Subject to subsection (4) below, a person shall have the same right to bring proceedings against that person's wife or husband for any offence (whether under this Act or otherwise) as if they were not married, and a person bringing any such proceedings shall be competent to give evidence for the prosecution at every stage of the proceedings.

(4) Proceedings shall not be instituted against a person for any offence of stealing or doing unlawful damage to property which at the time of the offence belongs to that person's wife or husband or civil partner, or for any attempt, incitement or conspiracy to commit such an offence, unless the proceedings are instituted by or with the consent of the Director of Public Prosecutions:

Provided that—

    (a) this subsection shall not apply to proceedings against a person for an offence—

        (i) if that person is charged with committing the offence jointly with the wife or husband or civil partner;

        (ii) if by virtue of any judicial decree or order (wherever made) that person and the wife or husband are at the time of the offence under no obligation to cohabit; or

        (iii) an order (wherever made) is in force providing for the separation of that person and his or her civil partner.

32 Effect on existing law and construction of references to offences

(1) The following offences are hereby abolished for all purposes not relating to offences committed before the commencement of this Act, that is to say—

    (a) any offence at common law of larceny, robbery, burglary, receiving stolen property, obtaining property by threats, extortion by colour of office or franchise, false accounting by public officers, concealment of treasure trove and, except as regards offences relating to the public revenue, cheating; . . .

34 Interpretation

(1) Sections 4(1) and 5 (1) of this Act shall apply generally for purposes of this Act as they apply for purposes of section 1.

(2) For purposes of this Act—

    (a) "gain" and "loss" are to be construed as extending only to gain or loss in money or other property, but as extending to any such gain or loss whether temporary or permanent; and—

        (i) "gain" includes a gain by keeping what one has, as well as a gain by getting what one has not; and

(ii) "loss" includes a loss by not getting what one might get, as well as a loss by parting with what one has;

(b) "goods" except in so far as the context otherwise requires, includes money and every other description of property except land, and includes things severed from the land by stealing.

(c) "mail bag" and "postal packet" have the meanings given by section 125(1) of the Postal Services Act 2000.

SCHEDULE 1   OFFENCES OF TAKING, ETC. FISH

Taking or destroying fish

2. (1) A person who unlawfully takes or destroys, or attempts to take or destroy, any fish in water which is private property or in which there is any private right of fishery shall on summary conviction be liable to a fine not exceeding level 5 on the standard scale.

Tattooing of Minors Act 1969

1   Prohibition of tattooing of minors

It shall be an offence to tattoo a person under the age of eighteen except when the tattoo is performed for medical reasons by a duly qualified medical practitioner or by a person working under his direction, but it shall be a defence for a person charged to show that at the time the tattoo was performed he had reasonable cause to believe that the person tattooed was of or over the age of eighteen and did in fact so believe. [S]

3   Definition

For the purposes of this Act "tattoo" shall mean the insertion into the skin of any colouring material designed to leave a permanent mark.

Administration of Justice Act 1970

40   Punishment for unlawful harassment of debtors

(1) A person commits an offence if, with the object of coercing another person to pay money claimed from the other as a debt due under a contract, he—

(a) harasses the other with demands for payment which, in respect of their frequency or the manner or occasion of making any such demand, or of any threat or publicity by which any demand is accompanied, are calculated to subject him or members of his family or household to alarm, distress or humiliation;

(b) falsely represents, in relation to the money claimed, that criminal proceedings lie for failure to pay it;

(c) falsely represents himself to be authorised in some official capacity to claim or enforce payment; or

(d) utters a document falsely represented by him to have some official character or purporting to have some official character which he knows it has not. [S]

(2) A person may be guilty of an offence by virtue of subsection 1 (a) above if he concerts with others in the taking of such action as is described in that paragraph, notwithstanding that his own course of conduct does not by itself amount to harassment.

(3) Subsection 1 (a) above does not apply to anything done by a person which is reasonable (and otherwise permissible in law) for the purpose—

(a) of securing the discharge of an obligation due, or believed by him to be due, to himself or to persons for whom he acts, or protecting himself or them from future loss; or

(b) of the enforcement of any liability by legal process.

(3A) Subsection (1) above does not apply to anything done by a person to another in circumstances where what is done is a commercial practice within the meaning of the Consumer Protection from Unfair Trading Regulations 2008 and the other is a consumer in relation to that practice.

Taxes Management Act 1970

106A Offence of fraudulent evasion of income tax

(1) A person commits an offence if that person is knowingly concerned in the fraudulent evasion of income tax by that or any other person.

(4) This section does not apply to things done or omitted before 1st January 2001. [E]

Criminal Damage Act 1971

1 Destroying or damaging property

(1) A person who without lawful excuse destroys or damages any property belonging to another intending to destroy or damage any such property or being reckless as to whether any such property would be destroyed or damaged shall be guilty of an offence. [E]

(2) A person who without lawful excuse destroys or damages any property, whether belonging to himself or another—

(a) intending to destroy or damage any property or being reckless as to whether any property would be destroyed or damaged; and

(b) intending by the destruction or damage to endanger the life of another or being reckless as to whether the life of another would be thereby endangered;

shall be guilty of an offence. [I]

(3) An offence committed under this section by destroying or damaging property by fire shall be charged as arson.

2 Threats to destroy or damage property

A person who without lawful excuse makes to another a threat, intending that that other would fear it would be carried out,—

(a) to destroy or damage any property belonging to that other or a third person; or

(b) to destroy or damage his own property in a way which he knows is likely to endanger the life of that other or a third person;

shall be guilty of an offence. [E]

3 Possessing anything with intent to destroy or damage property

A person who has anything in his custody or under his control intending without lawful excuse to use it or cause or permit another to use it—

(a) to destroy or damage any property belonging to some other person; or

(b) to destroy or damage his own or the user's property in a way which he knows is likely to endanger the life of some other person;

shall be guilty of an offence. [E]

4 Punishment of offences

(1) A person guilty of arson under section 1 above or of an offence under section 1(2) above (whether arson or not) shall on conviction on indictment be liable to imprisonment for life.

(2) A person guilty of any other offence under this Act shall on conviction on indictment be liable to imprisonment for a term not exceeding ten years.

5 "Without lawful excuse"

(1) This section applies to any offence under section 1(1) above and any offence under section 2 or 3 above other than one involving a threat by the person charged to destroy or damage property in a way which he knows is likely to endanger the life of another or involving an intent by the person charged to use or cause or permit the use of something in his custody or under his control so to destroy or damage property.

(2) A person charged with an offence to which this section applies shall whether or not he would be treated for the purposes of this Act as having a lawful excuse apart from this subsection, be treated for those purposes as having a lawful excuse—

(a) if at the time of the act or acts alleged to constitute the offence he believed that the person or persons whom he believed to be entitled to consent to the destruction of or damage to the property in question had so consented, or would have so consented to it if he or they had known of the destruction or damage and its circumstances; or

(b) if he destroyed or damaged or threatened to destroy or damage the property in question or, in the case of a charge of an offence under section 3 above, intended to use or cause or permit the use of something to destroy or damage it, in order to protect property belonging to himself or another or a right or interest in property which was or which he believed to be vested in himself or another, and at the time of the act or acts alleged to constitute the offence he believed—

(i) that the property, right or interest was in immediate need of protection; and

(ii) that the means of protection adopted or proposed to be adopted were or would be reasonable having regard to all the circumstances.

(3) For the purposes of this section it is immaterial whether a belief is justified or not if it is honestly held.

(4) For the purposes of subsection (2) above a right or interest in property includes any right or privilege in or over land, whether created by grant, licence or otherwise.

(5) This section shall not be construed as casting doubt on any defence recognised by law as a defence to criminal charges.

10 Interpretation

(1) In this Act "property" means property of a tangible nature, whether real or personal, including money and—

(a) including wild creatures which have been tamed or are ordinarily kept in captivity, and any other wild creatures or their carcasses if, but only if, they have been reduced into possession which has not been lost or abandoned or are in the course of being reduced into possession; but

(b) not including mushrooms growing wild on any land or flowers, fruit or foliage of a plant growing wild on any land.

For the purposes of this subsection "mushroom" includes any fungus and "plant" includes any shrub or tree.

(2) Property shall be treated for the purposes of this Act as belonging to any person—

(a) having the custody or control of it;

(b) having in it any proprietary right or interest (not being an equitable interest arising only from an agreement to transfer or grant an interest); or

(c) having a charge on it.

(3) Where property is subject to a trust, the persons to whom it belongs shall be so treated as including any person having a right to enforce the trust.

(4) Property of a corporation sole shall be so treated as belonging to the corporation not-withstanding a vacancy in the corporation.

(5) For the purposes of this Act a modification of the contents of a computer shall not be regarded as damaging any computer or computer storage medium unless its effect on that computer or computer storage medium impairs its physical condition.

Immigration Act 1971

24   Illegal entry and similar offences

(1) A person who is not a British citizen shall be guilty of an offence . . . in any of the following cases:—

   (a) if contrary to this Act he knowingly enters the United Kingdom in breach of a deportation order or without leave;

   (b) if, having only a limited leave to enter or remain in the United Kingdom, he knowingly either—

      (i)   remains beyond the time limited by the leave; or

      (ii) fails to observe a condition of the leave;

   (c) if, having lawfully entered the United Kingdom without leave by virtue of section 8(1) above, he remains without leave beyond the time allowed by section 8(1);

   (d) if, without reasonable excuse, he fails to comply with any requirement imposed on him under Schedule 2 to this Act to report to a medical officer of health, or to attend, or submit to a test or examination, as required by such an officer;

   (f) if he disembarks in the United Kingdom from a ship or aircraft after being placed on board under Schedule 2 or 3 to this Act with a view to his removal from the United Kingdom;

   (g) if he embarks in contravention of a restriction imposed by or under an Order in Council under section 3(7) of this Act; [S]

   (h) if the person is on immigration bail within the meaning of Schedule 10 to the Immigration Act 2016 and, without reasonable excuse, the person breaches a bail condition within the meaning of that Schedule.

(1A) A person commits an offence under subsection (1)(b)(i) above on the day when he first knows that the time limited by his leave has expired and continues to commit it throughout any period during which he is in the United Kingdom thereafter; but a person shall not be prosecuted under that provision more than once in respect of the same limited leave.

(4) In proceedings for an offence against subsection (1)(a) above of entering the United Kingdom without leave,—

   (a) any stamp purporting to have been imprinted on a passport or other travel document by an immigration officer on a particular date for the purpose of giving leave shall be presumed to have been duly so imprinted, unless the contrary is proved;

   (b) proof that a person had leave to enter the United Kingdom shall lie on the defence if, but only if, he is shown to have entered within six months before the date when the proceedings were commenced.

24A   Deception

(1) A person who is not a British citizen is guilty of an offence if, by means which include deception by him—

   (a) he obtains or seeks to obtain leave to enter or remain in the United Kingdom; or

   (b) he secures or seeks to secure the avoidance, postponement or revocation of enforcement action against him. [E]

(2) "Enforcement action", in relation to a person, means—

   (a) the giving of directions for his removal from the United Kingdom ("directions") under Schedule 2 to this Act or section 10 of the Immigration and Asylum Act 1999;

   (b) the making of a deportation order against him under section 5 of this Act; or

   (c) his removal from the United Kingdom in consequence of directions or a deportation order.

24B   Illegal working

(1) A person ("P") who is subject to immigration control commits an offence if—

   (a) P works at a time when P is disqualified from working by reason of P's immigration status, and

(b) at that time P knows or has reasonable cause to believe that P is disqualified from working by reason of P's immigration status.

(2) For the purposes of subsection (1) a person is disqualified from working by reason of the person's immigration status if—

(a) the person has not been granted leave to enter or remain in the United Kingdom, or

(b) the person's leave to enter or remain in the United Kingdom—

(i) is invalid,

(ii) has ceased to have effect (whether by reason of curtailment, revocation, cancellation, passage of time or otherwise), or

(iii) is subject to a condition preventing the person from doing work of that kind.

(8) The reference in subsection (1) to a person who is subject to immigration control is to a person who under this Act requires leave to enter or remain in the United Kingdom.

(9) Where a person is on immigration bail within the meaning of Part 1 of Schedule 10 to the Immigration Act 2016—

(a) the person is to be treated for the purposes of subsection (2) as if the person had been granted leave to enter the United Kingdom, but

(b) any condition as to the person's work in the United Kingdom to which the person's immigration bail is subject is to be treated for those purposes as a condition of leave.

(10) The reference in subsection (1) to a person working is to that person working—

(a) under a contract of employment,

(b) under a contract of apprenticeship,

(c) under a contract personally to do work,

(d) under or for the purposes of a contract for services,

(e) for a purpose related to a contract to sell goods,

(f) as a constable,

(g) in the course of Crown employment,

(h) as a relevant member of the House of Commons staff, or

(i) as a relevant member of the House of Lords staff.

(11) In subsection (10)—

"contract to sell goods" means a contract by which a person acting in the course of a trade, business, craft or profession transfers or agrees to transfer the property in goods to another person (and for this purpose "goods" means any tangible moveable items);

"Crown employment"—

(a) in relation to England and Wales and Scotland, has the meaning given by section 191(3) of the Employment Rights Act 1996;

"relevant member of the House of Commons staff" has the meaning given by section 195(5) of the Employment Rights Act 1996;

"relevant member of the House of Lords staff" has the meaning given by section 194(6) of the Employment Rights Act 1996.

(12) Subsection (1) does not apply to—

(a) service as a member of the naval, military or air forces of the Crown, or

(b) employment by an association established for the purposes of Part 11 of the Reserve Forces Act 1996.

(13) In this section "contract" means a contract whether express or implied and, if express, whether oral or in writing.

25 Assisting unlawful immigration to member State or the United Kingdom

(1) A person commits an offence if he—

(a) does an act which facilitates the commission of a breach or attempted breach of immigration law by an individual who is not a national of the United Kingdom,

(b) knows or has reasonable cause for believing that the act facilitates the commission of a breach or attempted breach of immigration law by the individual, and

(c) knows or has reasonable cause for believing that the individual is not a national of the United Kingdom. [E]

(2) In subsection (1) "immigration law" means a law which has effect in a member State or the United Kingdom and which controls, in respect of some or all persons who are not nationals of the State or, as the case may be, of the United Kingdom, entitlement to—

(a) enter the State or the United Kingdom,

(b) transit across the State or the United Kingdom, or

(c) be in the State or the United Kingdom.

(2A) In subsections (1) and (2), "national of the United Kingdom" means—

(a) a British citizen;

(b) a person who is a British subject by virtue of Part 4 of the British Nationality Act 1981 and who has the right of abode in the United Kingdom; or

(c) a person who is a British overseas territories citizen by virtue of a connection with Gibraltar.

(3) A document issued by the government of a member State certifying a matter of law in that State—

(a) shall be admissible in proceedings for an offence under this section, and

(b) shall be conclusive as to the matter certified.

(4) Subsection (1) applies to things done whether inside or outside the United Kingdom.

(7) In this section—

(a) a reference to a member State includes a reference to Norway or Iceland.

25A   Helping asylum-seeker to enter United Kingdom

(1) A person commits an offence if—

(a) he knowingly and for gain facilitates the arrival or the attempted arrival in, or the entry or the attempted entry into, the United Kingdom of an individual, and

(b) he knows or has reasonable cause to believe that the individual is an asylum-seeker. [E]

(2) In this section "asylum-seeker" means a person who intends to claim that to remove him from or require him to leave the United Kingdom would be contrary to the United Kingdom's obligations under—

(a) the Refugee Convention (within the meaning given by section 167(1) of the Immigration and Asylum Act 1999 (interpretation)), or

(b) the Human Rights Convention (within the meaning given by that section).

(3) Subsection (1) does not apply to anything done by a person acting on behalf of an organisation which—

(a) aims to assist asylum-seekers, and

(b) does not charge for its services.

(4) Subsections (4) to (6) of section 25 apply for the purpose of the offence in subsection (1) of this section as they apply for the purpose of the offence in subsection (1) of that section.

25B   Assisting entry to United Kingdom in breach of deportation order

(1) A person commits an offence if he—

(a) does an act which facilitates a breach or attempted breach of a deportation order in force against an individual who is a citizen of the European Union, and

(b) knows or has reasonable cause for believing that the act facilitates a breach or attempted breach of the deportation order. [E]

(2) Subsection (3) applies where the Secretary of State has made an order excluding an individual from the United Kingdom on the grounds of public policy, public security or public health, other than a temporary exclusion order.

(3) A person commits an offence if he—

(a) does an act which assists the individual to arrive in, enter or remain, or attempt to arrive in, enter or remain, in the United Kingdom,

(b) knows or has reasonable cause for believing that the act assists the individual to arrive in, enter or remain, or attempt to arrive in, enter or remain, in the United Kingdom, and

(c) knows or has reasonable cause for believing that the Secretary of State has made an order excluding the individual from the United Kingdom on the grounds of public policy, public security or public health. [E]

(4) Subsections (4) and (6) of section 25 apply for the purpose of an offence under this section as they apply for the purpose of an offence under that section.

(5) In this section a "temporary exclusion order" means an order under section 2 of the Counter-Terrorism and Security Act 2015.

Misuse of Drugs Act 1971

2   Controlled drugs and their classification for purposes of this Act

(1) In this Act—
- (a) the expression "controlled drug" means any substance or product for the time being specified—
  - (i)   in Part I, II or III of Schedule 2, or
  - (ii) in a temporary class drug order as a drug subject to temporary control (but this is subject to section 2A(6));
- (b) the expressions "Class A drug", "Class B drug", and "Class C drug" mean any of the substances and products for the time being specified respectively in Part I, Part II and Part III of that Schedule; and
- (c) the expression "temporary class drug" means any substance or product which is for the time being a controlled drug by virtue of a temporary class drug order;

and the provisions of Part IV of that Schedule shall have effect with respect to the meanings of expressions used in that Schedule.

3   Restriction of importation and exportation of controlled drugs

(1) Subject to subsection (2) below—
- (a) the importation of a controlled drug; and
- (b) the exportation of a controlled drug,

are hereby prohibited.

(2) Subsection (1) above does not apply—
- (a) to the importation or exportation of a controlled drug which is for the time being excepted from paragraph (a) or, as the case may be, paragraph (b) of subsection (1) above by regulations under section 7 of this Act or by provision made in a temporary class drug order by virtue of section 7A; or
- (b) to the importation or exportation of a controlled drug under and in accordance with the terms of a licence issued by the Secretary of State and in compliance with any conditions attached thereto.

4   Restriction of production and supply of controlled drugs

(1) Subject to any regulations under section 7 of this Act, or any provision made in a temporary class drug order by virtue of section 7A, for the time being in force, it shall not be lawful for a person—
- (a) to produce a controlled drug; or
- (b) to supply or offer to supply a controlled drug to another.

(2) Subject to section 28 of this Act, it is an offence for a person—
- (a) to produce a controlled drug in contravention of subsection (1) above; or
- (b) to be concerned in the production of such a drug in contravention of that subsection by another. [E]

(3) Subject to section 28 of this Act, it is an offence for a person—
- (a) to supply or offer to supply a controlled drug to another in contravention of subsection (1) above; or
- (b) to be concerned in the supplying of such a drug to another in contravention of that subsection; or
- (c) to be concerned in the making to another in contravention of that subsection of an offer to supply such a drug. [E]

4A   Aggravation of offence of supply of controlled drug

(8) In this section—

"school premises" means land used for the purposes of a school excluding any land occupied solely as a dwelling by a person employed at the school; and

"school" has the same meaning—

      (a) in England and Wales, as in section 4 of the Education Act 1996; . . .

5   Restriction of possession of controlled drugs

(1) Subject to any regulations under section 7 of this Act for the time being in force, it shall not be lawful for a person to have a controlled drug in his possession.

(2) Subject to section 28 of this Act and to subsection (4) below, it is an offence for a person to have a controlled drug in his possession in contravention of subsection (1) above. [E]

(2A) Subsections (1) and (2) do not apply in relation to a temporary class drug.

(3) Subject to section 28 of this Act, it is an offence for a person to have a controlled drug in his possession, whether lawfully or not, with intent to supply it to another in contravention of section 4(1) of this Act. [E]

(4) In any proceedings for an offence under subsection (2) above in which it is proved that the accused had a controlled drug in his possession, it shall be a defence for him to prove—

      (a) that, knowing or suspecting it to be a controlled drug, he took possession of it for the purpose of preventing another from committing or continuing to commit an offence in connection with that drug and that as soon as possible after taking possession of it he took all such steps as were reasonably open to him to destroy the drug or to deliver it into the custody of a person lawfully entitled to take custody of it; or

      (b) that, knowing or suspecting it to be a controlled drug, he took possession of it for the purpose of delivering it into the custody of a person lawfully entitled to take custody of it and that as soon as possible after taking possession of it he took all such steps as were reasonably open to him to deliver it into the custody of such a person.

(6) Nothing in subsection (4) above shall prejudice any defence which is open to a person charged with an offence under this section to raise apart from that subsection.

6   Restriction of cultivation of cannabis plants

(1) Subject to any regulations under section 7 of this Act for the time being in force, it shall not be lawful for a person to cultivate any plant of the genus Cannabis.

(2) Subject to section 28 of this Act, it is an offence to cultivate any such plant in contravention of subsection (1) above. [E]

7   Authorisation of activities otherwise unlawful under foregoing provisions

(1) The Secretary of State may by regulations—

      (a) except from section 3(1)(a) or (b), 4(1)(a) or (b) or 5(1) of this Act such controlled drugs as may be specified in the regulations; and

      (b) make such other provision as he thinks fit for the purpose of making it lawful for persons to do things which under any of the following provisions of this Act, that is to say sections 4(1), 5(1) and 6(1), it would otherwise be unlawful for them to do.

(2) Without prejudice to the generality of paragraph (b) of subsection (1) above, regulations under that subsection authorising the doing of any such thing as is mentioned in that paragraph may in particular provide for the doing of that thing to be lawful—

      (a) if it is done under and in accordance with the terms of a licence or other authority issued by the Secretary of State and in compliance with any conditions attached thereto; or

      (b) if it is done in compliance with such conditions as may be prescribed.

(3) Subject to subsection (4) below, the Secretary of State shall so exercise his power to make regulations under subsection (1) above as to secure—

      (a) that it is not unlawful under section 4(1) of this Act for a doctor, dentist, veterinary practitioner or veterinary surgeon, acting in his capacity as such, to prescribe, administer, manufacture, compound or supply a controlled drug, or for a pharmacist or a person lawfully conducting a retail pharmacy business, acting in either case in his capacity as such, to manufacture, compound or supply a controlled drug; and

(b) that it is not unlawful under section 5(1) of this Act for a doctor, dentist, veterinary practitioner, veterinary surgeon, pharmacist or person lawfully conducting a retail pharmacy business to have a controlled drug in his possession for the purpose of acting in his capacity as such.

(4) If in the case of any controlled drug the Secretary of State is of the opinion that it is in the public interest—

(a) for production, supply and possession of that drug to be either wholly unlawful or unlawful except for purposes of research or other special purposes; or

(b) for it to be unlawful for practitioners, pharmacists and persons lawfully conducting retail pharmacy business to do in relation to that drug any of the things mentioned in subsection (3) above except under a licence or other authority issued by the Secretary of State,

he may by order designate that drug as a drug to which this subsection applies; and while there is in force an order under this subsection designating a controlled drug as one to which this subsection applies subsection (3) above shall not apply as regards that drug.

(8) References in this section to a person's "doing" things include references to his having things in his possession.

8 Occupiers, etc., of premises to be punishable for permitting certain activities to take place there

A person commits an offence if, being the occupier or concerned in the management of any premises, he knowingly permits or suffers any of the following activities to take place on those premises, that is to say—

(a) producing or attempting to produce a controlled drug in contravention of section 4 (1) of this Act;

(b) supplying or attempting to supply a controlled drug to another in contravention of section 4(1) of this Act, or offering to supply a controlled drug to another in contravention of section 4(1);

(c) preparing opium for smoking;

(d) smoking cannabis, cannabis resin or prepared opium.

9 Prohibition of certain activities, etc., relating to opium

Subject to section 28 of this Act, it is an offence for a person—

(a) to smoke or otherwise use prepared opium; or

(b) to frequent a place used for the purpose of opium smoking; or

(c) to have in his possession

(i) any pipes or other utensils made or adapted for use in connection with the smoking of opium, being pipes or utensils which have been used by him or with his knowledge and permission in that connection or which he intends to use or permit others to use in that connection; or

(ii) any utensils which have been used by him or with his knowledge and permission in connection with the preparation of opium for smoking. [E]

9A Prohibition of supply, etc., of articles for administering or preparing controlled drugs

(1) A person who supplies or offers to supply any article which may be used or adapted to be used (whether by itself or in combination with another article or other articles) in the administration by any person of a controlled drug to himself or another, believing that the article (or the article as adapted) is to be so used in circumstances where the administration is unlawful, is guilty of an offence. [S]

(2) It is not an offence under subsection (1) above to supply or offer to supply a hypodermic syringe, or any part of one.

(3) A person who supplies or offers to supply any article which may be used to prepare a controlled drug for administration by any person to himself or another believing that the article is to be so used in circumstances where the administration is unlawful is guilty of an offence. [S]

(4) For the purposes of this section, any administration of a controlled drug is unlawful except—

(a) the administration by any person of a controlled drug to another in circumstances where the administration of the drug is not unlawful under section 4(1) of this Act,

(b) the administration by any person of a controlled drug, other than a temporary class drug, to himself in circumstances where having the controlled drug in his possession is not unlawful under section 5(1) of this Act, or

(c) the administration by any person of a temporary class drug to himself in circumstances where having the drug in his possession is to be treated as excepted possession for the purposes of this Act (see section 7A(2)(c)).

(5) In this section, references to administration by any person of a controlled drug to himself include a reference to his administering it to himself with the assistance of another.

19   Attempts, etc., to commit offences

It is an offence for a person to incite another to commit an offence under any other provision of this Act. [E] and [S]

20   Assisting in or inducing commission outside United Kingdom of offence punishable under a corresponding law

A person commits an offence if in the United Kingdom he assists in or induces the commission in any place outside the United Kingdom of an offence punishable under the provisions of a corresponding law in force in that place. [E]

28   Proof of lack of knowledge, etc., to be a defence in proceedings for certain offences

(1) This section applies to offences under any of the following provisions of this Act; that is to say section 4(2) and (3), section 5(2) and (3), section 6(2) and section 9.

(2) Subject to subsection (3) below, in any proceedings for an offence to which this section applies it shall be a defence for the accused to prove that he neither knew of nor suspected nor had reason to suspect the existence of some fact alleged by the prosecution which is necessary for the prosecution to prove if he is to be convicted of the offence charged.

(3) Where in any proceedings for an offence to which this section applies it is necessary, if the accused is to be convicted of the offence charged, for the prosecution to prove that some substance or product involved in the alleged offence was the controlled drug which the prosecution alleges it to have been, and it is proved that the substance or product in question was that controlled drug, the accused—

(a) shall not be acquitted of the offence charged by reason only of proving that he neither knew or suspected nor had reason to suspect that the substance or product in question was the particular controlled drug alleged; but

(b) shall be acquitted thereof—

(i) if he proves that he neither believed nor suspected nor had reason to suspect that the substance or product in question was a controlled drug; or

(ii) if he proves that he believed the substance or product in question to be a controlled drug, or a controlled drug of a description, such that, if it had in fact been that controlled drug or a controlled drug of that description, he would not at the material time have been committing any offence to which this section applies.

(4) Nothing in this section shall prejudice any defence which it is open to a person charged with an offence to which this section applies to raise apart from this section.

36 Meaning of "corresponding law", and evidence of certain matters by certificate

(1) In this Act the expression "corresponding law" means a law stated in a certificate purporting to be issued by or on behalf of the government of a country outside the United Kingdom to be a law providing for the control and regulation in that country of the production, supply, use, export and import of drugs and other substances in accordance with the provisions of the Single Convention on Narcotic Drugs signed at New York on 30th March 1961 or a law providing for the control and regulation in that country of the production, supply, use, export and import of dangerous or otherwise harmful drugs in pursuance of any treaty, convention or other agreement or arrangement to which the government of that country and Her Majesty's Government in the United Kingdom are for the time being parties.

37 Interpretation

(1) In this Act, except in so far as the context otherwise requires, the following expressions have the meanings hereby assigned to them respectively, that is to say:—

"produce", where the reference is to producing a controlled drug, means producing it by manufacture, cultivation or any other method and "production" has a corresponding meaning;

"supplying" includes distributing; . . .

(2) References in this Act to misusing a drug are references to misusing it by taking it; and the reference in the foregoing provision to the taking of a drug is a reference to the taking of it by a human being by way of any form of self-administration, whether or not involving assistance by another.

(3) For the purposes of this Act the things which a person has in his possession shall be taken to include any thing subject to his control which is in the custody of another.

Unsolicited Goods and Services Act 1971

4 Unsolicited publications

(1) A person shall be guilty of an offence if he sends or causes to be sent to another person any book, magazine or leaflet (or advertising material for any such publication) which he knows or ought reasonably to know is unsolicited and which describes or illustrates human sexual techniques. [S]

6 Interpretation

(1) In this Act, unless the context or subject matter otherwise requires,—

"send" includes deliver and "sender" shall be construed accordingly;

"unsolicited" means, in relation to goods sent to any person, that they are sent without any prior request made by him or on his behalf.

Health and Safety at Work etc. Act 1974

2 General duties of employers to their employees

(1) It shall be the duty of every employer to ensure, so far as is reasonably practicable, the health, safety and welfare at work of all his employees.

(2) Without prejudice to the generality of an employer's duty under the preceding subsection, the matters to which that duty extends include in particular—

    (a) the provision and maintenance of plant and systems of work that are, so far as is reasonably practicable, safe and without risks to health;

(b) arrangements for ensuring, so far as is reasonably practicable, safety and absence of risks to health in connection with the use, handling, storage and transport of articles and substances;

(c) the provision of such information, instruction, training and supervision as is necessary to ensure, so far as is reasonably practicable, the health and safety at work of his employees;

(d) so far as is reasonably practicable as regards any place of work under the employer's control, the maintenance of it in a condition that is safe and without risks to health and the provision and maintenance of means of access to and egress from it that are safe and without such risks;

(e) the provision and maintenance of a working environment for his employees that is, so far as is reasonably practicable, safe, without risks to health, and adequate as regards facilities and arrangements for their welfare at work.

(3) Except in such cases as may be prescribed, it shall be the duty of every employer to prepare and as often as may be appropriate revise a written statement of his general policy with respect to the health and safety at work of his employees and the organisation and arrangements for the time being in force for carrying out that policy, and to bring the statement and any revision of it to the notice of all of his employees.

3   General duties of employers and self-employed to persons other than their employees

(1) It shall be the duty of every employer to conduct his undertaking in such a way as to ensure, so far is reasonably practicable, that persons not in his employment who may be affected thereby are not thereby exposed to risks to their health or safety.

(2) It shall be the duty of every self-employed person who conducts an undertaking of a prescribed description to conduct the undertaking in such a way as to ensure, so far as is reasonably practicable, that he and other persons (not being his employees) who may be affected thereby are not thereby exposed to risks to their health or safety.

(2A) A description of undertaking included in regulations under subsection (2) may be framed by reference to—

(a) the type of activities carried out by the undertaking, where those activities are carried out or any other feature of the undertaking;

(b) whether persons who may be affected by the conduct of the undertaking, other than the self-employed person (or his employees), may thereby be exposed to risks to their health or safety.

(3) In such cases as may be prescribed, it shall be the duty of every employer and every self-employed person, in the prescribed circumstances and in the prescribed manner, to give to persons (not being his employees) who may be affected by the way in which he conducts his undertaking the prescribed information about such aspects of the way in which he conducts his undertaking as might affect their health or safety.

4   General duties of persons concerned with premises to persons other than their employees

(1) This section has effect for imposing on persons duties in relation to those who—

(a) are not their employees; but (b) use non-domestic premises made available to them as a place of work or as a place where they may use plant or substances provided for their use there,

and applies to premises so made available and other non-domestic premises used in connection with them.

(2) It shall be the duty of each person who has, to any extent, control of premises to which this section applies or of the means of access thereto or egress therefrom or of any plant or substance in such premises to take such measures as it is reasonable for a person in his position to take to ensure, so far as is reasonably practicable, that the premises, all means of access thereto or egress therefrom

available for use by persons using the premises, and any plant or substance in the premises or, as the case may be, provided for use there, is or are safe and without risks to health.

(3) Where a person has, by virtue of any contract or tenancy, an obligation of any extent in relation to—

(a) the maintenance or repair of any premises to which this section applies or any means of access thereto or egress therefrom; or

(b) the safety of or the absence of risks to health arising from plant or substances in any such premises;

that person shall be treated, for the purposes of subsection (2) above, as being a person who has control of the matters to which his obligation extends.

(4) Any reference in this section to a person having control of any premises or matter is a reference to a person having control of the premises or matter in connection with the carrying on by him of a trade, business or other undertaking (whether for profit or not).

6   General duties of manufacturers etc., as regards articles and substances for use at work

(1) It shall be the duty of any person who designs, manufactures, imports or supplies any article for use at work or any article of fairground equipment—

(a) to ensure, so far as is reasonably practicable, that the article is so designed and constructed that it will be safe and without risks to health at all times when it is being set, used, cleaned or maintained by a person at work;

(b) to carry out or arrange for the carrying out of such testing and examination as may be necessary for the performance of the duty imposed on him by the preceding paragraph;

(c) to take such steps as are necessary to secure that persons supplied by that person with the article are provided with adequate information about the use for which the article is designed or has been tested and about any conditions necessary to ensure that it will be safe and without risks to health at all such times as are mentioned in paragraph (a) above and when it is being dismantled or disposed of; and

(d) to take such steps as are necessary to secure, so far as is reasonably practicable, that persons so supplied are provided with all such revisions of information provided to them by virtue of the preceding paragraph as are necessary by reason of its becoming known that anything gives rise to a serious risk to health and safety.

(1A) It shall be the duty of any person who designs, manufactures, imports or supplies any article of fairground equipment—

(a) to ensure, so far as is reasonably practicable, that the article is so designed and constructed that it will be safe and without risks to health at all times when it is being used for or in connection with the entertainment of members of the public;

(b) to carry out or arrange for the carrying out of such testing and examination as may be necessary for the performance of the duty imposed on him by the preceding paragraph;

(c) to take such steps as are necessary to secure that persons supplied by that person with the article are provided with adequate information about the use for which the article is designed or has been tested and about any conditions necessary to ensure that it will be safe and without risks to health at all times when it is being used for or in connection with the entertainment of members of the public; and

(d) to take such steps as are necessary to secure, so far as is reasonably practicable, that persons so supplied are provided with all such revisions of information provided to them by virtue of the preceding paragraph as are necessary by reason of its becoming known that anything gives rise to a serious risk to health or safety.

(2) It shall be the duty of any person who undertakes the design or manufacture of any article for use at work or of any article of fairground equipment to carry out or arrange for the carrying out of any necessary research with a view to the discovery and, so far as is reasonably practicable, the elimination or minimisation of any risks to health or safety to which the design or article may give rise.

(3) It shall be the duty of any person who erects or installs any article for use at work in any premises where that article is to be used by persons at work or who erects or installs any article of fairground equipment to ensure, so far as is reasonably practicable, that nothing about the way in which the article is erected or installed makes it unsafe or a risk to health at any such time as is mentioned in paragraph (a) of subsection (1) or, as the case may be, in paragraph (a) of subsection (1) or (1A).

(4) It shall be the duty of any person who manufactures, imports or supplies any substance—

    (a) to ensure, so far as is reasonably practicable, that the substance will be safe and without risks to health at all times when it is being used, handled, processed, stored or transported by a person at work or in premises to which section 4 above applies;

    (b) to carry out or arrange for the carrying out of such testing and examination as may be necessary for the performance of the duty imposed on him by the preceding paragraph;

    (c) to take such steps as are necessary to secure that persons supplied by that person with the substance are provided with adequate information about any risks to health or safety to which the inherent properties of the substance may give rise, about the results of any relevant tests which have been carried out on or in connection with the substance and about any conditions necessary to ensure that the substance will be safe and without risks to health at all such times as are mentioned in paragraph (a) above and when the substance is being disposed of; and

    (d) to take such steps as are necessary to secure, so far as is reasonably practicable, that persons so supplied are provided with all such revisions of information provided to them by virtue of the preceding paragraph as are necessary by reason of its becoming known that anything gives rise to a serious risk to health or safety.

(5) It shall be the duty of any person who undertakes the manufacture of any substance to carry out or arrange for the carrying out of any necessary research with a view to the discovery and, so far as is reasonable practicable, the elimination or minimisation of any risks to health or safety to which the substance may give rise at all such times as are mentioned in paragraph (a) of subsection (4) above.

(6) Nothing in the preceding provisions of this section shall be taken to require a person to repeat any testing, examination or research which has been carried out otherwise than by him or at his instance, in so far as it is reasonable for him to rely on the results thereof for the purposes of those provisions.

(7) Any duty imposed on any person by any of the preceding provisions of this section shall extend only to things done in the course of a trade, business or other undertaking carried on by him (whether for profit or not) and to matters within his control.

(8) Where a person designs, manufactures, imports or supplies an article for use at work or an article of fairground equipment and does so for or to another on the basis of a written undertaking by that other to take specified steps sufficient to ensure, so far as is reasonably practicable, that the article will be safe and without risks to health at all such times as are mentioned in paragraph (a) of subsection (1) or, as the case may be, in paragraph (a) of subsection (1) or (1A) above, the undertaking shall have the effect of relieving the first-mentioned person from the duty imposed by virtue of that paragraph to such extent as is reasonable having regard to the terms of the undertaking.

(8A) Nothing in subsection (7) or (8) above shall relieve any person who imports any article or substance from any duty in respect of anything which—

    (a) in the case of an article designed outside the United Kingdom, was done by and in the course of any trade, profession or other undertaking carried on by, or was within the control of, the person who designed the article; or

    (b) in the case of an article or substance manufactured outside the United Kingdom, was done by and in the course of any trade, profession or other undertaking carried on by, or was within the control of, the person who manufactured the article or substance.

(9) Where a person ("the ostensible supplier") supplies any article or substance to another ("the customer") under a hire-purchase agreement, conditional sale agreement or credit-sale agreement, and the ostensible supplier—

    (a) carries on the business of financing the acquisition of goods by others by means of such agreements; and

    (b) in the course of that business acquired his interest in the article or substance supplied to the customer as a means of financing its acquisition by the customer from a third person ("the effective supplier"),

the effective supplier and not the ostensible supplier shall be treated for the purposes of this section as supplying the article or substance to the customer, and any duty imposed by the preceding provisions of this section on suppliers shall accordingly fall on the effective supplier and not on the ostensible supplier.

    (10) For the purposes of this section an absence of safety or a risk to health shall be disregarded in so far as the case in or in relation to which it would arise is shown to be one the occurrence of which could not reasonably be foreseen; and in determining whether any duty imposed by virtue of paragraph (a) of subsection (1), (1A) or (4) above has been performed regard shall be had to any relevant information or advice which has been provided to any person by the person by whom the article has been designed, manufactured, imported or supplied or, as the case may be, by the person by whom the substance has been manufactured, imported or supplied.

7   General duties of employees at work

It shall be the duty of every employee while at work—

    (a) to take reasonable care for the health and safety of himself and of other persons who may be affected by his acts or omissions at work; and

    (b) as regards any duty or requirement imposed on his employer or any other person by or under any of the relevant statutory provisions, to co-operate with him so far as is necessary to enable that duty or requirement to be performed or complied with.

8   Duty not to interfere with or misuse things provided pursuant to certain provisions

No person shall intentionally or recklessly interfere with or misuse anything provided in the interests of health, safety or welfare in pursuance of any of the relevant statutory provisions.

33   Offences

    (1) It is an offence for a person—

    (a) to fail to discharge a duty to which he is subject by virtue of section 2 to 7;

    (b) to contravene section 8 or 9;

    (c) to contravene any health and safety regulations or any requirement or prohibition imposed under any such regulations (including any requirement or prohibition to which he is subject by virtue of the terms of or any condition or restriction attached to any licence, approval, exemption or other authority issued, given or granted under the regulations);

    (k) to make a statement which he knows to be false or recklessly to make a statement which is false where the statement is made—

        (i) in purported compliance with a requirement to furnish any information imposed by or under any of the relevant statutory provisions; or

        (ii) for the purpose of obtaining the issue of a document under any of the relevant statutory provisions to himself or another person;

    (l) intentionally to make a false entry in any register, book, notice or other document required by or under any of the relevant statutory provisions to be kept, served or given or, with intent to deceive, to make use of any such entry which he knows to be false;

    (m) with intent to deceive, to use a document issued or authorised to be issued under any of the relevant statutory provisions or required for any purpose there under or to make or have in his possession a document so closely resembling any such document as to be calculated to deceive; [E]

(n) falsely to pretend to be an inspector; [S]

(o) to fail to comply with an order made by a court under section 42.

(2) Schedule 3A (which specifies the mode of trial and maximum penalty applicable to offences under this section and the existing statutory provisions) has effect.

(3) Schedule 3A is subject to any provision made by virtue of section 15(6)(c) or (d).

36   Offences due to fault of other person

(1) Where the commission by any person of an offence under any of the relevant statutory provisions is due to the act or default of some other person, that other person shall be guilty of the offence, and a person may be charged with and convicted of the offence by virtue of this subsection whether or not proceedings are taken against the first-mentioned person. [E]

(2) Where there would be or have been the commission of an offence under section 33 by the Crown but for the circumstance that that section does not bind the Crown, and that fact is due to the act or default of a person other than the Crown, that person shall be guilty of the offence which, but for that circumstance, the Crown would be committing or would have committed, and may be charged with and convicted of that offence accordingly. [E]

40   Onus of proving limits of what is practicable etc.

In any proceedings for an offence under any of the relevant statutory provisions consisting of a failure to comply with a duty or requirement to do something so far as is practicable or so far as is reasonably practicable, or to use the best means to do something, it shall be for the accused to prove (as the case may be) that it was not practicable or not reasonably practicable to do more than was in fact done to satisfy the duty or requirement, or that there was no better practicable means than was in fact used to satisfy the duty or requirement.

Juries Act 1974

20   Offences: failure to attend, serving while disqualified etc.

(1) Subject to the provisions of subsections (2) to (4) below—

(a) if a person duly summoned under this Act fails to attend (on the first or on any subsequent day on which he is required to attend by the summons or by the appropriate officer) in compliance with the summons, or

(b) if a person, after attending in pursuance of a summons, is not available when called on to serve as a juror, or is unfit for service by reason of drink or drugs,

he shall be liable to a fine not exceeding level 4 on the standard scale. [E]

(2) An offence under subsection (1) above shall be punishable either on summary conviction or as if it were criminal contempt of court committed in the face of the court.

(3) Subsection (1)(a) above shall not apply to a person summoned, otherwise than under section 6 of this Act, unless the summons was duly served on him on a date not later than fourteen days before the date fixed by the summons for his first attendance.

(4) A person shall not be liable to be punished under the preceding provisions of this section if he can show some reasonable cause for his failure to comply with the summons, or for not being available when called on to serve, and those provisions have effect subject to the provisions of this Act about the withdrawal or alteration of a summons and about the granting of any excusal or deferral.

(5) If any person—

(a) having been summoned under this Act makes, or causes or permits to be made on his behalf, any false representation to the appropriate officer with the intention of evading jury service; or

    (b) makes or causes to be made on behalf of another person who has been so summoned any false representation to that officer with the intention of enabling the other to evade jury service; or

    (c) when any question is put to him in pursuance of section 2(5) of this Act, refuses without reasonable excuse to answer, or gives an answer which he knows to be false in a material particular, or recklessly gives an answer which is false in a material particular;

    (d) knowing that he is disqualified under Part 2 of Schedule 1 to this Act, serves on a jury; or

    (e) knowing that he is not qualified for jury service by reason of section 40 of the Criminal Justice and Public Order Act 1994, serves on a jury,

he shall be liable on summary conviction to a fine of not more than level 5 on the standard scale in the case of an offence of serving on a jury when disqualified and, in any other case, a fine of not more than level 4 on the standard scale. [S]

20A Offence: research by jurors

    (1) It is an offence for a member of a jury that tries an issue in a case before a court to research the case during the trial period, subject to the exceptions in subsections (6) and (7). [I]

    (2) A person researches a case if (and only if) the person—

    (a) intentionally seeks information, and

    (b) when doing so, knows or ought reasonably to know that the information is or may be relevant to the case.

    (3) The ways in which a person may seek information include—

    (a) asking a question,

    (b) searching an electronic database, including by means of the internet,

    (c) visiting or inspecting a place or object,

    (d) conducting an experiment, and

    (e) asking another person to seek the information.

    (4) Information relevant to the case includes information about—

    (a) a person involved in events relevant to the case,

    (b) the judge dealing with the issue,

    (c) any other person involved in the trial, whether as a lawyer, a witness or otherwise,

    (d) the law relating to the case,

    (e) the law of evidence, and

    (f) court procedure.

    (5) "The trial period", in relation to a member of a jury that tries an issue, is the period—

    (a) beginning when the person is sworn to try the issue, and

    (b) ending when the judge discharges the jury or, if earlier, when the judge discharges the person.

    (6) It is not an offence under this section for a person to seek information if the person needs the information for a reason which is not connected with the case.

    (7) It is not an offence under this section for a person—

    (a) to attend proceedings before the court on the issue;

    (b) to seek information from the judge dealing with the issue;

    (c) to do anything which the judge dealing with the issue directs or authorises the person to do;

    (d) to seek information from another member of the jury, unless the person knows or ought reasonably to know that the other member of the jury contravened this section in the process of obtaining the information;

    (e) to do anything else which is reasonably necessary in order for the jury to try the issue.

20B Offence: sharing research with other jurors

    (1) It is an offence for a member of a jury that tries an issue in a case before a court intentionally to disclose information to another member of the jury during the trial period if—

(a) the member contravened section 20A in the process of obtaining the information, and

(b) the information has not been provided by the court.

(2) Information has been provided by the court if (and only if) it has been provided as part of—

(a) evidence presented in the proceedings on the issue, or

(b) other information provided to the jury or a juror during the trial period by, or with the permission of, the judge dealing with the issue.

(5) In this section, "the trial period" has the same meaning as in section 20A. [I]

20C   Offence: jurors engaging in other prohibited conduct

(1) It is an offence for a member of a jury that tries an issue in a case before a court intentionally to engage in prohibited conduct during the trial period, subject to the exceptions in subsections (4) and (5).

(2) "Prohibited conduct" means conduct from which it may reasonably be concluded that the person intends to try the issue otherwise than on the basis of the evidence presented in the proceedings on the issue.

(3) An offence under this section is committed whether or not the person knows that the conduct is prohibited conduct.

(4) It is not an offence under this section for a member of the jury to research the case (as defined in section 20A(2) to (4)).

(5) It is not an offence under this section for a member of the jury to disclose information to another member of the jury.

(8) In this section, "the trial period" has the same meaning as in section 20A. [I]

20D   Offence: disclosing jury's deliberations

(1) It is an offence for a person intentionally—

(a) to disclose information about statements made, opinions expressed, arguments advanced or votes cast by members of a jury in the course of their deliberations in proceedings before a court, or

(b) to solicit or obtain such information,

subject to the exceptions in sections 20E to 20G. [I]

20E   Offence of disclosing jury's deliberations: initial exceptions

(1) It is not an offence under section 20D for a person to disclose information in the proceedings mentioned in section 20D(1) for the purposes of enabling the jury to arrive at their verdict or in connection with the delivery of that verdict.

(2) It is not an offence under section 20D for the judge dealing with those proceedings to disclose information—

(a) for the purposes of dealing with the case, or

(b) for the purposes of an investigation by a relevant investigator into whether an offence or contempt of court has been committed by or in relation to a juror in the proceedings mentioned in section 20D(1).

(3) It is not an offence under section 20D for a person who reasonably believes that a disclosure described in subsection (2)(b) has been made to disclose information for the purposes of the investigation.

(4) It is not an offence under section 20D to publish information disclosed as described in subsection (1) or (2)(a) in the proceedings mentioned in section 20D(1).

(5) In this section—

"publish" means make available to the public or a section of the public;

"relevant investigator" means—

(a) a police force;

(b) the Attorney General;

(c) any other person or class of person specified by the Lord Chancellor for the purposes of this section by regulations made by statutory instrument.

20F Offence of disclosing jury's deliberations: further exceptions

(1) It is not an offence under section 20D for a person to disclose information to a person listed in subsection (2) if—

    (a) the disclosure is made after the jury in the proceedings mentioned in section 20D(1) has been discharged, and

    (b) the person making the disclosure reasonably believes that—

        (i) an offence or contempt of court has been, or may have been, committed by or in relation to a juror in connection with those proceedings, or

        (ii) conduct of a juror in connection with those proceedings may provide grounds for an appeal against conviction or sentence.

(2) Those persons are—

    (a) a member of a police force;

    (b) a judge of the Court of Appeal;

    (c) the registrar of criminal appeals;

    (d) a judge of the court where the proceedings mentioned in section 20D(1) took place;

    (e) a member of staff of that court who would reasonably be expected to disclose the information only to a person mentioned in paragraphs (b) to (d).

(3) It is not an offence under section 20D for a member of a police force to disclose information for the purposes of obtaining assistance in deciding whether to submit the information to a judge of the Court of Appeal or the registrar of criminal appeals, provided that the disclosure does not involve publishing the information.

(4) It is not an offence under section 20D for a judge of the Court of Appeal or the registrar of criminal appeals to disclose information for the purposes of an investigation by a relevant investigator into—

    (a) whether an offence or contempt of court has been committed by or in relation to a juror in connection with the proceedings mentioned in section 20D(1), or

    (b) whether conduct of a juror in connection with those proceedings may provide grounds for an appeal against conviction or sentence.

(5) It is not an offence under section 20D for a judge of the Court of Appeal or the registrar of criminal appeals to disclose information for the purposes of enabling or assisting—

    (a) a person who was the defendant in the proceedings mentioned in section 20D(1), or

    (b) a legal representative of such a person,

to consider whether conduct of a juror in connection with those proceedings may provide grounds for an appeal against conviction or sentence.

(6) It is not an offence under section 20D for a person who reasonably believes that a disclosure described in subsection (4) or (5) has been made to disclose information for the purposes of the investigation or consideration in question.

(7) It is not an offence under section 20D for a person to disclose information in evidence in—

    (a) proceedings for an offence or contempt of court alleged to have been committed by or in relation to a juror in connection with the proceedings mentioned in section 20D(1),

    (b) proceedings on an appeal, or an application for leave to appeal, against a decision in the proceedings mentioned in section 20D(1) where an allegation relating to conduct of or in relation to a juror forms part of the grounds of appeal, or

    (c) proceedings on any further appeal or reference arising out of proceedings mentioned in paragraph (a) or (b).

(8) It is not an offence under section 20D for a person to disclose information in the course of taking reasonable steps to prepare for proceedings described in subsection (7)(a) to (c).

(9) It is not an offence under section 20D to publish information disclosed as described in sub-section (7).

(10) In this section—

"publish" means make available to the public or a section of the public;

"relevant investigator" means—

(a) a police force;

(b) the Attorney General;

(c) the Criminal Cases Review Commission;

(d) the Crown Prosecution Service;

(e) any other person or class of person specified by the Lord Chancellor for the purposes of this section by regulations made by statutory instrument.

20G   Offence of disclosing jury's deliberations: exceptions for soliciting disclosures or obtaining information

(1) It is not an offence under section 20D to solicit a disclosure described in section 20E(1) to (4) or section 20F(1) to (9).

(2) It is not an offence under section 20D to obtain information—

(a) by means of a disclosure described in section 20E(1) to (4) or section 20F(1) to (9), or

(b) from a document that is available to the public or a section of the public.

Rehabilitation of Offenders Act 1974

9   Unauthorized disclosure of spent convictions

(1) In this section—

"official record" means a record kept for the purposes of its functions by any court, police force, Government department, local or other public authority in Great Britain, or a record kept, in Great Britain or elsewhere, for the purposes of any of Her Majesty's forces, being in either case a record containing information about persons convicted of offences; and

"specified information" means information imputing that a named or otherwise identifiable reha-bilitated living person has committed or been charged with or prosecuted for or convicted of or sentenced for any offence which is the subject of a spent conviction.

(2) Subject to the provisions of any order made under subsection (5) below, any person who, in the course of his official duties, has or at any time has had custody of or access to any official record or the information contained therein, shall be guilty of an offence if, knowing or having reasonable cause to suspect that any specified information he has obtained in the course of those duties is specified information, he discloses it, otherwise than in the course of those duties, to another person. [S]

(3) In any proceedings for an offence under subsection (2) above it shall be a defence for the defendant to show that the disclosure was made—

(a) to the rehabilitated person or to another person at the express request of the rehabili-tated person; or

(b) to a person whom he reasonably believed to be the rehabilitated person or to another person at the express request of a person whom he reasonably believed to be the reha-bilitated person.

(4) Any person who obtains any specified information from any official record by means of any fraud, dishonesty or bribe shall be guilty of an offence. [E]

9A   Unauthorised disclosure of spent cautions

(1) In this section—

(a) "official record" means a record which—

        (i)   contains information about persons given a caution for any offence or offences; and

       (ii) is kept for the purposes of its functions by any court, police force, Government department or other public authority in England and Wales;

    (b) "caution information" means information imputing that a named or otherwise identifiable living person ("the named person") has committed, been charged with or prosecuted or cautioned for any offence which is the subject of a spent caution; and

    (c) "relevant person" means any person who, in the course of his official duties (anywhere in the United Kingdom), has or at any time has had custody of or access to any official record or the information contained in it.

(2) Subject to the terms of any order made under subsection (5), a relevant person shall be guilty of an offence if, knowing or having reasonable cause to suspect that any caution information he has obtained in the course of his official duties is caution information, he discloses it, otherwise than in the course of those duties, to another person. [S]

(3) In any proceedings for an offence under subsection (2) it shall be a defence for the defendant to show that the disclosure was made—

    (a) to the named person or to another person at the express request of the named person;

    (b) to a person whom he reasonably believed to be the named person or to another person at the express request of a person whom he reasonably believed to be the named person.

(4) Any person who obtains any caution information from any official record by means of any fraud, dishonesty or bribe shall be guilty of an offence. [S]

Bail Act 1976

6 Offence of absconding by person released on bail

(1) If a person who has been released on bail in criminal proceedings fails without reasonable cause to surrender to custody he shall be guilty of an offence. [S]

(2) If a person who—

    (a) has been released on bail in criminal proceedings, and

    (b) having reasonable cause therefor, has failed to surrender to custody,

fails to surrender to custody at the appointed place as soon after the appointed time as is reasonably practicable he shall be guilty of an offence.

(3) It shall be for the accused to prove that he had reasonable cause for his failure to surrender to custody.

(4) A failure to give to a person granted bail in criminal proceedings a copy of the record of the decision shall not constitute a reasonable cause for that person's failure to surrender to custody.

9 Offence of agreeing to indemnify sureties in criminal proceedings

(1) If a person agrees with another to indemnify that other against any liability which that other may incur as a surety to secure the surrender to custody of a person accused or convicted of or under arrest for an offence, he and that other person shall be guilty of an offence. [E]

(2) An offence under subsection (1) above is committed whether the agreement is made before or after the person to be indemnified becomes a surety and whether or not he becomes a surety and whether the agreement contemplates compensation in money or in money's worth.

Criminal Law Act 1977

1 The offence of conspiracy

(1) Subject to the following provisions of this Part of this Act, if a person agrees with any other person or persons that a course of conduct shall be pursued which, if the agreement is carried out in accordance with their intentions, either—

(a) will necessarily amount to or involve the commission of any offence or offences by one or more parties to the agreement, or

(b) would do so but for the existence of facts which render the commission of the offence or any offences impossible,

he is guilty of conspiracy to commit the offence or offences in question. [I] [E]

(2) Where liability for any offence may be incurred without knowledge on the part of the person committing it of any particular fact or circumstance necessary for the commission of the offence, a person shall nevertheless not be guilty of conspiracy to commit that offence by virtue of subsection (1) above unless he and at least one other party to the agreement intend or know that that fact or circumstance shall or will exist at the time when the conduct constituting the offence is to take place.

(4) In this Part of this Act "offence" means an offence triable in England and Wales.

1A Conspiracy to commit offences outside England and Wales

(1) Where each of the following conditions is satisfied in the case of an agreement, this Part of this Act has effect in relation to the agreement as it has effect in relation to an agreement falling within section 1(1) above.

(2) The first condition is that the pursuit of the agreed course of conduct would at some stage involve—

(a) an act by one or more of the parties, or

(b) the happening of some other event,

intended to take place in a country or territory outside England and Wales.

(3) The second condition is that that act or other event constitutes an offence under the law in force in that country or territory.

(4) The third condition is that the agreement would fall within section 1(1) above as an agreement relating to the commission of an offence but for the fact that the offence would not be an offence triable in England and Wales if committed in accordance with the parties' intentions.

(5) The fourth condition is that—

(a) a party to the agreement, or a party's agent, did anything in England and Wales in relation to the agreement before its formation, or

(b) a party to the agreement became a party in England and Wales (by joining it either in person or through an agent), or

(c) a party to the agreement, or a party's agent, did or omitted anything in England and Wales in pursuance of the agreement.

(6) In the application of this Part of this Act to an agreement in the case of which each of the above conditions is satisfied, a reference to an offence is to be read as a reference to what would be the offence in question but for the fact that it is not an offence triable in England and Wales.

(7) Conduct punishable under the law in force in any country or territory is an offence under that law for the purposes of this section, however it is described in that law.

(8) Subject to subsection (9) below, the second condition is to be taken to be satisfied unless, not later than rules of court may provide, the defence serve on the prosecution a notice—

(a) stating that, on the facts as alleged with respect to the agreed course of conduct, the condition is not in their opinion satisfied,

(b) showing their grounds for that opinion, and

(c) requiring the prosecution to show that it is satisfied.

(9) The court may permit the defence to require the prosecution to show that the second condition is satisfied without the prior service of a notice under subsection (8) above.

(10) In the Crown Court the question whether the second condition is satisfied shall be decided by the judge alone, and shall be treated as a question of law for the purposes of—

(a) section 9(3) of the Criminal Justice Act 1987 (preparatory hearing in fraud cases), and

(b) section 31(3) of the Criminal Procedure and Investigations Act 1996 (preparatory hearing in other cases).

(11) Any act done by means of a message (however communicated) is to be treated for the purposes of the fourth condition as done in England and Wales if the message is sent or received in England and Wales.

(12) In any proceedings in respect of an offence triable by virtue of this section, it is immaterial to guilt whether or not the accused was a British citizen at the time of any act or other event proof of which is required for conviction of the offence.

(13) References in any enactment, instrument or document (except those in this Part of this Act) to an offence of conspiracy to commit an offence include an offence triable in England and Wales as such a conspiracy by virtue of this section (without prejudice to subsection (6)).

(14) Nothing in this section applies to an agreement entered into before 4 September 1998.

(15) In relation to an agreement entered into during the period beginning with that date and ending with the commencement of section 72(1) of the Coroners and Justice Act 2009, this section applies as if in subsection (2) for "England and Wales" there were substituted "the United Kingdom".

(16) Nothing in this section imposes criminal liability on any person acting on behalf of, or holding office under, the Crown.

2   Exemptions from liability for conspiracy

(1) A person shall not by virtue of section 1 above be guilty of conspiracy to commit any offence if he is an intended victim of that offence.

(2) A person shall not by virtue of section 1 above be guilty of conspiracy to commit any offence or offences if the only other person or persons with whom he agrees are (both initially and at all times during the currency of the agreement) persons of any one or more of the following descriptions, that is to say—

(a) his spouse or civil partner;

(b) a person under the age of criminal responsibility; and

(c) an intended victim of that offence or of each of those offences.

(3) A person is under the age of criminal responsibility for the purposes of subsection (2)(b) above so long as it is conclusively presumed, by virtue of section 50 of the Children and Young Persons Act 1933, that he cannot be guilty of any offence.

3   Penalties for conspiracy

(1) A person guilty by virtue of section 1 above of conspiracy to commit any offence or offences shall be liable on conviction on indictment—

(a) in a case falling within subsection (2) or (3) below, to imprisonment for a term related in accordance with that subsection to the gravity of the offence or offences in question (referred to below in this section as the relevant offence or offences); and

(b) in any other case, to a fine.

Paragraph (b) above shall not be taken as prejudicing the application of section 120 of the Sentencing Code (general power of court to fine offender convicted on indictment) in a case falling within subsection (2) or (3) below.

(2) Where the relevant offence or any of the relevant offences is an offence of any of the following descriptions, that is to say—

(a) murder, or any other offence the sentence for which is fixed by law;

(b) an offence for which a sentence extending to imprisonment for life is provided; or

(c) an indictable offence punishable with imprisonment for which no maximum term of imprisonment is provided,

the person convicted shall be liable to imprisonment for life.

(3) Where in a case other than one to which subsection (2) above applies the relevant offence or any of the relevant offences is punishable with imprisonment, the person convicted shall be liable to imprisonment for a term not exceeding the maximum term provided for that offence or (where more than one such offence is in question) for any one of those offences (taking the longer or the longest term as the limit for the purposes of this section where the terms provided differ).

In the case of an offence triable either way the references above in this subsection to the maximum term provided for that offence are references to the maximum term so provided on conviction on indictment.

4   Restrictions on the institution of proceedings for conspiracy

(1) Subject to subsection (2) below proceedings under section 1 above for conspiracy to commit any offence shall not be instituted against any person except by or with the consent of the Director of Public Prosecutions if the offence or (as the case may be) each of the offences in question is a summary offence.

(4) Where—

(a) an offence has been committed in pursuance of any agreement; and

(b) proceedings may not be instituted for that offence because any time limit applicable to the institution of any such proceedings has expired,

proceedings under section 1 above for conspiracy to commit that offence shall not be instituted against any person on the basis of that agreement.

5   Abolitions, savings, transitional provisions, consequential amendment and repeals

(1) Subject to the following provisions of this section, the offence of conspiracy at common law is hereby abolished.

(2) Subsection (1) above shall not affect the offence of conspiracy at common law so far as relates to conspiracy to defraud.

(3) Subsection (1) above shall not affect the offence of conspiracy at common law if and in so far as it may be committed by entering into an agreement to engage in conduct which—

(a) tends to corrupt public morals or outrages public decency; but

(b) would not amount to or involve the commission of an offence if carried out by a single person otherwise than in pursuance of an agreement.

(6) The rules laid down by sections 1 and 2 above shall apply for determining whether a person is guilty of an offence of conspiracy under any enactment other than section 1 above, but conduct which is an offence under any such other enactment shall not also be an offence under section 1 above.

(8) The fact that the person or persons who, so far as appears from the indictment on which any person has been convicted of conspiracy, were the only other parties to the agreement on which his conviction was based have been acquitted of conspiracy by reference to that agreement (whether after being tried with the person convicted or separately) shall not be a ground for quashing his conviction unless under all the circumstances of the case his conviction is inconsistent with the acquittal of the other person or persons in question.

(9) Any rule of law or practice inconsistent with the provisions of subsection (8) above is hereby abolished.

PART II   OFFENCES RELATING TO ENTERING AND REMAINING ON PROPERTY

6   Violence for securing entry

(1) Subject to the following provisions of this section, any person who, without lawful authority, uses or threatens violence for the purpose of securing entry into any premises for himself or for any other person is guilty of an offence, provided that—

(a) there is someone present on those premises at the time who is opposed to the entry which the violence is intended to secure; and

(b) the person using or threatening the violence knows that that is the case. [S]

(1A) Subsection (1) above does not apply to a person who is a displaced residential occupier or a protected intending occupier of the premises in question or who is acting on behalf of such an occupier; and if the accused adduces sufficient evidence that he was, or was acting on behalf of, such an occupier he shall be presumed to be, or to be acting on behalf of, such an occupier unless the contrary is proved by the prosecution.

(2) Subject to subsection (1A) above, the fact that a person has any interest in or right to possession or occupation of any premises shall not for the purposes of subsection (1) above constitute

lawful authority for the use or threat of violence by him or anyone else for the purpose of securing his entry into those premises.

(4) It is immaterial for the purposes of this section—

(a) whether the violence in question is directed against the person or against the property; and

(b) whether the entry which the violence is intended to secure is for the purpose of acquiring possession of the premises in question or for any other purpose.

7 Adverse occupation of residential premises

(1) Subject to the following provisions of this section and to section 12A(9) below, any person who is on any premises as a trespasser after having entered as such is guilty of an offence if he fails to leave those premises on being required to do so by or on behalf of—

(a) a displaced residential occupier of the premises; or

(b) an individual who is a protected intending occupier of the premises. [S]

(2) In any proceedings for an offence under this section it shall be a defence for the accused to prove that he believed that the person requiring him to leave the premises was not a displaced residential occupier or protected intending occupier of the premises or a person acting on behalf of a displaced residential occupier or protected intending occupier.

(3) In any proceedings for an offence under this section it shall be a defence for the accused to prove—

(a) that the premises in question are or form part of premises used mainly for non-residential purposes; and

(b) that he was not on any part of the premises used wholly or mainly for residential purposes.

(4) Any reference in the preceding provisions of this section to any premises includes a reference to any access to them, whether or not any such access itself constitutes premises, within the meaning of this Part of this Act.

(7) Section 12 below contains provisions which apply for determining when any person is to be regarded for the purposes of this Part of this Act as a displaced residential occupier of any premises or of any access to any premises and section 12A below contains provisions which apply for determining when any person is to be regarded for the purposes of this Part of this Act as a protected intending occupier of any premises or of any access to any premises.

8 Trespassing with a weapon of offence

(1) A person who is on any premises as a trespasser, after having entered as such, is guilty of an offence if, without lawful authority or reasonable excuse, he has with him on the premises any weapon of offence. [S]

(2) In subsection (1) above "weapon of offence" means any article made or adapted for use for causing injury to or incapacitating a person, or intended by the person having it with him for such use.

9 Trespassing on premises of foreign missions, etc.

(1) Subject to subsection (3) below, a person who enters or is on any premises to which this section applies as a trespasser is guilty of an offence. [S]

(2) This section applies to any premises which are or form part of—

(a) the premises of a diplomatic mission within the meaning of the definition in Article 1(i) of the Vienna Convention on Diplomatic Relations signed in 1961 as that Article has effect in the United Kingdom by virtue of section 2 of and Schedule 1 to the Diplomatic Privileges Act 1964;

(aa) the premises of a closed diplomatic mission;

(b) consular premises within the meaning of the definition in paragraph 1(j) of Article 1 of the Vienna Convention on Consular Relations signed in 1963 as that Article has effect in the United Kingdom by virtue of section 1 of and Schedule 1 to the Consular Relations Act 1968;

(bb) the premises of a closed consular post;

(c)   any other premises in respect of which any organisation or body is entitled to inviolability by or under any enactment; and

(d)   any premises which are the private residence of a diplomatic agent (within the meaning of Article 1(e) of the Convention mentioned in paragraph (a) above) or of any other
person who is entitled to inviolability of residence by or under any enactment.

(3) In any proceedings for an offence under this section it shall be a defence for the accused to
prove that he believed that the premises in question were not premises to which this section applies.

12   Supplementary provisions

(1) In this Part of this Act—

(a)   "premises" means any building, any part of a building under separate occupation, any land
ancillary to a building, the site comprising any building or buildings together with any land
ancillary thereto, and (for the purposes only of sections 10 and 11 above) any other place; and

(b)   "access" means, in relation to any premises, any part of any site or building within which
those premises are situated which constitutes an ordinary means of access to those
premises (whether or not that is its sole or primary use).

(2) References in this section to a building shall apply also to any structure other than a movable one, and to any movable structure, vehicle or vessel designed or adapted for use for residential
purposes; and for the purposes of subsection (1) above—

(a)   part of a building is under separate occupation if anyone is in occupation or entitled to
occupation of that part as distinct from the whole; and

(b)   land is ancillary to a building if it is adjacent to it and used (or intended for use) in connection with the occupation of that building or any part of it.

(3) Subject to subsection (4) below, any person who was occupying any premises as a residence
immediately before being excluded from occupation by anyone who entered those premises, or any
access to those premises, as a trespasser is a displaced residential occupier of the premises for the
purposes of this Part of this Act so long as he continues to be excluded from occupation of the premises by the original trespasser or by any subsequent trespasser.

(4) A person who was himself occupying the premises in question as a trespasser immediately
before being excluded from occupation shall not by virtue of subsection above be a displaced residential occupier of the premises for the purposes of this Part of this Act.

(5) A person who by virtue of subsection (3) above is a displaced residential occupier of any
premises shall be regarded for the purposes of this Part of this Act as a displaced residential occupier
also of any access to those premises.

12A   Protected intending occupiers: supplementary provisions

(1) For the purposes of this Part of this Act an individual is a protected intending occupier of
any premises at any time if at that time he falls within subsections (2), (4) or (6) below.

(2) An individual is a protected occupier of any premises if—

(a)   he has in those premises a freehold interest or a leasehold interest with not less than two
years still to run;

(b)   he requires the premises for his own occupation as a residence;

(c)   he is excluded from occupation of the premises by a person who entered them, or any
access to them, as a trespasser; and

(d)   he or a person acting on his behalf holds a written statement—

(i)   which specifies his interest in the premises;

(ii)   which states that he requires the premises for occupation as a residence for himself; and

(iii)   with respect to which the requirements in subsection (3) below are fulfilled.

(3) The requirements referred to in subsection (2)(d)(iii) above are—

(a)   that the statement is signed by the person whose interest is specified in it in the presence
of a justice of the peace or commissioner for oaths; and

(b)   that the justice of the peace or commissioner for oaths has subscribed his name as a witness to the signature.

(4) An individual is also a protected intending occupier of any premises if—
- (a) he has a tenancy of those premises (other than a tenancy falling within subsection (2)(a) above or (6)(a) below) or a licence to occupy those premises granted by a person with a freehold interest or a leasehold interest with not less than two years still to run in the premises;
- (b) he requires the premises for his own occupation as a residence;
- (c) he is excluded from occupation of the premises by a person who entered them, or any access to them, as a trespasser; and
- (d) he or a person acting on his behalf holds a written statement—
  - (i) which states that he has been granted a tenancy of those premises or a licence to occupy those premises;
  - (ii) which specifies the interest in the premises of the person who granted that tenancy or licence to occupy ("the landlord");
  - (iii) which states that he requires the premises for occupation as a residence for himself; and
  - (iv) with respect to which the requirements in subsection (5) below are fulfilled.

(5) The requirements referred to in subsection (4)(d)(iv) above are—
- (a) that the statement is signed by the landlord and by the tenant or licensee in the presence of a justice of the peace or commissioner for oaths;
- (b) that the justice of the peace or commissioner for oaths has subscribed his name as a witness to the signatures.

(6) An individual is also a protected intending occupier of any premises if—
- (a) he has a tenancy of those premises (other than a tenancy falling within subsection (2)(a) or (4)(a) above) or a licence to occupy those premises granted by an authority to which this subsection applies;
- (b) he requires the premises for his own occupation as a residence;
- (c) he is excluded from occupation of the premises by a person who entered the premises, or any access to them, as a trespasser; and
- (d) there has been issued to him by or on behalf of the authority referred to in paragraph (a) above a certificate stating that—
  - (i) he has been granted a tenancy of those premises or a licence to occupy those premises as a residence by the authority; and
  - (ii) the authority which granted that tenancy or licence to occupy is one to which this subsection applies, being of a description specified in the certificate.

(7) Subsection (6) above applies to the following authorities—
- (a) any body mentioned in section 14 of the Rent Act 1977 (landlord's interest belonging to local authority etc.);
- (b) the Regulator of Social Housing;
- (ba) a non-profit registered provider of social housing;
- (bb) a profit-making registered provider of social housing, but only in relation to premises which are social housing within the meaning of Part 2 of the Housing and Regeneration Act 2008; and
- (d) a registered social landlord within the meaning of the Housing Act 1985 (see section 5(4) and (5) of that Act).

(8) A person is guilty of an offence if he makes a statement for the purposes of subsection (2)(d) or (4)(d) above which he knows to be false in a material particular or if he recklessly makes such a statement which is false in a material particular. [S]

(9) In any proceedings for an offence under section 7 of this Act where the accused was requested to leave the premises by a person claiming to be or to act on behalf of a protected intending occupier of the premises—
- (a) it shall be a defence for the accused to prove that, although asked to do so by the accused at the time the accused was requested to leave, that person failed at that time to produce

to the accused such a statement as is referred to in subsection (2)(d) or (4)(d) above or such a certificate as is referred to in subsection (6)(d) above; and

(b) any document purporting to be a certificate under subsection (6)(d) above shall be received in evidence and, unless the contrary is proved, shall be deemed to have been issued by or on behalf of the authority stated in the certificate.

(11) A person who is protected intending occupier of any premises shall be regarded for the purposes of this Part of this Act as a protected intending occupier also of any access to those premises.

PART IV   MISCELLANEOUS PROVISIONS

51   Bomb hoaxes

(1) A person who—

(a) places any article in any place whatever; or

(b) dispatches any article by post, rail or any other means whatever of sending things from one place to another,

with the intention (in either case) of inducing in some other person a belief that it is likely to explode or ignite and thereby cause personal injury or damage to property is guilty of an offence.

In this subsection "article" includes substance. [E]

(2) A person who communicates any information which he knows or believes to be false to another person with the intention of inducing in him or any other person a false belief that a bomb or other thing liable to explode or ignite is present in any place or location whatever is guilty of an offence. [E]

(3) For a person to be guilty of an offence under subsection (1) or (2) above it is not necessary for him to have any particular person in mind as the person in whom he intends to induce the belief mentioned in that subsection.

Protection from Eviction Act 1977

1   Unlawful eviction and harassment of occupier

(1) In this section "residential occupier", in relation to any premises, means a person occupying the premises as a residence, whether under a contract or by virtue of any enactment or rule of law giving him the right to remain in occupation or restricting the right of any person to recover possession of the premises.

(2) If any person unlawfully deprives the residential occupier of any premises of his occupation of the premises or any part thereof, or attempts to do so, he shall be guilty of an offence unless he proves that he believed, and had reasonable cause to believe, that the residential occupier had ceased to reside in the premises. [E]

(3) If any person with intent to cause the residential occupier of any premises—

(a) to give up the occupation of the premises or any part thereof; or

(b) to refrain from exercising any right or pursuing any remedy in respect of the premises or part thereof;

does acts likely to interfere with the peace or comfort of the residential occupier or members of his household, or persistently withdraws or withholds services reasonably required for the occupation of the premises as a residence, he shall be guilty of an offence. [E]

(3A) Subject to subsection (3B) below, the landlord of a residential occupier or an agent of the landlord shall be guilty of an offence if—

(a) he does acts likely to interfere with the peace or comfort of the residential occupier or members of his household, or

(b) he persistently withdraws or withholds services reasonably required for the occupation of the premises in question as a residence, and (in either case) he knows, or has reasonable cause to believe, that that conduct is likely to cause the residential occupier to give up the occupation of the whole or part of the premises or to refrain from exercising any right or pursuing any remedy in respect of the whole or part of the premises. [E]

(3B) A person shall not be guilty of an offence under subsection (3A) above if he proves that he had reasonable grounds for doing the acts or withdrawing or withholding the services in question.

(3C) In subsection (3A) above "landlord", in relation to a residential occupier of any premises, means the person who, but for—

(a) the residential occupier's right to remain in occupation of the premises, or

(b) a restriction on the person's right to recover possession of the premises,

would be entitled to occupation of the premises and any superior landlord under whom that person derives title.

Interpretation Act 1978

5 Definitions
In any Act, unless the contrary intention appears, words and expressions listed in Schedule 1 to this Act are to be construed according to that Schedule.

6 Gender and number
In any Act, unless the contrary intention appears,—

(a) words importing the masculine gender include the feminine;

(b) words importing the feminine gender include the masculine;

(c) words in the singular include the plural and words in the plural include the singular.

15 Repeal of repeal
Where an Act repeals a repealing enactment, the repeal does not revive any enactment previously repealed unless words are added reviving it.

16 General savings
(1) Without prejudice to section 15, where an Act repeals an enactment, the repeal does not, unless the contrary intention appears,—

(a) revive anything not in force or existing at the time at which the repeal takes effect;

(b) affect the previous operation of the enactment repealed or anything duly done or suffered under that enactment;

(c) affect any right, privilege, obligation or liability acquired, accrued, or incurred under that enactment;

(d) affect any penalty, forfeiture or punishment incurred in respect of any offence committed against that enactment;

(e) affect any investigation, legal proceeding or remedy in respect of any such right, privilege, obligation, liability, penalty, forfeiture or punishment;

and any such investigation, legal proceeding or remedy may be instituted, continued or enforced, and any such penalty, forfeiture or punishment may be imposed, as if the repealing Act had not been passed.

(2) This section applies to the expiry of a temporary enactment as if it were repealed by an Act.

18 Duplicated offences
Where an act or omission constitutes an offence under two or more Acts, or both under an Act and at common law, the offender shall, unless the contrary intention appears, be liable to be prosecuted and punished under either or any of those Acts or at common law, but shall not be liable to be punished more than once for the same offence.

SCHEDULE 1

"Person" includes a body of persons corporate or unincorporate.

In relation to England and Wales—

    (a) "indictable offence" means an offence which, if committed by an adult, is triable on indictment, whether it is exclusively so triable or triable either way;

    (b) "summary offence" means an offence which, if committed by an adult, is triable only summarily;

    (c) "offence triable either way" means an offence (other than an offence triable on indictment only by virtue of Part V of the Criminal Justice Act 1988) which, if committed by an adult, is triable either on indictment or summarily;

and the terms "indictable", "summary" and "triable either way", in their application to offences, are to be construed accordingly.

In the above definitions references to the way or ways in which an offence is triable are to be construed without regard to the effect, if any, of section 22 of the Magistrates' Courts Act 1980 on the mode of trial in a particular case.

Protection of Children Act 1978

1   Indecent photographs of children

    (1) Subject to sections 1A and 1B, it is an offence for a person—

        (a) to take, or permit to be taken, or to make, any indecent photograph or pseudo-photograph of a child; or

        (b) to distribute or show such indecent photographs or pseudo-photographs; or

        (c) to have in his possession such indecent photographs, or pseudo-photographs with a view to their being distributed or shown by himself or others; or

        (d) to publish or cause to be published any advertisement likely to be understood as conveying that the advertiser distributes or shows such indecent photographs or pseudo-photographs, or intends to do so. [E]

    (2) For purposes of this Act, a person is to be regarded as distributing an indecent photograph or pseudo-photograph if he parts with possession of it to, or exposes or offers it for acquisition by, another person.

    (4) Where a person is charged with an offence under subsection (1)(b) or (c), it shall be a defence for him to prove—

        (a) that he had a legitimate reason for distributing or showing the photographs or pseudo-photographs or (as the case may be) having them in his possession; or

        (b) that he had not himself seen the photographs or pseudo-photographs and did not know, nor had any cause to suspect, them to be indecent.

1A   Marriage and other relationships

    (1) This section applies where, in proceedings for an offence under section 1(1)(a) of taking or making an indecent photograph or pseudo-photograph of a child, or for an offence under section 1(1)(b) or (c) relating to an indecent photograph or pseudo-photograph of a child, the defendant proves that the photograph or pseudo-photograph was of the child aged 16 or over, and that at the time of the offence charged the child and he—

        (a) were married or civil partners of each other, or

        (b) lived together as partners in an enduring family relationship.

    (2) Subsections (5) and (6) also apply where, in proceedings for an offence under section 1(1)(b) or (c) relating to an indecent photograph or pseudo-photograph of a child, the defendant proves that the photograph or pseudo-photograph was of the child aged 16 or over, and that at the time when he obtained it the child and he—

(a) were married or civil partners of each other, or

(b) lived together as partners in an enduring family relationship.

(3) This section applies whether the photograph or pseudo-photograph showed the child alone or with the defendant, but not if it showed any other person.

(4) In the case of an offence under section 1(1)(a), if sufficient evidence is adduced to raise an issue as to whether the child consented to the photograph or pseudo-photograph being taken or made, or as to whether the defendant reasonably believed that the child so consented, the defendant is not guilty of the offence unless it is proved that the child did not so consent and that the defendant did not reasonably believe that the child so consented.

(5) In the case of an offence under section 1(1)(b), the defendant is not guilty of the offence unless it is proved that the showing or distributing was to a person other than the child.

(6) In the case of an offence under section 1(1)(c), if sufficient evidence is adduced to raise an issue both—

(a) as to whether the child consented to the photograph or pseudo-photograph being in the defendant's possession, or as to whether the defendant reasonably believed that the child so consented, and

(b) as to whether the defendant had the photograph or pseudo-photograph in his possession with a view to its being distributed or shown to anyone other than the child,

the defendant is not guilty of the offence unless it is proved either that the child did not so consent and that the defendant did not reasonably believe that the child so consented, or that the defendant had the photograph or pseudo-photograph in his possession with a view to its being distributed or shown to a person other than the child.

1B   Exception for criminal proceedings, investigations, etc.

(1) In proceedings for an offence under section 1(1)(a) of making an indecent photograph or pseudo-photograph of a child, the defendant is not guilty of the offence if he proves that—

(a) it was necessary for him to make the photograph or pseudo-photograph for the purposes of the prevention, detection or investigation of crime, or for the purposes of criminal proceedings, in any part of that world,

(b) at the time of the offence charged he was a member of the Security Service or the Secret Intelligence Service, and it was necessary for him to make the photograph or pseudo-photograph for the exercise of any of the functions of that Service, or

(c) at the time of the offence charged he was a member of GCHQ, and it was necessary for him to make the photograph or pseudo-photograph for the exercise of any of the functions of GCHQ.

(2) In this section "GCHQ" has the same meaning as in the Intelligence Services Act 1994.

2   Evidence

(3) In proceedings under this Act [relating to indecent photographs of children] a person is to be taken as having been a child at any material time if it appears from the evidence as a whole that he was then under the age of 18.

7   Interpretation

(1) The following subsections apply for the interpretation of this Act.

(2) References to an indecent photograph include an indecent film, a copy of an indecent photograph or film, and an indecent photograph comprised in a film.

(3) Photographs (including those comprised in a film) shall, if they show children and are indecent, be treated for all purposes of this Act as indecent photographs of children, and so as respects pseudo-photographs.

(4) References to a photograph include—

(a) the negative as well as the positive version; and

(b) data stored on a computer disc or by other electronic means which is capable of conversion into a photograph.

(4A) References to a photograph also include—

(a) a tracing or other image, whether made by electronic or other means (of whatever nature)—

(i) which is not itself a photograph or pseudo-photograph, but

(ii) which is derived from the whole or part of a photograph or pseudo-photograph (or a combination of either or both); and

(b) data stored on a computer disc or by other electronic means which is capable of conversion into an image within paragraph (a);

and subsection (8) applies in relation to such an image as it applies in relation to a pseudo-photograph.

(5) "Film" includes any form of video-recording.

(6) "Child", subject to subsection (8), means a person under the age of 18.

(7) "Pseudo-photograph" means an image, whether made by computer-graphics or otherwise howsoever, which appears to be a photograph.

(8) If the impression conveyed by a pseudo-photograph is that the person shown is a child, the pseudo-photograph shall be treated for all purposes of this Act as showing a child and so shall a pseudo-photograph where the predominant impression conveyed is that the person shown is a child notwithstanding that some of the physical characteristics shown are those of an adult.

(9) References to an indecent pseudo-photograph include—

(a) a copy of an indecent pseudo-photograph; and

(b) data stored on a computer disc or by other electronic means which is capable of conversion into an indecent pseudo-photograph.

Suppression of Terrorism Act 1978

4   Jurisdiction in respect of offences committed outside United Kingdom

(1) If a person, whether a citizen of the United Kingdom and Colonies or not, does in a convention country any act which, if he had done it in a part of the United Kingdom, would have made him guilty in that part of the United Kingdom of—

(a) an offence mentioned in paragraph 1, 2, 4, 5, 10, 11B, 12, 13, 14 or 15 of Schedule 1 to this Act; or

(b) an offence of attempting to commit any offence so mentioned,

he shall, in that part of the United Kingdom, be guilty of the offence or offences aforesaid of which the act would have made him guilty if he had done it there.

(3) If a person who is a national of a convention country but not a citizen of the United Kingdom and Colonies does outside the United Kingdom and that convention country any act which makes him in that convention country guilty of an offence and which, if he had been a citizen of the United Kingdom and Colonies, would have made him in any part of the United Kingdom guilty of an offence mentioned in paragraph 1, 2 or 13 of Schedule 1 to this Act, he shall, in any part of the United Kingdom, be guilty of the offence or offences aforesaid of which the act would have made him guilty if he had been such a citizen.

(7) For the purposes of this section any act done—

(a) on board a ship registered in a convention country, being an act which, if the ship had been registered in the United Kingdom, would have constituted an offence within the jurisdiction of the Admiralty; or

(b) on board an aircraft registered in a convention country while the aircraft is in flight elsewhere than in or over that country; or

(c) on board a hovercraft registered in a convention country while the hovercraft is in journey elsewhere than in or over that country, shall be treated as done in that convention country; and subsection (4) of section 92 of the Civil Aviation Act 1982 (definition of "in flight" or, as applied to hovercraft, "in journey") shall apply for the purposes of this subsection as it applies for the purposes of that section.

8   Provisions as to interpretation and orders

(1) In this Act—

"act" includes omission;

"convention country" means a country for the time being designated in an order made by the Secretary of State as a party to the European Convention on the Suppression of Terrorism signed at Strasbourg on the 27th January 1977;

"country" includes any territory; . . .

SCHEDULE 1

Common law offences

1. Murder.
2. Manslaughter or culpable homicide.
4. Kidnapping, abduction or plagium.
5. False imprisonment.
6. Assault occasioning actual bodily harm or causing injury.
7. Wilful fire-raising.

Offences against the person

8. An offence under any of the following provisions of the Offences against the Person Act 1861—

(za) section 4 (soliciting etc. to commit murder);

(a)   section 18 (wounding with intent to cause grievous bodily harm);

(b)   section 20 (causing grievous bodily harm);

(c)   section 21 (attempting to choke etc. in order to commit or assist in the committing of any indictable offence);

(d)   section 22 (using chloroform etc. to commit or assist in the committing of any indictable offence);

(e)   section 23 (maliciously administering poison etc. so as to endanger life or inflict grievous bodily harm);

(f)   section 24 (maliciously administering poison etc. with intent to injure etc.);

(g)   section 48 (rape).

9. An offence under any of the following provisions of the Sexual Offences Act 2003—

(a)   sections 1 or 2 (rape, assault by penetration);

(b)   section 4 (causing a person to engage in sexual activity without consent), where the activity caused involved penetration within subsection (4)(a) to (d) of that section;

(c)   section 5 or 6 (rape of a child under 13, assault of a child under 13 by penetration);

(d)   section 8 (causing or inciting a child under 13 to engage in sexual activity), where an activity involving penetration within subsection (3)(a) to (d) of that section was caused;

(e)   section 30 (sexual activity with a person with a mental disorder impeding choice), where the touching involved penetration within subsection (3)(a) to (d) of that section;

(f)   section 31 (causing or inciting a person, with a mental disorder impeding choice, to engage in sexual activity), where an activity involving penetration within subsection (3)(a) to (d) of that section was caused.

9A. The offence of torture under section 134 of the Criminal Justice Act 1988.

Abduction

10. An offence under any of the following provisions of the Offences against the Person Act 1861—
   (a) section 55 (abduction of unmarried girl under 16);
   (b) section 56 (child-stealing or receiving stolen child).

11A. An offence under the Taking of Hostages Act 1982.

11B. An offence under section 2 of the Child Abduction Act 1984 (abduction of child by person other than parent etc.) or any corresponding provision in force in Northern Ireland.

Explosives

12. An offence under any of the following provisions of the Offences against the Person Act 1861—
   (a) section 28 (causing bodily injury by gunpowder);
   (b) section 29 (causing gunpowder to explode etc. with intent to do grievous bodily harm);
   (c) section 30 (placing gunpowder near a building etc. with intent to cause bodily injury).

13. An offence under any of the following provisions of the Explosive Substances Act 1883—
   (a) section 2 (causing explosion likely to endanger life or property);
   (b) section 3 (doing any act with intent to cause such an explosion, conspiring to cause such an explosion, or making or possessing explosive with intent to endanger life or property).

13A. An offence under any provision of the Nuclear Material (Offences) Act 1983.

Firearms

14. The following offences under the Firearms Act 1968—
   (a) an offence under section 16 (possession of firearm with intent to injure);
   (b) an offence under subsection (1) of section 17 (use of firearm or imitation firearm to resist arrest) involving the use or attempted use of a firearm within the meaning of that section.

Theft Act 1978

3   Making off without payment

(1) Subject to subsection (3) below, a person who, knowing that payment on the spot for any goods supplied or service done is required or expected from him, dishonestly makes off without having paid as required or expected and with intent to avoid payment of the amount due shall be guilty of an offence. [E]

(2) For purposes of this section "payment on the spot" includes payment at the time of collecting goods on which work has been done or in respect of which service has been provided.

(3) Subsection (1) above shall not apply where the supply of the goods or the doing of the service is contrary to law, or where the service done is such that payment is not legally enforceable.

5   Supplementary

(2) Sections 30(1) (husband and wife), 31(1) (effect on civil proceedings) and 34 (interpretation) of the Theft Act 1968, so far as they are applicable in relation to this Act, shall apply as they apply in relation to that Act.

Customs and Excise Management Act 1979

50   Penalty for improper importation of goods

(1) Subsection (2) below applies to goods of the following descriptions, that is to say—

(a) goods chargeable with a duty which has not been paid; and

(b) goods the importation, landing or unloading of which is for the time being prohibited or restricted by or under any enactment.

(2) If any person with intent to defraud Her Majesty of any such duty or to evade any such prohibition or restriction as is mentioned in subsection (1) above—

(a) unships or lands in any port or unloads from any aircraft in the United Kingdom or from any other vehicle which has entered the United Kingdom any goods to which this subsection applies, or assists or is otherwise concerned in such unshipping, landing or unloading; or

(b) removes from their place of importation or from any approved wharf, examination station, temporary storage facility, any place specified by an officer of Revenue and Customs under Part 1 of the Taxation (Cross-border Trade) Act 2018 as a place where the goods are required to be kept or customs and excise station any goods to which this subsection applies or assists or is otherwise concerned in such removal,

he shall be guilty of an offence under this subsection and may be arrested. [E]

(3) If any person imports or is concerned in importing any goods contrary to any prohibition or restriction for the time being in force under or by virtue of any enactment with respect to those goods, whether or not the goods are unloaded, and does so with intent to evade the prohibition or restriction, he shall be guilty of an offence under this subsection and may be arrested. [E]

(6) If any person—

(a) imports or causes to be imported any goods concealed in a container holding goods of a different description; or

(b) directly or indirectly imports, or causes to be imported, any chargeable goods found, whether before or after being released to a Customs procedure, not to correspond with any information provided under Part 1 of the Taxation (Cross-border Trade) Act 2018,

he shall be liable on summary conviction to a penalty of three times the value of the goods or level 3 on the standard scale, whichever is the greater. [S]

(7) In any case where a person would, apart from this subsection, be guilty of—

(a) an offence under this section in connection with the importation of goods contrary to a prohibition or restriction; and

(b) a corresponding offence under the enactment or other instrument imposing the prohibition or restriction, being an offence for which a fine or other penalty is expressly provided by that enactment or other instrument,

he shall not be guilty of the offence mentioned in paragraph (a) of this subsection.

170   Penalty for fraudulent evasion of duty, etc.

(1) Without prejudice to any other provision of the Customs and Excise Acts 1979, if any person—

(a) knowingly acquires possession of any of the following goods, that is to say—

(i)   goods which have been unlawfully removed from a warehouse or Queen's warehouse;

(ii) goods which are chargeable with a duty which has not been paid;

(iii) goods with respect to the importation or exportation of which any prohibition or restriction is for the time being in force under or by virtue of any enactment; or

(b) is in any way knowingly concerned in carrying, removing, depositing, harbouring, keeping or concealing or in any manner dealing with any such goods,

and does so with intent to defraud Her Majesty of any duty payable on the goods, or to evade any such prohibition or restriction with respect to the goods shall be guilty of an offence under this section and may be arrested. [E]

(2) Without prejudice to any other provision of the Customs and Excise Acts 1979, if any person is, in relation to any goods, in any way knowingly concerned in any fraudulent evasion or attempt at evasion—

    (a) of any duty chargeable on the goods;

    (b) of any prohibition or restriction for the time being in force with respect to the goods under or by virtue of any enactment; or

    (c) of any provision of the Customs and Excise Acts 1979, or Part 1 or section 40A or 40B of the Taxation (Cross-border Trade) Act 2018 applicable to the goods,

he shall be guilty of an offence under this section and may be arrested. [E]

(5) In any case where a person would, apart from this subsection, be guilty of—

    (a) an offence under this section in connection with a prohibition or restriction; and

    (b) a corresponding offence under the enactment or other instrument imposing the prohibition or restriction, being an offence for which a fine or other penalty is expressly provided by that enactment or other instrument,

he shall not be guilty of the offence mentioned in paragraph (a) of this subsection.

(6) Where any person is guilty of an offence under this section, the goods in respect of which the offence was committed shall be liable to forfeiture.

Highways Act 1980

137   Penalty for wilful obstruction

(1) If a person, without lawful authority or excuse, in any way wilfully obstructs the free passage along a highway he is guilty of an offence and liable to a fine not exceeding level 3 on the standard scale. [S]

161   Penalties for causing certain kinds of danger or annoyance

(1) If a person, without lawful authority or excuse, deposits any thing whatsoever on a highway in consequence of which a user of the highway is injured or endangered, that person is guilty of an offence and liable to a fine not exceeding level 3 on the standard scale. [S]

(2) If a person, without lawful authority or excuse,

    (a) lights any fire on or over a highway which consists of or comprises a carriageway; or

    (b) discharges any firearm or firework within 50 feet of the centre of such a highway,

and in consequence a user of the highway is injured, interrupted or endangered, that person is guilty of an offence and liable to a fine not exceeding level 3 on the standard scale. [S]

(3) If a person plays at football or any other game on a highway to the annoyance of a user of the highway he is guilty of an offence and liable to a fine not exceeding level 1 on the standard scale. [S]

(4) If a person, without lawful authority or excuse, allows any filth, dirt, lime or other offensive matter or thing to run or flow on to a highway from any adjoining premises, he is guilty of an offence and liable to a fine not exceeding level 1 on the standard scale. [S]

162   Penalty for placing rope, etc., across highway

A person who for any purpose places any rope, wire or other apparatus across a highway in such a manner as to be likely to cause danger to persons using the highway is, unless he proves that he had taken all necessary means to give adequate warning of the danger, guilty of an offence and liable, to a fine not exceeding level 3 on the standard scale. [S]

Magistrates' Courts Act 1980

44   Aiders and abettors

(1) A person who aids, abets, counsels or procures the commission by another person of a summary offence shall be guilty of the like offence and may be tried (whether or not he is charged as a principal) either by a court having jurisdiction to try that other person or by a court having by virtue of his own offence jurisdiction to try him.

(2) Any offence consisting in aiding, abetting, counselling or procuring the commission of an offence triable either way (other than an offence listed in Schedule 1 to this Act) shall by virtue of this subsection be triable either way.

101   Onus of proving exceptions, etc.

Where the defendant to an information or complaint relies for his defence on any exception, exemption, proviso, excuse or qualification, whether or not it accompanies the description of the offence or matter of complaint in the enactment creating the offence or on which the complaint is founded, the burden of proving the exception, exemption, proviso, excuse or qualification shall be on him; and this notwithstanding that the information or complaint contains an allegation negativing the exception, exemption, proviso, excuse or qualification.

108   Right of appeal to the Crown Court

(1) A person convicted by a magistrates' court may appeal to the Crown Court—
  (a) if he pleaded guilty, against his sentence;
  (b) if he did not, against the conviction or sentence.

(1A) Section 82 of the Sentencing Code (under which a conviction of an offence for which an order for conditional or absolute discharge is made is deemed not to be a conviction except for certain purposes) shall not prevent an appeal under this Act, whether against conviction or otherwise.

111   Statement of case by magistrates' court

(1) Any person who was a party to any proceeding before a magistrates' court or is aggrieved by the conviction, order, determination or other proceeding of the court may question the proceeding on the ground that it is wrong in law or is in excess of jurisdiction by applying to the justices composing the court to state a case for the opinion of the High Court on the question of law or jurisdiction involved; but a person shall not make an application under this section in respect of a decision against which he has a right of appeal to the High Court or which by virtue of any enactment passed after 31st December 1879 is final.

(2) An application under subsection (1) above shall be made within 21 days after the day on which the decision of the magistrates' court was given.

(3) For the purpose of subsection (2) above, the day on which the decision of the magistrates' court is given shall, where the court has adjourned the trial of an information after conviction, be the day on which the court sentences or otherwise deals with the offender.

(4) On the making of an application under this section in respect of a decision any right of the applicant to appeal against the decision to the Crown Court shall cease.

(5) If the justices are of opinion that an application under this section is frivolous, they may refuse to state a case, and, if the applicant so requires, shall give him a certificate stating that the application has been refused; but the justices shall not refuse to state a case if the application is made by or under the direction of the Attorney General.

(6) Where justices refuse to state a case, the High Court may, on the application of the person who applied for the case to be stated, make an order of mandamus requiring the justices to state a case.

Contempt of Court Act 1981

1   The strict liability rule

In this Act "the strict liability rule" means the rule of law whereby conduct may be treated as a contempt of court as tending to interfere with the course of justice in particular legal proceedings regardless of intent to do so.

2   Limitation of scope of strict liability

(1) The strict liability rule applies only in relation to publications, and for this purpose "publication" includes any speech, writing, programme included in a programme service or other

communication in whatever form, which is addressed to the public at large or any section of the public.

(2) The strict liability rule applies only to a publication which creates a substantial risk that the course of justice in the proceedings in question will be seriously impeded or prejudiced.

(3) The strict liability rule applies to a publication only if the proceedings in question are active within the meaning of this section at the time of the publication.

(4) Schedule 1 applies for determining the times at which proceedings are to be treated as active within the meaning of this section.

(5) In this section "programme service" has the same meaning as in the Broadcasting Act 1990.

3   Defence of innocent publication or distribution

(1) A person is not guilty of contempt of court under the strict liability rule as the publisher of any matter to which that rule applies if at the time of publication (having taken all reasonable care) he does not know and has no reason to suspect that relevant proceedings are active.

(2) A person is not guilty of contempt of court under the strict liability rule as the distributor of a publication containing any such matter if at the time of distribution (having taken all reasonable care) he does not know that it contains such matter and has no reason to suspect that it is likely to do so.

(3) The burden of proof of any fact tending to establish a defence afforded by this section to any person lies upon that person.

4   Contemporary reports of proceedings

(1) Subject to this section a person is not guilty of contempt of court under the strict liability rule in respect of a fair and accurate report of legal proceedings held in public, published contemporaneously and in good faith.

(2) In any such proceedings the court may, where it appears to be necessary for avoiding a substantial risk of prejudice to the administration of justice in those proceedings, or in any other proceedings pending or imminent, order that the publication of any report of the proceedings, or any part of the proceedings, be postponed for such period as the court thinks necessary for that purpose.

(2A) Where in proceedings for any offence which is an administration of justice offence for the purposes of section 54 of the Criminal Procedure and Investigations Act 1996 (acquittal tainted by an administration of justice offence) it appears to the court that there is a possibility that (by virtue of that section) proceedings may be taken against a person for an offence of which he has been acquitted, subsection (2) of this section shall apply as if those proceedings were pending or imminent.

(3) For the purposes of subsection (1) of this section a report of proceedings shall be treated as published contemporaneously—

    (a) in the case of a report of which publication is postponed pursuant to an order under subsection (2) of this section, if published as soon as practicable after that order expires;

    (b) in the case of a report of allocation or sending proceedings of which publication is permitted by virtue only of subsection (6) of section 52A of the Crime and Disorder Act 1998 ("The 1998 Act") if published as soon as practicable after publication is so permitted;

    (c) in the case of a report of an application of which publication is permitted by virtue only of sub-paragraph (5) or (7) of paragraph 3 of Schedule 3 to the 1998 Act, if published as soon as practicable after publication is so permitted.

5   Discussion of public affairs

A publication made as or as part of a discussion in good faith of public affairs or other matters of general public interest is not to be treated as a contempt of court under the strict liability rule if the risk of impediment or prejudice to particular legal proceedings is merely incidental to the discussion.

6 Savings

Nothing in the foregoing provisions of this Act—

 (a) prejudices any defence available at common law to a charge of contempt of court under the strict liability rule;

 (b) implies that any publication is punishable as contempt of court under that rule which would not be so punishable apart from those provisions;

 (c) restricts liability for contempt of court in respect of conduct intended to impede or prejudice the administration of justice.

9 Use of tape recorders

 (1) Subject to subsection (4) below, it is a contempt of court—

 (a) to use in court, or bring into court for use, any tape recorder or other instrument for recording sound, except with the leave of the court;

 (b) to publish a recording of legal proceedings made by means of any such instrument, or any recording derived directly or indirectly from it, by playing it in the hearing of the public or any section of the public, or to dispose of it or any recording so derived, with a view to such publication;

 (c) to use any such recording in contravention of any conditions of leave granted under paragraph (a).

 (d) to publish or dispose of any recording in contravention of any conditions of leave granted under subsection (1A).

 (1A) In the case of a recording of Supreme Court proceedings, subsection (1)(b) does not apply to its publication or disposal with the leave of the Court.

 (2) Leave under paragraph (a) of subsection (1) or under subsection (1A), may be granted or refused at the discretion of the court, and if granted—

 (a) may, in the case of leave under subsection (1)(a), be granted subject to such conditions as the court thinks proper with respect to the use of any recording made pursuant to the leave; and

 (b) may, in the case of leave under subsection (1A), be granted subject to such conditions as the Supreme Court thinks proper with respect to publication or disposal of any recording to which the leave relates;

and where leave has been granted the court may at the like discretion withdraw or amend it either generally or in relation to any particular part of the proceedings.

 (3) Without prejudice to any other power to deal with an act of contempt under paragraph (a) of subsection (1), the court may order the instrument, or any recording made with it, or both, to be forfeited; and any object so forfeited shall (unless the court otherwise determines on application by a person appearing to be the owner) be sold or otherwise disposed of in such manner as the court may direct.

 (4) This section does not apply to the making or use of sound recordings for purposes of official transcripts of proceedings.

 (5) See section 32 of the Crime and Courts Act 2013 for power to provide for further exceptions.

Criminal Attempts Act 1981

1 Attempting to commit an offence

 (1) If, with intent to commit an offence to which this section applies, a person does an act which is more than merely preparatory to the commission of the offence, he is guilty of attempting to commit the offence. [I] [E]

 (1A) Subject to section 8 of the Computer Misuse Act 1990 (relevance of external law), if this subsection applies to an act, what the person doing it had in view shall be treated as an offence to which this section applies.

(1B) Subsection (1A) above applies to an act if—

(a) it is done in England and Wales; and

(b) it would fall within subsection (1) above as more than merely preparatory to the commission of an offence under section 3 of the Computer Misuse Act 1990 but for the fact that the offence, if completed, would not be an offence triable in England and Wales.

(2) A person may be guilty of attempting to commit an offence to which this section applies even though the facts are such that the commission of the offence is impossible.

(3) In any case where—

(a) apart from this subsection a person's intention would not be regarded as having amounted to an intent to commit an offence: but

(b) if the facts of the case had been as he believed them to be, his intention would be so regarded,

then, for the purposes of subsection (1) above, he shall be regarded as having had an intent to commit that offence.

(4) This section applies to any offence which, if it were completed, would be triable in England and Wales as an indictable offence, other than—

(a)   conspiracy (at common law or under section 1 of the Criminal Law Act 1977 or any other enactment);

(b)   aiding, abetting, counselling, procuring or suborning the commission of an offence;

(ba) an offence under section 2(1) of the Suicide Act 1961 (encouraging or attempting suicide);

(c)   offences under section 4(1) (assisting offenders) or 5(1) (accepting or agreeing to accept consideration for not disclosing information about an arrestable offence) of the Criminal Law Act 1967.

(5) This section also applies to low-value shoplifting (which is defined in, and is triable only summarily by virtue of, section 22A of the Magistrates' Courts Act 1980).

1A   Extended jurisdiction in relation to certain attempts

(1) If this section applies to an act, what the person doing the act had in view shall be treated as an offence to which section 1(1) above applies.

(2) This section applies to an act if—

(a) it is done in England and Wales, and

(b) it would fall within section 1(1) above as more than merely preparatory to the commission of a Group A offence but for the fact that that offence, if completed, would not be an offence triable in England and Wales.

(3) In this section "Group A offence" has the same meaning as in Part 1 of the Criminal Justice Act 1993.

(4) Subsection (1) above is subject to the provisions of section 6 of the Act of 1993 (relevance of external law).

(5) Where a person does any act to which this section applies, the offence which he commits shall for all purposes be treated as the offence of attempting to commit the relevant Group A offence.

4   Trial and penalties

(1) A person guilty by virtue of section 1 above of attempting to commit an offence shall—

(a) if the offence attempted is murder or any other offence the sentence for which is fixed by law, be liable on conviction on indictment to imprisonment for life; and

(b) if the offence attempted is indictable but does not fall within paragraph (a) above, be liable on conviction on indictment to any penalty to which he would have been liable on conviction on indictment of that offence; and

(c) if the offence attempted is triable either way, or is low-value shoplifting (which is defined in, and is triable only summarily by virtue of, section 22A of the Magistrates' Courts Act 1980), be liable on summary conviction to any penalty to which he would have been liable on summary conviction of that offence.

(3) Where, in proceedings against a person for an offence under section 1 above, there is evidence sufficient in law to support a finding that he did an act falling within subsection (1) of that section, the question whether or not his act fell within that subsection is a question of fact.

6   Effect on common law

(1) The offence of attempt at common law and any offence at common law of procuring materials for crime are hereby abolished for all purposes not relating to acts done before the commencement of this Act.

(2) Except as regards offences committed before the commencement of this Act, references in any enactment passed before this Act which fall to be construed as references to the offence of attempt at common law shall be construed as references to the offence under section 1 above.

9   Interference with vehicles

(1) A person is guilty of the offence of vehicle interference if he interferes with a motor vehicle or trailer or with anything carried in or on a motor vehicle or trailer with the intention that any offence specified in subsection (2) below shall be committed by himself or some other person. [S]

(2) The offences mentioned in subsection (1) above are—

(a) theft of the motor vehicle or trailer or part of it;

(b) theft of anything carried in or on the motor vehicle or trailer; and

(c) an offence under section 12(1) of the Theft Act 1968 (taking and driving away without consent);

and, if it is shown that a person accused of an offence under this section intended that one of those offences should be committed, it is immaterial that it cannot be shown which it was.

(5) In this section "motor vehicle" and "trailer" have the meanings assigned to them by section 185(1) of the Road Traffic Act 1988.

Forgery and Counterfeiting Act 1981

PART I   FORGERY AND KINDRED OFFENCES

1   The offence of forgery

A person is guilty of forgery if he makes a false instrument, with the intention that he or another shall use it to induce somebody to accept it as genuine, and by reason of so accepting it to do or not to do some act to his own or any other person's prejudice. [E]

2   The offence of copying a false instrument

It is an offence for a person to make a copy of an instrument which is, and which he knows or believes to be, a false instrument, with the intention that he or another shall use it to induce somebody to accept it as a copy of a genuine instrument, and by reason of so accepting it to do or not to do some act to his own or any other person's prejudice. [E]

3   The offence of using a false instrument

It is an offence for a person to use an instrument which is, and which he knows or believes to be, false, with the intention of inducing somebody to accept it as genuine, and by reason of so accepting it to do or not to do some act to his own or any other person's prejudice. [E]

4   The offence of using a copy of a false instrument

It is an offence for a person to use a copy of an instrument which is, and which he knows or believes to be, a false instrument, with the intention of inducing somebody to accept it as a copy of a genuine instrument, and by reason of so accepting it to do or not to do some act to his own or any other person's prejudice. [E]

5   Offences relating to money orders, share certificates, passports, etc.

(1) It is an offence for a person to have in his custody or under his control an instrument to which this section applies which is, and which he knows or believes to be, false, with the intention that he or another shall use it to induce somebody to accept it as genuine, and by reason of so accepting it to do or not to do some act to his own or any other person's prejudice. [E]

(2) It is an offence for a person to have in his custody or under his control, without lawful authority or excuse, an instrument to which this section applies which is, and which he knows or believes to be, false. [E]

(3) It is an offence for a person to make or to have in his custody or under his control a machine or implement, or paper or any other material, which to his knowledge is or has been specially designed or adapted for the making of an instrument to which this section applies, with the intention that he or another shall make an instrument to which this section applies which is false and that he or another shall use the instrument to induce somebody to accept it as genuine, and by reason of so accepting it to do or not to do some act to his own or any other person's prejudice. [E]

(4) It is an offence for a person to make or to have in his custody or under his control any such machine, implement, paper or material, without lawful authority or excuse. [E]

(5) The instruments to which this section applies are—
  (a)   money orders;
  (b)   postal orders;
  (c)   United Kingdom postage stamps;
  (d)   Inland Revenue stamps;
  (e)   share certificates;
  (g)   cheques and other bills of exchange;
  (h)   travellers' cheques;
  (ha) bankers' drafts;
  (hb) promissory notes;
  (j)   cheque cards;
  (ja) debit cards;
  (k)   credit cards;
  (l)   Certified copies relating to an entry in a register of births, adoptions, marriages, civil partnerships, conversions or deaths and issued by the Registrar General, the Registrar General for Northern Ireland, a registration officer or person lawfully authorised to issue Certified copies relating to such entries; and
  (m)   certificates relating to entries in such registers.

(6) In subsection (5)(e) above "share certificate" means an instrument entitling or evidencing the title of a person to a share or interest—
  (a)   in any public stock, annuity, fund or debt of any government or state, including a state which forms part of another state; or
  (b)   in any stock, fund or debt of a body (whether corporate or unincorporated) established in the United Kingdom or elsewhere.

(6A) In subsection (5)(l) above, "conversion" means the conversion of a civil partnership into a marriage under section 9 of the Marriage (Same Sex Couples) Act 2013 and regulations made under that section.

(7) An instrument is also an instrument to which this section applies if it is a monetary instrument specified for the purposes of this section by the Secretary of State.

8   Meaning of "instrument"

(1) Subject to subsection (2) below, in this Part of this Act "instrument" means—
  (a)   any document, whether of a formal or informal character;
  (b)   any stamp issued or sold by a postal operator;
  (c)   any Inland Revenue stamp; and
  (d)   any disc, tape, sound track or other device on or in which information is recorded or stored by mechanical, electronic or other means.

(2) A currency note within the meaning of Part II of this Act is not an instrument for the purposes of this Part of this Act.

(3) A mark denoting payment of postage which a postal operator authorises to be used instead of an adhesive stamp is to be treated for the purposes of this Part of this Act as if it were a stamp issued by the postal operator concerned.

(3A) In this section "postal operator" has the meaning given by section 27 of the Postal Services Act 2011.

(4) In this Part of this Act "Inland Revenue stamp" means a stamp as defined in section 27 of the Stamp Duties Management Act 1891.

9　Meaning of "false" and "making"

(1) An instrument is false for the purposes of this Part of this Act—

    (a) if it purports to have been made in the form in which it is made by a person who did not in fact make it in that form; or

    (b) if it purports to have been made in the form in which it is made on the authority of a person who did not in fact authorise its making in that form; or

    (c) if it purports to have been made in the terms in which it is made by a person who did not in fact make it in those terms; or

    (d) if it purports to have been made in the terms in which it is made on the authority of a person who did not in fact authorise its making in those terms; or

    (e) if it purports to have been altered in any respect by a person who did not in fact alter it in that respect; or

    (f) if it purports to have been altered in any respect on the authority of a person who did not in fact authorise the alteration in that respect; or

    (g) if it purports to have been made or altered on a date on which, or at a place at which, or otherwise in circumstances in which, it was not in fact made or altered; or

    (h) if it purports to have been made or altered by an existing person but he did not in fact exist.

(2) A person is to be treated for the purposes of this Part of this Act as making a false instrument if he alters an instrument so as to make it false in any respect (whether or not it is false in some other respect apart from that alteration).

10　Meaning of "prejudice" and "induce"

(1) Subject to subsections (2) and (4) below, for the purposes of this Part of this Act an act or omission intended to be induced is to a person's prejudice if, and only if, it is one which if it occurs—

    (a) will result—

        (i)　in his temporary or permanent loss of property; or

        (ii)　in his being deprived of an opportunity to earn remuneration or greater remuneration; or

        (iii)　in his being deprived of an opportunity to gain a financial advantage otherwise than by way of remuneration; or

    (b) will result in somebody being given an opportunity—

        (i)　to earn remuneration or greater remuneration from him; or

        (ii)　to gain a financial advantage from him otherwise than by way of remuneration; or

    (c) will be the result of his having accepted a false instrument as genuine, or a copy of a false instrument as a copy of a genuine one, in connection with his performance of any duty.

(2) An act which a person has an enforceable duty to do and an omission to do an act which a person is not entitled to do shall be disregarded for the purposes of this Part of this Act.

(3) In this Part of this Act references to inducing somebody to accept a false instrument as genuine, or a copy of a false instrument as a copy of a genuine one, include references to inducing a machine to respond to the instrument or copy as if it were a genuine instrument or, as the case may be, a copy of a genuine one.

(4) Where subsection (3) above applies, the act or omission intended to be induced by the machine responding to the instrument or copy shall be treated as an act or omission to a person's prejudice.

(5) In this section "loss" includes not getting what one might get as well as parting with what one has.

PART II COUNTERFEITING AND KINDRED OFFENCES

14 Offences of counterfeiting notes and coins

(1) It is an offence for a person to make a counterfeit of a currency note or of a protected coin, intending that he or another shall pass or tender it as genuine. [E]

(2) It is an offence for a person to make a counterfeit of a currency note or of a protected coin without lawful authority or excuse. [E]

15 Offences of passing, etc., counterfeit notes and coins

(1) It is an offence for a person—

(a) to pass or tender as genuine any thing which is, and which he knows or believes to be, a counterfeit of a currency note or of a protected coin; or

(b) to deliver to another any thing which is, and which he knows or believes to be, such a counterfeit, intending that the person to whom it is delivered or another shall pass or tender it as genuine. [E]

(2) It is an offence for a person to deliver to another, without lawful authority or excuse, any thing which is, and which he knows or believes to be, a counterfeit of a currency note or of a protected coin. [E]

16 Offences involving the custody or control of counterfeit notes and coins

(1) It is an offence for a person to have in his custody or under his control any thing which is, and which he knows or believes to be, a counterfeit of a currency note or of a protected coin, intending either to pass or tender it as genuine or to deliver it to another with the intention that he or another shall pass or tender it as genuine. [E]

(2) It is an offence for a person to have in his custody or under his control, without lawful authority or excuse, any thing which is, and which he knows or believes to be, a counterfeit of a currency note or of a protected coin. [E]

(3) It is immaterial for the purposes of subsections (1) and (2) above that a coin or note is not in a fit state to be passed or tendered or that the making or counterfeiting of a coin or note has not been finished or perfected.

17 Offences involving the making or custody or control of counterfeiting materials and implements

(1) It is an offence for a person to make, or to have in his custody or under his control, anything which he intends to use, or to permit any other person to use, for the purpose of making a counterfeit of a currency note or of a protected coin with the intention that it be passed or tendered as genuine. [E]

(2) It is an offence for a person without lawful authority or excuse—

(a) to make; or

(b) to have in his custody or under his control,

anything which, to his knowledge, is or has been specially designed or adapted for the making of a counterfeit of a currency note. [E]

(3) Subject to subsection (4) below, it is an offence for a person to make, or to have in his custody or under his control, any implement which, to his knowledge, is capable of imparting to anything a resemblance—

(a) to the whole or part of either side of a protected coin; or

(b) to the whole or part of the reverse of the image on either side of a protected coin. [E]

(4) It shall be a defence for a person charged with an offence under subsection (3) above to show—

(a) that he made the implement or, as the case may be, had it in his custody or under his control, with the written consent of the Treasury; or

(b) that he had lawful authority otherwise than by virtue of paragraph (4) above, or a lawful excuse, for making it or having it in his custody or under his control.

18   The offence of reproducing British currency notes

(1) It is an offence for any person, unless the relevant authority has previously consented in writing, to reproduce on any substance whatsoever, and whether or not on the correct scale, any British currency note or any part of a British currency note. [E]

(2) In this section—

"British currency note" means any note which—

(a) has been lawfully issued in England and Wales, Scotland or Northern Ireland; and

(b) is or has been customarily used as money in the country where it was issued; and

(c) is payable on demand; and

"the relevant authority", in relation to a British currency note of any particular description, means the authority empowered by law to issue notes of that description.

19   Offences in making, etc., imitation British coins

(1) It is an offence for a person—

(a) to make an imitation British coin in connection with a scheme intended to promote the sale of any product or the making of contracts for the supply of any service; or

(b) to sell or distribute imitation British coins in connection with any such scheme, or to have imitation British coins in his custody or under his control with a view to such sale or distribution,

unless the Treasury have previously consented in writing to the sale or distribution of such imitation British coins in connection with that scheme. [E]

(2) In this section—

"'British coin" means any coin which is legal tender in any part of the United Kingdom; and "imitation British coin" means any thing which resembles a British coin in shape, size and the substance of which it is made.

20   Prohibition of importation of counterfeit notes and coins

The importation, landing or unloading of a counterfeit of a currency note or of a protected coin without the consent of the Treasury is hereby prohibited.

21   Prohibition of exportation of counterfeit notes and coins

(1) The exportation of a counterfeit of a currency note or of a protected coin without the consent of the Treasury is hereby prohibited.

27   Meaning of "currency note" and "protected coin"

(1) In this Part of this Act—

"currency note" means—

(a) any note which—

(i) has been lawfully issued in England and Wales, Scotland, Northern Ireland, any of the Channel Islands, the Isle of Man or the Republic of Ireland; and

(ii) is or has been customarily used as money in the country where it was issued; and

(iii) is payable on demand; or

(b) any note which—

(i) has been lawfully issued in some country other than those mentioned in paragraph (a)(i) above; and

(ii) is customarily used as money in that country; and

"protected coin" means any coin which—

    (a) is customarily used as money in any country; or

    (b) is specified in an order made by the Treasury for the purposes of this Part of this Act.

28 Meaning of "counterfeit"

(1) For the purposes of this Part of this Act a thing is a counterfeit of a currency note or of a protected coin—

    (a) if it is not a currency note or a protected coin but resembles a currency note or protected coin (whether on one side only or on both) to such an extent that it is reasonably capable of passing for a currency note or protected coin of that description; or

    (b) if it is a currency note or protected coin which has been so altered that it is reasonably capable of passing for a currency note or protected coin of some other description.

(2) For the purposes of this Part of this Act—

    (a) a thing consisting of one side only of a currency note, with or without the addition of other material, is a counterfeit of such a note;

    (b) a thing consisting—

        (i)   of parts of two or more currency notes; or

        (ii) of parts of a currency note, or of parts of two or more currency notes, with the addition of other material,

is capable of being a counterfeit of a currency note.

(3) References in this Part of this Act to passing or tendering a counterfeit of a currency note or a protected coin are not to be construed as confined to passing or tendering it as legal tender.

Indecent Displays (Control) Act 1981

1 Indecent displays

(1) If any indecent matter is publicly displayed the person making the display and any person causing or permitting the display to be made shall be guilty of an offence. [E]

(2) Any matter which is displayed in or so as to be visible from any public place shall, for the purposes of this section, be deemed to be publicly displayed.

(3) In subsection (2) above, "public place", in relation to the display of any matter, means any place to which the public have or are permitted to have access (whether on payment or otherwise) while that matter is displayed except—

    (a) a place to which the public are permitted to have access only on payment which is or includes payment for that display; or

    (b) a shop or any part of a shop to which the public can only gain access by passing beyond an adequate warning notice;

but the exclusions contained in paragraphs (a) and (b) above shall only apply where persons under the age of 18 years are not permitted to enter while the display in question is continuing.

(4) Nothing in this section applies in relation to any matter—

    (a) included by any person in a television broadcasting service or other television programme service (within the meaning of Part I of the Broadcasting Act 1990); or

    (b) included in the display of an art gallery or museum and visible only from within the gallery or museum; or

    (c) displayed by or with the authority of, and visible only from within a building occupied by, the Crown or any local authority; or

    (d) included in a performance of a play (within the meaning of paragraph 14(1) of Schedule 1 to the Licensing Act 2003) . . . ; or

    (e) included in an exhibition of a film within the meaning of paragraph 15 of Schedule 1 to the Licensing Act 2003 . . . —

     (i)   given in a place which as regards that exhibition is required to be licensed under section 1 of that Act or by virtue only of section 5, 7 or 8 of that Act, is not required to be so licensed; or

     (ii)   which is an exempted exhibition to which section 6 of that Act applies given by an exempted organisation as defined in subsection (6) of that section.

(5) In this section "matter" includes anything capable of being displayed, except that it does not include an actual human body or any part thereof; and in determining for the purpose of this section whether any displayed matter is indecent—

    (a) there shall be disregarded any part of that matter which is not exposed to view; and

    (b) account may be taken of the effect of juxtaposing one thing with another.

(6) A warning notice shall not be adequate for the purposes of this section unless it complies with the following requirements—

    (a) The warning notice must contain the following words, and no others—
"WARNING
Persons passing beyond this notice will find material on display which they may consider indecent. No admittance to persons under 18 years of age."

    (b) The word "WARNING" must appear as a heading.

    (c) No pictures or other matter shall appear on the notice.

    (d) The notice must be so situated that no one could reasonably gain access to the shop or part of the shop in question without being aware of the notice and it must be easily legible by any person gaining such access.

Wildlife and Countryside Act 1981

PART I   WILDLIFE

1 Protection of wild birds, their nests and eggs

(1) Subject to the provisions of this Part, if any person intentionally—

    (a)   kills, injures or takes any wild bird;

    (aa)   takes, damages or destroys the nest of a wild bird included in Schedule ZA1;

    (b)   takes, damages or destroys the nest of any wild bird while that nest is in use or being built; or

    (c)   takes or destroys an egg of any wild bird,

he shall be guilty of an offence. [S]

(2) Subject to the provisions of this Part, if any person has in his possession or control—

    (a) any live or dead wild bird or any part of, or anything derived from, such a bird; or

    (b) an egg of a wild bird or any part of such an egg,

he shall be guilty of an offence. [S]

(3) A person shall not be guilty of an offence under subsection (2) if he shows that—

    (a) the bird or egg had not been killed or taken, or had been killed or taken . . . ; or

    (b) the bird, egg or other thing in his possession or control had been sold (whether to him or any other person);

(3ZA) A person shall not be guilty of an offence under subsection (2)(b) if the person shows that the egg, or the part of the egg, was in any person's possession or control before 28th September 1982.

(3A) In subsection (3) "lawfully" means without any contravention of—

    (a) this Part and order made under it,

    (b) the Protection of Birds Acts 1954 to 1967 and orders made under those Acts,

    (c) any other legislation which implements the Wild Birds Directive and extends to any part of the United Kingdom, to any area designated in accordance with section 1(7) of the Continental Shelf Act 1964, or to any area to which British fishery limits extend in accordance with section 1 of the Fishery Limits Act 1976, and

(d) the provisions of the law of any member State (other than the United Kingdom) implementing the Wild Birds Directive.

(5) Subject to the provisions of this Part, if any person intentionally or recklessly—

(a) disturbs any wild bird included in Schedule 1 while it is building a nest or is in, on or near a nest containing eggs or young; or

(b) disturbs dependent young of such a bird,

he shall be guilty of an offence.

(6) For the purposes of this section the definition of "wild bird" in section 27(1) is to be read as not including any bird which is shown to have been bred in captivity unless it has been lawfully released into the wild as part of a re-population or re-introduction programme.

(6A) "Re-population" and "re-introduction" have the same meaning as in the Wild Birds Directive.

(7) Any reference in this Part to any bird included in Schedule 1 is a reference to any bird included in Part I and, during the close season for the bird in question, any bird included in Part II of that Schedule.

2   Exceptions to s. 1

(1) Subject to the provisions of this section, a person shall not be guilty of an offence under section 1 by reason of the killing or taking of a bird included in Part I of Schedule 2 outside the close season for that bird, or the injuring of such a bird outside that season in the course of an attempt to kill it.

(2) Subject to the provisions of this section, an authorised person shall not be guilty of an offence under section 1 by reason of—

(a) the killing or taking of a bird included in Part II of Schedule 2, or the injuring of such a bird in the course of an attempt to kill it;

(b) the taking, damaging or destruction of a nest of such a bird; or

(c) the taking or destruction of an egg of such a bird.

(3) Subsections (1) shall not apply in Scotland on Sundays or on Christmas Day; and subsection (1) shall not apply on Sundays in any area of England and Wales which the Secretary of State may by order prescribe for the purposes of that subsection.

(4) In this section and section 1 "close season" means—

(a) in the case of capercaillie and . . . woodcock, the period in any year commencing with 1st February and ending with 30th September;

(b) in the case of snipe, the period in any year commencing with 1st February and ending with 11th August;

(c) in the case of wild duck and wild geese in or over any area below high-water mark of ordinary spring tides, the period in any year commencing with 21st February and ending with 31st August;

(d) in any other case, subject to the provisions of this Part, the period in any year commencing with 1st February and ending with 31st August.

5   Prohibition of certain methods of killing or taking wild birds

(1) Subject to the provisions of this Part, if any person—

(a) sets in position any of the following articles, being an article which is of such a nature and is so placed as to be calculated to cause bodily injury to any wild bird coming into contact therewith, that is to say, any springe, trap, gin, snare, hook and line, any electrical device for killing, stunning or frightening or any poisonous, poisoned or stupefying substance;

(b) uses for the purpose of killing or taking any wild bird any such article as aforesaid, whether or not of such a nature and so placed as aforesaid, or any net, baited board, bird-lime or substance of a like nature to bird-lime;

(c) uses for the purpose of killing or taking any wild bird—

(i)   any bow or crossbow;

(ii)   any explosive other than ammunition for a firearm;

(iii) any automatic or semi-automatic weapon;

(iv) any shot-gun of which the barrel has an internal diameter at the muzzle of more than one and three-quarter inches;

(v) any device for illuminating a target or any sighting device for night shooting;

(vi) any form of artificial lighting or any mirror or other dazzling device;

(vii) any gas or smoke not falling within paragraphs (a) and (b); or

(viii) any chemical wetting agent;

(d) uses as a decoy, for the purpose of killing or taking any wild bird, any sound recording or any live bird or other animal whatever which is tethered, or which is secured by means of braces or other similar appliances, or which is blind, maimed or injured;

(e) uses any mechanically propelled vehicle in immediate pursuit of a wild bird for the purpose of killing or taking that bird; or

(f) knowingly causes or permits to be done an act which is mentioned in the foregoing provisions of this subsection and which is not lawful under subsection (5),

he shall be guilty of an offence. [S]

(4) In any proceedings under subsection (1)(a) it shall be a defence to show that the article was set in position for the purpose of killing or taking, in the interests of public health, agriculture, forestry, fisheries or nature conservation, any wild animals which could be lawfully killed or taken by those means and that he took all reasonable precautions to prevent injury thereby to wild birds.

(4A) In any proceedings under subsection (1)(f) relating to an act which is mentioned in subsection (1)(a) it shall be a defence to show that the article was set in position for the purpose of killing or taking, in the interests of public health, agriculture, forestry, fisheries or nature conservation, any wild animals which could be lawfully killed or taken by those means and that he took or caused to be taken all reasonable precautions to prevent injury thereby to wild birds.

(5) Nothing in subsection (1) shall make unlawful—

(a) the use of a cage-trap or net by an authorised person for the purpose of taking a bird included in Part II of Schedule 2;

(b) the use of nets for the purpose of taking wild duck in a duck decoy which is shown to have been in use immediately before the passing of the Protection of Birds Act 1954; or

(c) the use of a cage-trap or net for the purpose of taking any game bird if it is shown that the taking of the bird is solely for the purpose of breeding;

but nothing in this subsection shall make lawful the use of any net for taking birds in flight or the use for taking birds on the ground of any net which is projected or propelled otherwise than by hand.

6 Sale etc. of live or dead wild birds, eggs etc.

(1) Subject to the provisions of this Part, if any person—

(a) sells, offers or exposes for sale, or has in his possession or transports for the purpose of sale, any live wild bird other than a bird included in Part I of Schedule 3, or an egg of a wild bird or any part of such an egg; or

(b) publishes or causes to be published any advertisement likely to be understood as conveying that he buys or sells, or intends to buy or sell, any of those things,

he shall be guilty of an offence. [S]

(2) Subject to the provisions of this Part, if any person . . . —

(a) sells, offers or exposes for sale, or has in his possession or transports for the purpose of sale, any dead wild bird other than a bird included in Part II or III of Schedule 3, or any part of, or anything derived from, such a wild bird; or

(b) publishes or causes to be published any advertisement likely to be understood as conveying that he buys or sells, or intends to buy or sell, any of those things,

he shall be guilty of an offence. [S]

(3) Subject to the provisions of this Part, if any person shows or causes or permits to be shown for the purposes of any competition or in any premises in which a competition is being held—

(a) any live wild bird other than a bird included in Part I of Schedule 3; or

(b) any live bird one of whose parents was such a wild bird,

he shall be guilty of an offence. [S]

(5) Any reference in this section to any bird included in Part I of Schedule 3 is a reference to any bird included in that Part which

(a) was bred in captivity,

(b) has been ringed or marked in accordance with regulations made by the Secretary of State, and

(c) has not been lawfully released into the wild as part of a re-population or re-introduction programme.

(5A) "Re-population" and "re-introduction" have the same meaning as in the Wild Birds Directive.

(6) Any reference in this section to any bird included in Part II or III of Schedule 3 is a reference to any bird included in Part II and, during the period commencing with 1st September in any year and ending with 28th February of the following year, any bird included in Part III of that Schedule.

7 Registration etc. of certain captive birds

(1) If any person keeps or has in his possession or under his control any bird included in Schedule 4 which has not been registered and ringed or marked in accordance with regulations made by the Secretary of State, he shall be guilty of an offence. [S]

(3) If any person keeps or has in his possession or under his control any bird included in Schedule 4—

(a) within five years of his having been convicted of an offence under this Part which falls within subsection (3A); or

(b) within three years of his having been convicted of any other offence under this Part so far as it relates to the protection of birds or other animals or any offence involving their ill-treatment,

he shall be guilty of an offence. [S]

(3A) The offences falling within this subsection are—

(a) any offence under section 1(1) or (2) in respect of—

(i) a bird included in Schedule ZA1 or 1 or any part of, or anything derived from, such a bird,

(ii) the nest of such a bird, or

(iii) an egg of such a bird or any part of such an egg;

(b) any offence under section 1(5) or 5;

(c) any offence under section 6 in respect of—

(i) a bird included in Schedule ZA1 or 1 or any part of, or anything derived from, such a bird, or

(ii) an egg of such a bird or any part of such an egg;

(ca) any offence under subsection (1);

(d) any offence under section 8.

(4) If any person knowingly disposes of or offers to dispose of any bird included in Schedule 4 to any person—

(a) within five years of that person's having been convicted of such an offence as is mentioned in paragraph (a) of subsection (3); or

(b) within three years of that person's having been convicted of such an offence as is mentioned in paragraph (b) of that subsection,

he shall be guilty of an offence. [S]

(5) No account shall be taken for the purposes of subsections (3) and (4) of any conviction which has become spent for the purpose of the Rehabilitation of Offenders Act 1974.

8 Protection of captive birds

(1) If any person keeps or confines any bird whatever in any cage or other receptacle which is not sufficient in height, length or breadth to permit the bird to stretch its wings freely, he shall be guilty of an offence. [S]

(2) Subsection (1) does not apply to poultry, or to the keeping or confining of any bird—

(a) while that bird is in the course of conveyance, by whatever means;

(b) while that bird is being shown for the purposes of any public exhibition or competition if the time during which the bird is kept or confined for those purposes does not in the aggregate exceed 72 hours; or

(c) while that bird is undergoing examination or treatment by a veterinary surgeon or veterinary practitioner.

(3) Every person who—

(a) promotes, arranges, conducts, assists in, receives money for, or takes part in, any event whatever at or in the course of which captive birds are liberated by hand or by any other means whatever for the purpose of being shot immediately after their liberation; or

(b) being the owner or occupier of any land, permits that land to be used for the purposes of such an event,

shall be guilty of an offence. [S]

9 Protection of certain wild animals

(1) Subject to the provisions of this Part, if any person intentionally kills, injures or takes any wild animal included in Schedule 5, he shall be guilty of an offence. [S]

(2) Subject to the provisions of this Part, if any person has in his possession or control any live or dead wild animal included in Schedule 5 or any part of, or anything derived from, such an animal, he shall be guilty of an offence. [S]

(3) A person shall not be guilty of an offence under subsection (2) if he shows that—

(a) the animal had not been killed or taken, or had been killed or taken otherwise than in contravention of the relevant provisions; or

(b) the animal or other thing in his possession or control had been sold (whether to him or any other person) otherwise than in contravention of those provisions;

and in this subsection "the relevant provisions" means the provisions of this Part and of the Conservation of Wild Creatures and Wild Plants Act 1975.

(4) Subject to the provisions of this Part, a person is guilty of an offence if intentionally or recklessly—

(a) he damages or destroys any structure or place which any wild animal included in Schedule 5 uses for shelter or protection;

(b) he disturbs any such animal while it is occupying a structure or place which it uses for that purpose; or

(c) he obstructs access to any structure or place which any such animal uses for shelter or protection. [S]

(4A) Subject to the provisions of this Part, if any person intentionally or recklessly disturbs any wild animal included in Schedule 5 as—

(a) a dolphin or whale (cetacea), or

(b) a basking shark (cetorhinus maximus),

he shall be guilty of an offence. [S]

(5) Subject to the provisions of this Part, if any person—

(a) sells, offers or exposes for sale, or has in his possession or transports for the purpose of sale, any live or dead wild animal included in Schedule 5, or any part of, or anything derived from, such an animal; or

(b) publishes or causes to be published any advertisement likely to be understood as conveying that he buys or sells, or intends to buy or sell, any of those things,

he shall be guilty of an offence. [S]

(6) In any proceedings for an offence under subsection (1), (2) or (5)(a), the animal in question shall be presumed to have been a wild animal unless the contrary is shown.

10   Exceptions to s. 9

(1)   Nothing in section 9 shall make unlawful—

  (a)   anything done in pursuance of a requirement by the Minister of Agriculture, Fisheries and Food or the Secretary of State under section 98 of the Agriculture Act 1947 . . . , or

  (b)   anything done under, or in pursuance of an order made under, the Animal Health Act 1981.

(2)   Nothing in subsection (4) of section 9 shall make unlawful anything done within a dwelling-house.

(3)   Notwithstanding anything in section 9, a person shall not be guilty of an offence by reason of—

  (a)   the taking of any such animal if he shows that the animal had been disabled otherwise than by his unlawful act and was taken solely for the purpose of tending it and releasing it when no longer disabled;

  (b)   the killing of any such animal if he shows that the animal had been so seriously disabled otherwise than by his unlawful act that there was no reasonable chance of its recovering; or

  (c)   any act made unlawful by that section if he shows that the act was the incidental result of a lawful operation and could not reasonably have been avoided.

(4)   Notwithstanding anything in section 9, an authorised person shall not be guilty of an offence by reason of the killing or injuring of a wild animal included in Schedule 5 if he shows that his action was necessary for the purpose of preventing serious damage to livestock, foodstuffs for livestock, crops, vegetables, fruit, growing timber or any other form of property or to fisheries.

(5)   A person shall not be entitled to rely on the defence provided by subsection (2) or (3)(c) as respects anything done in relation to a bat otherwise than in the living area of a dwelling house unless he had notified the conservation body for the area in which the house is situated or, as the case may be, the act is to take place of the proposed action or operation and allowed them a reasonable time to advise him as to whether it should be carried out and, if so, the method to be used.

(6)   An authorised person shall not be entitled to rely on the defence provided by subsection (4) as respects any action taken at any time if it had become apparent, before that time, that that action would prove necessary for the purpose mentioned in that subsection and either—

  (a)   a licence under section 16 authorising that action had not been applied for as soon as reasonably practicable after that fact had become apparent; or

  (b)   an application for such a licence had been determined.

11   Prohibition of certain methods of killing or taking wild animals

(1)   Subject to the provisions of this Part, if any person—

  (a)   sets in position any self-locking snare which is of such a nature and so placed as to be calculated to cause bodily injury to any wild animal coming into contact therewith;

  (b)   uses for the purpose of killing or taking any wild animal any self-locking snare, whether or not of such a nature or so placed as aforesaid, any bow or cross-bow or any explosive other than ammunition for a firearm;

  (c)   uses as a decoy, for the purpose of killing or taking any wild animal, any live mammal or bird whatever, or

  (d)   knowingly causes or permits to be done an act which is mentioned in the foregoing provisions of this section,

he shall be guilty of an offence. [S]

(2)   Subject to the provisions of this Part, a person shall be guilty of an offence if that person—

  (a)   uses any trap or snare for the purpose of killing or taking or restraining any wild animal included in Schedule 6 or 6ZA;

  (b)   sets in position any trap or snare of such a nature and so placed as to be—

    (i)   in England and Wales, calculated to cause bodily injury to any wild animal included in Schedule 6 or 6ZA;

  (c)   sets in position any electrical device for killing or stunning, or any poisonous, poisoned or stupefying substance, of such a nature and so placed as to be—

    (i)   in England and Wales, calculated to cause bodily injury to any wild animal included in Schedule 6;

  (d)   uses for the purpose of killing or taking any wild animal included in Schedule 6—

    (i)   any electrical device for killing or stunning;

(ii)   any poisonous, poisoned or stupefying substance;

(iii)   any net;

(iv)   any automatic or semi-automatic weapon;

(v)   any device for illuminating a target or sighting device for night shooting;

(vi)   any form of artificial light or any mirror or other dazzling device;

(vii)   any gas or smoke not falling within sub-paragraph (ii);

(viii) any sound recording used as a decoy; or

(ix)   any mechanically propelled vehicle in immediate pursuit of any such animal;

(e) uses any mechanically propelled vehicle for the purpose of driving any wild animal included in Schedule 6; or

(f) knowingly causes or permits to be done an act mentioned in paragraphs (a) to (e).

(3) Subject to the provisions of this Part, if any person—

(a) sets in position or knowingly causes or permits to be set in position any snare which is of such a nature and so placed as to be calculated to cause bodily injury to any wild animal coming into contact therewith; and

(b) while the snare remains in position fails, without reasonable excuse, to inspect it, or cause it to be inspected, at least once every day,

he shall be guilty of an offence. [S]

(5) In any proceedings for an offence under subsection (1)(b) or (c) or (2)(a), (d) or (e), and in any proceedings for an offence under subsection (1)(d) or (2)(f) relating to an act which is mentioned in any of those paragraphs the animal in question shall be presumed to have been a wild animal unless the contrary is shown.

(6) In any proceedings for an offence under subsection (2)(b) or (c) it shall be a defence to show that the article was set in position by the accused for the purpose of killing or taking, in the interests of public health, agriculture, forestry, fisheries or nature conservation, any wild animals which could be lawfully killed or taken by those means and that he took all reasonable precautions to prevent injury thereby to any wild animals included in the relevant Schedule.

(7) In any proceedings for an offence under subsection (2)(f) relating to an act which is mentioned in subsection (2)(b) or (c) it shall be a defence to show that the article was set in position for the purpose of killing or taking, in the interests of public health, agriculture, forestry, fisheries or nature conservation, any wild animals which could be lawfully killed or taken by those means and that he took or caused to be taken all reasonable precautions to prevent injury thereby to any wild animals included in the relevant Schedule.

(7A) In subsections (6) and (7), "the relevant Schedule" means—

(a) where proceedings relate to an offence under subsection (2)(b), Schedule 6 or 6ZA;

(b) where proceedings relate to an offence under subsection (2)(c), Schedule 6.

13 Protection of wild plants

(1) Subject to the provisions of this Part, if any person—

(a) intentionally picks, uproots or destroys any wild plant included in Schedule 8; or

(b) not being an authorised person, intentionally uproots any wild plant not included in that Schedule,

he shall be guilty of an offence.

(2) Subject to the provisions of this Part, if any person—

(a) sells, offers or exposes for sale, or has in his possession or transports for the purpose of sale, any live or dead wild plant included in Schedule 8, or any part of, or anything derived from, such a plant; or

(b) publishes or causes to be published any advertisement likely to be understood as conveying that he buys or sells, or intends to buy or sell, any of those things,

he shall be guilty of an offence. [S]

(3) Notwithstanding anything in subsection (1), a person shall not be guilty of an offence by reason of any act made unlawful by that subsection if he shows that the act was an incidental result of a lawful operation and could not reasonably have been avoided.

(4) In any proceedings for an offence under subsection (2)(a), the plant in question shall be presumed to have been a wild plant unless the contrary is shown.

Aviation Security Act 1982

1 Hijacking

(1) A person on board an aircraft in flight who unlawfully, by the use of force or by threats of any kind, seizes the aircraft or exercises control of it commits the offence of hijacking, whatever his nationality, whatever the State in which the aircraft is registered and whether the aircraft is in the United Kingdom or elsewhere, but subject to subsection (2) below. [I]

(2) If—

(a) the aircraft is used in military, customs or police service, or

(b) both the place of take-off and the place of landing are in the territory of the State in which the aircraft is registered,

subsection (1) above shall not apply unless—

(i)   the person seizing or exercising control of the aircraft is a United Kingdom national; or

(ii) his act is committed in the United Kingdom; or

(iii) the aircraft is registered in the United Kingdom or is used in the military or customs service of the United Kingdom or in the service of any police force in the United Kingdom.

(5) For the purposes of this section the territorial waters of any State shall be treated as part of its territory.

2 Destroying, damaging or endangering safety of aircraft

(1) It shall, subject to subsection (4) below, be an offence for any person unlawfully and intentionally—

(a) to destroy an aircraft in service or so to damage such an aircraft as to render it incapable of flight or as to be likely to endanger its safety in flight; or

(b) to commit on board an aircraft in flight any act of violence which is likely to endanger the safety of the aircraft. [I]

(2) It shall also, subject to subsection (4) below, be an offence for any person unlawfully and intentionally to place, or cause to be placed, on an aircraft in service any device or substance which is likely to destroy the aircraft, or is likely so to damage it as to render it incapable of flight or as to be likely to endanger its safety in flight; but nothing in this subsection shall be construed as limiting the circumstances in which the commission of any act—

(a) may constitute an offence under subsection (1) above, or

(b) may constitute attempting or conspiring to commit, or aiding, abetting, counselling or procuring, or being art and part in, the commission of such an offence. [I]

(3) Except as provided by subsection (4) below, subsections (1) and (2) above shall apply whether any such act as is therein mentioned is committed in the United Kingdom or elsewhere, whatever the nationality of the person committing the act and whatever the State in which the aircraft is registered.

(4) Subsections (1) and (2) above shall not apply to any act committed in relation to an aircraft used in military, customs or police service unless—

(a) the act is committed in the United Kingdom, or

(b) where the act is committed outside the United Kingdom, the person committing it is a United Kingdom national.

(6) In this section "unlawfully"—

(a) in relation to the commission of an act in the United Kingdom, means so as (apart from this Act) to constitute an offence under the law of the part of the United Kingdom in which the act is committed, and

(b) in relation to the commission of an act outside the United Kingdom, means so that the commission of the act would (apart from this Act) have been an offence under the law of England and Wales if it had been committed in England and Wales or of Scotland if it had been committed in Scotland.

(7) In this section "act of violence" means—

(a) any act done in the United Kingdom which constitutes the offence of murder, attempted murder, manslaughter, culpable homicide or assault or an offence under section 18, 20, 21, 22, 23, 24, 28 or 29 of the Offences against the Person Act 1861 or under section 2 of the Explosive Substances Act 1883, and

(b) any act done outside the United Kingdom which, if done in the United Kingdom, would constitute such an offence as is mentioned in paragraph (a) above.

3   Other acts endangering or likely to endanger safety of aircraft

(1) It shall, subject to subsections (5) and (6) below, be an offence for any person unlawfully and intentionally to destroy or damage any property to which this subsection applies, or to interfere with the operation of any such property, where the destruction, damage or interference is likely to endanger the safety of aircraft in flight. [I]

(2) Subsection (1) above applies to any property used for the provision of air navigation facilities, including any land, building or ship so used, and including any apparatus or equipment so used, whether it is on board an aircraft or elsewhere.

(3) It shall also, subject to subsections (4) and (5) below, be an offence for any person intentionally to communicate any information which is false, misleading or deceptive in a material particular, where the communication of the information endangers the safety of an aircraft in flight or is likely to endanger the safety of aircraft in flight. [I]

(4) It shall be a defence for a person charged with an offence under subsection (3) above to prove—

(a) that he believed, and had reasonable grounds for believing, that the information was true; or

(b) that, when he communicated the information, he was lawfully employed to perform duties which consisted of or included the communication of information and that he communicated the information in good faith in the performance of those duties.

(5) Subsections (1) and (3) above shall not apply to the commission of any act unless either the act is committed in the United Kingdom, or, where it is committed outside the United Kingdom—

(a) the person committing it is a United Kingdom national; or

(b) the commission of the act endangers or is likely to endanger the safety in flight of a civil aircraft registered in the United Kingdom or chartered by demise to a lessee whose principal place of business, or (if he has no place of business) whose permanent residence, is in the United Kingdom; or

(c) the act is committed on board a civil aircraft which is so registered or so chartered; or

(d) the act is committed on board a civil aircraft which lands in the United Kingdom with the person who committed the act still on board.

(6) Subsection (1) above shall also not apply to any act committed outside the United Kingdom and so committed in relation to property which is situated outside the United Kingdom and is not used for the provision of air navigation facilities in connection with international air navigation, unless the person committing the act is a United Kingdom national.

(8) In this section "civil aircraft" means any aircraft other than an aircraft used in military, customs or police service and "unlawfully" has the same meaning as in section 2 of this Act.

4 Offences in relation to certain dangerous articles

(1) It shall be an offence for any person without lawful authority or reasonable excuse (the proof of which shall lie on him) to have with him—

    (a) in any aircraft registered in the United Kingdom, whether at a time when the aircraft is in the United Kingdom or not, or

    (b) in any other aircraft at a time when it is in, or in flight over, the United Kingdom, or

    (c) in any part of an aerodrome in the United Kingdom, or

    (d) in any air navigation installation in the United Kingdom which does not form part of an aerodrome,

any article to which this section applies. [E]

(2) This section applies to the following articles, that is to say—

    (a) any firearm, or any article having the appearance of being a firearm, whether capable of being discharged or not;

    (b) any explosive, any article manufactured or adapted (whether in the form of a bomb, grenade or otherwise) so as to have the appearance of being an explosive, whether it is capable of producing a practical effect by explosion or not, or any article marked or labelled so as to indicate that it is or contains an explosive; and

    (c) any article (not falling within either of the preceding paragraphs) made or adapted for use for causing injury to or incapacitating a person or for destroying or damaging property, or intended by the person having it with him for such use, whether by him or by any other person.

(3) For the purposes of this section a person who is for the time being in an aircraft, or in part of an aerodrome, shall be treated as having with him in the aircraft, or in that part of the aerodrome, as the case may be, an article to which this section applies if—

    (a) where he is in an aircraft, the article, or an article in which it is contained, is in the aircraft and has been caused (whether by him or by any other person) to be brought there as being, or as forming part of, his baggage on a flight in the aircraft or has been caused by him to be brought there as being, or as forming part of, any other property to be carried on such a flight, or

    (b) where he is in part of an aerodrome (otherwise than in an aircraft), the article, or an article in which it is contained, is in that or any other part of the aerodrome and has been caused (whether by him or by any other person) to be brought into the aerodrome as being, or as forming part of, his baggage on a flight from that aerodrome or has been caused by him to be brought there as being, or as forming part of, any other property to be carried on such a flight on which he is also to be carried,

notwithstanding that the circumstances may be such that (apart from this subsection) he would not be regarded as having the article with him in the aircraft or in a part of the aerodrome, as the case may be.

(5) Nothing in subsection (3) above shall be construed as limiting the circumstances in which a person would, apart from that subsection, be regarded as having an article with him as mentioned in subsection (1) above.

38 Interpretation, etc.

(1) In this Act, except in so far as the context otherwise requires—

"aerodrome" means the aggregate of the land, buildings and works comprised in an aerodrome within the meaning of the Civil Aviation Act 1982 and (if and so far as not comprised in an aerodrome as defined in that Act) any land, building or works situated within the boundaries of an area designated, by an order made by the Secretary of State which is for the time being in force, as constituting the area of an aerodrome for the purposes of this Act;

"air navigation installation" means any building, works, apparatus or equipment used wholly or mainly for the purpose of assisting air traffic control or as an aid to air navigation, together with any land contiguous or adjacent to any such building, works, apparatus or equipment and used wholly or mainly for purposes connected therewith;

"aircraft registered or operating in the United Kingdom" means any aircraft which is either—

    (a) an aircraft registered in the United Kingdom, or

    (b) an aircraft not so registered which is for the time being allocated for use on a flight any part of which is in the United Kingdom;

"article" includes any substance, whether in solid or liquid form or in the form of a gas or vapour;

"constable" includes any person having the powers and privileges of a constable;

"explosive" means any article manufactured for the purpose of producing a practical effect by explosion, or intended for that purpose by a person having the article with him;

"firearm" includes an airgun or air pistol;

"manager", in relation to an aerodrome, means the person (whether the Civil Aviation Authority, a local authority or any other person) by whom the aerodrome is managed;

"military service" includes naval and air force service;

"measures" (without prejudice to the generality of that expression) includes the construction, execution, alteration, demolition or removal of buildings or other works and also includes the institution or modification, and the supervision and enforcement, of any practice or procedure;

"operator" has the same meaning as in the Civil Aviation Act 1982;

"property" includes any land, buildings or works, any aircraft or vehicle and any baggage, cargo or other article of any description;

"United Kingdom national" means an individual who is—

    (a) a British citizen, a British Overseas Territories citizen, a British National (Overseas) or a British Overseas citizen;

    (b) a person who under the British Nationality Act 1981 is a British subject; or

    (c) a British protected person (within the meaning of that Act).

(1A) Subject to subsection (1D), a reference in this Act to an aircraft includes a reference to a medium-range rocket.

(1B) In subsection (1A) "rocket" means a projectile of mainly cylindrical or similar shape that can be propelled from or above the earth by combustion of its fuel (or fuel and oxidant).

(1C) For the purposes of subsection (1A) a rocket is a "medium-range" rocket if—

    (a) the total impulse of its motor or combination of motors exceeds 160 Newton-seconds, but

    (b) it is not capable of operating above the stratosphere.

(2) For the purposes of this Act—

    (a) in the case of an air navigation installation provided by, or used wholly or mainly by, the Civil Aviation Authority, that Authority, and

    (b) in the case of any other air navigation installation, the person by whom it is provided, or by whom it is wholly or mainly used,

shall be taken to be the authority responsible for that air navigation installation.

(3) For the purposes of this Act—

    (a) the period during which an aircraft is in flight shall be deemed to include any period from the moment when all its external doors are closed following embarkation until the moment when any such door is opened for disembarkation, and, in the case of a forced landing, any period until the competent authorities take over responsibility for the aircraft and for persons and property on board; and

    (b) an aircraft shall be taken to be in service during the whole of the period which begins with the pre-flight preparation of the aircraft for a flight and ends 24 hours after the aircraft lands having completed that flight, and also at any time (not falling within that period) while, in accordance with the preceding paragraph, the aircraft is in flight,

and anything done on board an aircraft while in flight over any part of the United Kingdom shall be treated as done in that part of the United Kingdom.

(4) For the purposes of this Act the territorial waters adjacent to any part of the United Kingdom shall be treated as included in that part of the United Kingdom.

Civil Aviation Act 1982

92   Application of criminal law to aircraft

(1) Any act or omission taking place on board a British-controlled aircraft or (subject to subsection (1A) below) a foreign aircraft while in flight elsewhere than in or over the United Kingdom which, if taking place in, or in a part of, the United Kingdom, would constitute an offence under the law in force in, or in that part of, the United Kingdom shall constitute that offence; but this subsection shall not apply to any act or omission which is expressly or impliedly authorised by or under that law when taking place outside the United Kingdom.

(1A) Subsection (1) above shall only apply to an act or omission which takes place on board a foreign aircraft where—

    (a) the next landing of the aircraft is in the United Kingdom, and

    (b) in the case of an aircraft registered in a country other than the United Kingdom, the act or omission would, if taking place there, also constitute an offence under the law in force in that country.

(1B) Any act or omission punishable under the law in force in any country is an offence under that law for the purposes of subsection (1A) above, however it is described in that law.

(4) For the purposes of this section the period during which an aircraft is in flight shall be deemed to include any period from the moment when power is applied for the purpose of the aircraft taking off on a flight until the moment when the landing run (if any) at the termination of that flight ends; and any reference in this section to an aircraft in flight shall include a reference to an aircraft during any period when it is on the surface of the sea or land but not within the territorial limits of any country.

(5) In this section, except where the context otherwise requires—

"aircraft" means any aircraft, whether or not a British-controlled aircraft, other than—

    (a) a military aircraft; or

    (b) subject to section 101(1)(b) below, an aircraft which, not being a military aircraft, belongs to or is exclusively employed in the service of Her Majesty in right of the United Kingdom;

"British-controlled aircraft" means an aircraft—

    (a) which is for the time being registered in the United Kingdom; or

    (b) which is not for the time being registered in any country but in the case of which either the operator of the aircraft or each person entitled as owner to any legal or beneficial interest in it satisfies the following requirements, namely—

        (i) that he is a person qualified to be the owner of a legal or beneficial interest in an aircraft registered in the United Kingdom; and

        (ii) that he resides or has his principal place of business in the United Kingdom; or

    (c) which, being for the time being registered in some other country, is for the time being chartered by demise to a person who, or to persons each of whom, satisfies the requirements aforesaid; . . .

"foreign aircraft" means any aircraft other than a British-controlled aircraft.

"military aircraft" means—

    (a) an aircraft of the naval, military or air forces of any country; or

    (b) any other aircraft in respect of which there is in force a certificate issued in accordance with any Order in Council in force under section 60, 87, 89, 91, 101(1)(a) or 107(2) of this Act that the aircraft is to be treated for the purposes of that Order in Council as a military aircraft;

and a certificate of the Secretary of State that any aircraft is or is not a military aircraft for the purposes of this section shall be conclusive evidence of the fact certified.

Taking of Hostages Act 1982

1   Hostage-taking

(1) A person, whatever his nationality, who, in the United Kingdom or elsewhere,—

    (a) detains any other person ("the hostage"), and

    (b) in order to compel a State, international governmental organisation or person to do or abstain from doing any act, threatens to kill, injure or continue to detain the hostage,

commits an offence. [I]

Mental Health Act 1983

PART IV   CONSENT TO TREATMENT

56   Patients to whom Part IV applies

(1) Section 57 and, so far as relevant to that section, sections 59 to 62 below apply to any patient.

(2) Subject to that and to subsection (5) below, this Part of this Act applies to a patient only if he falls within subsection (3) or (4) below.

(3) A patient falls within this subsection if he is liable to be detained under this Act but not if—

    (a) he is so liable by virtue of an emergency application and the second medical recommendation referred to in section 4(4)(a) above has not been given and received;

    (b) he is so liable by virtue of section 5(2) or (4) or 35 above or section 135 or 136 below or by virtue of a direction for his detention in a place of safety under section 37(4) or 45A(5) above; or

    (c) he has been conditionally discharged under section 42(2) above or section 73 or 74 below and he is not recalled to hospital.

(4) A patient falls within this subsection if—

    (a) he is a community patient; and

    (b) he is recalled to hospital under section 17E above.

(5) Section 58A and, so far as relevant to that section, sections 59 to 62 below also apply to any patient who—

    (a) does not fall within subsection (3) above;

    (b) is not a community patient; and

    (c) has not attained the age of 18 years.

57   Treatment requiring consent and a second opinion

(1) This section applies to the following forms of medical treatment for mental disorder—

    (a) any surgical operation for destroying brain tissue or for destroying the functioning of brain tissue; and

    (b) such other forms of treatment as may be specified for the purposes of this section by regulations made by the Secretary of State.

(2) Subject to section 62 below, a patient shall not be given any form of treatment to which this section applies unless he has consented to it and—

    (a) a registered medical practitioner appointed for the purposes of this Part of this Act by the regulatory authority (not being the responsible clinician (if there is one) or, the person in charge of the treatment in question) and two other persons appointed for the purposes of this paragraph by the regulatory authority (not being registered medical practitioners) have certified in writing that the patient is capable of understanding the nature, purpose and likely effects of the treatment in question and has consented to it; and

    (b) the registered medical practitioner referred to in paragraph (a) above has certified in writing that it is appropriate for the treatment to be given.

(3) Before giving a certificate under subsection (2)(b) above the registered medical practitioner concerned shall consult two other persons who have been professionally concerned with the patient's medical treatment, but, of those persons—

    (a) one shall be a nurse and the other shall be neither a nurse nor a registered medical practitioner; and

    (b) neither shall be the responsible clinician (if there is one) or the person in charge of the treatment in question.

58   Treatment requiring consent or a second opinion

(1) This section applies to the following forms of medical treatment for mental disorder—

    (a) such forms of treatment as may be specified for the purposes of this section by regulations made by the Secretary of State;

    (b) the administration of medicine to a patient by any means (not being a form of treatment specified under paragraph (a) above or section 57 above or section 58A(1)(b)) below at any time during a period for which he is liable to be detained as a patient to whom this Part of this Act applies if three months or more have elapsed since the first occasion in that period when medicine was administered to him by any means for his mental disorder.

(3) Subject to section 62 below, a patient shall not be given any form of treatment to which this section applies unless—

    (a) he has consented to that treatment and either the approved clinician in charge of it or a registered medical practitioner appointed for the purposes of this Part of this Act by the regulatory authority has certified in writing that the patient is capable of understanding its nature, purpose and likely effects and has consented to it; or

    (b) a registered medical practitioner appointed as aforesaid (not being the responsible clinician or the approved clinician in charge of the treatment in question) has certified in writing that the patient is not capable of understanding the nature, purpose and likely effects of that treatment or being so capable has not consented to it but that it is appropriate for the treatment to be given.

(4) Before giving a certificate under subsection (3)(b) above the registered medical practitioner concerned shall consult two other persons who have been professionally concerned with the patient's medical treatment but, of those persons—

    (a) one shall be a nurse and the other shall be neither a nurse nor a registered medical practitioner; and

    (b) neither shall be the responsible clinician or the approved clinician in charge of the treatment in question.

58A   Electro-convulsive therapy, etc.

(1) This section applies to the following forms of medical treatment for mental disorder—

    (a) electro-convulsive therapy; and

    (b) such other forms of treatment as may be specified for the purposes of this section by regulations made by the appropriate national authority.

(2) Subject to section 62 below, a patient shall be not be given any form of treatment to which this section applies unless he falls within subsection (3), (4) or (5) below.

(3) A patient falls within this subsection if—

    (a) he has attained the age of 18 years;

    (b) he has consented to the treatment in question; and

    (c) either the approved clinician in charge of it or a registered medical practitioner appointed as mentioned in section 58(3) above has certified in writing that the patient is capable of understanding the nature, purpose and likely effects of the treatment and has consented to it.

(4) A patient falls within this subsection if—

(a) he has not attained the age of 18 years; but

(b) he has consented to the treatment in question; and

(c) a registered medical practitioner appointed as aforesaid (not being the approved clinician in charge of the treatment) has certified in writing—

    (i) that the patient is capable of understanding the nature, purpose and likely effects of the treatment and has consented to it; and

    (ii) that it is appropriate for the treatment to be given.

(5) A patient falls within this subsection if a registered medical practitioner appointed as aforesaid (not being the responsible clinician (if there is one) or the approved clinician in charge of the treatment in question) has certified in writing—

(a) that the patient is not capable of understanding the nature, purpose and likely effects of the treatment; but

(b) that it is appropriate for the treatment to be given; and

(c) that giving him the treatment would not conflict with—

    (i) an advance decision which the registered medical practitioner concerned is satisfied is valid and applicable; or

    (ii) a decision made by a donee or deputy or by the Court of Protection.

(6) Before giving a certificate under subsection (5) above the registered medical practitioner concerned shall consult two other persons who have been professionally concerned with the patient's medical treatment but, of those persons—

(a) one shall be a nurse and the other shall be neither a nurse nor a registered medical practitioner; and

(b) neither shall be the responsible clinician (if there is one) or the approved clinician in charge of the treatment in question.

(7) This section shall not by itself confer sufficient authority for a patient who falls within section 56(5) above to be given a form of treatment to which this section applies if he is not capable of understanding the nature, purpose and likely effects of the treatment (and cannot therefore consent to it).

(9) In this section—

(a) a reference to an advance decision is to an advance decision (within the meaning of the Mental Capacity Act 2005) made by the patient;

(b) "valid and applicable", in relation to such a decision, means valid and applicable to the treatment in question in accordance with section 25 of that Act;

(c) a reference to a donee is to a donee of a lasting power of attorney (within the meaning of section 9 of that Act) created by the patient, where the donee is acting within the scope of his authority and in accordance with that Act; and

(d) a reference to a deputy is to a deputy appointed for the patient by the Court of Protection under section 16 of that Act, where the deputy is acting within the scope of his authority and in accordance with that Act.

59 Plans of treatment

Any consent or certificate under section 57, 58 or 58A above may relate to a plan of treatment under which the patient is to be given (whether within a specified period or otherwise) one or more of the forms of treatment to which that section applies.

60 Withdrawal of consent

(1) Where the consent of a patient to any treatment has been given for the purposes of section 57, 58 or 58A above, the patient may, subject to section 62 below, at any time before the completion of the treatment withdraw his consent, and those sections shall then apply as if the remainder of the treatment were a separate form of treatment.

(1A) Subsection (1B) below applies where—

(a) the consent of a patient to any treatment has been given for the purposes of section 57, 58 or 58A above; but

    (b) before the completion of the treatment, the patient ceases to be capable of understanding its nature, purpose and likely effects.

(1B) The patient shall, subject to section 62 below, be treated as having withdrawn his consent, and those sections shall then apply as if the remainder of the treatment were a separate form of treatment.

(1C) Subsection (1D) below applies where—

    (a) a certificate has been given under section 58 or 58A above that a patient is not capable of understanding the nature, purpose and likely effects of the treatment to which the certificate applies; but

    (b) before the completion of the treatment, the patient becomes capable of understanding its nature, purpose and likely effects.

(1D) The certificate shall, subject to section 62 below, cease to apply to the treatment and those sections shall then apply as if the remainder of the treatment were a separate form of treatment.

(2) Without prejudice to the application of subsections (1) to (1D) above to any treatment given under the plan of treatment to which a patient has consented, a patient who has consented to such a plan may, subject to section 62 below, at any time withdraw his consent to further treatment, or to further treatment of any description, under the plan.

62 Urgent treatment

(1) Sections 57 and 58 above shall not apply to any treatment—

    (a) which is immediately necessary to save the patient's life; or

    (b) which (not being irreversible) is immediately necessary to prevent a serious deterioration of his condition; or

    (c) which (not being irreversible or hazardous) is immediately necessary to alleviate serious suffering by the patient; or

    (d) which (not being irreversible or hazardous) is immediately necessary and represents the minimum interference necessary to prevent the patient from behaving violently or being a danger to himself or to others.

(1A) Section 58A above, in so far as it relates to electro-convulsive therapy by virtue of subsection (1)(a) of that section, shall not apply to any treatment which falls within paragraph (a) or (b) of subsection (1) above.

(1B) Section 58A above, in so far as it relates to a form of treatment specified by virtue of subsection (1)(b) of that section, shall not apply to any treatment which falls within such of paragraphs (a) to (d) of subsection (1) above as may be specified in regulations under that section.

(1C) For the purposes of subsection (1B) above, the regulations—

    (a) may make different provision for different cases (and may, in particular, make different provision for different forms of treatment);

    (b) may make provision which applies subject to specified exceptions; and

    (c) may include transitional, consequential, incidental or supplemental provision.

(2) Sections 60 and 61(3) above shall not preclude the continuation of any treatment or of treatment under any plan pending compliance with section 57, 58 or 58A above if the approved clinician in charge of the treatment considers that the discontinuance of the treatment or of treatment under the plan would cause serious suffering to the patient.

(3) For the purposes of this section treatment is irreversible if it has unfavourable irreversible physical or psychological consequences and hazardous if it entails significant physical hazard.

63 Treatment not requiring consent

The consent of a patient shall not be required for any medical treatment given to him for the mental disorder from which he is suffering, not being a form of treatment to which section 57, 58 or 58A applies, if the treatment is given by or under the direction of the approved clinician in charge of the treatment.

PART IX   OFFENCES

127   Ill-treatment of patients

(1) It shall be an offence for any person who is an officer on the staff of or otherwise employed in, or who is one of the managers of, a hospital, independent hospital or care home—

    (a) to ill-treat or wilfully to neglect a patient for the time being receiving treatment for mental disorder as an in-patient in that hospital or home; or

    (b) to ill-treat or wilfully to neglect, on the premises of which the hospital or home forms part, a patient for the time being receiving such treatment there as an out-patient. [E]

(2) It shall be an offence for any individual to ill-treat or wilfully to neglect a mentally disordered patient who is for the time being subject to his guardianship under this Act or otherwise in his custody or care (whether by virtue of a legal or moral obligation or otherwise). [E]

Child Abduction Act 1984

PART I   OFFENCES UNDER THE LAW OF ENGLAND AND WALES

1   Offence of abduction of child by parent, etc.

(1) Subject to subsections (5) and (8) below, a person connected with a child under the age of sixteen commits an offence if he takes or sends the child out of the United Kingdom without the appropriate consent. [E]

(2) A person is connected with a child for the purposes of this section if—

    (a) he is a parent of the child; or

    (b) in the case of a child whose parents were not married to, or civil partners of, each other at the time of his birth, there are reasonable grounds for believing that he is the father of the child; or

    (c) he is a guardian of the child; or

    (ca) he is a special guardian of the child; or

    (d) he is a person named in a child arrangements order as a person with whom the child is to live; or

    (e) he has custody of the child.

(3) In this section "the appropriate consent" in relation to a child, means—

    (a) the consent of each of the following—

        (i)   the child's mother;

        (ii)   the child's father, if he has parental responsibility for him;

        (iii)   any guardian of the child;

        (iiia)   any special guardian of the child;

        (iv)   any person named in a child arrangements order as a person with whom the child is to live;

        (v)   any person who has custody of the child; or

    (b) the leave of the court granted under or by virtue of any provision of Part II of the Children Act 1989; or

    (c) if any person has custody of the child, the leave of the court which awarded custody to him.

(4) A person does not commit an offence under this section by taking or sending a child out of the United Kingdom without obtaining the appropriate consent if—

    (a) he is a person named in a child arrangements order as a person with whom the child is to live and he takes or sends the child out of the United Kingdom for a period of less than one month; or

    (b) he is a special guardian of the child and he takes or sends the child out of the United Kingdom for a period of less than three months.

(4A) Subsection (4) above does not apply if the person taking or sending the child out of the United Kingdom does so in breach of an order under Part II of the Children Act 1989.

(5) A person does not commit an offence under this section by doing anything without the consent of another person whose consent is required under the foregoing provisions if—

    (a) he does it in the belief that the other person—

        (i)   has consented; or

        (ii) would consent if he was aware of all the relevant circumstances; or

    (b) he has taken all reasonable steps to communicate with the other person but has been unable to communicate with him; or

    (c) the other person has unreasonably refused to consent.

(5A) Subsection (5)(c) above does not apply if—

    (a) the person who refused to consent is a person—

        (i)   named in a child arrangements order as a person with whom the child is to live;

        (ia) who is a special guardian of the child; or

        (ii) who has custody of the child; or

    (b) the person taking or sending the child out of the United Kingdom is, by so acting, in breach of an order made by a court in the United Kingdom.

(6) Where, in proceedings for an offence under this section, there is sufficient evidence to raise an issue as to the application of subsection (5) above, it shall be for the prosecution to prove that the subsection does not apply.

(7) For the purposes of this section—

    (a) "guardian of a child", "special guardian", "child arrangements order" and "parental responsibility" have the same meaning as in the Children Act 1989; and

    (b) a person shall be treated as having custody of a child if there is in force an order of a court in the United Kingdom awarding him (whether solely or jointly with another person) custody, legal custody or care and control of the child.

(8) This section shall have effect subject to the provisions of the Schedule to this Act in relation to a child who is in the care of a local authority detained in a place of safety, remanded otherwise than on bail or the subject of proceedings or an order relating to adoption.

2   Offence of abduction of child by other persons

(1) Subject to subsection (3) below, a person, other than one mentioned in subsection (2) below, commits an offence if, without lawful authority or reasonable excuse, he takes or detains a child under the age of sixteen—

    (a) so as to remove him from the lawful control of any person having lawful control of the child; or

    (b) so as to keep him out of the lawful control of any person entitled to lawful control of the child. [E]

(2) The persons are—

    (a) where the father and mother of the child in question were married to, or civil partners of, each other at the time of his birth, the child's father and mother;

    (b) where the father and mother of the child in question were not married to, or civil partners of, each other at the time of his birth, the child's mother; and

    (c) any other person mentioned in section 1(2)(c) to (e) above.

(3) In proceedings against any person for an offence under this section, it shall be a defence for that person to prove—

    (a) where the father and mother of the child in question were not married to, or civil partners of, each other at the time of his birth—

        (i)   that he is the child's father; or

        (ii) that, at the time of the alleged offence, he believed, on reasonable grounds, that he was the child's father; or

    (b) that, at the time of the alleged offence, he believed that the child had attained the age of sixteen.

3 Construction of references to taking, sending and detaining

For the purposes of this Part of this Act—

(a) a person shall be regarded as taking a child if he causes or induces the child to accompany him or any other person or causes the child to be taken;

(b) a person shall be regarded as sending a child if he causes the child to be sent;

(c) a person shall be regarded as detaining a child if he causes the child to be detained or induces the child to remain with him or any other person; and

(d) references to a child's parents and to a child whose parents were (or were not) married to, or civil partners of, each other at the time of his birth shall be construed in accordance with section 1 of the Family Law Reform Act 1987 (which extends their meaning).

Police and Criminal Evidence Act 1984

24 Arrest without warrant: constables

(1) A constable may arrest without a warrant—

(a) anyone who is about to commit an offence;

(b) anyone who is in the act of committing an offence;

(c) anyone whom he has reasonable grounds for suspecting to be about to commit an offence;

(d) anyone whom he has reasonable grounds for suspecting to be committing an offence.

(2) If a constable has reasonable grounds for suspecting that an offence has been committed, he may arrest without a warrant anyone whom he has reasonable grounds to suspect of being guilty of it.

(3) If an offence has been committed, a constable may arrest without a warrant—

(a) anyone who is guilty of the offence;

(b) anyone whom he has reasonable grounds for suspecting to be guilty of it.

(4) But the power of summary arrest conferred by subsection (1), (2) or (3) is exercisable only if the constable has reasonable grounds for believing that for any of the reasons mentioned in subsection (5) it is necessary to arrest the person in question.

(5) The reasons are—

(a) to enable the name of the person in question to be ascertained (in the case where the constable does not know, and cannot readily ascertain, the person's name, or has reasonable grounds for doubting whether a name given by the person as his name is his real name);

(b) correspondingly as regards the person's address;

(c) to prevent the person in question—

(i) causing physical injury to himself or any other person;

(ii) suffering physical injury;

(iii) causing loss of or damage to property;

(iv) committing an offence against public decency (subject to subsection (6)); or

(v) causing an unlawful obstruction of the highway;

(d) to protect a child or other vulnerable person from the person in question;

(e) to allow the prompt and effective investigation of the offence or of the conduct of the person in question;

(f) to prevent any prosecution for the offence from being hindered by the disappearance of the person in question.

(6) Subsection (5)(c)(iv) applies only where members of the public going about their normal business cannot reasonably be expected to avoid the person in question.

24A Arrest without warrant: other persons

(1) A person other than a constable may arrest without a warrant—

(a) anyone who is in the act of committing an indictable offence;

(b) anyone whom he has reasonable grounds for suspecting to be committing an indictable offence.

(2) Where an indictable offence has been committed, a person other than a constable may arrest without a warrant—

  (a) anyone who is guilty of the offence;

  (b) anyone whom he has reasonable grounds for suspecting to be guilty of it.

(3) But the power of summary arrest conferred by subsection (1) or (2) is exercisable only if—

  (a) the person making the arrest has reasonable grounds for believing that for any of the reasons mentioned in subsection (4) it is necessary to arrest the person in question; and

  (b) it appears to the person making the arrest that it is not reasonably practicable for a constable to make it instead.

(4) The reasons are to prevent the person in question—

  (a) causing physical injury to himself or any other person;

  (b) suffering physical injury;

  (c) causing loss of or damage to property; or

  (d) making off before a constable can assume responsibility for him.

(5) This section does not apply in relation to an offence under Part 3 or 3A of the Public Order Act 1986.

117   Power of constable to use reasonable force

Where any provision of this Act—

  (a) confers a power on a constable; and

  (b) does not provide that the power may only be exercised with the consent of some person, other than a police officer,

the officer may use reasonable force, if necessary, in the exercise of the power.

Road Traffic Regulation Act 1984

47   Offences relating to designated parking places

(3) A person who, with intent to defraud, interferes with a parking meter, or operates or attempts to operate a parking meter by the insertion of objects other than current coins or bank notes of the appropriate denomination, or the appropriate credit or debit cards, shall be guilty of an offence. [S]

81   General speed limit for restricted roads

(1) It shall not be lawful for a person to drive a motor vehicle on a restricted road at a speed exceeding 30 miles per hour. [S]

82   What roads are restricted roads

(1) Subject to the provisions of this section and of section 84(3) of this Act, a road is a restricted road for the purposes of section 81 of this Act if—

  (a) in England and Wales, there is provided on it a system of street lighting furnished by means of lamps placed not more than 200 yards apart.

84   Speed limits on roads other than restricted roads

(1) An order made under this subsection as respects any road may prohibit—

  (a) the driving of motor vehicles on that road at a speed exceeding that specified in the order,

  (b) the driving of motor vehicles on that road at a speed exceeding that specified in the order during periods specified in the order, or

  (c) the driving of motor vehicles on that road at a speed exceeding the speed for the time being indicated by traffic signs in accordance with the order.

(1A) An order made by virtue of subsection (1)(c) above may—

(a) make provision restricting the speeds that may be indicated by traffic signs or the periods during which the indication may be given, and

(b) provide for the indications to be given only in such circumstances as may be determined by or under the order;

but any such order must comply with regulations made under subsection (1B) below, except where the national authority authorises otherwise in a particular case.

(3) While an order made by virtue of subsection (1)(a) above is in force as respects a road, that road shall not be a restricted road for the purposes of section 81 of this Act.

85   Traffic signs for indicating speed restrictions

(4) Where no such system of street or carriageway lighting as is mentioned in section 82(1) is provided on a road, but a limit of speed is to be observed on the road, a person shall not be convicted of driving a motor vehicle on the road at a speed exceeding the limit unless the limit is indicated by means of such traffic signs as are mentioned in subsection (1) or subsection (2) above.

(5) In any proceedings for a contravention of section 81 of this Act, where the proceedings relate to driving on a road provided with such a system of street or carriageway lighting, evidence of the absence of traffic signs displayed in pursuance of this section to indicate that the road is not a restricted road for the purposes of that section shall be evidence that the road is a restricted road for those purposes.

86   Speed limits for particular classes of vehicles

(1) It shall not be lawful for a person to drive a motor vehicle of any class on a road at a speed greater than the speed specified in Schedule 6 to this Act as the maximum speed in relation to a vehicle of that class. [S]

87   Exemption of fire brigade, ambulance and police vehicles from speed limits

(1) No statutory provision imposing a speed limit on motor vehicles shall apply to any vehicle on an occasion when it is being used for fire and rescue authority, ambulance or police purposes, if the observance of that provision would be likely to hinder the use of the vehicle for the purpose for which it is being used on that occasion.

(1A) Subsection (1) above applies in relation to a vehicle that, although not being used for ambulance purposes, is being used for the purpose of providing a response to an emergency at the request of an NHS ambulance service.

(1B) In subsection (1A), "an NHS ambulance service" means—

(a) an NHS trust or NHS foundation trust established under the National Health Service Act 2006 which has a function of providing ambulance services; . . .

(2) Subsection (1) above applies in relation to a vehicle being used—

(a) for National Crime Agency purposes, or

(b) for training persons to drive vehicles for use for National Crime Agency purposes,

as it applies in relation to a vehicle being used for police purposes.

(3) But (except where it is being used for training the person by whom it is being driven) subsection (1) above does not apply in relation to a vehicle by virtue of subsection (2) above unless it is being driven by a person who has been trained in driving vehicles at high speeds.

89   Speeding offences generally

(1) A person who drives a motor vehicle on a road at a speed exceeding a limit imposed by or under any enactment to which this section applies shall be guilty of an offence. [S]

(4) If a person who employs other persons to drive motor vehicles on roads publishes or issues any time-table or schedule, or gives any directions, under which any journey, or any stage or part of any journey, is to be completed within some specified time, and it is not practicable in the circumstances of the case for that journey (or that stage or part of it) to be completed in the specified time without the commission of such an offence as is mentioned in subsection (1) above, the publication or issue of the time-table or schedule, or the giving of the directions may be produced as prima facie evidence that the employer procured or (as the case may be) incited the persons employed by him to drive the vehicles to commit such an offence.

Video Recordings Act 1984

1 Interpretation of terms

(1) The provisions of this section shall have effect for the interpretation of terms used in this Act.

(2) "Video work" means any series of visual images (with or without sound)—

(a) produced electronically by the use of information contained on any disc, magnetic tape or any other device capable of storing data electronically, and

(b) shown as a moving picture.

(3) "Video recording" means any disc, magnetic tape or any other device capable of storing data electronically containing information by the use of which the whole or a part of a video work may be produced.

(4) "Supply" means supply in any manner, whether or not for reward, and, therefore, includes supply by way of sale, letting on hire, exchange or loan; and references to a supply are to be interpreted accordingly.

2 Exempted works

(1) Subject to subsection (1ZA) below, a video work other than a video game is for the purposes of this Act an exempted work if, taken as a whole—

(a) it is designed to inform, educate or instruct; or

(b) it is concerned with sport, religion or music.

(1A) Subject to subsection (2) or (3) below, a video game is for the purposes of this Act an exempted work if—

(a) it is, taken as a whole, designed to inform, educate or instruct;

(b) it is, taken as a whole, concerned with sport, religion or music; or

(c) it satisfies one or more of the conditions in section 2A.

(1ZA) A video work other than a video game is not an exempted work for those purposes if it does one or more of the following—

(a) it depicts or promotes violence or threats of violence;

(b) it depicts the immediate aftermath of violence on human or animal characters;

(c) it depicts an imitable dangerous activity without also depicting that the activity may endanger the welfare or health of a human or animal character;

(d) it promotes an imitable dangerous activity;

(e) it depicts or promotes activities involving illegal drugs or the misuse of drugs;

(f) it promotes the use of alcohol or tobacco;

(g) it depicts or promotes suicide or attempted suicide, or depicts the immediate aftermath of such an event;

(h) it depicts or promotes any act of scarification or mutilation of a person, or of self-harm, or depicts the immediate aftermath of such an act;

(i) it depicts techniques likely to be useful in the commission of offences or, through its depiction of criminal activity, promotes the commission of offences;

(j) it includes words or images intended or likely to convey a sexual message (ignoring words or images depicting any mild sexual behaviour);

(k) it depicts human sexual activity (ignoring any depictions of mild sexual activity);

(l) it depicts or promotes acts of force or restraint associated with human sexual activity;

(m) it depicts human genital organs or human urinary or excretory functions (unless the depiction is for a medical, scientific or educational purpose);

(n) it includes swearing (ignoring any mild bad language); or

(o) it includes words or images that are intended or likely (to any extent) to cause offence, whether on the grounds of race, gender, disability, religion or belief or sexual orientation, or otherwise.

(1ZB) For the purposes of subsection (1ZA), a video work promotes something if the work is likely (to any extent) to stimulate or encourage that thing.

(1ZC) In subsection (1ZA)—

"human or animal character" means a character that is or whose appearance is similar to that of—

 (a) a human being, or

 (b) an animal that exists or has existed in real life,

but does not include a simple stick character or any equally basic representation of a human being or animal;

"imitable dangerous activity" means an activity which—

 (a) if imitated by a person, may endanger the welfare or health of any person or animal, and

 (b) may be easily imitated by a person; and

"violence" does not include any violence that is—

 (a) mild, or

 (b) not directed towards human or animal characters,

unless it is sexual violence.

(1A) Subject to subsection (2) or (3) below, a video game is for the purposes of this Act an exempted work if—

 (a) it is, taken as a whole, designed to inform, educate or instruct;

 (b) it is, taken as a whole, concerned with sport, religion or music; or

 (c) it satisfies one or more of the conditions in section 2A.

(2) A video game is not an exempted work for those purposes if, to any significant extent, it depicts—

 (a) a human sexual activity or acts of force or restraint associated with such activity;

 (b) mutilation or torture of, or other acts of gross violence towards, humans or animals;

 (c) human genital organs or human urinary or excretory functions;

 (d) techniques likely to be useful in the commission of offences;

or is likely to any significant extent to stimulate or encourage anything falling within paragraph (a) or, in the case of anything falling within paragraph (b), is likely to any extent to do so.

(3) A video game is not an exempted work for those purposes if, to any significant extent, it depicts criminal activity which is likely to any significant extent to stimulate or encourage the commission of offences.

2A Conditions relating to video games

(1) The conditions referred to in section 2(1A)(c) are as follows.

(2) The first condition is that the video game does not include any of the following—

 (a) depictions of violence towards human or animal characters, whether or not the violence looks realistic and whether or not the violence results in obvious harm,

 (b) depictions of violence towards other characters where the violence looks realistic,

 (c) depictions of criminal activity that are likely, to any extent, to stimulate or encourage the commission of offences,

 (d) depictions of activities involving illegal drugs or the misuse of drugs,

 (e) words or images that are likely, to any extent, to stimulate or encourage the use of alcohol or tobacco,

 (f) words or images that are intended to convey a sexual message,

 (g) swearing, or

 (h) words or images that are intended or likely, to any extent, to cause offence, whether on the grounds of race, gender, disability, religion or belief or sexual orientation or otherwise.

(3) In subsection (2) "human or animal character" means a character that is, or whose appearance is similar to that of—

 (a) a human being, or

 (b) an animal that exists or has existed in real life,

but does not include a simple stick character or any equally basic representation of a human being or animal.

(4) The second condition is that the designated authority, or a person nominated by the designated authority for the purposes of this section, has confirmed in writing that the video game is suitable for viewing by persons under the age of 12.

3   Exempted supplies

(1) The provisions of this section apply to determine whether or not a supply of a video recording is an exempted supply for the purposes of this Act.

(2) The supply of a video recording by any person is an exempted supply if it is neither—

(a) a supply for reward, nor

(b) a supply in the course of furtherance of a business.

(3) Where on any premises facilities are provided in the course or furtherance of a business for supplying video recordings, the supply by any person of a video recording on those premises is to be treated for the purposes of subsection (2) above as a supply in the course or furtherance of a business.

(4) Where a person (in this subsection referred to as the "original supplier") supplies a video recording to a person who, in the course of a business, makes video works or supplies video recordings, the supply is an exempted supply—

(a) if it is not made with a view to any further supply of that recording, or

(b) if it is so made, but is not made with a view to the eventual supply of that recording to the public or is made with a view to the eventual supply of that recording to the original supplier.

For the purposes of this subsection, any supply is a supply to the public unless it is—

(i) a supply to a person who, in the course of a business, makes video works or supplies video recordings,

(ii) an exempted supply by virtue of subsection (2) above or subsections (5) to (10) below, or

(iii) a supply outside the United Kingdom.

(5) Where a video work—

(a) is designed to provide a record of an event or occasion for those who took part in the event or occasion or are connected with those who did so,

(b) does not, to any significant extent, depict any of the following—

(i) human sexual activity or acts of force or restraint associated with such activity,

(ii) mutilation or torture of, or other acts of gross violence towards, humans or animals, or

(iii) human genital organs or human urinary or excretory functions, and

(c) is not designed—

(i) to any significant extent to stimulate or encourage anything falling within paragraph (b)(i), or

(ii) to any extent to stimulate or encourage anything falling within paragraph (b)(ii),

the supply of a video recording containing only that work to a person who took part in the event or occasion or is connected with someone who did so is an exempted supply.

(6) The supply of a video recording for the purpose only of the exhibition of any video work contained in the recording in premises other than a dwelling-house—

(a) being premises mentioned in subsection (7) below, or

(b) being an exhibition which in England and Wales or Scotland would be a film exhibition to which section 6 of the Cinemas Act 1985 applies (film exhibition to which public not admitted or are admitted without payment)

is an exempted supply.

(7) The premises referred to in subsection (6) above are—

(za) premises in England and Wales which by virtue of an authorisation within the meaning of section 136 of the Licensing Act 2003, may be used for the exhibition of a film within the meaning of paragraph 15 of Schedule 1 to that Act.

(8) The supply of a video recording with a view only to its use for or in connection with a programme service (within the meaning of the Broadcasting Act 1990) is an exempted supply.

(8A) The supply of a video recording in the form of a machine of a type designed primarily for use in an amusement arcade is an exempted supply unless the video game (or, if more than one, any of the video games) that it contains—

(a) depicts, to any significant extent, anything falling within section 2(2)(a), (b), (c) or (d) or (3), or

(b) is likely to any significant extent to stimulate or encourage anything falling within section 2(2)(a) or, in the case of anything falling within section 2(2)(b), is likely to any extent to do so.

(8B) The supply of any other video recording is an exempted supply if the recording is supplied for the purpose only of its use in connection with a supply that is an exempted supply under subsection (8A).

(9) The supply of a video recording for the purpose only of submitting a video work contained in the recording for the issue of a classification certificate or otherwise only for purposes of arrangements made by the designated authority is an exempted supply.

(10) The supply of a video recording with a view only to its use—

(a) in training for or carrying on any medical or related occupation,

(b) for the purpose of—

(i) services provided in pursuance of the National Health Service Act 2006 . . .

(c) in training persons employed in the course of services falling within paragraph (b) above,

is an exempted supply.

(11) For the purposes of subsection (10) above, an occupation is a medical or related occupation if, to carry on the occupation, a person is required to be registered under the Health Professions Order 2001, the Nursing and Midwifery Order 2001, the Medical Act 1983, the Osteopaths Act 1993 or the Chiropractors Act 1994.

(12) The supply of a video recording otherwise than for reward, being a supply made for the purpose only of supplying it to a person who previously made an exempted supply of the recording, is also an exempted supply.

7 Classification certificates

(1) In this Act "classification certificate" means a certificate—

(a) issued in respect of a video work in pursuance of arrangements made by the designated authority; and

(b) satisfying the requirements of subsection (2) below.

(2) Those requirements are that the certificate must contain the title assigned to the video work in accordance with section 4(1)(b)(ia) of this Act and—

(a) a statement that the video work concerned is suitable for general viewing and unrestricted supply (with or without any advice as to the desirability of parental guidance with regard to the viewing of the work by young children or as to the particular suitability of the work for viewing by children or young children); or

(b) a statement that the video work concerned is suitable for viewing only by persons who have attained the age (not being more than eighteen years) specified in the certificate and that no video recording containing that work is to be supplied to any person who has not attained the age so specified; or

(c) the statement mentioned in paragraph (b) above together with a statement that no video recording containing that work is to be supplied other than in a licensed sex shop.

(3) For the purposes of this Act, a video work is not a video work in respect of which a classification certificate has been issued if every classification certificate issued in respect of the video work has been revoked.

9 Supplying video recording of unclassified work

(1) A person who supplies or offers to supply a video recording containing a video work in respect of which no classification certificate has been issued is guilty of an offence unless—

(a) the supply is, or would if it took place be, an exempted supply, or

(b) the video work is an exempted work. [E]

(2) It is a defence to a charge of committing an offence under this section to prove that the accused believed on reasonable grounds—

   (a) that the video work concerned or, if the video recording contained more than one work to which the charge relates, each of those works was either an exempted work or a work in respect of which a classification certificate had been issued, or

   (b) that the supply was, or would if it took place be, an exempted supply by virtue of section 3(4) or (5) of this Act.

10   Possession of video recording of unclassified work for the purposes of supply

(1) Where a video recording contains a video work in respect of which no classification certificate has been issued, a person who has the recording in his possession for the purpose of supplying it is guilty of an offence unless—

   (a) he has it in his possession for the purpose only of a supply which, if it took place, would be an exempted supply, or

   (b) the video work is an exempted work. [E]

(2) It is a defence to a charge of committing an offence under this section to prove—

   (a) that the accused believed on reasonable grounds that the video work concerned or, if the video recording contained more than one work to which the charge relates, each of those works was either an exempted work or a work in respect of which a classification certificate had been issued,

   (b) that the accused had the video recording in his possession for the purpose only of a supply which he believed on reasonable grounds would, if it took place, be an exempted supply by virtue of section 3(4) or (5) of this Act, or

   (c) that the accused did not intend to supply the video recording until a classification certificate had been issued in respect of the video work concerned.

11   Supplying video recording of classified work in breach of classification

(1) Where a classification certificate issued in respect of a video work states that no video recording, or no video recording described in the certificate, that contains that work is to be supplied to any person who has not attained the age specified in the certificate, a person who supplies or offers to supply such a video recording to a person who has not attained the age so specified is guilty of an offence unless—

   (a) the video work is an exempted work, or

   (b) the supply is, or would if it took place be, an exempted supply. [S]

(2) It is a defence to a charge of committing an offence under this section to prove—

   (a)   that the accused neither knew nor had reasonable grounds to believe that the classification certificate contained the statement concerned,

   (b)   that the accused neither knew nor had reasonable grounds to believe that the person concerned had not attained that age,

  (ba) that the accused believed on reasonable grounds that the video work concerned or, if the video recording contained more than one work to which the charge relates, each of those works was an exempted work, or

   (c)   that the accused believed on reasonable grounds that the supply was, or would if it took place be, an exempted supply by virtue of section 3(4) or (5) of this Act.

12   Certain video recordings only to be supplied in licensed sex shops

(1) Where a classification certificate issued in respect of a video work states that no video recording, or no video recording described in the certificate, that contains that work is to be supplied other than in a licensed sex shop, a person who at any place other than in a sex shop for which a licence is in force under the relevant enactment—

   (a) supplies such a video recording, or

   (b) offers to do so,

is guilty of an offence unless the supply is, or would if it took place be, an exempted supply. [S]

(2) It is a defence to a charge of committing an offence under subsection (1) above to prove—

   (a) that the accused neither knew nor had reasonable grounds to believe that the classification certificate contained the statement concerned,

    (b) that the accused believed on reasonable grounds that the place concerned was a sex shop for which a licence was in force under the relevant enactment, or

    (c) that the accused believed on reasonable grounds that the supply was, or would if it took place be, an exempted supply by virtue of section 3(4) of this Act or subsection (6) below.

    (3) Where a classification certificate issued in respect of a video work states that no video recording, or no video recording described in the certificate, that contains that work is to be supplied other than in a licensed sex shop, a person who has such a video recording in his possession for the purpose of supplying it at any place other than in such a sex shop is guilty of an offence, unless he has it in his possession for the purpose only of a supply which, if it took place, would be an exempted supply.

    (4) It is a defence to a charge of committing an offence under subsection (3) above to prove—

    (a) that the accused neither knew nor had reasonable grounds to believe that the classification certificate contained the statement concerned,

    (b) that the accused believed on reasonable grounds that the place concerned was a sex shop for which a licence was in force under the relevant enactment, or

    (c) that the accused had the video recording in his possession for the purpose only of a supply which he believed on reasonable grounds would, if it took place, be an exempted supply by virtue of section 3(4) of this Act or subsection (6) below.

    (5) In this section "relevant enactment" means Schedule 3 to the Local Government (Miscellaneous Provisions) Act 1982 . . . and "sex shop" has the same meaning as in the relevant enactment.

    (6) For the purposes of this section, where a classification certificate issued in respect of a video work states that no video recording or no video recording described in the certificate, that contains that work is to be supplied other than in a licensed sex shop, the supply of such a video recording—

    (a) to a person who, in the course of a business, makes video works or supplies video recordings, and

    (b) with a view to its eventual supply in sex shops, being sex shops for which licences are in force under the relevant enactment,

is an exempted supply.

14A General defence to offences under this Act

Without prejudice to any defence specified in the preceding provisions of this Act in relation to a particular offence, it is a defence to a charge of committing any offence under this Act to prove—

    (a) that the commission of the offence was due to the act or default of a person other than the accused, and

    (b) that the accused took all reasonable precautions and exercised all due diligence to avoid the commission of the offence by any person under his control.

16 Offences by bodies corporate

    (1) Where an offence under this Act committed by a body corporate is proved to have been committed with the consent or connivance of, or to be attributable to any neglect on the part of, any director, manager, secretary or other similar officer of the body corporate, or any person who was purporting to act in any such capacity, he as well as the body corporate shall be guilty of the offence and shall be liable to be proceeded against and punished accordingly.

    (2) Where the affairs of a body corporate are managed by its members, subsection (1) above shall apply in relation to the acts and defaults of a member in connection with his functions of management as if he were a director of the body corporate.

22 Other interpretation

    (1) In this Act—

"business", except in section 3(4), includes any activity carried on by a club;

"premises" includes any vehicle, vessel or stall.

    (2) For the purposes of this Act (and subject to regulations under subsection (2A)), a video recording contains a video work if it contains information by the use of which the whole or a part of the work may be produced; but where a video work includes any extract from another video work, that extract is not to be regarded for the purposes of this subsection as a part of that other work.

(3) Where any alteration is made to a video work in respect of which a classification certificate has been issued, the classification certificate is not to be treated for the purposes of this Act as issued in respect of the altered work.

In this subsection, "alteration" includes addition.

Sporting Events (Control of Alcohol etc.) Act 1985

1   Offences in connection with alcohol on coaches and trains

(1) This section applies to a vehicle which—

   (a) is a public service vehicle or railway passenger vehicle, and

   (b) is being used for the principal purpose of carrying passengers for the whole or part of a journey to or from a designated sporting event.

(2) A person who knowingly causes or permits alcohol to be carried on a vehicle to which this section applies is guilty of an offence—

   (a) if the vehicle is a public service vehicle and he is the operator of the vehicle or the servant or agent of the operator, or

   (b) if the vehicle is a hired vehicle and he is the person to whom it is hired or the servant or agent of that person. [S]

(3) A person who has alcohol in his possession while on a vehicle to which this section applies is guilty of an offence. [S]

(4) A person who is drunk on a vehicle to which this section applies is guilty of an offence. [S]

(5) In this section "public service vehicle" and "operator" have the same meaning as in the Public Passenger Vehicles Act 1981.

1A   Alcohol on certain other vehicles

(1) This section applies to a motor vehicle which—

   (a) is not a public service vehicle but is adapted to carry more than 8 passengers, and

   (b) is being used for the principal purpose of carrying two or more passengers for the whole or part of a journey to or from a designated sporting event.

(2) A person who knowingly causes or permits alcohol to be carried on a motor vehicle to which this section applies is guilty of an offence—

   (a) if he is its driver, or

   (b) if he is not its driver but is its keeper, the servant or agent of its keeper, a person to whom it is made available (by hire, load or otherwise) by its keeper or the keeper's servant or agent, of the servant or agent of a person to whom it is so made available. [S]

(3) A person who has alcohol in his possession while on a motor vehicle to which this section applies is guilty of an offence. [S]

(4) A person who is drunk on a motor vehicle to which this section applies is guilty of an offence. [S]

(5) In this section—

"keeper", in relation to a vehicle, means the person having the duty to take out a licence for it under the Vehicle Excise and Registration Act 1994,

"motor vehicle" means a mechanically propelled vehicle intended or adapted for use on roads, and

"public service vehicle" has the same meaning as in the Public Passenger Vehicles Act 1981.

2   Offences in connection with alcohol, containers etc., at sports grounds

(1) A person who has alcohol or an article to which this section applies in his possession—

   (a) at any time during the period of a designated sporting event when he is in any area of a designated sports ground from which the event may be directly viewed, or

   (b) while entering or trying to enter a designated sports ground at any time during the period of a designated sporting event at that ground,

is guilty of an offence. [S]

(1A) Subsection (1)(a) above has effect subject to section 5A(1) of this Act.

(2) A person who is drunk in a designated sports ground at any time during the period of a designated sporting event at that ground or is drunk while entering or trying to enter such a ground at any time during the period of a designated sporting event at that ground is guilty of an offence. [S]

(3) This section applies to any article capable of causing injury to a person struck by it, being—

(a) a bottle, can or other portable container (including such an article when crushed or broken) which—

(i) is for holding any drink, and

(ii) is of a kind which, when empty, is normally discarded or returned to, or left to be recovered by, the supplier, or

(b) part of an article falling within paragraph (a) above;

but does not apply to anything that is for holding any medicinal product (within the meaning of the Medicines Act 1968) or any veterinary medicinal product (within the meaning of the Veterinary Medicines Regulations 2006).

9 Interpretation

(1) The following provisions shall have effect for the interpretation of this Act.

(2) "Designated sports ground" means any place—

(a) used (wholly or partly) for sporting events where accommodation is provided for spectators, and

(b) for the time being designated, or of a class designated, by order made by the Secretary of State;

and an order under this subsection may include provision for determining for the purposes of this Act the outer limit of any designated sports ground.

(3) "Designated sporting event"—

(a) means a sporting event or proposed sporting event for the time being designated, or of a class designated, by order made by the Secretary of State,

and an order under this subsection may apply to events or proposed events outside Great Britain as well as those in England and Wales.

(4) The period of a designated sporting event is the period beginning two hours before the start of the event or (if earlier) two hours before the time at which it is advertised to start and ending one hour after the end of the event, but—

(a) where an event advertised to start at a particular time on a particular day is postponed to a later day, the period includes the period in the day on which it is advertised to take place beginning two hours before and ending one hour after that time, and

(b) where an event advertised to start at a particular time on a particular day does not take place, the period is the period referred to in paragraph (a) above.

(6) This Act does not apply to any sporting event or proposed sporting event—

(a) where all competitors are to take part otherwise than for reward, and

(b) to which all spectators are to be admitted free of charge.

(7) An expression used in this Act and in the Licensing Act 2003 has the same meaning in this Act as in that Act.

Surrogacy Arrangements Act 1985

1 Meaning of "surrogate mother", "surrogacy arrangement" and other terms

(1) The following provisions shall have effect for the interpretation of this Act.

(2) "Surrogate mother" means a woman who carries a child in pursuance of an arrangement—

(a) made before she began to carry the child, and

(b) made with a view to any child carried in pursuance of it being handed over to, and parental responsibility being met (so far as practicable) by, another person or other persons.

(3) An arrangement is a surrogacy arrangement if, were a woman to whom the arrangement relates to carry a child in pursuance of it, she would be a surrogate mother.

(4) In determining whether an arrangement is made with such a view as is mentioned in subsection (2) above regard may be had to the circumstances as a whole (and, in particular, where there is a promise or understanding that any payment will or may be made to the woman or for her benefit in respect of the carrying of any child in pursuance of the arrangement, to that promise or understanding).

(5) An arrangement may be regarded as made with such a view though subject to conditions relating to the handing over of any child.

(6) A woman who carries a child is to be treated for the purposes of subsection (2)(a) above as beginning to carry it at the time of the insemination or of the placing in her of an embryo, of an egg in the process of fertilisation, or of sperm and eggs, as the case may be, that results in her carrying the child.

(7) "Body of persons" means a body of persons corporate or unincorporate.

(7A) "Non-profit making body" means a body of persons whose activities are not carried on for profit.

(8) "Payment" means payment in money or money's worth.

(9) This Act applies to arrangements whether or not they are lawful.

2   Negotiating surrogacy arrangements on a commercial basis, etc.

(1) No person shall on a commercial basis do any of the following acts in the United Kingdom, that is—

(a)   initiate any negotiations with a view to the making of a surrogacy arrangement,

(aa)   take part in any negotiations with a view to the making of a surrogacy arrangement,

(b)   offer or agree to negotiate the making of a surrogacy arrangement, or

(c)   compile any information with a view to its use in making, or negotiating the making of, surrogacy arrangements;

and no person shall in the United Kingdom knowingly cause another to do any of those acts on a commercial basis.

(2) A person who contravenes subsection (1) above is guilty of an offence; but it is not a contravention of that subsection—

(a)   for a woman, with a view to becoming a surrogate mother herself, to do any act mentioned in that subsection or to cause such an act to be done, or

(b)   for any person, with a view to a surrogate mother carrying a child for him, to do such an act or to cause such an act to be done. [S]

(2A) A non-profit making body does not contravene subsection (1) merely because—

(a)   the body does not act falling within subsection (1)(a) or (c) in respect of which any reasonable payment is at any time received by it or another, or

(b)   it does an act falling within subsection (1)(a) or (c) with a view to any reasonable payment being received by it or another in respect of facilitating the making of any surrogacy arrangement.

(2B) A person who knowingly causes a non-profit making body to do an act falling within subsection (1)(a) or (c) does not contravene subsection (1) merely because—

(a)   any reasonable payment is at any time received by the body or another in respect of the body doing the act, or

(b)   the body does the act with a view to any reasonable payment being received by it or another person in respect of the body facilitating the making of any surrogacy arrangement.

(2C) Any reference in subsection (2A) or (2B) to a reasonable payment in respect of the doing of an act by a non-profit making body is a reference to a payment not exceeding the body's cost reasonably attributable to the doing of the act.

(3) For the purpose of this section, a person does an act on a commercial basis (subject to subsection (4) below) if—

(a)   any payment is at any time received by himself or another in respect of it, or

(b)   he does it with a view to any payment being received by himself or another in respect of making, or negotiating or facilitating the making of, any surrogacy arrangement.

In this subsection "payment" does not include payment to or for the benefit of a surrogate mother or prospective surrogate mother.

(4) In proceedings against a person for an offence under subsection (1) above, he is not to be treated as doing an act on a commercial basis by reason of any payment received by another in respect of the act if it is proved that—

    (a) in a case where the payment was received before he did the act, he did not do the act knowing or having reasonable cause to suspect that any payment had been received in respect of the act; and

    (b) in any other case, he did not do the act with a view to any payment being received in respect of it.

(5) Where—

    (a) a person acting on behalf of a body of persons takes any part in negotiating or facilitating the making of a surrogacy arrangement in the United Kingdom, and

    (b) negotiating or facilitating the making of surrogacy arrangements is an activity of the body,

then, if the body at any time receives any payment made by or on behalf of—

    (i)   a woman who carries a child in pursuance of the arrangement,

    (ii)   the person or persons for whom she carries it, or

    (iii) any person connected with the woman or with that person or those persons,

the body is guilty of an offence. [S]

For the purposes of this subsection, a payment received by a person connected with a body is to be treated as received by the body.

(5A) A non-profit making body is not guilty of an offence under subsection (5), in respect of the receipt of any payment described in that subsection, merely because a person acting on behalf of the body takes part in facilitating the making of a surrogacy arrangement.

(6) In proceedings against a body for an offence under subsection (5) above, it is a defence to prove that the payment concerned was not made in respect of the arrangement mentioned in paragraph (a) of the subsection.

(7) A person who in the United Kingdom takes part in the management or control—

    (a) of any body of persons, or

    (b) of any of the activities of any body of persons,

is guilty of an offence if the activity described in subsection (8) below is an activity of the body concerned.

(8) The activity referred to in subsection (7) above is negotiating or facilitating the making of surrogacy arrangements in the United Kingdom, being—

    (a) arrangements the making of which is negotiated or facilitated on a commercial basis, or

    (b) arrangements in the case of which payments are received (or treated for the purposes of subsection (5) above as received) by the body concerned in contravention of subsection (5) above.

(8A) A person is not guilty of an offence under subsection (7) if—

    (a) the body of persons referred to in that subsection is a non-profit making body, and

    (b) the only activity of that body which falls within subsection (8) is facilitating the making of surrogacy arrangements in the United Kingdom.

(8B) In subsection (8A)(b) "facilitating the making of surrogacy arrangements" is to be construed in accordance with subsection (8).

(9) In proceedings against a person for an offence under subsection (7) above, it is a defence to prove that he neither knew nor had reasonable cause to suspect that the activity described in subsection (8) above was an activity of the body concerned; and for the purposes of such proceedings any arrangement falling within subsection (8)(b) above shall be disregarded if it is proved that the payment concerned was not made in respect of the arrangement.

3   Advertisement about surrogacy

(1) This section applies to any advertisement containing an indication (however expressed)—

    (a) that any person is or may be willing to enter into a surrogacy arrangement or to negotiate or facilitate the making of a surrogacy arrangement, or

(b) that any person is looking for a woman willing to become a surrogate mother or for persons wanting a woman to carry a child as a surrogate mother.

(1A) This section does not apply to any advertisement placed by, or on behalf of, a non-profit making body if the advertisement relates only to the doing by the body of acts that would not contravene section 2(1) even if done on a commercial basis (within the meaning of section 2).

(2) Where a newspaper or periodical containing an advertisement to which this section applies is published in the United Kingdom, any proprietor, editor or publisher of the newspaper or periodical is guilty of an offence. [S]

(3) Where an advertisement to which this section applies is conveyed by means of an electronic communication network so as to be seen or heard (or both) in the United Kingdom, any person who in the United Kingdom causes it to be so conveyed knowing it to contain such an indication as is mentioned in subsection (1) above is guilty of an offence. [S]

(4) A person who publishes or causes to be published in the United Kingdom an advertisement to which this section applies (not being an advertisement contained in a newspaper or periodical or conveyed by means of an electronic communication network) is guilty of an offence. [S]

(5) A person who distributes or causes to be distributed in the United Kingdom an advertisement to which this section applies (not being an advertisement contained in a newspaper or periodical published outside the United Kingdom or an advertisement conveyed by means of an electronic communication network) knowing it to contain such an indication as is mentioned in subsection (1) above is guilty of an offence. [S]

4   Offences

(3) Where an offence under this Act committed by a body corporate is proved to have been committed with the consent or connivance of, or to be attributable to any neglect on the part of, any director, manager, secretary or other similar officer of the body corporate or any person who was purporting to act in any such capacity, he as well as the body corporate is guilty of the offence and is liable to be proceeded against and punished accordingly.

(4) Where the affairs of a body corporate are managed by its members, subsection (3) above shall apply in relation to the acts and defaults of a member in connection with his functions of management as if he were a director of the body corporate.

(5) If any proceedings for an offence under section 2 of this Act, proof of things done or of words written, spoken or published (whether or not in the presence of any party to the proceedings) by any person taking part in the management or control of a body of persons or of any of the activities of the body, or by any person doing any of the acts mentioned in subsection (1)(a) to (c) of that section on behalf of the body, shall be admissible as evidence of the activities of the body.

Weights and Measures Act 1985

PART IV   REGULATION OF TRANSACTIONS IN GOODS

28   Short weight, etc.

(1) Subject to sections 33 to 37 below, any person who, in selling or purporting to sell any goods by weight or other measurement or by number, delivers or causes to be delivered to the buyer—
  (a) a lesser quantity than that purported to be sold, or
  (b) a lesser quantity than corresponds with the price charged, shall be guilty of an offence. [S]
(2) For the purposes of this section—
  (a) the quantity of the goods in a package, or of a loaf of bread, to which the packaged goods regulations apply shall be deemed to be the nominal quantity (within the meaning of those regulations) of the package or the loaf of bread; and
  (b) any statement, whether oral or in writing, as to the weight of any goods shall be taken, unless otherwise expressed, to be a statement as to the net weight of the goods.

30   Quantity less than stated

(1) If, in the case of any goods that are pre-packed within the meaning of this Act or are pre-packed food within the meaning of the FIC Regulation and (in either case) are in or on a container marked with a statement in writing with respect to the quantity of the goods, the quantity of the goods is at any time found to be less than that stated, then, subject to sections 33 to 37 below—

    (a) any person who has those goods in his possession for sale shall be guilty of an offence, and

    (b) if it is shown that the deficiency cannot be accounted for by anything occurring after the goods had been sold by retail and delivered to, or to a person nominated in that behalf by, the buyer, any person by whom or on whose behalf those goods have been sold or agreed to be sold at any time while they were pre-packed within the meaning of this Act or were pre-packed food within the meaning of the FIC Regulation and (in either case) were in or on the container in question, shall be guilty of an offence. [S]

(2) If—

    (a) in the case of a sale of or agreement to sell any goods which, not being pre-packed within the meaning of this Act or pre-packed food within the meaning of the FIC Regulation, are made up for sale or for delivery after sale in or on a container marked with a statement in writing with respect to the quantity of the goods, or

    (b) in the case of any goods which, in connection with their sale or an agreement for their sale, have associated with them a document containing such a statement,

the quantity of the goods is at any time found to be less than that stated, then, if it is shown that the deficiency cannot be accounted for by anything occurring after the goods had been delivered to, or to a person nominated in that behalf by, the buyer, and subject to sections 33 to 37 below and paragraph 10 of Schedule 4 to this Act, the person by whom, and any other person on whose behalf, the goods were sold or agreed to be sold shall be guilty of an offence.

(3) Subsections (1) and (2) above shall have effect notwithstanding that the quantity stated is expressed to be the quantity of the goods at a specified time falling before the time in question, or is expressed with some other qualification of whatever description, except where—

    (a) that quantity is so expressed in pursuance of an express requirement of this Part of this Act or any instrument made under this Part, or

    (b) the goods, although falling within subsection (1) or subsection (2)(a) above—

        (i) are not required by or under this Part of this Act to be pre-packed as mentioned in subsection (1) or required by the FIC Regulation to be pre-packed food as mentioned in that subsection or, as the case may be, to be made up for sale or for delivery after sale in or on a container only if the container is marked as mentioned in subsection (2)(a), and

        (ii) are not goods on a sale of which (whether any sale or a sale of any particular description) the quantity sold is required by or under any provision of this Part of this Act other than section 26 or required by the FIC Regulation, to be made known to the buyer at or before a particular time, or

    (c) the goods, although falling within subsection (2)(b) above, are not required by or under this Part of this Act to have associated with them such a document as is mentioned in that provision.

(4) In any case to which, by virtue of paragraph (a), (b) or (c) of subsection (3) above, the provisions of subsection (1) or (2) above do not apply, if it is found at any time that the quantity of the goods in question is less than that stated and it is shown that the deficiency is greater than can be reasonably justified on the ground justifying the qualification in question, then, subject to sections 33 to 37 below—

    (a) in the case of goods such as are mentioned in subsection (1) above, if it is further shown as mentioned in that subsection, then—

        (i) where the container in question was marked in Great Britain, the person by whom, and any other person on whose behalf, the container was marked, or

(ii)   where the container in question was marked outside Great Britain, the person by whom, and any other person on whose behalf, the goods were first sold in Great Britain,

shall be guilty of an offence; [S]

(b)   in the case of goods such as are mentioned in subsection (2) above, the person by whom, and any other person on whose behalf, the goods were sold or agreed to be sold shall be guilty of an offence if, but only if, he would, but for paragraph (a), (b) or (c) of subsection (3) above have been guilty of an offence under subsection (2). [S]

(5)   Subsection (2) of section 28 above shall have effect for the purposes of this section as it has effect for the purposes of that section.

31   Incorrect statements

(1)   Without prejudice to section 30(2) to (4) above, if in the case of any goods required by or under this Part of this Act to have associated with them a document containing particular statements, that document is found to contain any such statement which is materially incorrect, any person who, knowing or having reasonable cause to suspect that statement to be materially incorrect, inserted it or caused it to be inserted in the document, or used the document for the purposes of this Part of this Act while that statement was contained in the document, shall be guilty of an offence. [S]

(2)   Subsection (2) of section 28 above shall have effect for the purposes of this section as it has effect for the purposes of that section.

32   Offences due to default of third person

Where the commission by any person of an offence under this Part of this Act other than section 31A or an instrument made under this Part is due to the act or default of some other person, the other person shall be guilty of an offence and may be charged with and convicted of the offence whether or not proceedings are taken against the first-mentioned person. [S]

33   Warranty

(1)   Subject to the following provisions of this section, in any proceedings for an offence under this Part of this Act or any instrument made under this Part, being an offence relating to the quantity or pre-packing of any goods, it shall be a defence for the person charged to prove—

(a)   that he bought the goods from some other person—
   (i)   as being of the quantity which the person charged purported to sell or represented, or which was marked on any container or stated in any document to which the proceedings relate, or
   (ii)   as conforming with the statement marked on any container to which the proceedings relate, or with the requirements with respect to the pre-packing of goods of this Part of this Act or any instrument made under this Part,
   as the case may require, and

(b)   that he so bought the goods with a written warranty from that other person that they were of that quantity or, as the case may be, did so conform, and

(c)   that at the time of the commission of the offence he did in fact believe the statement contained in the warranty to be accurate and had no reason to believe it to be inaccurate, and

(d)   if the warranty was given by a person who at the time he gave it was resident outside Great Britain and any designated country, that the person charged had taken reasonable steps to check the accuracy of the statement contained in the warranty, and

(e)   in the case of proceedings relating to the quantity of any goods, that he took all reasonable steps to ensure that, while in his possession, the quantity of the goods remained unchanged and, in the case of such or any other proceedings, that apart from any change in their quantity the goods were at the time of the commission of the offence in the same state as when he bought them.

(2)   A warranty shall not be a defence in any such proceedings as are mentioned in subsection (1) above unless, not later than three days before the date of the hearing, the person charged has sent to the prosecutor a copy of the warranty with a notice stating that he intends to rely on it and

specifying the name and address of the person from whom the warranty was received, and has also sent a like notice to that person.

(3) Where the person charged is the employee of a person who, if he had been charged, would have been entitled to plead a warranty as a defence under this section, subsection (1) above shall have effect—

(a) with the substitution, for any reference (however expressed) in paragraphs (a), (b), (d), and (e) to the person charged, of a reference to his employer, and

(b) with the substitution for paragraph (c) of the following—

"(c) that at the time of the commission of the offence his employer did in fact believe the statement contained in the warranty to be accurate and the person charged had no reason to believe it to be inaccurate".

(4) The person by whom the warranty is alleged to have been given shall be entitled to appear at the hearing and to give evidence.

(5) If the person charged in any such proceedings as are mentioned in subsection (1) above wilfully attributes to any goods a warranty given in relation to any other goods, he shall be guilty of an offence.

(6) A person who, in respect of any goods sold by him in respect of which a warranty might be pleaded under this section, gives to the buyer a false warranty in writing shall be guilty of an offence unless he proves that when he gave the warranty he took all reasonable steps to ensure that the statements contained in it were, and would continue at all relevant times to be, accurate.

(7) Where in any such proceedings as are mentioned in subsection (1) above ("the original proceedings") the person charged relies successfully on a warranty given to him or to his employer, any proceedings under subsection (6) above in respect of the warranty may, at the option of the prosecutor, be taken either before a court having jurisdiction in the place where the original proceedings were taken or before a court having jurisdiction in the place where the warranty was given.

(8) For the purposes of this section, any statement with respect to any goods which is contained in any document required by or under this Part of this Act to be associated with the goods or in any invoice, and, in the case of goods made up in or on a container for sale or for delivery after sale, any statement with respect to those goods with which that container is marked, shall be taken to be a written warranty of the accuracy of that statement.

34   Reasonable precautions and due diligence

(1) In any proceedings for an offence under this Part of this Act or any instrument made under this Part, it shall be a defence for the person charged to prove that he took all reasonable precautions and exercised all due diligence to avoid the commission of the offence.

(2) If in any case the defence provided by subsection (1) above involves an allegation that the commission of the offence in question was due to the act or default of another person or due to reliance on information supplied by another person, the person charged shall not, without the leave of the court, be entitled to rely on the defence unless, before the beginning of the period of seven days ending with the date when the hearing of the charge began, he served on the prosecutor a notice giving such information identifying or assisting in the identification of the other person as was then in his possession.

35   Subsequent deficiency

(1) This subsection applies to any proceedings for an offence under this Part of this Act, or any instrument made under this Part, by reason of the quantity—

(a) of any goods made up for sale or for delivery after sale (whether by way of pre-packing or otherwise) in or on a container marked with an indication of quantity,

(b) of any goods which, in connection with their sale or an agreement for their sale, have associated with them a document purporting to state the quantity of the goods, or

(c) of any goods required by or under this Part of this Act to be pre-packed, or to be otherwise made up in or on a container for sale or for delivery after sale, or to be made for sale, only in particular quantities,

being less than that marked on the container or stated in the document in question or than the relevant particular quantity, as the case may be.

(2) In any proceedings to which subsection (1) above applies, it shall be a defence for the person charged to prove that the deficiency arose—

(a) in a case falling within paragraph (a) of subsection (1) above, after the making up of the goods and the marking of the container,

(b) in a case falling within paragraph (b) of that subsection, after the preparation of the goods for delivery in pursuance of the sale or agreement and after the completion of the document,

(c) in a case falling within paragraph (c) of that subsection, after the making up or making, as the case may be, of the goods for sale,

and was attributable wholly to factors for which reasonable allowance was made in stating the quantity of the goods in the marking or document or in making up or making the goods for sale, as the case may be.

(3) In the case of a sale by retail of food, other than food pre-packed in a container which is, or is required by or under this Part of this Act or the FIC Regulation to be, marked with an indication of quantity, in any proceedings for an offence under this Part of this Act or any instrument made under this Part, by reason of the quantity delivered to the buyer being less than that purported to be sold, it shall be a defence for the person charged to prove that the deficiency was due wholly to unavoidable evaporation or drainage since the sale and that due care and precaution were taken to minimise any such evaporation or drainage.

(4) If in any proceedings for an offence under this Part of this Act or any instrument made under this Part, being an offence in respect of any deficiency in the quantity of any goods sold, it is shown that between the sale and the discovery of the deficiency the goods were with the consent of the buyer subjected to treatment which could result in a reduction in the quantity of those goods for delivery to, or to any person nominated in that behalf by, the buyer, the person charged shall not be found guilty of that offence unless it is shown that the deficiency cannot be accounted for by the subjecting of the goods to that treatment.

36   Excess due to precautions

In any proceedings for an offence under this Part of this Act or any instrument made under this Part, being an offence in respect of any excess in the quantity of any goods, it shall be a defence for the person charged to prove that the excess was attributable to the taking of measures reasonably necessary in order to avoid the commission of an offence in respect of a deficiency in those or other goods.

37   Provisions as to testing

(1) If proceedings for an offence under this Part of this Act, or any instrument made under this Part, in respect of any deficiency or excess in the quantity—

(a) of any goods made up for sale (whether by way of pre-packing or otherwise) in or on a container marked with an indication of quantity, or

(b) of any goods which have been pre-packed or otherwise made up in or on a container for sale or for delivery after sale, or which have been made for sale, and which are required by or under this Part of this Act or the FIC Regulation to be prepacked, or to be otherwise so made up, or to be so made, as the case may be, only in particular quantities,

are brought with respect to any article, and it is proved that, at the time and place at which that article was tested, other articles of the same kind, being articles which, or articles containing goods which, had been sold by the person charged or were in that person's possession for sale or for delivery after sale, were available for testing, the person charged shall not be convicted of such an offence with respect to that article unless a reasonable number of those other articles was also tested.

(2) In any proceedings for such an offence as is mentioned in subsection (1) above, the court—

(a) if the proceedings are with respect to one or more of a number of articles tested on the same occasion, shall have regard to the average quantity in the articles tested,

(b) if the proceedings are with respect to a single article, shall disregard any inconsiderable deficiency or excess, and

(c) shall have regard generally to all the circumstances of the case.

(3) Subsections (1) and (2) above shall apply with the necessary modifications to proceedings for an offence in respect of the size, capacity or contents of a container as they apply to proceedings for an offence in respect of the excess or deficiency in the quantity of certain goods.

(4) Where by virtue of section 32 above a person is charged with an offence with which some other person might have been charged, the reference in subsection (1) above to articles or goods sold by or in the possession of the person charged shall be construed as a reference to articles or goods sold by or in the possession of that other person.

PART VII   GENERAL

82   Offences by corporations

(1) Where an offence under, or under any instrument made under, this Act which has been committed by a body corporate is proved to have been committed with the consent or connivance of, or to be attributable to any neglect on the part of, any director, manager, secretary or other similar officer of the body corporate, or any person who was purporting to act in any such capacity, he as well as the body corporate shall be guilty of that offence and shall be liable to be proceeded against and punished accordingly. [S]

(2) In subsection (1) above "director" in relation to any body corporate established by or under any enactment for the purpose of carrying on under national ownership any industry or part of an industry or undertaking, being a body corporate whose affairs are managed by its members, means a member of that body corporate.

Insolvency Act 1986

350   Scheme of this Chapter

(1) Subject to section 360(3) below, this Chapter applies—
   (a) where an adjudicator has made a bankruptcy order as a result of a bankruptcy application, or
   (b) where the court has made a bankruptcy order on a bankruptcy petition.

(2) This Chapter applies whether or not the bankruptcy order is annulled, but proceedings for an offence under this Chapter shall not be instituted after the annulment.

(3) Without prejudice to his liability in respect of a subsequent bankruptcy, the bankrupt is not guilty of an offence under this Chapter in respect of anything done after his discharge; but nothing in this Group of Parts prevents the institution of proceedings against a discharged bankrupt for an offence committed before his discharge.

(3A) Subsection (3) is without prejudice to any provision of this Chapter which applies to a person in respect of whom a bankruptcy restrictions order is in force.

(4) It is not a defence in proceedings for an offence under this Chapter that anything relied on, in whole or in part, as constituting that offence was done outside England and Wales.

351   Definitions

In the following provisions of this Chapter—
   (a) references to property comprised in the bankrupt's estate or to property possession of which is required to be delivered up to the official receiver or the trustee of the bankrupt's estate include any property which would be such property if a notice in respect of it were given under section 307 (after-acquired property), section 308 (personal property and effects of bankrupt having more than replacement value) or section 308A (vesting in trustee of certain tenancies);
   (b) "the initial period" means the period between the making of the bankruptcy application or (as the case may be) the presentation of the bankruptcy petition and the commencement of the bankruptcy.

352   Defence of innocent intention

Where in the case of an offence under any provision of this Chapter it is stated that this section applies, a person is not guilty of the offence if he proves that, at the time of the conduct constituting the offence, he had no intent to defraud or to conceal the state of his affairs.

353 Non-disclosure

(1) The bankrupt is guilty of an offence if—

    (a) he does not to the best of his knowledge and belief disclose all the property comprised in his estate to the official receiver or the trustee, or

    (b) he does not inform the official receiver or the trustee of any disposal of any property which but for the disposal would be so comprised, stating how, when, to whom and for what consideration the property was disposed of. [E]

(2) Subsection (1)(b) does not apply to any disposal in the ordinary course of a business carried on by the bankrupt or to any payment of the ordinary expenses of the bankrupt or his family.

(3) Section 352 applies to this offence.

354 Concealment of property

(1) The bankrupt is guilty of an offence if—

    (a) he does not deliver up possession to the official receiver or trustee, or as the official receiver or trustee may direct, of such part of the property comprised in his estate as is in his possession or under his control and possession of which he is required by law so to deliver up,

    (b) he conceals any property the value of which is not less than the prescribed amount and possession of which he is required to deliver up to the official receiver or trustee, or

    (c) in the 12 months before the making of the bankruptcy application or (as the case may be) the presentation of the bankruptcy petition, or in the initial period, he did anything which would have been an offence under paragraph (b) above if the bankruptcy order had been made immediately before he did it.

Section 352 applies to this offence. [E]

(2) The bankrupt is guilty of an offence if he removes, or in the initial period removed, any property the value of which was not less than the prescribed amount and possession of which he has or would have been required to deliver up to the official receiver or the trustee.

Section 352 applies to this offence. [E]

(3) The bankrupt is guilty of an offence if he without reasonable excuse fails, on being required to do so by the official receiver, the trustee, or the court—

    (a) to account for the loss of any substantial part of his property incurred in the 12 months before the making of the bankruptcy application or (as the case may be) the presentation of the bankruptcy petition or in the initial period, or

    (b) to give a satisfactory explanation of the manner in which such a loss was incurred. [E]

355 Concealment of books and papers; falsification

(1) The bankrupt is guilty of an offence if he does not deliver up possession to the official receiver or the trustee, or as the official receiver or trustee may direct, of all books, papers and other records of which he has possession or control and which relate to his estate or his affairs.

Section 352 applies to this offence. [E]

(2) The bankrupt is guilty of an offence if—

    (a) he prevents, or in the initial period prevented, the production of any books, papers or records relating to his estate or affairs;

    (b) he conceals, destroys, mutilates or falsifies, or causes or permits the concealment, destruction, mutilation or falsification of, any books, papers or other records relating to his estate or affairs;

    (c) he makes, or causes or permits the making of, any false entries in any book, document or record relating to his estate or affairs; or

    (d) in the 12 months before the making of the bankruptcy application or (as the case may be) the presentation of the bankruptcy petition, or in the initial period, he did anything which would have been an offence under paragraph (b) or (c) above if the bankruptcy order had been made before he did it.

Section 352 applies to this offence. [E]

(3) The bankrupt is guilty of an offence if—

(a) he disposes of, or alters or makes any omission in, or causes or permits the disposal, altering or making of any omission in, any book, document or record relating to his estate or affairs, or

(b) in the 12 months before the making of the bankruptcy application or (as the case may be) the presentation of the bankruptcy petition, or in the initial period he did anything which would have been an offence under paragraph (a) if the bankruptcy order had been made before he did it.

Section 352 applies to this offence. [E]

356   False statements

(1) The bankrupt is guilty of an offence if he makes or has made any material omission in any statement made under any provision in this Group of Parts and relating to his affairs.

Section 352 applies to this offence. [E]

(2) The bankrupt is guilty of an offence if—

(a) knowing or believing that a false debt has been proved by any person under the bankruptcy, he fails to inform the trustee as soon as practicable; or

(b) he attempts to account for any part of his property by fictitious losses or expenses; or

(c) in connection with any creditors' decision procedure or deemed consent procedure in the 12 months before the making of the bankruptcy application or (as the case may be) the presentation of the bankruptcy petition or (whether or not in connection with such a procedure) at any time in the initial period, he did anything which would have been an offence under paragraph (b) if the bankruptcy order had been made before he did it; or

(d) he is, or at any time has been, guilty of any false representation or other fraud for the purpose of obtaining the consent of his creditors, or any of them, to an agreement with reference to his affairs or to his bankruptcy. [E]

357   Fraudulent disposal of property

(1) The bankrupt is guilty of an offence if he makes or causes to be made, or has in the period of 5 years ending with the commencement of the bankruptcy made or caused to be made, any gift or transfer of, or any charge on, his property.

Section 352 applies to this offence. [E]

(2) The reference to making a transfer of or charge on any property includes causing or conniving at the levying of any execution against that property.

(3) The bankrupt is guilty of an offence if he conceals or removes, or has at any time before the commencement of the bankruptcy concealed or removed, any part of his property after, or within 2 months before, the date on which a judgment or order for the payment of money has been obtained against him, being a judgment or order which was not satisfied before the commencement of the bankruptcy.

Section 352 applies to this offence. [E]

358   Absconding

The bankrupt is guilty of an offence if—

(a) he leaves, or attempts or makes preparations to leave, England and Wales with any property the value of which is not less than the prescribed amount and possession of which he is required to deliver up to the official receiver or the trustee, or

(b) in the 6 months before the making of the bankruptcy application or (as the case may be) the presentation of the bankruptcy petition, or in the initial period, he did anything which would have been an offence under paragraph (a) if the bankruptcy order had been made immediately before he did it.

Section 352 applies to this offence. [E]

359   Fraudulent dealing with property obtained on credit

(1) The bankrupt is guilty of an offence if, in the 12 months before the making of the bankruptcy application or (as the case may be) the presentation of the bankruptcy petition, or in the initial period, he disposed of any property which he had obtained on credit and, at the time he disposed of it, had not paid for.

Section 352 applies to this offence. [E]

(2) A person is guilty of an offence if, in the 12 months before the making of the bankruptcy application or (as the case may be) the presentation of the bankruptcy petition or in the initial period, he acquired or received property from the bankrupt knowing or believing—

(a) that the bankrupt owed money in respect of the property, and

(b) that the bankrupt did not intend, or was unlikely to be able, to pay the money he so owed. [E]

(3) A person is not guilty of an offence under subsection (1) or (2) if the disposal, acquisition or receipt of the property was in the ordinary course of a business carried on by the bankrupt at the time of the disposal, acquisition or receipt.

(4) In determining for the purposes of this section whether any property is disposed of, acquired or received in the ordinary course of a business carried on by the bankrupt, regard may be had, in particular, to the price paid for the property.

(5) In this section references to disposing of property include pawning or pledging it; and references to acquiring or receiving property shall be read accordingly.

360   Obtaining credit; engaging in business

(1) The bankrupt is guilty of an offence if—

(a) either alone or jointly with any other person, he obtains credit to the extent of the prescribed amount or more without giving the person from whom he obtains it the relevant information about his status; or

(b) he engages (whether directly or indirectly) in any business under a name other than that in which he was made bankrupt without disclosing to all persons with whom he enters into any business transaction the name in which he was so made. [E]

(2) The reference to the bankrupt obtaining credit includes the following cases—

(a) where goods are bailed to him under a hire-purchase agreement, or agreed to be sold to him under a conditional sale agreement, and

(b) where he is paid in advance (whether in money or otherwise) for the supply of goods or services.

(3) A person whose estate has been sequestrated in Scotland, or who has been adjudged bankrupt in Northern Ireland, is guilty of an offence if, before his discharge, he does anything in England and Wales which would be an offence under subsection (1) if he were an undischarged bankrupt and the sequestration of his estate or the adjudication in Northern Ireland were an adjudication under this Part. [E]

(4) For the purposes of subsection (1)(a), the relevant information about the status of the person in question is the information that he is an undischarged bankrupt or, as the case may be, that his estate has been sequestrated in Scotland and that he has not been discharged.

(5) This section applies to the bankrupt after discharge while a bankruptcy restrictions order is in force in respect of him.

(6) For the purposes of subsection (1)(a) as it applies by virtue of subsection (5), the relevant information about the status of the person in question is the information that a bankruptcy restrictions order is in force in respect of him.

Public Order Act 1986

PART I   NEW OFFENCES

1   Riot

(1) Where 12 or more persons who are present together use or threaten unlawful violence for a common purpose and the conduct of them (taken together) is such as would cause a person of reasonable firmness present at the scene to fear for his personal safety, each of the persons using unlawful violence for the common purpose is guilty of riot. [I]

(2) It is immaterial whether or not the 12 or more use or threaten unlawful violence simultaneously.

(3) The common purpose may be inferred from conduct.

(4) No person of reasonable firmness need actually be, or be likely to be, present at the scene.

(5) Riot may be committed in private as well as in public places.

2 Violent disorder

(1) Where 3 or more persons who are present together use or threaten unlawful violence and the conduct of them (taken together) is such as would cause a person of reasonable firmness present at the scene to fear for his personal safety, each of the persons using or threatening unlawful violence is guilty of violent disorder. [E]

(2) It is immaterial whether or not the 3 or more use or threaten unlawful violence simultaneously.

(3) No person of reasonable firmness need actually be, or be likely to be, present at the scene.

(4) Violent disorder may be committed in private as well as in public places.

3 Affray

(1) A person is guilty of affray if he uses or threatens unlawful violence towards another and his conduct is such as would cause a person of reasonable firmness present at the scene to fear for his personal safety. [E]

(2) Where 2 or more persons use or threaten the unlawful violence, it is the conduct of them taken together that must be considered for the purposes of subsection (1).

(3) For the purposes of this section a threat cannot be made by the use of words alone.

(4) No person of reasonable firmness need actually be, or be likely to be, present at the scene.

(5) Affray may be committed in private as well as in public places.

4 Fear or provocation of violence

(1) A person is guilty of an offence if he—

    (a) uses towards another person threatening, abusive or insulting words or behaviour; or

    (b) distributes or displays to another person any writing, sign or other visible representation which is threatening, abusive or insulting,

with intent to cause that person to believe that immediate unlawful violence will be used against him or another by any person, or to provoke the immediate use of unlawful violence by that person or another, or whereby that person is likely to believe that such violence will be used or it is likely that such violence will be provoked. [S]

(2) An offence under this section may be committed in a public or a private place, except that no offence is committed where the words or behaviour are used, or the writing, sign or other visible representation is distributed or displayed, by a person inside a dwelling and the other person is also inside that or another dwelling.

4A Intentional harassment, alarm or distress

(1) A person is guilty of an offence if, with intent to cause a person harassment, alarm or distress, he—

    (a) uses threatening, abusive or insulting words or behaviour, or disorderly behaviour, or

    (b) displays any writing, sign or other visible representation which is threatening, abusive or insulting,

thereby causing that or another person harassment, alarm or distress. [S]

(2) An offence under this section may be committed in a public or a private place, except that no offence is committed where the words or behaviour are used, or the writing, sign or other visible representation is displayed, by a person inside a dwelling and the person who is harassed, alarmed or distressed is also inside that or another dwelling.

(3) It is a defence for the accused to prove—

    (a) that he was inside a dwelling and had no reason to believe that the words or behaviour used, or the writing, sign or other visible representation displayed would be heard or seen by a person outside that or any other dwelling, or

    (b) that his conduct was reasonable.

5   Harassment, alarm or distress

(1) A person is guilty of an offence if he—

(a) uses threatening or abusive words or behaviour, or disorderly behaviour, or

(b) displays any writing, sign or other visible representation which is threatening or abusive, within the hearing or sight of a person likely to be caused harassment, alarm or distress thereby. [S]

(2) An offence under this section may be committed in a public or a private place, except that no offence is committed where the words or behaviour are used, or the writing, sign or other visible representation is displayed, by a person inside a dwelling and the other person is also inside that or another dwelling.

(3) It is a defence for the accused to prove—

(a) that he had no reason to believe that there was any person within hearing or sight who was likely to be caused harassment, alarm or distress, or

(b) that he was inside a dwelling and had no reason to believe that the words or behaviour used, or the writing, sign or other visible representation displayed, would be heard or seen by a person outside that or any other dwelling, or

(c) that his conduct was reasonable.

6   Mental element: miscellaneous

(1) A person is guilty of riot only if he intends to use violence or is aware that his conduct may be violent.

(2) A person is guilty of violent disorder or affray only if he intends to use or threaten violence or is aware that his conduct may be violent or threaten violence.

(3) A person is guilty of an offence under section 4 only if he intends his words or behaviour, or the writing, sign or other visible representation, to be threatening, abusive or insulting, or is aware that it may be threatening, abusive or insulting.

(4) A person is guilty of an offence under section 5 only if he intends his words or behaviour, or the writing, sign or other visible representation, to be threatening or abusive, or is aware that it may be threatening or abusive or (as the case may be) he intends his behaviour to be or is aware that it may be disorderly.

(5) For the purposes of this section a person whose awareness is impaired by intoxication shall be taken to be aware of that of which he would be aware if not intoxicated, unless he shows either that his intoxication was not self-induced or that it was caused solely by the taking or administration of a substance in the course of medical treatment.

(6) In subsection (5) "intoxication" means any intoxication, whether caused by drink, drugs or other means, or by a combination of means.

(7) Subsections (1) and (2) do not affect the determination for the purposes of riot or violent disorder of the number of persons who use or threaten violence.

8   Interpretation

In this Part—

"dwelling" means any structure or part of a structure occupied as a person's home or as other living accommodation (whether the occupation is separate or shared with others) but does not include any part not so occupied, and for this purpose "structure" includes a tent, caravan, vehicle, vessel or other temporary or movable structure;

"violence" means any violent conduct, so that—

(a) except in the context of affray, it includes violent conduct towards property as well as violent conduct towards persons, and

(b) it is not restricted to conduct causing or intended to cause injury or damage but includes any other violent conduct (for example, throwing at or towards a person a missile of a kind capable of causing injury which does not hit or falls short).

PART III   RACIAL HATRED

17   Meaning of "racial hatred"

In this Part "racial hatred" means hatred against a group of persons defined by reference to colour, race, nationality (including citizenship) or ethnic or national origins.

18   Use of words or behaviour or display of written material

(1) A person who uses threatening, abusive or insulting words or behaviour, or displays any written material which is threatening, abusive or insulting, is guilty of an offence if—

    (a) he intends thereby to stir up racial hatred, or

    (b) having regard to all the circumstances racial hatred is likely to be stirred up thereby. [E]

(2) An offence under this section may be committed in a public or a private place, except that no offence is committed where the words or behaviour are used, or the written material is displayed, by a person inside a dwelling and are not heard or seen except by other persons in that or another dwelling.

(4) In proceedings for an offence under this section it is a defence for the accused to prove that he was inside a dwelling and had no reason to believe that the words or behaviour used, or the written material displayed, would be heard or seen by a person outside that or any other dwelling.

(5) A person who is not shown to have intended to stir up racial hatred is not guilty of an offence under this section if he did not intend his words or behaviour, or the written material, to be, and was not aware that it might be, threatening, abusive or insulting.

(6) This section does not apply to words or behaviour used, or written material displayed, solely for the purpose of being included in a programme service.

19   Publishing or distributing written material

(1) A person who publishes or distributes written material which is threatening, abusive or insulting is guilty of an offence if—

    (a) he intends thereby to stir up racial hatred, or

    (b) having regard to all the circumstances racial hatred is likely to be stirred up thereby. [E]

(2) In proceedings for an offence under this section it is a defence for an accused who is not shown to have intended to stir up racial hatred to prove that he was not aware of the content of the material and did not suspect, and had no reason to suspect, that it was threatening, abusive or insulting.

(3) References in this Part to the publication or distribution of written material are to its publication or distribution to the public or a section of the public.

20   Public performance of play

(1) If a public performance of a play is given which involves the use of threatening, abusive or insulting words or behaviour, any person who presents or directs the performance is guilty of an offence if—

    (a) he intends thereby to stir up racial hatred, or

    (b) having regard to all the circumstances (and, in particular, taking the performance as a whole) racial hatred is likely to be stirred up thereby.

(2) If a person presenting or directing the performance is not shown to have intended to stir up racial hatred, it is a defence for him to prove—

    (a) that he did not know and had no reason to suspect that the performance would involve the use of the offending words or behaviour, or

    (b) that he did not know and had no reason to suspect that the offending words or behaviour were threatening, abusive or insulting, or

    (c) that he did not know and had no reason to suspect that the circumstances in which the performance would be given would be such that racial hatred would be likely to be stirred up.

(3) This section does not apply to a performance given solely or primarily for one or more of the following purposes—

    (a) rehearsal,

    (b) making a recording of the performance, or

    (c) enabling the performance to be included in a programme service;

but if it is proved that the performance was attended by persons other than those directly connected with the giving of the performance or the doing in relation to it of the things mentioned in paragraph (b) or (c), the performance shall, unless the contrary is shown, be taken not to have been given solely or primarily for the purposes mentioned above.

    (4) For the purposes of this section—

        (a) a person shall not be treated as presenting a performance of a play by reason only of his taking part in it as a performer,

        (b) a person taking part as a performer in a performance directed by another shall be treated as a person who directed the performance if without reasonable excuse he performs otherwise than in accordance with that person's direction, and

        (c) a person shall be taken to have directed a performance of a play given under his direction notwithstanding that he was not present during the performance;

and a person shall not be treated as aiding or abetting the commission of an offence under this section by reason only of his taking part in a performance as a performer.

    (5) In this section "play" and "public performance" have the same meaning as in the Theatres Act 1968.

21   Distributing, showing or playing a recording

    (1) A person who distributes, or shows or plays, a recording of visual images or sounds which are threatening, abusive or insulting is guilty of an offence if—

        (a) he intends thereby to stir up racial hatred, or

        (b) having regard to all the circumstances racial hatred is likely to be stirred up thereby.

    (2) In this Part "recording" means any record from which visual images or sounds may, by any means, be reproduced; and references to the distribution, showing or playing of a recording are to its distribution, showing or playing of a recording are to its distribution, showing or playing to the public or a section of the public.

    (3) In proceedings for an offence under this section it is a defence for an accused who is not shown to have intended to stir up racial hatred to prove that he was not aware of the content of the recording and did not suspect, and had no reason to suspect, that it was threatening, abusive or insulting.

    (4) This section does not apply to the showing or playing of a recording solely for the purpose of enabling the recording to be included in a programme service.

22   Broadcasting or including programme in cable programme service

    (1) If a programme involving threatening, abusive or insulting visual images or sounds is included in a programme service, each of the persons mentioned in subsection (2) is guilty of an offence if—

        (a) he intends thereby to stir up racial hatred, or

        (b) having regard to all the circumstances racial hatred is likely to be stirred up thereby.

    (2) The persons are—

        (a) the person providing the programme service,

        (b) any person by whom the programme is produced or directed, and

        (c) any person by whom offending words or behaviour are used.

    (3) If the person providing the service, or a person by whom the programme was produced or directed, is not shown to have intended to stir up racial hatred, it is a defence for him to prove that—

        (a) he did not know and had no reason to suspect that the programme would involve the offending material, and

        (b) having regard to the circumstances in which the programme was included in a programme service, it was not reasonably practicable for him to secure the removal of the material.

    (4) It is a defence for a person by whom the programme was produced or directed who is not shown to have intended to stir up racial hatred to prove that he did not know and had no reason to suspect—

        (a) that the programme would be included in a programme service, or

(b) that the circumstances in which the programme would be so included would be such that racial hatred would be likely to be stirred up.

(5) It is a defence for a person by whom offending words or behaviour were used and who is not shown to have intended to stir up racial hatred to prove that he did not know and had no reason to suspect—

(a) that a programme involving the use of the offending material would be included in a programme service, or

(b) that the circumstances in which a programme involving the use of the offending material would be so included, or in which a programme so included would involve the use of the offending material, would be such that racial hatred would be likely to be stirred up.

(6) A person who is not shown to have intended to stir up racial hatred is not guilty of an offence under this section if he did not know, and had no reason to suspect, that the offending material was threatening, abusive or insulting.

23   Possession of racially inflammatory material

(1) A person who has in his possession written material which is threatening, abusive or insulting, or a recording of visual images or sounds which are threatening, abusive or insulting, with a view to—

(a) in the case of written material, its being displayed, published, distributed, or included in a programme service, whether by himself or another, or

(b) in the case of a recording, its being distributed, shown, played, or included in a programme service, whether by himself or another,

is guilty of an offence if he intends racial hatred to be stirred up thereby or, having regard to all the circumstances, racial hatred is likely to be stirred up thereby.

(2) For this purpose regard shall be had to such display, publication, distribution, showing, playing, or inclusion in a programme service as he has, or it may reasonably be inferred that he has, in view.

(3) In proceedings for an offence under this section it is a defence for an accused who is not shown to have intended to stir up racial hatred to prove that he was not aware of the content of the written material or recording and did not suspect, and had no reason to suspect, that it was threatening, abusive or insulting.

PART IIIA   HATRED AGAINST PERSONS ON RELIGIOUS GROUNDS OR GROUNDS OF SEXUAL ORIENTATION

29A   Meaning of "religious hatred"

In this Part "religious hatred" means hatred against a group of persons defined by reference to religious belief or lack of religious belief.

29AB   Meaning of "hatred on the grounds of sexual orientation"

In this Part "hatred on the grounds of sexual orientation" means hatred against a group of persons defined by reference to sexual orientation (whether towards persons of the same sex, the opposite sex or both).

29B   Use of words or behaviour or display of written material

(1) A person who uses threatening words or behaviour, or displays any written material which is threatening, is guilty of an offence if he intends thereby to stir up religious hatred or hatred on the grounds of sexual orientation. [E]

(2) An offence under this section may be committed in a public or a private place, except that no offence is committed where the words or behaviour are used, or the written material is displayed, by a person inside a dwelling and are not heard or seen except by other persons in that or another dwelling.

(4) In proceedings for an offence under this section it is a defence for the accused to prove that he was inside a dwelling and had no reason to believe that the words or behaviour used, or the written material displayed, would be heard or seen by a person outside that or any other dwelling.

(5) This section does not apply to words or behaviour used, or written material displayed, solely for the purpose of being included in a programme service.

29C   Publishing or distributing written material

(1) A person who publishes or distributes written material which is threatening is guilty of an offence if he intends thereby to stir up religious hatred or hatred on the grounds of sexual orientation. [E]

(2) References in this Part to the publication or distribution of written material are to its publication or distribution to the public or a section of the public.

29D   Public performance of play

(1) If a public performance of a play is given which involves the use of threatening words or behaviour, any person who presents or directs the performance is guilty of an offence if he intends thereby to stir up religious hatred or hatred on the grounds of sexual orientation. [E]

(2) This section does not apply to a performance given solely or primarily for one or more of the following purposes—

  (a) rehearsal,

  (b) making a recording of the performance, or

  (c) enabling the performance to be included in a programme service;

but if it is proved that the performance was attended by persons other than those directly connected with the giving of the performance or the doing in relation to it of the things mentioned in paragraph (b) or (c), the performance shall, unless the contrary is shown, be taken not to have been given solely or primarily for the purpose mentioned above.

(3) For the purposes of this section—

  (a) a person shall not be treated as presenting a performance of a play by reason only of his taking part in it as a performer,

  (b) a person taking part as a performer in a performance directed by another shall be treated as a person who directed the performance if without reasonable excuse he performs otherwise than in accordance with that person's direction, and

  (c) a person shall be taken to have directed a performance of a play given under his direction notwithstanding that he was not present during the performance;

and a person shall not be treated as aiding or abetting the commission of an offence under this section by reason only of his taking part in a performance as a performer.

(4) In this section "play" and "public performance" have the same meaning as in the Theatres Act 1968.

29E   Distributing, showing or playing a recording

(1) A person who distributes, or shows or plays, a recording of visual images or sounds which are threatening is guilty of an offence if he intends thereby to stir up religious hatred or hatred on the grounds of sexual orientation. [E]

(2) In this Part "recording" means any record from which visual images or sounds may, by any means, be reproduced; and references to the distribution, showing or playing of a recording are to its distribution, showing or playing to the public or a section of the public.

(3) This section does not apply to the showing or playing of a recording solely for the purpose of enabling the recording to be included in a programme service.

29F   Broadcasting or including programme in programme service

(1) If a programme involving threatening visual images or sounds is included in a programme service, each of the persons mentioned in subsection (2) is guilty of an offence if he intends thereby to stir up religious hatred or hatred on the grounds of sexual orientation.

(2) The persons are—

  (a) the person providing the programme service,

  (b) any person by whom the programme is produced or directed, and

  (c) any person by whom offending words or behaviour are used.

29G   Possession of inflammatory material

(1) A person who has in his possession written material which is threatening, or a recording of visual images or sounds which are threatening, with a view to—

    (a) in the case of written material, its being displayed, published, distributed, or included in a programme service whether by himself or another, or

    (b) in the case of a recording, its being distributed, shown, played, or included in a programme service, whether by himself or another,

is guilty of an offence if he intends thereby to stir up religious hatred or hatred on the grounds of sexual orientation. [E]

(2) For this purpose regard shall be had to such display, publication, distribution, showing, playing, or inclusion in a programme service as he has, or it may be reasonably be inferred that he has, in view.

29J   Protection of freedom of expression

Nothing in this Part shall be read or given effect in a way which prohibits or restricts discussion, criticism or expressions of antipathy, dislike, ridicule, insult or abuse of particular religions or the beliefs or practices of their adherents, or of any other belief system or the beliefs or practices of its adherents, or proselytising or urging adherents of a different religion or belief system to cease practising their religion or belief system.

29JA   Protection of freedom of expression (sexual orientation)

(1) In this Part, for the avoidance of doubt, the discussion or criticism of sexual conduct or practices or the urging of persons to refrain from or modify such conduct or practices shall not be taken of itself to be threatening or intended to stir up hatred.

(2) In this Part, for the avoidance of doubt, any discussion or criticism of marriage which concerns the sex of the parties to marriage shall not be taken of itself to be threatening or intended to stir up hatred.

29K   Savings for reports of parliamentary or judicial proceedings

(1) Nothing in this Part applies to a fair and accurate report of proceedings in Parliament, in the Scottish Parliament or in the National Assembly for Wales.

(2) Nothing in this Part applies to a fair and accurate report of proceedings publicly heard before a court or tribunal exercising judicial authority where the report is published contemporaneously with the proceedings or, if it is not reasonably practicable or would be unlawful to publish a report of them contemporaneously, as soon as publication is reasonably practicable and lawful.

29L   Procedure and punishment

(2) For the purposes of the rules against charging more than one offence in the same count or information, each of sections 29B to 29G creates one offence.

29M   Offences by corporations

(1) Where a body corporate is guilty of an offence under this Part and it is shown that the offence was committed with the consent or connivance of a director, manager, secretary or other similar officer of the body, or a person purporting to act in any such capacity, he as well as the body corporate is guilty of the offence and liable to be proceeded against and punished accordingly.

(2) Where the affairs of a body corporate are managed by its members, subsection (1) applies in relation to the acts and defaults of a member in connection with his functions of management as it applies to a director.

29N   Interpretation

In this Part—

"distribute", and related expressions, shall be construed in accordance with section 29C(2) (written material) and section 29E(2) (recordings);

"dwelling" means any structure or part of a structure occupied as a person's home or other living accommodation (whether the occupation is separate or shared with others) but does not include any part not so occupied, and for this purpose "structure" includes a tent, caravan, vehicle, vessel or other temporary or movable structure;

"hatred on the grounds of sexual orientation" has the meaning given by section 29AB;

"programme" means any item which is included in a programme service;

"programme service" has the same meaning as in the Broadcasting Act 1990;

"publish", and related expressions, in relation to written material, shall be construed in accordance with section 29C(2);

"religious hatred" has the meaning given by section 29A;

"recording" has the meaning given by section 29E(2), and "play" and "show", and related expressions, in relation to a recording, shall be construed in accordance with that provision;

"written material" includes any sign or other visible representation.

PART V   MISCELLANEOUS AND GENERAL

38   Contamination of or interference with goods with intention of causing public alarm or anxiety, etc.

(1) It is an offence for a person, with the intention—

(a) of causing public alarm or anxiety, or

(b) of causing injury to members of the public consuming or using the goods, or

(c) of causing economic loss to any person by reason of the goods being shunned by members of the public, or

(d) of causing economic loss to any person by reason of steps taken to avoid any such alarm or anxiety, injury or loss,

to contaminate or interfere with goods, or make it appear that goods have been contaminated or interfered with, or to place goods which have been contaminated or interfered with, or which appear to have been contaminated and interfered with, in a place where goods of that description are consumed, used, sold or otherwise supplied. [E]

(2) It is also an offence for a person, with any such intention as is mentioned in paragraph (a), (c) or (d) of subsection (1), to threaten that he or another will do, or claim that he or another has done, any of the acts mentioned in that subsection. [E]

(3) It is an offence for a person to be in possession of any of the following articles with a view to the commission of an offence under subsection (1)—

(a) materials to be used for contaminating or interfering with goods or making it appear that goods have been contaminated or interfered with, or

(b) goods which have been contaminated or interfered with, or which appear to have been contaminated or interfered with. [E]

(5) In this section "goods" includes substances whether natural or manufactured and whether or not incorporated in or mixed with other goods.

(6) The reference in subsection (2) to a person claiming that certain acts have been committed does not include a person who in good faith reports or warns that such acts have been, or appear to have been, committed.

Salmon Act 1986

32   Handling fish in suspicious circumstance

(1) Subject to subsections (3) and (4) below, a person shall be guilty of an offence if, at a time when he believes or it would be reasonable for him to suspect that a relevant offence has at any time been committed in relation to any fish to which this section applies, he receives that fish, or undertakes or assists in its retention, removal or disposal, or if he arranges to do so. [E]

(1A) This section applies to—

(a) salmon, trout, eels, lampreys, smelt and freshwater fish; and

(b) fish of such other description as may be specified for the purposes of this section by order under section 40A of the Salmon and Freshwater Fisheries Act 1975.

(2) For the purposes of this section an offence is a relevant offence in relation to a fish to which this section applies if—

(a) it is committed by taking, killing, landing or selling that fish, either in England and Wales or in Scotland; or

(b) that fish is taken, killed, landed, or sold, either in England and Wales or in Scotland, in the course of the commission of the offence.

(3) It shall be immaterial for the purposes of subsection (1) above that a person's belief or the grounds for suspicion relate neither specifically to a particular offence that has been committed nor exclusively to a relevant offence or to relevant offences; but it shall be a defence in proceedings for an offence under this section to show that no relevant offence had in fact been committed in relation to the fish in question.

(4) A person shall not be guilty of an offence under this section in respect of conduct which constitutes a relevant offence in relation to any fish to which this section applies or in respect of anything done in good faith for the purposes connected with the prevention or detection of crime or the investigation or treatment of disease.

(7) In this section "offence", in relation to the taking, killing, landing, or selling, of a fish to which this section applies either in England and Wales or in Scotland, means an offence under the law applicable to the place where the fish is taken, killed, landed or sold.

Consumer Protection Act 1987

11   Safety regulations

(1) The Secretary of State may by regulations under this section ("safety regulations") make such provision as he considers appropriate for the purpose of securing—

(a) that goods to which this section applies are safe;

(b) that goods to which this section applies which are unsafe, or would be unsafe in the hands of persons of a particular description, are not made available to persons generally or, as the case may be, to persons of that description; and

(c) that appropriate information is, and inappropriate information is not, provided in relation to goods to which this section applies.

12   Offences against the safety regulations

(1) Where safety regulations prohibit a person from supplying or offering or agreeing to supply any goods or from exposing or possessing any goods for supply, that person shall be guilty of an offence if he contravenes the prohibition. [S]

(2) Where safety regulations require a person who makes or processes any goods in the course of carrying on a business—

(a) to carry out a particular test or use a particular procedure in connection with the making or processing of the goods with a view to ascertaining whether the goods satisfy any requirements of such regulations; or

(b) to deal or not to deal in a particular way with a quantity of the goods of which the whole or part does not satisfy such a test or does not satisfy standards connected with such a procedure,

that person shall be guilty of an offence if he does not comply with the requirement. [S]

(3) If a person contravenes a provision of safety regulations which prohibits or requires the provision, by means of a mark or otherwise, of information of a particular kind in relation to goods, he shall be guilty of an offence. [S]

(4) Where safety regulations require any person to give information to another for the purpose of enabling that other to exercise any function, that person shall be guilty of an offence if—

(a) he fails without reasonable cause to comply with the requirement; or

(b) in giving the information which is required of him—

　(i)　he makes any statement which he knows is false in a material particular; or

　(ii)　he recklessly makes any statement which is false in a material particular. [S]

39　Defence of due diligence

(1)　Subject to the following provisions of this section, in proceedings against any person for an offence to which this section applies it shall be a defence for that person to show that he took all reasonable steps and exercised all due diligence to avoid committing the offence.

(2)　Where in any proceedings against any person for such an offence the defence provided by subsection (1) above involves an allegation that the commission of the offence was due—

(a)　to the act or default of another; or

(b)　to reliance on information given by another,

that person shall not, without the leave of the court, be entitled to rely on the defence unless, not less than seven clear days before the hearing of the proceedings, he has served a notice under subsection (3) below on the person bringing the proceedings.

(3)　A notice under this subsection shall give such information identifying or assisting in the identification of the person who committed the act or default or gave the information as is in the possession of the person serving the notice at the time he serves it.

(4)　It is hereby declared that a person shall not be entitled to rely on the defence provided by subsection (1) above by reason of his reliance on information supplied by another, unless he shows that it was reasonable in all the circumstances for him to have relied on the information, having regard in particular—

(a)　to the steps which he took, and those which might reasonably have been taken, for the purpose of verifying the information; and

(b)　to whether he had any reason to disbelieve the information.

(5)　This section shall apply to an offence under section 12(1), (2) or (3), 13(4) or 14(6) above.

40　Liability of persons other than the principal offender

(1)　Where the commission by any person of an offence to which section 39 above applies is due to an act or default committed by some other person in the course of any business of his, the other person shall be guilty of the offence and may be proceeded against and punished by virtue of this subsection whether or not proceedings are taken against the first-mentioned person. [S]

(2)　Where a body corporate is guilty of an offence under this Act (including where it is so guilty by virtue of subsection (1) above) in respect of any act or default which is shown to have been committed with the consent or connivance of, or to be attributable to any neglect on the part of, any director, manager, secretary or other similar officer of the body corporate or any person who was purporting to act in any such capacity he, as well as the body corporate, shall be guilty of that offence and shall be liable to be proceeded against and punished accordingly. [S]

(3)　Where the affairs of a body corporate are managed by its members, subsection (2) above shall apply in relation to the acts and defaults of a member in connection with his functions of management as if he were a director of the body corporate.

Criminal Justice Act 1987

12　Charges of and penalty for conspiracy to defraud

(1)　If—

(a)　a person agrees with any other person or persons that a course of conduct shall be pursued; and

(b)　that course of conduct will necessarily amount to or involve the commission of any offence or offences by one or more of the parties to the agreement if the agreement is carried out in accordance with their intentions,

the fact that it will do so shall not preclude a charge of conspiracy to defraud being brought against any of them in respect of the agreement. [I]

Copyright, Designs and Patents Act 1988

107   Criminal liability for making or dealing with infringing articles, etc.

(1) A person commits an offence who, without the licence of the copyright owner—

    (a) makes for sale or hire, [E] or

    (b) imports into the United Kingdom otherwise than for his private and domestic use, [E] or

    (c) possesses in the course of a business with a view to committing any act infringing the copyright [S], or

    (d) in the course of a business—

        (i)   sells or lets for hire, or

        (ii)   offers or exposes for sale or hire, or

        (iii) exhibits in public, or

        (iv) distributes, [E] or

    (e) distributes otherwise than in the course of a business to such an extent as to affect preju-dicially the owner of the copyright, [E]

an article which is, and which he knows or has reason to believe is, an infringing copy of a copyright work.

(2) A person commits an offence who—

    (a) makes an article specifically designed or adapted for making copies of a particular copy-right work, or

    (b) has such an article in his possession,

knowing or having reason to believe that it is to be used to make infringing copies for sale or hire or for use in the course of a business. [S]

(2A) A person ("P") who infringes copyright in a work by communicating the work to the public commits an offence if P—

    (a) knows or has reason to believe that P is infringing copyright in the work, and

    (b) either—

        (i)   intends to make a gain for P or another person, or

        (ii)   knows or has reason to believe that communicating the work to the public will cause loss to the owner of the copyright, or will expose the owner of the copyright to a risk of loss.

(2B) For the purposes of subsection (2A)—

    (a) "gain" and "loss"—

        (i)   extend only to gain or loss in money, and

        (ii)   include any such gain or loss whether temporary or permanent, and

    (b) "loss" includes a loss by not getting what one might get.

(3) Where copyright is infringed (otherwise than by reception of a communication to the public)—

    (a) by the public performance of a literary, dramatic or musical work, or

    (b) by the playing or showing in public of a sound recording or film,

any person who caused the work to be so performed, played or shown is guilty of an offence if he knew or had reason to believe that copyright would be infringed. [S]

Criminal Justice Act 1988

39   Common assault and battery to be summary offences

(1) Common assault and battery shall be summary offences and a person guilty of either of them shall be liable to a fine not exceeding level 5 on the standard scale, to imprisonment for a term not exceeding six months, or to both. [S]

134   Torture

(1) A public official or person acting in an official capacity, whatever his nationality, commits the offence of torture if in the United Kingdom or elsewhere he intentionally inflicts severe pain or suffering on another in the performance or purported performance of his official duties. [I]

(2) A person not falling within subsection (1) above commits the offence of torture, whatever his nationality, if—

  (a) in the United Kingdom or elsewhere he intentionally inflicts severe pain or suffering on another at the instigation or with the consent or acquiescence—

  (i) of a public official; or

  (ii) of a person acting in an official capacity; and

  (b) the official or other person is performing or purporting to perform his official duties when he instigates the commission of the offence or consents to or acquiesces in it. [I]

(3) It is immaterial whether the pain or suffering is physical or mental and whether it is caused by an act or an omission.

(4) It shall be a defence for a person charged with an offence under this section in respect of any conduct of his to prove that he had lawful authority, justification or excuse for that conduct.

(5) For the purposes of this section "lawful authority, justification or excuse" means—

  (a) in relation to pain or suffering inflicted in the United Kingdom, lawful authority, justification or excuse under the law of the part of the United Kingdom where it was inflicted;

  (b) in relation to pain or suffering inflicted outside the United Kingdom—

  (i) if it was inflicted by a United Kingdom official acting under the law of the United Kingdom or by a person acting in an official capacity under that law, lawful authority, justification or excuse under that law;

  (ii) if it was inflicted by a United Kingdom official acting under the law of any part of the United Kingdom or by a person acting in an official capacity under such law, lawful authority, justification or excuse under the law of the part of the United Kingdom under whose law he was acting; and

  (iii) in any other case, lawful authority, justification or excuse under the law of the place where it was inflicted.

139   Having article with blade or point in public place

(1) Subject to subsections (4) and (5) below, any person who has an article to which this section applies with him in a public place shall be guilty of an offence. [E]

(2) Subject to subsection (3) below, this section applies to any article which has a blade or is sharply pointed except a folding pocketknife.

(3) This section applies to a folding pocketknife if the cutting edge of its blade exceeds 3 inches.

(4) It shall be a defence for a person charged with an offence under this section to prove that he had good reason or lawful authority for having the article with him in a public place.

(5) Without prejudice to the generality of subsection (4) above, it shall be a defence for a person charged with an offence under this section to prove that he had the article with him—

  (a) for use at work;

  (b) for religious reasons; or

  (c) as part of any national costume.

(7) In this section "public place" includes any place to which at the material time the public have or are permitted access, whether on payment or otherwise.

139A   Offence of having article with blade or point (or offensive weapon) on education premises

(1) Any person who has an article to which section 139 of this Act applies with him on school premises or further education premises shall be guilty of an offence. [E]

(2) Any person who has an offensive weapon within the meaning of section 1 of the Prevention of Crime Act 1953 with him on school premises or further education premises shall be guilty of an offence. [E]

(3) It shall be a defence for a person charged with an offence under subsection (1) or (2) above to prove that he had good reason or lawful authority for having the article or weapon with him on the premises in question.

(4) Without prejudice to the generality of subsection (3) above, it shall be a defence for a person charged with an offence under subsection (1) or (2) above to prove that he had the article or weapon in question with him—

(a) for use at work,

(b) for educational purposes,

(c) for religious reasons, or

(d) as part of any national costume.

(6) In this section and section 139B, "school premises" means land used for the purposes of a school, excluding any land occupied solely as a dwelling by a person employed at the school; and "school" has the meaning given by; section 4 of the Education Act 1996.

(a) in relation to land in England and Wales,section 4 of the Education Act 1996.

(6A) In this section and section 139B "further education premises" means—

(a) in relation to England and Wales, land used solely for the purposes of—

(i)   an institution within the further education sector (within the meaning of section 91 of the Further and Higher Education Act 1992), or

(ii) a 16 to 19 Academy (within the meaning of section 1B of the Academies Act 2010), excluding any land occupied solely as a dwelling by a person employed at the institution or the 16 to 19 Academy;

139AA   Offence of threatening with article with blade or point or offensive weapon

(1) A person is guilty of an offence if that person—

(a) has an article to which this section applies with him or her in a public place or on school premises,

(b) unlawfully and intentionally threatens another person ("A") with the article, and

(c) does so in such a way that a reasonable person ("B") who was exposed to the same threat as A would think that there was an immediate risk of physical harm to B. [E]

(1A) A person is guilty of an offence if that person—

(a) has an article to which this section applies with them on further education premises,

(b) unlawfully and intentionally threatens another person ("A") with the article, and

(c) does so in such a way that a reasonable person ("B") who was exposed to the same threat as A would think that there was an immediate risk of physical harm to B.

(2) In relation to a public place this section applies to an article to which section 139 applies.

(3) In relation to school premises this section applies to each of these—

(a) an article which section 139 applies;

(b) an offensive weapon within the meaning of section 1 of the Prevention of Crime Act 1953.

(3A) In relation to further education premises this section applies to each of these—

(a) an article to which section 139 applies;

(b) an offensive weapon within the meaning of section 1 of the Prevention of Crime Act 1953.

(5) In this section—

"further education premises" means land used solely for the purposes of—

(a) an institution within the further education sector (within the meaning of section 91 of the Further and Higher Education Act 1992), or

(b) a 16 to 19 Academy (within the meaning of section 1B of the Academies Act 2010), excluding any land occupied solely as a dwelling by a person employed at the institution or the 16 to 19 Academy;

"public place" has the same meaning as in section 139;

"school premises" means land used for the purposes of a school, excluding any land occupied solely as a dwelling by a person employed at the school;

and "school" has the meaning given by section 4 of the Education Act 1996.

141 Offensive weapons

(1) Any person who manufactures, sells or hires or offers for sale or hire, exposes or has in his possession for the purpose of sale or hire, or lends or gives to any other person, a weapon to which this section applies shall be guilty of an offence . . . [S]

(1A) Any person who possesses a weapon to which this section applies in private is guilty of an offence ...

(1C) For the purposes of subsection (1A) as it has effect in relation to England and Wales, a person possesses a weapon to which this section applies in private if the person possesses the weapon in a place other than—

(a) a public place,

(b) school premises,

(c) further education premises, or

(d) a prison.

(1F) In subsections (1C)—

"further education premises", in relation to England and Wales, means land used solely for the purposes of—

(a) an institution within the further education sector (within the meaning of section 91 of the Further and Higher Education Act 1992), or

(b) a 16 to 19 Academy (within the meaning of section 1B of the Academies Act 2010),

excluding any land occupied solely as a dwelling by a person employed at the institution or the 16 to 19 Academy;

"prison" includes—

(a) a young offender institution,

(b) a secure training centre, and

(c) a secure college;

"public place" includes any place to which, at the time in question, the public have or are permitted access, whether on payment or otherwise;

"school premises" means land used for the purposes of a school, excluding any land occupied solely as a dwelling by a person employed at the school;

and "school" has the meaning given by—

(a) in relation to land in England and Wales, section 4 of the Education Act 1996;

(2) The Secretary of State may by order made by statutory instrument direct that this section shall apply to any description of weapon specified in the order except—

(a) any weapon subject to the Firearms Act 1968; and

(b) crossbows.

(4) The importation of a weapon to which this section applies is hereby prohibited.

(5) It shall be a defence for any person charged in respect of any conduct of his relating to a weapon to which this section applies—

(a) with an offence under subsection (1) or (1A) above; or

(b) with an offence under section 50(2) or (3) of the Customs and Excise Management Act 1979 (improper importation),

to show that his conduct was only for the purposes of functions carried out on behalf of the Crown or of a visiting force.

(7A) It is a defence for a person charged with an offence under subsection (1A) to show that the weapon in question is one of historical importance.

(8) It shall be a defence for any person charged in respect of any conduct of his relating to a weapon to which this section applies—

(a) with an offence under subsection (1) above; or

(b) with an offence under section 50(2) or (3) of the Customs and Excise Management Act 1979, to show that the conduct in question was only for the purposes of making the weapon available to a museum or gallery to which this subsection applies.

(8A) It is a defence for a person charged with an offence under subsection (1A) to show that they possessed the weapon in question only in their capacity as the operator of, or as a person acting on behalf of, a museum or gallery.

(9) If the operator of, or a person acting on behalf of a museum or gallery to which subsection (8) above applies is charged with hiring or lending a weapon to which this section applies, it shall be a defence for him to show that he had reasonable grounds for believing that the person to whom he lent or hired it would use it only for cultural, artistic or educational purposes.

(10) Subsection (8) above applies to a museum or gallery only if it does not distribute profits.

(11) In this section "museum or gallery" includes any institution which has as its purpose, or one of its purposes, the preservation, display and interpretation of material of historical, artistic or scientific interest and gives the public access to it.

(11ZA) It is a defence for a person charged with an offence under subsection (1A) to show that they possessed the weapon in question for educational purposes only.

(11A) It shall be a defence for a person charged in respect of conduct of his relating to a weapon to which this section applies—

(a) with an offence under subsection (1) or (1A) above, or

(b) with an offence under section 50(2) or (3) of the Customs and Excise Management Act 1979, to show that his conduct was for the purpose only of making the weapon in question available for one or more of the purposes specified in subsection (11B).

(11AA) It is a defence for a person charged with an offence under subsection (1A) to show that they possessed the weapon in question only for one or more of the purposes specified in subsection (11B).

(11B) Those purposes are—

(a) the purposes of theatrical performances and of rehearsals for such performances;

(b) the production of films (within the meaning of Part 1 of the Copyright, Designs and Patents Act 1988—see section 5B of that Act);

(c) the production of television programmes (within the meaning of the Communications Act 2003—see section 405(1) of that Act).

(11C) For the purposes of this section a person shall be taken to have shown a matter specified in subsection (5), (7A), (8), (8A), (9), (11ZA), (11A) or (11AA) if—

(a) sufficient evidence of that matter is adduced to raise an issue with respect to it; and

(b) the contrary is not proved beyond a reasonable doubt.

(12) This section shall not have effect in relation to anything done before it comes into force.

141A   Sale of knives and certain articles with blade or point to persons under eighteen

(1) Any person who sells to a person under the age of eighteen years an article to which this section applies shall be guilty of an offence. [S]

(2) Subject to subsection (3) below, this section applies to—

(a) any knife, knife blade or razor blade,

(b) any axe, and

(c) any other article which has a blade or which is sharply pointed and which is made or adapted for use for causing injury to the person.

(3) This section does not apply to any article described in—

    (a) section 1 of the Restriction of Offensive Weapons Act 1959; or

    (c) an order made by the Secretary of State under this section.

(4) Subject to section 141B, it shall be a defence for a person charged with an offence under subsection (1) above to prove that he took all reasonable precautions and exercised all due diligence to avoid the commission of the offence.

141B Limitations on defence to offence under section 141A: England and Wales

(1) This section applies if—

    (a) a person ("the seller") is charged with an offence under section 141A (sale of bladed articles to persons under 18), and

    (b) the seller was not in the presence of the person ("the buyer") to whom the article to which the charge relates was sold at the time of the sale.

(2) For the purposes of subsection (1)(b) the seller was not in the presence of the buyer at the time of the sale if—

    (a) where the seller is an individual, the seller or a person acting on the seller's behalf was not in the presence of the buyer at that time;

    (b) where the seller is not an individual, a person acting on the seller's behalf was not in the presence of the buyer at that time.

(3) The seller is not to be regarded as having proved that they took all reasonable precautions and exercised all due diligence to avoid the commission of the offence unless, as a minimum, they prove that the following conditions are met.

(4) Condition A is that, at the time the offence is alleged to have been committed—

    (a) the seller operated a system for checking that persons who bought articles to which section 141A applied by the same or a similar method of purchase to that used by the buyer were not under the age of 18, and

    (b) that system was likely to prevent persons under the age of 18 from buying such articles by that method.

(5) Condition B is that when the package containing the article was dispatched by the seller, it was clearly marked to indicate—

    (a) that it contained an article with a blade or which was sharply pointed (as the case may be), and

    (b) that, when finally delivered, it should only be delivered into the hands of a person aged 18 or over.

(6) Condition C is that the seller took all reasonable precautions and exercised all due diligence to ensure that, when finally delivered, the package would be delivered into the hands of a person aged 18 or over.

(7) Condition D is that the seller did not deliver the package, or arrange for its delivery, to a locker.

(8) Where the article to which section 141A applied was dispatched by the seller to a place from which it was to be collected by the buyer or a person acting on behalf of the buyer, references in subsections (5) and (6) to the final delivery of the article are to be read as its supply to the buyer or a person acting on behalf of the buyer from that place.

(9) In subsection (7) "locker" means a lockable container to which the package was delivered with a view to its collection by the buyer, or a person acting on behalf of the buyer, in accordance with arrangements made between the seller and the buyer.

160 Possession of indecent photograph of child

(1) Subject to section 160A, it is an offence for a person to have any indecent photograph or pseudo-photograph of a child in his possession. [I]

(2) Where a person is charged with an offence under subsection (1) above, it shall be a defence for him to prove—

    (a) that he had a legitimate reason for having the photograph or pseudo-photograph in his possession; or

    (b) that he had not himself seen the photograph or pseudo-photograph and did not know, nor had any cause to suspect, it to be indecent; or

    (c) that the photograph or pseudo-photograph was sent to him without any prior request made by him or on his behalf and that he did not keep it for an unreasonable time.

  (4) Sections 1(3), 2(3), 3 and 7 of the Protection of Children Act 1978 shall have effect as if any reference in them to that Act included a reference to this section.

160A   Marriage and other relationships

  (1) This section applies where, in proceedings for an offence under section 160 relating to an indecent photograph or pseudo-photograph of a child, the defendant proves that the photograph or pseudo-photograph was of the child aged 16 or over, and that at the time of the offence charged the child and he—

    (a) were married or civil partners of each other, or

    (b) lived together as partners in an enduring family relationship.

  (2) This section also applies where, in proceedings for an offence under section 160 relating to an indecent photograph or pseudo-photograph of a child, the defendant proves that the photograph or pseudo-photograph was of the child aged 16 or over, and that at the time when he obtained it the child and he—

    (a) were married or civil partners of each other, or

    (b) lived together as partners in an enduring family relationship.

  (3) This section applies whether the photograph or pseudo-photograph showed the child alone or with the defendant, but not if it showed any other person.

  (4) If sufficient evidence is adduced to raise an issue as to whether the child consented to the photograph or pseudo-photograph being in the defendant's possession, or as to whether the defendant reasonably believed that the child so consented, the defendant is not guilty of the offence unless it is proved that the child did not so consent and that the defendant did not reasonably believe that the child so consented.

Firearms (Amendment) Act 1988

5   Restriction on sale of ammunition for smooth-bore guns

  (1) This section applies to ammunition to which section 1 of the Firearms Act 1968 does not apply and which is capable of being used in a shot gun or in a smooth-bore gun to which that section applies.

  (2) It is an offence for a person to sell any such ammunition to another person in the United Kingdom who is neither a registered firearms dealer nor a person who sells such ammunition by way of trade or business unless that other person—

    (a) produces a certificate authorising him to possess a gun of a kind mentioned in subsection (1) above; or

    (b) shows that he is by virtue of that Act or this Act entitled to have possession of such a gun without holding a certificate; or

    (c) produces a certificate authorising another person to possess such a gun, together with that person's written authority to purchase the ammunition on his behalf. [S]

6   Shortening of barrels

  (1) Subject to subsection (2) below, it is an offence to shorten to a length less than 24 inches the barrel of any smooth-bore gun to which section 1 of the Firearms Act 1968 applies other than one which has a barrel with a bore exceeding 2 inches in diameter . . . [E]

  (2) It is not an offence under this section for a registered firearms dealer to shorten the barrel of a gun for the sole purpose of replacing a defective part of the barrel so as to produce a barrel not less than 24 inches in length.

14   Auctioneers, carriers and warehousemen

(1) It is an offence for an auctioneer, carrier or warehouseman—

(a) to fail to take reasonable precautions for the safe custody of any firearm or ammunition which, by virtue of section 9(1) of the Firearms Act 1968 he or any servant of his has in his possession without holding a certificate; or

(b) to fail to report forthwith to the police the loss or theft of any such firearm or ammunition. [S]

Malicious Communications Act 1988

1   Offence of sending letters etc. with intent to cause distress or anxiety

(1) Any person who sends to another person—

(a) a letter, electronic communication or article of any description which conveys—

(i)   a message which is indecent or grossly offensive;

(ii) a threat; or

(iii) information which is false and known or believed to be false by the sender; or

(b) any article or electronic communication which is, in whole or part, of an indecent or grossly offensive nature,

is guilty of an offence if his purpose, or one of his purposes, in sending it is that it should, so far as falling within paragraph (a) or (b) above, cause distress or anxiety to the recipient or to any other person to whom he intends that it or its contents or nature should be communicated. [S]

(2) A person is not guilty of an offence by virtue of subsection (1)(a)(ii) above if he shows—

(a) that the threat was used to reinforce a demand made by him on reasonable grounds; and

(b) that he believed, and had reasonable grounds for believing, that the use of the threat was a proper means of reinforcing the demand.

(2A) In this section "electronic communication" includes—

(a) any oral or other communication by means of an electronic communications network; and

(b) any communication (however sent) that is in electronic form.

(3) In this section references to sending include references to delivering or transmitting and to causing to be sent, delivered or transmitted and "sender" shall be construed accordingly.

Road Traffic Act 1988

PART I   PRINCIPAL ROAD SAFETY PROVISIONS

1   Causing death by dangerous driving

A person who causes the death of another person by driving a mechanically propelled vehicle dangerously on a road or other public place is guilty of an offence. [I]

1A   Causing serious injury by dangerous driving

(1) A person who causes serious injury to another person by driving a mechanically propelled vehicle dangerously on a road or other public place is guilty of an offence. [E]

(2) In this section "serious injury" means—

(a) In England and Wales, physical harm which amounts to grievous bodily harm for the purposes of the Offences against the Person Act 1861.

2   Dangerous driving

A person who drives a mechanically propelled vehicle dangerously on a road or other public place is guilty of an offence. [E]

2A   Meaning of dangerous driving

(1) For the purposes of sections 1, 1A and 2 above a person is to be regarded as driving dangerously if (and, subject to subsection (2) below, only if)—

(a) the way he drives falls far below what would be expected of a competent and careful driver, and

(b) it would be obvious to a competent and careful driver that driving in that way would be dangerous.

(2) A person is also to be regarded as driving dangerously for the purposes of sections 1, 1A and 2 above if it would be obvious to a competent and careful driver that driving the vehicle in its current state would be dangerous.

(3) In subsections (1) and (2) above "dangerous" refers to danger either of injury to any person or of serious damage to property; and in determining for the purposes of those subsections what would be expected of, or obvious to, a competent and careful driver in a particular case, regard shall be had not only to the circumstances of which he could be expected to be aware but also to any circumstances shown to have been within the knowledge of the accused.

(4) In determining for the purposes of subsection (2) above the state of a vehicle, regard may be had to anything attached to or carried on or in it and to the manner in which it is attached or carried.

2B   Causing death by careless or inconsiderate driving

A person who causes the death of another person by driving a mechanically propelled vehicle on a road or other public place without due care and attention, or without reasonable consideration for other persons using the road or place, is guilty of an offence. [E]

3   Careless, and inconsiderate, driving

If a person drives a mechanically propelled vehicle on a road or other public place without due care and attention, or without reasonable consideration for other persons using the road or place, he is guilty of an offence. [S]

3ZA   Meaning of careless, or inconsiderate, driving

(1) This section has effect for the purposes of sections 2B and 3 above and section 3A below.

(2) A person is to be regarded as driving without due care and attention if (and only if) the way he drives falls below what would be expected of a competent and careful driver.

(3) In determining for the purposes of subsection (2) above what would be expected of a careful and competent driver in a particular case, regard shall be had not only to the circumstances of which he could be expected to be aware but also to any circumstances shown to have been within the knowledge of the accused.

(4) A person is to be regarded as driving without reasonable consideration for other persons only if those persons are inconvenienced by his driving.

3ZB   Causing death by driving: unlicensed or uninsured drivers

A person is guilty of an offence under this section if he causes the death of another person by driving a motor vehicle on a road and, at the time when he is driving, the circumstances are such that he is committing an offence under—

(a) section 87(1) of this Act (driving otherwise than in accordance with a licence), or

(c) section 143 of this Act (using motor vehicle while uninsured). [E]

3ZC   Causing death by driving: disqualified drivers

A person is guilty of an offence under this section if he or she—

(a) causes the death of another person by driving a motor vehicle on a road, and

(b) at that time, is committing an offence under section 103(1)(b) of this Act (driving while disqualified). [I]

3ZD   Causing serious injury by driving: disqualified drivers

(1) A person is guilty of an offence under this section if he or she—

(a) causes serious injury to another person by driving a motor vehicle on a road, and

    (b) at that time, is committing an offence under section 103(1)(b) of this Act (driving while disqualified). [E]

(2) In this section "serious injury" means—

    (a) in England and Wales, physical harm which amounts to grievous bodily harm for the purposes of the Offences against the Person Act 1861, . . .

3A   Causing death by careless driving when under influence of drink or drugs

(1) If a person causes the death of another person by driving a mechanically propelled vehicle on a road or other public place without due care and attention, or without reasonable consideration for other persons using the road or place, and—

    (a) he is, at the time when he is driving, unfit to drive through drink or drugs, or

    (b) he has consumed so much alcohol that the proportion of it in his breath, blood or urine at that time exceeds the prescribed limit, or

    (ba) he has in his body a specified controlled drug and the proportion of it in his blood or urine at that time exceeds the specified limit for that drug, or

    (c) he is, within 18 hours after that time, required to provide a specimen in pursuance of section 7 of this Act, but without reasonable excuse fails to provide it, or

    (d) he is required by a constable to give his permission for a laboratory test of a specimen of blood taken from him under section 7A of this Act, but without reasonable excuse fails to do so

he is guilty of an offence. [I]

(2) For the purposes of this section a person shall be taken to be unfit to drive at any time when his ability to drive properly is impaired.

(3) Subsection (1)(b), (ba), (c) and (d) above shall not apply in relation to a person driving a mechanically propelled vehicle other than a motor vehicle.

4   Driving, or being in charge, when under influence of drink or drugs

(1) A person who, when driving or attempting to drive a mechanically propelled vehicle on a road or other public place, is unfit to drive through drink or drugs is guilty of an offence. [S]

(2) Without prejudice to subsection (1) above, a person who, when in charge of a mechanically propelled vehicle which is on a road or other public place, is unfit to drive through drink or drugs is guilty of an offence. [S]

(3) For the purposes of subsection (2) above, a person shall be deemed not to have been in charge of a mechanically propelled vehicle if he proves that at the material time the circumstances were such that there was no likelihood of his driving it so long as he remained unfit to drive through drink or drugs.

(4) The court may, in determining whether there was such a likelihood as is mentioned in subsection (3) above, disregard any injury to him and any damage to the vehicle.

(5) For the purposes of this section, a person shall be taken to be unfit to drive if his ability to drive properly is for the time being impaired.

5   Driving or being in charge of a motor vehicle with alcohol concentration above prescribed limit

(1) If a person—

    (a) drives or attempts to drive a motor vehicle on a road or other public place, or

    (b) is in charge of a motor vehicle on a road or other public place,

after consuming so much alcohol that the proportion of it in his breath, blood or urine exceeds the prescribed limit he is guilty of an offence. [S]

(2) It is a defence for a person charged with an offence under subsection (1)(b) above to prove that at the time he is alleged to have committed the offence the circumstances were such that there was no likelihood of his driving the vehicle whilst the proportion of alcohol in his breath, blood or urine remained likely to exceed the prescribed limit.

(3) The court may, in determining whether there was such a likelihood as is mentioned in subsection (2) above, disregard any injury to him and any damage to the vehicle.

5A   Driving or being in charge of a motor vehicle with concentration of specified controlled drug above specified limit

(1) This section applies where a person ("D")—

    (a) drives or attempts to drive a motor vehicle on a road or other public place, or

    (b) is in charge of a motor vehicle on a road or other public place,

and there is in D's body a specified controlled drug.

(2) D is guilty of an offence if the proportion of the drug in D's blood or urine exceeds the specified limit for that drug. [S]

(3) It is a defence for a person ("D") charged with an offence under this section to show that—

    (a) the specified controlled drug had been prescribed or supplied to D for medical or dental purposes,

    (b) D took the drug in accordance with any directions given by the person by whom the drug was prescribed or supplied, and with any accompanying instructions (so far as consistent with any such directions) given by the manufacturer or distributor of the drug, and

    (c) D's possession of the drug immediately before taking it was not unlawful under section 5(1) of the Misuse of Drugs Act 1971 (restriction of possession of controlled drugs) because of an exemption in regulations made under section 7 of that Act (authorisation of activities otherwise unlawful under foregoing provisions).

(4) The defence in subsection (3) is not available if D's actions were—

    (a) contrary to any advice, given by the person by whom the drug was prescribed or supplied, about the amount of time that should elapse between taking the drug and driving a motor vehicle, or

    (b) contrary to any accompanying instructions about that matter (so far as consistent with any such advice) given by the manufacturer or distributor of the drug.

(5) If evidence is adduced that is sufficient to raise an issue with respect to the defence in subsection (3), the court must assume that the defence is satisfied unless the prosecution proves beyond reasonable doubt that it is not.

(6) It is a defence for a person ("D") charged with an offence by virtue of subsection (1)(b) to prove that at the time D is alleged to have committed the offence the circumstances were such that there was no likelihood of D driving the vehicle whilst the proportion of the specified controlled drug in D's blood or urine remained likely to exceed the specified limit for that drug.

(7) The court may, in determining whether there was such a likelihood, disregard any injury to D and any damage to the vehicle.

(8) In this section, and in sections 3A, 6C(1), 6D and 10, "specified" means specified in regulations made—

    (a) by the Secretary of State, in relation to driving or attempting to drive, or being in charge of a vehicle, in England and Wales; . . .

(9) A limit specified under subsection (2) may be zero.

6   Power to administer preliminary tests

(1) If any of subsections (2) to (5) applies a constable may require a person to co-operate with any one or more preliminary tests administered to the person by that constable or another constable.

(2) This subsection applies if a constable reasonably suspects that the person—

    (a) is driving, is attempting to drive or is in charge of a motor vehicle on a road or other public place, and

    (b) has alcohol or a drug in his body or is under the influence of a drug.

(3) This subsection applies if a constable reasonably suspects that the person—

    (a) has been driving, attempting to drive or in charge of a motor vehicle on a road or other public place while having alcohol or a drug in his body or while unfit to drive because of a drug, and

    (b) still has alcohol or a drug in his body or is still under the influence of a drug.

(4) This subsection applies if a constable reasonably suspects that the person—

   (a) is or has been driving, attempting to drive or in charge of a motor vehicle on a road or other public place, and

   (b) has committed a traffic offence while the vehicle was in motion.

   (5) This subsection applies if—

   (a) an accident occurs owing to the presence of a motor vehicle on a road or other public place, and

   (b) a constable reasonably believes that the person was driving, attempting to drive or in charge of the vehicle at the time of the accident.

   (6) A person commits an offence if without reasonable excuse he fails to co-operate with a preliminary test in pursuance of a requirement imposed under this section. [S]

   (7) A constable may administer a preliminary test by virtue of any of subsections (2) to (4) only if he is in uniform.

   (8) In this section—

   (a) a reference to a preliminary test is to any of the tests described in sections 6A to 6C, and

   (b) "traffic offence" means an offence under—

      (i)   a provision of Part II of the Public Passenger Vehicles Act 1981,

      (ii) a provision of the Road Traffic Regulation Act 1984,

      (iii) a provision of the Road Traffic Offenders Act 1988 other than a provision of Part III, or

      (iv) a provision of this Act other than a provision of Part V.

7   Provision of specimens for analysis

   (1) In the course of an investigation into whether a person has committed an offence under section 3A, 4 or 5 of this Act a constable may, subject to the following provisions of this section and section 9 of this Act, require him—

   (a) to provide two specimens of breath for analysis by means of a device of a type approved by the Secretary of State, or

   (b) to provide a specimen of blood or urine for a laboratory test.

   (1A) In the course of an investigation into whether a person has committed an offence under section 5A of this Act a constable may, subject to the subsections (3) to (7) of this section and section 9 of this Act, require the person to provide a specimen of blood or urine for a laboratory test.

   (2) A constable may make a requirement under this section to provide specimens of breath only if—

   (a) the requirement is made at a police station or a hospital,

   (b) the requirement is imposed in circumstances where section 6(5) of this Act applies, or

   (c) the constable is in uniform.

   (2C) Where a constable has imposed a requirement on the person concerned to co-operate with a relevant breath test at any place, he is entitled to remain at or near that place in order to impose on him there a requirement under this section.

   (2CA) For the purposes of subsection (2C) "a relevant breath test" is a procedure involving the provision by the person concerned of a specimen of breath to be used for the purpose of obtaining an indication whether the proportion of alcohol in his breath or blood is likely to exceed the prescribed limit.

   (2D) If a requirement under subsection (1)(a) above has been made at a place other than at a police station, such a requirement may subsequently be made at a police station if (but only if)—

   (a) a device or a reliable device of the type mentioned in subsection (1)(a) above was not available at that place or it was for any other reason not practicable to use such a device there, or

   (b) the constable who made the previous requirement has reasonable cause to believe that the device used there has not produced a reliable indication of the proportion of alcohol in the breath of the person concerned.

   (3) A requirement under this section to provide a specimen of blood or urine can only be made at a police station or at a hospital; and it cannot be made at a police station unless—

(a)   the constable making the requirement has reasonable cause to believe that for medical reasons a specimen of breath cannot be provided or should not be required, or

(b)   specimens of breath have not been provided elsewhere and at the time the requirement is made a device or a reliable device of the type mentioned in subsection (1)(a) above is not available at the police station or it is then for any other reason not practicable to use such a device there, or

(bb) a device of the type mentioned in subsection (1)(a) above has been used (at the police station or elsewhere) but the constable who required the specimens of breath has reasonable cause to believe that the device has not produced a reliable indication of the proportion of alcohol in the breath of the person concerned, or

(bc) as a result of the administration of a preliminary drug test, the constable making the requirement has reasonable cause to believe that the person required to provide a specimen of blood or urine has a drug in his body, or

(c)   the suspected offence is one under section 3A, 4 or 5A of this Act and the constable making the requirement has been advised by a medical practitioner or a registered healthcare practitioner that the condition of the person required to provide the specimen might be due to some drug;

but may then be made notwithstanding that the person required to provide the specimen has already provided or been required to provide two specimens of breath.

(4) If the provision of a specimen other than a specimen of breath may be required in pursuance of this section the question whether it is to be a specimen of blood or a specimen of urine and, in the case of a specimen of blood, the question who is to be asked to take it shall be decided (subject to subsection (4A)) by the constable making the requirement.

(4A) Where a constable decides for the purposes of subsection (4) to require the provision of a specimen of blood, there shall be no requirement to provide such a specimen if—

(a) the medical practitioner who is asked to take the specimen is of the opinion that, for medical reasons, it cannot or should not be taken; or

(b) the registered health care professional who is asked to take it is of that opinion and there is no contrary opinion from a medical practitioner;

and, where by virtue of this subsection there can be no requirement to provide a specimen of blood, the constable may require a specimen of urine instead.

(5) A specimen of urine shall be provided within one hour of the requirement for its provision being made and after the provision of a previous specimen of urine.

(5A) A constable may arrest a person without warrant if—

(a) the person fails to provide a specimen of breath when required to do so in pursuance of this section, and

(b) the constable reasonably suspects that the person has alcohol in his body.

(6) A person who, without reasonable excuse, fails to provide a specimen when required to do so in pursuance of this section is guilty of an offence. [S]

(7) A constable must, on requiring any person to provide a specimen in pursuance of this section, warn him that a failure to provide it may render him liable to prosecution.

8   Breath specimen showing higher alcohol level to be disregarded

(1) Of any two specimens of breath provided by any person in pursuance of section 7 of this Act that with the lower proportion of alcohol in the breath shall be used and the other shall be disregarded.

9   Protection for hospital patients

(1) While a person is at a hospital as a patient he shall not be required to co-operate with a preliminary test or to provide a specimen under section 7 of this Act unless the medical practitioner in immediate charge of his case has been notified of the proposal to make the requirement; and—

(a) if the requirement is then made, it shall be for co-operation with a test administered, or for the provision of a specimen at the hospital, but

(b) if the medical practitioner objects on the ground specified in subsection (2) below, the requirement shall not be made.

(1A) While a person is at a hospital as a patient, no specimen of blood shall be taken from him under section 7A of this Act and he shall not be required to give his permission for a laboratory test of a specimen taken under that section unless the medical practitioner in immediate charge of his case—

(a) has been notified of the proposal to take the specimen or to make the requirement; and

(b) has not objected on the ground specified in subsection (2).

(2) The ground on which the medical practitioner may object is—

(a) in a case falling within subsection (1), that the requirement or the provision of the specimen or (if one is required) the warning required by section 7(7) of this Act would be prejudicial to the proper care and treatment of the patient; and

(b) in a case falling within subsection (1A), that the taking of the specimen, the requirement or the warning required by section 7A(5) of this Act would be so prejudicial.

11   Interpretation of sections 4 to 10

(1) The following provisions apply for the interpretation of sections 3A to 10 of this Act.

(2) In those sections—

"controlled drug" has the meaning given by section 2 of the Misuse of Drugs Act 1971,

"drug" includes any intoxicant other than alcohol,

"fail" includes refuse,

"hospital" means an institution which provides medical or surgical treatment for in-patients or out-patients,

"the prescribed limit" means, as the case may require—

(a) 35 microgrammes of alcohol in 100 millilitres of breath,

(b) 80 milligrammes of alcohol in 100 millilitres of blood, or

(c) 107 milligrammes of alcohol in 100 millilitres of urine,

or such other proportion as may be prescribed by regulations,

"registered health care professional" means a person (other than a medical practitioner) who is—

(a) a registered nurse; or

(b) a registered member of a health care profession which is designated for the purposes of this paragraph by an order made by the Secretary of State,

"specified" in relation to a controlled drug has the meaning given by section 5A(8).

(2A) A health care profession is any profession mentioned in section 60(2) of the Health Act 1999 other than the profession of practising medicine and the profession of nursing.

(3) A person does not co-operate with a preliminary test or provide a specimen of breath for analysis unless his co-operation or the specimen—

(a) is sufficient to enable the test or the analysis to be carried out, and

(b) is provided in such a way as to enable the objective of the test or analysis to be satisfactorily achieved.

(4) A person provides a specimen of blood if and only if—

(a) he consents to the taking of such a specimen from him; and

(b) the specimen is taken from him either by a medical practitioner or by a registered health care professional.

12   Motor racing on public ways

(1) A person who promotes or takes part in a race or trial of speed between motor vehicles on a public way is guilty of an offence. [S]

(1A) Subsection (1) is subject to—

(a) in relation to England and Wales, sections 12A to 12F (which make provision to allow the holding of races or trials of speed between motor vehicles on public ways in England and Wales);

(2) In this section "public way" means, in England and Wales, a highway . . .

13 Regulation of motoring events on public ways

(1) A person who promotes or takes part in a competition or trial (other than a race or trial of speed) involving the use of motor vehicles on a public way is guilty of an offence unless the competition or trial—

    (a) is authorised, and

    (b) is conducted in accordance with any conditions imposed,

by or under regulations under this section. [S]

(4) In this section "public way" means, in England and Wales, a highway . . .

13A Disapplication of sections 1 to 3 for authorised motoring events

(1) A person shall not be guilty of an offence under sections 1, 1A, 2, 2B, or 3 of this Act by virtue of driving a vehicle in a public place other than a road if he shows that he was driving in accordance with an authorisation for a motoring event given under regulations made by the Secretary of State.

14 Seat belts: adults

(1) The Secretary of State may make regulations requiring, subject to such exceptions as may be prescribed, persons who are driving or riding in motor vehicles on a road to wear seat belts of such description as may be prescribed.

(3) A person who drives or rides in a motor vehicle in contravention of regulations under this section is guilty of an offence; but, notwithstanding any enactment or rule of law, no person other than the person actually committing the contravention is guilty of an offence by reason of the contravention. [S]

(6) Regulations under this section requiring the wearing of seat belts by persons riding in motor vehicles shall not apply to children under the age of fourteen years.

15 Restriction on carrying children not wearing seat belts in motor vehicles

(1) Except as provided by regulations, where a child under the age of fourteen years is in the front of a motor vehicle, a person must not without reasonable excuse drive the vehicle on a road unless the child is wearing a seat belt in conformity with regulations.

(1A) Where—

    (a) a child is in the front of a motor vehicle other than a bus,

    (b) the child is in a rear-facing child restraining device, and

    (c) the passenger seat where the child is placed is protected by a front air bag,

a person must not without reasonable excuse drive the vehicle on a road unless the air bag is deactivated.

(2) It is an offence for a person to drive a motor vehicle in contravention of subsection (1) or (1A) above. [S]

(3) Except as provided by regulations, where—

    (a) a child under the age of three years is in the rear of a motor vehicle, or

    (b) a child of or over that age but under the age of fourteen years is in the rear of a motor vehicle and any seat belt is fitted in the rear of that vehicle,

a person must not without reasonable excuse drive the vehicle on a road unless the child is wearing a seat belt in conformity with regulations.

(3A) Except as provided by regulations, where—

    (a) a child who is under the age of 12 years and less than 150 centimetres in height is in the rear of a passenger car,

    (b) no seat belt is fitted in the rear of the passenger car, and

    (c) a seat in the front of the passenger car is provided with a seat belt but is not occupied by any person,

a person must not without reasonable excuse drive the passenger car on a road.

(4) It is an offence for a person to drive a motor vehicle in contravention of subsection (3) or (3A) above. [S]

(9) In this section—

"regulations" means regulations made by the Secretary of State under this section, "seat belt" includes any description of restraining device for a child and any reference to wearing a seat belt is to be construed accordingly.

16 Wearing of protective headgear

(1) The Secretary of State may make regulations requiring, subject to such exceptions as may be specified in the regulations, persons driving or riding (otherwise than in side-cars) on motor cycles of any class specified in the regulations to wear protective headgear of such description as may be so specified.

(2) A requirement imposed by regulations under this section shall not apply to any follower of the Sikh religion while he is wearing a turban.

(4) A person who drives or rides a motor cycle in contravention of regulations under this section is guilty of an offence; but notwithstanding any enactment or rule of law no person other than the person actually committing the contravention is guilty of an offence by reason of the contravention unless the person actually committing the contravention is a child under the age of sixteen years. [S]

18 Authorisation of head-worn appliances for use on motor cycles

(1) The Secretary of State may make regulations prescribing (by reference to shape, construction or any other quality) types of appliance of any description to which this section applies as authorised for use by persons driving or riding (otherwise than in sidecars) on motor cycles of any class specified in the regulations.

(3) If a person driving or riding on a motor cycle on a road uses an appliance of any description for which a type is prescribed under this section and that appliance—

    (a) is not of a type so prescribed, or

    (b) is otherwise used in contravention of regulations under this section, he is guilty of an offence. [S]

(4) If a person sells, or offers for sale, an appliance of any such description as authorised for use by persons on or in motor cycles, or motor cycles of any class, and that appliance is not of a type prescribed under this section as authorised for such use, he is, subject to subsection (5) below, guilty of an offence. [S]

(5) A person shall not be convicted of an offence under this section in respect of the sale or offer for sale of an appliance if he proves that it was sold or, as the case may be, offered for sale for export from Great Britain.

(7) This section applies to appliances of any description designed or adapted for use—

    (a) with any headgear, or

    (b) by being attached to or placed upon the head,

(as, for example, eye protectors or earphones).

(8) References in this section to selling or offering for sale include respectively references to letting on hire and offering to let on hire.

22 Leaving vehicles in dangerous positions

If a person in charge of a vehicle causes or permits the vehicle or a trailer drawn by it to remain at rest on a road in such a position or in such condition or in such circumstances as to involve a danger of injury to other persons using the road, he is guilty of an offence. [S]

22A Causing danger to road-users

(1) A person is guilty of an offence if he intentionally and without lawful authority or reasonable cause—

    (a) causes anything to be on or over a road, or

    (b) interferes with a motor vehicle, trailer or cycle, or

    (c) interferes (directly or indirectly) with traffic equipment,

in such circumstances that it would be obvious to a reasonable person that to do so would be dangerous. [E]

(2) In subsection (1) above "dangerous" refers to danger either of injury to any person while on or near a road, or of serious damage to property on or near a road; and in determining for the purposes of that subsection what would be obvious to a reasonable person in a particular case, regard shall be had not only to the circumstances of which he could be expected to be aware but also to any circumstances shown to have been within the knowledge of the accused.

(3) In subsection (1) above "traffic equipment" means—

    (a) anything lawfully placed on or near a road by a highway authority;

    (b) a traffic sign lawfully placed on or near a road by a person other than a highway authority;

    (c) any fence, barrier or light lawfully placed on or near a road—

        (i) in pursuance of section 174 of the Highways Act 1980, or section 65 of the New Roads and Street Works Act 1991 (which provide for guarding, lighting and signing in streets where works are undertaken), or

        (ii) by a constable or a person acting under the instructions (whether general or specific) of a chief officer of police.

(4) For the purposes of subsection (3) above anything placed on or near a road shall unless the contrary is proved be deemed to have been lawfully placed there.

(5) In this section "road" does not include a footpath or bridleway.

23 Restriction of carriage of persons on motor cycles

(1) Not more than one person in addition to the driver may be carried on a motor bicycle.

(2) No person in addition to the driver may be carried on a motor bicycle otherwise than sitting astride the motor cycle and on a proper seat securely fixed to the motor cycle behind the driver's seat.

(3) If a person is carried on a motor cycle in contravention of this section, the driver of the motor cycle is guilty of an offence. [S]

24 Restriction of carriage of persons on bicycles

(1) Not more than one person may be carried on a road on a bicycle not propelled by mechanical power unless it is constructed or adapted for the carriage of more than one person.

(2) In this section—

    (a) references to a person carried on a bicycle include references to a person riding the bicycle, and

    (b) "road" includes bridleway.

(3) If a person is carried on a bicycle in contravention of subsection (1) above, each of the persons carried is guilty of an offence. [S]

25 Tampering with motor vehicles

If, while a motor vehicle is on a road or on a parking place provided by a local authority, a person—

    (a) gets on to the vehicle, or

    (b) tampers with the brake or other part of its mechanism,

without lawful authority or reasonable cause he is guilty of an offence. [S]

26 Holding or getting on to vehicle in order to be towed or carried

(1) If, for the purpose of being carried, a person without lawful authority or reasonable cause takes or retains hold of, or gets on to, a motor vehicle or trailer while in motion on a road he is guilty of an offence.

(2) If, for the purpose of being drawn, a person takes or retains hold of a motor vehicle or trailer while in motion on a road he is guilty of an offence. [S]

27 Control of dogs on roads

(1) A person who causes or permits a dog to be on a designated road without the dog being held on a lead is guilty of an offence. [S]

(2) In this section "designated road" means a length of road specified by an order in that behalf of the local authority in whose area the length of road is situated.

(4) An order under this section may provide that subsection (1) above shall apply subject to such limitations or exceptions as may be specified in the order, and (without prejudice to the generality of this subsection) subsection (1) above does not apply to dogs proved—

    (a) to be kept for driving or tending sheep or cattle in the course of a trade or business, or

    (b) to have been at the material time in use under proper control for sporting purposes.

28   Dangerous cycling

(1) A person who rides a cycle on a road dangerously is guilty of an offence. [S]

(2) For the purposes of subsection (1) above a person is to be regarded as riding dangerously if (and only if)—

    (a) the way he rides falls far below what would be expected of a competent and careful cyclist, and

    (b) it would be obvious to a competent and careful cyclist that riding in that way would be dangerous.

(3) In subsection (2) above "dangerous" refers to danger either of injury to any person or of serious damage to property; and in determining for the purposes of that subsection what would be obvious to a competent and careful cyclist in a particular case, regard shall be had not only to the circumstances of which he could be expected to be aware but also to any circumstances shown to have been within the knowledge of the accused.

29   Careless, and inconsiderate, cycling

If a person rides a cycle on a road without due care and attention, or without reasonable consideration for other persons using the road, he is guilty of an offence. [S]

30   Cycling when under influence of drink or drugs

(1) A person who, when riding a cycle on a road or other public place, is unfit to ride through drink or drugs (that is to say, is under the influence of drink or a drug to such an extent as to be incapable of having proper control of the cycle) is guilty of an offence. [S]

31   Regulation of cycle racing on public ways

(1) A person who promotes or takes part in a race or trial of speed on a public way between cycles is guilty of an offence, unless the race or trial—

    (a) is authorised, and

    (b) is conducted in accordance with any conditions imposed,

by or under regulations under this section. [S]

(6) In this section "public way" means, in England and Wales, a highway . . .

34   Prohibition of driving mechanically propelled vehicles elsewhere than on roads

(1) Subject to the provisions of this section, if without lawful authority a person drives a motor vehicle—

    (a) on to or upon any common land, moorland or land of any other description, not being land forming part of a road, or

    (b) on any road being a footpath, bridleway, or restricted byway,

he is guilty of an offence. [S]

(3) It is not an offence under this section to drive a mechanically propelled vehicle on any land within fifteen yards of a road, being a road on which a motor vehicle may lawfully be driven, for the purpose only of parking the vehicle on that land.

(4) A person shall not be convicted of an offence under this section with respect to a vehicle if he proves to the satisfaction of the court that it was driven in contravention of this section for the purpose of saving life or extinguishing fire or meeting any other like emergency.

35   Drivers to comply with traffic directions

(1) Where a constable or traffic officer is for the time being engaged in the regulation of traffic in a road, a person driving or propelling a vehicle who neglects or refuses—

    (a) to stop the vehicle, or

    (b) to make it proceed in, or keep to, a particular line of traffic,

when directed to do so by the constable in the execution of his duty or the traffic officer (as the case may be) is guilty of an offence. [S]

    (2) Where—

    (a) a traffic survey of any description is being carried out on or in the vicinity of a road, and

    (b) a constable or traffic officer gives to a person driving or propelling a vehicle a direction—

        (i) to stop the vehicle,

        (ii) to make it proceed in, or keep to, a particular line of traffic, or

        (iii) to proceed to a particular point on or near the road on which the vehicle is being driven or propelled,

        being a direction given for the purposes of the survey (but not a direction requiring any person to provide any information for the purposes of a traffic survey),

the person is guilty of an offence if he neglects or refuses to comply with the direction.

36   Drivers to comply with traffic signs

    (1) Where a traffic sign, being a sign—

    (a) of the prescribed size, colour and type, or

    (b) of another character authorised by the relevant authority under the provisions in that behalf of the Road Traffic Regulation Act 1984,

has been lawfully placed on or near a road, a person driving or propelling a vehicle who fails to comply with the indication given by the sign is guilty of an offence. [S]

    (2) A traffic sign shall not be treated for the purposes of this section as having been lawfully placed unless either—

    (a) the indication given by the sign is an indication of a statutory prohibition, restriction or requirement, or

    (b) it is expressly provided by or under any provision of the Traffic Acts that this section shall apply to the sign or to signs of a type of which the sign is one;

and, where the indication mentioned in paragraph (a) of this subsection is of the general nature only of the prohibition, restriction or requirement to which the sign relates, a person shall not be convicted of failure to comply with the indication unless he has failed to comply with the prohibition, restriction or requirement to which the sign relates.

    (3) For the purposes of this section a traffic sign placed on or near a road shall be deemed—

    (a) to be of the prescribed size, colour and type, or of another character authorised by the relevant authority under the provisions in that behalf of the Road Traffic Regulation Act 1984, and

    (b) (subject to subsection (2) above) to have been lawfully so placed,

unless the contrary is proved.

    (4) Where a traffic survey of any description is being carried out on or in the vicinity of a road, this section applies to a traffic sign by which a direction is given—

    (a) to stop a vehicle,

    (b) to make it proceed in, or keep to, a particular line of traffic, or

    (c) to proceed to a particular point on or near the road on which the vehicle is being driven or propelled,

being a direction given for the purposes of the survey (but not a direction requiring any person to provide any information for the purposes of the survey).

37   Directions to pedestrians

Where a constable in uniform or traffic officer is for the time being engaged in the regulation of vehicular traffic in a road, a person on foot who proceeds across or along the carriageway in contravention of a direction to stop given by the constable in the execution of his duty or the traffic officer (as the case may be), either to persons on foot or to persons on foot and other traffic, is guilty of an offence. [S]

PART II   CONSTRUCTION AND USE OF VEHICLES AND EQUIPMENT

40A   Using vehicles in dangerous condition

A person is guilty of an offence if he uses, or causes or permits another to use, a motor vehicle or trailer on a road when—

(a) the condition of the motor vehicle or trailer, or of its accessories or equipment, or

(b) the purpose for which it is used, or

(c) the number of passengers carried by it or the manner in which they are carried, or

(d) the weight, position or distribution of its load, or the manner in which it is secured,

is such that the use of the motor vehicle or trailer involves a danger of injury to any person. [S]

41A   Breach of requirement as to brakes, steering-gear or tyres

A person who—

(a) contravenes or fails to comply with a construction and use requirement as to brakes, steering-gear or tyres, or

(b) uses on a road a motor vehicle or trailer which does not comply with such a requirement, or causes or permits a motor vehicle or trailer to be so used,

is guilty of an offence. [S]

41B   Breach of requirement as to weight: goods and passenger vehicles

(1) A person who—

(a) contravenes or fails to comply with a construction and use requirement as to any description of weight applicable to—

(i) a goods vehicle, or

(ii) a motor vehicle or trailer adapted to carry more than eight passengers, or

(b) uses on a road a vehicle which does not comply with such a requirement, or causes or permits a vehicle to be so used,

is guilty of an offence. [S]

(2) In any proceedings for an offence under this section in which there is alleged a contravention of or failure to comply with a construction and use requirement as to any description of weight applicable to a goods vehicle, it shall be a defence to prove either—

(a) that at the time when the vehicle was being used on the road—

(i) it was proceeding to a weighbridge which was the nearest available one to the place where the loading of the vehicle was completed for the purpose of being weighed, or

(ii) it was proceeding from a weighbridge after being weighed to the nearest point at which it was reasonably practicable to reduce the weight to the relevant limit, without causing an obstruction on any road, or

(b) in a case where the limit of that weight was not exceeded by more than 5 per cent—

(i) that that limit was not exceeded at the time when the loading of the vehicle was originally completed, and

(ii) that since that time no person has made any addition to the load.

42   Breach of other construction and use requirements

A person who—

(a) contravenes or fails to comply with any construction or use requirement other than one within section 41A(a) or 41B(1)(a) or 41D of this Act, or

(b) uses on a road a motor vehicle or trailer which does not comply with such a requirement, or causes or permits a motor vehicle or trailer to be so used,

is guilty of an offence. [S]

75   Vehicles not to be sold in unroadworthy condition or altered so as to be unroadworthy

(1) Subject to the provisions of this section no person shall supply a motor vehicle or trailer in an unroadworthy condition.

(2) In this section references to supply include—

(a) sell,

(b) offer to sell or supply, and

(c) expose for sale.

(3) For the purposes of subsection (1) above a motor vehicle or trailer is in an unroadworthy condition if—

(a) it is in such a condition that the use of it on a road in that condition would be unlawful by virtue of any provision made by regulations under section 41 of this Act as respects—

(i)   brakes, steering-gear or tyres, or

(ii)   the construction, weight or equipment of vehicles, or

(b) it is in such a condition that its use on a road would involve a danger of injury to any person.

(4) Subject to the provisions of this section no person shall alter a motor vehicle or trailer so as to render its condition such that the use of it on a road in that condition

(a) would be unlawful by virtue of any provision made as respects the construction, weight or equipment of vehicles by regulations under section 41, or

(b) would involve a danger of injury to any person.

(5) A person who supplies or alters a motor vehicle or trailer in contravention of this section, or causes or permits it to be so supplied or altered, is guilty of an offence. [S]

(6) A person shall not be convicted of an offence under this section in respect of the supply or alteration of a motor vehicle or trailer if he proves—

(a) that it was supplied or altered, as the case may be, for export from Great Britain, or

(b) that he had reasonable cause to believe that the vehicle or trailer would not be used on a road in Great Britain, or would not be so used until it had been put into a condition in which it might lawfully be so used.

(6A) Paragraph (b) of subsection (6) above shall not apply in relation to a person who, in the course of a trade or business—

(a) exposes a vehicle or trailer for sale, unless he also proves that he took all reasonable steps to ensure that any prospective purchaser would be aware that its use in its current condition on a road in Great Britain would be unlawful, or

(b) offers to sell a vehicle or trailer, unless he also proves that he took all reasonable steps to ensure that the person to whom the offer was made was aware of that fact.

76   Fitting and supply of defective or unsuitable vehicle parts

(1) If any person—

(a) fits a vehicle part to a vehicle, or

(b) causes or permits a vehicle part to be fitted to a vehicle,

in such circumstances that the use of the vehicle on a road would, by reason of that part being fitted to the vehicle involve a danger of injury to any person, or, constitute a contravention of or failure to comply with any of the construction and use requirements, he is guilty of an offence. [S]

(2) A person shall not be convicted of an offence under subsection (1) above if he proves—

(a) that the vehicle to which the part was fitted was to be exported from Great Britain, or

(b) that he had reasonable cause to believe that that vehicle—

(i)   would not be used on a road in Great Britain, or

(ii) that it would not be so used until it had been put into a condition in which its use on a road would not constitute a contravention of or a failure to comply with any of the construction and use requirements, and would not involve a danger of injury to any person.

(3) If a person—

(a) supplies a vehicle part or causes or permits a vehicle part to be supplied, and

(b) has reasonable cause to believe that the part is to be fitted to a motor vehicle, or to a vehicle of a particular class, or to a particular vehicle,

he is guilty of an offence if that part could not be fitted to a motor vehicle, or, as the case may require, to a vehicle of that class or of a class to which the particular vehicle belongs, except in such circumstances that the use of the vehicle on a road would, by reason of that part being fitted to the vehicle, constitute a contravention of or failure to comply with any of the construction and use requirement or involve a danger of injury to any person. [S]

(4) In this section references to supply include—

(a) sell, and

(b) offer to sell or supply.

(5) A person shall not be convicted of an offence under subsection (3) above in respect of the supply of a vehicle part if he proves—

(a) that the part was supplied for export from Great Britain, or

(b) that he had reasonable cause to believe that—

(i) it would not be fitted to a vehicle used on a road in Great Britain, or

(ii) it would not be so fitted until it had been put into such a condition that it could be fitted otherwise than in such circumstances that the use of the vehicle on a road would, by reason of that part being fitted to the vehicle, constitute a contravention of or failure to comply with any of the construction and use requirements, or involve a danger of injury to any person.

PART III   LICENSING OF DRIVERS OF VEHICLES

87   Drivers of motor vehicles to have driving licences

(1) It is an offence for a person to drive on a road a motor vehicle of any class otherwise than in accordance with a licence authorising him to drive a motor vehicle of that class.

(2) It is an offence for a person to cause or permit another person to drive on a road a motor vehicle of any class otherwise than in accordance with a licence authorising that other person to drive a motor vehicle of that class. [S]

103   Obtaining licence, or driving, while disqualified

(1) A person is guilty of an offence if, while disqualified for holding or obtaining a licence, he—

(a) obtains a licence, or

(b) drives a motor vehicle on a road. [S]

(2) A licence obtained by a person who is disqualified is of no effect (or, where the disqualification relates only to vehicles of a particular class, is of no effect in relation to vehicles of that class).

PART VI   THIRD PARTY LIABILITIES

143   Users of motor vehicles to be insured

(1) Subject to the provisions of this Part of this Act—

(a) a person must not use a motor vehicle on a road or other public place unless there is in force in relation to the use of the vehicle by that person such a policy of insurance as complies with the requirements of this Part of this Act, and

(b) a person must not cause or permit any other person to use a motor vehicle on a road or other public place unless there is in force in relation to the use of the vehicle by that other person such a policy of insurance as complies with the requirements of this Part of this Act.

(2) If a person acts in contravention of subsection (1) above he is guilty of an offence. [S]

(3) A person charged with using a motor vehicle in contravention of this section shall not be convicted if he proves—

(a) that the vehicle did not belong to him and was not in his possession under a contract of hiring or of loan,

(b) that he was using the vehicle in the course of his employment, and

(c) that he neither knew nor had reason to believe that there was not in force in relation to the vehicle such a policy of insurance as is mentioned in subsection (1) above.

(4) This Part of this Act does not apply to invalid carriages.

144A Offence of keeping vehicle which does not meet insurance requirements

(1) If a motor vehicle registered under the Vehicle Excise and Registration Act 1994 does not meet the insurance requirements, the person in whose name the vehicle is registered is guilty of an offence. [S]

(2) For the purposes of this section a vehicle meets the insurance requirements if—

(a) it is covered by such a policy of insurance as complies with the requirements of this Part of this Act, and

(b) either of the following conditions is satisfied.

(3) The first condition is that the policy or security, of the certificate of insurance which relates to it, identifies the vehicle by its registration mark as a vehicle which is covered by the policy or security.

(4) The second condition is that the vehicle is covered by the policy because—

(a) the policy covers any vehicle, or any vehicle of a particular description, the owner of which is a person named in the policy or in the certificate of insurance which relates to it, and

(b) the vehicle is owned by that person.

(5) For the purposes of this section a vehicle is covered by a policy of insurance if the policy of insurance is in force in relation to the use of the vehicle.

144B Exceptions to section 144A offence

(1) A person ("the registered keeper") in whose name a vehicle which does not meet the insurance requirements is registered at any particular time ("the relevant time") does not commit an offence under section 144A of this Act at that time if any of the following conditions are satisfied.

(2) The first condition is that at the relevant time the vehicle is owned as described—

(a) in subsection (1) of section 144 of this Act, or

(b) in paragraph (a), (b), (da), (db), (dc) or (g) of subsection (2) of that section,

(whether or not at the relevant time it is being driven as described in that provision).

(3) The second condition is that at the relevant time the vehicle is owned with the intention that it should be used as described in paragraph (c), (d), (e) or (f) of section 144(2) of this Act.

(4) The third condition is that the registered keeper—

(a) is not at the relevant time the person keeping the vehicle, and

(b) if previously he was the person keeping the vehicle, he has by the relevant time complied with any requirements under subsection (7)(a) below that he is required to have complied with by the relevant or any earlier time.

(5) The fourth condition is that—

(a) the registered keeper is at the relevant time the person keeping the vehicle,

(b) at the relevant time the vehicle is not used on a road or other public place, and

(c) the registered keeper has by the relevant time complied with any requirements under subsection (7)(a) below that he is required to have complied with by the relevant or any earlier time.

(6) The fifth condition is that—

(a) the vehicle has been stolen before the relevant time,

(b) the vehicle has not been recovered by the relevant time, and

(c) any requirements under subsection (7)(b) below that, in connection with the theft, are required to have been complied with by the relevant or any earlier time have been complied with by the relevant time.

(6A) The sixth condition is that—

(a) the registered keeper is at the relevant time the person keeping the vehicle,

(b) neither a licence nor a nil licence under the Vehicle Excise and Registration Act 1994 was in force for the vehicle on 31st January 1998,

(c) neither a licence nor a nil licence has been taken out for the vehicle for a period starting after that date, and

(d) the vehicle has not been used or kept on a public road after that date.

(9) A person accused of an offence under section 144A of this Act is not entitled to the benefit of an exception conferred by or under this section unless evidence is adduced that is sufficient to raise an issue with respect to that exception; but where evidence is so adduced it is for the prosecution to prove beyond reasonable doubt that the exception does not apply.

PART VII   MISCELLANEOUS AND GENERAL

168   Failure to give, or giving false, name and address in case of dangerous or careless or inconsiderate driving or cycling

Any of the following persons—

(a) the driver of a mechanically propelled vehicle who is alleged to have committed an offence under section 2 or 3 of this Act, or

(b) the rider of a cycle who is alleged to have committed an offence under section 28 or 29 of this Act,

who refuses, on being so required by any person having reasonable ground for so requiring, to give his name or address, or gives a false name or address, is guilty of an offence. [S]

169   Pedestrian contravening constable's direction to stop to give name and address

A constable may require a person committing an offence under section 37 of this Act to give his name and address, and if that person fails to do so he is guilty of an offence. [S]

170   Duty of driver to stop, report accident and give information or documents

(1) This section applies in a case where, owing to the presence of a mechanically propelled vehicle on a road or other public place, an accident occurs by which—

(a) personal injury is caused to a person other than the driver of that mechanically propelled vehicle, or

(b) damage is caused—

(i) to a vehicle other than that mechanically propelled vehicle or a trailer drawn by that mechanically propelled vehicle, or

(ii) to an animal other than an animal in or on that mechanically propelled vehicle or a trailer drawn by that mechanically propelled vehicle, or

(iii) to any other property constructed on, fixed to, growing in or otherwise forming part of the land on which the road or place in question is situated or land adjacent to such land.

(2) The driver of the mechanically propelled vehicle must stop and, if required to do so by any person having reasonable grounds for so requiring, give his name and address and also the name and address of the owner and the identification marks of the vehicle.

(3) If for any reason the driver of the mechanically propelled vehicle does not give his name and address under subsection (2) above, he must report the accident.

(4) A person who fails to comply with subsection (2) or (3) above is guilty of an offence. [S]

(5) If, in a case where this section applies by virtue of subsection (1)(a) above, the driver of a motor vehicle does not at the time of the accident produce such a certificate of insurance, or other evidence, as is mentioned in section 165(2)(a) of this Act—

(a) to a constable, or

(b) to some person who, having reasonable grounds for so doing, has required him to produce it,

the driver must report the accident and produce such a certificate or other evidence.

This subsection does not apply to the driver of an invalid carriage.

(6) To comply with a duty under this section to report an accident or to produce such a certificate of insurance, or other evidence, as is mentioned in section 165(2)(a) of this Act, the driver—

(a) must do so at a police station or to a constable, and

(b) must do so as soon as is reasonably practicable and, in any case, within twenty-four hours of the occurrence of the accident.

(7) A person who fails to comply with a duty under subsection (5) above is guilty of an offence, but he shall not be convicted by reason only of a failure to produce a certificate or other evidence if, within seven days after the occurrence of the accident, the certificate or other evidence is produced at a police station that was specified by him at the time when the accident was reported. [S]

(8) In this section "animal" means horse, cattle, ass, mule, sheep, pig, goat or dog.

171　Duty of owner of motor vehicle to give information for verifying compliance with requirement of compulsory insurance

(1) For the purpose of determining whether a motor vehicle was or was not being driven in contravention of section 143 of this Act on any occasion when the driver was required under section 165(1) or 170 of this Act to produce such a certificate of insurance, or other evidence, as is mentioned in section 165(2)(a) of this Act, the owner of the vehicle must give such information as he may be required, by or on behalf of a chief officer of police, to give.

(2) A person who fails to comply with the requirement of subsection (1) above is guilty of an offence. [S]

(3) In this section "owner", in relation to a vehicle which is the subject of a hiring agreement, includes each party to the agreement.

172　Duty to give information as to identity of driver, etc., in certain circumstances

(1) This section applies—

(a) to any offence under the preceding provisions of this Act except—

(i)　an offence under Part V, or

(ii)　an offence under section 13, 16, 51(2), 61(4), 67(9), 68(4), 96 or 120,

and to an offence under section 178 of this Act,

(b) to any offence under sections 25, 26 or 27 of the Road Traffic Offenders Act 1988,

(c) to any offence against any other enactment relating to the use of vehicles on roads, and

(d) to manslaughter . . . by the driver of a motor vehicle.

(2) Where the driver of a vehicle is alleged to be guilty of an offence to which this section applies—

(a) the person keeping the vehicle shall give such information as to the identity of the driver as he may be required to give by or on behalf of a chief officer of police or the Chief Constable of the British Transport Police Force, and

(b) any other person shall if required as stated above give any information which it is in his power to give and may lead to identification of the driver.

(3) Subject to the following provisions, a person who fails to comply with a requirement under subsection (2) above shall be guilty of an offence. [S]

(4) A person shall not be guilty of an offence by virtue of paragraph (a) of subsection (2) above if he shows that he did not know and could not with reasonable diligence have ascertained who the driver of the vehicle was.

(5) Where a body corporate is guilty of an offence under this section and the offence is proved to have been committed with the consent or connivance of, or to be attributable to neglect on the part of, a director, manager, secretary or other similar officer of the body corporate, or a person who was purporting to act in any such capacity, he, as well as the body corporate, is guilty of that offence and liable to be proceeded against and punished accordingly.

(6) Where the alleged offender is a body corporate, . . . or the proceedings are brought against him by virtue of subsection (5) above or subsection (11) below, subsection (4) above shall not apply unless, in addition to the matters there mentioned, the alleged offender shows that no record was kept of the persons who drove the vehicle and that the failure to keep a record was reasonable.

(7) A requirement under subsection (2) may be made by written notice served by post; and where it is so made—

(a) it shall have effect as a requirement to give the information within the period of 28 days beginning with the day on which the notice is served, and

(b) the person on whom the notice is served shall not be guilty of an offence under this section if he shows either that he gave the information as soon as reasonably practicable after the end of that period or that it has not been reasonably practicable for him to give it.

(8) Where the person on whom a notice under subsection (7) above is to be served is a body corporate, the notice is duly served if it is served on the secretary or clerk of that body.

(9) For the purposes of section 7 of the Interpretation Act 1978 as it applies for the purposes of this section the proper address of any person in relation to the service on him of a notice under subsection (7) above is—

(a) in the case of the secretary or clerk of a body corporate, that of the registered or principal office of that body or (if the body corporate is the registered keeper of the vehicle concerned) the registered address, and

(b) in any other case, his last known address at the time of service.

(10) In this section—

"registered address", in relation to the registered keeper of a vehicle, means the address recorded in the record kept under the Vehicles (Excise) and Registration Act 1994 with respect to that vehicle as being that person's address, and

"registered keeper", in relation to a vehicle, means the person in whose name the vehicle is registered under that Act;

and references to the driver of a vehicle include references to the rider of a cycle.

185 Meaning of "motor vehicle" and other expressions relating to vehicles

(1) In this Act—. . .

"invalid carriage" means a mechanically propelled vehicle the weight of which unladen does not exceed 254 kilograms and which is specially designed and constructed, and not merely adapted, for the use of a person suffering from some physical defect or disability and is used solely by such a person,

"motor car" means a mechanically propelled vehicle, not being a motor cycle or an invalid carriage, which is constructed itself to carry a load or passengers and the weight of which unladen—

(a) if it is constructed solely for the carriage of passengers and their effects, is adapted to carry not more than seven passengers exclusive of the driver and is fitted with tyres of such type as may be specified in regulations made by the Secretary of State, does not exceed 3050 kilograms,

(b) if it is constructed or adapted for use for the conveyance of goods or burden of any description, does not exceed 3050 kilograms, or 3500 kilograms if the vehicle carries a container or containers for holding for the purposes of its propulsion any fuel which is wholly gaseous at 17.5 degrees Celsius under a pressure of 1.013 bar or plant and materials for producing such fuel,

(c) does not exceed 2540 kilograms in a case not falling within sub-paragraph (a) or (b) above,

"motor cycle" means a mechanically propelled vehicle, not being an invalid carriage, with less than four wheels and the weight of which unladen does not exceed 410 kilograms,

. . .

"motor vehicle" means, subject to section 20 of the Chronically Sick and Disabled Persons Act 1970 (which makes special provision about invalid carriages, within the meaning of that Act), a mechanically propelled vehicle intended or adapted for use on roads, and

"trailer" means a vehicle drawn by a motor vehicle.

. . .

192 General interpretation of Act

(1) In this Act—

"bridleway" means a way over which the public have the following, but no other, rights of way: a right of way on foot and a right of way on horseback or leading a horse, with or without a right to drive animals of any description along the way,

"carriage of goods" includes the haulage of goods,

"cycle" means a bicycle, a tricycle, or a cycle having four or more wheels, not being in any case a motor vehicle,

"driver", where a separate person acts as a steersman of a motor vehicle, includes (except for the purposes of section 1 of this Act) that person as well as any other person engaged in the driving of the vehicle, and "drive" is to be interpreted accordingly,

"footpath", in relation to England and Wales, means a way over which the public have a right of way on foot only,

"goods" includes goods or burden of any description,

"goods vehicle" means a motor vehicle constructed or adapted for use for the carriage of goods, or a trailer so constructed or adapted,

"highway authority", in England and Wales, means—

(a) in relation to a road for which he is the highway authority within the meaning of the Highway Act 1980, the Secretary of State, and

(b) in relation to any other road, the council of the county, metropolitan district or London borough or the Common Council of the City of London as the case may be.

. . .

"owner", in relation to a vehicle which is the subject of a hiring agreement or hire-purchase agreement, means the person in possession of the vehicle under that agreement, "prescribed" (except in section 5A) means prescribed by regulations made by the Secretary of State,

"road", in relation to England and Wales, means any highway and any other road to which the public has access, and includes bridges over which a road passes,

"the Road Traffic Acts" means the Road Traffic Offenders Act 1988, the Road Traffic (Consequential Provisions) Act 1988 (so far as it reproduces the effect of provisions repealed by that Act) and this Act,

"statutory", in relation to any prohibition, restriction, requirement or provision, means contained in, or having effect under, any enactment (including any enactment contained in this Act),

"the Traffic Acts" means the Road Traffic Acts and the Road Traffic Regulation Act 1984,

"traffic sign" has the meaning given by section 64(1) of the Road Traffic Regulation Act 1984,

"tramcar" includes any carriage used on any road by virtue of an order under the Light Railways Act 1896, and

"trolley vehicle" means a mechanically propelled vehicle adapted for use on roads without rails under power transmitted to it from some external source whether or not there is in addition a source of power on board the vehicle.

...

(3) References in this Act to a class of vehicles are to be interpreted as references to a class defined or described by reference to any characteristics of the vehicles or to any other circumstances whatsoever, and accordingly as authorising the use of "category" to indicate a class of vehicles, however defined or described.

Road Traffic Offenders Act 1988

24   Alternate verdicts: general

(A1) Where—

(a) A person charged with manslaughter in connection with the driving of a mechanically propelled vehicle by him is found not guilty of that offence, but

(b) the allegations in the indictment amount to or include an allegation of any of the relevant offences,

he may be convicted of that offence.

(A2) For the purposes of subsection (A1) above the following are the relevant offences—

(a)   an offence under section 1 of the Road Traffic Act 1988 (causing death by dangerous driving),

(aa)   an offence under section 1A of that Act (causing serious injury by dangerous driving),

(b)   an offence under section 2 of that Act (dangerous driving),

(ba)   an offence under section 3ZC of that Act (causing death by driving: disqualified drivers),

(bb)   an offence under section 3ZD of that Act (causing serious injury by driving: disqualified drivers),

(c)   an offence under section 3A of that Act (causing death by careless driving when under influence of drink or drugs), and

(d)   an offence under section 35 of the Offence against the Person Act 1861 (furious driving).

(1) Where—

(a) a person charged with an offence under a provision of the Road Traffic Act 1988 specified in the first column of the Table below (where the general nature of the offences is also indicated) is found not guilty of that offence, but

(b) the allegations in the indictment or information (or in Scotland complaint) amount to or include an allegation of an offence under one or more of the provisions specified in the corresponding entry in the second column, he may be convicted of that offence or of one or more of those offences.

Offence charged	Alternative
Section 1 (causing death by dangerous driving)	Section 2 (dangerous driving)
	Section 2B (causing death by careless, or inconsiderate, driving)
	Section 3 (careless, and inconsiderate, driving)
Section 1A (causing serious injury by dangerous driving)	Section 2 (dangerous driving)
	Section 3 (careless, and inconsiderate, driving)
Section 2 (dangerous driving)	Section 3 (careless, and inconsiderate, driving)
Section 2B (causing death by careless, or inconsiderate, driving)	Section 3 (careless, and inconsiderate, driving)
Section 3A (causing death by careless driving when under influence of drink or drugs)	Section 2B (causing death by careless, or inconsiderate, driving)
	Section 3 (careless, and inconsiderate, driving)
	Section 4(1) (driving when unfit to drive through drink or drugs)
	Section 5(1)(a) (driving with excess alcohol in breath, blood or urine)
	Section 7(6) (failing to provide specimen)
	Section 7A(6) (failing to give permission for laboratory test)
Section 3ZC (causing death by driving: disqualified drivers)	Section 103(1)(b) (driving whilst disqualified)
Section 3ZD (causing serious injury by driving: disqualified drivers)	Section 103(1)(b) (driving while disqualified)
Section 4(1) (driving or attempting to drive when unfit to drive through drink or drugs)	Section 4(2) (being in charge of a vehicle when unfit to drive through drink or drugs)
Section 5(1)(a) (driving or attempting to drive with excess alcohol in breath, blood or urine)	Section 5(1)(b) (being in charge of a vehicle with excess alcohol in breath, blood or urine)
Section 5A(1)(a) and (2) (driving or attempting to drive with concentration of specified controlled drug above specified limit)	Section 5A(1)(b) and (2) (being in charge of a vehicle with concentration of specified controlled drug above specified limit)
Section 28 (dangerous cycling)	Section 29 (careless, and inconsiderate, cycling)

(2)   Where the offence with which a person is charged is an offence under section 3A of the Road Traffic Act 1988, subsection (1) above shall not authorise his conviction of any offence of attempting to drive.

(3)   Where a person is charged with having committed an offence under section 4(1), 5(1)(a) or 5A(1)(a) of the Road Traffic Act 1988 by driving a vehicle, he may be convicted of having committed an offence under the provision in question by attempting to drive.

(6)   This section has effect without prejudice to section 6(3) of the Criminal Law Act 1967 (alternative verdicts on trial on indictment) . . .

Official Secrets Act 1989

1 Security and intelligence

(1) A person who is or has been—

(a) a member of the security and intelligence services; or

(b) a person notified that he is subject to the provisions of this subsection,

is guilty of an offence if without lawful authority he discloses any information, document or other article relating to security or intelligence which is or has been in his possession by virtue of his position as a member of any of those services or in the course of his work while the notification is or was in force. [E]

(2) The reference in subsection (1) above to disclosing information relating to security or intelligence includes a reference to making any statement which purports to be a disclosure of such information or is intended to be taken by those to whom it is addressed as being such a disclosure.

(3) A person who is or has been a Crown servant or government contractor is guilty of an offence if without lawful authority he makes a damaging disclosure of any information, document or other article relating to security or intelligence which is or has been in his possession by virtue of his position as such but otherwise than as mentioned in subsection (1) above. [E]

(4) For the purposes of subsection (3) above a disclosure is damaging if—

(a) it causes damage to the work of, or of any part of, the security and intelligence services; or

(b) it is of information or a document or other article which is such that its unauthorised disclosure would be likely to cause such damage or which falls within a class or description of information, documents or articles the unauthorised disclosure of which would be likely to have that effect.

(5) It is a defence for a person charged with an offence under this section to prove that at the time of the alleged offence he did not know, and had no reasonable cause to believe, that the information, document or article in question related to security or intelligence or, in the case of an offence under subsection (2), that the disclosure would be damaging within the meaning of that subsection.

(6) Notification that a person is subject to subsection (1) above shall be effected by a notice in writing served on him by a Minister of the Crown; and such a notice may be served if, in the Minister's opinion, the work undertaken by the person in question is or includes work connected with the security and intelligence services and its nature is such that the interests of national security require that he should be subject to the provisions of that subsection.

(7) Subject to subsection (8) below, a notification for the purposes of subsection (1) above shall be in force for the period of five years beginning with the day on which it is served but may be renewed by further notices under subsection (6) above for periods of five years at a time.

(8) A notification for the purposes of subsection (1) above may at any time be revoked by a further notice in writing served by the Minister on the person concerned; and the Minister shall serve such a further notice as soon as, in his opinion, the work undertaken by that person ceases to be such as is mentioned in subsection (6) above.

(9) In this section "security or intelligence" means the work of, or in support of, the security and intelligence services or any part of them, and references to information relating to security or intelligence include references to information held or transmitted by those services or by persons in support of, or of any part of, them.

2 Defence

(1) A person who is or has been a Crown servant or government contractor is guilty of an offence if without lawful authority he makes a damaging disclosure of any information, document or other article relating to defence which is or has been in his possession by virtue of his position as such. [E]

(2) For the purposes of subsection (1) above a disclosure is damaging if—

    (a) it damages the capability of, or of any part of, the armed forces of the Crown to carry out their tasks or leads to loss of life or injury to members of those forces or serious damage to the equipment or installations of those forces; or

    (b) otherwise than as mentioned in paragraph (a) above, it endangers the interests of the United Kingdom abroad, seriously obstructs the promotion or protection by the United Kingdom of those interests or endangers the safety of British citizens abroad; or

    (c) it is of information or of a document or article which is such that its unauthorised disclosure would be likely to have any of those effects.

(3) It is a defence for a person charged with an offence under this section to prove that at the time of the alleged offence he did not know, and had no reasonable cause to believe, that the information, document or article in question related to defence or that its disclosure would be damaging within the meaning of subsection (1) above.

(4) In this section "defence" means—

    (a) the size, shape, organisation, logistics, order of battle, deployment, operations, state of readiness and training of the armed forces of the Crown;

    (b) the weapons, stores or other equipment of those forces and the invention, development, production and operation of such equipment and research relating to it;

    (c) defence policy and strategy and military planning and intelligence;

    (d) plans and measures for the maintenance of essential supplies and services that are or would be needed in time of war.

3 International relations

(1) A person who is or has been a Crown servant or government contractor is guilty of an offence if without lawful authority he makes a damaging disclosure of—

    (a) any information, document or other article relating to international relations; or

    (b) any confidential information, document or other article which was obtained from a State other than the United Kingdom or an international organisation,

being information or a document or article which is or has been in his possession by virtue of his position as a Crown servant or government contractor. [E]

(2) For the purposes of subsection (1) above a disclosure is damaging if—

    (a) it endangers the interests of the United Kingdom abroad, seriously obstructs the promotion or protection by the United Kingdom of those interests or endangers the safety of British citizens abroad; or

    (b) it is of information or of a document or article which is such that its unauthorised disclosure would be likely to have any of those effects.

(3) In the case of information or a document or article within subsection (1)(b) above—

    (a) the fact that it is confidential, or

    (b) its nature or contents,

may be sufficient to establish for the purposes of subsection (2)(b) above that the information, document or article is such that its unauthorised disclosure would be likely to have any of the effects there mentioned.

(4) It is a defence for a person charged with an offence under this section to prove that at the time of the alleged offence he did not know, and had no reasonable cause to believe, that the information, document or article in question was such as is mentioned in subsection (1) above or that its disclosure would be damaging within the meaning of that subsection.

(5) In this section "international relations" means the relations between States, between international organisations or between one or more States and one or more such organisations and includes any matter relating to a State other than the United Kingdom or to an international organisation which is capable of affecting the relations of the United Kingdom with another State or with an international organisation.

(6) For the purposes of this section any information, document or article obtained from a State or organisation is confidential at any time while the terms on which it was obtained require it to be held in confidence or while the circumstances in which it was obtained make it reasonable for the State or organisation to expect that it would be so held.

4   Crime and special investigation powers

(1) A person who is or has been a Crown servant or government contractor is guilty of an offence if without lawful authority he discloses any information, document or other article to which this section applies and which is or has been in his possession by virtue of his position as such. [E]

(2) This section applies to any information, document or other article—

    (a) the disclosure of which—

        (i)   results in the commission of an offence; or

        (ii) facilitates an escape from legal custody or the doing of any other act prejudicial to the safekeeping of persons in legal custody; or

        (iii) impedes the prevention or detection of offences or the apprehension or prosecution of suspected offenders; or

    (b) which is such that its unauthorised disclosure would be likely to have any of those effects.

(3) This section also applies to—

    (a) any information obtained by reason of the interception of any communication in obedience to a warrant issued under section 2 of the Interception of Communications Act 1985 or under the authority of an interception warrant under section 5 of the Regulation of Investigatory Powers Act 2000, any information relating to the obtaining of information by reason of any such interception and any document or other article which is or has been used or held for use in, or has been obtained by reason of, any such interception;

    (b) any information obtained by reason of action authorised by a warrant issued under section 3 of the Security Service Act 1989 or under section 5 of the Intelligence Services Act 1994 or by an authorisation given under section 7 of that Act, any information relating to the obtaining of information by reason of any such action and any document or other article which is or has been used or held for use in, or has been obtained by reason of, any such action; and

    (c) any information obtained under a warrant under Chapter 1 of Part 2 or Chapter 1 of Part 6 of the Investigatory Powers Act 2016, any information relating to the obtaining of information under such a warrant and any document or other article which is or has been used or held for use in, or has been obtained by reason of, the obtaining of information under such a warrant.

(4) It is a defence for a person charged with an offence under this section in respect of a disclosure falling within subsection (2)(a) above to prove that at the time of the alleged offence he did not know, and had no reasonable cause to believe, that the disclosure would have any of the effects there mentioned.

(5) It is a defence for a person charged with an offence under this section in respect of any other disclosure to prove that at the time of the alleged offence he did not know, and had no reasonable cause to believe, that the information, document or article in question was information or a document or article to which this section applies.

(6) In this section "legal custody" includes detention in pursuance of any enactment or any instrument made under an enactment.

5   Information resulting from unauthorised disclosures or entrusted in confidence

(1) Subsection (2) below applies where—

    (a) any information, document or other article protected against disclosure by the foregoing provisions of this Act has come into a person's possession as a result of having been—

        (i)   disclosed (whether to him or another) by a Crown servant or government contractor without lawful authority; or (ii)　entrusted to him by a Crown servant or government contractor on terms requiring it to be held in confidence or in circumstances in which the Crown servant or government contractor could reasonably expect that it would be so held; or

(iii)　disclosed (whether to him or another) without lawful authority by a person to whom it was entrusted as mentioned in sub-paragraph (ii) above; and

(b)　the disclosure without lawful authority of the information, document or article by the person into whose possession it has come is not an offence under any of those provisions.

(2)　Subject to subsections (3) and (4) below, the person into whose possession the information, document or article has come is guilty of an offence if he discloses it without lawful authority knowing, or having reasonable cause to believe, that it is protected against disclosure by the foregoing provisions of this Act and that it has come into his possession as mentioned in subsection (1) above. [E]

(3)　In the case of information or a document or article protected against disclosure by sections 1 to 3 above, a person does not commit an offence under subsection (2) above unless—

(a)　the disclosure by him is damaging; and

(b)　he makes it knowing, or having reasonable cause to believe, that it would be damaging; and the question whether a disclosure is damaging shall be determined for the purposes of this subsection as it would be in relation to a disclosure of that information, document or article by a Crown servant in contravention of section 1(3), 2(1) or 3(1) above.

(4)　A person does not commit an offence under subsection (2) above in respect of information or a document or other article which has come into his possession as a result of having been disclosed—

(a)　as mentioned in subsection (1)(a)(i) above by a government contractor; or

(b)　as mentioned in subsection (1)(a)(iii) above,

unless that disclosure was by a British citizen or took place in the United Kingdom, in any of the Channel Islands or in the Isle of Man or a colony.

(5)　For the purposes of this section information or a document or article is protected against disclosure by the foregoing provisions of this Act if—

(a)　it relates to security or intelligence, defence or international relations within the meaning of section 1, 2 or 3 above or is such as is mentioned in section 3(1)(b) above; or

(b)　it is information or a document or article to which section 4 above applies;

and information or a document or article is protected against disclosure by sections 1 to 3 above if it falls within paragraph (a) above.

(6)　A person is guilty of an offence if without lawful authority he discloses any information, document or other article which he knows, or has reasonable cause to believe, to have come into his possession as a result of a contravention of section 1 of the Official Secrets Act 1911. [E]

6　Information entrusted in confidence to other States or international organisations

(1)　This section applies where—

(a)　any information, document or other article which—

(i)　relates to security or intelligence, defence or international relations; and

(ii)　has been communicated in confidence by or on behalf of the United Kingdom to another State or to an international organisation,

has come into a person's possession as a result of having been disclosed (whether to him or another) without the authority of that State or organisation or, in the case of an organisation, of a member of it; and

(b)　the disclosure without lawful authority of the information, document or article by the person into whose possession it has come is not an offence under any of the foregoing provisions of this Act.

(2) Subject to subsection (2) below, the person into whose possession the information, document or article has come is guilty of an offence if he makes a damaging disclosure of it knowing, or having reasonable cause to believe, that it is such as is mentioned in subsection (1) above, that it has come into his possession as there mentioned and that its disclosure would be damaging. [E]

(3) A person does not commit an offence under subsection (2) above if the information, document or article is disclosed by him with lawful authority or has previously been made available to the public with the authority of the State or organisation concerned or, in the case of an organisation, of a member of it.

(4) For the purposes of this section "security or intelligence", "defence" and "international relations" have the same meaning as in sections 1, 2 and 3 above and the question whether a disclosure is damaging shall be determined as it would be in relation to a disclosure of the information, document or article in question by a Crown servant in contravention of sections 1(3), 2 (1) and 3(1) above.

(5) For the purposes of this section information or a document or article is communicated in confidence if it is communicated on terms requiring it to be held in confidence or in circumstances in which the person communicating it could reasonably expect that it would be so held.

7   Authorised disclosures

(1) For the purposes of this Act a disclosure by—
  (a) a Crown servant; or
  (b) a person, not being a Crown servant or government contractor, in whose case a notification for the purposes of section 1(1) above is in force,
is made with lawful authority if, and only if, it is made in accordance with his official duty.

(2) For the purposes of this Act a disclosure by a government contractor is made with lawful authority if, and only if, it is made—
  (a) in accordance with an official authorisation; or
  (b) for the purposes of the functions by virtue of which he is a government contractor and without contravening an official restriction.

(3) For the purposes of this Act a disclosure made by any other person is made with lawful authority if, and only if, it is made—
  (a) to a Crown servant for the purposes of his functions as such; or
  (b) in accordance with an official authorisation.

(4) It is a defence for a person charged with an offence under any of the foregoing provisions of this Act to prove that at the time of the alleged offence he believed that he had lawful authority to make the disclosure in question and had no reasonable cause to believe otherwise.

(5) In this section "official authorisation" and "official restriction" mean, subject to subsection (6) below, an authorisation or restriction duly given or imposed by a Crown servant or government contractor or by or on behalf of a prescribed body or a body of a prescribed class.

(6) In relation to section 6 above "official authorisation" includes an authorisation duly given by or on behalf of the State or organisation concerned or, in the case of an organisation, a member of it.

8   Safeguarding of information

(1) Where a Crown servant or government contractor, by virtue of his position as such, has in his possession or under his control any document or other article which it would be an offence under any of the foregoing provisions of this Act for him to disclose without lawful authority he is guilty of an offence if—
  (a) being a Crown servant, he retains the document or article contrary to his official duty; or
  (b) being a government contractor, he fails to comply with an official direction for the return or disposal of the document or article,
or if he fails to take such care to prevent the unauthorised disclosure of the document or article as a person in his position may reasonably be expected to take. [E]

(2) It is a defence for a Crown servant charged with an offence under subsection (1)(a) above to prove that at the time of the alleged offence he believed that he was acting in accordance with his official duty and had no reasonable cause to believe otherwise.

(3) In subsections (1) and (2) above references to a Crown servant include any person, not being a Crown servant or government contractor, in whose case a notification for the purposes of section 1(1) above is in force.

(4) Where a person has in his possession or under his control any document or other article which it would be an offence under section 5 above for him to disclose without lawful authority, he is guilty of an offence if—

    (a) he fails to comply with an official direction for its return or disposal; or

    (b) where he obtained it from a Crown servant or government contractor on terms requiring it to be held in confidence or in circumstances in which that servant or contractor could reasonably expect that it would be so held, he fails to take such care to prevent its unauthorised disclosure as a person in his position may reasonably be expected to take.

(5) Where a person has in his possession or under his control any document or other article which it would be an offence under section 6 above for him to disclose without lawful authority, he is guilty of an offence if he fails to comply with an official direction for its return or disposal.

(6) A person is guilty of an offence if he discloses any official information, document or other article which can be used for the purpose of obtaining access to any information, document or other article protected against disclosure by the foregoing provisions of this Act and the circumstances in which it is disclosed are such that it would be reasonable to expect that it might be used for that purpose without authority.

(7) For the purposes of subsection (6) above a person discloses information or a document or article which is official if—

    (a) he has or has had it in his possession by virtue of his position as a Crown servant or government contractor; or

    (b) he knows or has reasonable cause to believe that a Crown servant or government contractor has or has had it in his possession by virtue of his position as such.

(8) Subsection (5) of section 5 above applies for the purposes of subsection (6) above as it applies for the purposes of that section.

(9) In this section "official direction" means a direction duly given by a Crown servant or government contractor or by or on behalf of a prescribed body or a body of a prescribed class.

12   "Crown servant" and "government contractor"

(1) In this Act "Crown servant" means—

    (a) a Minister of the Crown;

    (ab) The First Minister for Wales, a Welsh Minister appointed under section 48 of the Government of Wales Act 2006, the Counsel General to the Welsh Government or a Deputy Welsh Minister;

    (c) any person employed in the civil service of the Crown, including Her Majesty's Diplomatic Service, Her Majesty's Overseas Civil Service, the civil service of Northern Ireland and the Northern Ireland Court Service;

    (d) any member of the naval, military or air forces of the Crown, including any person employed by an association established for the purposes of Part XI the Reserve Forces Act 1996;

    (e) any constable and any other person employed or appointed in or for the purposes of any police force (including the Police Service of Northern Ireland and the Police Service of Northern Ireland Reserve) or an NCA special (within the meaning of Part 1 of the Crime and Courts Act 2013);

    (f) any person who is a member or employee of a prescribed body or a body of a prescribed class and either is prescribed for the purposes of this paragraph or belongs to a prescribed class of members or employees of any such body;

    (g) any person who is the holder of a prescribed office or who is an employee of such a holder and either is prescribed for the purposes of this paragraph or belongs to a prescribed class of such employees.

(2) In this Act "government contractor" means, subject to subsection (3) below, any person who is not a Crown servant but who provides, or is employed in the provision of, goods or services—

    (a) for the purposes of any Minister or person mentioned in paragraph (a), (ab) or (b) of subsection (1) above, ... of any of the services, forces or bodies mentioned in that subsection or of the holder of any office prescribed under that subsection;

    (b) under an agreement or arrangement certified by the Secretary of State as being one to which the government of a State other than the United Kingdom or an international organisation is a party or which is subordinate to, or made for the purposes of implementing, any such agreement or arrangement.

(3) Where an employee or class of employees of any body, or of any holder of an office, is prescribed by an order made for the purposes of subsection (1) above—

    (a) any employee of that body, or of the holder of that office, who is not prescribed or is not within the prescribed class; and

    (b) any person who does not provide, or is not employed in the provision of, goods or services for the purposes of the performance of those functions of the body or the holder of the office in connection with which the employee or prescribed class of employees is engaged,

shall not be a government contractor for the purposes of this Act.

(4A) In this section the reference to a police force includes a reference to the Civil Nuclear Constabulary.

13 Other interpretation provisions

(1) In this Act—

"disclose" and "disclosure", in relation to a document or other article, include parting with possession of it;

"international organisation" means, subject to subsections (2) and (3) below, an organisation of which only States are members and includes a reference to any organ of such an organisation;

"prescribed" means prescribed by an order made by the Secretary of State;

"State" includes the government of a State and any organ of its government and references to a State other than the United Kingdom include references to any territory outside the United Kingdom.

(2) In section 12(2)(b) above the reference to an international organisation includes a reference to any such organisation whether or not one of which only States are members and includes a commercial organisation.

(3) In determining for the purposes of subsection (1) above whether only States are members of an organisation, any member which is itself an organisation of which only States are members, or which is an organ of such an organisation, shall be treated as a State.

15 Acts done abroad

(1) Any act—

    (a) done by a British citizen or Crown servant; or

    (b) done by any person in any of the Channel Islands or the Isle of Man or any colony,

shall, if it would be an offence by that person under any provision of this Act other than section 8(1), (4) or (5) when done by him in the United Kingdom, be an offence under that provision.

Aviation and Maritime Security Act 1990

PART I   AVIATION SECURITY

1   Endangering safety at aerodromes

(1) It is an offence for any person by means of any device, substance or weapon intentionally to commit at an aerodrome serving international civil aviation any act of violence which—

(a) causes or is likely to cause death or serious personal injury, and

(b) endangers or is likely to endanger the safe operation of the aerodrome or the safety of persons at the aerodrome. [I]

(2) It is also, subject to subsection (4) below, an offence for any person by means of any device, substance or weapon unlawfully and intentionally—

(a) to destroy or seriously to damage—

(i) property used for the provision of any facilities at an aerodrome serving international civil aviation (including any apparatus or equipment so used), or

(ii) any aircraft which is at such an aerodrome but is not in service, or

(b) to disrupt the services of such an aerodrome,

in such a way as to endanger or be likely to endanger the safe operation of the aerodrome or the safety of persons at the aerodrome. [I]

(3) Except as provided by subsection (4) below, subsections (1) and (2) above apply whether any such act as is referred to in those subsections is committed in the United Kingdom or elsewhere and whatever the nationality of the person committing the act.

(4) Subsection (2)(a)(ii) above does not apply to any act committed in relation to an aircraft used in military, customs or police service unless—

(a) the act is committed in the United Kingdom, or

(b) where the act is committed outside the United Kingdom, the person committing it is a United Kingdom national.

(9) In this section—

"act of violence" means—

(a) any act done in the United Kingdom which constitutes the offence of murder, attempted murder, manslaughter, culpable homicide or assault or an offence under section 18, 20, 21, 22, 23, 24, 28 or 29 of the Offences against the Person Act 1861 or under section 2 of the Explosive Substances Act 1883, and

(b) any act done outside the United Kingdom which, if done in the United Kingdom, would constitute such an offence as is mentioned in paragraph (a) above;

"aerodrome" has the same meaning as in the Civil Aviation Act 1982;

"military service" and "United Kingdom national" have the same meaning as in the Aviation Security Act 1982; and

"unlawfully"—

(a) in relation to the commission of an act in the United Kingdom, means so as (apart from this section) to constitute an offence under the law of the part of the United Kingdom in which the act is committed, and

(b) in relation to the commission of an act outside the United Kingdom, means so that the commission of the act would (apart from this section) have been an offence under the law of England and Wales if it had been committed in England and Wales . . .

PART II   OFFENCES AGAINST THE SAFETY OF SHIPS AND FIXED PLATFORMS

9 Hijacking of ships

(1) A person who unlawfully, by the use of force or by threats of any kind, seizes a ship or exercises control of it, commits the offence of hijacking a ship, whatever his nationality and whether the ship is in the United Kingdom or elsewhere, but subject to subsection (2) below.

(2) Subsection (1) above does not apply in relation to a warship or any other ship used as a naval auxiliary or in customs or police service unless—

(a) the person seizing or exercising control of the ship is a United Kingdom national, or

(b) his act is committed in the United Kingdom, or

(c) the ship is used in the naval or customs service of the United Kingdom or in the service of any police force in the United Kingdom. [I]

10 Seizing or exercising control of fixed platforms

(1) A person who unlawfully, by the use of force or by threats of any kind, seizes a fixed platform or exercises control of it, commits an offence, whatever his nationality and whether the fixed platform is in the United Kingdom or elsewhere. [I]

11 Destroying ships or fixed platforms or endangering their safety

(1) Subject to subsection (5) below, a person commits an offence if he unlawfully and intentionally—

    (a) destroys a ship or a fixed platform,

    (b) damages a ship, its cargo or a fixed platform so as to endanger, or to be likely to endanger, the safe navigation of the ship, or as the case may be, the safety of the platform, or

    (c) commits on board a ship or on a fixed platform an act of violence which is likely to endanger the safe navigation of the ship, or as the case may be, the safety of the platform. [I]

(2) Subject to subsection (5) below, a person commits an offence if he unlawfully and intentionally places, or causes to be placed, on a ship or fixed platform any device or substance which—

    (a) in the case of a ship, is likely to destroy the ship or is likely so to damage it or its cargo as to endanger its safe navigation, or

    (b) in the case of a fixed platform, is likely to destroy the fixed platform or so to damage it as to endanger its safety.

(3) Nothing in subsection (2) above is to be construed as limiting the circumstances in which the commission of any act—

    (a) may constitute an offence under subsection (1) above, or

    (b) may constitute attempting or conspiring to commit, or aiding, abetting, counselling, procuring or inciting, or being art and part in, the commission of such an offence.

(4) Except as provided by subsection (5) below, subsections (1) and (2) above apply whether any such act as is mentioned in those subsections is committed in the United Kingdom or elsewhere and whatever the nationality of the person committing the act.

(5) Subsections (1) and (2) above do not apply in relation to any act committed in relation to a warship or any other ship used as a naval auxiliary or in customs or police service unless—

    (a) the person committing the act is a United Kingdom national, or

    (b) his act is committed in the United Kingdom, or

    (c) the ship is used in the naval or customs service of the United Kingdom or in the service of any police force in the United Kingdom.

(7) In this section—

"act of violence" means—

    (a) any act done in the United Kingdom which constitutes the offence of murder, attempted murder, manslaughter, culpable homicide or assault or an offence under section 18, 20, 21, 22, 23, 24, 28 or 29 of the Offences against the Person Act 1861 or under section 2 of the Explosive Substances Act 1883, and

    (b) any act done outside the United Kingdom which, if done in the United Kingdom, would constitute such an offence as is mentioned in paragraph (a) above, and

"unlawfully"—

    (a) in relation to the commission of an act in the United Kingdom, means so as (apart from this Act) to constitute an offence under the law of the part of the United Kingdom in which the act is committed, and

    (b) in relation to the commission of an act outside the United Kingdom means so that the commission of the act would (apart from this Act) have been an offence under the law of England and Wales if it had been committed in England and Wales . . .

12 Other acts endangering or likely to endanger safe navigation

(1) Subject to subsection (6) below, it is an offence for any person unlawfully and intentionally—

    (a) to destroy or damage any property to which this subsection applies, or

(b) seriously to interfere with the operation of any such property,

where the destruction, damage or interference is likely to endanger the safe navigation of any ship. [I]

(2) Subsection (1) above applies to any property used for the provision of maritime navigation facilities, including any land, building or ship so used, and including any apparatus or equipment so used, whether it is on board a ship or elsewhere.

(3) Subject to subsection (6) below, it is also an offence for any person intentionally to communicate any information which he knows to be false in a material particular, where the communication of the information endangers the safe navigation of any ship.

(4) It is a defence for a person charged with an offence under subsection (3) above to prove that, when he communicated the information, he was lawfully employed to perform duties which consisted of or included the communication of information and that he communicated the information in good faith in performance of those duties.

(5) Except as provided by subsection (6) below, subsections (1) and (3) above apply whether any such act as is mentioned in those subsections is committed in the United Kingdom or elsewhere and whatever the nationality of the person committing the act.

(6) For the purposes of subsections (1) and (3) above any danger, or likelihood of danger, to the safe navigation of a warship or any other ship used as a naval auxiliary or in customs or police service is to be disregarded unless—

(a) the person committing the act is a United Kingdom national, or

(b) his act is committed in the United Kingdom, or

(c) the ship is used in the naval or customs service of the United Kingdom or in the service of any police force in the United Kingdom.

(8) In this section "unlawfully" has the same meaning as in section 11 of this Act.

13   Offences involving threats

(1) A person commits an offence if—

(a) in order to compel any other person to do or abstain from doing any act, he threatens that he or some other person will do in relation to any ship or fixed platform an act which is an offence by virtue of section 11(1) of this Act, and

(b) the making of that threat is likely to endanger the safe navigation of the ship or, as the case may be, the safety of the fixed platform. [I]

(2) Subject to subsection (4) below, a person commits an offence if—

(a) in order to compel any other person to do or abstain from doing any act, he threatens that he or some other person will do an act which is an offence by virtue of section 12(1) of this Act, and

(b) the making of that threat is likely to endanger the safe navigation of any ship. [I]

(3) Except as provided by subsection (4) below, subsections (1) and (2) above apply whether any such act as is mentioned in those subsections is committed in the United Kingdom or elsewhere and whatever the nationality of the person committing the act.

(4) Section 12(6) of this Act applies for the purposes of subsection (2)(b) above as it applies for the purposes of section 12(1) and (3) of this Act.

17   Interpretation of Part II

(1) In this Part of this Act—

"fixed platform" means—

(a) any offshore installation, within the meaning of the Mineral Workings (Offshore Installations) Act 1971, which is not a ship, and

(b) any other artificial island, installation or structure which—

(i) permanently rests on, or is permanently attached to, the seabed,

(ii) is maintained for the purposes of the exploration or exploitation of resources or for other economic purposes, and

(iii) is not connected with dry land by a permanent structure providing access at all times and for all purposes;

"naval service" includes military and air force service;

"ship" means any vessel (including hovercraft, submersible craft and other floating craft) other than one which—

    (a) permanently rests on, or is permanently attached to, the seabed, or

    (b) has been withdrawn from navigation or laid up; and

"United Kingdom national" means an individual who is—

    (a) a British citizen, a British Overseas Territories citizen, a British National (Overseas) or a British Overseas citizen,

    (b) a person who under the British Nationality Act 1981 is a British subject, or

    (c) a British protected person (within the meaning of that Act).

(2) For the purposes of this Part of this Act the territorial waters adjacent to any part of the United Kingdom shall be treated as included in that part of the United Kingdom.

Computer Misuse Act 1990

1   Unauthorised access to computer material

(1) A person is guilty of an offence if—

    (a) he causes a computer to perform any function with intent to secure access to any program or data held in any computer, or to enable any such access to be secured;

    (b) the access he intends to secure, or to enable to be secured, is unauthorised; and

    (c) he knows at the time when he causes the computer to perform the function that that is the case. [E]

(2) The intent a person has to have to commit an offence under this section need not be directed at—

    (a) any particular program or data;

    (b) a program or data of any particular kind; or

    (c) a program or data held in any particular computer.

2   Unauthorised access with intent to commit or facilitate commission of further offences

(1) A person is guilty of an offence under this section if he commits an offence under section 1 above ("the unauthorised access offence") with intent—

    (a) to commit an offence to which this section applies; or

    (b) to facilitate the commission of such an offence (whether by himself or by any other person);

and the offence he intends to commit or facilitate is referred to below in this section as the further offence. [E]

(2) This section applies to offences—

    (a) for which the sentence is fixed by law; or

    (b) for which a person of twenty-one years of age or over (not previously convicted) may be sentenced to imprisonment for a term of five years (or, in England and Wales, might be so sentenced but for the restrictions imposed by section 33 of the Magistrates' Courts Act 1980).

(3) It is immaterial for the purposes of this section whether the further offence is to be committed on the same occasion as the unauthorised access offence or on any future occasion.

(4) A person may be guilty of an offence under this section even though the facts are such that the commission of the further offence is impossible.

3   Unauthorised acts with intent to impair, or with recklessness as to impairing, operation of computer, etc.

(1) A person is guilty of an offence if—

    (a) he does any unauthorised act in relation to a computer;

    (b) at the time when he does the act he knows that it is unauthorised; and

    (c) either subsection (2) or subsection (3) below applies. [E]

(2) This subsection applies if the person intends by doing the act—

   (a) to impair the operation of any computer;

   (b) to prevent or hinder access to any program or data held in any computer; or

   (c) to impair the operation of any such program or the reliability of any such data.

(3) This subsection applies if the person is reckless as to whether the act will do any of the things mentioned in paragraphs (a) to (c) of subsection (2) above.

(4) The intention referred to in subsection (2) above, or the recklessness referred to in sub-section (3) above, need not relate to—

   (a) any particular computer;

   (b) any particular program or data; or

   (c) a program or data of any particular kind.

(5) In this section—

   (a) a reference to doing an act includes a reference to causing an act to be done;

   (b) "act" includes a series of acts;

   (c) a reference to impairing, preventing or hindering something includes a reference to doing so temporarily.

3ZA   Unauthorised acts causing, or creating risk of, serious damage

(1) A person is guilty of an offence if—

   (a) the person does any unauthorised act in relation to a computer;

   (b) at the time of doing the act the person knows that it is unauthorised;

   (c) the act causes, or creates a significant risk of, serious damage of a material kind; and

   (d) the person intends by doing the act to cause serious damage of a material kind or is reckless as to whether such damage is caused. [I]

(2) Damage is of a "material kind" for the purposes of this section if it is—

   (a) damage to human welfare in any place;

   (b) damage to the environment of any place;

   (c) damage to the economy of any country; or

   (d) damage to the national security of any country.

(3) For the purposes of subsection (2)(a) an act causes damage to human welfare only if it causes—

   (a) loss to human life;

   (b) human illness or injury;

   (c) disruption of a supply of money, food, water, energy or fuel;

   (d) disruption of a system of communication;

   (e) disruption of facilities for transport; or

   (f) disruption of services relating to health.

(4) It is immaterial for the purposes of subsection (2) whether or not an act causing damage—

   (a) does so directly;

   (b) is the only or main cause of the damage.

(5) In this section—

   (a) a reference to doing an act includes a reference to causing an act to be done;

   (b) "act" includes a series of acts;

   (c) a reference to a country includes a reference to a territory, and to any place in, or part or region of, a country or territory.

3A   Making, supplying or obtaining articles for use in offence under section 1, 3 or 3ZA

(1) A person is guilty of an offence if he makes, adapts, supplies or offers to supply any article intending it to be used to commit, or to assist in the commission of, an offence under section 1, 3 or 3ZA. [E]

(2) A person is guilty of an offence if he supplies or offers to supply any article believing that it is likely to be used to commit, or to assist in the commission of, an offence under section 1, 3 or 3ZA. [E]

(3) A person is guilty of an offence if he obtains any article—

    (a) intending to use it to commit, or to assist in the commission of, an offence under section 1, 3 or 3ZA, or

    (b) with a view to its being supplied for use to commit, or to assist in the commission of, an offence under section 1, 3 or 3ZA. [E]

(4) In this section "article" includes any program or data held in electronic form.

4   Territorial scope of offences under this Act

(1) Except as provided below in this section, it is immaterial for the purposes of any offence under section 1, 3 or 3ZA above—

    (a) whether any act or other event proof of which is required for conviction of the offence occurred in the home country concerned; or

    (b) whether the accused was in the home country concerned at the time of any such act or event.

(2) Subject to subsection (3) below, in the case of such an offence at least one significant link with domestic jurisdiction must exist in the circumstances of the case for the offence to be committed.

(3) There is no need for any such link to exist for the commission of an offence under section 1 above to be established in proof of an allegation to that effect in proceedings for an offence under section 2 above.

(4) Subject to section 8 below, where—

    (a) any such link does in fact exist in the case of an offence under section 1 above; and

    (b) commission of that offence is alleged in proceedings for an offence under section 2 above;

section 2 above shall apply as if anything the accused intended to do or facilitate in any place outside the home country concerned which would be an offence to which section 2 applies if it took place in the home country concerned were the offence in question.

(4A) It is immaterial for the purposes of an offence under section 3A whether the accused was in the home country concerned at the time of any act or other event proof of which is required for conviction of the offence if there is a significant link with domestic jurisdiction in relation to the offence.

(6) References in this Act to the home country concerned are references—

    (a) in application of this Act to England and Wales, to England and Wales; . . .

5   Significant links with domestic jurisdiction

(1) The following provisions of this section apply for the interpretation of section 4 above.

(1A) In relation to an offence under section 1, 3, 3ZA or 3A, where the accused was in a country outside the United Kingdom at the time of the act constituting the offence there is a significant link with domestic jurisdiction if—

    (a) the accused was a United Kingdom national at that time; and

    (b) the act constituted an offence under the law of the country in which it occurred.

(1B) In subsection (1A)—

"country" includes territory;

"United Kingdom national" means an individual who is—

    (a) a British citizen, a British overseas territories citizen, a British National (Overseas) or a British Overseas citizen;

    (b) a person who under the British Nationality Act 1981 is a British subject; or

    (c) a British protected person within the meaning of that Act.

(2) In relation to an offence under section 1, either of the following is a significant link with domestic jurisdiction—

    (a) that the accused was in the home country concerned at the time when he did the act which caused the computer to perform the function; or

(b) that any computer containing any program or data to which the accused by doing that act secured or intended to secure unauthorised access, or enabled or intended to enable unauthorised access to be secured, was in the home country concerned at that time.

(3) In relation to an offence under section 3, either of the following is a significant link with domestic jurisdiction—

(a) that the accused was in the home country concerned at the time when he did the unauthorised act (or caused it to be done); or

(b) that the unauthorised act was done in relation to a computer in the home country concerned.

(3A) In relation to an offence under section 3ZA, any of the following is also a significant link with domestic jurisdiction—

(a) that the accused was in the home country concerned at the time when he did the unauthorised act (or caused it to be done);

(b) that the unauthorised act was done in relation to a computer in the home country concerned;

(c) that the unauthorised act caused, or created a significant risk of, serious damage of a material kind (within the meaning of that section) in the home country concerned.

6 Territorial scope of inchoate offences related to offences under this Act

(1) On a charge of conspiracy to commit an offence under this Act the following questions are immaterial to the accused's guilt—

(a) the question where any person became a party to the conspiracy; and

(b) the question whether any act, omission or other event occurred in the home country concerned.

(2) On a charge of attempting to commit an offence under this Act the following questions are immaterial to the accused's guilt—

(a) the question where the attempt was made; and

(b) the question whether it had an effect in the home country concerned.

8 Relevance of external law

(1) A person is guilty of an offence triable by virtue of section 4(4) above only if what he intended to do or facilitate would involve the commission of an offence under the law in force where the whole or any part of it was intended to take place.

(3) A person is guilty of an offence triable by virtue of section 1(1A) of the Criminal Attempts Act 1981 only if what he had in view would involve the commission of an offence under the law in force where the whole or any part of it was intended to take place.

(4) Conduct punishable under the law in force in any place is an offence under that law for the purposes of this section, however it is described in that law.

(5) Subject to subsection (7) below, a condition specified in subsections (1) or (3) above shall be taken to be satisfied unless not later than rules of court may provide the defence serve on the prosecution a notice—

(a) stating that, on the facts as alleged with respect to the relevant conduct, the condition is not in their opinion satisfied;

(b) showing their grounds for that opinion; and

(c) requiring the prosecution to show that it is satisfied.

(6) In subsection (5) above "the relevant conduct" means—

(a) where the condition in subsection (1) above is in question, what the accused intended to do or facilitate; and

(c) where the condition in subsection (3) above is in question, what the accused had in view.

(7) The court, if it thinks fit, may permit the defence to require the prosecution to show that the condition is satisfied without the prior service of a notice under subsection (5) above.

(9) In the Crown Court the question whether the condition is satisfied shall be decided by the judge alone.

9   British citizenship immaterial

(1) Except as provided by section 5(1A), in any proceedings brought in England and Wales in respect of any offence to which this section applies it is immaterial to guilt whether or not the accused was a British citizen at the time of any act, omission or other event proof of which is required for conviction of the offence.

(2) This section applies to the following offences—

    (a) any offence under this Act; and

    (c) any attempt to commit an offence under this Act.

17   Interpretation

(1) The following provisions of this section apply for the interpretation of this Act.

(2) A person secures access to any program or data held in a computer if by causing a computer to perform any function he—

    (a) alters or erases the program or data;

    (b) copies or moves it to any storage medium other than that in which it is held or to a different location in the storage medium in which it is held;

    (c) uses it; or

    (d) has it output from the computer in which it is held (whether by having it displayed or in any other manner);

and references to access to a program or data (and to an intent to secure such access or to enable such access to be secured) shall be read accordingly.

(3) For the purposes of subsection (2)(c) above a person uses a program if the function he causes the computer to perform—

    (a) causes the program to be executed; or

    (b) is itself a function of the program.

(4) For the purposes of subsection (2)(d) above—

    (a) a program is output if the instructions of which it consists are output; and

    (b) the form in which any such instructions or any other data is output (and in particular whether or not it represents a form in which, in the case of instructions, they are capable of being executed or, in the case of data, it is capable of being processed by a computer) is immaterial.

(5) Access of any kind by any person to any program or data held in a computer is unauthorised if—

    (a) he is not himself entitled to control access of the kind in question to the program or data; and

    (b) he does not have consent to access by him of the kind in question to the program or data from any person who is so entitled

but this subsection is subject to section 10.

(6) References to any program or data held in a computer include references to any program or data held in any removable storage medium which is for the time being in the computer; and a computer is to be regarded as containing any program or data held in any such medium.

(8) An act done in relation to a computer is unauthorised if the person doing the act (or causing it to be done)—

    (a) is not himself a person who has responsibility for the computer and is entitled to determine whether the act may be done; and

    (b) does not have consent to the act from any such person.

In this subsection "act" includes a series of acts.

(9) References to the home country concerned shall be read in accordance with section 4(6) above.

(10) References to a program include references to part of a program.

Environmental Protection Act 1990

PART IV   LITTER ETC.

87   Offence of leaving litter

(1) A person is guilty of an offence if he throws down, drops or otherwise deposits any litter in any place to which this section applies and leaves it. [S]

(2) This section applies to any place in the area of a principal litter authority which is open to the air, subject to subject (3) below.

(3) This section does not apply to a place which is "open to the air" for the purposes of this Part by virtue of section 86(13) above if the public does not have access to it, with or without payment.

(4) It is immaterial for the purposes of this section whether the litter is deposited on land or in water.

(4A) No offence is committed under subsection (1) above where the depositing of litter is—

    (a) authorised by law; or

    (b) done by or with the consent of the owner, occupier or other person having control of the place where it is deposited.

(4B) A person may only give consent under subsection (4A)(b) above in relation to the depositing of litter in a lake or pond or watercourse if he is the owner, occupier or other person having control of—

    (a) all the land adjoining that lake or pond or watercourse; and

    (b) all the land through or into which water in that lake or pond or watercourse directly or indirectly discharges, otherwise than by means of a public sewer.

(4C) In subsection (4B) above, "lake or pond", "watercourse" and "public sewer" have the same meanings as in section 104 of the Water Resources Act 1991.

(4D) No proceedings may be instituted for an offence under subsection (1) which is a littering offence in respect of a vehicle within the meaning of section 88A(2) if—

    (a) a penalty notice has been given under section 88A to the keeper of the vehicle in respect of which the offence was committed, and

    (b) the fixed penalty has been paid or recovered in full.

98   Definitions

(5A) "Litter" includes—

    (a) the discarded ends of cigarettes, cigars and like produces, and

    (b) discarded chewing-gum and the discarded remains of other products designed for chewing.

Food Safety Act 1990

PART I   PRELIMINARY

1   Meaning of "food" and other basic expressions

(1) In this Act "food" has the same meaning as it has in Regulation (EC) No 178/2002.

(3) In this Act, unless the context otherwise requires—

"business" includes the undertaking of a canteen, club, school, hospital or institution, whether carried on for profit or not, and any undertaking or activity carried on by a public or local authority;

"commercial operation", in relation to any food or contact material, means any of the following, namely—

    (a) selling, possessing for sale and offering, exposing or advertising for sale;

    (b) consigning, delivering or serving by way of sale;

    (c) preparing for sale or presenting, labelling or wrapping for the purpose of sale;

    (d) storing or transporting for the purpose of sale;

    (e) importing and exporting;

and, in relation to any food source, means deriving food from it for the purpose of sale or for purposes connected with sale;

"contact material" means any article or substance which is intended to come into contact with food;

"food business" means any business in the course of which commercial operations with respect to food or food sources are carried out;

"food premises" means any premises used for the purposes of a food business;

"food source" means any growing crop or live animal, bird or fish from which food is intended to be derived (whether by harvesting, slaughtering, milking, collecting eggs or otherwise);

"premises" includes any place, any vehicle, stall or moveable structure and, for such purposes as may be specified in an order made by the Secretary of State, any ship or aircraft of a description so specified.

    (4) The reference in subsection (3) above to preparing for sale shall be construed, in relation to any contact material, as a reference to manufacturing or producing for the purpose of sale.

2   Extended meaning of "sale", etc.

    (1) For the purposes of this Act—

    (a) the supply of food, otherwise than on sale, in the course of a business; and

    (b) any other thing which is done with respect to food and is specified in an order made by the Secretary of State,

shall be deemed to be a sale of the food, and references to purchasers and purchasing shall be construed accordingly.

    (2) This Act shall apply—

    (a) in relation to any food which is offered as a prize or reward or given away in connection with any entertainment to which the public are admitted, whether on payment of money or not, as if the food were, or had been, exposed for sale by each person concerned in the organisation of the entertainment;

    (b) in relation to any food which, for the purpose of advertisement or in furtherance of any trade or business, is offered as a prize or reward or given away, as if the food were, or had been, exposed for sale by the person offering or giving away the food; and

    (c) in relation to any food which is exposed or deposited in any premises for the purpose of being so offered or given away as mentioned in paragraph (a) or (b) above, as if the food were, or had been, exposed for sale by the occupier of the premises;

and in this subsection "entertainment" includes any social gathering, amusement, exhibition, performance, game, sport or trial of skill.

3   Presumptions that food intended for human consumption

    (1) The following provisions shall apply for the purposes of this Act.

    (2) Any food commonly used for human consumption shall, if sold or offered, exposed or kept for sale, be presumed, until the contrary is proved, to have been sold or, as the case may be, to have been or to be intended for sale for human consumption.

    (3) The following, namely—

(a) any food commonly used for human consumption which is found on premises used for the preparation, storage, or sale of that food; and

(b) any article or substance commonly used in the manufacture of food for human consumption which is found on premises used for the preparation, storage or sale of that food,

shall be presumed, until the contrary is proved, to be intended for sale, or for manufacturing food for sale, for human consumption.

(4) Any article or substance capable of being used in the composition or preparation of any food commonly used for human consumption which is found on premises on which that food is prepared shall, until the contrary is proved, be presumed to be intended for such use.

PART II   MAIN PROVISIONS

7   Rendering food injurious to health

(1) Any person who renders any food injurious to health by means of any of the following operations, namely—

(a) adding any article or substance to the food;

(b) using any article or substance as an ingredient in the preparation of the food;

(c) abstracting any constituent from the food; and

(d) subjecting the food to any other process or treatment,

with intent that it shall be sold for human consumption, shall be guilty of an offence. [E]

(2) In determining for the purposes of this section whether any food is injurious to health, regard shall be had to the matters specified in sub-paragraphs (a) to (c) of Article 14(4) of Regulation (EC) No 178/2002.

8   Selling food not complying with food safety requirements

(2) For the purposes of this Part food fails to comply with food safety requirements if it is unsafe within the meaning of Article 14 of Regulation (EC) No 178/2002 and references to such requirements or to food complying with such requirements shall be construed accordingly.

(4) For the purposes of this Part, any part of, or product derived wholly or partly from, an animal—

(a) which has been slaughtered in a knacker's yard, or of which the carcase has been brought into a knacker's yard; . . .

shall be deemed to be unfit for human consumption.

14   Selling food not of the nature or substance or quality demanded

(1) Any person who sells to the purchaser's prejudice any food which is not of the nature or substance or quality demanded by the purchaser shall be guilty of an offence. [E]

(2) In subsection (1) above the reference to sale shall be construed as a reference to sale for human consumption; and in proceedings under that subsection it shall not be a defence that the purchaser was not prejudiced because he bought for analysis or examination.

15   Falsely describing or presenting food

(1) Any person who gives with any food sold by him, or displays with any food offered or exposed by him for sale or in his possession for the purpose of sale, a label, whether or not attached to or printed on the wrapper or container, which—

(a) falsely described the food; or

(b) is likely to mislead as to the nature or substance or quality of the food, shall be guilty of an offence. [E]

(2) Any person who publishes, or is a party to the publication of, an advertisement (not being such a label given or displayed by him as mentioned in subsection (1) above) which—

(a) falsely describes any food; or

(b) is likely to mislead as to the nature or substance or quality of any food,

shall be guilty of an offence. [E]

(3) Any person who sells, or offers or exposes for sale, or has in his possession for the purpose of sale, any food the presentation of which is likely to mislead as to the nature or substance or quality of the food shall be guilty of an offence. [E]

(4) In proceedings for an offence under subsection (1) or (2) above, the fact that a label or advertisement in respect of which the offence is alleged to have been committed contained an accurate statement of the composition of the food shall not preclude the court from finding that the offence was committed.

(5) In this section references to sale shall be construed as references to sale for human consumption.

20   Offences due to fault of another person

Where the commission by any person of an offence under any of the preceding provisions of this Part is due to an act or default of some other person, that other person shall be guilty of the offence; and a person may be charged with and convicted of the offence by virtue of this section whether or not proceedings are taken against the first-mentioned person.

21   Defence of due diligence

(1) In any proceedings for an offence under any of the preceding provisions of this Part (in this section referred to as "the relevant provision"), it shall, subject to subsection (5) below, be a defence for the person charged to prove that he took all reasonable precautions and exercised all due diligence to avoid the commission of the offence by himself or by a person under his control.

(2) Without prejudice to the generality of subsection (1) above, a person charged with an offence under section 14 or 15 above who neither—

(a) prepared the food in respect of which the offence is alleged to have been committed; nor

(b) imported it into Great Britain,

shall be taken to have established the defence provided by that subsection if he satisfies the requirements of subsection (3) or (4) below.

(3) A person satisfies the requirements of this subsection if he proves—

(a) that the commission of the offence was due to an act or default of another person who was not under his control, or to reliance on information supplied by such a person;

(b) that he carried out all such checks of the food in question as were reasonable in all the circumstances, or that it was reasonable in all the circumstances for him to rely on checks carried out by the person who supplied the food to him; and

(c) that he did not know and had no reason to suspect at the time of the commission of the alleged offence that his act or omission would amount to an offence under the relevant provision.

(4) A person satisfies the requirements of this subsection if he proves—

(a) that the commission of the offence was due to an act or default of another person who was not under his control, or to reliance on information supplied by such a person;

(b) that the sale or intended sale of which the alleged offence consisted was not a sale or intended sale under his name or mark; and

(c) that he did not know, and could not reasonably have been expected to know, at the time of the commission of the alleged offence that his act or omission would amount to an offence under the relevant provision.

(5) If in any case the defence provided by subsection (1) above involves the allegation that the commission of the offence was due to an act or default of another person, or to reliance on information supplied by another person, the person charged shall not, without leave of the court, be entitled to rely on that defence unless—

(a) at least seven clear days before the hearing; and

(b) where he has previously appeared before a court in connection with the alleged offence, within one month of his first such appearance,

he has served on the prosecutor a notice in writing giving such information identifying or assisting in the identification of that other person as was then in his possession.

(6) In subsection (5) above any reference to appearing before a court shall be construed as including a reference to being brought before a court.

22   Defence of publication in the course of business

In proceedings for an offence under any of the preceding provisions of this Part consisting of the advertisement for sale of any food, it shall be a defence for the person charged to prove—

(a) that he is a person whose business it is to publish or arrange for the publication of advertisements; and

(b) that he received the advertisement in the ordinary course of business and did not know and had no reason to suspect that its publication would amount to an offence under that provision.

PART III ADMINISTRATION AND ENFORCEMENT

33   Obstruction, etc., of officers

(1) Any person who—

(a) intentionally obstructs any person acting in the execution of this Act; or

(b) without reasonable cause, fails to give to any person acting in the execution of this Act any assistance or information which that person may reasonably require of him for the performance of his functions under this Act,

shall be guilty of an offence. [S]

(2) Any person who, in purported compliance with any such requirement as is mentioned in subsection (1)(b) above—

(a) furnishes information which he knows to be false or misleading in a material particular; or

(b) recklessly furnishes information which is false or misleading in a material particular,

shall be guilty of an offence. [E]

(3) Nothing in subsection (1)(b) above shall be construed as requiring any person to answer any question or give information if to do so might incriminate him.

36   Offences by bodies corporate

(1) Where an offence under this Act which has been committed by a body corporate is proved to have been committed with the consent or connivance of, or to be attributable to any neglect on the part of—

(a) any director, manager, secretary or other similar officer of the body corporate; or

(b) any person who was purporting to act in any such capacity,

he as well as the body corporate shall be deemed to be guilty of that offence and shall be liable to be proceeded against and punished accordingly.

(2) In subsection (1) above "director", in relation to any body corporate established by or under any enactment for the purpose of carrying on under national ownership any industry or part of an industry or undertaking, being a body corporate whose affairs are managed by its members, means a member of that body corporate.

Children and Young Persons (Protection from Tobacco) Act 1991

3 Sale of unpackaged cigarettes

(1) It shall be an offence for any person carrying on a retail business to sell cigarettes to any person other than in their original package. [S]

(3) In this section, "original package" means the package in which the cigarettes were supplied for the purpose of retail sale by the manufacturer or importer; and "package" means any box, carton or other container.

4 Display of warning statements in retail premises and on vending machines

(1) A notice displaying the following statement—

"It is illegal to sell tobacco products to anyone under the age of 18"

shall be exhibited at every premises at which tobacco is sold by retail, and shall be so exhibited in a prominent position where the statement is readily visible to persons at the point of sale of the tobacco; and where—

(a) any person carries on a business involving the sale of tobacco by retail at any premises, and

(b) no notice is exhibited at those premises in accordance with this subsection,

that person shall be guilty of an offence. [S]

(2) A notice displaying the following statement—

"This machine is only for the use of people aged 18 or over"

shall be exhibited on every automatic machine for the sale of tobacco which is kept available for use as such at any premises, and shall be so exhibited in such a way that the statement is readily visible to persons using the machine and where—

(a) any person is the owner of any such machine which is so kept or the owner of the premises at which any such machine is so kept, and

(b) no notice is exhibited on the machine in accordance with this subsection,

that person shall be guilty of an offence. [S]

(5) It shall be a defence for a person charged with any such offence to prove that he took all reasonable precautions and exercised all due diligence to avoid the commission of the offence.

(6) Where any such offence is committed by a body corporate and is proved to have been committed with the consent or connivance of, or to be attributable to any neglect on the part of, any director, manager, secretary or other similar officer of the body corporate, or any person who was purporting to act in any such capacity, he as well as the body corporate shall be guilty of that offence and shall be liable to be proceeded against and punished accordingly. In relation to a body corporate whose affairs are managed by its members, "director" means a member of the body corporate.

(8) In this section—

"premises" includes any place and any vehicle, vessel, aircraft, hovercraft, stall or moveable structure; and

"tobacco" (except where it appears in the statement required by subsection (1)) has the same meaning as in section 7 of the Children and Young Persons Act 1933.

Criminal Procedure (Insanity and Unfitness to Plead) Act 1991

1 Acquittals on grounds of insanity

(1) A jury shall not return a special verdict under section 2 of the Trial of Lunatics Act 1883 (acquittal on ground of insanity) except on the written or oral evidence of two or more registered medical practitioners at least one of whom is duly approved.

6 Interpretation etc.

(1) In this Act—

"duly approved", in relation to a registered medical practitioner, means approved for the purposes of section 12 of the 1983 Act by the Secretary of State, or by another person by virtue of section 12ZA or 12ZB of that Act, as having special experience in the diagnosis or treatment of mental disorder.

Dangerous Dogs Act 1991

1 Dogs bred for fighting

(1) This section applies to—

(a) any dog of the type known as the pit bull terrier;

(b) any dog of the type known as the Japanese tosa; and

(c) any dog of any type designated for the purposes of this section by an order of the Secretary of State, being a type appearing to him to be bred for fighting or to have the characteristics of a type bred for that purpose.

(2) No person shall—

(a) breed, or breed from, a dog to which this section applies;

(b) sell or exchange such a dog or offer, advertise or expose such a dog for sale or exchange;

(c) make or offer to make a gift of such a dog or advertise or expose such a dog as a gift;

(d) allow such a dog of which he is the owner or of which he is for the time being in charge to be in a public place without being muzzled and kept on a lead; or

(e) abandon such a dog of which he is the owner or, being the owner or for the time being in charge of such a dog, allow it to stray.

(7) Any person who contravenes this section is guilty of an offence and liable on summary conviction to imprisonment for a term not exceeding six months or a fine not exceeding level 5 on the standard scale or both except that a person who publishes an advertisement in contravention of subsection (2)(b) or (c)—

(a) shall not on being convicted be liable to imprisonment if he shows that he published the advertisement to the order of someone else and did not himself devise it; and

(b) shall not be convicted if, in addition, he shows that he did not know and had no reasonable cause to suspect that it related to a dog to which this section applies. [S]

3 Keeping dogs under proper control

(1) If a dog is dangerously out of control in any place in England or Wales (whether or not a public place)—

(a) the owner; and

(b) if different, the person for the time being in charge of the dog,

is guilty of an offence [S], or, if the dog while so out of control injures any person or assistance dog, an aggravated offence [E], under this subsection.

(1A) A person ("D") is not guilty of an offence under subsection (1) in a case which is a householder case.

(1B) For the purposes of subsection (1A) "a householder case" is a case where—

(a) the dog is dangerously out of control while in or partly in a building, or part of a building, that is a dwelling or is forces accommodation (or is both), and

(b) at that time—

(i) the person in relation to whom the dog is dangerously out of control ("V") is in, or is entering, the building or part as a trespasser, or

(ii) D (if present at the time) believed V to be in, or entering, the building or part as a trespasser.

Section 76(8B) to (8F) of the Criminal Justice and Immigration Act 2008 (use of force at place of residence) apply for the purposes of this subsection as they apply for the purposes of subsection (8A) of that section (and for those purposes the reference in section 76(8D) to subsection (8A)(d) is to be read as if it were a reference to paragraph (b)(ii) of this subsection).

(2) In proceedings for an offence under subsection (1) above against a person who is the owner of a dog but was not at the material time in charge of it, it shall be a defence for the accused to prove that the dog was at the material time in the charge of a person whom he reasonably believed to be a fit and proper person to be in charge of it.

6   Dogs owned by young persons

Where a dog is owned by a person who is less than sixteen years old any reference to its owner in section 1(2)(d) or (e) or 3 above shall include a reference to the head of the household, if any, of which that person is a member . . .

7   Muzzling and leads

(1) In this Act—

(a) references to a dog being muzzled are to its being securely fitted with a muzzle sufficient to prevent it biting any person; and

(b) references to its being kept on a lead are to its being securely held on a lead by a person who is not less than sixteen years old.

10   Interpretation

(2) In this Act—

"advertisement" includes any means of bringing a matter to the attention of the public and "advertise" shall be construed accordingly;

"assistance dog" has the meaning given by section 173(1) of the Equality Act 2010;

"public place" means any street, road or other place (whether or not enclosed) to which the public have or are permitted to have access whether for payment or otherwise and includes the common parts of a building containing two or more separate dwellings.

(3) For the purposes of this Act a dog shall be regarded as dangerously out of control on any occasion on which there are grounds for reasonable apprehension that it will injure any person or assistance dog whether or not it actually does so, but references to a dog injuring a person or assistance dog or there being grounds for reasonable apprehension that it will do so do not include references to any case in which the dog is being used for a lawful purpose by a constable or a person in the service of the Crown.

Football (Offences) Act 1991

1   Designated football matches

(1) In this Act a "designated football match" means an association football match designated, or of a description designated, for the purposes of this Act by order of the Secretary of State.

Any such order shall be made by statutory instrument which shall be subject to annulment in pursuance of a resolution of either House of Parliament.

(2) References in this Act to things done at a designated football match include anything done at the ground—

(a) within the period beginning two hours before the start of the match or (if earlier) two hours before the time at which it is advertised to start and ending one hour after the end of the match; or

(b) where the match is advertised to start at a particular time on a particular day but does not take place on that day, within the period beginning two hours before and ending one hour after the advertised starting time.

2   Throwing of missiles

It is an offence for a person at a designated football match to throw anything at or towards—

(a) the playing area, or any area adjacent to the playing area to which spectators are not generally admitted, or

(b) any area in which spectators or other persons are or may be present,

without lawful authority or lawful excuse (which shall be for him to prove). [S]

3   Indecent or racialist chanting

(1) It is an offence to engage or take part in chanting of an indecent or racialist nature at a designated football match. [S]

(2) For this purpose—

(a) "chanting" means the repeated uttering of any words or sounds (whether alone or in concert with one or more others); and

(b) "of a racialist nature" means consisting of or including matter which is threatening, abusive or insulting to a person by reason of his colour, race, nationality (including citizenship) or ethnic or national origins.

4   Going onto the playing area

It is an offence for a person at a designated football match to go onto the playing area, or any area adjacent to the playing area to which spectators are not generally admitted, without lawful authority or lawful excuse (which shall be for him to prove). [S]

War Crimes Act 1991

1   Jurisdiction over certain war crimes

(1) Subject to the provisions of this section, proceedings for murder, manslaughter or culpable homicide may be brought against a person in the United Kingdom irrespective of his nationality at the time of the alleged offence if that offence—

(a) was committed during the period beginning with 1st September 1939 and ending with 5th June 1945 in a place which at the time was part of Germany or under German occupation; and

(b) constituted a violation of the laws and customs of war.

(2) No proceedings shall by virtue of this section be brought against any person unless he was on 8th March 1990, or has subsequently become, a British citizen or resident in the United Kingdom, the Isle of Man or any of the Channel Islands.

Prison Security Act 1992

1   Offence of prison mutiny

(1) Any prisoner who takes part in a prison mutiny shall be guilty of an offence and liable, on conviction on indictment, to imprisonment for a term not exceeding ten years or to a fine or to both. [I]

(2) For the purposes of this section there is a prison mutiny where two or more prisoners, while on the premises of any prison, engage in conduct which is intended to further a common purpose of overthrowing lawful authority in that prison.

(3) For the purposes of this section the intentions and common purpose of prisoners may be inferred from the form and circumstances of their conduct and it shall be immaterial that conduct falling within subsection (2) above takes a different form in the case of different prisoners.

(4) Where there is a prison mutiny, a prisoner who has or is given a reasonable opportunity of submitting to lawful authority and fails, without reasonable excuse, to do so shall be regarded for the purposes of this section as taking part in the mutiny.

(6) In this section—

"conduct" includes acts and omissions;

"prison" means any prison, young offender institution, or remand centre which is under the general superintendence of, or is provided by, the Secretary of State under the Prison Act 1952, including a contracted out prison within the meaning of Part IV of the Criminal Justice Act 1991;

"prisoner" means any person for the time being in a prison as a result of any requirement imposed by a court or otherwise that he be detained in legal custody.

Social Security Administration Act 1992

111A   Dishonest representations for obtaining benefit etc.

(1) If a person dishonestly—

    (a) makes a false statement or representation; or

    (b) produces or furnishes, or causes or allows to be produced or furnished, any document or information which is false in a material particular;

with a view to obtaining any benefit or other payment or advantage under the relevant social security legislation (whether for himself or for some other person), he shall be guilty of an offence. [E]

(1A) A person shall be guilty of an offence if—

    (a) there has been a change of circumstances affecting any entitlement of his to any benefit or other payment or advantage under any provision of the relevant social security legislation;

    (b) the change is not a change that is excluded by regulations from the changes that are required to be notified;

    (c) he knows that the change affects an entitlement of his to such a benefit or other payment or advantage; and

    (d) he dishonestly fails to give a prompt notification of that change in the prescribed manner to the prescribed person. [E]

(1B) A person shall be guilty of an offence if—

    (a) there has been a change of circumstances affecting any entitlement of another person to any benefit or other payment or advantage under any provision of the relevant social security legislation;

    (b) the change is not a change that is excluded by regulations from the changes that are required to be notified;

    (c) he knows that the change affects an entitlement of that other person to such a benefit or other payment or advantage; and

    (d) he dishonestly causes or allows that other person to fail to give a prompt notification of that change in the prescribed manner to the prescribed person. [E]

(1C) This subsection applies where—

    (a) there has been a change of circumstances affecting any entitlement of a person ("the claimant") to any benefit or other payment or advantage under any provision of the relevant social security legislation;

    (b) the benefit, payment or advantage is one in respect of which there is another person ("the recipient") who for the time being has a right to receive payments to which the claimant has, or (but for the arrangements under which they are payable to the recipient) would have, an entitlement; and

    (c) the change is not a change that is excluded by regulations from the changes that are required to be notified.

(1D) In a case where subsection (1C) above applies, the recipient is guilty of an offence if—

(a) he knows that the change affects an entitlement of the claimant to a benefit or other payment or advantage under a provision of the relevant social security legislation;

(b) the entitlement is one in respect of which he has a right to receive payments to which the claimant has, or (but for the arrangements under which they are payable to the recipient) would have, an entitlement; and

(c) he dishonestly fails to give a prompt notification of that change in the prescribed manner to the prescribed person. [E]

(1E) In a case where that subsection applies, a person other than the recipient is guilty of an offence if—

(a) he knows that the change affects an entitlement of the claimant to a benefit or other payment or advantage under a provision of the relevant social security legislation;

(b) the entitlement is one in respect of which the recipient has a right to receive payments to which the claimant has, or (but for the arrangements under which they are payable to the recipient) would have, an entitlement; and

(c) he dishonestly causes or allows the recipient to fail to give a prompt notification of that change in the prescribed manner to the prescribed person. [E]

(1F) In any case where subsection (1C) above applies but the right of the recipient is confined to a right, by reason of his being a person to whom the claimant is required to make payments in respect of a dwelling, to receive payments of housing benefit—

(a) a person shall not be guilty of an offence under subsection (1D) or (1E) above unless the change is one relating to one or both of the following—

(i)   the claimant's occupation of that dwelling;

(ii)   the claimant's liability to make payments in respect of that dwelling; but

(b) subsections (1D)(a) and (1E)(a) above shall each have effect as if after "knows" there were inserted "or could reasonably be expected to know".

(1G) For the purposes of subsections (1A) to (1E) above a notification of a change is prompt if, and only if, it is given as soon as reasonably practicable after the change occurs.

112   Making false statements for the purpose of obtaining benefit

(1) If a person for the purpose of obtaining any benefit or other payment under the relevant social security legislation whether for himself or some other person, or for any purpose connected with that legislation—

(a) makes a statement or representation which he knows to be false; or

(b) produces or furnishes or knowingly causes or knowingly allows to be produced or furnished any document or information which he knows to be false in any material particular;

he shall be guilty of an offence. [S]

(1A) A person shall be guilty of an offence if—

(a) there has been a change of circumstances affecting any entitlement of his to any benefit or other payment or advantage under any provision of the relevant social security legislation;

(b) the change is not a change that is excluded by regulations from the changes that are required to be notified;

(c) he knows that the change affects an entitlement of his to such a benefit or other payment or advantage; and

(d) he fails to give a prompt notification of that change in the prescribed manner to the prescribed person. [E]

(1B) A person is guilty of an offence under this section if—

(a) there has been a change of circumstances affecting any entitlement of another person to any benefit or other payment or advantage under any provision of the relevant social security legislation;

(b) the change is not a change that is excluded by regulations from the changes that are required to be notified;

(c) he knows that the change affects an entitlement of that other person to such a benefit or other payment or advantage; and

(d) he causes or allows that other person to fail to give a prompt notification of that change in the prescribed manner to the prescribed person. [E]

(1C) In a case where subsection (1C) of section 111A above applies, the recipient is guilty of an offence if—

(a) he knows that the change affects an entitlement of the claimant to a benefit or other payment or advantage under a provision of the relevant social security legislation;

(b) the entitlement is one in respect of which he has a right to receive payments to which the claimant has, or (but for the arrangements under which they are payable to the recipient) would have, an entitlement; and

(c) he fails to give a prompt notification of that change in the prescribed manner to the prescribed person. [E]

(1D) In a case where that subsection applies, a person other than the recipient is guilty of an offence if—

(a) he knows that the change affects an entitlement of the claimant to a benefit or other payment or advantage under a provision of the relevant social security legislation;

(b) the entitlement is one in respect of which the recipient has a right to receive payments to which the claimant has, or (but for the arrangements under which they are payable to the recipient) would have, an entitlement; and

(c) he causes or allows the recipient to fail to give a prompt notification of that change in the prescribed manner to the prescribed person. [E]

(1E) Subsection (1F) of section 111A above applies in relation to subsections (1C) and (1D) above as it applies in relation to subsections (1D) and (1E) of that section.

(1F) For the purposes of subsections (1A) to (1D) above a notification of a change is prompt if, and only if, it is given as soon as reasonably practicable after the change occurs.

Trade Union and Labour Relations (Consolidation) Act 1992

PART V   INDUSTRIAL ACTION

241   Intimidation or annoyance by violence or otherwise

(1) A person commits an offence who, with a view to compelling another person to abstain from doing or to do any act which that person has a legal right to do or abstain from doing, wrongfully and without legal authority—

(a) uses violence to or intimidates that person or his spouse or civil partner or children, or injures his property,

(b) persistently follows that person about from place to place,

(c) hides any tools, clothes or other property owned or used by that person, or deprives him of or hinders him in the use thereof,

(d) watches or besets the house or other place where that person resides, works, carries on business or happens to be, or the approach to any such house or place, or

(e) follows that person with two or more other persons in a disorderly manner in or through any street or road. [E]

242   Restriction of offence of conspiracy: England and Wales

(1) Where in pursuance of any such agreement as is mentioned in section 1(1) of the Criminal Law Act 1977 (which provides for the offence of conspiracy) the acts in question in relation to an offence are to be done in contemplation or furtherance of a trade dispute, the offence shall be disregarded for the purposes of that subsection if it is a summary offence which is not punishable with imprisonment.

244   Meaning of "trade dispute"

(1) In this Part a "trade dispute" means a dispute between workers and their employer which relates wholly or mainly to one or more of the following—

    (a) terms and conditions of employment, or the physical conditions in which any workers are required to work;

    (b) engagement or non-engagement, or termination or suspension of employment or the duties of employment, of one or more workers;

    (c) allocation of work or the duties of employment between workers or groups of workers;

    (d) matters of discipline;

    (e) a worker's membership or non-membership of a trade union;

    (f) facilities for officials of trade unions; and

    (g) machinery for negotiation or consultation, and other procedures, relating to any of the above matters, including the recognition by employers or employers' associations of the right of a trade union to represent workers in such negotiations of the right of a trade union to represent workers in such negotiation or consultation or in the carrying out of such procedures.

(2) A dispute between a Minister of the Crown and any workers shall, notwithstanding that he is not the employer of those workers, be treated as a dispute between those workers and their employer if the dispute relates to matters which—

    (a) have been referred for consideration by a joint body on which, by virtue of provision made by or under any enactment, he is represented, or

    (b) cannot be settled without him exercising a power conferred on him by or under an enactment.

(3) There is a trade dispute even though it relates to matters occurring outside the United Kingdom, so long as the person or persons whose actions in the United Kingdom are said to be in contemplation or furtherance of a trade dispute relating to matters occurring outside the United Kingdom are likely to be affected in respect of one or more of the matters specified in subsection (1) by the outcome of the dispute.

(4) An act, threat or demand done or made by one person or organisation against another which, if resisted, would have led to a trade dispute with that other, shall be treated as being done or made in contemplation of a trade dispute with that other, notwithstanding that because that other submits to the act or threat or accedes to the demand no dispute arises.

(5) In this section—

"employment" includes any relationship whereby one person personally does work or performs services for another; and

"worker", in relation to a dispute with an employer, means—

    (a) a worker employed by that employer; or

    (b) a person who has ceased to be so employed if his employment was terminated in connection with the dispute or if the termination of his employment was one of the circumstances giving rise to the dispute.

Criminal Justice Act 1993

PART I JURISDICTION

1 Offences to which this Part applies

(1) This Part applies to two groups of offences—

(a) any offence mentioned in subsection (2) (a "Group A offence"); and

(b) any offence mentioned in subsection (3) (a "Group B offence").

(2) The Group A offences are—

(a) an offence under any of the following provisions of the Theft Act 1968—

section 1 (theft);

section 17 (false accounting);

section 19 (false statements by company directors etc.);

section 21 (blackmail);

section 22 (handling stolen goods);

section 24A (retaining credits from dishonest sources, etc.);

(bb) an offence under any of the following provisions of the Fraud Act 2006—

(i) section 1 (fraud);

(ii) section 6 (possession etc. of articles for use in frauds);

(iii) section 7 (making or supplying articles for use in frauds);

(iv) section 9 (participating in fraudulent business carried on by sole trader etc.);

(v) section 11 (obtaining services dishonestly).

(c) an offence under any of the following provisions of the Forgery and Counterfeiting Act 1981—

section 1 (forgery);

section 2 (copying a false instrument);

section 3 (using a false instrument);

section 4 (using a copy of a false instrument);

section 5 (offences which relate to money orders, share certificates, passports, etc.);

section 14 (offences of counterfeiting notes and coins);

section 15 (offences of passing etc. counterfeit notes and coins);

section 16 (offences involving the custody or control of counterfeit notes and coins);

section 17 (offences involving the making or custody or control of counterfeiting materials and implements);

section 20 (prohibition of importation of counterfeit notes and coins);

section 21 (prohibition of exportation of counterfeit notes and coins);

(ca) an offence under sections 4 to 6 of the Identity Documents Act 2010;

(d) the common law offence of cheating in relation to the public revenue.

(3) The Group B offences are—

(a) conspiracy to commit a Group A offence;

(b) conspiracy to defraud;

(c) attempting to commit a Group A offence;

(d) incitement to commit a Group A offence.

2 Jurisdiction in respect of Group A offences

(1) For the purposes of this Part, "relevant event", in relation to any Group A offence, means (subject to subsection (1A)) any act or omission or other event (including any result of one or more acts or omissions) proof of which is required for conviction of the offence.

(1A) In relation to an offence under section 1 of the Fraud Act 2006 (fraud), "relevant event" includes—

    (a) if the fraud involved an intention to make a gain and the gain occurred, that occurrence;

    (b) if the fraud involved an intention to cause a loss or to expose another to a risk of loss and the loss occurred, that occurrence.

(2) For the purpose of determining whether or not a particular event is a relevant event in relation to a Group A offence, any question as to where it occurred is to be disregarded.

(3) A person may be guilty of a Group A offence if any of the events which are relevant events in relation to the offence occurred in England and Wales.

3 Questions immaterial to jurisdiction in the case of certain offences

(1) A person may be guilty of a Group A or Group B offence whether or not—

    (a) he was a British citizen at any material time;

    (b) he was in England and Wales at any such time.

(2) On a charge of conspiracy to commit a Group A offence, or on a charge of conspiracy to defraud in England and Wales, the defendant may be guilty of the offence whether or not—

    (a) he became a party to the conspiracy in England and Wales;

    (b) any act or omission or other event in relation to the conspiracy occurred in England and Wales.

(3) On a charge of attempting to commit a Group A offence, the defendant may be guilty of the offence whether or not—

    (a) the attempt was made in England and Wales;

    (b) it had an effect in England and Wales.

(4) Subsection (1)(a) does not apply where jurisdiction is given to try the offence in question by an enactment which makes provision by reference to the nationality of the person charged.

(5) Subsection (2) does not apply in relation to any charge under the Criminal Law Act 1977 brought by virtue of section 1A of that Act.

(6) Subsection (3) does not apply in relation to any charge under the Criminal Attempts Act 1981 brought by virtue of section 1A of that Act.

4 Rules for determining certain jurisdictional questions relating to the location of events

In relation to a Group A or Group B offence—

    (a) there is an obtaining of property in England and Wales if the property is either despatched from or received at a place in England and Wales; and

    (b) there is a communication in England and Wales of any information, instruction, request, demand or other matter if it is sent by any means—

        (i) from a place in England and Wales to a place elsewhere; or

        (ii) from a place elsewhere to a place in England and Wales.

5 Extended jurisdiction over conspiracies to defraud and incitement

(3) A person may be guilty of conspiracy to defraud if—

    (a) a party to the agreement constituting the conspiracy, or a party's agent, did anything in England and Wales in relation to the agreement before its formation, or

    (b) a party to it became a party in England and Wales (by joining it either in person or through an agent), or

    (c) a party to it, or a party's agent, did or omitted anything in England and Wales in pursuance of it,

and the conspiracy would be triable in England and Wales but for the fraud which the parties to it had in view not being intended to take place in England and Wales.

(4) A person may be guilty of incitement to commit a Group A offence if—

    (a) the incitement takes place in England and Wales; and

   (b) a charge in respect of incitement would be triable in England and Wales but for what the person charged had in view not being an offence triable in England and Wales.

   (5) Subsections (3) and (4) are subject to section 6.

6   Relevance of external law

   (1) A person is guilty of an offence triable by virtue of section 5(3), only if the pursuit of the agreed course of conduct would at some stage involve—

   (a) an act or omission by one or more of the parties, or

   (b) the happening of some other event,

constituting an offence under the law in force where the act, omission or other event was intended to take place.

   (2) A person is guilty of an offence triable by virtue of section 1A of the Criminal Attempts Act 1981, or by virtue of section 5(4), only if what he had in view would involve the commission of an offence under the law in force where the whole or any part of it was intended to take place.

   (3) Conduct punishable under the law in force in any place is an offence under that law for the purposes of this section, however it is described in that law.

   (4) Subject to subsection (6), a condition specified in subsection (1) or (2) shall be taken to be satisfied unless, not later than rules of court may provide, the defence serve on the prosecution a notice—

   (a) stating that, on the facts as alleged with respect to the relevant conduct, the condition is not in their opinion satisfied;

   (b) showing their grounds for that opinion; and

   (c) requiring the prosecution to show that it is satisfied.

   (5) In subsection (4) "the relevant conduct" means—

   (a) where the condition in subsection (1) is in question, the agreed course of conduct; and

   (b) where the condition in subsection (2) is in question, what the defendant had in view.

   (6) The court, if it thinks fit, may permit the defence to require the prosecution to show that the condition is satisfied without the prior service of a notice under subsection (4).

   (7) In the Crown Court, the question whether the condition is satisfied shall be decided by the judge alone.

PART V   INSIDER DEALING

52   The offence of insider dealing

   (1) An individual who has information as an insider is guilty of insider dealing if, in the circumstances mentioned in subsection (3), he deals in securities that are price-affected securities in relation to the information. [E]

   (2) An individual who has information as an insider is also guilty of insider dealing if—

   (a) he encourages another person to deal in securities that are (whether or not that other knows it) price-affected securities in relation to the information, knowing or having reasonable cause to believe that the dealing would take place in the circumstances mentioned in subsection (3); or

   (b) he discloses the information, otherwise than in the proper performance of the functions of his employment, office or profession, to another person. [E]

   (3) The circumstances referred to above are that the acquisition or disposal in question occurs on a regulated market, or that the person dealing relies on a professional intermediary or is himself acting as a professional intermediary.

   (4) This section has effect subject to section 53.

53   Defences

   (1) An individual is not guilty of insider dealing by virtue of dealing in securities if he shows—

   (a) that he did not at the time expect the dealing to result in a profit attributable to the fact that the information in question was price-sensitive information in relation to the securities, or

    (b) that at the time he believed on reasonable grounds that the information had been disclosed widely enough to ensure that none of those taking part in the dealing would be prejudiced by not having the information, or

    (c) that he would have done what he did even if he had not had the information.

(2) An individual is not guilty of insider dealing by virtue of encouraging another person to deal in securities if he shows—

    (a) that he did not at the time expect the dealing to result in a profit attributable to the fact that the information in question was price-sensitive information in relation to the securities, or

    (b) that at the time he believed on reasonable grounds that the information had been or would be disclosed widely enough to ensure that none of those taking part in the dealing would be prejudiced by not having the information, or

    (c) that he would have done what he did even if he had not had the information.

(3) An individual is not guilty of insider dealing by virtue of a disclosure of information if he shows—

    (a) that he did not at the time expect any person, because of the disclosure, to deal in securities in the circumstances mentioned in subsection (3) of section 52; or

    (b) that, although he had such an expectation at the time, he did not expect the dealing to result in a profit attributable to the fact that the information was price-sensitive information in relation to the securities.

(4) Schedule 1 (special defences) shall have effect.

(6) In this section references to a profit include references to the avoidance of a loss.

54 Securities to which Part V applies

(1) This Part applies to any security which—

    (a) falls within any paragraph of Schedule 2; and

    (b) satisfies any conditions applying to it under an order made by the Treasury for the purposes of this subsection;

and in the provisions of this Part (other than that Schedule) any reference to a security is a reference to a security to which this Part applies.

55 Meaning of "dealing"

(1) For the purposes of this Part, a person deals in securities if—

    (a) he acquires or disposes of the securities (whether as principal or agent); or

    (b) he procures, directly or indirectly, an acquisition or disposal of the securities by any other person.

(2) For the purposes of this Part, "acquire", in relation to a security, includes—

    (a) agreeing to acquire the security; and

    (b) entering into a contract which creates the security.

(3) For the purposes of this Part, "dispose", in relation to a security, includes—

    (a) agreeing to dispose of the security; and

    (b) bringing to an end a contract which created the security.

(4) For the purposes of subsection (1), a person procures an acquisition or disposal of a security if the security is acquired or disposed of by a person who is—

    (a) his agent,

    (b) his nominee, or

    (c) a person who is acting at his direction, in relation to the acquisition or disposal.

(5) Subsection (4) is not exhaustive as to the circumstances in which one person may be regarded as procuring an acquisition or disposal of securities by another.

56 Meaning of "inside information"

(1) For the purposes of this section and section 57, "inside information" means information which—

(a) relates to particular securities or to a particular issuer of securities or to particular issuers of securities and not to securities generally or to the issuers of securities generally;

(b) is specific or precise;

(c) has not been made public; and

(d) if it were made public would be likely to have a significant effect on the price of any securities.

(2) For the purposes of this Part, securities are "price-affected securities" in relation to inside information, and inside information is "price-sensitive information" in relation to securities, if and only if the information would, if made public, be likely to have a significant effect on the price of the securities.

(3) For the purpose of this section "price" includes value.

57   "Insiders"

(1) For the purposes of this Part, a person has information as an insider if and only if—

(a) it is, and he knows that it is, inside information, and

(b) he has it, and knows that he has it, from an inside source.

(2) For the purposes of subsection (1), a person has information from an inside source if and only if—

(a) he has it through—

(i) being a director, employee or shareholder of an issuer of securities; or

(ii) having access to the information by virtue of his employment, office or profession; or

(b) the direct or indirect source of his information is a person within paragraph (a).

58   Information "made public"

(1) For the purposes of section 56, "made public", in relation to information, shall be construed in accordance with the following provisions of this section; but those provisions are not exhaustive as to the meaning of that expression.

(2) Information is made public if—

(a) it is published in accordance with the rules of a regulated market for the purpose of informing investors and their professional advisers;

(b) it is contained in records which by virtue of any enactment are open to inspection by the public;

(c) it can be readily acquired by those likely to deal in any securities—

(i) to which the information relates, or

(ii) of an issuer to which the information relates; or

(d) it is derived from information which has been made public.

(3) Information may be treated as made public even though—

(a) it can be acquired only by persons exercising diligence or expertise;

(b) it is communicated to a section of the public and not to the public at large;

(c) it can be acquired only by observation;

(d) it is communicated only on payment of a fee; or

(e) it is published only outside the United Kingdom.

59   "Professional intermediary"

(1) For the purposes of this Part, a "professional intermediary" is a person—

(a) who carries on a business consisting of an activity mentioned in subsection (2) and who holds himself out to the public or any section of the public (including a section of the public constituted by persons such as himself) as willing to engage in any such business; or

(b) who is employed by a person falling within paragraph (a) to carry out any such activity.

(2) The activities referred to in subsection (1) are—

(a) acquiring or disposing of securities (whether as principal or agent); or

(b) acting as an intermediary between persons taking part in any dealing in securities.

(3) A person is not to be treated as carrying on a business consisting of an activity mentioned in subsection (2)—

(a) if the activity in question is merely incidental to some other activity not falling within subsection (2); or

(b) merely because he occasionally conducts one of those activities.

(4) For the purposes of section 52, a person dealing in securities relies on a professional intermediary if and only if a person who is acting as a professional intermediary carries out an activity mentioned in subsection (2) in relation to that dealing.

60   Other interpretation provisions

(1) For the purposes of this Part, "regulated market" means any market, however operated, which, by an order made by the Treasury, is identified (whether by name or by reference to criteria prescribed by the order) as a regulated market for the purposes of this Part.

(2) For the purposes of this Part an "issuer", in relation to any securities, means any company, public sector body or individual by which or by whom the securities have been or are to be issued.

(3) For the purposes of this Part—

(a) "company" means any body (whether or not incorporated and wherever incorporated or constituted) which is not a public sector body; and

(b) "public sector body" means—

(i)   the government of the United Kingdom, of Northern Ireland or of any country or territory outside the United Kingdom;

(ii)   a local authority in the United Kingdom or elsewhere;

(iii) any international organisation the members of which include the United Kingdom or another member state;

(iv)   the Bank of England; or

(v)   the central bank of any sovereign State.

(4) For the purposes of this Part, information shall be treated as relating to an issuer of securities which is a company not only where it is about the company but also where it may affect the company's business prospects.

62   Territorial scope of offence of insider dealing

(1) An individual is not guilty of an offence falling within subsection (1) of section 52 unless—

(a) he was within the United Kingdom at the time when he is alleged to have done any act constituting or forming part of the alleged dealing;

(b) the regulated market on which the dealing is alleged to have occurred is one which is declared by an order made by the Treasury to be a market which for the purposes of this Part is to be treated as regulated in the United Kingdom; or

(c) the professional intermediary was within the United Kingdom at the time when he is alleged to have done anything by means of which the offence is alleged to have been committed.

(2) An individual is not guilty of an offence falling within subsection (2) of section 52 unless—

(a) he was within the United Kingdom at the time when he is alleged to have disclosed the information or encouraged the dealing; or

(b) the alleged recipient of the information or encouragement was within the United Kingdom at the time when he is alleged to have received the information or encouragement.

63   Limits on section 52

(1) Section 52 does not apply to anything done by an individual acting on behalf of a public sector body in pursuit of monetary policies or policies with respect to exchange rates or the management of public debt or foreign exchange reserves.

(2) No contract shall be void or unenforceable by reason only of section 52.

SCHEDULE 1 SPECIAL DEFENCES

Market makers

1. (1) An individual is not guilty of insider dealing by virtue of dealing in securities or encouraging another person to deal if he shows that he acted in good faith in the course of—

(a) his business as a market maker, or

(b) his employment in the business of a market maker.

(2) A market maker is a person who—

(a) holds himself out at all normal times in compliance with the rules of a regulated market or an approved organisation as willing to acquire or dispose of securities; and

(b) is recognised as doing so under those rules.

(3) In this paragraph "approved organisation" means an international securities self-regulating organisation approved by the Treasury under any relevant order under section 22 of the Financial Services and Markets Act 2000.

Market information

2. (1) An individual is not guilty of insider dealing by virtue of dealing in securities or encouraging another person to deal if he shows that—

(a) the information which he had as an insider was market information; and

(b) is was reasonable for an individual in his position to have acted as he did despite having that information as an insider at the time.

(2) In determining whether it is reasonable for an individual to do any act despite having market information at the time, there shall, in particular, be taken into account—

(a) the content of the information;

(b) the circumstances in which he first had the information and in what capacity; and

(c) the capacity in which he now acts.

3. An individual is not guilty of insider dealing by virtue of dealing in securities or encouraging another person to deal if he shows—

(a) that he acted—

(i)   in connection with an acquisition or disposal which was under consideration or the subject of negotiation, or in the course of a series of such acquisitions or disposals; and

(ii) with a view to facilitating the accomplishment of the acquisition or disposal or the series of acquisitions or disposals; and

(b) that the information which he had as an insider was market information arising directly out of his involvement in the acquisition or disposal or series of acquisitions or disposals.

4. For the purposes of paragraphs 2 and 3 market information is information consisting of one or more of the following facts—

(a) that securities of a particular kind have been or are to be acquired or disposed of, or that their acquisition or disposal is under consideration or the subject of negotiation;

(b) that securities of a particular kind have not been or are not to be acquired or disposed of;

(c) the number of securities acquired or disposed of or to be acquired or disposed of or whose acquisition or disposal is under consideration or the subject of negotiation;

(d) the price (or range of prices) at which securities have been or are to be acquired or disposed of or the price (or range of prices) at which securities whose acquisition or disposal is under consideration or the subject of negotiation may be acquired or disposed of;

(e) the identity of the persons involved or likely to be involved in any capacity in an acquisition or disposal.

Price stabilisation

5. (1) An individual is not guilty of insider dealing by virtue of dealing in securities or encouraging another person to deal if he shows that he acted in conformity with—

(a) Article 5 of Regulation (EU) No 596/2014 of the European Parliament and of the Council of 16 April 2014 on market abuse (market abuse regulation), as that Article has effect at the time mentioned in sub-paragraph (2), and

(i) each EU regulation, originally made under that Article before that time, which is retained direct EU legislation; and

(ii) all subordinate legislation (within the meaning of the Interpretation Act 1978) made under that Article on or after IP completion day.

(b) rules made under section 137Q(1) of the Financial Services and Markets Act 2000.

(2) The time is the beginning of the day on which the Market Abuse (Amendment) (EU Exit) Regulations 2019 are made.

SCHEDULE 2 SECURITIES

Shares

1. Shares and stock in the share capital of a company ("shares").

Debt securities

2. Any instrument creating or acknowledging indebtedness which is issued by a company or public sector body, including, in particular, debentures, debenture stock, loan stock, bonds and certificates of deposit ("debt securities").

Warrants

3. Any right (whether conferred by warrant or otherwise) to subscribe for shares or debt securities ("warrants").

Depositary receipts

4. (1) The rights under any depositary receipt.

(2) For the purposes of sub-paragraph (1)a "depositary receipt" means a certificate or other record (whether or not in the form of a document)—

(a) which is issued by or on behalf of a person who holds any relevant securities of a particular issuer; and

(b) which acknowledges that another person is entitled to rights in relation to the relevant securities or relevant securities of the same kind.

(3) In sub-paragraph (2) "relevant securities" means shares, debt securities and warrants.

Options

5. Any option to acquire or dispose of any security falling within any other paragraph of this Schedule.

Futures

6. (1) Rights under a contract for the acquisition or disposal at a future date of any relevant securities at a price agreed when the contract is made.

(2) In sub-paragraph (1)—

(a) the references to a future date and to a price agreed when the contract is made include references to a date and a price determined in accordance with terms of the contract; and

(b) "relevant securities" means any security falling within any other paragraph of this Schedule.

Contracts, for differences

7. (1) Rights under a contract which does not provide for the delivery of securities but whose purpose or pretended purpose is to secure a profit or avoid a loss by reference to fluctuations in—

(a) a share index or other similar factor connected with relevant securities;

(b) the price of particular relevant securities; or

(c) the interest rate offered on money placed on deposit.

(2) In sub-paragraph (1) "relevant securities" means any security falling within any other paragraph of this Schedule.

Sexual Offences Act 1993

1   Abolition of presumption of sexual incapacity

The presumption of criminal law that a boy under the age of fourteen is incapable of sexual intercourse (whether natural or unnatural) is hereby abolished.

Criminal Justice and Public Order Act 1994

51   Intimidation, etc., of witnesses, jurors and others

(1) A person commits an offence if—
   (a) he does an act which intimidates, and is intended to intimidate, another person ("the victim"),
   (b) he does the act knowing or believing that the victim is assisting in the investigation of an offence or is a witness or potential witness or a juror or potential juror in proceedings for an offence, and
   (c) he does it intending thereby to cause the investigation or the course of justice to be obstructed, perverted or interfered with. [E]

(2) A person commits an offence if—
   (a) he does an act which harms, and is intended to harm, another person or, intending to cause another person to fear harm, he threatens to do an act which would harm that other person,
   (b) he does or threatens to do the act knowing or believing that the person harmed or threatened to be harmed ("the victim"), or some other person, has assisted in an investigation into an offence or has given evidence or particular evidence in proceedings for an offence, or has acted as a juror or concurred in a particular verdict in proceedings for an offence, and
   (c) he does or threatens to do it because of that knowledge or belief. [E]

(3) For the purposes of subsections (1) and (2) it is immaterial that the act is or would be done, or that the threat is made—
   (a) otherwise than in the presence of the victim, or
   (b) to a person other than the victim.

(4) The harm that may be done or threatened may be financial as well as physical (whether to the person or a person's property) and similarly as respects an intimidatory act which consists of threats.

(5) The intention required by subsection (1)(c) and the motive required by subsection (2)(c) above need not be the only or the predominating intention or motive with which the act is done or, in the case of subsection (2), threatened.

(7) If, in proceedings against a person for an offence under subsection (1) above, it is proved that he did an act falling within paragraph (a) with the knowledge or belief required by paragraph (b), he shall be presumed, unless the contrary is proved, to have done the act with the intention required by paragraph (c) of that subsection.

(8) If, in proceedings against a person for an offence under subsection (2) above, it is proved that within the relevant period—
   (a) he did an act which harmed, and was intended to harm, another person, or
   (b) intending to cause another person fear of harm, he threatened to do an act which would harm that other person,

and that he did the act, or (as the case may be) threatened to do the act, with the knowledge or belief required by paragraph (b), he shall be presumed, unless the contrary is proved, to have done the act or (as the case may be) threatened to do the act with the motive required by paragraph (c) of that subsection.

(9) In this section—

"investigation into an offence" means such an investigation by the police or other person charged with the duty of investigating offences or charging offenders;

"offence" includes an alleged or suspected offence;

"potential", in relation to a juror, means a person who has been summoned for jury service at the court at which proceedings for the offence are pending; and

"the relevant period"—

    (a) in relation to a witness or juror in any proceedings for an offence, means the period beginning with the institution of the proceedings and ending with the first anniversary of the conclusion of the trial or, if there is an appeal or a reference under section 9 or 11 of the Criminal Appeal Act 1995, of the conclusion of the appeal;

    (b) in relation to a person who has, or is believed by the accused to have assisted in an investigation into an offence, but was not also a witness in proceedings for an offence, means the period of one year beginning with any act of his, or any act believed by the accused to be an act of his, assisting in the investigation; and

    (c) in relation to a person who both has, or is believed by the accused to have, assisted in the investigation into an offence and was a witness in proceedings for the offence, means the period beginning with any act of his, or any act believed by the accused to be an act of his, assisting in the investigation and ending with the anniversary mentioned in paragraph (a) above.

(10) For the purposes of the definition of the relevant period in subsection (9) above—

    (a) proceedings for an offence are instituted at the earliest of the following times—

        (i)   when a justice of the peace issues a summons or warrant under section 1 of the Magistrates' Courts Act 1980 in respect of the offence;

        (ii) when a person is charged with the offence after being taken into custody without a warrant;

        (iii) when a bill of indictment is preferred by virtue of section 2(2)(b) or (ba) of the Administration of Justice (Miscellaneous Provisions) Act 1933;

    (b) proceedings at a trial of an offence are concluded with the occurrence of any of the following, the discontinuance of the prosecution, the discharge of the jury without a finding, otherwise than in circumstances where the proceedings are continued without a jury, the acquittal of the accused or the sentencing of or other dealing with the accused for the offence of which he was convicted; and

    (c) proceedings on an appeal are concluded on the determination of the appeal or the abandonment of the appeal.

(11) This section is in addition to, and not in derogation of, any offence subsisting at common law.

61 Power to remove trespassers on land

(1) If the senior police officer present at the scene reasonably believes that two or more persons are trespassing on land and are present there with the common purpose of residing there for any period, that reasonable steps have been taken by or on behalf of the occupier to ask them to leave and—

    (a) that any of those persons has caused damage to the land or to property on the land or used threatening, abusive or insulting words or behaviour towards the occupier, a member of his family or an employee or agent of his, or

    (b) that those persons have between them six or more vehicles on the land,

he may direct those persons, or any of them, to leave the land and to remove any vehicles or other property they have with them on the land.

(2) Where the persons in question are reasonably believed by the senior police officer to be persons who were not originally trespassers but have become trespassers on the land, the officer must reasonably believe that the other conditions specified in subsection (1) are satisfied after those persons became trespassers before he can exercise the power conferred by that subsection.

(3) A direction under subsection (1) above, if not communicated to the persons referred to in subsection (1) by the police officer giving the direction, may be communicated to them by any constable at the scene.

(4) If a person knowing that a direction under subsection (1) above has been given which applies to him—

    (a) fails to leave the land as soon as reasonably practicable, or

    (b) having left again enters the land as a trespasser within the period of three months beginning with the day on which the direction was given,

he commits an offence ... [S]

(6) In proceedings for an offence under this section it is a defence for the accused to show—

    (a) that he was not trespassing on the land, or

    (b) that he had a reasonable excuse for failing to leave the land as soon as reasonably practicable or, as the case may be, for again entering the land as a trespasser.

(7) In its application in England and Wales to common land this section has effect as if in the preceding subsections of it—

    (a) references to trespassing or trespassers were references to acts and persons doing acts which constitute either a trespass as against the occupier or an infringement of the commoners' rights; and

    (b) references to "the occupier" included the commoners or any of them or, in the case of common land to which the public has access, the local authority as well as any commoner.

(8) Subsection (7) above does not—

    (a) require action by more than one occupier; or

    (b) constitute persons trespassers as against any commoner or the local authority if they are permitted to be there by the other occupier.

(9) In this section—

"common land" means

    (a) land registered as common land is a register of common land kept under Part I of the Commons Act 2006; and

    (b) land to which Part I of that Act does not apply and which is subject to rights of common as defined in that Act;

"commoner" means a person with rights of common as so defined

"land" does not include—

    (a) buildings other than—

        (i) agricultural buildings within the meaning of, in England and Wales, paragraphs 3 to 8 of Schedule 5 to the Local Government Finance Act 1988 ... or

        (ii) scheduled monuments within the meaning of the Ancient Monuments and Archaeological Areas Act 1979;

    (b) land forming part of—

        (i) a highway unless it is a footpath, bridleway or byway open to all traffic within the meaning of Part III of the Wildlife and Countryside Act 1981, is a restricted byway within the meaning of Part II of the Countryside and Rights of Way Act 2000 or is a cycle track under the Highways Act 1980 or the Cycle Tracks Act 1984;

"the local authority", in relation to common land, means any local authority which has powers in relation to the land under section 45 of the Commons Act 2006;

"occupier" (and in subsection (8) "the other occupier") means—

    (a) in England and Wales, the person entitled to possession of the land by virtue of an estate or interest held by him;

"property" in relation to damage to property on land, means—
- (a) in England and Wales, property within the meaning of section 10(1) of the Criminal Damage Act 1971;

and "damage" includes the deposit of any substance capable of polluting the land;

"trespass" means, in the application of this section—
- (a) In England and Wales, subject to the extensions effected by subsection (7) above, trespass as against the occupier of the land;

"trespassing" and "trespasser" shall be construed accordingly;

"vehicle" includes—
- (a) any vehicle, whether or not it is in a fit state for use on roads, and includes any chassis or body, with or without wheels, appearing to have formed part of such a vehicle, and any load carried by, and anything attached to, such a vehicle; and
- (b) a caravan as defined in section 29(1) of the Caravan Sites and Control of Development Act 1960;

and a person may be regarded for the purposes of this section as having a purpose of residing in a place notwithstanding that he has a home elsewhere.

63   Powers to remove persons attending or preparing for a rave

(1) This section applies to a gathering on land in the open air of 20 or more persons (whether or not trespassers) at which amplified music is played during the night (with or without intermissions) and is such as, by reason of its loudness and duration and the time at which it is played, is likely to cause serious distress to the inhabitants of the locality; and for this purpose—
- (a) such a gathering continues during intermissions in the music and, where the gathering extends over several days, throughout the period during which amplified music is played at night (with or without intermissions); and
- (b) "music" includes sounds wholly or predominantly characterised by the emission of a succession of repetitive beats.

(2) If, as respects any land, a police officer of at least the rank of superintendent reasonably believes that—
- (a) two or more persons are making preparations for the holding there of a gathering to which this section applies,
- (b) ten or more persons are waiting for such a gathering to begin there, or
- (c) ten or more persons are attending such a gathering which is in progress,

he may give a direction that those persons and any other persons who come to prepare or wait for or to attend the gathering are to leave the land and remove any vehicles or other property which they have with them on the land.

(3) A direction under subsection (2) above, if not communicated to the persons referred to in subsection (2) by the police officer giving the direction, may be communicated to them by any constable at the scene.

(4) Persons shall be treated as having had a direction under subsection (2) above communicated to them if reasonable steps have been taken to bring it to their attention.

(5) A direction under subsection (2) above does not apply to an exempt person.

(6) If a person knowing that a direction has been given which applies to him—
- (a) fails to leave the land as soon as reasonably practicable, or
- (b) having left again enters the land within the period of 7 days beginning with the day on which the direction was given,

he commits an offence . . . [S]

(7) In proceedings for an offence under subsection 6 above it is a defence for the accused to show that he had a reasonable excuse for failing to leave the land as soon as reasonably practicable or, as the case may be, for again entering the land.

(10) In this section—

"exempt person", in relation to land (or any gathering on land), means the occupier, any member of his family and any employee or agent of his and any person whose home is situated on the land;

"land in the open air" includes a place partly open to the air;

"occupier", "trespasser" and "vehicle" have the same meaning as in section 61.

68   Offence of aggravated trespass

(1) A person commits the offence of aggravated trespass if he trespasses on land and, in relation to any lawful activity which persons are engaging in or are about to engage in on that or adjoining land, does there anything which is intended by him to have the effect—

(a) of intimidating those persons or any of them so as to deter them or any of them from engaging in that activity,

(b) of obstructing that activity, or

(c) of disrupting that activity. [S]

(2) Activity on any occasion on the part of a person or persons on land is "lawful" for the purposes of this section if he or they may engage in the activity on the land on that occasion without committing an offence or trespassing on the land.

69   Powers to remove persons committing or participating in aggravated trespass

(1) If the senior police officer present at the scene reasonably believes—

(a) that a person is committing, has committed or intends to commit the offence of aggravated trespass on land; or

(b) that two or more persons are trespassing on land and are present there with the common purpose of intimidating persons so as to deter them from engaging in a lawful activity or of obstructing or disrupting a lawful activity,

he may direct that person or (as the case may be) those persons (or any of them) to leave the land.

(2) A direction under subsection (1) above, if not communicated to the persons referred to in subsection (1) by the police officer giving the direction, may be communicated to them by any constable at the scene.

(3) If a person knowing that a direction under subsection (1) above has been given which applies to him—

(a) fails to leave the land as soon as practicable, or

(b) having left again enters the land as a trespasser within the period of three months beginning with the day on which the direction was given,

he commits an offence . . . [S]

(4) In proceedings for an offence under subsection (3) it is a defence for the accused to show—

(a) that he was not trespassing on the land, or

(b) that he had a reasonable excuse for failing to leave the land as soon as practicable or, as the case may be, for again entering the land as a trespasser.

Intelligence Services Act 1994

7   Authorisation of otherwise unlawful acts outside the British Islands

(1) If, apart from this section, a person would be liable in the United Kingdom for any act done outside the British Islands, he shall not be so liable if the act is one which is authorised to be done by virtue of an authorisation given by the Secretary of State under this section.

(2) In subsection (1) above "liable in the United Kingdom" means liable under the criminal or civil law of any part of the United Kingdom.

(3) The Secretary of State shall not give an authorisation under this section unless he is satisfied—

(a) that any acts which may be done in reliance on the authorization or, as the case may be, the operation in the course of which the acts may be done will be necessary for the proper discharge of a function of the Intelligence Service or GCHQ; and

(b) that there are satisfactory arrangements in force to secure—

    (i)   that nothing will be done in reliance on the authorisation beyond what is necessary for the proper discharge of a function of the Intelligence Service or GCHQ; and

    (ii)   that, in so far as any acts may be done in reliance on the authorisation, their nature and likely consequences will be reasonable, having regard to the purposes for which they are carried out; and

(c) that there are satisfactory arrangements in force under section 2(2)(a) or 4(2)(a) above with respect to the disclosure of information obtained by virtue of this section and that any information obtained by virtue of anything done in reliance on the authorisation will be subject to those arrangements.

(4) Without prejudice to the generality of the power of the Secretary of State to give an authorisation under this section, such an authorisation—

(a) may relate to a particular act or acts, to acts of a description specified in the authorisation or to acts undertaken in the course of an operation so specified;

(b) may be limited to a particular person or persons of a description so specified; and

(c) may be subject to conditions so specified.

(5) An authorisation shall not be given under this section except—

(a) under the hand of the Secretary of State; or

(b) in an urgent case where the Secretary of State has expressly authorised it to be given and a statement of that fact is endorsed on it, under the hand of a senior official.

(6) An authorisation shall, unless renewed under subsection (7) below, cease to have effect—

(a) if the authorisation was given under the hand of the Secretary of State, at the end of the period of six months beginning with the day on which it was given;

(b) in any case, at the end of the period ending with the fifth working day following the day on which it was given.

(7) If at any time before the day on which an authorisation would cease to have effect the Secretary of State considers it necessary for the authorisation to continue to have effect for the purpose for which it was given, he may by an instrument under his hand renew it for a period of six months beginning with that day.

(8) The Secretary of State shall cancel an authorisation if he is satisfied that any act authorised by it is no longer necessary.

Trade Marks Act 1994

92   Unauthorised use of trade mark, etc., in relation to goods

(1) A person commits an offence who with a view to gain for himself or another, or with intent to cause loss to another, and without the consent of the proprietor—

(a) applies to goods or their packaging a sign identical to or likely to be mistaken for, a registered trade mark, or

(b) sells or lets for hire, offers or exposes for sale or hire or distributes goods which bear, or the packaging of which bears, such a sign, or

(c) has in his possession, custody or control in the course of a business any such goods with a view to the doing of anything, by himself or another, which would be an offence under paragraph (b). [E]

(2) A person commits an offence who with a view to gain for himself or another, or with intent to cause loss to another, and without the consent of the proprietor—

    (a) applies a sign identical to, or likely to be mistaken for, a registered trade mark to material intended to be used—

        (i) for labelling or packaging goods

        (ii) as a business paper in relation to goods, or

        (iii) for advertising goods, or

    (b) uses in the course of a business material bearing such a sign for labelling or packaging goods, as a business paper in relation to goods, or for advertising goods, or

    (c) has in his possession, custody or control in the course of a business any such material with a view to the doing of anything, by himself or another, which would be an offence under paragraph (b). [E]

(3) A person commits an offence who with a view to gain for himself or another, or with intent to cause loss to another, and without the consent of the proprietor—

    (a) makes an article specifically designed or adapted for making copies of a sign identical to, or likely to be mistaken for, a registered trade mark, or

    (b) has such an article in his possession, custody or control in the course of a business,

knowing or having reason to believe that it has been, or is to be, used to produce goods, or material for labelling or packaging goods, as a business paper in relation to goods, or for advertising goods. [E]

(4) A person does not commit an offence under this section unless—

    (a) the goods are goods in respect of which the trade mark is registered, or

    (b) the trade mark has a reputation in the United Kingdom and the use of the sign takes or would take unfair advantage of, or is or would be detrimental to, the distinctive character or the repute of the trade mark.

(5) It is a defence for a person charged with an offence under this section to show that he believed on reasonable grounds that the use of the sign in the manner in which it was used, or was to be used, was not an infringement of the registered trade mark.

Gas Act 1995

SCHEDULE 2

Injury to gas fittings and interference with meters

10. (1) If any person intentionally or by culpable negligence—

    (a) injures or allows to be injured any gas fitting provided by a public gas transporter or gas supplier or any service pipe by which any premises are connected to such transporter's mains;

    (b) alters the index to any meter used for measuring the quantity of gas supplied by such a transporter or supplier; or

    (c) prevents any such meter from duly registering the quantity of gas conveyed or supplied,

he shall be guilty of an offence and liable on summary conviction to a fine not exceeding level 3 on the standard scale. [S]

(2) In the case of any offence under sub-paragraph (1) above, the transporter or supplier may disconnect the premises or cut off the supply of gas to the person so offending.

(3) Where any person is prosecuted for an offence under sub-paragraph (1)(b) or (c) above, the possession by him of artificial means for causing an alteration of the index of the meter or, as the case may be, the prevention of the meter from duly registering shall, if the meter was in his custody or under his control, be prima facie evidence that the alteration or prevention was intentionally caused by him.

Restoration of supply without consent

11. (1) Where a consumer's premises have been disconnected by a public gas transporter or a supply of gas to a consumer's premises has been cut off by a gas supplier otherwise than in the exercise of a power conferred by—

(a) paragraph 20, 21 or 22 below;

(b) regulations under section 18(2) or 18A(1) of this Act; or

(c) regulations under section 15 of the Health and Safety at Work etc. Act 1974 (health and safety regulations),

no person shall, without the relevant consent, reconnect the premises or restore the supply.

(2) If any person acts in contravention of sub-paragraph (1) above—

(a) he shall be guilty of an offence and liable on summary conviction to a fine not exceeding level 3 on the standard scale; and

(b) the transporter or supplier may again disconnect the premises or, as the case may be, cut off the supply. [S]

Merchant Shipping Act 1995

58 Conduct endangering ships, structures or individuals

(1) This section applies—

(a) to the master of, or any seaman employed in, a United Kingdom ship; and

(b) to the master of, or any seaman employed in, a ship which—

(i) is registered under the law of any country outside the United Kingdom, and

(ii) is in a port in the United Kingdom or within the United Kingdom while proceeding to or from any such port.

(2) If a person to whom this section applies, while on board his ship or in its immediate vicinity—

(a) does any act which causes or is likely to cause—

(i) the loss or destruction of or serious damage to his ship or its machinery, navigational equipment or safety equipment, or

(ii) the loss or destruction of or serious damage to any other ship or any structure, or

(iii) the death of or serious injury to any person, or

(b) omits to do anything required—

(i) to preserve his ship or its machinery, navigational equipment or safety equipment from being lost, destroyed or seriously damaged, or

(ii) to preserve any person on board his ship from death or serious injury, or

(iii) to prevent his ship from causing the loss or destruction of or serious damage to any other ship or any structure, or the death of or serious injury to any person not on board his ship,

and either of the conditions specified in subsection (3) below is satisfied with respect to that act or omission, he shall (subject to subsections (6) and (7) below) be guilty of an offence. [E]

(3) Those conditions are—

(a) that the act or omission was deliberate or amounted to a breach or neglect of duty;

(b) that the master or seaman in question was under the influence of drink or a drug at the time of the act or omission.

(4) If a person to whom this section applies—

(a) discharges any of his duties, or performs any other function in relation to the operation of his ship or its machinery or equipment, in such a manner as to cause, or to be likely to cause, any such loss, destruction, death or injury as is mentioned in subsection (2)(a) above, or

(b) fails to discharge any of his duties, or to perform any such function, properly to such an extent as to cause, or to be likely to cause, any of those things,

he shall (subject to subsections (6) and (7) below) be guilty of an offence. [E]

(6) In proceedings for an offence under this section it shall be a defence to prove—

    (a) in the case of an offence under subsection (2) above where the act or omission alleged against the defendant constituted a breach or neglect of duty, that the defendant took all reasonable steps to discharge that duty;

    (b) in the case of an offence under subsection (2) above, that at the time of the act or omission alleged against the accused he was under the influence of a drug taken by him for medical purposes and either that he took it on medical advice and complied with any directions given as part of that advice, or that he had no reason to believe the drug might have the influence it had;

    (c) in the case of an offence under subsection (4) above, that the defendant took all reasonable precautions and exercised all due diligence to avoid committing the offence; or

    (d) in the case of an offence under either of those subsections—

        (i) that he could have avoided committing the offence only by disobeying a lawful command, or

        (ii) that in all the circumstances the loss, destruction, damage, death or injury in question, or (as the case may be) the likelihood of its being caused, either could not reasonably have been foreseen by the defendant or could not reasonably have been avoided by him.

(7) In the application of this section to any person falling within subsection (1)(b) above, subsections (2) and (4) shall have effect as if subsection (2)(a)(i) and (b)(i) were omitted . . .

(8) In this section—

"breach or neglect of duty", except in relation to a master, includes any disobedience to a lawful command;

"duty"—

    (a) in relation to a master or seaman, means any duty falling to be discharged by him in his capacity as such; and

    (b) in relation to a master, includes his duty with respect to the good management of his ship and his duty with respect to the safety of operation of his ship, its machinery and equipment; and

"structure" means any fixed or movable structure (of whatever description) other than a ship.

59   Concerted disobedience and neglect of duty

(1) If a seaman employed in a United Kingdom ship combines with other seamen employed in that ship—

    (a) to disobey lawful commands which are required to be obeyed at a time while the ship is at sea;

    (b) to neglect any duty which is required to be discharged at such a time; or

    (c) to impede, at such a time, the progress of a voyage or the navigation of the ship,

he shall be liable—

        (i) on summary conviction, to a fine not exceeding the statutory maximum;

        (ii) on conviction on indictment, to imprisonment for a term not exceeding two years or a fine or both. [E]

(2) For the purposes of this section a ship shall be treated as being at sea at any time when it is not securely moored in a safe berth.

92   Duty of ship to assist the other in case of collision

(1) In every case of collision between two ships, it shall be the duty of the master of each ship, if and so far as he can do so without danger to his own ship, crew and passengers (if any)—

    (a) to render to the other ship, its master, crew and passengers (if any) such assistance as may be practicable, and may be necessary to save them from any danger caused by the collision, and to stay by the other ship until he has ascertained that it has no need of further assistance; and

(b) to give to the master of the other ship the name of his own ship and also the names of the ports from which it comes and to which it is bound.

(2) The duties imposed on the master of a ship by subsection (1) above apply to the masters of United Kingdom ships and to the masters of foreign ships when in United Kingdom waters.

(3) The failure of the master of a ship to comply with the provisions of this section shall not raise any presumption of law that the collision was caused by his wrongful act, neglect, or default.

(4) If the master fails without reasonable excuse to comply with this section, he shall—

    (a) in the case of a failure to comply with subsection (1)(a) above, be liable—

        (i) on summary conviction, to a fine or imprisonment for a term not exceeding six months or both;

        (ii) on conviction on indictment, to a fine or imprisonment for a term not exceeding two years or both; and

    (b) in the case of a failure to comply with subsection (1)(b) above, be liable—

        (i) on summary conviction, to a fine not exceeding the statutory maximum;

        (ii) on conviction on indictment, to a fine;

    and in either case if he is a certified officer, an inquiry into his conduct may be held, and his certificate cancelled or suspended. [E]

93 Duty to assist aircraft in distress

(1) The master of a ship, on receiving at sea a signal of distress from an aircraft or information from any source that an aircraft is in distress, shall proceed with all speed to the assistance of the persons in distress (informing them if possible that he is doing so) unless he is unable, or in the special circumstances of the case considers it unreasonable or unnecessary, to do so, or unless he is released from this duty under subsection (5) below.

(3) The duties imposed on the master of a ship by subsection (1) above apply to the masters of United Kingdom ships and to the masters of foreign ships when in United Kingdom waters.

(5) A master shall be released from the duty imposed by subsection (1) above, if he is informed by the persons in distress, or by the master of any ship that has reached the persons in distress, that assistance is no longer required. [E]

94 Meaning of "dangerously unsafe ship"

(1) For the purposes of sections 95, 96, 97 and 98 a ship in port is "dangerously unsafe" if, having regard to the nature of the service for which it is intended, the ship is, by reason of the matters mentioned in subsection (2) below, unfit to go to sea without serious danger to human life.

(1A) For the purposes of those sections a ship at sea is "dangerously unsafe" if, having regard to the nature of the service for which it is being used or is intended, the ship is, by reason of the matters mentioned in subsection (2) below either—

    (a) unfit to remain at sea without serious danger to human life, or

    (b) unfit to go on a voyage without serious danger to human life.

(2) Those matters are—

    (a) the condition, or the unsuitability for its purpose, of—

        (i) the ship or its machinery or equipment, or

        (ii) any part of the ship or its machinery or equipment;

    (b) undermanning;

    (c) overloading or unsafe or improper loading;

    (d) any other matter relevant to the safety of the ship;

and are referred to in those sections, in relation to any ship, as "the matters relevant to its safety".

(3) Any reference in those sections to "going to sea" shall, in a case where the service for which the ship is intended consists of going on voyages or excursions that do not involve going to sea, be construed as a reference to going on such a voyage or excursion.

98 Owner and master liable in respect of dangerously unsafe ship

(1) If a ship which—

    (a) is in a port in the United Kingdom, or

    (b) is a United Kingdom ship and is in any other port,

is dangerously unsafe, then, subject to subsections (4) and (5) below, the master and the owner of the ship shall each be guilty of an offence. [E]

(2) Where, at the time when a ship is dangerously unsafe, any responsibilities of the owner with respect to the matters relevant to its safety have been assumed (whether wholly or in part) by any person or persons other than the owner, and have been so assumed by that person or (as the case may be) by each of those persons either—

    (a) directly, under the terms of a charter-party or management agreement made with the owner, or

    (b) indirectly, under the terms of a series of charter-parties or management agreements,

the reference to the owner in subsection (1) above shall be construed as a reference to that other person or (as the case may be) to each of those other persons.

(4) It shall be a defence in proceedings for an offence under this section to prove that at the time of the alleged offence—

    (a) arrangements had been made which were appropriate to ensure that before the ship went to sea it was made fit to do so without serious danger to human life by reason of the matters relevant to its safety which are specified in the charge . . . ; or

    (b) it was reasonable for such arrangements not to have been made.

(5) It shall also be a defence in proceedings for an offence under this section to prove—

    (a) that, under the terms of one or more charter-parties or management agreements entered into by the accused, the relevant responsibilities, namely—

        (i) where the accused is the owner, his responsibilities with respect to the matters relevant to the ship's safety, or

        (ii) where the accused is liable to proceedings under this section by virtue of subsection (2) above, so much of those responsibilities as had been assumed by him as mentioned in that subsection,

    had at the time of the alleged offence been wholly assumed by some other person or persons party thereto; and

    (b) that in all the circumstances of the case the accused had taken such steps as it was reasonable for him to take, and exercised such diligence as it was reasonable for him to exercise, to secure the proper discharge of the relevant responsibilities during the period during which they had been assumed by some other person or persons as mentioned in paragraph (a) above;

and, in determining whether the accused had done so, regard shall be had in particular to the matters mentioned in subsection (6) below.

(6) Those matters are—

    (a) whether prior to the time of the alleged offence the accused was, or in all the circumstances ought reasonably to have been, aware of any deficiency in the discharge of the relevant responsibilities; and

    (b) the extent to which the accused was or was not able, under the terms of any such charter-party or management agreement as is mentioned in subsection (5)(a) above—

        (i) to terminate it, or

        (ii) to intervene in the management of the ship,

    in the event of any such deficiency, and whether it was reasonable for the accused to place himself in that position.

(8) In this section—

"management agreement", in relation to a ship, means any agreement (other than a charter-party or a contract of employment) under which the ship is managed, either wholly or in part, by a person other than the owner (whether on behalf of the owner or on behalf of some other person); and

"relevant responsibilities" shall be construed in accordance with subsection (5) above.

(9) References in this section to responsibilities being assumed by a person under the terms of a charter-party or management agreement are references to their being so assumed by him whether or not he has entered into a further charter-party or management agreement providing for them to be assumed by some other person.

100   Owner liable for unsafe operation of ship

(1) It shall be the duty of the owner of a ship to which this section applies to take all reasonable steps to secure that the ship is operated in a safe manner.

(2) This section applies to—

(a) any United Kingdom ship; and

(b) any ship which—

(i)   is registered under the law of any country outside the United Kingdom, and

(ii) is within United Kingdom waters while proceeding to or from a port in the United Kingdom,

unless the ship would not be so proceeding but for weather conditions or any other unavoidable circumstances. [E]

(4) Where any such ship—

(a) is chartered by demise, or

(b) is managed, either wholly or in part, by a person other than the owner under the terms of a management agreement within the meaning of section 98,

any reference to the owner of the ship in subsection (1) or (3) above shall be construed as including a reference—

(i)   to the charterer under the charter by demise, or

(ii) to any such manager as is referred to in paragraph (b) above, or

(iii) (if the ship is both chartered and managed as mentioned above) to both the charterer and any such manager,

and accordingly the reference in subsection (1) above to the taking of all reasonable steps shall, in relation to the owner, the charterer or any such manager, be construed as a reference to the taking of all such steps as it is reasonable for him to take in the circumstances of the case.

101   Offences in connection with passenger ships

(1) A person commits an offence if, in relation to a ship to which this section applies, he does any of the following things, that is to say—

(a) if, being drunk or disorderly, he has been on that account refused admission to the ship by the owner or any person in his employment, and, after having the amount of his fare (if he has paid it) returned or tendered to him, nevertheless persists in attempting to enter the ship;

(b) if, being drunk or disorderly on board the ship, he is requested by the owner or any person in his employment to leave the ship at any place in the United Kingdom at which he can conveniently do so, and, after having the amount of his fare (if he has paid it) returned or tendered to him, does not comply with the request;

(c) if, on board the ship, after warning by the master or other officer thereof, he molests or continues to molest any passenger;

(d) if, after having been refused admission to the ship by the owner or any person in his employment on account of the ship being full, and having had the amount of his fare (if he has paid it) returned or tendered to him, he nevertheless persists in attempting to enter the ship;

(e) if, having gone on board the ship at any place, and being requested, on account of the ship being full, by the owner or any person in his employment to leave the ship before it has left that place, and having had the amount of his fare (if he has paid it) returned or tendered to him, he does not comply with that request;

(f) if, on arriving in the ship at a point to which he has paid his fare, he knowingly and intentionally refuses or neglects to leave the ship; and

(g) if, on board the ship he fails, when requested by the master or other officer thereof, either to pay his fare or show such ticket or other receipt, if any, showing the payment of his fare, as is usually given to persons travelling by and paying their fare for the ship;

but his liability in respect of any such offence shall not prejudice the recovery of any fare payable by him. [S]

(2) A person commits an offence if, on board any ship to which this section applies he intentionally does or causes to be done anything in such a manner as to—

(a) obstruct or damage any part of the machinery or equipment of the ship, or

(b) obstruct, impede or molest the crew, or any of them, in the navigation or management of the ship, or otherwise in the execution of their duty on or about the ship. [S]

(3) The master or other officer of any ship to which this section applies, and all persons called by him to his assistance, may, without any warrant, detain any person who commits any offence against subsection (1) or (2) above and whose name and address are unknown to the master or officer, and deliver that person to a constable.

(5) If any person commits an offence against subsection (1) or (2) above and on the application of the master of the ship, or any other person in the employment of the owner thereof, refuses to give his name and address, or gives a false name or address, that person shall be liable, on summary conviction, to a fine not exceeding level 2 on the standard scale. [S]

(6) This section applies to a ship for which there is in force a Passenger Ship Safety Certificate or Passenger Certificate, as the case may be, issued under or recognised by safety regulations.

103 Stowaways

(1) If a person, without the consent of the master or of any other person authorised to give it, goes to sea or attempts to go to sea in a United Kingdom ship, he shall be liable on summary conviction to a fine not exceeding level 3 on the standard scale. [S]

104 Unauthorised presence on board ship

Where a United Kingdom ship or a ship registered in any other country is in a port in the United Kingdom and a person who is neither in Her Majesty's service nor authorised by law to do so—

(a) goes on board the ship without the consent of the master or of any other persons authorised to give it; or

(b) remains on board the ship after being requested to leave by the master, a constable, an officer authorised by the Secretary of State or an officer of customs and excise,

he shall be liable on summary conviction to a fine not exceeding level 5 on the standard scale. [S]

131 Discharge of oil from ships into certain United Kingdom waters

(A1) In this section "relevant discharge" means—

(a) a discharge of oil or a mixture containing oil which is made—

(i)   from a ship which is an offshore installation, and

(ii)   into United Kingdom national waters which are navigable by sea-going ships, or

(b) a discharge of oil or a mixture containing oil which is made—

(i)   from a ship which is not an offshore installation, and

(ii)   into United Kingdom national waters which are navigable by sea-going ships but which do not form part of the sea.

(1) If there is a relevant discharge, subject to the following provisions of this Chapter, the following shall be guilty of an offence, that is to say—

(a) the owner or master of the ship, unless he proves that the discharge took place and was caused as mentioned in paragraph (b) below;

(b) if the discharge from the ship takes place in the course of a transfer of oil to or from another ship or a place on land and is caused by the act or omission of any person in charge of any apparatus in that other ship or that place, the owner or master of that other ship or, as the case may be, the occupier of that place. [E]

(2) Subsection (1) above does not apply to any discharge from an offshore installation which—

(a) is made into the sea; and

(b) is of a kind or is made in circumstances for the time being prescribed by regulations made by the Secretary of State.

(3A) In this section "offshore installation" means any mobile or fixed drilling or production platform or any other platform used in connection with the exploration, exploitation or associated offshore processing of sea bed mineral resources.

(4) In this section "sea" includes any estuary or arm of the sea.

(5) In this section "place on land" includes anything resting on the bed or shore of the sea, or of any other waters included in United Kingdom national waters, and also includes anything afloat (other than a ship) if it is anchored or attached to the bed or shore of the sea or any such waters.

(6) In this section "occupier", in relation to any such thing as is mentioned in subsection (5) above, if it has no occupier, means the owner thereof.

132   Defences of owner or master charged with offence under section 131

(1) Where a person is charged with an offence under section 131 as the owner or master of a ship, it shall be a defence to prove that the oil or mixture was discharged for the purpose of—

(a) securing the safety of any ship;

(b) preventing damage to any ship or cargo, or

(c) saving life,

unless the court is satisfied that the discharge of the oil or mixture was not necessary for that purpose or was not a reasonable step to take in the circumstances.

(2) Where a person is charged with an offence under section 131 as the owner or master of a ship, it shall also be a defence to prove—

(a) that the oil or mixture escaped in consequence of damage to the ship, and that as soon as practicable after the damage occurred all reasonable steps were taken for preventing, or (if it could not be prevented) for stopping or reducing, the escape of the oil or mixture; or

(b) that the oil or mixture escaped by reason of leakage, that neither the leakage nor any delay in discovering it was due to any want of reasonable care, and that as soon as practicable after the escape was discovered all reasonable steps were taken for stopping or reducing it.

133   Defences of occupier charged with offence under section 131

Where a person is charged, in respect of the escape of any oil or mixture containing oil, with an offence under section 131 as the occupier of a place on land, it shall be a defence to prove that neither the escape nor any delay in discovering it was due to any want of reasonable care and that as soon as practicable after it was discovered all reasonable steps were taken for stopping or reducing it.

282   Offences committed by British seamen

(1) Any act in relation to property or person done in or at any place (ashore or afloat) outside the United Kingdom by any master or seaman who at the time is employed in a United Kingdom ship, which, if done in any part of the United Kingdom, would be an offence under the law of any part of the United Kingdom, shall—

(a) be an offence under that law, and

(b) be treated for the purposes of jurisdiction and trial, as if it had been done within the jurisdiction of the Admiralty of England.

(2) Subsection (1) above also applies in relation to a person who had been so employed within the period of three months expiring with the time when the act was done.

(3) Subsections (1) and (2) above apply to omissions as they apply to acts.

Education Act 1996

444   Failure to secure regular attendance at school of registered pupil

(1) If a child of compulsory school age who is a registered pupil at a school fails to attend regularly at the school, his parent is guilty of an offence. [S]

(1A) If in the circumstances mentioned in subsection (1) the parent knows that his child is failing to attend regularly at the school and fails to cause him to do so, he is guilty of an offence. [S]

(1B) It is a defence for a person charged with an offence under subsection (1A) to prove that he had a reasonable justification for his failure to cause the child to attend regularly at the school.

(2) Subsections (2A) to (6) below apply in proceedings for an offence under this section in respect of a child who is not a boarder at the school at which he is a registered pupil.

(2A) The child shall not be taken to have failed to attend regularly at the school by reason of his absence from the school at any time if the parent proves that at that time the child was prevented from attending by reason of sickness or any unavoidable cause.

(3) The child shall not be taken to have failed to attend regularly at the school by reason of his absence from the school—

(a) with leave, or

(c) on any day exclusively set apart for religious observance by the religious body to which his parent belongs.

(3A) Subsections (3B) and (3D) apply where the child's home is in England.

(3B) The child shall not be taken to have failed to attend regularly at the school if the parent proves that—

(a) the local authority have a duty to make travel arrangements in relation to the child under section 508B(1) for the purpose of facilitating the child's attendance at the school and have failed to discharge that duty, or

(b) the local authority have a duty to make travel arrangements in relation to the child by virtue of subsection (2)(c) of section 508E (school travel schemes) for the purpose of facilitating the child's attendance at the school and have failed to discharge that duty.

(3C) For the purposes of subsection (3B)—

(a) the reference to "travel arrangements" in paragraph (a) has the same meaning as in section 508B, and

(b) the reference to "travel arrangements" in paragraph (b) has the same meaning as in paragraph 3 of Schedule 35C.

(3D) Where the school is an independent school which is not a qualifying school, the child shall not be taken to have failed to attend regularly at the school if the parent proves—

(a) that the school is not within walking distance of the child's home,

(b) that no suitable arrangements have been made by the local authority for boarding accommodation for him at or near the school, and

(c) that no suitable arrangements have been made by the local authority for enabling him to become a registered pupil at a qualifying school nearer to his home.

(3E) For the purposes of subsection (3D), "qualifying school" has the same meaning as it has for the purposes of Schedule 35B (meaning of "eligible child" for the purposes of section 508B).

(5) In subsection (3D) above, "walking distance" means—

(a) in relation to a child who is under the age of eight years, means 3.218688 kilometres (two miles), and

(b) in relation to a child who has attained the age of eight years, means 4.828032 kilometres (three miles),

in each case measured by the nearest available route.

(6) If it is proved that the child has no fixed abode, subsections 3B, 3D . . . above shall not apply, but it is a defence for the parent to prove—

(a) that he is engaged in a trade or business of such a nature as to require him to travel from place to place,

(b) that the child has attended at a school as a registered pupil as regularly as the nature of that trade or business permits, and

(c) if the child has attained the age of six years, that he has made at least two hundred attendances during the period of twelve months ending with the date on which the proceedings were instituted.

(7) In proceedings for an offence under this section in respect of a child who is a boarder at the school at which he is a registered pupil, the child shall be taken to have failed to attend regularly at the school if he is absent from it without leave during any part of the school term unless the parent proves that at that time the child was prevented from being present by reason of sickness or any unavoidable cause.

(8B) If, on the trial of an offence under subsection (1A), the court finds the defendant not guilty of that offence but is satisfied that he is guilty of an offence under subsection (1), the court may find him guilty of that offence.

(9) In this section "leave", in relation to a school, means leave granted by any person authorised to do so by the governing body or proprietor of the school.

547   Nuisance or disturbance on school premises

(1) Any person who without lawful authority is present on premises to which this section applies and causes or permits nuisance or disturbance to the annoyance of persons who lawfully use those premises (whether or not any such persons are present at the time) is guilty of an offence. [S]

(2) This section applies to premises, including playgrounds, playing fields and other premises for outdoor recreation, of—

    (a) any school maintained by a local authority,

      (aa) any special school not so maintained,

      (ab) any independent school, and

      (ac) any alternative provision Academy that is not an independent school

(2A) This section also applies to any premises which are—

    (a) provided by a local authority under section 507A or 507B (if the authority are in England) . . . and

    (b) used wholly or mainly in connection with the provision of instruction or leadership in sporting, recreational or outdoor activities.

548   No right to give corporal punishment

(1) Corporal punishment given by, or on the authority of, a member of staff to a child—

    (a) for whom education is provided at any school, or

    (b) for whom education is provided, otherwise than at school, under any arrangements made by a local authority, or

    (c) for whom specified early years education is provided otherwise than at school,

cannot be justified in any proceedings on the ground that it was given in pursuance of a right exercisable by the member of staff by virtue of his position as such.

(2) Subsection (1) applies to corporal punishment so given to a child at any time, whether at the school or other place at which education is provided for the child, or elsewhere.

(3) The following provisions have effect for the purposes of this section.

(4) Any reference to giving corporal punishment to a child is to doing anything for the purpose of punishing that child (whether or not there are other reasons for doing it) which, apart from any justification, would constitute battery.

(5) However, corporal punishment shall not be taken to be given to a child by virtue of anything done for reasons that include averting—

    (a) an immediate danger of personal injury to, or

    (b) an immediate danger to the property of,

any person (including the child himself).

(6) "Member of staff", in relation to the child concerned, means—

    (a) any person who works as a teacher at the school or other place at which education is provided for the child, or

    (b) any other person who (whether in connection with the provision of education for the child or otherwise)—

      (i)   works at that school or place, or—

(ii) otherwise provides his services there (whether or not for payment), and has lawful control or charge of the child.

(7) "Child" (except in subsection (8)) means a person under the age of 18.

(8) "Specified early years education" means—

(a) in relation to England, early years provision as defined by section 20 of the Childcare Act 2006 which is

(i) provided under arrangements made by a local authority in England in pursuance of the duty imposed by section 7 of that Act (whether or not the local authority provides the early years provision); or

(ii) provided under arrangements made by a local authority in pursuance of any duty imposed under section 2 of the Childcare Act 2016 (whether or not the local authority provides the early years provision).

550ZA Power of members of staff to search pupils for prohibited items

(1) This section applies where a member of staff of a school in England—

(a) has reasonable grounds for suspecting that a pupil at the school may have a prohibited item with him or her or in his or her possessions; and

(b) falls within section 550ZB(1).

(2) The member of staff may search the pupil ("P") or P's possessions for that item.

(3) For the purposes of this section and section 550ZC each of the following is a "prohibited item"—

(a) an article to which section 139 of the Criminal Justice Act 1988 applies (knives and blades etc.);

(b) an offensive weapon, within the meaning of the Prevention of Crime Act 1953;

(c) alcohol, within the meaning of section 191 of the Licensing Act 2003;

(d) a controlled drug, within the meaning of section 2 of the Misuse of Drugs Act 1971, which section 5(1) of that Act makes it unlawful for P to have in P's possession;

(e) a stolen article;

(ea) an article that the member of staff reasonably suspects has been, or is likely to be, used—

(i) to commit an offence, or

(ii) to cause personal injury to, or damage to the property of, any person (including P);

(f) an article of a kind specified in regulations;

(g) any other item which the school rules identify as an item for which a search may be made.

(4) In subsection (3)(e) "stolen", in relation to an article, has the same meaning as it has by virtue of section 24 of the Theft Act 1968 in the provisions of that Act relating to goods which have been stolen.

(4A) In subsection (3)(ea)(i), "offence" includes anything that would be an offence but for the operation of any presumption that a person under a particular age is incapable of committing an offence.

(4B) In subsection (3)(g), the "school rules" means—

(a) in the case of a maintained school or a non-maintained special school, rules in force at the school that are made under measures determined and publicised by the head teacher under section 89 of the Education and Inspections Act 2006;

(b) in the case of any other school, measures relating to discipline in the school that are determined and publicised in accordance with regulations.

(4C) In subsection (4B)(a)—

"maintained school" means—

(a) a community, foundation or voluntary school,

(b) a community or foundation special school,

(c) a maintained nursery school, or

(d) a pupil referral unit;

"non-maintained special school" means a school that is approved under section 342.

(5) In this section and section 550ZB—

"member of staff", in relation to a school, means—

    (a) any teacher who works at the school; and

    (b) any other person who, with the authority of the head teacher, has lawful control or charge of pupils for whom education is being provided at the school;

"possessions", in relation to P, includes any goods over which P has or appears to have control.

(6) The powers conferred by this section and sections 550ZB and 550ZC are in addition to any powers exercisable by the member of staff in question apart from those sections and are not to be construed as restricting such powers.

550ZB   Power of search under section 550ZA: supplementary

(1) A person may carry out a search under section 550ZA only if that person—

    (a) is the head teacher of the school; or

    (b) has been authorised by the head teacher to carry out the search.

(2) An authorisation for the purposes of subsection (1)(b) may be given in relation to—

    (a) searches under section 550ZA generally;

    (b) a particular search under that section;

    (c) a particular description of searches under that section.

(3) Nothing in any enactment, instrument or agreement shall be construed as authorising a head teacher of a school in England to require a person other than a member of security staff of the school to carry out a search under section 550ZA.

(4) A search under section 550ZA may be carried out only where—

    (a) the member of staff and P are on the premises of the school; or

    (b) they are elsewhere and the member of staff has lawful control or charge of P.

(5) A person exercising the power in section 550ZA to search for an item within section 550ZA(3)(a) to (f) may use such force as is reasonable in the circumstances for exercising that power.

(6) A person carrying out a search of P under section 550ZA—

    (a) may not require P to remove any clothing other than outer clothing;

    (b) must be of the same sex as P unless the condition in subsection (6A) is satisfied;

    (c) may carry out the search only in the presence of another member of staff unless the conditions in subsection (6A) is satisfied; and

    (d) must ensure that the other member of staff is of the same sex as P if it is reasonably practicable to do so.

(6A) The condition is satisfied if—

    (a) the person carrying out the search reasonably believes that there is a risk that serious harm will be caused to a person if the search is not carried out as a matter of urgency, and

    (b) in the time available it is not reasonably practicable for the search to be carried out by a person of the same sex as P or in the presence of another member of staff (as the case may be).

(7) P's possessions may not be searched under section 550ZA except in the presence of—

    (a) P; and

    (b) another member of staff unless the condition in subsection (7A) is satisfied.

(7A) The condition is satisfied if—

    (a) the person carrying out the search reasonably believes that there is a risk that serious harm will be caused to a person if the search is not carried out as a matter of urgency, and

    (b) in the time available it is not reasonably practicable for the search to be carried out in the presence of another member of staff.

(8) In this section—

"outer clothing" means—

    (a) any item of clothing that is being worn otherwise than wholly next to the skin or immediately over a garment being worn as underwear; or

    (b) a hat, shoes, boots, gloves or a scarf.

Family Law Act 1996

42A   Offence of breaching non-molestation order

(1) A person who without reasonable excuse does anything that he is prohibited from doing by a non-molestation order is guilty of an offence. [E]

(2) In the case of a non-molestation order made by virtue of section 45(1), a person can be guilty of an offence under this section only in respect of conduct engaged in at a time when he was aware of the existence of the order.

(3) Where a person is convicted of an offence under this section in respect of any conduct, that conduct is not punishable as a contempt of court.

(4) A person cannot be convicted of an offence under this section in respect of any conduct which has been punished as a contempt of court.

63CA   Offence of breaching forced marriage protection order

(1) A person who without reasonable excuse does anything that the person is prohibited from doing by a forced marriage protection order is guilty of an offence. [E]

(2) In the case of a forced marriage protection order made by virtue of section 63D(1), a person can be guilty of an offence under this section only in respect of conduct engaged in at a time when the person was aware of the existence of the order.

(3) Where a person is convicted of an offence under this section in respect of any conduct, that conduct is not punishable as a contempt of court.

(4) A person cannot be convicted of an offence under this section in respect of any conduct which has been punished as a contempt of court.

Law Reform (Year and a Day Rule) Act 1996

1   Abolition of "year and a day rule"

The rule known as the "year and a day rule" (that is, the rule that, for the purposes of offences involving death and of suicide, an act or omission is conclusively presumed not to have caused a person's death if more than a year and a day elapsed before he died) is abolished for all purposes.

2   Restriction on institution of proceedings for a fatal offence

(1) Proceedings to which this section applies may only be instituted by or with the consent of the Attorney General.

(2) This section applies to proceedings against a person for a fatal offence if—

   (a) the injury alleged to have caused the death was sustained more than three years before the death occurred, or

   (b) the person has previously been convicted of an offence committed in circumstances alleged to be connected with the death.

(3) In subsection (2) "fatal offence" means—

   (a) murder, manslaughter, infanticide or any other offence of which one of the elements is causing a person's death,

   (b) an offence under section 2(1) of the Suicide Act 1961 (offence of encouraging or assisting suicide) in connection with the death of a person, or

   (c) an offence under section 5 of the Domestic Violence, Crime and Victims Act 2004 of causing or allowing the death of a child or vulnerable adult.

Police Act 1996

89   Assaults on constables

(1) Any person who assaults a constable in the execution of his duty, or a person assisting a constable in the execution of his duty, shall be guilty of an offence . . . [S]

(2) Any person who resists or wilfully obstructs a constable in the execution of his duty, or a person assisting a constable in the execution of his duty shall be guilty of an offence . . . [S]

90   Impersonation, etc.

(1) Any person who with intent to deceive impersonates a member of a police force or special constable, or makes any statement or does any act calculated falsely to suggest that he is such a member or constable, shall be guilty of an offence . . . [S]

(2) Any person who, not being a constable, wears any article of police uniform in circumstances where it gives him an appearance so nearly resembling that of a member of a police force as to be calculated to deceive shall be guilty of an offence . . . [S]

(3) Any person who, not being a member of a police force or special constable, has in his possession any article of police uniform shall, unless he proves that he obtained possession of that article lawfully and has possession of it for a lawful purpose, be guilty of an offence . . . [S]

(4) In this section—

    (a) "article of police uniform" means any article of uniform or any distinctive badge or mark or document of identification usually issued to members of police forces or special constables, or anything having the appearance of such an article, badge, mark or document; and

    (b) "special constable" means a special constable appointed for a police area.

91   Causing disaffection

(1) Any person who causes, or attempts to cause, or does any act calculated to cause, disaffection amongst the members of any police force, or induces or attempts to induce, or does any act calculated to induce, any member of a police force to withhold his services, shall be guilty of an offence . . . [E]

(2) This section applies in the case of—

    (a) special constables appointed for a police area,

    (b) members of the Civil Nuclear Constabulary, and

    (c) members of the British Transport Police Force,

as it applies in the case of members of a police force.

(3) Liability under subsection (1) for any behaviour is in addition to any civil liability for that behaviour.

Treasure Act 1996

8   Duty of finder of treasure to notify coroner

(1) A person who finds an object which he believes or has reasonable grounds for believing is treasure must notify the coroner for the district in which the object was found before the end of the notice period.

(2) The notice period is fourteen days beginning with—

    (a) the day after the find; or

    (b) if later, the day on which the finder first believes or has reason to believe the object is treasure.

(3) Any person who fails to comply with subsection (1) is guilty of an offence . . . [S]

(4) In proceedings for an offence under this section, it is a defence for the defendant to show that he had, and has continued to have, a reasonable excuse for failing to notify the coroner.

Wild Mammals (Protection) Act 1996

1   Offences

If, save as permitted by this Act, any person mutilates, kicks, beats, nails or otherwise impales, stabs, burns, stones, crushes, drowns, drags or asphyxiates any wild mammal with intent to inflict unnecessary suffering he shall be guilty of an offence. [S]

2 Exceptions from offences under the Act

(1) A person shall not be guilty of an offence under this Act by reason of—

    (a) the attempted killing of any such wild mammal as an act of mercy if he shows that the mammal had been so seriously disabled otherwise than by his unlawful act that there was no reasonable chance of its recovering;

    (b) the killing in a reasonably swift and humane manner of any such wild mammal if he shows that the wild mammal had been injured or taken in the course of either lawful shooting, hunting, coursing or lawful pest control activity;

    (c) doing anything which is authorised by or under any enactment;

    (d) any act made unlawful by section 1 if the act was done by means of any snare, trap, dog, or bird lawfully used for the purpose of killing or taking any wild mammal; or

    (e) the lawful use of any poisonous or noxious substance on any wild mammal.

3 Interpretation

In this Act "wild mammal" means any mammal which is not a "protected animal" within the meaning of the Animal Welfare Act 2006.

Firearms (Amendment) Act 1997

2 Slaughtering instruments

The authority of the Secretary of State. . . is not required by virtue of subsection (1)(aba) of section 5 of the 1968 Act—

    (a) for a person to have in his possession, or to purchase or acquire, or to sell or transfer, a slaughtering instrument if he is authorised by a firearm certificate to have the instrument in his possession, or to purchase or acquire it;

    (b) for a person to have a slaughtering instrument in his possession if he is entitled, under section 10 of the 1968 Act, to have it in his possession without a firearm certificate.

3 Firearms used for humane killing of animals

The authority of the Secretary of State . . . is not required by virtue of subsection (1)(aba) of section 5 of the 1968 Act for a person to have in his possession, or to purchase or acquire, or to sell or transfer, a firearm if he is authorised by a firearm certificate to have the firearm in his possession, or to purchase or acquire it, subject to a condition that it is only for use in connection with the humane killing of animals.

4 Shot pistols used for shooting vermin

(1) The authority of the Secretary of State . . . is not required by virtue of subsection (1)(aba) of section 5 of the 1968 Act for a person to have in his possession, or to purchase or acquire, or to sell or transfer, a shot pistol if he is authorised by a firearm certificate to have the shot pistol in his possession, or to purchase or acquire it, subject to a condition that it is only for use in connection with the shooting of vermin.

(2) For the purposes of this section, "shot pistol" means a smooth-bored gun which is chambered for .410 cartridges or 9mm rim-fire cartridges.

5 Races at athletic meetings

The authority of the Secretary of State . . . is not required by virtue of subsection (1)(aba) of section 5 of the 1968 Act—

    (a) for a person to have a firearm in his possession at an athletic meeting for the purpose of starting races at that meeting; or

    (b) for a person to have in his possession, or to purchase or acquire, or to sell or transfer, a firearm if he is authorised by a firearm certificate to have the firearm in his possession, or to purchase or acquire it, subject to a condition that it is only for use in connection with starting races at athletic meetings.

6 Trophies of war

The authority of the Secretary of State . . . is not required by virtue of subsection (1)(aba) of section 5 of the 1968 Act for a person to have in his possession a firearm which was acquired as a trophy of war before 1st January 1946 if he is authorised by a firearm certificate to have it in his possession.

7 Firearms of historic interest

(1) The authority of the Secretary of State . . . is not required by virtue of subsection (1)(aba) of section 5 of the 1968 Act for a person to have in his possession, or to purchase or acquire, or to sell or transfer, a firearm which—

(a) was manufactured before 1st January 1919; and

(b) is of a description specified under subsection (2) below,

if he is authorised by a firearm certificate to have the firearm in his possession, or to purchase or acquire it, subject to a condition that he does so only for the purpose of its being kept or exhibited as part of a collection.

(2) The Secretary of State may by order made by statutory instrument specify a description of firearm for the purposes of subsection (1) above if it appears to him that—

(a) firearms of that description were manufactured before 1st January 1919, and

(b) ammunition for firearms of that type is not readily available.

(3) The authority of the Secretary of State . . . is not required by virtue of subsection (1)(aba) of section 5 of the 1968 Act for a person to have in his possession, or to purchase or acquire, or to sell or transfer, a firearm which—

(a) is of particular rarity, aesthetic quality or technical interest, or

(b) is of historical importance,

if he is authorised by a firearm certificate to have the firearm in his possession subject to a condition requiring it to be kept and used only at a place designated for the purposes of this subsection by the Secretary of State . . .

(4) This section has effect without prejudice to section 58(2) of the 1968 Act (antique firearms).

8 Weapons and ammunition used for treating animals

The authority of the Secretary of State . . . is not required by virtue of subsection (1)(aba), (b) or (c) of section 5 of the 1968 Act for a person to have in his possession, or to purchase or acquire, or to sell or transfer, any firearm, weapon or ammunition designed or adapted for the purpose of tranquillising or otherwise treating any animal, if he is authorised by a firearm certificate to possess, or to purchase or acquire, the firearm, weapon or ammunition subject to a condition restricting its use to use in connection with the treatment of animals.

48 Firearms powered by compressed carbon dioxide

Any reference to an air rifle, air pistol or air gun—

(a) in the Firearms Acts 1968 to 1997; or

(b) in the Firearms (Dangerous Air Weapons) Rules 1969 . . . ,

shall include a reference to a rifle, pistol or gun powered by compressed carbon dioxide.

Knives Act 1997

1 Unlawful marketing of knives

(1) A person is guilty of an offence if he markets a knife in a way which—

(a) indicates, or suggests, that it is suitable for combat; or

(b) is otherwise likely to stimulate or encourage violent behaviour involving the use of the knife as a weapon. [E]

(2) "Suitable for combat" and "violent behaviour" are defined in section 10.

(3) For the purposes of this Act, an indication or suggestion that a knife is suitable for combat may, in particular, be given or made by a name or description—

    (a) applied to the knife;

    (b) on the knife or on any packaging in which it is contained; or

    (c) included in any advertisement which, expressly or by implication, relates to the knife.

  (4) For the purposes of this Act, a person markets a knife if—

    (a) he sells or hires it;

    (b) he offers, or exposes, it for sale or hire; or

    (c) he has it in his possession for the purpose of sale or hire.

2   Publications

  (1) A person is guilty of an offence if he publishes any written, pictorial or other material in connection with the marketing of any knife and that material—

    (a) indicates, or suggests, that the knife is suitable for combat; or

    (b) is otherwise likely to stimulate or encourage violent behaviour involving the use of the knife as a weapon. [E]

3   Exempt trades

  (1) It is a defence for a person charged with an offence under section 1 to prove that—

    (a) the knife was marketed—

      (i)   for use by the armed forces of any country;

      (ii) as an antique or curio; or

      (iii) as falling within such other category (if any) as may be prescribed;

    (b) it was reasonable for the knife to be marketed in that way; and

    (c) there were no reasonable grounds for suspecting that a person into whose possession the knife might come in consequence of the way in which it was marketed would use it for an unlawful purpose.

  (2) It is a defence for a person charged with an offence under section 2 to prove that—

    (a) the material was published in connection with marketing a knife—

      (i)   for use by the armed forces of any country;

      (ii) as an antique or curio; or

      (iii) as falling within such other category (if any) as may be prescribed.

    (b) it was reasonable for the knife to be marketed in that way; and

    (c) there were no reasonable grounds for suspecting that a person into whose possession the knife might come in consequence of the publishing of the material would use it for an unlawful purpose.

  (3) In this section "prescribed" means prescribed by regulations made by the Secretary of State.

4   Other defences

  (1) It is a defence for a person charged with an offence under section 1 to prove that he did not know or suspect, and had no reasonable grounds for suspecting, that the way in which the knife was marketed—

    (a) amounted to an indication or suggestion that the knife was suitable for combat; or

    (b) was likely to stimulate or encourage violent behaviour involving the use of the knife as a weapon.

  (2) It is a defence for a person charged with an offence under section 2 to prove that he did not know or suspect, and had no reasonable grounds for suspecting, that the material—

    (a) amounted to an indication or suggestion that the knife was suitable for combat; or

    (b) was likely to stimulate or encourage violent behaviour involving the use of the knife as a weapon.

  (3) It is a defence for a person charged with an offence under section 1 or 2 to prove that he took all reasonable precautions and exercised all due diligence to avoid committing the offence.

9   Offences by bodies corporate

  (1) If an offence under this Act committed by a body corporate is proved—

    (a) to have been committed with the consent or connivance of an officer, or

(b) to be attributable to any neglect on his part,

he as well as the body corporate is guilty of be offence and liable to be proceeded against and punished accordingly.

(2) In subsection (1) "officer", in relation to a body corporate, means a director, manager, secretary or other similar officer of the body, or a person purporting to act in any such capacity.

(3) If the affairs of a body corporate are managed by its members, subsection (1) applies in relation to the acts and defaults of a member in connection with his functions of management as if he were a director of the body corporate.

10   Interpretation

In this Act—

"the court" means—

(a) in relation to England and Wales or Northern Ireland, the Crown Court or a magistrate's court;

"knife" means an instrument which has a blade or is sharply pointed;

"marketing" and related expressions are to be read with section 1(4);

"publication" includes a publication in electronic form and, in the case of a publication which is, or may be, produced from electronic data, any medium on which the data are stored;

"suitable for combat" means suitable for use as a weapon for inflicting injury on a person or causing a person to fear injury;

"violent behaviour" means an unlawful act inflicting injury on a person or causing a person to fear injury.

Protection from Harassment Act 1997

1   Prohibition of harassment

(1) A person must not pursue a course of conduct—

(a) which amounts to harassment of another, and

(b) which he knows or ought to know amounts to harassment of the other.

(1A) A person must not pursue a course of conduct—

(a) which involves harassment of two or more persons, and

(b) which he knows or ought to know involves harassment of those persons, and

(c) by which he intends to persuade any person (whether or not one of those mentioned above)—

(i) not to do something that he is entitled or required to do, or

(ii) to do something that he is not under any obligation to do.

(2) For the purposes of this section or section 2A(2)(c), the person whose course of conduct is in question ought to know that it amounts to or involves harassment of another if a reasonable person in possession of the same information would think the course of conduct amounted to or involved harassment of the other.

(3) Subsection (1) or (1A) does not apply to a course of conduct if the person who pursued it shows—

(a) that it was pursued for the purpose of preventing or detecting crime,

(b) that it was pursued under any enactment or rule of law or to comply with any condition or requirement imposed by any person under any enactment, or

(c) that in the particular circumstances the pursuit of the course of conduct was reasonable.

2   Offence of harassment

(1) A person who pursues a course of conduct in breach of section 1(1) or (1A) is guilty of an offence. [S]

2A   Offence of stalking

(1) A person is guilty of an offence if—

(a) the person pursues a course of conduct in breach of section 1(1), and

(b) the course of conduct amounts to stalking. [S]

(2) For the purposes of subsection (1)(b) (and section 4A(1)(a)) a person's course of conduct amounts to stalking of another person if—

(a) it amounts to harassment of that person,

(b) the acts or omissions involved are ones associated with stalking, and

(c) the person whose course of conduct it is knows or ought to know that the course of conduct amounts to harassment of the other person.

(3) The following are examples of acts or omissions which, in particular circumstances, are ones associated with stalking—

(a) following a person,

(b) contacting, or attempting to contact, a person by any means,

(c) publishing any statement or other material—

(i)   relating or purporting to relate to a person, or

(ii)   purporting to originate from a person,

(d) monitoring the use by a person of the internet, email or any other form of electronic communication,

(e) loitering in any place (whether public or private),

(f) interfering with any property in the possession of a person,

(g) watching or spying on a person.

(6) This section is without prejudice to the generality of section 2.

4   Putting people in fear of violence

(1) A person whose course of conduct causes another to fear, on at least two occasions, that violence will be used against him is guilty of an offence if he knows or ought to know that his course of conduct will cause the other so to fear on each of those occasions. [E]

(2) For the purposes of this section, the person whose course of conduct is in question ought to know that it will cause another to fear that violence will be used against him on any occasion if a reasonable person in possession of the same information would think the course of conduct would cause the other so to fear on that occasion.

(3) It is a defence for a person charged with an offence under this section to show that—

(a) his course of conduct was pursued for the purpose of preventing or detecting crime,

(b) his course of conduct was pursued under any enactment or rule of law or to comply with any condition or requirement imposed by any person under any enactment, or

(c) the pursuit of his course of conduct was reasonable for the protection of himself or another or for the protection of his or another's property.

(5) If on the trial on indictment of a person charged with an offence under this section the jury find him not guilty of the offence charged, they may find him guilty of an offence under section 2 or 2A.

(6) The Crown Court has the same powers and duties in relation to a person who is by virtue of subsection (5) convicted before it of an offence under section 2 or 2A as a magistrates' court would have on convicting him of the offence.

4A   Stalking involving fear of violence or serious alarm or distress

(1) A person ("A") whose course of conduct—

(a) amounts to stalking, and

(b) either—

(i)   causes another ("B") to fear, on at least two occasions, that violence will be used against B, or

(ii)   causes B serious alarm or distress which has a substantial adverse effect on B's usual day-to-day activities,

is guilty of an offence if A knows or ought to know that A's course of conduct will cause B so to fear on each of those occasions or (as the case may be) will cause such alarm or distress. [E]

(2) For the purposes of this section A ought to know that A's course of conduct will cause B to fear that violence will be used against B on any occasion if a reasonable person in possession of the same information would think the course of conduct would cause B so to fear on that occasion.

(3) For the purposes of this section A ought to know that A's course of conduct will cause B serious alarm or distress which has a substantial adverse effect on B's usual day-to-day activities if a reasonable person in possession of the same information would think the course of conduct would cause B such alarm or distress.

(4) It is a defence for A to show that—

(a) A's course of conduct was pursued for the purpose of preventing or detecting crime,

(b) A's course of conduct was pursued under any enactment or rule of law or to comply with any condition or requirement imposed by any person under any enactment, or

(c) the pursuit of A's course of conduct was reasonable for the protection of A or another or for the protection of A's or another's property.

(9) This section is without prejudice to the generality of section 4.

4B Offences under sections 4 and 4A committed outside the United Kingdom

(1) If—

(a) a person's course of conduct consists of or includes conduct in a country outside the United Kingdom,

(b) the course of conduct would constitute an offence under section 4 or 4A if it occurred in England and Wales, and

(c) the person is a United Kingdom national or is habitually resident in England and Wales,

the person is guilty in England and Wales of that offence.

(2) In this section—

"country" includes territory;

"United Kingdom national" means an individual who is—

(a) a British citizen, a British overseas territories citizen, a British National (Overseas) or a British Overseas citizen,

(b) a person who under the British Nationality Act 1981 is a British subject, or

(c) a British protected person within the meaning of that Act.

5A Restraining orders on acquittal

(1) A court before which a person ("the defendant") is acquitted of an offence may, if it considers it necessary to do so to protect a person from harassment by the defendant, make an order prohibiting the defendant from doing anything described in the order.

(2) The order may have effect for a specified period or until further order.

(2A) In proceedings under this section both the prosecution and the defence may lead, as further evidence, any evidence that would be admissible in proceedings for an injunction under section 3.

(2B) The prosecutor, the defendant or any other person mentioned in the order may apply to the court that made the order for it to be varied or discharged by a further order.

(2C) Any person mentioned in the order is entitled to be heard on the hearing of an application under subsection (2B).

(2D) It is an offence for the defendant, without reasonable excuse, to do anything that the defendant is prohibited from doing by an order under this section. [E]

(2F) A court dealing with a person for an offence under this section may vary or discharge the order in question by a further order.

(3) Where the Court of Appeal allow an appeal against conviction they may remit the case to the Crown Court to consider whether to proceed under this section.

(4) Where—

(a) the Crown Court allows an appeal against conviction, or

(b) a case is remitted to the Crown Court under subsection (3),

the reference in subsection (1) to a court before which a person is acquitted of an offence is to be read as referring to that court.

(5) A person made subject to an order under this section has the same right of appeal against the order as if—

(a) he had been convicted of the offence in question before the court which made the order, and

(b) the order had been made under section 5.

7   Interpretation of this group of sections

(1) This section applies for the interpretation of sections 1 to 5A.

(2) References to harassing a person include alarming the person or causing the person distress.

(3) A "course of conduct" must involve—

    (a) in the case of conduct in relation to a single person (see section 1(1)), conduct on at least two occasions in relation to that person, or

    (b) in the case of conduct in relation to two or more persons (see section 1(1A)), conduct on at least one occasion in relation to each of those persons.

(3A) A person's conduct on any occasion shall be taken, if aided, abetted, counselled or procured by another—

    (a) to be conduct on that occasion of the other (as well as conduct of the person whose conduct it is); and

    (b) to be conduct in relation to which the other's knowledge and purpose, and what he ought to have known, are the same as they were in relation to what was contemplated or reasonably foreseeable at the time of the aiding, abetting, counselling or procuring.

(4) "Conduct" includes speech.

12   National security, etc.

(1) If the Secretary of State certifies that in his opinion anything done by a specified person on a specified occasion related to—

    (a) national security,

    (b) the economic well-being of the United Kingdom, or

    (c) the prevention or detection of serious crime,

and was done on behalf of the Crown, the certificate is conclusive evidence that this Act does not apply to any conduct of that person on that occasion.

(2) In subsection (1), "specified" means specified in the certificate in question.

Crime and Disorder Act 1998

28   Meaning of "racially or religiously aggravated"

(1) An offence is racially or religiously aggravated for the purposes of sections 29 to 32 below if—

    (a) at the time of committing the offence, or immediately before or after doing so, the offender demonstrates towards the victim of the offence hostility based on the victim's membership (or presumed membership) of a racial or religious group; or

    (b) the offence is motivated (wholly or partly) by hostility towards members of a racial or religious group based on their membership of that group.

(2) In subsection (1)(a) above—

"membership", in relation to a racial or religious group, includes association with members of that group;

"presumed" means presumed by the offender.

(3) It is immaterial for the purposes of paragraph (a) or (b) of subsection (1) above whether or not the offender's hostility is also based, to any extent, on any other factor not mentioned in that paragraph.

(4) In this section "racial group" means a group of persons defined by reference to race, colour, nationality (including citizenship) or ethnic or national origins.

(5) In this section "religious group" means a group of persons defined by reference to religious belief or lack of religious belief.

29   Racially or religiously aggravated assaults

(1) A person is guilty of an offence under this section if he commits—

(a) an offence under section 20 of the Offences Against the Person Act 1861 (malicious wounding or grievous bodily harm);

(b) an offence under section 47 of that Act (actual bodily harm); or

(c) common assault,

which is racially or religiously aggravated for the purposes of this section. [E]

30   Racially or religiously aggravated criminal damage

(1) A person is guilty of an offence under this section if he commits an offence under section 1(1) of the Criminal Damage Act 1971 (destroying or damaging property belonging to another) which is racially or religiously aggravated for the purposes of this section. [E]

(3) For the purposes of this section, section 28(1)(a) above shall have effect as if the person to whom the property belongs or is treated as belonging for the purposes of that Act were the victim of the offence.

31   Racially or religiously aggravated public order offences

(1) A person is guilty of an offence under this section if he commits—

(a) an offence under section 4 of the Public Order Act 1986 (fear or provocation of violence) [E];

(b) an offence under section 4A of that Act (intentional harassment, alarm or distress) [E] or

(c) an offence under section 5 of that Act (harassment, alarm or distress) [S],

which is racially or religiously aggravated for the purposes of this section.

(6) If, on the trial on indictment of a person charged with an offence falling within subsection (1)(a) or (b) above, the jury find him not guilty of the offence charged, they may find him guilty of the basic offence mentioned in that provision.

(7) For the purposes of subsection (1)(c) above, section 28(1)(a) above shall have effect as if the person likely to be caused harassment, alarm or distress were the victim of the offence.

32   Racially or religiously aggravated harassment, etc.

(1) A person is guilty of an offence under this section if he commits—

(a) an offence under section 2 or 2A of the Protection from Harassment Act 1997 (offences of harassment and stalking); or

(b) an offence under section 4 or 4A of that Act (putting people in fear of violence and stalking involving fear of violence or serious alarm or distress),

which is racially or religiously aggravated for the purposes of this section. [E]

(5) If, on the trial on indictment of a person charged with an offence falling within subsection (1)(a) above, the jury find him not guilty of the offence charged, they may find him guilty of the basic offence mentioned in that provision.

(6) If, on the trial on indictment of a person charged with an offence falling within subsection (1)(b) above, the jury find him not guilty of the offence charged, they may find him guilty of an offence failing within subsection (1)(a) above.

34   Abolition of rebuttable presumption that a child is doli incapax

The rebuttable presumption of criminal law that a child aged 10 or over is incapable of committing an offence is hereby abolished.

Human Rights Act 1998

1   The Convention Rights

(1) In this Act "the Convention rights" means the rights and fundamental freedoms set out in—

(a) Articles 2 to 12 and 14 of the Convention,

(b) Articles 1 to 3 of the First Protocol, and

(c) Articles 1 of the Thirteenth Protocol,

as read with Articles 16 to 18 of the Convention.

(2) Those Articles are to have effect for the purposes of this Act subject to any designated derogation or reservation (as to which see sections 14 and 15).

(3) The Articles are set out in Schedule 1.

2   Interpretation of Convention rights

(1) A court or tribunal determining a question which has arisen in connection with a Convention right must take into account any—

    (a) judgment, decision, declaration or advisory opinion of the European Court of Human Rights,

    (b) opinion of the Commission given in a report adopted under Article 31 of the Convention,

    (c) decision of the Commission in connection with Article 26 or 27(2) of the Convention, or

    (d) decision of the Committee of Ministers taken under Article 46 of the Convention,

whenever made or given, so far as, in the opinion of the court or tribunal, it is relevant to the proceedings in which that question has arisen.

(2) Evidence of any judgment, decision, declaration or opinion of which account may have to be taken under this section is to be given in proceedings before any court or tribunal in such manner as may be provided by rules.

3   Interpretation of legislation

(1) So far as it is possible to do so, primary legislation and subordinate legislation must be read and given effect in a way which is compatible with the Convention rights.

(2) This section—

    (a) applies to primary legislation and subordinate legislation whenever enacted;

    (b) does not affect the validity, continuing operation or enforcement of any incompatible primary legislation; and

    (c) does not affect the validity, continuing operation or enforcement of any incompatible subordinate legislation if (disregarding any possibility of revocation) primary legislation prevents removal of the incompatibility.

4   Declaration of incompatibility

(1) Subsection (2) applies in any proceedings in which a court determines whether a provision of primary legislation is compatible with a Convention right.

(2) If the court is satisfied that the provision is incompatible with a Convention right, it may make a declaration of that incompatibility.

(3) Subsection (4) applies in any proceedings in which a court determines whether a provision of subordinate legislation, made in the exercise of a power conferred by primary legislation, is compatible with a Convention right.

(4) If the court is satisfied—

    (a) that the provision is incompatible with a Convention right, and

    (b) that (disregarding any possibility of revocation) the primary legislation concerned prevents removal of the incompatibility,

it may make a declaration of that incompatibility.

(5) In this section "court" means—

    (a) the Supreme Court;

    (b) the Judicial Committee of the Privy Council;

    (c) the Court Martial Appeal Court;

    (e) in England and Wales or Northern Ireland, the High Court or the Court of Appeal;

    (f) the Court of Protection, in any matter being dealt with by the President of the Family Division, the Chancellor of the High Court or a puisne judge of the High Court.

(6) A declaration under this section ("a declaration of incompatibility")—

(a) does not affect the validity, continuing operation or enforcement of the provision in respect of which it is given; and

(b) is not binding on the parties to the proceedings in which it is made.

6 Acts of public authorities

(1) It is unlawful for a public authority to act in a way which is incompatible with a Convention right.

(2) Subsection (1) does not apply to an act if—

(a) as the result of one or more provisions of primary legislation, the authority could not have acted differently; or

(b) in the case of one or more provisions of, or made under, primary legislation which cannot be read or given effect in a way which is compatible with the Convention rights, the authority was acting so as to give effect to or enforce those provisions.

(3) In this section "public authority" includes—

(a) a court or tribunal, and

(b) any person certain of whose functions are functions of a public nature,

but does not include either House of Parliament or a person exercising functions in connection with proceedings in Parliament.

(5) In relation to a particular act, a person is not a public authority by virtue only of subsection (3)(b) if the nature of the act is private.

(6) "An act" includes a failure to act but does not include a failure to—

(a) introduce in, or lay before, Parliament a proposal for legislation; or

(b) make any primary legislation or remedial order.

7 Proceedings

(1) A person who claims that a public authority has acted (or proposes to act) in a way which is made unlawful by section 6(1) may—

(a) bring proceedings against the authority under this Act in the appropriate court or tribunal, or

(b) rely on the Convention right or rights concerned in any legal proceedings,

but only if he is (or would be) a victim of the unlawful act.

(2) In subsection (1)(a) "appropriate court or tribunal" means such court or tribunal as may be determined in accordance with rules; and proceedings against an authority include a counterclaim or similar proceeding.

(3) If the proceedings are brought on an application for judicial review, the applicant is to be taken to have a sufficient interest in relation to the unlawful act only if he is, or would be, a victim of that act.

(6) In subsection (1)(b) "legal proceedings" includes—

(a) proceedings brought by or at the instigation of a public authority; and

(b) an appeal against the decision of a court or tribunal.

(7) For the purposes of this section, a person is a victim of an unlawful act only if he would be a victim for the purposes of Article 34 of the Convention if proceedings were brought in the European Court of Human Rights in respect of that act.

(8) Nothing in this Act creates a criminal offence.

(9) In this section "rules" means —

(a) in relation to proceedings before a court or tribunal outside Scotland, rules made by the Lord Chancellor or the Secretary of State for the purposes of this section or rules of court,

and includes provision made by order under section 1 of the Courts and Legal Services Act 1990.

(10) In making rules, regard must be had to section 9.

SCHEDULE 1 THE ARTICLES

PART I THE CONVENTION

Rights and freedoms

Article 2 Right to life

1. Everyone's right to life shall be protected by law. No one shall be deprived of his life intentionally save in the execution of a sentence of a court following his conviction of a crime for which this penalty is provided by law.

2. Deprivation of life shall not be regarded as inflicted in contravention of this Article when it results from the use of force which is no more than absolutely necessary:

   (a) in defence of any person from unlawful violence;

   (b) in order to effect a lawful arrest or to prevent the escape of a person lawfully detained;

   (c) in action lawfully taken for the purpose of quelling a riot or insurrection.

Article 3 Prohibition of torture

No one shall be subjected to torture or to inhuman or degrading treatment or punishment.

Article 4 Prohibition of slavery and forced labour

1. No one shall be held in slavery or servitude.

2. No one shall be required to perform forced or compulsory labour.

3. For the purpose of this Article the term "forced or compulsory labour" shall not include:

   (a) any work required to be done in the ordinary course of detention imposed according to the provisions of Article 5 of this Convention or during conditional release from such detention;

   (b) any service of a military character or, in case of conscientious objectors in countries where they are recognised, service exacted instead of compulsory military service;

   (c) any service exacted in case of an emergency or calamity threatening the life or well-being of the community;

   (d) any work or service which forms part of normal civic obligations.

Article 5 Right to liberty and security

1. Everyone has the right to liberty and security of person. No one shall be deprived of his liberty save in the following cases and in accordance with a procedure prescribed by law:

   (a) the lawful detention of a person after conviction by a competent court;

   (b) the lawful arrest or detention of a person for non-compliance with the lawful order of a court or in order to secure the fulfilment of any obligation prescribed by law;

   (c) the lawful arrest or detention of a person effected for the purpose of bringing him before the competent legal authority on reasonable suspicion of having committed an offence or when it is reasonably considered necessary to prevent his committing an offence or fleeing after having done so;

   (d) the detention of a minor by lawful order for the purpose of educational supervision or his lawful detention for the purpose of bringing him before the competent legal authority;

   (e) the lawful detention of persons for the prevention of the spreading of infectious diseases, of persons of unsound mind, alcoholics or drug addicts or vagrants;

   (f) the lawful arrest or detention of a person to prevent his effecting an unauthorised entry into the country or of a person against whom action is being taken with a view to deportation or extradition.

2. Everyone who is arrested shall be informed promptly, in a language which he understands, of the reasons for his arrest and of any charge against him.

4. Everyone who is deprived of his liberty by arrest or detention shall be entitled to take proceedings by which the lawfulness of his detention shall be decided speedily by a court and his release ordered if the detention is not lawful.

Article 6   Right to a fair trial

1. In the determination of his civil rights and obligations or of any criminal charge against him, everyone is entitled to a fair and public hearing within a reasonable time by an independent and impartial tribunal established by law. Judgment shall be pronounced publicly but the press and public may be excluded from all or part of the trial in the interest of morals, public order or national security in a democratic society, where the interests of juveniles or the protection of the private life of the parties so require, or to the extent strictly necessary in the opinion of the court in special circumstances where publicity would prejudice the interests of justice.

2. Everyone charged with a criminal offence shall be presumed innocent until proved guilty according to law.

Article 7   No punishment without law

1. No one shall be held guilty of any criminal offence on account of any act or omission which did not constitute a criminal offence under national or international law at the time when it was committed. Nor shall a heavier penalty be imposed than the one that was applicable at the time the criminal offence was committed.

2. This Article shall not prejudice the trial and punishment of any person for any act or omission which, at the time when it was committed, was criminal according to the general principles of law recognised by civilised nations.

Article 8   Right to respect for private and family life

1. Everyone has the right to respect for his private and family life, his home and his correspondence.

2. There shall be no interference by a public authority with the exercise of this right except such as is in accordance with the law and is necessary in a democratic society in the interests of national security, public safety or the economic well being of the country, for the prevention of disorder or crime, for the protection of health or morals, or for the protection of the rights and freedoms of others.

Article 9   Freedom of thought, conscience and religion

1. Everyone has the right to freedom of thought, conscience and religion; this right includes freedom to change his religion or belief and freedom, either alone or in community with others and in public or private, to manifest his religion or belief, in worship, teaching, practice and observance.

2. Freedom to manifest one's religion or beliefs shall he subject only to such limitations as are prescribed by law and are necessary in a democratic society in the interests of public safety, for the protection of public order, health or morals, or for the protection of the rights and freedoms of others.

Article 10   Freedom of expression

1. Everyone has the right to freedom of expression. This right shall include freedom to hold opinions and to receive and impart information and ideas without interference by public authority and regardless of frontiers. This Article shall not prevent States from requiring the licensing of broadcasting television or cinema enterprises.

2. The exercise of these freedoms, since it carries with it duties and responsibilities, may be subject to such formalities, conditions, restrictions or penalties as are prescribed by law and are necessary in a democratic society, in the interests of national security, territorial integrity or public safety, for the prevention of disorder or crime, for the protection of health or morals, for the protection of the reputation or rights of others, for preventing the disclosure of information received in confidence, or for maintaining the authority and impartiality of the judiciary.

Article 11   Freedom of assembly and association

1. Everyone has the right to freedom of peaceful assembly and to freedom of association with others, including the right to form and to join trade unions for the protection of his interests.

2. No restrictions shall be placed on the exercise of these rights other than such as are prescribed by law and are necessary in a democratic society in the interests of national security or public safety, for the prevention of disorder or crime, for the protection of health or morals or for the protection of the rights and freedoms of others. This Article shall not prevent the imposition of lawful restrictions on the exercise of these rights by members of the armed forces, of the police or of the administration of the State.

Article 14   Prohibition of discrimination
The enjoyment of the rights and freedoms set forth in this Convention shall be secured without discrimination on any ground such as sex, race, colour, language, religion, political or other opinion, national or social origin, association with a national minority, property, birth or other status.

Article 16   Restrictions on political activity of aliens
Nothing in Articles 10, 11 and 14 shall be regarded as preventing the High Contracting Parties from imposing restrictions on the political activity of aliens.

Article 17   Prohibition of abuse of rights
Nothing in this Convention may be interpreted as implying for any State, group or person any right to engage in any activity or perform any act aimed at the destruction of any of the rights and freedoms set forth herein or at their limitation to a greater extent than is provided for in the Convention.

Article 18   Limitation on use of restrictions on rights
The restrictions permitted under this Convention to the said rights and freedoms shall not be applied for any purpose other than those for which they have been prescribed.

PART II THE FIRST PROTOCOL

Article 1   Protection of property
Every natural or legal person is entitled to the peaceful enjoyment of his possessions. No one shall be deprived of his possessions except in the public interest and subject to the conditions provided for by law and by the general principles of international law.

The preceding provisions shall not, however, in any way impair the right of a State to enforce such laws as it deems necessary to control the use of property in accordance with the general interest or to secure the payment of taxes or other contributions or penalties.

PART III ARTICLE 1 OF THE THIRTEENTH PROTOCOL

Article 1   Abolition of the death penalty
The death penalty shall be abolished. No one shall be condemned to such penalty or executed.

Postal Services Act 2000

83   Interfering with the mail: postal operators
(1) A person who is engaged in the business of a postal operator commits an offence if, contrary to his duty and without reasonable excuse, he—

(a) intentionally delays or opens a postal packet in the course of its transmission by post, or

(b) intentionally opens a mail-bag. [E]

(2) Subsection (1) does not apply to the delaying or opening of a postal packet or the opening of a mail-bag under the authority of—

(a) this Act or any other enactment (including, in particular, in pursuance of a warrant issued under any other enactment).

(3) Subsection (1) does not apply to the delaying or opening of a postal packet in accordance with any terms and conditions applicable to its transmission by post.

(4) Subsection (1) does not apply to the delaying of a postal packet as a result of industrial action in contemplation or furtherance of a trade dispute.

84   Interfering with the mail: general

(1) A person commits an offence if, without reasonable excuse, he—

(a) intentionally delays or opens a postal packet in the course of its transmission by post, or

(b) intentionally opens a mail-bag. [S]

(2) Subsections (2) to (5) of section 83 apply to subsection (1) above as they apply to subsection (1) of that section.

(3) A person commits an offence if, intending to act to a person's detriment and without reasonable excuse, he opens a postal packet which he knows or reasonably suspects has been incorrectly delivered to him. [S]

(4) Subsections (2) and (3) of section 83 (so far as they relate to the opening of postal packets) apply to subsection (3) above as they apply to subsection (1) of that section.

85   Prohibition on sending certain articles by post

(1) A person commits an offence if he sends by post a postal packet which encloses any creature, article or thing of any kind which is likely to injure other postal packets in course of their transmission by post or any person engaged in the business of a postal operator. [E]

(2) Subsection (1) does not apply to postal packets which enclose anything permitted (whether generally or specifically) by the postal operator concerned.

(3) A person commits an offence if he sends by post a postal packet which encloses—

(a) any indecent or obscene print, painting, photograph, lithograph, engraving, cinematograph film or other record of a picture or pictures, book, card or written communication, or

(b) any other indecent or obscene article (whether or not of a similar kind to those mentioned in paragraph (a)). [E]

(4) A person commits an offence if he sends by post a postal packet which has on the packet, or on the cover of the packet, any words, marks or designs which are of an indecent or obscene character. [E]

86   Additional protection for universal postal service

(1) A person commits an offence if, without due authority, he affixes any advertisement, document, board or thing in or on any universal postal service post office, universal postal service letter box or other property belonging to, or used by, a universal service provider in connection with the provision of a universal postal service. [S]

(2) A person commits an offence if, without due authority, he paints or in any way disfigures any such office, box or property. [S]

(4) In this Act—

"universal postal service letter box" means any box or receptacle provided by a universal service provider for the purpose of receiving postal packets, or any class of postal packets, for onwards transmission in connection with the provision of a universal postal service, and

"universal postal service post office" includes any house, building, room, vehicle or place used for the provision of any postal services in connection with the provision of a universal postal service or a part of such a service.

88 Obstruction of business of universal service providers

(1) A person commits an offence if, without reasonable excuse, he—

(a) obstructs a person engaged in the business of a universal service provider in the execution of his duty in connection with the provision of a universal postal service, or

(b) obstructs, while in any universal postal service post office or related premises, the course of business of a universal service provider. [S]

Terrorism Act 2000

1 Terrorism: interpretation

(1) In this Act "terrorism" means the use or threat of action where—

(a) the action falls within subsection (2),

(b) the use or threat is designed to influence the government or an international governmental organisation or to intimidate the public or a section of the public, and

(c) the use or threat is made for the purpose of advancing a political, religious, racial or ideological cause.

(2) Action falls within this subsection if it—

(a) involves serious violence against a person,

(b) involves serious damage to property,

(c) endangers a person's life, other than that of the person committing the action,

(d) creates a serious risk to the health or safety of the public or a section of the public, or

(e) is designed seriously to interfere with or seriously to disrupt an electronic system.

(3) The use or threat of action falling within subsection (2) which involves the use of firearms or explosives is terrorism whether or not subsection (1)(b) is satisfied.

(4) In this section—

(a) "action" includes action outside the United Kingdom,

(b) a reference to any person or to property is a reference to any person, or to property, wherever situated,

(c) a reference to the public includes a reference to the public of a country other than the United Kingdom, and

(d) "the government" means the government of the United Kingdom, of a part of the United Kingdom or of a country other than the United Kingdom.

(5) In this Act a reference to action taken for the purposes of terrorism includes a reference to action taken for the benefit of a proscribed organisation.

3 Proscription

(1) For the purposes of this Act an organisation is proscribed if—

(a) it is listed in Schedule 2, or

(b) it operates under the same name as an organisation listed in that Schedule.

11 Membership

(1) A person commits an offence if he belongs or professes to belong to a proscribed organisation. [I]

(2) It is a defence for a person charged with an offence under subsection (1) to prove—

(a) that the organisation was not proscribed on the last (or only) occasion on which he became a member or began to profess to be a member, and

(b) that he has not taken part in the activities of the organisation at any time while it was proscribed.

(4) In subsection (2) "proscribed" means proscribed for the purposes of any of the following—

(a) this Act;

(b) the Northern Ireland (Emergency Provisions) Act 1996;

(c) the Northern Ireland (Emergency Provisions) Act 1991;

(d) the Prevention of Terrorism (Temporary Provisions) Act 1989;

(e) the Prevention of Terrorism (Temporary Provisions) Act 1984;

(f) the Northern Ireland (Emergency Provisions) Act 1978;

(g) the Prevention of Terrorism (Temporary Provisions) Act 1976;

(h) the Prevention of Terrorism (Temporary Provisions) Act 1974;

(i) the Northern Ireland (Emergency Provisions) Act 1973.

12 Support

(1) A person commits an offence if—

(a) he invites support for a proscribed organisation, and

(b) the support is not, or is not restricted to, the provision of money or other property (within the meaning of section 15). [I]

(1A) A person commits an offence if the person—

(a) expresses an opinion or belief that is supportive of a proscribed organisation, and

(b) in doing so is reckless as to whether a person to whom the expression is directed will be encouraged to support a proscribed organisation.

(2) A person commits an offence if he arranges, manages or assists in arranging or managing a meeting which he knows is—

(a) to support a proscribed organisation,

(b) to further the activities of a proscribed organisation, or

(c) to be addressed by a person who belongs or professes to belong to a proscribed organisation. [I]

(3) A person commits an offence if he addresses a meeting and the purpose of his address is to encourage support for a proscribed organisation or to further its activities. [I]

(4) Where a person is charged with an offence under subsection (2)(c) in respect of a private meeting it is a defence for him to prove that he had no reasonable cause to believe that the address mentioned in subsection (2)(c) would support a proscribed organisation or further its activities.

(5) In subsections (2) to (4)—

(a) "meeting" means a meeting of three or more persons, whether or not the public are admitted, and

(b) a meeting is private if the public are not admitted.

13 Uniform and publication of images

(1) A person in a public place commits an offence if he—

(a) wears an item of clothing, or

(b) wears, carries or displays an article,

in such a way or in such circumstances as to arouse reasonable suspicion that he is a member or supporter of a proscribed organisation. [E]

(1A) A person commits an offence if the person publishes an image of—

(a) an item of clothing, or

(b) any other article,

in such a way or in such circumstances as to arouse reasonable suspicion that the person is a member or supporter of a proscribed organisation.

(1B) In subsection (1A) the reference to an image is a reference to a still or moving image (produced by any means).

14 Terrorist property

(1) In this Act "terrorist property" means—

(a) money or other property which is likely to be used for the purposes of terrorism (including any resources of a proscribed organisation),

(b) proceeds of the commission of acts of terrorism, and

(c) proceeds of acts carried out for the purposes of terrorism.

(2) In subsection (1)—

    (a) a reference to proceeds of an act includes a reference to any property which wholly or partly, and directly or indirectly, represents the proceeds of the act (including payments or other rewards in connection with its commission), and

    (b) the reference to an organisation's resources includes a reference to any money or other property which is applied or made available, or is to be applied or made available, for use by the organisation.

15 Fund-raising

(1) A person commits an offence if he—

    (a) invites another to provide money or other property, and

    (b) intends that it should be used, or has reasonable cause to suspect that it may be used, for the purposes of terrorism. [I]

(2) A person commits an offence if he—

    (a) receives money or other property, and

    (b) intends that it should be used, or has reasonable cause to suspect that it may be used, for the purposes of terrorism. [I]

(3) A person commits an offence if he—

    (a) provides money or other property, and

    (b) knows or has reasonable cause to suspect that it will or may be used for the purposes of terrorism. [I]

(4) In this section a reference to the provision of money or other property is a reference to its being given, lent or otherwise made available, whether or not for consideration.

16 Use and possession

(1) A person commits an offence if he uses money or other property for the purposes of terrorism.

(2) A person commits an offence if he—

    (a) possesses money or other property, and

    (b) intends that it should be used, or has reasonable cause to suspect that it may be used, for the purposes of terrorism. [I]

17 Funding arrangements

A person commits an offence if—

    (a) he enters into or becomes concerned in an arrangement as a result of which money or other property is made available or is to be made available to another, and

    (b) he knows or has reasonable cause to suspect that it will or may be used for the purposes of terrorism. [I]

18 Money laundering

(1) A person commits an offence if he enters into or becomes concerned in an arrangement which facilitates the retention or control by or on behalf of another person of terrorist property—

    (a) by concealment,

    (b) by removal from the jurisdiction,

    (c) by transfer to nominees, or

    (d) in any other way. [I]

(2) It is a defence for a person charged with an offence under subsection (1) to prove that he did not know and had no reasonable cause to suspect that the arrangement related to terrorist property.

19 Disclosure of information: duty

(1) This section applies where a person—

    (a) believes or suspects that another person has committed an offence under any of sections 15 to 18, and

    (b) bases his belief or suspicion on information which comes to his attention—

(i)   in the course of a trade, profession or business, or

(ii) in the course of his employment (whether or not in the course of a trade, profession or business).

(1A) But this section does not apply if the information came to the person in the course of a business in the regulated sector.

(2) The person commits an offence if he does not disclose to a constable as soon as is reasonably practicable—

(a) his belief or suspicion, and

(b) the information on which it is based. [E]

(3) It is a defence for a person charged with an offence under subsection (2) to prove that he had a reasonable excuse for not making the disclosure.

(4) Where—

(a) a person is in employment,

(b) his employer has established a procedure for the making of disclosures of the matters specified in subsection (2), and

(c) he is charged with an offence under that subsection,

it is a defence for him to prove that he disclosed the matters specified in that subsection in accordance with the procedure.

(5) Subsection (2) does not require disclosure by a professional legal adviser of—

(a) information which he obtains in privileged circumstances, or

(b) a belief or suspicion based on information which he obtains in privileged circumstances.

(6) For the purpose of subsection (5) information is obtained by an adviser in privileged circumstances if it comes to him, otherwise than with a view to furthering a criminal purpose—

(a) from a client or a client's representative, in connection with the provision of legal advice by the adviser to the client,

(b) from a person seeking legal advice from the adviser, or from the person's representative, or

(c) from any person, for the purpose of actual or contemplated legal proceedings.

(7) For the purposes of subsection (1)(a) a person shall be treated as having committed an offence under one of sections 15 to 18 if—

(a) he has taken an action or been in possession of a thing, and

(b) he would have committed an offence under one of those sections if he had been in the United Kingdom at the time when he took the action or was in possession of the thing.

(7A) The reference to a business in the regulated sector must be construed in accordance with Schedule 3A.

(7B) The reference to a constable includes a reference to a National Crime Agency officer authorised for the purposes of this section by the Director General of that Agency.

21   Cooperation with police

(1) A person does not commit an offence under any of sections 15 to 18 if he is acting with the express consent of a constable.

(2) Subject to subsections (3) and (4), a person does not commit an offence under any of sections 15 to 18 by involvement in a transaction or arrangement relating to money or other property if he discloses to a constable—

(a) his suspicion or belief that the money or other property is terrorist property, and

(b) the information on which his suspicion or belief is based.

(3) Subsection (2) applies only where a person makes a disclosure—

(a) after he becomes concerned in the transaction concerned,

(b) on his own initiative, and

(c) as soon as is reasonably practicable.

(4) Subsection (2) does not apply to a person if—

(a) a constable forbids him to continue his involvement in the transaction or arrangement to which the disclosure relates, and

(b) he continues his involvement.

(5) It is a defence for a person charged with an offence under any of sections 15(2) and (3) and 16 to 18 to prove that—

(a) he intended to make a disclosure of the kind mentioned in subsections (2) and (3), and

(b) there is reasonable excuse for his failure to do so.

(6) Where—

(a) a person is in employment, and

(b) his employer has established a procedure for the making of disclosures of the same kind as may be made to a constable under subsection (2),

this section shall have effect in relation to that person as if any reference to disclosure to a constable included a reference to disclosure in accordance with the procedure.

(7) A reference in this section to a transaction or arrangement relating to money or other property includes a reference to use or possession.

21ZA   Arrangements with prior consent

(1) A person does not commit an offence under any of sections 15 to 18 by involvement in a transaction or an arrangement relating to money or other property if, before becoming involved, the person—

(a) discloses to an authorised officer the person's suspicion or belief that the money or other property is terrorist property and the information on which the suspicion or belief is based, and

(b) has the authorised officer's consent to becoming involved in the transaction or arrangement.

(2) A person is treated as having an authorised officer's consent if before the end of the notice period the person does not receive notice from an authorised officer that consent is refused.

(3) The notice period is the period of 7 working days starting with the first working day after the person makes the disclosure.

(4) A working day is a day other than a Saturday, a Sunday, Christmas Day, Good Friday or a day that is a bank holiday under the Banking and Financial Dealings Act 1971 in the part of the United Kingdom in which the person is when making the disclosure.

(5) In this section "authorised officer" means a National Crime Agency officer authorised for the purposes of this section by the Director General of that Agency.

(6) The reference in this section to a transaction or arrangement relating to money or other property includes a reference to use or possession.

21ZB   Disclosure after entering into arrangements

(1) A person does not commit an offence under any of sections 15 to 18 by involvement in a transaction or an arrangement relating to money or other property if, after becoming involved, the person discloses to an authorised officer—

(a) the person's suspicion or belief that the money or other property is terrorist property, and

(b) the information on which the suspicion or belief is based.

(2) This section applies only where—

(a) there is a reasonable excuse for the person's failure to make the disclosure before becoming involved in the transaction or arrangement, and

(b) the disclosure is made on the person's own initiative and as soon as it is reasonably practicable for the person to make it.

(3) This section does not apply to a person if—

(a) an authorised officer forbids the person to continue involvement in the transaction or arrangement to which the disclosure relates, and

(b) the person continues that involvement.

(4) In this section "authorised officer" means a National Crime Agency officer authorised for the purposes of this section by the Director General of that Agency.

(5) The reference in this section to a transaction or arrangement relating to money or other property includes a reference to use or possession.

21ZC　Reasonable excuse for failure to disclose

It is a defence for a person charged with an offence under any of sections 15 to 18 to prove that—

- (a) the person intended to make a disclosure of the kind mentioned in section 21ZA or 21ZB, and
- (b) there is a reasonable excuse for the person's failure to do so.

21A　Failure to disclose: regulated sector

(1) A person commits an offence if each of the following three conditions is satisfied. [E]

(2) The first condition is that he—

- (a) knows or suspects, or
- (b) has reasonable grounds for knowing or suspecting,

that another person has committed or attempted to commit an offence under any of sections 15 to 18.

(3) The second condition is that the information or other matter—

- (a) on which his knowledge or suspicion is based, or
- (b) which gives reasonable grounds for such knowledge or suspicion,

came to him in the course of a business in the regulated sector.

(4) The third condition is that he does not disclose the information or other matter to a constable or a nominated officer as soon as is practicable after it comes to him.

(5) But a person does not commit an offence under this section if—

- (a) he has a reasonable excuse for not disclosing the information or other matter;
- (b) he is a professional legal adviser or relevant professional adviser and the information or other matter came to him in privileged circumstances;
- (c) subsection (5A) applies to him.

(5A) This subsection applies to a person if—

- (a) the person is employed by, or is in partnership with, a professional legal adviser or relevant professional adviser to provide the adviser with assistance or support,
- (b) the information or other matter comes to the person in connection with the provision of such assistance or support, and
- (c) the information or other matter came to the adviser in privileged circumstances.

(6) In deciding whether a person committed an offence under this section the court must consider whether he followed any relevant guidance which was at the time concerned—

- (a) issued by a supervisory authority or any other appropriate body,
- (b) approved by the Treasury, and
- (c) published in a manner it approved as appropriate in its opinion to bring the guidance to the attention of persons likely to be affected by it.

(7) A disclosure to a nominated officer is a disclosure which—

- (a) is made to a person nominated by the alleged offender's employer to receive disclosures under this section, and
- (b) is made in the course of the alleged offender's employment and in accordance with the procedure established by the employer for the purpose.

(8) Information or other matter comes to a professional legal adviser or relevant professional adviser in privileged circumstances if it is communicated or given to him—

- (a) by (or by a representative of) a client of his in connection with the giving by the adviser of legal advice to the client,
- (b) by (or by a representative of) a person seeking legal advice from the adviser, or
- (c) by a person in connection with legal proceedings or contemplated legal proceedings.

(9) But subsection (8) does not apply to information or other matter which is communicated or given with a view to furthering a criminal purpose.

(10) Schedule 3A has effect for the purpose of determining what is—

- (a) a business in the regulated sector;
- (b) a supervisory authority.

(11) For the purposes of subsection (2) a person is to be taken to have committed an offence there mentioned if—

    (a) he has taken an action or been in possession of a thing, and

    (b) he would have committed the offence if he had been in the United Kingdom at the time when he took the action or was in possession of the thing.

(13) An appropriate body is any body which regulates or is representative of any trade, profession, business or employment carried on by the alleged offender.

(14) The reference to a constable includes a reference to a National Crime Agency officer authorised for the purposes of this section by the Director General of that Agency.

(15) In this section "relevant professional adviser" means an accountant, auditor or tax adviser who is a member of a professional body which is established for accountants, auditors or tax advisers (as the case may be) and which makes provision for—

    (a) testing the competence of those seeking admission to membership of such a body as a condition for such admission; and

    (b) imposing and maintaining professional and ethical standards for its members, as well as imposing sanctions for non-compliance with those standards.

22A Meaning of "employment"

In sections 19 to 21B—

    (a) "employment" means any employment (whether paid or unpaid) and includes—

        (i) work under a contract for services or as an office-holder,

        (ii) work experience provided pursuant to a training course or programme or in the course of training for employment, and

        (iii) voluntary work;

    (b) "employer" has a corresponding meaning.

38B Information about acts of terrorism

(1) This section applies where a person has information which he knows or believes might be of material assistance—

    (a) in preventing the commission by another person of an act of terrorism, or

    (b) in securing the apprehension, prosecution or conviction of another person, in the United Kingdom, for an offence involving the commission, preparation or instigation of an act of terrorism.

(2) The person commits an offence if he does not disclose the information as soon as reasonably practicable in accordance with subsection (3). [E]

(3) Disclosure is in accordance with this subsection if it is made—

    (a) in England and Wales, to a constable,

(4) It is a defence for a person charged with an offence under subsection (2) to prove that he had a reasonable excuse for not making the disclosure.

(6) Proceedings for an offence under this section may be taken, and the offence may for the purposes of those proceedings be treated as having been committed, in any place where the person to be charged is or has at any time been since he first knew or believed that the information might be of material assistance as mentioned in subsection (1).

39 Disclosure of information, etc.

(1) Subsection (2) applies where a person knows or has reasonable cause to suspect that a constable is conducting or proposes to conduct a terrorist investigation.

(2) The person commits an offence if he—

    (a) discloses to another anything which is likely to prejudice the investigation, or

    (b) interferes with material which is likely to be relevant to the investigation. [E]

(3) Subsection (4) applies where a person knows or has reasonable cause to suspect that a disclosure has been or will be made under any of sections 19 to 21B or 38B.

(4) The person commits an offence if he—

(a) discloses to another anything which is likely to prejudice an investigation resulting from the disclosure under that section, or

(b) interferes with material which is likely to be relevant to an investigation resulting from the disclosure under that section. [E]

(5) It is a defence for a person charged with an offence under subsection (2) or (4) to prove—

(a) that he did not know and had no reasonable cause to suspect that the disclosure or interference was likely to affect a terrorist investigation, or

(b) that he had a reasonable excuse for the disclosure or interference.

(6) Subsections (2) and (4) do not apply to a disclosure which is made by a professional legal adviser—

(a) to his client or to his client's representative in connection with the provision of legal advice by the adviser to the client and not with a view to furthering a criminal purpose, or

(b) to any person for the purpose of actual or contemplated legal proceedings and not with a view to furthering a criminal purpose.

(8) For the purposes of this section—

(a) a reference to conducting a terrorist investigation includes a reference to taking part in the conduct of, or assisting, a terrorist investigation, and

(b) a person interferes with material if he falsifies it, conceals it, destroys it or disposes of it, or if he causes or permits another to do any of those things.

48   Authorisations

(1) An authorisation under this section authorises any constable in uniform to prohibit or restrict the parking of vehicles on a road specified in the authorisation.

(2) An authorisation may be given only if the person giving it considers it expedient for the prevention of acts of terrorism.

(3) An authorisation may be given—

(a) where the road specified is in England and Wales and is wholly or partly within a police area other than one mentioned in paragraphs (b) or (c), by a police officer for the area who is of at least the rank of assistant chief constable;

(b) where the road specified is wholly or partly in the metropolitan police district, by a police officer for the district who is of at least the rank of commander of the metropolitan police;

(c) where the road specified is wholly or partly in the City of London, by a police officer for the City who is of at least the rank of commander in the City of London police force; . . .

(4) If an authorisation is given orally, the person giving it shall confirm it in writing as soon as is reasonably practicable.

49   Exercise of power

(1) The power conferred by an authorisation under section 48 shall be exercised by placing a traffic sign on the road concerned.

51   Offences

(1) A person commits an offence if he parks a vehicle in contravention of a prohibition or restriction imposed by virtue of section 48. [S]

(2) A person commits an offence if—

(a) he is the driver or other person in charge of a vehicle which has been permitted to remain at rest in contravention of any prohibition or restriction imposed by virtue of section 48, and

(b) he fails to move the vehicle when ordered to do so by a constable in uniform. [S]

(3) It is a defence for a person charged with an offence under this section to prove that he had a reasonable excuse for the act or omission in question.

(4) Possession of a current disabled person's badge shall not itself constitute a reasonable excuse for the purposes of subsection (3).

52 Interpretation

In sections 48 to 51—

"disabled person's badge" means a badge issued, or having effect as if issued, under any regulations for the time being in force under section 21 of the Chronically Sick and Disabled Persons Act 1970 . . . ;

"driver" means, in relation to a vehicle which has been left on any road, the person who was driving it when it was left there;

"parking" means leaving a vehicle or permitting it to remain at rest;

"traffic sign" has the meaning given in section 142(1) of the Road Traffic Regulation Act 1984 . . . ;

"vehicle" has the same meaning as in section 99(5) of the Road Traffic Regulation Act 1984 . . .

54 Weapons training

(1) A person commits an offence if he provides instruction or training in the making or use of—
   (a) firearms,
   (aa) radioactive material or weapons designed or adapted for the discharge of any radioactive material,
   (b) explosives, or
   (c) chemical, biological or nuclear weapons. [E]

(2) A person commits an offence if he receives instruction or training in the making or use of—
   (a) firearms,
   (aa) radioactive material or weapons designed or adapted for the discharge of any radioactive material,
   (b) explosives, or
   (c) chemical, biological or nuclear weapons. [E]

(3) A person commits an offence if he invites another to receive instruction or training and the receipt—
   (a) would constitute an offence under subsection (2), or
   (b) would constitute an offence under subsection (2) but for the fact that it is to take place outside the United Kingdom. [E]

(4) For the purpose of subsections (1) and (3)—
   (a) a reference to the provision of instruction includes a reference to making it available either generally or to one or more specific persons, and
   (b) an invitation to receive instruction or training may be either general or addressed to one or more specific persons.

(5) It is a defence for a person charged with an offence under this section in relation to instruction or training to prove that his action or involvement was wholly for a purpose other than assisting, preparing for or participating in terrorism.

55 Weapons training: interpretation

In section 54—

"biological weapon" means a biological agent or toxin (within the meaning of the Biological Weapons Act 1974) in a form capable of use for hostile purposes or anything to which section 1(1)(b) of that Act applies,

"chemical weapon" has the meaning given by section 1 of the Chemical Weapons Act 1996, and

"radioactive material" means radioactive material capable of endangering life or causing harm to human health.

56 Directing terrorist organisation

(1) A person commits an offence if he directs, at any level, the activities of an organisation which is concerned in the commission of acts of terrorism. [I]

57 Possession for terrorist purposes

(1) A person commits an offence if he possesses an article in circumstances which give rise to a reasonable suspicion that his possession is for a purpose connected with the commission, preparation or instigation of an act of terrorism. [E]

(2) It is a defence for a person charged with an offence under this section to prove that his possession of the article was not for a purpose connected with the commission, preparation or instigation of an act of terrorism.

(3) In proceedings for an offence under this section, if it is proved that an article—

    (a) was on any premises at the same time as the accused, or

    (b) was on premises of which the accused was the occupier or which he habitually used otherwise than as a member of the public,

the court may assume that the accused possessed the article, unless he proves that he did not know of its presence on the premises or that he had no control over it.

58 Collection of information

(1) A person commits an offence if—

    (a) he collects or makes a record of information of a kind likely to be useful to a person committing or preparing an act of terrorism,

    (b) he possesses a document or record containing information of that kind, or [E]

    (c) the person views, or otherwise accesses, by means of the internet a document or record containing information of that kind.

(1A) The cases in which a person collects or makes a record for the purposes of subsection (1)(a) include (but are not limited to) those in which the person does so by means of the internet (whether by downloading the record or otherwise).

(2) In this section "record" includes a photographic or electronic record.

(3) It is a defence for a person charged with an offence under this section to prove that he had a reasonable excuse for his action or possession.

(3A) The cases in which a person has a reasonable excuse for the purposes of subsection (3) include (but are not limited to) those in which—

    (a) at the time of the person's action or possession the person did not know, and had no reason to believe, that the document or record in question contained, or was likely to contain, information of a kind likely to be useful to a person committing or preparing an act of terrorism, or

    (b) the person's action or possession was for the purposes of—

        (i) carrying out work as a journalist, or

        (ii) academic research.

58A Eliciting, publishing or communicating information about members of armed forces etc.

(1) A person commits an offence who—

    (a) elicits or attempts to elicit information about an individual who is or has been—

        (i) a member of Her Majesty's forces,

        (ii) a member of any of the intelligence services, or

        (iii) a constable,

    which is of a kind likely to be useful to a person committing or preparing an act of terrorism, or

    (b) publishes or communicates any such information.

(2) It is a defence for a person charged with an offence under this section to prove that they had a reasonable excuse for their action. [E]

(4) In this section "the intelligence services" means the Security Service, the Secret Intelligence Service and GCHQ (within the meaning of section 3 of the Intelligence Services Act 1994).

58B Entering or remaining in a designated area

(1) Subject to subsections (3) and (4), a person commits an offence if—

    (a) the person enters, or remains in, a designated area, and

    (b) the person is a United Kingdom national, or a United Kingdom resident, at the time of entering the area or at any time during which the person remains there.

(2) It is a defence for a person charged with an offence under this section to prove that the person had a reasonable excuse for entering, or remaining in, the designated area.

(3) A person does not commit an offence under this section of entering, or remaining in, a designated area if—

> (a) the person is already travelling to, or is already in, the area on the day on which it becomes a designated area, and
>
> (b) the person leaves the area before the end of the period of one month beginning with that day.

(4) A person does not commit an offence under this section of entering, or remaining in, a designated area if—

> (a) the person enters, or remains in, a designated area involuntarily, or
>
> (b) the person enters, or remains in, a designated area for or in connection with one or more of the purposes mentioned in subsection (5).

(5) The purposes are—

> (a) providing aid of a humanitarian nature;
>
> (b) satisfying an obligation to appear before a court or other body exercising judicial power;
>
> (c) carrying out work for the government of a country other than the United Kingdom (including service in or with the country's armed forces);
>
> (d) carrying out work for the United Nations or an agency of the United Nations;
>
> (e) carrying out work as a journalist;
>
> (f) attending the funeral of a relative or visiting a relative who is terminally ill;
>
> (g) providing care for a relative who is unable to care for themselves without such assistance.

(6) But a person does not commit an offence of entering or remaining in a designated area by virtue of subsection (4)(b) only if—

> (a) the person enters or remains in the area exclusively for or in connection with one or more of the purposes mentioned in subsection (5), or
>
> (b) in a case where the person enters or remains in the area for or in connection with any other purpose or purposes (in addition to one or more of the purposes mentioned in subsection (5)), the other purpose or purposes provide a reasonable excuse for doing so under subsection (2).

(8) For the purposes of subsection (5)—

> (a) the reference to the provision of aid of a humanitarian nature does not include the provision of aid in contravention of internationally recognised principles and standards applicable to the provision of humanitarian aid;
>
> (b) references to the carrying out of work do not include the carrying out of any act which constitutes an offence in a part of the United Kingdom or would do so if the act occurred in a part of the United Kingdom;
>
> (c) a person is "terminally ill" at any time if at that time the person suffers from a progressive disease and the person's death in consequence of that disease can reasonably be expected within 6 months.

(10) In this section—

"designated area" means an area outside the United Kingdom that is for the time being designated for the purposes of this section in regulations under section 58C;

"relative" means spouse or civil partner, brother, sister, ancestor or lineal descendant;

"United Kingdom national" means an individual who is—

> (a) a British citizen, a British overseas territories citizen, a British National (Overseas) or a British Overseas citizen,
>
> (b) a person who under the British Nationality Act 1981 is a British subject, or
>
> (c) a British protected person within the meaning of that Act;

"United Kingdom resident" means an individual who is resident in the United Kingdom.

(12) Nothing in this section imposes criminal liability on any person acting on behalf of, or holding office under, the Crown.

59   Inciting terrorism overseas

(1) A person commits an offence if—

    (a) he incites another person to commit an act of terrorism wholly or partly outside the United Kingdom, and

    (b) the act would, if committed in England and Wales, constitute one of the offences listed in subsection (2).

(2) Those offences are—

    (a) murder,

    (b) an offence under section 18 of the Offences against the Person Act 1861 (wounding with intent),

    (c) an offence under section 23 or 24 of that Act (poison),

    (d) an offence under section 28 or 29 of that Act (explosions), and

    (e) an offence under section 1(2) of the Criminal Damage Act 1971 (endangering life by damaging property).

(3) A person guilty of an offence under this section shall be liable to any penalty to which he would be liable on conviction of the offence listed in subsection (2) which corresponds to the act which he incites.

(4) For the purposes of subsection (1) it is immaterial whether or not the person incited is in the United Kingdom at the time of the incitement.

(5) Nothing in this section imposes criminal liability on any person acting on behalf of, or holding office under, the Crown.

62   Terrorist bombing: jurisdiction

(1) If—

    (a) a person does anything outside the United Kingdom as an act of terrorism or for the purposes of terrorism, and

    (b) his action would have constituted the commission of one of the offences listed in subsection (2) if it had been done in the United Kingdom,

he shall be guilty of the offence.

(2) The offences referred to in subsection (1)(b) are—

    (a) an offence under section 2, 3 or 5 of the Explosive Substances Act 1883 (causing explosions etc.),

    (b) an offence under section 1 of the Biological Weapons Act 1974 (biological weapons), and

    (c) an offence under section 2 of the Chemical Weapons Act 1996 (chemical weapons).

118   Defences

(1) Subsection (2) applies where in accordance with a provision mentioned in subsection (5) it is a defence for a person charged with an offence to prove a particular matter.

(2) If the person adduces evidence which is sufficient to raise an issue with respect to the matter the court or jury shall assume that the defence is satisfied unless the prosecution proves beyond reasonable doubt that it is not.

(3) Subsection (4) applies where in accordance with a provision mentioned in subsection (5) a court—

    (a) may make an assumption in relation to a person charged with an offence unless a particular matter is proved, or

    (b) may accept a fact as sufficient evidence unless a particular matter is proved.

(4) If evidence is adduced which is sufficient to raise an issue with respect to the matter mentioned in subsection (3)(a) or (b) the court shall treat it as proved unless the prosecution disproves it beyond reasonable doubt.

(5) The provisions in respect of which subsections (2) and (4) apply are—

(a) sections 12(4), 39(5)(a), 54, 57, 58, 58A, 58B, 77 and 103 of this Act, . . .

121   Interpretation

In this Act—

"act" and "action" include omission,

"article" includes substance and any other thing,

"counter-terrorism financial investigator" is to be read in accordance with section 63F,

"customs officer" means an officer of Revenue and Customs,

"dwelling" means a building or part of a building used as a dwelling, and a vehicle which is habitually stationary and which is used as a dwelling,

"explosive" means—

(a) an article or substance manufactured for the purpose of producing a practical effect by explosion,

(b) materials for making an article or substance within paragraph (a),

(c) anything used or intended to be used for causing or assisting in causing an explosion, and

(d) a part of anything within paragraph (a) or (c),

"firearm" includes an air gun or air pistol,

"immigration officer" means a person appointed as an immigration officer under paragraph 1 of Schedule 2 to the Immigration Act 1971,

"the Islands" means the Channel Islands and the Isle of Man,

"organisation" includes any association or combination of persons,

"premises", except in section 63D, includes any place and in particular includes—

(a) a vehicle,

(b) an offshore installation within the meaning given in section 44 of the Petroleum Act 1998, and

(c) a tent or moveable structure,

"property" includes property wherever situated and whether real or personal, heritable or moveable, and things in action and other intangible or incorporeal property,

"public place" means a place to which members of the public have or are permitted to have access, whether or not for payment,

"road" has the same meaning as in the Road Traffic Act 1988 (in relation to England and Wales), . . . and includes part of a road, and

"vehicle", except in sections 48 to 52 and Schedule 7, includes an aircraft, hovercraft, train or vessel.

Anti-Terrorism, Crime and Security Act 2001

113   Use of noxious substances or things to cause harm and intimidate

(1) A person who takes any action which—

(a) involves the use of a noxious substance or other noxious thing;

(b) has or is likely to have an effect falling within subsection (2); and

(c) is designed to influence the government or an international governmental organisation or to intimidate the public or a section of the public,

is guilty of an offence. [E]

(2) Action has an effect falling within this subsection if it—

(a) causes serious violence against a person anywhere in the world;

(b) causes serious damage to real or personal property anywhere in the world;

(c) endangers human life or creates a serious risk to the health or safety of the public or a section of the public; or

(d) induces in members of the public the fear that the action is likely to endanger their lives or create a serious risk to their health or safety;

but any effect on the person taking the action is to be disregarded.

(3) A person who—

(a) makes a threat that he or another will take any action which constitutes an offence under subsection (1); and

(b) intends thereby to induce in a person anywhere in the world the fear that the threat is likely to be carried out,

is guilty of an offence. [E]

(5) In this section—

"the government" means the government of the United Kingdom, of a part of the United Kingdom or of a country other than the United Kingdom; and

"the public" includes the public of a country other than the United Kingdom.

114 Hoaxes involving noxious substances or things

(1) A person is guilty of an offence if he—

(a) places any substance or other thing in any place; or

(b) sends any substance or other thing from one place to another (by post, rail or any other means whatever);

with the intention of inducing in a person anywhere in the world a belief that it is likely to be (or contain) a noxious substance or other noxious thing and thereby endanger human life or create a serious risk to human health. [E]

(2) A person is guilty of an offence if he communicates any information which he knows or believes to be false with the intention of inducing in a person anywhere in the world a belief that a noxious substance or other noxious thing is likely to be present (whether at the time the information is communicated or later) in any place and thereby endanger human life or create a serious risk to human health. [E]

115 Sections 113 and 114: supplementary

(1) For the purposes of sections 113 and 114 "substance" includes any biological agent and any other natural or artificial substance (whatever its form, origin or method of production).

(2) For a person to be guilty of an offence under section 113(3) or 114 it is not necessary for him to have any particular person in mind as the person in whom he intends to induce the belief in question.

Criminal Justice and Police Act 2001

39 Intimidation of witnesses

(1) A person commits an offence if—

(a) he does an act which intimidates, and is intended to intimidate, another person ("the victim");

(b) he does the act—

(i) knowing or believing that the victim is or may be a witness in any relevant proceedings; and

(ii) intending, by his act, to cause the course of justice to be obstructed, perverted or interfered with; and

(c) the act is done after the commencement of those proceedings. [E]

(2) For the purposes of subsection (1) it is immaterial—

(a) whether or not the act that is done is done in the presence of the victim;

(b) whether that act is done to the victim himself or to another person; and

(c) whether or not the intention to cause the course of justice to be obstructed, perverted or interfered with is the predominating intention of the person doing the act in question.

(3) If, in proceedings against a person for an offence under this section, it is proved—

(a) that he did any act that intimidated, and was intended to intimidate, another person, and

(b) that he did that act knowing or believing that that other person was or might be a witness in any relevant proceedings that had already commenced,

he shall be presumed, unless the contrary is shown, to have done the act with the intention of causing the course of justice to be obstructed, perverted or interfered with.

(5) References in this section to a witness, in relation to any proceedings, include references to a person who provides, or is able to provide, any information or any document or other thing which might be used as evidence in those proceedings or which (whether or not admissible as evidence in those proceedings)—

(a) might tend to confirm evidence which will be or might be admitted in those proceedings;

(b) might be referred to in evidence given in those proceedings by another witness; or

(c) might be used as the basis for any cross examination in the course of those proceedings.

(6) References in this section to doing an act include references to issuing any threat (whether against a person or his finances or property or otherwise), or making any other statement.

(7) This section is in addition to, and not in derogation of, any offence subsisting at common law.

40 Harming witnesses etc.

(1) A person commits an offence if, in circumstances falling within subsection (2)—

(a) he does an act which harms, and is intended to harm, another person; or

(b) intending to cause another person to fear harm, he threatens to do an act which would harm that other person. [E]

(2) The circumstances fall within this subsection if—

(a) the person doing or threatening to do the act does so knowing or believing that some person (whether or not the person harmed or threatened or the person against whom harm is threatened) has been a witness in relevant proceedings; and

(b) he does or threatens to do that act because of that knowledge or belief.

(3) If, in proceedings against a person for an offence under this section, it is proved that, within the relevant period—

(a) he did an act which harmed, and was intended to harm, another person, or

(b) intending to cause another person to fear harm, he threatened to do an act which would harm that other person,

and that he did the act, or (as the case may be) threatened to do the act, with the knowledge or belief required by paragraph (a) of subsection (2), he shall be presumed, unless the contrary is shown, to have done the act, or (as the case may be) threatened to do the act, because of that knowledge or belief.

(4) For the purposes of this section it is immaterial—

(a) whether or not the act that is done or threatened, or the threat that is made, is or would be done or is made in the presence of the person who is or would be harmed or of the person who is threatened;

(b) whether or not the motive mentioned in subsection (2)(b) is the predominating motive for the act or threat; and

(c) whether the harm that is done or threatened is physical or financial or is harm to a person or to his property.

(6) In this section "the relevant period", in relation to an act done, or threat made, with the knowledge or belief that a person has been a witness in any relevant proceedings, means the period that begins with the commencement of those proceedings and ends one year after they are finally concluded.

(7) References in this section to a witness, in relation to any proceedings, include references to a person who has provided any information or any document or other thing which was or might have been used as evidence in those proceedings or which (whether or not it was admissible as evidence in those proceedings)—

    (a) tended to confirm or might have tended to confirm any evidence which was or could have been given in those proceedings;

    (b) was or might have been referred to in evidence given in those proceedings by another witness; or

    (c) was or might have been used as the basis for any cross examination in the course of those proceedings.

(8) This section is in addition to, and not in derogation of, any offence subsisting at common law.

41 Relevant proceedings

(1) A reference in section 39 or 40 to relevant proceedings is a reference to any proceedings in or before the Court of Appeal, the High Court, the Crown Court or any county court or magistrates' court which—

    (a) are not proceedings for an offence; and

    (b) were commenced after the coming into force of that section.

(2) For the purposes of any reference in section 39 or 40 or this section to the commencement of any proceedings relevant proceedings are commenced (subject to subsection (5)) at the earliest time at which one of the following occurs—

    (a) an information is laid or application, claim form, complaint, petition, summons or other process made or issued for the purpose of commencing the proceedings;

    (b) any other step is taken by means of which the subject matter of the proceedings is brought for the first time (whether as part of the proceedings or in anticipation of them) before the court.

(3) For the purposes of any reference in section 39 or 40 to the time when any proceedings are finally concluded, relevant proceedings are finally concluded (subject to subsection (4))—

    (a) if proceedings for an appeal against, or an application for a review of, those proceedings or of any decision taken in those proceedings are brought or is made, at the time when proceedings on that appeal or application are finally concluded;

    (b) if the proceedings are withdrawn or discontinued, at the time when they are withdrawn or discontinued; and

    (c) in any other case, when the court in or before which the proceedings are brought finally disposes of all the matters arising in those proceedings.

(4) Relevant proceedings shall not be taken to be finally concluded by virtue of subsection (3)(a) where—

    (a) the matters to which the appeal or application relate are such that the proceedings in respect of which it is brought or made continue or resume after the making of any determination on that appeal or application; or

    (b) a determination made on that appeal or application requires those proceedings to continue or to be resumed.

(5) Where, after having appeared to be finally concluded, any relevant proceedings continue by reason of—

    (a) the giving of permission to bring an appeal after a fixed time for appealing has expired,

    (b) the lifting of any stay in the proceedings,

    (c) the setting aside, without an appeal, of any judgment or order, or

(d) the revival of any discontinued proceedings,

sections 39 and 40 and this section shall have effect as if the proceedings had concluded when they appeared to, but as if the giving of permission, the lifting of the stay, the setting aside of the judgment or order or, as the case may be, the revival of the discontinued proceedings were the commencement of new relevant proceedings.

42   Police directions stopping the harassment etc. of a person in his home

(1) Subject to the following provisions of this section, a constable who is at the scene may give a direction under this section to any person if—

(a) that person is present outside or in the vicinity of any premises that are used by any individual ("the resident") as his dwelling;

(b) that constable believes, on reasonable grounds, that that person is present there for the purpose (by his presence or otherwise) of representing to the resident or another individual (whether or not one who uses the premises as his dwelling), or of persuading the resident or such another individual—

(i) that he should not do something that he is entitled or required to do; or

(ii) that he should do something that he is not under any obligation to do; and

(c) that constable also believes, on reasonable grounds, that the presence of that person (either alone or together with that of any other persons who are also present)—

(i) amounts to, or is likely to result in, the harassment of the resident; or

(ii) is likely to cause alarm or distress to the resident.

(2) A direction under this section is a direction requiring the person to whom it is given to do all such things as the constable giving it may specify as the things he considers necessary to prevent one or both of the following—

(a) the harassment of the resident; or

(b) the causing of any alarm or distress to the resident.

(3) A direction under this section may be given orally; and where a constable is entitled to give a direction under this section to each of several persons outside, or in the vicinity of, any premises, he may give that direction to those persons by notifying them of his requirements either individually or all together.

(4) The requirements that may be imposed by a direction under this section include—

(a) a requirement to leave the vicinity of the premises in question, and

(b) a requirement to leave that vicinity and not to return to it within such period as the constable may specify, not being longer than 3 months;

and (in either case) the requirement to leave the vicinity may be to do so immediately or after a specified period of time.

(7) Any person who knowingly fails to comply with a requirement in a direction given to him under this section (other than a requirement under subsection (4)(b)) shall be guilty of an offence . . . [S]

(7A) Any person to whom a constable has given a direction including a requirement under subsection (4)(b) commits an offence if he—

(a) returns to the vicinity of the premises in question within the period specified in the direction beginning with the date on which the direction is given; and

(b) does so for the purpose described in subsection (1)(b). [S]

(9) In this section "dwelling" has the same meaning as in Part I of the Public Order Act 1986.

42A   Offence of harassment etc. of a person in his home

(1) A person commits an offence if—

(a) that person is present outside or in the vicinity of any premises that are used by any individual ("the resident") as his dwelling;

  (b) that person is present there for the purpose (by his presence or otherwise) of represent-ing to the resident or another individual (whether or not one who uses the premises as his dwelling), or of persuading the resident or such another individual—

    (i) that he should not do something that he is entitled or required to do; or

    (ii) that he should do something that he is not under any obligation to do;

  (c) that person—

    (i) intends his presence to amount to the harassment of, or to cause alarm or distress to, the resident; or

    (ii) knows or ought to know that his presence is likely to result in the harassment of, or to cause alarm or distress to, the resident; and

  (d) the presence of that person—

    (i) amounts to the harassment of, or causes alarm or distress to, any person falling within subsection (2); or

    (ii) is likely to result in the harassment of, or to cause alarm or distress to, any such person. [S]

 (2) A person falls within this subsection if he is—

  (a) the resident,

  (b) a person in the resident's dwelling, or

  (c) a person in another dwelling in the vicinity of the resident's dwelling.

 (3) The references in subsection (1)(c) and (d) to a person's presence are references to his pres-ence either alone or together with that of any other persons who are also present.

 (4) For the purposes of this section a person (A) ought to know that his presence is likely to re-sult in the harassment of, or to cause alarm or distress to, a resident if a reasonable person in posses-sion of the same information would think that A's presence was likely to have that effect.

 (7) In this section "dwelling" has the same meaning as in Part 1 of the Public Order Act 1986.

46 Placing of advertisement relating to prostitution

 (1) A person commits an offence if—

  (a) he places on, or in the immediate vicinity of, a public telephone an advertisement re-lating to prostitution, and

  (b) he does so with the intention that the advertisement should come to the attention of any other person or persons. [S]

 (2) For the purposes of this section, an advertisement is an advertisement relating to prostitu-tion if it—

  (a) is for the services of a prostitute, whether male or female; or

  (b) indicates that premises are premises at which such services are offered.

 (3) In any proceedings for an offence under this section, any advertisement which a reasonable person would consider to be an advertisement relating to prostitution shall be presumed to be such an advertisement unless it is shown not to be.

 (5) In this section—

"public telephone" means—

  (a) any telephone which is located in a public place and made available for use by the public, or a section of the public, and

  (b) where such a telephone is located in or on, or attached to, a kiosk, booth, acoustic hood, shelter or other structure, that structure; and

"public place" means any place to which the public have or are permitted to have access, whether on payment or otherwise, other than—

  (a) any place to which children under the age of 16 years are not permitted to have access, whether by law or otherwise, and

  (b) any premises which are wholly or mainly used for residential purposes.

International Criminal Court Act 2001

PART 5   OFFENCES UNDER DOMESTIC LAW

51   Genocide, crimes against humanity and war crimes

(1) It is an offence against the law of England and Wales for a person to commit genocide, a crime against humanity or a war crime. [I]

(2) This section applies to acts committed—

  (a) in England or Wales, or

  (b) outside the United Kingdom by a United Kingdom national, a United Kingdom resident or a person subject to UK service jurisdiction.

52   Conduct ancillary to genocide, etc. committed outside jurisdiction

(1) It is an offence against the law of England and Wales for a person to engage in conduct ancillary to an act to which this section applies. [I]

(2) This section applies to an act that if committed in England or Wales would constitute—

  (a) an offence under section 51 (genocide, crime against humanity or war crime), or

  (b) an offence under this section,

but which, being committed (or intended to be committed) outside England and Wales, does not constitute such an offence.

(3) The reference in subsection (1) to conduct ancillary to such an act is to conduct that would constitute an ancillary offence in relation to that act if the act were committed in England or Wales.

(4) This section applies where the conduct in question consists of or includes an act committed—

  (a) in England or Wales, or

  (b) outside the United Kingdom by a United Kingdom national, a United Kingdom resident or a person subject to UK service jurisdiction.

55   Meaning of "ancillary offence"

(1) References in this Part to an ancillary offence under the law of England and Wales are to—

  (a) aiding, abetting, counselling or procuring the commission of an offence,

  (b) inciting a person to commit an offence,

  (c) attempting or conspiring to commit an offence, or

  (d) assisting an offender or concealing the commission of an offence.

(2) In subsection (1)(a) the reference to aiding, abetting, counselling or procuring is to conduct that in relation to an indictable offence would be punishable under section 8 of the Accessories and Abettors Act 1861.

(4) In subsection (1)(c)—

  (a) the reference to an attempt is to conduct amounting to an offence under section 1 of the Criminal Attempts Act 1981; and

  (b) the reference to conspiracy is to conduct amounting to an offence of conspiracy under section 1 of the Criminal Law Act 1977.

(5) In subsection (1)(d)—

  (a) the reference to assisting an offender is to conduct that in relation to a relevant offence would amount to an offence under section 4(1) of the Criminal Law Act 1967; and

  (b) the reference to concealing an offence is to conduct that in relation to a relevant offence would amount to an offence under section 5(1) of that Act.

65   Responsibility of commanders and other superiors

(1) This section applies in relation to—

  (a) offences under this Part, and

  (b) offences ancillary to such offences.

(2) A military commander, or a person effectively acting as a military commander, is responsible for offences committed by forces under his effective command and control, or (as the case may be) his effective authority and control, as a result of his failure to exercise control properly over such forces where—

    (a) he either knew, or owing to the circumstances at the time, should have known that the forces were committing or about to commit such offences, and

    (b) he failed to take all necessary and reasonable measures within his power to prevent or repress their commission or to submit the matter to the competent authorities for investigation and prosecution.

(3) With respect to superior and subordinate relationships not described in subsection (2), a superior is responsible for offences committed by subordinates under his effective authority and control, as a result of his failure to exercise control properly over such subordinates where—

    (a) he either knew, or consciously disregarded information which clearly indicated, that the subordinates were committing or about to commit such offences,

    (b) the offences concerned activities that were within his effective responsibility and control, and

    (c) he failed to take all necessary and reasonable measures within his power to prevent or repress their commission or to submit the matter to the competent authorities for investigation and prosecution.

(4) A person responsible under this section for an offence is regarded as aiding, abetting, counselling or procuring the commission of the offence.

(5) In interpreting and applying the provisions of this section (which corresponds to article 28) the court shall take into account any relevant judgment or decision of the International Criminal Court.

Account may also be taken of any other relevant international jurisprudence.

(6) Nothing in this section shall be read as restricting or excluding—

    (a) any liability of the commander or superior apart from this section, or

    (b) the liability of persons other than the commander or superior.

65A Retrospective application of certain offences

(1) Sections 51 and 58 apply to acts committed on or after 1 January 1991.

(2) But those sections do not apply to a crime against humanity, or a war crime within article 8.2(b) or (e), committed by a person before 1 September 2001 unless, at the time the act constituting that crime was committed, the act amounted in the circumstances to a criminal offence under international law.

(3) Section 52 applies to conduct in which a person engaged on or after 1 January 1991, and in subsections (2) and (3) of that section references to an offence include an act or conduct which would not constitute an offence under the law of England and Wales but for this section.

(5) Any enactment or rule of law relating to an offence ancillary to a relevant Part 5 offence—

    (a) applies to conduct in which a person engaged on or after 1 January 1991, and

    (b) applies even if the act or conduct constituting the relevant Part 5 offence would not constitute such an offence but for this section.

(6) But sections 52 and 59, and any enactment or rule of law relating to an offence ancillary to a relevant Part 5 offence, do not apply to—

    (a) conduct in which the person engaged before 1 September 2001, or

    (b) conduct in which the person engaged on or after that date which was ancillary to an act or conduct which—

        (i) was committed or engaged in before that date, and

        (ii) would not constitute a relevant Part 5 offence, or fall within section 52(2) or 59(2), but for this section, unless, at the time the person engaged in the conduct, it amounted in the circumstances to a criminal offence under international law.

(7) Section 65, so far as it has effect in relation to relevant Part 5 offences—

(a) applies to failures to exercise control of the kind mentioned in section 65(2) or (3) which occurred on or after 1 January 1991, and

(b) applies even if the act or conduct constituting the relevant Part 5 offence would not constitute such an offence but for this section.

(8) But section 65, so far as it has effect in relation to relevant Part 5 offences, does not apply to a failure to exercise control of the kind mentioned in section 65(2) or (3) which occurred before 1 September 2001 unless, at the time the failure occurred, it amounted in the circumstances to a criminal offence under international law.

(9) In this section "relevant Part 5 offence" means an offence under section 51, 52, 58 or 59 or an offence ancillary to such an offence.

67 Meaning of "UK national", "UK resident" and "person subject to UK service jurisdiction"

(1) In this Part a "United Kingdom national" means an individual who is—

(a) a British citizen, a British Overseas Territories citizen, a British National (Overseas) or a British Overseas Citizen,

(b) a person who under the British Nationality Act 1981 is a British subject, or

(c) a British protected person within the meaning of that Act.

(2) In this Part a "United Kingdom resident" means a person who is resident in the United Kingdom.

(3) In this Part a "person subject to UK service jurisdiction" means a person subject to service law, or a civilian subject to service discipline, within the meaning of the Armed Forces Act 2006.

67A Supplemental provision about UK residents

(1) To the extent that it would not otherwise be the case, the following individuals are to be treated for the purposes of this Part as being resident in the United Kingdom—

(a) an individual who has indefinite leave to remain in the United Kingdom;

(b) any other individual who has made an application for such leave (whether or not it has been determined) and who is in the United Kingdom;

(c) an individual who has leave to enter or remain in the United Kingdom for the purposes of work or study and who is in the United Kingdom;

(d) an individual who has made an asylum claim, or a human rights claim, which has been granted;

(e) any other individual who has made an asylum claim or human rights claim (whether or not the claim has been determined) and who is in the United Kingdom;

(f) an individual named in an application for indefinite leave to remain, an asylum claim or a human rights claim as a dependant of the individual making the application or claim if—

(i) the application or claim has been granted, or

(ii) the named individual is in the United Kingdom (whether or not the application or claim has been determined);

(g) an individual who would be liable to removal or deportation from the United Kingdom but cannot be removed or deported because of section 6 of the Human Rights Act 1998 or for practical reasons;

(h) an individual—

(i) against whom a decision to make a deportation order under section 5(1) of the Immigration Act 1971 by virtue of section 3(5)(a) of that Act (deportation conducive to the public good) has been made,

(ii) who has appealed against the decision to make the order (whether or not the appeal has been determined), and

(iii) who is in the United Kingdom;

(i) an individual who is an illegal entrant within the meaning of section 33(1) of the Immigration Act 1971 or who is liable to removal under section 10 of the Immigration and Asylum Act 1999;

(j) an individual who is detained in lawful custody in the United Kingdom.

(2) When determining for the purposes of this Part whether any other individual is resident in the United Kingdom regard is to be had to all relevant considerations including—

(a) the periods during which the individual has been or intends to be in the United Kingdom,

(b) the purposes for which the individual is, has been or intends to be in the United Kingdom,

(c) whether the individual has family or other connections to the United Kingdom and the nature of those connections, and

(d) whether the individual has an interest in residential property located in the United Kingdom.

(3) In this section—

"asylum claim" means—

(a) a claim that it would be contrary to the United Kingdom's obligations under the Refugee Convention for the claimant to be removed from, or required to leave, the United Kingdom, or

(b) a claim that the claimant would face a real risk of serious harm if removed from the United Kingdom;

"Convention rights" means the rights identified as Convention rights by section 1 of the Human Rights Act 1998;

"detained in lawful custody" means—

(a) detained in pursuance of a sentence of imprisonment, detention or custody for life or a detention and training order,

(b) remanded in or committed to custody by an order of a court,

(c) detained pursuant to an order under section 2 of the Colonial Prisoners Removal Act 1884 or a warrant under section 1 or 4A of the Repatriation of Prisoners Act 1984,

(d) detained under Part 3 of the Mental Health Act 1983 or by virtue of an order under section 5 of the Criminal Procedure (Insanity) Act 1964 or section 6 or 14 of the Criminal Appeal Act 1968 (hospital orders, etc.),

"human rights claim" means a claim that to remove the claimant from, or to require the claimant to leave, the United Kingdom would be unlawful under section 6 of the Human Rights Act 1998 (public authority not to act contrary to Convention) as being incompatible with the person's Convention rights;

"the Refugee Convention" means the Convention relating to the Status of Refugees done at Geneva on 28 July 1951 and the Protocol to the Convention;

"serious harm" has the meaning given by article 15 of Council Directive 2004/83/EC on minimum standards for the qualification and status of third country nationals or stateless persons as refugees or as persons who otherwise need international protection and the content of the protection granted;

and a reference to having leave to enter or remain in the United Kingdom is to be construed in accordance with the Immigration Act 1971.

(4) This section applies in relation to any offence under this Part (whether committed before or after the coming into force of this section).

Enterprise Act 2002

188   Cartel offence

(1) An individual is guilty of an offence if he agrees with one or more other persons to make or implement, or to cause to be made or implemented, arrangements of the following kind relating to at least two undertakings (A and B). [E]

(2) The arrangements must be ones which, if operating as the parties to the agreement intend, would—

(a) directly or indirectly fix a price for the supply by A in the United Kingdom (otherwise than to B) of a product or service,

(b) limit or prevent supply by A in the United Kingdom of a product or service,

(c) limit or prevent production by A in the United Kingdom of a product,

(d) divide between A and B the supply in the United Kingdom of a product or service to a customer or customers,

(e) divide between A and B customers for the supply in the United Kingdom of a product or service, or

(f) be bid-rigging arrangements.

(3) Unless subsection (2)(d), (e) or (f) applies, the arrangements must also be ones which, if operating as the parties to the agreement intend, would—

(a) directly or indirectly fix a price for the supply by B in the United Kingdom (otherwise than to A) of a product or service,

(b) limit or prevent supply by B in the United Kingdom of a product or service, or

(c) limit or prevent production by B in the United Kingdom of a product.

(4) In subsections (2)(a) to (d) and (3), references to supply or production are to supply or production in the appropriate circumstances (for which see section 189).

(5) "Bid-rigging arrangements" are arrangements under which, in response to a request for bids for the supply of a product or service in the United Kingdom, or for the production of a product in the United Kingdom—

(a) A but not B may make a bid, or

(b) A and B may each make a bid but, in one case or both, only a bid arrived at in accordance with the arrangements.

(7) "Undertaking" has the same meaning as in Part 1 of the 1998 Act.

(8) This section is subject to section 188A.

188A   Circumstances in which cartel offence not committed

(1) An individual does not commit an offence under section 188(1) if, under the arrangements—

(a) in a case where the arrangements would (operating as the parties intend) affect the supply in the United Kingdom of a product or service, customers would be given relevant information about the arrangements before they enter into agreements for the supply to them of the product or service so affected,

(b) in the case of bid-rigging arrangements, the person requesting bids would be given relevant information about them at or before the time when a bid is made, or

(c) in any case, relevant information about the arrangements would be published, before the arrangements are implemented, in the manner specified at the time of the making of the agreement in an order made by the Secretary of State.

(2) In subsection (1), "relevant information" means—

(a) the names of the undertakings to which the arrangements relate,

(b) a description of the nature of the arrangements which is sufficient to show why they are or might be arrangements of the kind to which section 188(1) applies,

(c) the products or services to which they relate, and

(d) such other information as may be specified in an order made by the Secretary of State.

(3) An individual does not commit an offence under section 188(1) if the agreement is made in order to comply with a legal requirement.

(4) In subsection (3), "legal requirement" has the same meaning as in paragraph 5 of Schedule 3 to the Competition Act 1998.

188B   Defences to commission of cartel offence

(1) In a case where the arrangements would (operating as the parties intend) affect the supply in the United Kingdom of a product or service, it is a defence for an individual charged with an offence under section 188(1) to show that, at the time of the making of the agreement, he or she did not intend that the nature of the arrangements would be concealed from customers at all times before they enter into agreements for the supply to them of the product or service.

(2) It is a defence for an individual charged with an offence under section 188(1) to show that, at the time of the making of the agreement, he or she did not intend that the nature of the arrangements would be concealed from the CMA.

(3) It is a defence for an individual charged with an offence under section 188(1) to show that, before the making of the agreement, he or she took reasonable steps to ensure that the nature of the arrangements would be disclosed to professional legal advisers for the purposes of obtaining advice about them before their making or (as the case may be) their implementation.

189   Cartel offence: supplementary

(1) For section 188(2)(a), the appropriate circumstances are that A's supply of the product or service would be at a level in the supply chain at which the product or service would at the same time be supplied by B in the United Kingdom.

(2) For section 188(2)(b), the appropriate circumstances are that A's supply of the product or service would be at a level in the supply chain—

(a) at which the product or service would at the same time be supplied by B in the United Kingdom, or

(b) at which supply by B in the United Kingdom of the product or service would be limited or prevented by the arrangements.

(3) For section 188(2)(c), the appropriate circumstances are that A's production of the product would be at a level in the production chain—

(a) at which the product would at the same time be produced by B in the United Kingdom, or

(b) at which production by B in the United Kingdom of the product would be limited or prevented by the arrangements.

(4) For section 188(2)(d), the appropriate circumstances are that A's supply of the product or service would be at the same level in the supply chain as B's.

(5) For section 188(3)(a), the appropriate circumstances are that B's supply of the product or service would be at a level in the supply chain at which the product or service would at the same time be supplied by A in the United Kingdom.

(6) For section 188(3)(b), the appropriate circumstances are that B's supply of the product or service would be at a level in the supply chain—

(a) at which the product or service would at the same time be supplied by A in the United Kingdom, or

(b) at which supply by A in the United Kingdom of the product or service would be limited or prevented by the arrangements.

(7) For section 188(3)(c), the appropriate circumstances are that B's production of the product would be at a level in the production chain—

(a) at which the product would at the same time be produced by A in the United Kingdom, or

(b) at which production by A in the United Kingdom of the product would be limited or prevented by the arrangements.

Proceeds of Crime Act 2002

PART 7 MONEY LAUNDERING

327 Concealing etc.

(1) A person commits an offence if he—

    (a) conceals criminal property;

    (b) disguises criminal property;

    (c) converts criminal property;

    (d) transfers criminal property;

    (e) removes criminal property from England and Wales or from Scotland or from Northern Ireland. [E]

(2) But a person does not commit such an offence if—

    (a) he makes an authorised disclosure under section 338 and (if the disclosure is made before he does the act mentioned in subsection (1)) he has the appropriate consent;

    (b) he intended to make such a disclosure but had a reasonable excuse for not doing so;

    (c) the act he does is done in carrying out a function he has relating to the enforcement of any provision of this Act or of any other enactment relating to criminal conduct or benefit from criminal conduct.

(2A) Nor does a person commit an offence under subsection (1) if—

    (a) he knows, or believes on reasonable grounds, that the relevant criminal conduct occurred in a particular country or territory outside the United Kingdom, and

    (b) the relevant criminal conduct—

        (i) was not, at the time it occurred, unlawful under the criminal law then applying in that country or territory, and

        (ii) is not of a description prescribed by an order made by the Secretary of State.

(2B) In subsection (2A) "the relevant criminal conduct" is the criminal conduct by reference to which the property concerned is criminal property.

(2C) A deposit-taking body, electronic money institution or payment institution that does an act mentioned in paragraph (c) or (d) of subsection (1) does not commit an offence under that subsection if—

    (a) it does the act in operating an account maintained with it, and

    (b) the value of the criminal property concerned is less than the threshold amount determined under section 339A for the act.

(3) Concealing or disguising criminal property includes concealing or disguising its nature, source, location, disposition, movement or ownership or any rights with respect to it.

328 Arrangements

(1) A person commits an offence if he enters into or becomes concerned in an arrangement which he knows or suspects facilitates (by whatever means) the acquisition, retention, use or control of criminal property by or on behalf of another person. [E]

(2) But a person does not commit such an offence if—

    (a) he makes an authorised disclosure under section 338 and (if the disclosure is made before he does the act mentioned in subsection (1)) he has the appropriate consent;

    (b) he intended to make such a disclosure but had a reasonable excuse for not doing so;

    (c) the act he does is done in carrying out a function he has relating to the enforcement of any provision of this Act or of any other enactment relating to criminal conduct or benefit from criminal conduct.

(3) Nor does a person commit an offence under subsection (1) if—

    (a) he knows, or believes on reasonable grounds, that the relevant criminal conduct occurred in a particular country or territory outside the United Kingdom, and

    (b) the relevant criminal conduct—

        (i) was not, at the time it occurred, unlawful under the criminal law then applying in that country or territory, and

(ii) is not of a description prescribed by an order made by the Secretary of State.

(4) In subsection (3) "the relevant criminal conduct" is the criminal conduct by reference to which the property concerned is criminal property.

(5) A deposit-taking body, electronic money institution or payment institution that does an act mentioned in subsection (1) does not commit an offence under that subsection if—

(a) it does the act in operating an account maintained with it, and

(b) the arrangement facilitates the acquisition, retention, use or control of criminal property of a value that is less than the threshold amount determined under section 339A for the act.

329 Acquisition, use and possession

(1) A person commits an offence if he—

(a) acquires criminal property;

(b) uses criminal property;

(c) has possession of criminal property. [E]

(2) But a person does not commit such an offence if—

(a) he makes an authorised disclosure under section 338 and (if the disclosure is made before he does the act mentioned in subsection (1)) he has the appropriate consent;

(b) he intended to make such a disclosure but had a reasonable excuse for not doing so;

(c) he acquired or used or had possession of the property for adequate consideration;

(d) the act he does is done in carrying out a function he has relating to the enforcement of any provision of this Act or of any other enactment relating to criminal conduct or benefit from criminal conduct.

(2A) Nor does a person commit an offence under subsection (1) if—

(a) he knows, or believes on reasonable grounds, that the relevant criminal conduct occurred in a particular country or territory outside the United Kingdom, and

(b) the relevant criminal conduct—

(i) was not, at the time it occurred, unlawful under the criminal law then applying in that country or territory, and

(ii) is not of a description prescribed by an order made by the Secretary of State.

(2B) In subsection (2A) "the relevant criminal conduct" is the criminal conduct by reference to which the property concerned is criminal property.

(2C) A deposit-taking body, electronic money institution or payment institution that does an act mentioned in subsection (1) does not commit an offence under that subsection if—

(a) it does the act in operating an account maintained with it, and

(b) the value of the criminal property concerned is less than the threshold amount determined under section 339A for the act.

(3) For the purposes of this section—

(a) a person acquires property for inadequate consideration if the value of the consideration is significantly less than the value of the property;

(b) a person uses or has possession of property for inadequate consideration if the value of the consideration is significantly less than the value of the use or possession;

(c) the provision by a person of goods or services which he knows or suspects may help another to carry out criminal conduct is not consideration.

330 Failure to disclose: regulated sector

(1) A person commits an offence if the conditions in subsections (2) to (4) are satisfied. [E]

(2) The first condition is that he—

(a) knows or suspects, or

(b) has reasonable grounds for knowing or suspecting,

that another person is engaged in money laundering.

(3) The second condition is that the information or other matter—

(a) on which his knowledge or suspicion is based, or

(b) which gives reasonable grounds for such knowledge or suspicion, came to him in the course of a business in the regulated sector.

    (3A) The third condition is—

        (a) that he can identify the other person mentioned in subsection (2) or the whereabouts of any of the laundered property, or

        (b) that he believes, or it is reasonable to expect him to believe, that the information or other matter mentioned in subsection (3) will or may assist in identifying that other person or the whereabouts of any of the laundered property.

    (4) The fourth condition is that he does not make the required disclosure to—

        (a) a nominated officer, or

        (b) a person authorised for the purposes of this Part by the Director General of the National Crime Agency,

as soon as is practicable after the information or other matter mentioned in subsection (3) comes to him.

    (5) The required disclosure is a disclosure of—

        (a) the identity of the other person mentioned in subsection (2), if he knows it,

        (b) the whereabouts of the laundered property, so far as he knows it, and

        (c) the information or other matter mentioned in subsection (3).

    (5A) The laundered property is the property forming the subject-matter of the money laundering that he knows or suspects, or has reasonable grounds for knowing or suspecting, that other person to be engaged in.

    (6) But he does not commit an offence under this section if—

        (a) he has a reasonable excuse for not making the required disclosure,

        (b) he is a professional legal adviser or relevant professional adviser and—

            (i) if he knows either of the things mentioned in subsection (5)(a) and (b), he knows the thing because of information or other matter that came to him in privileged circumstances, or

            (ii) the information or other matter mentioned in subsection (3) came to him in privileged circumstances, or

        (c) subsection (7) or (7B) applies to him.

    (7) This subsection applies to a person if—

        (a) he does not know or suspect that another person is engaged in money laundering, and

        (b) he has not been provided by his employer with such training as is specified by the Secretary of State by order for the purposes of this section.

    (7A) Nor does a person commit an offence under this section if—

        (a) he knows, or believes on reasonable grounds, that the money laundering is occurring in a particular country or territory outside the United Kingdom, and

        (b) the money laundering—

             (i) is not unlawful under the criminal law applying in that country or territory, and

            (ii) is not of a description prescribed in an order made by the Secretary of State.

    (7B) This subsection applies to a person if—

        (a) he is employed by, or is in partnership with, a professional legal adviser or a relevant professional adviser to provide the adviser with assistance or support,

        (b) the information or other matter mentioned in subsection (3) comes to the person in connection with the provision of such assistance or support, and

        (c) the information or other matter came to the adviser in privileged circumstances.

    (8) In deciding whether a person committed an offence under this section the court must consider whether he followed any relevant guidance which was at the time concerned—

        (a) issued by a supervisory authority or any other appropriate body,

        (b) approved by the Treasury, and

        (c) published in a manner it approved as appropriate in its opinion to bring the guidance to the attention of persons likely to be affected by it.

(9) A disclosure to a nominated officer is a disclosure which—

    (a) is made to a person nominated by the alleged offender's employer to receive disclosures under this section, and

    (b) is made in the course of the alleged offender's employment.

(9A) But a disclosure which satisfies paragraphs (a) and (b) of subsection (9) is not to be taken as a disclosure to a nominated officer if the person making the disclosure—

    (a) is a professional legal adviser or relevant professional adviser,

    (b) makes it for the purpose of obtaining advice about making a disclosure under this section, and

    (c) does not intend it to be a disclosure under this section.

(10) Information or other matter comes to a professional legal adviser or relevant professional advisor in privileged circumstances if it is communicated or given to him—

    (a) by (or by a representative of) a client of his in connection with the giving by the adviser of legal advice to the client,

    (b) by (or by a representative of) a person seeking legal advice from the adviser, or

    (c) by a person in connection with legal proceedings or contemplated legal proceedings.

(11) But subsection (10) does not apply to information or other matter which is communicated or given with the intention of furthering a criminal purpose.

(12) Schedule 9 has effect for the purpose of determining what is—

    (a) a business in the regulated sector;

    (b) a supervisory authority.

(13) An appropriate body is any body which regulates or is representative of any trade, profession, business or employment carried on by the alleged offender.

(14) A relevant professional adviser is an accountant, auditor or tax adviser who is a member of a professional body which is established for accountants, auditors or tax advisers (as the case may be) and which makes provision for—

    (a) testing the competence of those seeking admission to membership of such a body as a condition for such admission; and

    (b) imposing and maintaining professional and ethical standards for its members, as well as imposing sanctions for non-compliance with those standards.

331 Failure to disclose: nominated officers in the regulated sector

(1) A person nominated to receive disclosures under section 330 commits an offence if the conditions in subsections (2) to (4) are satisfied. [E]

(2) The first condition is that he—

    (a) knows or suspects, or

    (b) has reasonable grounds for knowing or suspecting,

that another person is engaged in money laundering.

(3) The second condition is that the information or other matter—

    (a) on which his knowledge or suspicion is based, or

    (b) which gives reasonable grounds for such knowledge or suspicion,

came to him in consequence of a disclosure made under section 330.

(3A) The third condition is—

    (a) that he knows the identity of the other person mentioned in subsection (2), or the whereabouts of any of the laundered property, in consequence of a disclosure made under section 330,

    (b) that that other person, or the whereabouts of any of the laundered property, can be identified from the information or other matter mentioned in subsection (3), or

    (c) that he believes, or it is reasonable to expect him to believe, that the information or other matter will or may assist in identifying that other person or the whereabouts of any of the laundered property.

(4) The fourth condition is that he does not make the required disclosure to a person authorised for the purposes of this Part by the Director General of the National Crime Agency as soon as is practicable after the information or other matter mentioned in subsection (3) comes to him.

(5) The required disclosure is a disclosure of—

    (a) the identity of the other person mentioned in subsection (2), if disclosed to him under section 330,

    (b) the whereabouts of the laundered property, so far as disclosed to him under section 330, and

    (c) the information or other matter mentioned in subsection (3).

(5A) The laundered property is the property forming the subject-matter of the money laundering that he knows or suspects, or has reasonable grounds for knowing or suspecting, that other person to be engaged in.

(6) But he does not commit an offence under this section if he has a reasonable excuse for not making the required disclosure.

(6A) Nor does a person commit an offence under this section if—

    (a) he knows, or believes on reasonable grounds, that the money laundering is occurring in a particular country or territory outside the United Kingdom, and

    (b) the money laundering—

        (i) is not unlawful under the criminal law applying in that country or territory, and

        (ii) is not of a description prescribed in an order made by the Secretary of State.

(7) In deciding whether a person committed an offence under this section the court must consider whether he followed any relevant guidance which was at the time concerned—

    (a) issued by a supervisory authority or any other appropriate body,

    (b) approved by the Treasury, and

    (c) published in a manner it approved as appropriate in its opinion to bring the guidance to the attention of persons likely to be affected by it.

(8) Schedule 9 has effect for the purpose of determining what is a supervisory authority.

(9) An appropriate body is a body which regulates or is representative of a trade, profession, business or employment.

332 Failure to disclose: other nominated officers

(1) A person nominated to receive disclosures under section 337 or 338 commits an offence if the conditions in subsections (2) to (4) are satisfied. [E]

(2) The first condition is that he knows or suspects that another person is engaged in money laundering.

(3) The second condition is that the information or other matter on which his knowledge or suspicion is based came to him in consequence of a disclosure made under the applicable section.

(3A) The third condition is—

    (a) that he knows the identity of the other person mentioned in subsection (2), or the whereabouts of any of the laundered property, in consequence of a disclosure made under the applicable section,

    (b) that that other person, or the whereabouts of any of the laundered property, can be identified from the information or other matter mentioned in subsection (3), or

    (c) that he believes, or it is reasonable to expect him to believe, that the information or other matter will or may assist in identifying that other person or the whereabouts of any of the laundered property.

(4) The fourth condition is that he does not make the required disclosure to a person authorised for the purposes of this Part by the Director General of the National Crime Agency as soon as is practicable after the information or other matter mentioned in subsection (3) comes to him.

(5) The required disclosure is a disclosure of—

    (a) the identity of the other person mentioned in subsection (2), if disclosed to him under section,

    (b) the whereabouts of the laundered property, so far as disclosed to him under the applicable section, and

    (c) the information or other matter mentioned in subsection (3).

  (5A) The laundered property is the property forming the subject-matter of the money laundering that he knows or suspects, or has reasonable grounds for knowing or suspecting, that other person to be engaged in.

  (5B) The applicable section is section 337 or, as the case may be, section 338.

  (6) But he does not commit an offence under this section if he has a reasonable excuse for not making the required disclosure.

  (7) Nor does a person commit an offence under this section if—

    (a) he knows, or believes on reasonable grounds, that the money laundering is occurring in a particular country or territory outside the United Kingdom, and

    (b) the money laundering—

      (i) is not unlawful under the criminal law applying in that country or territory, and

      (ii) is not of a description prescribed in an order made by the Secretary of State.

333A   Tipping off: regulated sector

  (1) A person commits an offence if—

    (a) the person discloses any matter within subsection (2);

    (b) the disclosure is likely to prejudice any investigation that might be conducted following the disclosure referred to in that subsection; and

    (c) the information on which the disclosure is based came to the person in the course of a business in the regulated sector. [E]

  (2) The matters are that the person or another person has made a disclosure under this Part—

    (a) to a constable,

    (b) to an officer of Revenue and Customs,

    (c) to a nominated officer, or

    (d) to a National Crime Agency officer authorised for the purposes of this Part by the Director General of that Agency,

of information that came to that person in the course of a business in the regulated sector.

  (3) A person commits an offence if—

    (a) the person discloses that an investigation into allegations that an offence under this Part has been committed is being contemplated or is being carried out;

    (b) the disclosure is likely to prejudice that investigation; and

    (c) the information on which the disclosure is based came to the person in the course of a business in the regulated sector. [E]

  (5) This section is subject to—

    (a) section 333B (disclosures within an undertaking or group etc.),

    (b) section 333C (other permitted disclosures between institutions etc.), and

    (c) section 333D (other permitted disclosures etc.).

333B   Disclosures within an undertaking or group etc.

  (1) An employee, officer or partner of an undertaking does not commit an offence under section 333A if the disclosure is to an employee, officer or partner of the same undertaking.

  (2) A person does not commit an offence under section 333A in respect of a disclosure by a credit institution or a financial institution if—

    (a) the disclosure is to a credit institution or a financial institution,

    (b) the institution to whom the disclosure is made is situated in the United Kingdom or an EEA State or in a country or territory imposing equivalent money laundering requirements, and

    (c) both the institution making the disclosure and the institution to whom it is made belong to the same group.

  (3) In subsection (2) "group" has the same meaning as in Directive 2002/87/EC of the European Parliament and of the Council of 16th December 2002 on the supplementary supervision of credit institutions, insurance undertakings and investment firms in a financial conglomerate.

(4) A professional legal adviser or a relevant professional adviser does not commit an offence under section 333A if—

    (a) the disclosure is to professional legal adviser or a relevant professional adviser,

    (b) both the person making the disclosure and the person to whom it is made carry on business in the United Kingdom or an EEA State or in a country or territory imposing equivalent money laundering requirements, and

    (c) those persons perform their professional activities within different undertakings that share common ownership, management or control.

333C Other permitted disclosures between institutions etc.

(1) This section applies to a disclosure—

    (a) by a credit institution to another credit institution,

    (b) by a financial institution to another financial institution,

    (c) by a professional legal adviser to another professional legal adviser, or

    (d) by a relevant professional adviser of a particular kind to another relevant professional adviser of the same kind.

(2) A person does not commit an offence under section 333A in respect of a disclosure to which this section applies if—

    (a) the disclosure relates to—

      (i) a client or former client of the institution or adviser making the disclosure and the institution or adviser to whom it is made,

      (ii) a transaction involving them both, or

      (iii) the provision of a service involving them both;

    (b) the disclosure is for the purpose only of preventing an offence under this Part of this Act;

    (c) the institution or adviser to whom the disclosure is made is situated in the United Kingdom or an EEA State or in a country or territory imposing equivalent money laundering requirements; and

    (d) the institution or adviser making the disclosure and the institution or adviser to whom it is made are subject to equivalent duties of professional confidentiality and the protection of personal data (within the meaning of Parts 5 to 7 of the Data Protection Act 2018 (see section 3(2) and (14) of that Act)).

333D Other permitted disclosures etc.

(1) A person does not commit an offence under section 333A if the disclosure is—

    (a) to the authority that is the supervisory authority for that person by virtue of the Money Laundering, Terrorist Financing and Transfer of Funds (Information on the Payer) Regulations 2017;

    (aa) for the purposes of proceedings under section 336A (power of court to extend moratorium period);

    (ab) made in good faith by virtue of section 339ZB (disclosures within the regulated sector); or

    (b) for the purpose of—

      (i) the detection, investigation or prosecution of a criminal offence (whether in the United Kingdom or elsewhere),

      (ii) an investigation under this Act, or

      (iii) the enforcement of any order of a court under this Act.

(2) A professional legal adviser or a relevant professional adviser does not commit an offence under section 333A if the disclosure—

    (a) is to the adviser's client, and

    (b) is made for the purpose of dissuading the client from engaging in conduct amounting to an offence.

(3) A person does not commit an offence under section 333A(1) if the person does not know or suspect that the disclosure is likely to have the effect mentioned in section 333A(1)(b).

(4) A person does not commit an offence under section 333A(3) if the person does not know or suspect that the disclosure is likely to have the effect mentioned in section 333A(3)(b).

333E   Interpretation of sections 333A to 333D

    (1) For the purposes of sections 333A to 333D, Schedule 9 has effect for determining—

        (a) what is a business in the regulated sector, and

        (b) what is a supervisory authority.

    (2) In those sections—

    "credit institution" has the same meaning as in Schedule 9;

    "financial institution" means an undertaking that carries on a business in the regulated sector by virtue of any of paragraphs (b) to (i) of paragraph 1(1) of that Schedule.

    (3) References in those sections to a disclosure by or to a credit institution or a financial institution include disclosure by or to an employee, officer or partner of the institution acting on its behalf.

    (4) For the purposes of those sections a country or territory imposes "equivalent money laundering requirements" if it imposes requirements equivalent to those laid down in Directive 2015/849/EU of the European Parliament and of the Council of 20th May 2015 on the prevention of the use of the financial system for the purpose of money laundering and terrorist financing, as amended by Directive 2018/843 of the European Parliament and of the Council of 30th May 2018.

    (5) In those sections "relevant professional adviser" means an accountant, auditor or tax adviser who is a member of a professional body which is established for accountants, auditors or tax advisers (as the case may be) and which makes provision for—

        (a) testing the competence of those seeking admission to membership of such a body as a condition for such admission; and

        (b) imposing and maintaining professional and ethical standards for its members, as well as imposing sanctions for non-compliance with those standards.

335   Appropriate consent

    (1) The appropriate consent is—

        (a) the consent of a nominated officer to do a prohibited act if an authorised disclosure is made to the nominated officer;

        (b) the consent of a constable to do a prohibited act if an authorised disclosure is made to a constable;

        (c) the consent of a customs officer to do a prohibited act if an authorised disclosure is made to a customs officer.

    (2) A person must be treated as having the appropriate consent if—

        (a) he makes an authorised disclosure to a constable or a customs officer, and

        (b) the condition in subsection (3) or the condition in subsection (4) is satisfied.

    (3) The condition is that before the end of the notice period he does not receive notice from a constable or customs officer that consent to the doing of the act is refused.

    (4) The condition is that—

        (a) before the end of the notice period he receives notice from a constable or customs officer that consent to the doing of the act is refused, and

        (b) the moratorium period has expired.

    (5) The notice period is the period of seven working days starting with the first working day after the person makes the disclosure.

    (6) The moratorium period is the period of 31 days starting with the day on which the person receives notice that consent to the doing of the act is refused.

    (6A) Subsection (6) is subject to—

        (a) section 336A, which enables the moratorium period to be extended by court order in accordance with that section, and

        (b) section 336C, which provides for an automatic extension of the moratorium period in certain cases (period extended if it would otherwise end before determination of application or appeal proceedings etc.).

    (7) A working day is a day other than a Saturday, a Sunday, Christmas Day, Good Friday or a day which is a bank holiday under the Banking and Financial Dealings Act 1971 in the part of the United Kingdom in which the person is when he makes the disclosure.

(8) References to a prohibited act are to an act mentioned in section 327(1), 328(1) or 329(1) (as the case may be).

(9) A nominated officer is a person nominated to receive disclosures under section 338.

(10) Subsections (1) to (4) apply for the purposes of this Part.

336   Nominated officer: consent

(1) A nominated officer must not give the appropriate consent to the doing of a prohibited act unless the condition in subsection (2), the condition in subsection (3) or the condition in subsection (4) is satisfied.

(2) The condition is that—

    (a) he makes a disclosure that property is criminal property to a person authorised for the purposes of this Part by the Director General of the National Crime Agency, and

    (b) such a person gives consent to the doing of the act.

(3) The condition is that—

    (a) he makes a disclosure that property is criminal property to a person authorised for the purposes of this Part by the Director General of the National Crime Agency, and

    (b) before the end of the notice period he does not receive notice from such a person that consent to the doing of the act is refused.

(4) The condition is that—

    (a) he makes a disclosure that property is criminal property to a person authorised for the purposes of this Part by the Director General of the National Crime Agency,

    (b) before the end of the notice period he receives notice from such a person that consent to the doing of the act is refused, and

    (c) the moratorium period has expired.

(5) A person who is a nominated officer commits an offence if—

    (a) he gives consent to a prohibited act in circumstances where none of the conditions in subsections (2), (3) and (4) is satisfied, and

    (b) he knows or suspects that the act is a prohibited act. [E]

(7) The notice period is the period of seven working days starting with the first working day after the nominated officer makes the disclosure.

(8) The moratorium period is the period of 31 days starting with the day on which the nominated officer is given notice that consent to the doing of the act is refused.

(8A) Subsection (8) is subject to—

    (a) section 336A, which enables the moratorium period to be extended by court order in accordance with that section, and

    (b) section 336C, which provides for an automatic extension of the moratorium period in certain cases (period extended if it would otherwise end before determination of application or appeal proceedings etc.).

(9) A working day is a day other than a Saturday, a Sunday, Christmas Day, Good Friday or a day which is a bank holiday under the Banking and Financial Dealings Act 1971 in the part of the United Kingdom in which the nominated officer is when he gives the appropriate consent.

(10) References to a prohibited act are to an act mentioned in section 327(1), 328(1) or 329(1) (as the case may be).

(11) A nominated officer is a person nominated to receive disclosures under section 338.

337   Protected disclosures

(1) A disclosure which satisfies the following three conditions is not to be taken to breach any restriction on the disclosure of information (however imposed).

(2) The first condition is that the information or other matter disclosed came to the person making the disclosure (the discloser) in the course of his trade, profession, business or employment.

(3) The second condition is that the information or other matter—

    (a) causes the discloser to know or suspect, or

    (b) gives him reasonable grounds for knowing or suspecting,

that another person is engaged in money laundering.

(4) The third condition is that the disclosure is made to a constable, a customs officer or a nominated officer as soon as is practicable after the information or other matter comes to the discloser.

(4A) Where a disclosure consists of a disclosure protected under subsection (1) and a disclosure of either or both of—

(a) the identity of the other person mentioned in subsection (3), and

(b) the whereabouts of property forming the subject-matter of the money laundering that the discloser knows or suspects, or has reasonable grounds for knowing or suspecting, that other person to be engaged in,

the disclosure of the thing mentioned in paragraph (a) or (b) (as well as the disclosure protected under subsection (1)) is not to be taken to breach any restriction on the disclosure of information (however imposed).

(5) A disclosure to a nominated officer is a disclosure which—

(a) is made to a person nominated by the discloser's employer to receive disclosures under section 330 or this section, and

(b) is made in the course of the discloser's employment.

338   Authorised disclosures

(1) For the purposes of this Part a disclosure is authorised if—

(a) it is a disclosure to a constable, a customs officer or a nominated officer by the alleged offender that property is criminal property, and

(c) the first, second or third condition set out below is satisfied.

(2) The first condition is that the disclosure is made before the alleged offender does the prohibited act.

(2A) The second condition is that—

(a) the disclosure is made while the alleged offender is doing the prohibited act,

(b) he began to do the act at a time when, because he did not then know or suspect that the property constituted or represented a person's benefit from criminal conduct, the act was not a prohibited act, and

(c) the disclosure is made on his own initiative and as soon as is practicable after he first knows or suspects that the property constitutes or represents a person's benefit from criminal conduct.

(3) The third condition is that—

(a) the disclosure is made after the alleged offender does the prohibited act,

(b) he has a reasonable excuse for his failure to make the disclosure before he did the act, and

(c) the disclosure is made on his own initiative and as soon as it is practicable for him to make it.

(4) An authorised disclosure is not to be taken to breach any restriction on the disclosure of information (however imposed).

(4A) Where an authorised disclosure is made in good faith, no civil liability arises in respect of the disclosure on the part of the person by or on whose behalf it is made.

(5) A disclosure to a nominated officer is a disclosure which—

(a) is made to a person nominated by the alleged offender's employer to receive authorised disclosures, and

(b) is made in the course of the alleged offender's employment.

(6) References to the prohibited act are to an act mentioned in section 327(1), 328(1) or 329(1) (as the case may be).

339A   Threshold amounts

(1) This section applies for the purposes of sections 327(2C), 328(5) and 329(2C).

(2) The threshold amount for acts done by a deposit-taking body, electronic money institution or payment institution in operating an account is £250 unless a higher amount is specified under the following provisions of this section (in which event it is that higher amount).

(3) An officer of Revenue and Customs, or a constable, may specify the threshold amount for acts done by a deposit-taking body, electronic money institution or payment institution in operating an account—

> (a) when he gives consent, or gives notice refusing consent, to the body's or institution's doing of an act mentioned in section 327(1), 328(1) or 329(1) in opening, or operating, the account or a related account, or
> (b) on a request from the body or institution.

(4) Where the threshold amount for acts done in operating an account is specified under subsection (3) or this subsection, an officer of Revenue and Customs, or a constable, may vary the amount (whether on a request from the deposit-taking body, electronic money institution or payment institution or otherwise) by specifying a different amount.

(5) Different threshold amounts may be specified under subsections (3) and (4) for different acts done in operating the same account.

(6) The amount specified under subsection (3) or (4) as the threshold amount for acts done in operating an account must, when specified, not be less than the amount specified in subsection (2).

(7) The Secretary of State may by order vary the amount for the time being specified in subsection (2).

(8) For the purposes of this section, an account is related to another if each is maintained with the same deposit-taking body, electronic money institution or payment institution and there is a person who, in relation to each account, is the person or one of the persons entitled to instruct the body as respects the operation of the account.

340 Interpretation

(1) This section applies for the purposes of this Part.

(2) Criminal conduct is conduct which—

> (a) constitutes an offence in any part of the United Kingdom, or
> (b) would constitute an offence in any part of the United Kingdom if it occurred there.

(3) Property is criminal property if—

> (a) it constitutes a person's benefit from criminal conduct or it represents such a benefit (in whole or part and whether directly or indirectly), and
> (b) the alleged offender knows or suspects that it constitutes or represents such a benefit.

(4) It is immaterial—

> (a) who carried out the conduct;
> (b) who benefited from it;
> (c) whether the conduct occurred before or after the passing of this Act.

(5) A person benefits from conduct if he obtains property as a result of or in connection with the conduct.

(6) If a person obtains a pecuniary advantage as a result of or in connection with conduct, he is to be taken to obtain as a result of or in connection with the conduct a sum of money equal to the value of the pecuniary advantage.

(7) References to property or a pecuniary advantage obtained in connection with conduct include references to property or a pecuniary advantage obtained in both that connection and some other.

(8) If a person benefits from conduct his benefit is the property obtained as a result of or in connection with the conduct.

(9) Property is all property wherever situated and includes—

> (a) money;
> (b) all forms of property, real or personal, heritable or moveable;
> (c) things in action and other intangible or incorporeal property.

(10) The following rules apply in relation to property—

> (a) property is obtained by a person if he obtains an interest in it;
> (b) references to an interest, in relation to land in England and Wales..., are to any legal estate or equitable interest or power;

(d) references to an interest, in relation to property other than land, include references to a right (including a right to possession).

(11) Money laundering is an act which—

    (a) constitutes an offence under section 327, 328 or 329,

    (b) constitutes an attempt, conspiracy or incitement to commit an offence specified in paragraph (a),

    (c) constitutes aiding, abetting, counselling or procuring the commission of an offence specified in paragraph (a), or

    (d) would constitute an offence specified in paragraph (a), (b) or (c) if done in the United Kingdom.

(12) For the purposes of a disclosure to a nominated officer—

    (a) references to a person's employer include any body, association or organisation (including a voluntary organisation) in connection with whose activities the person exercises a function (whether or not for gain or reward), and

    (b) references to employment must be construed accordingly.

(13) References to a constable include references to a person authorised for the purposes of this Part by the Director General of the National Crime Agency.

(14) "Deposit-taking body" means—

    (a) a business which engages in the activity of accepting deposits

    (b) the National Savings Bank, or

    (c) a person specified, or of a description specified, in regulations made by the Treasury or the Secretary of State.

(14A) In subsection (14)(a)—

    (a) the reference to the activity of accepting deposits is a reference to that activity so far as it is, for the time being, a regulated activity for the purposes of the Financial Services and Markets Act 2000 by virtue of an order under section 22 of that Act, but

    (b) the reference to a business which engages in that activity does not include a person specified, or of a description specified, in regulations made by the Treasury or the Secretary of State.

(14B) Before making regulations under subsection (14A)(b), the Treasury or the Secretary of State (as appropriate) must consult such persons likely to be affected by the regulations, or such representatives of such persons, as they consider appropriate.

(14C) "Electronic money institution" has the same meaning as in the Electronic Money Regulations 2011 (S.I. 2011/99) (see regulation 2 of those Regulations).

(15) "Further information order" means an order made under section 339ZH.

(16) "Payment institution" means an authorised payment institution or a small payment institution (each as defined in regulation 2 of the Payment Services Regulations 2017 (S.I. 2017/752)).

Anti-social Behaviour Act 2003

54 Sale of aerosol paint to children

(1) A person commits an offence if he sells an aerosol paint container to a person under the age of sixteen.

(2) In subsection (1) "aerosol paint container" means a device which—

    (a) contains paint stored under pressure, and

    (b) is designed to permit the release of the paint as a spray.

(4) It is a defence for a person charged with an offence under this section in respect of a sale to prove that—

    (a) he took all reasonable steps to determine the purchaser's age, and

    (b) he reasonably believed that the purchaser was not under the age of sixteen.

(5) It is a defence for a person charged with an offence under this section in respect of a sale effected by another person to prove that he (the defendant) took all reasonable steps to avoid the commission of an offence under this section. [S]

Communications Act 2003

125 Dishonestly obtaining electronic communications services

(1) A person who—

    (a) dishonestly obtains an electronic communications service, and

    (b) does so with intent to avoid payment of a charge applicable to the provision of that service,

is guilty of an offence. [E]

(2) It is not an offence under this section to obtain a service mentioned in section 297(1) of the Copyright, Designs and Patents Act 1988 (dishonestly obtaining a broadcasting service provided from a place in the UK).

126 Possession or supply of apparatus etc. for contravening s. 125

(1) A person is guilty of an offence if, with an intention falling within subsection (3), he has in his possession or under his control anything that may be used—

    (a) for obtaining an electronic communications service; or

    (b) in connection with obtaining such a service. [E]

(2) A person is guilty of an offence if—

    (a) he supplies or offers to supply anything which may be used as mentioned in subsection (1); and

    (b) he knows or believes that the intentions in relation to that thing of the person to whom it is supplied or offered fall within subsection (3). [E]

(3) A person's intentions fall within this subsection if he intends—

    (a) to use the thing to obtain an electronic communications service dishonestly;

    (b) to use the thing for a purpose connected with the dishonest obtaining of such a service;

    (c) dishonestly to allow the thing to be used to obtain such a service; or

    (d) to allow the thing to be used for a purpose connected with the dishonest obtaining of such a service.

(4) An intention does not fall within subsection (3) if it relates exclusively to the obtaining of a service mentioned in section 297(1) of the Copyright, Designs and Patents Act 1988.

(6) In this section, references, in the case of a thing used for recording data, to the use of that thing include references to the use of data recorded by it.

127 Improper use of public electronic communications network

(1) A person is guilty of an offence if he—

    (a) sends by means of a public electronic communications network a message or other matter that is grossly offensive or of an indecent, obscene or menacing character; or

    (b) causes any such message or matter to be so sent. [S]

(2) A person is guilty of an offence if, for the purpose of causing annoyance, inconvenience or needless anxiety to another, he—

    (a) sends by means of a public electronic communications network, a message that he knows to be false,

    (b) causes such a message to be sent; or

    (c) persistently makes use of a public electronic communications network. [S]

(4) Subsections (1) and (2) do not apply to anything done in the course of providing a programme service (within the meaning of the Broadcasting Act 1990).

Dealing in Cultural Objects (Offences) Act 2003

1 Offence of dealing in tainted cultural objects

(1) A person is guilty of an offence if he dishonestly deals in a cultural object that is tainted, knowing or believing that the object is tainted.

(2) It is immaterial whether he knows or believes that the object is a cultural object. [E]

2 Meaning of "tainted cultural object"

(1) "Cultural object" means an object of historical, architectural or archaeological interest.

(2) A cultural object is tainted if, after the commencement of this Act—

    (a) a person removes the object in a case falling within subsection (4) or he excavates the object, and

    (b) the removal or excavation constitutes an offence.

(3) It is immaterial whether—

    (a) the removal or excavation was done in the United Kingdom or elsewhere,

    (b) the offence is committed under the law of a part of the United Kingdom or under the law of any other country or territory.

(4) An object is removed in a case falling within this subsection if—

    (a) it is removed from a building or structure of historical, architectural or archaeological interest where the object has at any time formed part of the building or structure, or

    (b) it is removed from a monument of such interest.

(5) "Monument" means—

    (a) any work, cave or excavation,

    (b) any site comprising the remains of any building or structure or of any work, cave or excavation,

    (c) any site comprising, or comprising the remains of, any vehicle, vessel, aircraft or other movable structure, or part of any such thing.

(6) "Remains" includes any trace or sign of the previous existence of the thing in question.

(7) It is immaterial whether—

    (a) a building, structure or work is above or below the surface of the land,

    (b) a site is above or below water.

(8) This section has effect for the purposes of section 1.

3 Meaning of "deals in"

(1) A person deals in an object if (and only if) he—

    (a) acquires, disposes of, imports or exports it,

    (b) agrees with another to do an act mentioned in paragraph (a), or

    (c) makes arrangements under which another person does such an act or under which another person agrees with a third person to do such an act.

(2) "Acquires" means buys, hires, borrows or accepts.

(3) "Disposes of" means sells, lets on hire, lends or gives.

(4) In relation to agreeing or arranging to do an act, it is immaterial whether the act is agreed or arranged to take place in the United Kingdom or elsewhere.

(5) This section has effect for the purposes of section 1.

5 Offences by bodies corporate

(1) If an offence under section 1 committed by a body corporate is proved—

    (a) to have been committed with the consent or connivance of an officer, or

    (b) to be attributable to any neglect on his part,

he (as well as the body corporate) is guilty of the offence and liable to be proceeded against and punished accordingly.

(2) "Officer", in relation to a body corporate, means—
    (a) a director, manager, secretary or other similar officer of the body,
    (b) a person purporting to act in any such capacity.

(3) If the affairs of a body corporate are managed by its members, subsection (1) applies in relation to the acts and defaults of a member in connection with his functions of management as if he were a director of the body.

Female Genital Mutilation Act 2003

1   Offence of female genital mutilation

(1) A person is guilty of an offence if he excises, infibulates or otherwise mutilates the whole or any part of a girl's labia majora, labia minora or clitoris. [E]

(2) But no offence is committed by an approved person who performs—
    (a) a surgical operation on a girl which is necessary for her physical or mental health, or
    (b) a surgical operation on a girl who is in any stage of labour, or has just given birth, for purposes connected with the labour or birth.

(3) The following are approved persons—
    (a) in relation to an operation falling within subsection (2)(a), a registered medical practitioner,
    (b) in relation to an operation falling within subsection (2)(b), a registered medical practitioner, a registered midwife or a person undergoing a course of training with a view to becoming such a practitioner or midwife.

(4) There is also no offence committed by a person who—
    (a) performs a surgical operation falling within subsection (2)(a) or (b) outside the United Kingdom, and
    (b) in relation to such an operation exercises functions corresponding to those of an approved person.

(5) For the purpose of determining whether an operation is necessary for the mental health of a girl it is immaterial whether she or any other person believes that the operation is required as a matter of custom or ritual.

2   Offence of assisting a girl to mutilate her own genitalia

A person is guilty of an offence if he aids, abets, counsels or procures a girl to excise, infibulate or otherwise mutilate the whole or any part of her own labia majora, labia minora or clitoris. [E]

3   Offence of assisting a non-UK person to mutilate overseas a girl's genitalia

(1) A person is guilty of an offence if he aids, abets, counsels or procures a person who is not a United Kingdom national or United Kingdom resident to do a relevant act of female genital mutilation outside the United Kingdom. [E]

(2) An act is a relevant act of female genital mutilation if—
    (a) it is done in relation to a United Kingdom national or United Kingdom resident, and
    (b) it would, if done by such a person, constitute an offence under section 1.

(3) But no offence is committed if the relevant act of female genital mutilation—
    (a) is a surgical operation falling within section 1(2)(a) or (b), and
    (b) is performed by a person who, in relation to such an operation, is an approved person or exercises functions corresponding to those of an approved person.

3A   Offence of failing to protect girl from risk of genital mutilation

(1) If a genital mutilation offence is committed against a girl under the age of 16, each person who is responsible for the girl at the relevant time is guilty of an offence.
This is subject to subsection (5).

(2) For the purposes of this section a person is "responsible" for a girl in the following two cases.

(3) The first case is where the person—
    (a) has parental responsibility for the girl, and

    (b) has frequent contact with her.

  (4) The second case is where the person—

    (a) is aged 18 or over, and

    (b) has assumed (and not relinquished) responsibility for caring for the girl in the manner of a parent.

  (5) It is a defence for the defendant to show that—

    (a) at the relevant time, the defendant did not think that there was a significant risk of a genital mutilation offence being committed against the girl, and could not reasonably have been expected to be aware that there was any such risk, or

    (b) the defendant took such steps as he or she could reasonably have been expected to take to protect the girl from being the victim of a genital mutilation offence.

  (6) A person is taken to have shown the fact mentioned in subsection (5)(a) or (b) if—

    (a) sufficient evidence of the fact is adduced to raise an issue with respect to it, and

    (b) the contrary is not proved beyond reasonable doubt.

  (7) For the purposes of subsection (3)(b), where a person has frequent contact with a girl which is interrupted by her going to stay somewhere temporarily, that contact is treated as continuing during her stay there.

  (8) In this section—

"genital mutilation offence" means an offence under section 1, 2 or 3 (and for the purposes of subsection (1) the prosecution does not have to prove which section it is);

"parental responsibility"—

    (a) in England Wales, has the same meaning as in the Children Act 1989;

"the relevant time" means the time when the mutilation takes place.

4   Extension of sections 1 to 3A to extra-territorial acts or omissions

  (1) Sections 1 to 3 extend to any act done outside the United Kingdom by a United Kingdom national or United Kingdom resident.

  (1A) An offence under section 3A can be committed wholly or partly outside the United Kingdom by a person who is a United Kingdom national or a United Kingdom resident.

  (2) If an offence under this Act is committed outside the United Kingdom—

    (a) proceedings may be taken, and

    (b) the offence may for incidental purposes be treated as having been committed,

in any place in England and Wales or Northern Ireland.

6   Definitions

  (1) Girl includes woman.

  (2) A United Kingdom national is an individual who is—

    (a) a British citizen, a British overseas territories citizen, a British National (Overseas) or a British Overseas citizen,

    (b) a person who under the British Nationality Act 1981 is a British subject, or

    (c) a British protected person within the meaning of that Act.

  (3) A "United Kingdom resident" is an individual who is habitually resident in the United Kingdom.

  (4) This section has effect for the purposes of this Act.

Licensing Act 2003

PART 7   OFFENCES

136   Unauthorised licensable activities

  (1) A person commits an offence if—

    (a) he carries on or attempts to carry on a licensable activity on or from any premises otherwise than under and in accordance with an authorisation, or

(b) he knowingly allows a licensable activity to be so carried on. [S]

(2) Where the licensable activity in question is the provision of regulated entertainment, a person does not commit an offence under this section if his only involvement in the provision of the entertainment is that he—

(a) performs in a play,

(b) participates as a sportsman in an indoor sporting event,

(c) boxes or wrestles in a boxing or wrestling entertainment,

(d) performs live music,

(e) plays recorded music,

(f) performs dance, or

(g) does something coming within paragraph 2(1)(h) of Schedule 1 (entertainment similar to music, dance, etc.).

(5) In this Part "authorisation" means—

(a) a premises licence,

(b) a club premises certificate, or

(c) a temporary event notice in respect of which the conditions of section 98(2) to (4) are satisfied.

137   Exposing alcohol for unauthorised sale

(1) A person commits an offence if, on any premises, he exposes for sale by retail any alcohol in circumstances where the sale by retail of that alcohol on those premises would be an unauthorised licensable activity.

(2) For that purpose a licensable activity is unauthorised unless it is under and in accordance with an authorisation. [S]

138   Keeping alcohol on premises for unauthorised sale

(1) A person commits an offence if he has in his possession or under his control alcohol which he intends to sell by retail or supply in circumstances where that activity would be an unauthorised licensable activity.

(2) For that purpose a licensable activity is unauthorised unless it is under and in accordance with an authorisation.

(3) In subsection (1) the reference to the supply of alcohol is a reference to the supply of alcohol by or on behalf of a club to, or to the order of, a member of the club. [S]

139   Defence of due diligence

(1) In proceedings against a person for an offence to which subsection (2) applies, it is a defence that—

(a) his act was due to a mistake, or to reliance on information given to him, or to an act or omission by another person, or to some other cause beyond his control, and

(b) he took all reasonable precautions and exercised all due diligence to avoid committing the offence.

(2) This subsection applies to an offence under—

(a) section 136(1)(a) (carrying on unauthorised licensable activity),

(b) section 137 (exposing alcohol for unauthorised sale), or

(c) section 138 (keeping alcohol on premises for unauthorised sale).

140   Allowing disorderly conduct on licensed premises, etc.

(1) A person to whom subsection (2) applies commits an offence if he knowingly allows disorderly conduct on relevant premises.

(2) This subsection applies—

(a) to any person who works at the premises in a capacity, whether paid or unpaid, which authorises him to prevent the conduct,

(b) in the case of licensed premises, to—

(i)   the holder of a premises licence in respect of the premises, and

(ii) the designated premises supervisor (if any) under such a licence,

(c) in the case of premises in respect of which a club premises certificate has effect, to any member or officer of the club which holds the certificate who at the time the conduct takes place is present on the premises in a capacity which enables him to prevent it, and

(d) in the case of premises which may be used for a permitted temporary activity by virtue of Part 5, to the premises user in relation to the temporary event notice in question. [S]

141   Sale of alcohol to a person who is drunk

(1) A person to whom subsection (2) applies commits an offence if, on relevant premises, he knowingly—

(a) sells or attempts to sell alcohol to a person who is drunk, or

(b) allows alcohol to be sold to such a person.

(2) This subsection applies—

(a) to any person who works at the premises in a capacity, whether paid or unpaid, which gives him authority to sell the alcohol concerned,

(b) in the case of licensed premises, to—

(i)   the holder of a premises licence in respect of the premises, and

(ii)   the designated premises supervisor (if any) under such a licence,

(c) in the case of premises in respect of which a club premises certificate has effect, to any member or officer of the club which holds the certificate who at the time the sale (or attempted sale) takes place is present on the premises in a capacity which enables him to prevent it, and

(d) in the case of premises which may be used for a permitted temporary activity by virtue of Part 5, to the premises user in relation to the temporary event notice in question.

(3) This section applies in relation to the supply of alcohol by or on behalf of a club to or to the order of a member of the club as it applies in relation to the sale of alcohol. [S]

142   Obtaining alcohol for a person who is drunk

(1) A person commits an offence if, on relevant premises, he knowingly obtains or attempts to obtain alcohol for consumption on those premises by a person who is drunk. [S]

143   Failure to leave licensed premises etc.

(1) A person who is drunk or disorderly commits an offence if, without reasonable excuse—

(a) he fails to leave relevant premises when requested to do so by a constable or by a person to whom subsection (2) applies, or

(b) he enters or attempts to enter relevant premises after a constable or a person to whom subsection (2) applies has requested him not to enter.

(2) This subsection applies—

(a) to any person who works at the premises in a capacity, whether paid or unpaid, which authorises him to make such a request,

(b) in the case of licensed premises, to—

(i)   the holder of a premises licence in respect of the premises, or

(ii)   the designated premises supervisor (if any) under such a licence,

(c) in the case of premises in respect of which a club premises certificate has effect, to any member or officer of the club which holds the certificate who is present on the premises in a capacity which enables him to make such a request, and

(d) in the case of premises which may be used for a permitted temporary activity by virtue of Part 5, to the premises user in relation to the temporary event notice in question. [S]

146   Sale of alcohol to children

(1) A person commits an offence if he sells alcohol to an individual aged under 18.

(2) A club commits an offence if alcohol is supplied by it or on its behalf—

    (a) to, or to the order of, a member of the club who is aged under 18, or

    (b) on the order of a member of the club, to an individual who is aged under 18.

  (3) A person commits an offence if he supplies alcohol on behalf of a club—

    (a) to, or to the order of, a member of the club who is aged under 18, or

    (b) to the order of a member of the club, to an individual who is aged under 18.

  (4) Where a person is charged with an offence under this section by reason of his own conduct it is a defence that—

    (a) he believed that the individual was aged 18 or over, and

    (b) either—

      (i) he had taken all reasonable steps to establish the individual's age, or

      (ii) nobody could reasonably have suspected from the individual's appearance that he was aged under 18.

  (5) For the purposes of subsection (4), a person is treated as having taken all reasonable steps to establish an individual's age if—

    (a) he asked the individual for evidence of his age, and

    (b) the evidence would have convinced a reasonable person.

  (6) Where a person ("the accused") is charged with an offence under this section by reason of the act or default of some other person it is a defence that the accused exercised all due diligence to avoid committing it. [S]

147 Allowing the sale of alcohol to children

  (1) A person to whom subsection (2) applies commits an offence if he knowingly allows the sale of alcohol on relevant premises to an individual aged under 18.

  (2) This subsection applies to a person who works at the premises in a capacity, whether paid or unpaid, which authorises him to prevent the sale.

  (3) A person to whom subsection (4) applies commits an offence if he knowingly allows alcohol to be supplied on relevant premises by or on behalf of a club—

    (a) to or to the order of a member of the club who is aged under 18, or

    (b) to the order of a member of the club, to an individual who is aged under 18.

  (4) This subsection applies to—

    (a) a person who works on the premises in a capacity, whether paid or unpaid, which authorises him to prevent the supply, and

    (b) any member or officer of the club who at the time of the supply is present on the relevant premises in a capacity which enables him to prevent it. [S]

147A Persistently selling alcohol to children

  (1) A person is guilty of an offence if—

    (a) on 2 or more different occasions within a period of 3 consecutive months alcohol is unlawfully sold on the same premises to an individual aged under 18;

    (b) at the time of each sale the premises were either licensed premises or premises authorised to be used for a permitted temporary activity by virtue of Part 5; and

    (c) that person was a responsible person in relation to the premises at each such time. [S]

  (2) For the purposes of this section alcohol sold to an individual aged under 18 is unlawfully sold to him if—

    (a) the person making the sale believed the individual to be aged under 18; or

    (b) that person did not have reasonable grounds for believing the individual to be aged 18 or over.

  (3) For the purposes of subsection (2) a person has reasonable grounds for believing an individual to be aged 18 or over only if—

    (a) he asked the individual for evidence of his age and that individual produced evidence that would have convinced a reasonable person; or

    (b) nobody could reasonably have suspected from the individual's appearance that he was aged under 18.

  (4) A person is, in relation to premises and a time, a responsible person for the purposes of subsection (1) if, at that time, he is—

    (a) the person or one of the persons holding a premises licence in respect of the premises; or

    (b) the person or one of the persons who is the premises user in respect of a temporary event notice by reference to which the premises are authorised to be used for a permitted temporary activity by virtue of Part 5.

  (5) The individual to whom the sales mentioned in subsection (1) are made may, but need not be, the same in each case.

  (6) The same sale may not be counted in respect of different offences for the purpose—

    (a) of enabling the same person to be convicted of more than one offence under this section; or

    (b) of enabling the same person to be convicted of both an offence under this section and an offence under section 146 or 147.

  (7) In determining whether an offence under this section has been committed, the following shall be admissible as evidence that there has been an unlawful sale of alcohol to an individual aged under 18 on any premises on any occasion—

    (a) the conviction of a person for an offence under section 146 in respect of a sale to that individual on those premises on that occasion;

    (b) the giving to a person of a caution (within the meaning of Part 5 of the Police Act 1997) in respect of such an offence; or

    (c) the payment by a person of a fixed penalty under Part 1 of the Criminal Justice and Police Act 2001 in respect of such a sale.

149 Purchase of alcohol by or on behalf of children

  (1) An individual aged under 18 commits an offence if—

    (a) he buys or attempts to buy alcohol, or

    (b) where he is a member of a club—

        (i)   alcohol is supplied to him or to his order by or on behalf of the club, as a result of some act or default of his, or

        (ii) he attempts to have alcohol supplied to him or to his order by or on behalf of the club.

  (2) But subsection (1) does not apply where the individual buys or attempts to buy the alcohol at the request of—

    (a) a constable, or

    (b) a weights and measures inspector,

who is acting in the course of his duty.

  (3) A person commits an offence if—

    (a) he buys or attempts to buy alcohol on behalf of an individual aged under 18, or

    (b) where he is a member of a club, on behalf of an individual aged under 18 he—

        (i)   makes arrangements whereby alcohol is supplied to him or to his order by or on behalf of the club, or

        (ii) attempts to make such arrangements.

  (4) A person ("the relevant person") commits an offence if—

    (a) he buys or attempts to buy alcohol for consumption on relevant premises by an individual aged under 18, or

    (b) where he is a member of a club—

        (i)   by some act or default of his, alcohol is supplied to him, or to his order, by or on behalf of the club for consumption on relevant premises by an individual aged under 18, or

        (ii) he attempts to have alcohol so supplied for such consumption.

  (5) But subsection (4) does not apply where—

    (a) the relevant person is aged 18 or over,

    (b) the individual is aged 16 or 17,

    (c) the alcohol is beer, wine or cider,

    (d) its purchase or supply is for consumption at a table meal on relevant premises, and

    (e) the individual is accompanied at the meal by an individual aged 18 or over.

  (6) Where a person is charged with an offence under subsection (3) or (4) it is a defence that he had no reason to suspect that the individual was aged under 18. [S]

150   Consumption of alcohol by children

(1) An individual aged under 18 commits an offence if he knowingly consumes alcohol on relevant premises.

(2) A person to whom subsection (3) applies commits an offence if he knowingly allows the consumption of alcohol on relevant premises by an individual aged under 18.

(3) This subsection applies—

   (a) to a person who works at the premises in a capacity, whether paid or unpaid, which authorises him to prevent the consumption, and

   (b) where the alcohol was supplied by a club to or to the order of a member of the club, to any member or officer of the club who is present at the premises at the time of the consumption in a capacity which enables him to prevent it.

(4) Subsections (1) and (2) do not apply where—

   (a) the individual is aged 16 or 17,

   (b) the alcohol is beer, wine or cider,

   (c) its consumption is at a table meal on relevant premises, and

   (d) the individual is accompanied at the meal by an individual aged 18 or over. [S]

151   Delivering alcohol to children

(1) A person who works on relevant premises in any capacity, whether paid or unpaid, commits an offence if he knowingly delivers to an individual aged under 18—

   (a) alcohol sold on the premises, or

   (b) alcohol supplied on the premises by or on behalf of a club to or to the order of a member of the club.

(2) A person to whom subsection (3) applies commits an offence if he knowingly allows anybody else to deliver to an individual aged under 18 alcohol sold on relevant premises.

(3) This subsection applies to a person who works on the premises in a capacity, whether paid or unpaid, which authorises him to prevent the delivery of the alcohol.

(4) A person to whom subsection (5) applies commits an offence if he knowingly allows anybody else to deliver to an individual aged under 18 alcohol supplied on relevant premises by or on behalf of a club to or to the order of a member of the club.

(5) This subsection applies—

   (a) to a person who works on the premises in a capacity, whether paid or unpaid, which authorises him to prevent the sale, and

   (b) to any member or officer of the club who at the time of the supply in question is present on the premises in a capacity which enables him to prevent the supply.

(6) Subsections (1), (2) and (4) do not apply where—

   (a) the alcohol is delivered at a place where the buyer or, as the case may be, person supplied lives or works, or

   (b) the individual aged under 18 works on the relevant premises in a capacity, whether paid or unpaid, which involves the delivery of alcohol, or

   (c) the alcohol is sold or supplied for consumption on the relevant premises. [S]

152   Sending a child to obtain alcohol

(1) A person commits an offence if he knowingly sends an individual aged under 18 to obtain—

   (a) alcohol sold or to be sold on relevant premises for consumption off the premises, or

   (b) alcohol supplied or to be supplied by or on behalf of a club to or to the order of a member of the club for such consumption.

(2) For the purposes of this section, it is immaterial whether the individual aged under 18 is sent to obtain the alcohol from the relevant premises or from other premises from which it is delivered in pursuance of the sale or supply.

(3) Subsection (1) does not apply where the individual aged under 18 works on the relevant premises in a capacity, whether paid or unpaid, which involves the delivery of alcohol.

(4) Subsection (1) also does not apply where the individual aged under 18 is sent by—
   (a) a constable, or
   (b) a weights and measures inspector,
who is acting in the course of his duty. [S]

153 Prohibition of unsupervised sales by children

(1) A responsible person commits an offence if on any relevant premises he knowingly allows an individual aged under 18 to make on the premises—
   (a) any sale of alcohol, or
   (b) any supply of alcohol by or on behalf of a club to or to the order of a member of the club,
unless the sale or supply has been specifically approved by that or another responsible person.

(2) But subsection (1) does not apply where—
   (a) the alcohol is sold or supplied for consumption with a table meal,
   (b) it is sold or supplied in premises which are being used for the service of table meals (or in a part of any premises which is being so used), and
   (c) the premises are (or the part is) not used for the sale or supply of alcohol otherwise than to persons having table meals there and for consumption by such a person as an ancillary to his meal.

(4) In this section "responsible person" means—
   (a) in relation to licensed premises—
      (i)   the holder of the premises licence,
      (ii) the designated premises supervisor, or
      (iii) any individual aged 18 or over who is authorised for the purposes of this section by such a holder or supervisor,
   (b) in relation to premises in respect of which there is in force a club premises certificate, any member or officer of the club present on the premises in a capacity which enables him to prevent the supply in question, and
   (c) in relation to premises which may be used for a permitted temporary activity by virtue of Part 5—
      (i)   the premises user, or
      (ii) any individual aged 18 or over who is authorised for the purposes of this section by the premises user. [S]

159 Interpretation of this Part of this Act

In this Part—
   "authorisation" has the meaning given in section 136(5);
   "relevant premises" means—
      (a) licensed premises, or
      (b) premises in respect of which there is in force a club premises certificate, or
      (c) premises which may be used for a permitted temporary activity by virtue of Part 5;
   "table meal" means a meal eaten by a person seated at a table, or at a counter or other structure which serves the purpose of a table and is not used for the service of refreshments for consumption by persons not seated at a table or structure serving the purpose of a table
   "weights and measures inspector" means an inspector of weights and measures appointed under section 72(1) of the Weights and Measures Act 1985.

PART 9   MISCELLANEOUS AND SUPPLEMENTARY

187 Offences by bodies corporate etc.

(1) If an offence committed by a body corporate is shown—
   (a) to have been committed with the consent or connivance of an officer, or
   (b) to be attributable to any neglect on his part,

the officer as well as the body corporate is guilty of the offence and liable to be proceeded against and punished accordingly.

(2) If the affairs of a body corporate are managed by its members, subsection (1) applies in relation to the acts and defaults of a member in connection with his functions of management as if he were a director of the body.

(3) In subsection (1) "officer", in relation to a body corporate, means—

(a) a director, member of the committee of management, chief executive, manager, secretary or other similar officer of the body, or a person purporting to act in any such capacity, and

(b) an individual who is a controller of the body.

(4) If an offence committed by a partnership is shown—

(a) to have been committed with the consent or connivance of a partner, or

(b) to be attributable to any neglect on his part,

the partner as well as the partnership is guilty of the offence and liable to be proceeded against and punished accordingly.

(5) In subsection (4) "partner" includes a person purporting to act as a partner.

(6) If an offence committed by an unincorporated association (other than a partnership) is shown—

(a) to have been committed with the consent or connivance of an officer of the association or a member of its governing body, or

(b) to be attributable to any neglect on the part of such an officer or member,

that officer or member as well as the association is guilty of the offence and liable to be proceeded against and punished accordingly.

(8) In this section "offence" means an offence under this Act.

191   Meaning of "alcohol"

(1) In this Act, "alcohol" means spirits, wine, beer, cider or any other fermented, distilled or spirituous liquor (in any state), but does not include—

(a) alcohol which is of a strength not exceeding 0.5% at the time of the sale or supply in question,

(b) perfume,

(c) flavouring essences recognised by the Commissioners of Customs and Excise as not being intended for consumption as or with dutiable alcoholic liquor,

(d) the aromatic flavouring essence commonly known as Angostura bitters,

(e) alcohol which is, or is included in, a medicinal product or a veterinary medicinal product,

(f) denatured alcohol,

(g) methyl alcohol,

(h) naphtha, or

(i) alcohol contained in liqueur confectionery.

(2) In this section—

"denatured alcohol" has the same meaning as in section 5 of the Finance Act 1995;

"dutiable alcoholic liquor" has the same meaning as in the Alcoholic Liquor Duties Act 1979;

"liqueur confectionery" means confectionery which—

(a) contains alcohol in a proportion not greater than 0.2 litres of alcohol (of a strength not exceeding 57%) per kilogram of the confectionery, and

(b) either consists of separate pieces weighing not more than 42g or is designed to be broken into such pieces for the purpose of consumption;

"medicinal product" has the same meaning as in section 130 of the Medicines Act 1968;

"strength" is to be construed in accordance with section 2 of the Alcoholic Liquor Duties Act 1979, and

"veterinary medicinal product" has the same meaning as in regulation 2 of the Veterinary Medicines Regulations 2006.

192   Meaning of "sale by retail"

(1) For the purposes of this Act "sale by retail", in relation to any alcohol, means a sale of alcohol to any person, other than a sale of alcohol that—

    (a) is within subsection (2),

    (b) is made from premises owned by the person making the sale, or occupied by him under a lease to which the provisions of Part 2 of the Landlord and Tenant Act 1954 (security of tenure) apply, and

    (c) is made for consumption off the premises.

  (2) A sale of alcohol is within this subsection if it is—

    (a) to a trader for the purposes of his trade,

    (b) to a club, which holds a club premises certificate, for the purposes of that club,

    (c) to the holder of a personal licence for the purpose of making sales authorised by a premises licence,

    (d) to the holder of a premises licence for the purpose of making sales authorised by that licence, or

    (e) to the premises user in relation to a temporary event notice for the purpose of making sales authorised by that notice.

193   Other definitions

  (1) In this Act—

"beer" has the same meaning as in the Alcoholic Liquor Duties Act 1979;

"cider" has the same meaning as in that Act;

"licensed premises" means premises in respect of which a premises licence has effect;

"licensing functions" is to be construed in accordance with section 4(1);

"premises" means any place and includes a vehicle, vessel or moveable structure;

"recognised club" means a club which satisfies conditions 1 to 3 of the general conditions in section 62;

"vehicle" means a vehicle intended or adapted for use on roads;

"vessel" includes a ship, boat, raft or other apparatus constructed or adapted for floating on water;

"wine" means—

    (a) "wine" within the meaning of the Alcoholic Liquor Duties Act 1979, and

    (b) "made-wine" within the meaning of that Act.

  (2) For the purposes of references in this Act to the prevention of illegal working in licensed premises, a person is working illegally if by doing that work at that time the person is committing an offence under section 24B of the Immigration Act 1971.

Sexual Offences Act 2003

PART 1   SEXUAL OFFENCES

1   Rape

  (1) A person (A) commits an offence if—

    (a) he intentionally penetrates the vagina, anus or mouth of another person (B) with his penis,

    (b) B does not consent to the penetration, and

    (c) A does not reasonably believe that B consents. [I]

  (2) Whether a belief is reasonable is to be determined having regard to all the circumstances, including any steps A has taken to ascertain whether B consents.

  (3) Sections 75 and 76 apply to an offence under this section.

2   Assault by penetration

  (1) A person (A) commits an offence if—

    (a) he intentionally penetrates the vagina or anus of another person (B) with a part of his body or anything else,

    (b) the penetration is sexual,

(c) B does not consent to the penetration, and

(d) A does not reasonably believe that B consents. [I]

(2) Whether a belief is reasonable is to be determined having regard to all the circumstances, including any steps A has taken to ascertain whether B consents.

(3) Sections 75 and 76 apply to an offence under this section.

3   Sexual assault

(1) A person (A) commits an offence if—

(a) he intentionally touches another person (B),

(b) the touching is sexual,

(c) B does not consent to the touching, and

(d) A does not reasonably believe that B consents.

(2) Whether a belief is reasonable is to be determined having regard to all the circumstances, including any steps A has taken to ascertain whether B consents.

(3) Sections 75 and 76 apply to an offence under this section. [E]

4   Causing a person to engage in sexual activity without consent

(1) A person (A) commits an offence if—

(a) he intentionally causes another person (B) to engage in an activity,

(b) the activity is sexual,

(c) B does not consent to engaging in the activity, and

(d) A does not reasonably believe that B consents.

(2) Whether a belief is reasonable is to be determined having regard to all the circumstances, including any steps A has taken to ascertain whether B consents.

(3) Sections 75 and 76 apply to an offence under this section.

(4) A person guilty of an offence under this section, if the activity caused involved—

(a) penetration of B's anus or vagina,

(b) penetration of B's mouth with a person's penis,

(c) penetration of a person's anus or vagina with a part of B's body or by B with anything else, or

(d) penetration of a person's mouth with B's penis,

is liable, on conviction on indictment, to imprisonment for life. [E] and [I]

(5) Unless subsection (4) applies, a person guilty of an offence under this section is liable—

(a) on summary conviction, to imprisonment for a term not exceeding 6 months or to a fine not exceeding the statutory maximum or both;

(b) on conviction on indictment, to imprisonment for a term not exceeding 10 years.

5   Rape of a child under 13

(1) A person commits an offence if—

(a) he intentionally penetrates the vagina, anus or mouth of another person with his penis, and

(b) the other person is under 13. [I]

6   Assault of a child under 13 by penetration

(1) A person commits an offence if—

(a) he intentionally penetrates the vagina or anus of another person with a part of his body or anything else,

(b) the penetration is sexual, and

(c) the other person is under 13. [I]

7   Sexual assault of a child under 13

(1) A person commits an offence if—

(a) he intentionally touches another person,

(b) the touching is sexual, and

(c) the other person is under 13. [E]

8   Causing or inciting a child under 13 to engage in sexual activity

(1) A person commits an offence if—

(a) he intentionally causes or incites another person (B) to engage in an activity,

(b) the activity is sexual, and

(c) B is under 13. [E]

(2) A person guilty of an offence under this section, if the activity caused or incited involved—

(a) penetration of B's anus or vagina,

(b) penetration of B's mouth with a person's penis,

(c) penetration of a person's anus or vagina with a part of B's body or by B with anything else, or

(d) penetration of a person's mouth with B's penis,

is liable, on conviction on indictment, to imprisonment for life.

9   Sexual activity with a child

(1) A person aged 18 or over (A) commits an offence if—

(a) he intentionally touches another person (B),

(b) the touching is sexual, and

(c) either—

(i)   B is under 16 and A does not reasonably believe that B is 16 or over, or

(ii) B is under 13. [E]

(2) A person guilty of an offence under this section, if the touching involved—

(a) penetration of B's anus or vagina with a part of A's body or anything else,

(b) penetration of B's mouth with A's penis,

(c) penetration of A's anus or vagina with a part of B's body, or

(d) penetration of A's mouth with B's penis,

is liable, on conviction on indictment, to imprisonment for a term not exceeding 14 years.

10   Causing or inciting a child to engage in sexual activity

(1) A person aged 18 or over (A) commits an offence if—

(a) he intentionally causes or incites another person (B) to engage in an activity,

(b) the activity is sexual, and

(c) either—

(i)   B is under 16 and A does not reasonably believe that B is 16 or over, or

(ii) B is under 13. [E]

(2) A person guilty of an offence under this section, if the activity caused or incited involved—

(a) penetration of B's anus or vagina,

(b) penetration of B's mouth with a person's penis,

(c) penetration of a person's anus or vagina with a part of B's body or by B with anything else, or

(d) penetration of a person's mouth with B's penis,

is liable, on conviction on indictment, to imprisonment for a term not exceeding 14 years.

11   Engaging in sexual activity in the presence of a child

(1) A person aged 18 or over (A) commits an offence if—

(a) he intentionally engages in an activity,

(b) the activity is sexual,

(c) for the purpose of obtaining sexual gratification, he engages in it—

(i)   when another person (B) is present or is in a place from which A can be observed, and,

(ii) knowing or believing that B is aware, or intending that B should be aware, that he is engaging in it, and

(d) either—

(i)   B is under 16 and A does not reasonably believe that B is 16 or over, or

(ii) B is under 13. [E]

12   Causing a child to watch a sexual act

(1) A person aged 18 or over (A) commits an offence if—

    (a) for the purpose of obtaining sexual gratification, he intentionally causes another person (B) to watch a third person engaging in an activity, or to look at an image of any person engaging in an activity,

    (b) the activity is sexual, and

    (c) either—

        (i)   B is under 16 and A does not reasonably believe that B is 16 or over, or

        (ii) B is under 13. [E]

13   Child sex offences committed by children or young persons

(1) A person under 18 commits an offence if he does anything which would be an offence under any of sections 9 to 12 if he were aged 18. [E]

14   Arranging or facilitating commission of a child sex offence

(1) A person commits an offence if—

    (a) he intentionally arranges or facilitates something that he intends to do, intends another person to do, or believes that another person will do, in any part of the world, and

    (b) doing it will involve the commission of an offence under any of sections 9 to 13.

(2) A person does not commit an offence under this section if—

    (a) he arranges or facilitates something that he believes another person will do, but that he does not intend to do or intend another person to do, and

    (b) any offence within subsection (1)(b) would be an offence against a child for whose protection he acts.

(3) For the purposes of subsection (2), a person acts for the protection of a child if he acts for the purpose of—

    (a) protecting the child from sexually transmitted infection,

    (b) protecting the physical safety of the child,

    (c) preventing the child from becoming pregnant, and

    (d) promoting the child's emotional well-being by the giving of advice,

and not for the purpose of obtaining sexual gratification or for the purpose of causing or encouraging the activity constituting the offence within subsection (1)(b) or the child's participation in it. [E]

15   Meeting a child following sexual grooming, etc.

(1) A person aged 18 or over (A) commits an offence if—

    (a) A has met or communicated with another person (B) on one or more occasions and subsequently—

        (i)   A intentionally meets B,

        (ii) A travels with the intention of meeting B in any part of the world or arranges to meet B in any part of the world, or

        (iii) B travels with the intention of meeting A in any part of the world,

    (b) A intends to do anything to or in respect of B, during or after the meeting mentioned in paragraph (a)(i) to (iii) and in any part of the world, which if done will involve the commission by A of a relevant offence,

    (c) B is under 16, and

    (d) A does not reasonably believe that B is 16 or over.

(2) In subsection (1)—

    (a) the reference to A having met or communicated with B is a reference to A having met B in any part of the world or having communicated with B by any means from, to or in any part of the world;

    (b) "relevant offence" means—

        (i)   an offence under this Part, or

(iii) anything done outside England and Wales which is not an offence within sub-paragraph (i) or (ii) but would be an offence within sub-paragraph (i) if done in England and Wales. [E]

15A   Sexual communication with a child

(1) A person aged 18 or over (A) commits an offence if—

(a) for the purpose of obtaining sexual gratification, A intentionally communicates with another person (B),

(b) the communication is sexual or is intended to encourage B to make (whether to A or to another) a communication that is sexual, and

(c) B is under 16 and A does not reasonably believe that B is 16 or over.

(2) For the purposes of this section, a communication is sexual if—

(a) any part of it relates to sexual activity, or

(b) a reasonable person would, in all the circumstances but regardless of any person's purpose, consider any part of the communication to be sexual;

and in paragraph (a) "sexual activity" means an activity that a reasonable person would, in all the circumstances but regardless of any person's purpose, consider to be sexual.

16   Abuse of position of trust: sexual activity with a child

(1) A person aged 18 or over (A) commits an offence if—

(a) he intentionally touches another person (B),

(b) the touching is sexual,

(c) A is in a position of trust in relation to B, and

(d) where subsection (2) applies, A knows or could reasonably be expected to know of the circumstances by virtue of which he is in a position of trust in relation to B, and

(e) either—

(i)   B is under 18 and A does not reasonably believe that B is 18 or over, or

(ii) B is under 13.

(2) This subsection applies where A—

(a) is in a position of trust in relation to B by virtue of circumstances within section 21 (2), (3), (4) or (5), and

(b) is not in such a position of trust by virtue of other circumstances.

(3) Where in proceedings for an offence under this section it is proved that the other person was under 18, the defendant is to be taken not to have reasonably believed that that person was 18 or over unless sufficient evidence is adduced to raise an issue as to whether he reasonably believed it.

(4) Where in proceedings for an offence under this section—

(a) it is proved that the defendant was in a position of trust in relation to the other person by virtue of circumstances within section 21(2), (3), (4) or (5), and

(b) it is not proved that he was in such a position of trust by virtue of other circumstances,

it is to be taken that the defendant knew or could reasonably have been expected to know of the circumstances by virtue of which he was in such a position of trust unless sufficient evidence is adduced to raise an issue as to whether he knew or could reasonably have been expected to know of those circumstances. [E]

17   Abuse of position of trust: causing or inciting a child to engage in sexual activity

(1) A person aged 18 or over (A) commits an offence if—

(a) he intentionally causes or incites another person (B) to engage in an activity,

(b) the activity is sexual,

(c) A is in a position of trust in relation to B,

(d) where subsection (2) applies, A knows or could reasonably be expected to know of the circumstances by virtue of which he is in a position of trust in relation to B, and

(e) either—

(i) B is under 18 and A does not reasonably believe that B is 18 or over, or

(ii) B is under 13.

(2) This subsection applies where A—

(a) is in a position of trust in relation to B by virtue of circumstances within section 21 (2), (3), (4) or (5), and

(b) is not in such a position of trust by virtue of other circumstances.

(3) Where in proceedings for an offence under this section it is proved that the other person was under 18, the defendant is to be taken not to have reasonably believed that that person was 18 or over unless sufficient evidence is adduced to raise an issue as to whether he reasonably believed it.

(4) Where in proceedings for an offence under this section—

(a) it is proved that the defendant was in a position of trust in relation to the other person by virtue of circumstances within section 21(2), (3), (4) or (5), and

(b) it is not proved that he was in such a position of trust by virtue of other circumstances,

it is to be taken that the defendant knew or could reasonably have been expected to know of the circumstances by virtue of which he was in such a position of trust unless sufficient evidence is adduced to raise an issue as to whether he knew or could reasonably have been expected to know of those circumstances. [E]

18 Abuse of position of trust: sexual activity in the presence of a child

(1) A person aged 18 or over (A) commits an offence if—

(a) he intentionally engages in an activity,

(b) the activity is sexual,

(c) for the purpose of obtaining sexual gratification, he engages in it

(i) when another person (B) is present, or is in a place from which A can be observed, and

(ii) knowing or believing that B is aware, or intending that B should be aware, that he is engaging in it,

(d) A is in a position of trust in relation to B,

(e) where subsection (2) applies, A knows or could reasonably be expected to know of the circumstances by virtue of which he is in a position of trust in relation to B, and

(f) either—

(i) B is under 18 and A does not reasonably believe that B is 18 or over, or

(ii) B is under 13.

(2) This subsection applies where A—

(a) is in a position of trust in relation to B by virtue of circumstances within section 21 (2), (3), (4) or (5), and

(b) is not in such a position of trust by virtue of other circumstances.

(3) Where in proceedings for an offence under this section it is proved that the other person was under 18, the defendant is to be taken not to have reasonably believed that that person was 18 or over unless sufficient evidence is adduced to raise an issue as to whether he reasonably believed it.

(4) Where in proceedings for an offence under this section—

(a) it is proved that the defendant was in a position of trust in relation to the other person by virtue of circumstances within section 21(2), (3), (4) or (5), and

(b) it is not proved that he was in such a position of trust by virtue of other circumstances,

it is to be taken that the defendant knew or could reasonably have been expected to know of the circumstances by virtue of which he was in such a position of trust unless sufficient evidence is adduced to raise an issue as to whether he knew or could reasonably have been expected to know of those circumstances. [E]

19 Abuse of position of trust: causing a child to watch a sexual act

(1) A person aged 18 or over (A) commits an offence if—

(a) for the purpose of obtaining sexual gratification, he intentionally causes another person (B) to watch a third person engaging in an activity, or to look at an image of any person engaging in an activity,

    (b) the activity is sexual,

    (c) A is in a position of trust in relation to B,

    (d) where subsection (2) applies, A knows or could reasonably be expected to know of the circumstances by virtue of which he is in a position of trust in relation to B, and

    (e) either—

        (i) B is under 18 and A does not reasonably believe that B is 18 or over, or

        (ii) B is under 13.

  (2) This subsection applies where A—

    (a) is in a position of trust in relation to B by virtue of circumstances within section 21(2), (3), (4) or (5), and

    (b) is not in such a position of trust by virtue of other circumstances.

  (3) Where in proceedings for an offence under this section it is proved that the other person was under 18, the defendant is to be taken not to have reasonably believed that that person was 18 or over unless sufficient evidence is adduced to raise an issue as to whether he reasonably believed it.

  (4) Where in proceedings for an offence under this section—

    (a) it is proved that the defendant was in a position of trust in relation to the other person by virtue of circumstances within section 21(2), (3), (4) or (5), and

    (b) it is not proved that he was in such a position of trust by virtue of other circumstances,

it is to be taken that the defendant knew or could reasonably have been expected to know of the circumstances by virtue of which he was in such a position of trust unless sufficient evidence is adduced to raise an issue as to whether he knew or could reasonably have been expected to know of those circumstances. [E]

20　Abuse of position of trust: acts done in Scotland

Anything which, if done in England and Wales, would constitute an offence under any of sections 16 to 19 also constitutes that offence if done in Scotland or Northern Ireland.

21　Positions of trust

  (1) For the purposes of sections 16 to 19, a person (A) is in a position of trust in relation to another person (B) if—

    (a) any following subsections applies, or

    (b) any condition specified in an order made by the Secretary of State is met.

  (2) This subsection applies if A looks after persons under 18 who are detained in an institution by virtue of a court order or under an enactment, and B is so detained in that institution.

  (3) This subsection applies if A looks after persons under 18 who are resident in a home or other place in which—

    (a) accommodation and maintenance are provided by an authority in accordance with section 22C(6) of the Children Act 1989 . . . , or

    (b) accommodation is provided by a voluntary organisation under section 59(1) of the Children Act 1989,

and B is resident, and is so provided with accommodation and maintenance or accommodation, in that place.

  (4) This subsection applies if A looks after persons under 18 who are accommodated and cared for in one of the following institutions—

    (a) a hospital,

    (b) in Wales, an independent clinic,

    (c) a care home,

    (d) a community home, voluntary home or children's home, or

    (e) a home provided under section 82(5) of the Children Act 1989,

    (g) a place in Wales at which a care home service is provided,

    (h) premises in Wales at which a secure accommodation service is provided,

and B is accommodated and cared for in that institution.

  (5) This subsection applies if A looks after persons under 18 who are receiving education at an educational institution and B is receiving, and A is not receiving, education at that institution.

(7) This subsection applies if A is engaged in the provision of services under, or pursuant to anything done under—

    (a) sections 8 to 10 of the Employment and Training Act 1973, or

    (b) section 68, 70(1)(b) or 74 of the Education and Skills Act 2008,

and, in that capacity, looks after B on an individual basis.

(8) This subsection applies if A regularly has unsupervised contact with B (whether face to face or by any other means)—

    (a) in the exercise of functions of a local authority under section 20 or 21 of the Children Act 1989 . . .

(9) This subsection applies if A, as a person who is to report to the court under section 7 of the Children Act 1989 on matters relating to the welfare of B, regularly has unsupervised contact with B (whether face to face or by any other means).

(10) This subsection applies if A is a personal adviser appointed for B under—

    (a) section 23B(2) of, or paragraph 19C of Schedule 2 to, the Children Act 1989 and, in that capacity, looks after B on an individual basis.

(11) This subsection applies if—

    (a) B is subject to a care order, a supervision order or an education supervision order, and

    (b) in the exercise of functions conferred by virtue of the order on an authorised person or the authority designated by the order, A looks after B on an individual basis.

(12) This subsection applies if A—

    (a) is an officer of the Service . . . appointed for B under section 41(1) of the Children Act 1989,

    (b) is appointed a children's guardian of B under rule 6 or rule 18 of the Adoption Rules 1984,

    (c) is appointed to be the guardian ad litem of B under rule 9.5 of the Family Proceedings Rules 1991, or

    (d) is appointed to be the children's guardian of B under rule 59 of the Family Procedure (Adoption) Rules 2005 or rule 16.3(1)(ii) or rule 16.4 of the Family Procedure Rules 2010,

and, in that capacity, regularly has unsupervised contact with B (whether face to face or by any other means).

(13) This subsection applies if—

    (a) B is subject to requirements imposed by or under an enactment on his release from detention for a criminal offence, or is subject to requirements imposed by a court order made in criminal proceedings, and

    (b) A looks after B on an individual basis in pursuance of the requirements.

22   Positions of trust: interpretation

(1) The following provisions apply for the purposes of section 21.

(2) Subject to subsection (3), a person looks after persons under 18 if he is regularly involved in caring for, training, supervising or being in sole charge of such persons.

(3) A person (A) looks after another person (B) on an individual basis if—

    (a) A is regularly involved in caring for, training or supervising B, and

    (b) in the course of his involvement, A regularly has unsupervised contact with B alone (whether face to face or by any other means).

(4) A person receives education at an educational institution if—

    (a) he is registered or otherwise enrolled as a pupil or student at the institution, or

    (b) he receives education at the institution under arrangements with another educational institution at which he is so registered or otherwise enrolled.

(5) In section 21—

"authority"—

    (a) in relation to England and Wales, means a local authority;

"care home" means an establishment in England which is a care home for the purposes of the Care Standards Act 2000;

"care order" has—

    (a) in relation to England and Wales, the same meaning as in the Children Act 1989

"children's home" has—

    (a) in relation to England and Wales, the meaning given by section 1 of the Care Standards Act 2000,

"community home" has, in relation to England, the meaning given by section 53 of the Children Act 1989;

"education supervision order" has—

    (a) in relation to England and Wales, the meaning given by section 36 of the Children Act 1989,

"hospital" means—

    (a) a hospital as defined by section 275 of the National Health Service Act 2006, or section 206 of the National Health Service (Wales) Act 2006; or

    (b) any other establishment—

        (i)   in England, in which any of the services listed in subsection (6) are provided; and

        (ii) in Wales, which is a hospital within the meaning given by section 2(3) of the Care Standards Act 2000;

"independent clinic" has—

    (a) the meaning given by section 2 of the Care Standards Act 2000;

"supervision order" has—

    (a) in relation to England and Wales, the meaning given by section 31(11) of the Children Act 1989

"voluntary home" has—

    (a) in relation to England, the meaning given by section 60(3) of the Children Act 1989.

  (6) The services referred to in paragraph (b)(i) of the definition of "hospital" are as follows—

    (a) medical treatment under anaesthesia or intravenously administered sedation;

    (b) dental treatment under general anaesthesia;

    (c) obstetric services and, in connection with childbirth, medical services;

    (d) termination of pregnancies;

    (e) cosmetic surgery, other than—

        (i)   ear and body piercing;

        (ii) tattooing;

        (iii) the subcutaneous injection of a substance or substances into the skin for cosmetic purposes; or

        (iv) the removal of hair roots or small blemishes on the skin by the application of heat using an electric current.

23 Sections 16 to 19: exception for spouses and civil partners

  (1) Conduct by a person (A) which would otherwise be an offence under any of sections 16 to 19 against another person (B) is not an offence under that section if at the time—

    (a) B is 16 or over, and

    (b) A and B are lawfully married or civil partners of each other.

  (2) In proceedings for such an offence it is for the defendant to prove that A and B were at the time lawfully married or civil partners of each other.

24 Sections 16 to 19: sexual relationships which pre-date position of trust

  (1) Conduct by a person (A) which would otherwise be an offence under any of sections 16 to 19 against another person (B) is not an offence under that section if, immediately before the position of trust arose, a sexual relationship existed between A and B.

  (2) Subsection (1) does not apply if at that time sexual intercourse between A and B would have been unlawful.

  (3) In proceedings for an offence under any of sections 16 to 19 it is for the defendant to prove that such a relationship existed at that time.

25 Sexual activity with a child family member

(1) A person (A) commits an offence if—

(a) he intentionally touches another person (B),

(b) the touching is sexual,

(c) the relation of A to B is within section 27,

(d) A knows or could reasonably be expected to know that his relation to B is of a description falling within that section, and

(e) either—

(i) B is under 18 and A does not reasonably believe that B is 18 or over, or

(ii) B is under 13. [E]

(2) Where in proceedings for an offence under this section it is proved that the other person was under 18, the defendant is to be taken not to have reasonably believed that that person was 18 or over unless sufficient evidence is adduced to raise an issue as to whether he reasonably believed it.

(3) Where in proceedings for an offence under this section it is proved that the relation of the defendant to the other person was of a description falling within section 27, it is to be taken that the defendant knew or could reasonably have been expected to know that his relation to the other person was of that description unless sufficient evidence is adduced to raise an issue as to whether he knew or could reasonably have been expected to know that it was.

(6) This section applies where the touching involved—

(a) penetration of B's anus or vagina with a part of A's body or anything else,

(b) penetration of B's mouth with A's penis,

(c) penetration of A's anus or vagina with a part of B's body, or

(d) penetration of A's mouth with B's penis.

26 Inciting a child family member to engage in sexual activity

(1) A person (A) commits an offence if—

(a) he intentionally incites another person (B) to touch, or allow himself to be touched by, A,

(b) the touching is sexual,

(c) the relation of A to B is within section 27,

(d) A knows or could reasonably be expected to know that his relation to B is of a description falling within that section, and

(e) either—

(i) B is under 18 and A does not reasonably believe that B is 18 or over, or

(ii) B is under 13. [E]

(2) Where in proceedings for an offence under this section it is proved that the other person was under 18, the defendant is to be taken not to have reasonably believed that that person was 18 or over unless sufficient evidence is adduced to raise an issue as to whether he reasonably believed it.

(3) Where in proceedings for an offence under this section it is proved that the relation of the defendant to the other person was of a description falling within section 27, it is to be taken that the defendant knew or could reasonably have been expected to know that his relation to the other person was of that description unless sufficient evidence is adduced to raise an issue as to whether he knew or could reasonably have been expected to know that it was.

(6) This section applies where the touching to which the incitement related involved—

(a) penetration of B's anus or vagina with a part of A's body or anything else,

(b) penetration of B's mouth with A's penis,

(c) penetration of A's anus or vagina with a part of B's body, or

(d) penetration of A's mouth with B's penis.

27 Family relationships

(1) The relation of one person (A) to another (B) is within this section if—

(a) it is within any of subsections (2) to (4), or

(b) it would be within one of those subsections but for section 39 of the Adoption Act 1976 or section 67 of the Adoption and Children Act 2002 (status conferred by adoption).

(2) The relation of A to B is within this subsection if—

    (a) one of them is the other's parent, grandparent, brother, sister, half-brother, half-sister, aunt or uncle, or

    (b) A is or has been B's foster parent.

(3) The relation of A to B is within this subsection if A and B live or have lived in the same household, or A is or has been regularly involved in caring for, training, supervising or being in sole charge of B, and—

    (a) one of them is or has been the partner of the other's step-parent,

    (b) A and B are cousins, or

    (c) one of them is or has been the other's stepbrother or stepsister, or

    (d) the parent or present or former foster parent of one of them is or has been the other's foster parent.

(4) The relation of A to B is within this subsection if—

    (a) A and B live in the same household, and

    (b) A is regularly involved in caring for, training, supervising or being in sole charge of B.

(5) For the purposes of this section—

    (a) "aunt" means the sister or half-sister of a person's parent, and "uncle" has a corresponding meaning;

    (b) "cousin" means the child of an aunt or uncle;

    (c) a person is a child's foster parent if—

        (i) he is a person with whom the child has been placed under section 22C of the Children Act 1989 in a placement falling within subsection (6)(a) or (b) of that section (placement with local authority foster parent)

        (ia) he is a person with whom the child has been placed under section 59(1)(a) of that Act (placement by voluntary organisation), or

        (ii) he fosters the child privately, within the meaning given by section 66(1)(b) of that Act;

    (d) a person is another's partner (whether they are of different sexes or the same sex) if they live together as partners in an enduring family relationship;

    (e) "step-parent" includes a parent's partner and "stepbrother" and "stepsister" include the child of a parent's partner.

28 Sections 25 and 26: exception for spouses and civil partners

(1) Conduct by a person (A) which would otherwise be an offence under section 25 or 26 against another person (B) is not an offence under that section if at the time—

    (a) B is 16 or over, and

    (b) A and B are lawfully married or civil partners of each other.

(2) In proceedings for such an offence it is for the defendant to prove that A and B were at the time lawfully married or civil partners of each other.

29 Sections 25 and 26: sexual relationships which pre-date family relationships

(1) Conduct by a person (A) which would otherwise be an offence under section 25 or 26 against another person (B) is not an offence under that section if—

    (a) the relation of A to B is not within subsection (2) of section 27,

    (b) it would not be within that subsection if section 39 of the Adoption Act 1976 or section 67 of the Adoption and Children Act 2002 did not apply, and

    (c) immediately before the relation of A to B first became such as to fall within section 27, a sexual relationship existed between A and B.

(2) Subsection (1) does not apply if at the time referred to in subsection (1)(c) sexual intercourse between A and B would have been unlawful.

(3) In proceedings for an offence under section 25 or 26 it is for the defendant to prove the matters mentioned in subsection (1)(a) to (c).

30   Sexual activity with a person with a mental disorder impeding choice

(1) A person (A) commits an offence if—

  (a) he intentionally touches another person (B),

  (b) the touching is sexual,

  (c) B is unable to refuse because of or for a reason related to a mental disorder, and

  (d) A knows or could reasonably be expected to know that B has a mental disorder and that because of it or for a reason related to it B is likely to be unable to refuse.

(2) B is unable to refuse if—

  (a) he lacks the capacity to choose whether to agree to the touching (whether because he lacks sufficient understanding of the nature or reasonably foreseeable consequences of what is being done, or for any other reason), or

  (b) he is unable to communicate such a choice to A. [E]

(3) A person guilty of an offence under this section, if the touching involved—

  (a) penetration of B's anus or vagina with a part of A's body or anything else,

  (b) penetration of B's mouth with A's penis,

  (c) penetration of A's anus or vagina with a part of B's body, or

  (d) penetration of A's mouth with B's penis,

is liable, on conviction on indictment, to imprisonment for life.

31   Causing or inciting a person with a mental disorder impeding choice to engage in sexual activity

(1) A person (A) commits an offence if—

  (a) he intentionally causes or incites another person (B) to engage in an activity,

  (b) the activity is sexual,

  (c) B is unable to refuse because of or for a reason related to a mental disorder, and

  (d) A knows or could reasonably be expected to know that B has a mental disorder and that because of or for a reason related to it B is likely to be unable to refuse.

(2) B is unable to refuse if—

  (a) he lacks the capacity to choose whether to agree to engaging in the activity caused or incited (whether because he lacks sufficient understanding of the nature or reasonably foreseeable consequences of the activity, or for any other reason), or

  (b) he is unable to communicate such a choice to A. [E]

(3) A person guilty of an offence under this section, if the activity caused or incited involved—

  (a) penetration of B's anus or vagina,

  (b) penetration of B's mouth with a person's penis,

  (c) penetration of a person's anus or vagina with a part of B's body or by B with anything else, or

  (d) penetration of a person's mouth with B's penis,

is liable, on conviction on indictment, to imprisonment for life.

32   Engaging in sexual activity in the presence of a person with a mental disorder impeding choice

(1) A person (A) commits an offence if—

  (a) he intentionally engages in an activity,

  (b) the activity is sexual,

  (c) for the purpose of obtaining sexual gratification, he engages in it—

    (i)   when another person (B) is present or is in a place from which A can be observed, and

    (ii) knowing or believing that B is aware, or intending that B should be aware, that he is engaging in it,

  (d) B is unable to refuse because of a mental disorder, and

  (e) A knows or could reasonably be expected to know that B has a mental disorder and that because of it B is likely to be unable to refuse.

(2) B is unable to refuse if—

(a) he lacks the capacity to choose whether to agree to being present (whether because he lacks sufficient understanding of the nature of the activity, or for any other reason), or

(b) he is unable to communicate such a choice to A. [E]

33 Causing a person with a mental disorder impeding choice to watch a sexual act

(1) A person (A) commits an offence if—

(a) for the purpose of obtaining sexual gratification, he intentionally causes another person (B) to watch a third person engaging in an activity, or to look at an image of any person engaging in an activity,

(b) the activity is sexual,

(c) B is unable to refuse because of or for a reason related to a mental disorder, and

(d) A knows or could reasonably be expected to know that B has a mental disorder and that because of it or for a reason related to it B is likely to be unable to refuse.

(2) B is unable to refuse if—

(a) he lacks the capacity to choose whether to agree to watching or looking (whether because he lacks sufficient understanding of the nature of the activity, or for any other reason), or

(b) he is unable to communicate such a choice to A. [E]

34 Inducement, threat or deception to procure sexual activity with a person with a mental disorder

(1) A person (A) commits an offence if—

(a) with the agreement of another person (B) he intentionally touches that person,

(b) the touching is sexual,

(c) A obtains B's agreement by means of an inducement offered or given, a threat made or a deception practised by A for that purpose,

(d) B has a mental disorder, and

(e) A knows or could reasonably be expected to know that B has a mental disorder. [E]

(2) A person guilty of an offence under this section, if the touching involved—

(a) penetration of B's anus or vagina with a part of A's body or anything else,

(b) penetration of B's mouth with A's penis,

(c) penetration of A's anus or vagina with a part of B's body, or

(d) penetration of A's mouth with B's penis,

is liable, on conviction on indictment, to imprisonment for life.

35 Causing a person with a mental disorder to engage in sexual activity by inducement, threat or deception

(1) A person (A) commits an offence if—

(a) by means of an inducement offered or given, a threat made or a deception practised by him for this purpose, he intentionally causes a person (B) to engage in, or to agree to engage in, an activity,

(b) the activity is sexual,

(c) B has a mental disorder, and

(d) A knows or could reasonably be expected to know that B has a mental disorder. [E]

(2) A person guilty of an offence under this section, if the activity caused involved—

(a) penetration of B's anus or vagina,

(b) penetration of B's mouth with a person's penis,

(c) penetration of a person's anus or vagina with a part of B's body or by B with anything else, or

(d) penetration of a person's mouth with B's penis, is liable, on conviction on indictment, to imprisonment for life.

36 Engaging in sexual activity in the presence, procured by inducement, threat or deception, of a person with a mental disorder

(1) A person (A) commits an offence if—

(a) he intentionally engages in an activity,

(b) the activity is sexual,

(c) for the purpose of obtaining sexual gratification, he engages in it—

    (i) when another person (B) is present or is in a place from which A can be observed, and

    (ii) knowing or believing that B is aware, or intending that B should be aware, that he is engaging in it,

(d) B agrees to be present or in the place referred to in paragraph (c)(i) because of an inducement offered or given, a threat made or a deception practised by A for the purpose of obtaining that agreement,

(e) B has a mental disorder, and

(f) A knows or could reasonably be expected to know that B has a mental disorder. [E]

37 Causing a person with a mental disorder to watch a sexual act by inducement, threat or deception

(1) A person (A) commits an offence if—

(a) for the purpose of obtaining sexual gratification, he intentionally causes another person (B) to watch a third person engaging in an activity, or to look at an image of any person engaging in an activity,

(b) the activity is sexual,

(c) B agrees to watch or look because of an inducement offered or given, a threat made or a deception practised by A for the purpose of obtaining that agreement,

(d) B has a mental disorder, and

(e) A knows or could reasonably be expected to know that B has a mental disorder. [E]

38 Care workers: sexual activity with a person with a mental disorder

(1) A person (A) commits an offence if—

(a) he intentionally touches another person (B),

(b) the touching is sexual,

(c) B has a mental disorder,

(d) A knows or could reasonably be expected to know that B has a mental disorder, and

(e) A is involved in B's care in a way that falls within section 42.

(2) Where in proceedings for an offence under this section it is proved that the other person had a mental disorder, it is to be taken that the defendant knew or could reasonably have been expected to know that that person had a mental disorder unless sufficient evidence is adduced to raise an issue as to whether he knew or could reasonably have been expected to know it. [E]

(3) A person guilty of an offence under this section, if the touching involved—

(a) penetration of B's anus or vagina with a part of A's body or anything else,

(b) penetration of B's mouth with A's penis,

(c) penetration of A's anus or vagina with a part of B's body, or

(d) penetration of A's mouth with B's penis,

is liable, on conviction on indictment, to imprisonment for a term not exceeding 14 years.

39 Care workers: causing or inciting sexual activity

(1) A person (A) commits an offence if—

(a) he intentionally causes or incites another person (B) to engage in an activity,

(b) the activity is sexual,

(c) B has a mental disorder,

(d) A knows or could reasonably be expected to know that B has a mental disorder, and

(e) A is involved in B's care in a way that falls within section 42.

(2) Where in proceedings for an offence under this section it is proved that the other person had a mental disorder, it is to be taken that the defendant knew or could reasonably have been expected to know that that person had a mental disorder unless sufficient evidence is adduced to raise an issue as to whether he knew or could reasonably have been expected to know it. [E]

(3) A person guilty of an offence under this section, if the activity caused or incited involved—

(a) penetration of B's anus or vagina,

(b) penetration of B's mouth with a person's penis,

(c) penetration of a person's anus or vagina with a part of B's body or by B with anything else, or

(d) penetration of a person's mouth with B's penis,

is liable, on conviction on indictment, to imprisonment for a term not exceeding 14 years.

40   Care workers: sexual activity in the presence of a person with a mental disorder

(1) A person (A) commits an offence if—

(a) he intentionally engages in an activity,

(b) the activity is sexual,

(c) for the purpose of obtaining sexual gratification, he engages in it—

(i)   when another person (B) is present or is in a place from which A can be observed, and

(ii)   knowing or believing that B is aware, or intending that B should be aware, that he is engaging in it,

(d) B has a mental disorder,

(e) A knows or could reasonably be expected to know that B has a mental disorder, and

(f) A is involved in B's care in a way that falls within section 42.

(2) Where in proceedings for an offence under this section it is proved that the other person had a mental disorder, it is to be taken that the defendant knew or could reasonably have been expected to know that that person had a mental disorder unless sufficient evidence is adduced to raise an issue as to whether he knew or could reasonably have been expected to know it. [E]

41   Care workers: causing a person with a mental disorder to watch a sexual act

(1) A person (A) commits an offence if—

(a) for the purpose of obtaining sexual gratification, he intentionally causes another person (B) to watch a third person engaging in an activity, or to look at an image of any person engaging in an activity,

(b) the activity is sexual,

(c) B has a mental disorder,

(d) A knows or could reasonably be expected to know that B has a mental disorder, and

(e) A is involved in B's care in a way that falls within section 42.

(2) Where in proceedings for an offence under this section it is proved that the other person had a mental disorder, it is to be taken that the defendant knew or could reasonably have been expected to know that that person had a mental disorder unless sufficient evidence is adduced to raise an issue as to whether he knew or could reasonably have been expected to know it. [E]

42   Care workers: interpretation

(1) For the purposes of sections 38 to 41, a person (A) is involved in the care of another person (B) in a way that falls within this section if any of subsections (2) to (4) applies.

(2) This subsection applies if—

(a) B is accommodated and cared for in a care home, community home, voluntary home or children's home, and

(b) A has functions to perform in the course of employment in the home or the premises which have brought him or are likely to bring him into regular face to face contact with B.

(3) This subsection applies if B is a patient for whom services are provided—

(a) by a National Health Service body or an independent medical agency, or

(b) in an independent hospital; or

(c) in Wales, in an independent clinic,

and A has functions to perform for the body or agency or in the clinic or hospital in the course of employment which have brought A or are likely to bring A into regular face to face contact with B.

(4) This subsection applies if A—

(a) is, whether or not in the course of employment, a provider of care, assistance or services to B in connection with B's mental disorder, and

(b) as such, has had or is likely to have regular face to face contact with B.

(5) In this section—

"care home" means

(a) an establishment in England which is a care home for the purposes of the Care Standards Act 2000;

"children's home"

(a) has the meaning given by section 1 of the Care Standards Act 2000 in relation to a children's home in England;

"community home" has the meaning given by section 53(1) of the Children Act 1989;

"employment" means any employment, whether paid or unpaid and whether under a contract of service or apprenticeship, under a contract for services, or otherwise than under a contract;

"independent clinic" has the meaning given by section 2 of the Care Standards Act 2000;

"independent hospital"—

(a) in England, means—

(i) a hospital as defined by section 275 of the National Health Service Act 2006 that is not a health service hospital as defined by that section; or

(ii) any other establishment in which any of the services listed in section 22(6) are provided and which is not a health service hospital as so defined; and

(b) in Wales, has the meaning given by section 2 of the Care Standards Act 2000;

"independent medical agency" means an undertaking (not being an independent hospital, or in Wales an independent clinic) which consists of or includes the provision of services by medical practitioners;

"National Health Service body" means—

(a) a Local Health Board,

(b) a National Health Service trust,

(ba) the Secretary of State in relation to the exercise of functions under section 2A or 2B of, or paragraph 7C, 8 or 12 of Schedule 1 to, the National Health Service Act 2006,

(bb) a local authority in relation to the exercise of functions under section 2B or 111 of, or any of paragraphs 1 to 7B, or 13 of Schedule 1 to, the National Health Service Act 2006, or

(d) a Special Health Authority;

"voluntary home" has the meaning given by section 60(3) of the Children Act 1989.

(6) In subsection (5), in the definition of "independent medical agency", "undertaking" includes any business or profession and—

(a) in relation to a public or local authority, includes the exercise of any functions of that authority; and

(b) in relation to any other body of persons, whether corporate or unincorporate, includes any of the activities of that body.

43 Sections 38 to 41: exception for spouses and civil partners

(1) Conduct by a person (A) which would otherwise be an offence under any of sections 38 to 41 against another person (B) is not an offence under that section if at the time—

(a) B is 16 or over, and

(b) A and B are lawfully married or civil partners of each other.

(2) In proceedings for such an offence it is for the defendant to prove that A and B were at the time lawfully married or civil partners of each other.

44 Sections 38 to 41: sexual relationships which pre-date care relationships

(1) Conduct by a person (A) which would otherwise be an offence under any of sections 38 to 41 against another person (B) is not an offence under that section if, immediately before A became involved in B's care in a way that falls within section 42, a sexual relationship existed between A and B.

(2) Subsection (1) does not apply if at that time sexual intercourse between A and B would have been unlawful.

(3) In proceedings for an offence under any of sections 38 to 41 it is for the defendant to prove that such a relationship existed at that time.

47   Paying for sexual services of a child

(1) A person (A) commits an offence if—
- (a) he intentionally obtains for himself the sexual services of another person (B),
- (b) before obtaining those services, he has made or promised payment for those services to B or a third person, or knows that another person has made or promised such a payment, and
- (c) either—
    - (i)   B is under 18, and A does not reasonably believe that B is 18 or over, or
    - (ii)   B is under 13.

(2) In this section, "payment" means any financial advantage, including the discharge of an obligation to pay or the provision of goods or services (including sexual services) gratuitously or at a discount. [E]

(3) A person guilty of an offence under this section against a person under 13, where subsection (6) applies, is liable on conviction on indictment to imprisonment for life.

(6) This subsection applies where the offence involved—
- (a) penetration of B's anus or vagina with a part of A's body or anything else,
- (b) penetration of B's mouth with A's penis,
- (c) penetration of A's anus or vagina with a part of B's body or by B with anything else, or
- (d) penetration of A's mouth with B's penis.

48   Causing or inciting sexual exploitation of a child

(1) A person (A) commits an offence if—
- (a) he intentionally causes or incites another person (B) to be sexually exploited, in any part of the world, and
- (b) either—
    - (i)   B is under 18, and A does not reasonably believe that B is 18 or over, or
    - (ii)   B is under 13. [E]

49   Controlling a child in relation to sexual exploitation

(1) A person (A) commits an offence if—
- (a) he intentionally controls any of the activities of another person (B) relating to B's sexual exploitation in any part of the world, and
- (b) either—
    - (i)   B is under 18, and A does not reasonably believe that B is 18 or over, or
    - (ii)   B is under 13. [E]

50   Arranging or facilitating sexual exploitation of a child

(1) A person (A) commits an offence if—
- (a) he intentionally arranges or facilitates the sexual exploitation in any part of the world of another person (B), and
- (b) either—
    - (i)   B is under 18, and A does not reasonably believe that B is 18 or over, or
    - (ii)   B is under 13. [E]

51   Sections 48 to 50: interpretation

(2) For the purposes of sections 48 to 50, a person (B) is sexually exploited if—
- (a) on at least one occasion and whether or not compelled to do so, B offers or provides sexual services to another person in return for payment or a promise of payment to B or a third person, or
- (b) an indecent image of B is recorded or streamed or otherwise transmitted;

and "sexual exploitation" is to be interpreted accordingly.

(3) In subsection (2), "payment" means any financial advantage, including the discharge of an obligation to pay or the provision of goods or services (including sexual services) gratuitously or at a discount.

51A   Soliciting

(1) It is an offence for a person in a street or public place to solicit another (B) for the purpose of obtaining B's sexual services as a prostitute. [S]

(2) The reference to a person in a street or public place includes a person in a vehicle in a street or public place.

(4) In this section "street" has the meaning given by section 1(4) of the Street Offences Act 1959.

52   Causing or inciting prostitution for gain

(1) A person commits an offence if—

    (a) he intentionally causes or incites another person to become a prostitute in any part of the world, and

    (b) he does so for or in the expectation of gain for himself or a third person. [E]

53   Controlling prostitution for gain

(1) A person commits an offence if—

    (a) he intentionally controls any of the activities of another person relating to that person's prostitution in any part of the world, and

    (b) he does so for or in the expectation of gain for himself or a third person. [E]

53A   Paying for sexual services of a prostitute subjected to force etc.

(1) A person (A) commits an offence if—

    (a) A makes or promises payment for the sexual services of a prostitute (B),

    (b) a third person (C) has engaged in exploitative conduct of a kind likely to induce or encourage B to provide the sexual services for which A has made or promised payment, and

    (c) C engaged in that conduct for or in the expectation of gain for C or another person (apart from A or B). [S]

(2) The following are irrelevant—

    (a) where in the world the sexual services are to be provided and whether those services are provided,

    (b) whether A is, or ought to be, aware that C has engaged in exploitative conduct.

(3) C engages in exploitative conduct if—

    (a) C uses force, threats (whether or not relating to violence) or any other form of coercion, or

    (b) C practises any form of deception.

54   Sections 51A to 53A: interpretation

(1) In sections 52, 53 and 53A, "gain" means—

    (a) any financial advantage, including the discharge of an obligation to pay or the provision of goods or services (including sexual services) gratuitously or at a discount; or

    (b) the goodwill of any person which is or appears likely, in time, to bring financial advantage.

(2) In sections 51A, 52, 53 and 53A "prostitute" means a person (A) who, on at least one occasion and whether or not compelled to do so, offers or provides sexual services to another person in return for payment or a promise of payment to A or a third person; and "prostitution" is to be interpreted accordingly.

(3) In subsection (2) and section 53A, "payment" means any financial advantage, including the discharge of an obligation to pay or the provision of goods or services (including sexual services) gratuitously or at a discount.

61   Administering a substance with intent

(1) A person commits an offence if he intentionally administers a substance to, or causes a substance to be taken by, another person (B)—

(a) knowing that B does not consent, and

(b) with the intention of stupefying or overpowering B, so as to enable any person to engage in a sexual activity that involves B. [E]

62 Committing an offence with intent to commit a sexual offence

(1) A person commits an offence under this section if he commits any offence with the intention of committing a relevant sexual offence.

(2) In this section, "relevant sexual offence" means any offence under this Part (including an offence of aiding, abetting, counselling or procuring such an offence). [I] and [E]

(3) A person guilty of an offence under this section is liable on conviction on indictment, where the offence is committed by kidnapping or false imprisonment, to imprisonment for life.

63 Trespass with intent to commit a sexual offence

(1) A person commits an offence if—

(a) he is a trespasser on any premises,

(b) he intends to commit a relevant sexual offence on the premises, and

(c) he knows that, or is reckless as to whether, he is a trespasser.

(2) In this section—

"premises" includes a structure or part of a structure;

"relevant sexual offence" has the same meaning as in section 62;

"structure" includes a tent, vehicle or vessel or other temporary or movable structure. [E]

64 Sex with an adult relative: penetration

(1) A person aged 16 or over (A) (subject to subsection (3A)) commits an offence if—

(a) he intentionally penetrates another person's vagina or anus with a part of his body or anything else, or penetrates another person's mouth with his penis,

(b) the penetration is sexual, and

(c) the other person (B) is aged 18 or over,

(d) A is related to B in a way mentioned in subsection (2), and

(e) A knows or could reasonably be expected to know that he is related to B in that way.

(2) The ways that A may be related to B are as parent, grandparent, child, grandchild, brother, sister, half-brother, half-sister, uncle, aunt, nephew or niece.

(3) In subsection (2)—

(za) "parent" includes an adoptive parent;

(zb) "child" includes an adopted person within the meaning of Chapter 4 of Part 1 of the Adoption and Children Act 2002;

(a) "uncle" means the brother of a person's parent, and "aunt" has a corresponding meaning;

(b) "nephew" means the child of a person's brother or sister, and "niece" has a corresponding meaning.

(3A) Where subsection (1) applies in a case where A is related to B as B's child by virtue of subsection (3)(zb), A does not commit an offence under this section unless A is 18 or over.

(4) Where in proceedings for an offence under this section it is proved that the defendant was related to the other person in any of those ways, it is to be taken that the defendant knew or could reasonably have been expected to know that he was related in that way unless sufficient evidence is adduced to raise an issue as to whether he knew or could reasonably have been expected to know that he was. [E]

(6) Nothing in—

(a) section 47 of the Adoption Act 1976 (which disapplies the status provisions in section 39 of that Act for the purposes of this section in relation to adoptions before 30 December 2005), or

(b) section 74 of the Adoption and Children Act 2002 (which disapplies the status provisions in section 67 of that Act for those purposes in relation to adoptions on or after that date),

is to be read as preventing the application of section 39 of the Adoption Act 1976 or section 67 of the Adoption and Children Act 2002 for the purposes of subsection (3)(za) and (zb) above.

65 Sex with an adult relative: consenting to penetration

(1) A person aged 16 or over (A) (subject to subsection (3A)) commits an offence if—

    (a) another person (B) penetrates A's vagina or anus with a part of B's body or anything else, or penetrates A's mouth with B's penis,

    (b) A consents to the penetration,

    (c) the penetration is sexual,

    (d) B is aged 18 or over,

    (e) A is related to B in a way mentioned in subsection (2), and

    (f) A knows or could reasonably be expected to know that he is related to B in that way.

(2) The ways that A may be related to B are as parent, grandparent, child, grandchild, brother, sister, half-brother, half-sister, uncle, aunt, nephew or niece.

(3) In subsection (2)—

    (za) "parent" includes an adoptive parent;

    (zb) "child" includes an adopted person within the meaning of Chapter 4 of Part 1 of the Adoption and Children Act 2002;

    (a) "uncle" means the brother of a person's parent, and "aunt" has a corresponding meaning;

    (b) "nephew" means the child of a person's brother or sister, and "niece" has a corresponding meaning.

(3A) Where subsection (1) applies in a case where A is related to B as B's child by virtue of subsection (3)(zb), A does not commit an offence under this section unless A is 18 or over.

(4) Where in proceedings for an offence under this section it is proved that the defendant was related to the other person in any of those ways, it is to be taken that the defendant knew or could reasonably have been expected to know that he was related in that way unless sufficient evidence is adduced to raise an issue as to whether he knew or could reasonably have been expected to know that he was. [E]

(6) Nothing in—

    (a) section 47 of the Adoption Act 1976 (which disapplies the status provisions in section 39 of that Act for the purposes of this section in relation to adoptions before 30 December 2005), or

    (b) section 74 of the Adoption and Children Act 2002 (which disapplies the status provisions in section 67 of that Act for those purposes in relation to adoptions on or after that date),

is to be read as preventing the application of section 39 of the Adoption Act 1976 or section 67 of the Adoption and Children Act 2002 for the purposes of subsection (3)(za) and (zb) above.

66 Exposure

(1) A person (A) commits an offence if—

    (a) he intentionally exposes his genitals, and

    (b) he knows or intends that someone will see them and be caused alarm or distress. [E]

67 Voyeurism

(1) A person commits an offence if—

    (a) for the purpose of obtaining sexual gratification, he observes another person doing a private act, and

    (b) he knows that the other person does not consent to being observed for his sexual gratification.

(2) A person commits an offence if—

    (a) he operates equipment with the intention of enabling another person to observe, for the purpose of obtaining sexual gratification, a third person (B) doing a private act, and

    (b) he knows that B does not consent to his operating equipment with that intention.

(3) A person commits an offence if—

    (a) he records another person (B) doing a private act,

    (b) he does so with the intention that he or a third person will, for the purpose of obtaining sexual gratification, look at an image of B doing the act, and

    (c) he knows that B does not consent to his recording the act with that intention.

(4) A person commits an offence if he installs equipment, or constructs or adapts a structure or part of a structure, with the intention of enabling himself or another person to commit an offence under subsection (1). [E]

67A Voyeurism: additional offences

(1) A person (A) commits an offence if—

(a) A operates equipment beneath the clothing of another person (B),

(b) A does so with the intention of enabling A or another person (C), for a purpose mentioned in subsection (3), to observe—

(i) B's genitals or buttocks (whether exposed or covered with underwear), or

(ii) the underwear covering B's genitals or buttocks,

in circumstances where the genitals, buttocks or underwear would not otherwise be visible, and

(c) A does so—

(i) without B's consent, and

(ii) without reasonably believing that B consents.

(2) A person (A) commits an offence if—

(a) A records an image beneath the clothing of another person (B),

(b) the image is of—

(i) B's genitals or buttocks (whether exposed or covered with underwear), or

(ii) the underwear covering B's genitals or buttocks,

in circumstances where the genitals, buttocks or underwear would not otherwise be visible,

(c) A does so with the intention that A or another person (C) will look at the image for a purpose mentioned in subsection (3), and

(d) A does so—

(i) without B's consent, and

(ii) without reasonably believing that B consents.

(3) The purposes referred to in subsections (1) and (2) are—

(a) obtaining sexual gratification (whether for A or C);

(b) humiliating, alarming or distressing B.

68 Voyeurism: interpretation

(1) For the purposes of section 67, a person is doing a private act if the person is in a place which, in the circumstances, would reasonably be expected to provide privacy, and—

(a) the person's genitals, buttocks or breasts are exposed or covered only with underwear,

(b) the person is using a lavatory, or

(c) the person is doing a sexual act that is not of a kind ordinarily done in public.

(1A) For the purposes of sections 67 and 67A, operating equipment includes enabling or securing its activation by another person without that person's knowledge.

(2) In section 67, "structure" includes a tent, vehicle or vessel or other temporary or movable structure.

69 Intercourse with an animal

(1) A person commits an offence if—

(a) he intentionally performs an act of penetration with his penis,

(b) what is penetrated is the vagina or anus of a living animal, and

(c) he knows that, or is reckless as to whether, that is what is penetrated.

(2) A person (A) commits an offence if—

(a) A intentionally causes, or allows, A's vagina or anus to be penetrated,

(b) the penetration is by the penis of a living animal, and

(c) A knows that, or is reckless as to whether, that is what A is being penetrated by. [E]

70 Sexual penetration of a corpse

(1) A person commits an offence if—

(a) he intentionally performs an act of penetration with a part of his body or anything else,

(b) what is penetrated is a part of the body of a dead person,

    (c) he knows that, or is reckless as to whether, that is what is penetrated, and

    (d) the penetration is sexual. [E]

71   Sexual activity in a public lavatory

(1) A person commits an offence if—

    (a) he is in a lavatory to which the public or a section of the public has or is permitted to have access, whether on payment or otherwise,

    (b) he intentionally engages in an activity, and,

    (c) the activity is sexual.

(2) For the purposes of this section, an activity is sexual if a reasonable person would, in all the circumstances but regardless of any person's purpose, consider it to be sexual. [S]

72   Offences outside the United Kingdom

(1) If—

    (a) a United Kingdom national does an act in a country outside the United Kingdom, and

    (b) the act, if done in England and Wales, would constitute a sexual offence to which this subsection applies,

the United Kingdom national is guilty in England and Wales of that sexual offence.

(2) If—

    (a) a United Kingdom resident does an act in a country outside the United Kingdom,

    (b) the act constitutes an offence under the law in force in that country, and

    (c) the act, if done in England and Wales, would constitute a sexual offence to which this subsection applies,

the United Kingdom resident is guilty in England and Wales of that sexual offence.

(3) If—

    (a) a person does an act in a country outside the United Kingdom at a time when the person was not a United Kingdom national or a United Kingdom resident,

    (b) the act constituted an offence under the law in force in that country,

    (c) the act, if done in England and Wales, would have constituted a sexual offence to which this subsection applies, and

    (d) the person meets the residence or nationality condition at the relevant time,

proceedings may be brought against the person in England and Wales for that sexual offence as if the person had done the act there.

(4) The person meets the residence or nationality condition at the relevant time if the person is a United Kingdom national or a United Kingdom resident at the time when the proceedings are brought.

(5) An act punishable under the law in force in any country constitutes an offence under that law for the purposes of subsections (2) and (3) however it is described in that law.

(6) The condition in subsection (2)(b) or (3)(b) is to be taken to be met unless, not later than rules of court may provide, the defendant serves on the prosecution a notice—

    (a) stating that, on the facts as alleged with respect to the act in question, the condition is not in the defendant's opinion met,

    (b) showing the grounds for that opinion, and

    (c) requiring the prosecution to prove that it is met.

(7) But the court, if it thinks fit, may permit the defendant to require the prosecution to prove that the condition is met without service of a notice under subsection (6).

(8) In the Crown Court the question whether the condition is met is to be decided by the judge alone.

(9) In this section—

"country" includes territory;

"United Kingdom national" means an individual who is—

    (a) a British citizen, a British overseas territories citizen, a British National (Overseas) or a British Overseas citizen;

(b) a person who under the British Nationality Act 1981 is a British subject; or

(c) a British protected person within the meaning of that Act;

"United Kingdom resident" means an individual who is resident in the United Kingdom.

(10) Schedule 2 lists the sexual offences to which subsections (1) to (3) apply.

73 Exceptions to aiding, abetting and counselling

(1) A person is not guilty of aiding, abetting or counselling the commission against a child of an offence to which this section applies if he acts for the purpose of—

(a) protecting the child from sexually transmitted infection,

(b) protecting the physical safety of the child,

(c) preventing the child from becoming pregnant, or

(d) promoting the child's emotional well-being by the giving of advice,

and not for the purpose of obtaining sexual gratification or for the purpose of causing or encouraging either the activity constituting the offence or the child's participation in it.

(2) This section applies to—

(a) an offence under any of sections 5 to 7 (offences against children under 13);

(b) an offence under section 9 (sexual activity with a child);

(c) an offence under section 13 which would be an offence under section 9 if the offender were aged 18;

(d) an offence under any of sections 16, 25, 30, 34 and 38 (sexual activity) against a person under 16.

(3) This section does not affect any other enactment or any rule of law restricting the circumstances in which a person is guilty of aiding, abetting or counselling an offence under this Part.

74 "Consent"

For the purposes of this Part, a person consents if he agrees by choice, and has the freedom and capacity to make that choice.

75 Evidential presumptions about consent

(1) If in proceedings for an offence to which this section applies it is proved—

(a) that the defendant did the relevant act,

(b) that any of the circumstances specified in subsection (2) existed, and

(c) that the defendant knew that those circumstances existed,

the complainant is to be taken not to have consented to the relevant act unless sufficient evidence is adduced to raise an issue as to whether he consented, and the defendant is to be taken not to have reasonably believed that the complainant consented unless sufficient evidence is adduced to raise an issue as to whether he reasonably believed it.

(2) The circumstances are that—

(a) any person was, at the time of the relevant act or immediately before it began, using violence against the complainant or causing the complainant to fear that immediate violence would be used against him;

(b) any person was, at the time of the relevant act or immediately before it began, causing the complainant to fear that violence was being used, or that immediate violence would be used, against another person;

(c) the complainant was, and the defendant was not, unlawfully detained at the time of the relevant act;

(d) the complainant was asleep or otherwise unconscious at the time of the relevant act;

(e) because of the complainant's physical disability, the complainant would not have been able at the time of the relevant act to communicate to the defendant whether the complainant consented;

(f) any person had administered to or caused to be taken by the complainant, without the complainant's consent, a substance which, having regard to when it was administered or taken, was capable of causing or enabling the complainant to be stupefied or overpowered at the time of the relevant act.

(3) In subsection (2)(a) and (b), the reference to the time immediately before the relevant act began is, in the case of an act which is one of a continuous series of sexual activities, a reference to the time immediately before the first sexual activity began.

76 Conclusive presumptions about consent

(1) If in proceedings for an offence to which this section applies it is proved that the defendant did the relevant act and that any of the circumstances specified in subsection (2) existed, it is to be conclusively presumed—

    (a) that the complainant did not consent to the relevant act, and

    (b) that the defendant did not believe that the complainant consented to the relevant act.

(2) The circumstances are that—

    (a) the defendant intentionally deceived the complainant as to the nature or purpose of the relevant act;

    (b) the defendant intentionally induced the complainant to consent to the relevant act by impersonating a person known personally to the complainant.

77 Sections 75 and 76: relevant acts

In relation to an offence to which sections 75 and 76 apply, references in those sections to the relevant act and to the complainant are to be read as follows—

Offence	Relevant Act
An offence under section 1 (rape).	The defendant intentionally penetrating, with his penis, the vagina, anus or mouth of another person ("the complainant").
An offence under section 2 (assault by penetration).	The defendant intentionally penetrating, with a part of his body or anything else, the vagina or anus of another person ("the complainant"), where the penetration is sexual.
An offence under section 3 (sexual assault).	The defendant intentionally touching another person ("the complainant"), where the touching is sexual.
An offence under section 4 (causing a person to engage in sexual activity without consent).	The defendant intentionally causing another person ("the complainant") to engage in an activity, where the activity is sexual.

78 "Sexual"

For the purposes of this Part (except sections 15A and 71) penetration, touching or any other activity is sexual if a reasonable person would consider that—

    (a) whatever the circumstances or any person's purpose in relation to it, it is because of its nature sexual, or

    (b) because of its nature it may be sexual and because of the circumstances or the purpose of any person in relation to it (or both) it is sexual.

79 General interpretation

(1) The following apply for the purposes of this Part.

(2) Penetration is a continuing act from entry to withdrawal.

(3) References to a part of the body include references to a part surgically constructed (in particular, through gender reassignment surgery).

(4) "Image" means a moving or still image and includes an image produced by any means and, where the context permits, a three-dimensional image.

(5) References to an image of a person include references to an image of an imaginary person.

(6) "Mental disorder" has the meaning given by section 1 of the Mental Health Act 1983.

(7) References to observation (however expressed) are to observation whether direct or by looking at an image.

(8) Touching includes touching—
    (a) with any part of the body,
    (b) with anything else,
    (c) through anything,
and in particular includes touching amounting to penetration.
(9) "Vagina" includes vulva.
(10) In relation to an animal, references to the vagina or anus include references to any similar part.

SCHEDULE 2

1. In relation to England and Wales, the following are sexual offences to which subsections (1), (2) and (3) of section 72 apply—
    (a) an offence under any of sections 5 to 19, 25 and 26, and 47 to 50;
    (b) an offence under any of sections 1 to 4, 30–41, and 61 where the victim of the offence was under 18 at the time of the offence;
    (c) an offence under section 62 or 63 where the intended offence was an offence against a person under 18;
    (d) an offence under—
        (i) section 1 of the Protection of Children Act 1978 (indecent photographs of children), or
        (ii) section 160 of the Criminal Justice Act 1988 (possession of indecent photograph of child).
1A. In relation to England and Wales, subsections (1) and (2) of section 72 also apply to an offence under any of sections 1 to 4 where the victim of the offence was 18 or over at the time of the offence.

General

3. A reference in paragraph 1 or 1A to an offence includes—
    (a) a reference to an attempt, conspiracy or incitement to commit that offence; and
    (b) a reference to aiding and abetting, counselling or procuring the commission of that offence.

Children Act 2004

58   Reasonable punishment: England

(1) In relation to any offence specified in subsection (2), battery of a child taking place in England cannot be justified on the ground that it constituted reasonable punishment.
(2) The offences referred to in subsection (1) are—
    (a) an offence under section 18 or 20 of the Offences against the Person Act 1861 (wounding and causing grievous bodily harm);
    (b) an offence under section 47 of that Act (assault occasioning actual bodily harm);
    (c) an offence under section 1 of the Children and Young Persons Act 1933 (cruelty to persons under 16).
(4) For the purposes of subsection (3) "actual bodily harm" has the same meaning as it has for the purposes of section 47 of the Offences against the Person Act 1861.

Domestic Violence, Crime and Victims Act 2004

5   Causing or allowing the death or serious physical harm of a child or vulnerable adult

(1) A person ("D") is guilty of an offence if—
    (a) a child or vulnerable adult ("V") dies or suffers serious physical harm as a result of the unlawful act of a person who—
        (i) was a member of the same household as V, and
        (ii) had frequent contact with him,

(b) D was such a person at the time of that act,

(c) at that time there was a significant risk of serious physical harm being caused to V by the unlawful act of such a person, and

(d) either D was the person whose act caused the death or serious physical harm or—

    (i) D was, or ought to have been, aware of the risk mentioned in paragraph (c),

    (ii) D failed to take such steps as he could reasonably have been expected to take to protect V from the risk, and

    (iii) the act occurred in circumstances of the kind that D foresaw or ought to have foreseen.

(2) The prosecution does not have to prove whether it is the first alternative in subsection (1)(d) or the second (sub-paragraphs (i) to (iii)) that applies.

(3) If D was not the mother or father of V—

(a) D may not be charged with an offence under this section if he was under the age of 16 at the time of the act that caused the death or serious physical harm;

(b) for the purposes of subsection (1)(d)(ii) D could not have been expected to take any such step as is referred to there before attaining that age.

(4) For the purposes of this section—

(a) a person is to be regarded as a "member" of a particular household, even if he does not live in that household, if he visits it so often and for such periods of time that it is reasonable to regard him as a member of it;

(b) where V lived in different households at different times, "the same household as V" refers to the household in which V was living at the time of the act that caused the death or serious physical harm.

(5) For the purposes of this section an "unlawful" act is one that—

(a) constitutes an offence, or

(b) would constitute an offence but for being the act of—

    (i) a person under the age of ten, or

    (ii) a person entitled to rely on a defence of insanity.

Paragraph (b) does not apply to an act of D.

(6) In this section—

"act" includes a course of conduct and also includes omission;

"child" means a person under the age of 16;

"serious" harm means harm that amounts to grievous bodily harm for the purposes of the Offences against the Person Act 1861;

"vulnerable adult" means a person aged 16 or over whose ability to protect himself from violence, abuse or neglect is significantly impaired through physical or mental disability or illness, through old age or otherwise. [I]

Fire and Rescue Services Act 2004

44 Powers of fire-fighters etc. in an emergency etc.

(1) An employee of a fire and rescue authority who is authorised in writing by the authority for the purposes of this section may do anything he reasonably believes to be necessary—

(a) if he reasonably believes a fire to have broken out or to be about to break out, for the purpose of extinguishing or preventing the fire or protecting life or property;

(b) if he reasonably believes a road traffic accident to have occurred, for the purpose of rescuing people or protecting them from serious harm;

(c) if he reasonably believes an emergency of another kind to have occurred, for the purpose of discharging any function conferred on the fire and rescue authority in relation to the emergency;

(d) for the purpose of preventing or limiting damage to property resulting from action taken as mentioned in paragraph (a), (b) or (c).

(2) In particular, an employee of a fire and rescue authority who is authorised as mentioned in subsection (1) may under that subsection—

(a) enter premises or a place, by force if necessary, without the consent of the owner or occupier of the premises or place;

(b) move or break into a vehicle without the consent of its owner;

(c) close a highway;

(d) stop and regulate traffic;

(e) restrict the access of persons to premises or a place.

49   False alarms of fire

(1) A person commits an offence if he knowingly gives or causes to be given a false alarm of fire to a person acting on behalf of a fire and rescue authority. [S]

Gender Recognition Act 2004

9   General

(1) Where a full gender recognition certificate is issued to a person, the person's gender becomes for all purposes the acquired gender (so that, if the acquired gender is the male gender, the person's sex becomes that of a man and, if it is the female gender, the person's sex becomes that of a woman).

(2) Subsection (1) does not affect things done, or events occurring, before the certificate is issued; but it does operate for the interpretation of enactments passed, and instruments and other documents made, before the certificate is issued (as well as those passed or made afterwards).

(3) Subsection (1) is subject to provision made by this Act or any other enactment or any subordinate legislation.

20   Gender-specific offences

(1) Where (apart from this subsection) a relevant gender-specific offence could be committed or attempted only if the gender of a person to whom a full gender recognition certificate has been issued were not the acquired gender, the fact that the person's gender has become the acquired gender does not prevent the offence being committed or attempted.

(2) An offence is a "relevant gender-specific offence" if—

(a) either or both of the conditions in subsection (3) are satisfied, and

(b) the commission of the offence involves the accused engaging in sexual activity.

(3) The conditions are—

(a) that the offence may be committed only by a person of a particular gender, and

(b) that the offence may be committed only on, or in relation to, a person of a particular gender,

and the references to a particular gender include a gender identified by reference to the gender of the other person involved.

Human Tissue Act 2004

32   Prohibition of commercial dealings in human material for transplantation

(1) A person commits an offence if he—

(a) gives or receives a reward for the supply of, or for an offer to supply, any controlled material;

(b) seeks to find a person willing to supply any controlled material for reward;

(c) offers to supply any controlled material for reward;

(d) initiates or negotiates any arrangement involving the giving of a reward for the supply of, or for an offer to supply, any controlled material;

(e) takes part in the management or control of a body of persons corporate or unincorporate whose activities consist of or include the initiation or negotiation of such arrangements. [E]

(2) Without prejudice to subsection (1)(b) and (c), a person commits an offence if he causes to be published or distributed, or knowingly publishes or distributes, an advertisement—

(a) inviting persons to supply, or offering to supply, any controlled material for reward, or

(b) indicating that the advertiser is willing to initiate or negotiate any such arrangement as is mentioned in subsection (1)(d). [S]

(3) A person who engages in an activity to which subsection (1) or (2) applies does not commit an offence under that subsection if he is designated by the Authority as a person who may lawfully engage in the activity.

(3A) The Authority may not designate a person under subsection (3) if doing so would be incompatible with the principles set out in—

(a) Article 12 of Directive 2004/23/EC of the European Parliament and of the Council on setting standards of quality and safety for the donation, procurement, testing, processing, preservation, storage and distribution of human tissues and cells, or

(b) Article 13 of Directive 2010/53/EU of the European Parliament and of the Council on standards of quality and safety of human organs intended for transplantation,

and for the purposes of this subsection as it applies in relation to Great Britain, those Articles of those Directives are to be read subject to the modifications set out in subsections (3B) and (3C).

(3B) Article 12 of Directive 2004/23/EC3 is to be read as if—

(a) in paragraph 1—

(i) for the first subparagraph there were substituted—

"Donations of tissues and cells shall be voluntary and unpaid.";

(ii) in the second subparagraph, the second sentence were omitted;

(iii) the third subparagraph were omitted;

(b) in paragraph 2, for the first subparagraph there were substituted—

"Any promotion and publicity activities in support of the donation of human tissues and cells shall comply with any directions of the Authority or any provision of any enactment which relates to such activities.";

(c) also in paragraph 2, in the second subparagraph—

(i) "Member States shall endeavour to ensure that" were omitted;

(ii) for "is" there were substituted "shall be".

(3C) Article 13 of Directive 2010/53/EU is to be read as if—

(a) in paragraph 1—

(i) "Member States shall ensure that" were omitted; and

(ii) for "are" there were substituted "shall be".

(b) in paragraph 2, the second sentence were omitted;

(c) in paragraph 3—

(i) "Member States shall prohibit" were omitted; and

(ii) at the end there were inserted "shall be prohibited";

(d) in paragraph 4—

(i) "Member States shall ensure that" were omitted; and

(ii) for "is" there were substituted "shall be".

(6) For the purposes of subsections (1) and (2), payment in money or money's worth to the holder of a licence shall be treated as not being a reward where—

(a) it is in consideration for transporting, removing, preparing, preserving or storing controlled material, and

(b) its receipt by the holder of the licence is not expressly prohibited by the terms of the licence.

(7) References in subsections (1) and (2) to reward, in relation to the supply of any controlled material, do not include payment in money or money's worth for defraying or reimbursing—

(a) any expenses incurred in, or in connection with, transporting, removing, preparing, preserving or storing the material,

(b) any liability incurred in respect of—

(i) expenses incurred by a third party in, or in connection with, any of the activities mentioned in paragraph (a), or

(ii) a payment in relation to which subsection (6) has effect, or

(c) any expenses or loss of earnings incurred by the person from whose body the material comes so far as reasonably and directly attributable to his supplying the material from his body.

(8) For the purposes of this section, controlled material is any material which—

(a) consists of or includes human cells,

(b) is, or is intended to be removed, from a human body,

(c) is intended to be used for the purpose of transplantation, and

(d) is not of a kind excepted under subsection (9).

(9) The following kinds of material are excepted—

(a) gametes,

(b) embryos, and

(c) material which is the subject of property because of an application of human skill.

(10) Where the body of a deceased person is intended to be used to provide material which—

(a) consists of or includes human cells, and

(b) is not of a kind excepted under subsection (9),

for use for the purpose of transplantation, the body shall be treated as controlled material for the purposes of this section.

(11) In this section—

"advertisement" includes any form of advertising whether to the public generally, to any section of the public or individually to selected persons;

"reward" means any description of financial or other material advantage.

33 Restriction on transplants involving a live donor

(1) Subject to subsections (3) and (5), a person commits an offence if—

(a) he removes any transplantable material from the body of a living person intending that the material be used for the purpose of transplantation, and

(b) when he removes the material, he knows, or might reasonably be expected to know, that the person from whose body he removes the material is alive. [S]

(2) Subject to subsections (3) and (5), a person commits an offence if—

(a) he uses for the purpose of transplantation any transplantable material which has come from the body of a living person, and

(b) when he does so, he knows, or might reasonably be expected to know, that the transplantable material has come from the body of a living person. [S]

(3) The Secretary of State may by regulations provide that subsection (1) or (2) shall not apply in a case where—

(a) the Authority is satisfied—

(i) that no reward has been or is to be given in contravention of section 32, and

(ii) that such other conditions as are specified in the regulations are satisfied, and

(b) such other requirements as are specified in the regulations are complied with.

(4) Regulations under subsection (3) shall include provision for decisions of the Authority in relation to matters which fall to be decided by it under the regulations to be subject, in such circumstances as the regulations may provide, to reconsideration in accordance with such procedure as the regulations may provide.

(5) Where under subsection (3) an exception from subsection (1) or (2) is in force, a person does not commit an offence under that subsection if he reasonably believes that the exception applies.

(7) In this section—

"reward" has the same meaning as in section 32;

"transplantable material" means material of a description specified by regulations made by the Secretary of State.

49 Offences by bodies corporate

(1) Where an offence under this Act is committed by a body corporate and is proved to have been committed with the consent or connivance of or to be attributable to any neglect on the part of—

(a) any director, manager, secretary or other similar officer of the body corporate, or

(b) any person who was purporting to act in any such capacity,

he (as well as the body corporate) commits the offence and shall be liable to be proceeded against and punished accordingly.

(2) Where the affairs of a body corporate are managed by its members, subsection (1) applies in relation to the acts and defaults of a member in connection with his functions of management as if he were a director of the body corporate.

54 General interpretation

(2) In this Act—

(a) references to material from the body of a living person are to material from the body of a person alive at the point of separation, and

(b) references to material from the body of a deceased person are to material from the body of a person not alive at the point of separation.

(3) In this Act, references to transplantation are to transplantation to a human body and include transfusion.

(6) In the Act "embryo" and "gametes" have the same meaning as they have by virtue of section 1(1), (4) and (6) of the Human Fertilisation and Embryology Act 1990 in the other provisions of that Act (apart from section 4A).

(7) For the purposes of this Act, material shall not be regarded as from a human body if it is created outside the human body.

Hunting Act 2004

1 Hunting wild mammals with dogs

A person commits an offence if he hunts a wild mammal with a dog, unless his hunting is exempt. [S]

2 Exempt hunting

(1) Hunting is exempt if it is within a class specified in Schedule 1.

3 Hunting: assistance

(1) A person commits an offence if he knowingly permits land which belongs to him to be entered or used in the course of the commission of an offence under section 1.

(2) A person commits an offence if he knowingly permits a dog which belongs to him to be used in the course of the commission of an offence under section 1.

4 Hunting: defence

It is a defence for a person charged with an offence under section 1 in respect of hunting to show that he reasonably believed that the hunting was exempt.

5 Hare coursing

(1) A person commits an offence if he—

(a) participates in a hare coursing event,

(b) attends a hare coursing event,

(c) knowingly facilitates a hare coursing event, or

(d) permits land which belongs to him to be used for the purposes of a hare coursing event.

(2) Each of the following persons commits an offence if a dog participates in a hare coursing event—

(a) any person who enters the dog for the event,

(b) any person who permits the dog to be entered, and

(c) any person who controls or handles the dog in the course of or for the purposes of the event.

(3) A "hare coursing event" is a competition in which dogs are, by the use of live hares, assessed as to skill in hunting hares.

10   Offence by body corporate

(1) This section applies where an offence under this Act is committed by a body corporate with the consent or connivance of an officer of the body.

(2) The officer, as well as the body, shall be guilty of the offence.

(3) In subsection (1) a reference to an officer of a body corporate includes a reference to—

(a) a director, manager or secretary,

(b) a person purporting to act as a director, manager or secretary, and

(c) if the affairs of the body are managed by its members, a member.

11   Interpretation

(1) In this Act "wild mammal" includes, in particular—

(a) a wild mammal which has been bred or tamed for any purpose,

(b) a wild mammal which is in captivity or confinement,

(c) a wild mammal which has escaped or been released from captivity or confinement, and

(d) any mammal which is living wild.

(2) For the purposes of this Act a reference to a person hunting a wild mammal with a dog includes, in particular, any case where—

(a) a person engages or participates in the pursuit of a wild mammal, and

(b) one or more dogs are employed in that pursuit (whether or not by him and whether or not under his control or direction).

(3) For the purposes of this Act land belongs to a person if he—

(a) owns an interest in it,

(b) manages or controls it, or

(c) occupies it.

(4) For the purposes of this Act a dog belongs to a person if he—

(a) owns it,

(b) is in charge of it, or

(c) has control of it.

SCHEDULE 1   EXEMPT HUNTING

Stalking and flushing out

1. (1) Stalking a wild mammal, or flushing it out of cover, is exempt hunting if the conditions in this paragraph are satisfied.

(2) The first condition is that the stalking or flushing out is undertaken for the purpose of—

(a) preventing or reducing serious damage which the wild mammal would otherwise cause—

(i)   to livestock,

(ii)   to game birds or wild birds (within the meaning of section 27 of the Wildlife and Countryside Act 1981),

(iii)   to food for livestock,

(iv)   to crops (including vegetables and fruit),

(v)   to growing timber,

(vi)   to fisheries,

(vii)   to other property, or

(viii) to the biological diversity of an area (within the meaning of the United Nations Environmental Programme Convention on Biological Diversity of 1992),

(b) obtaining meat to be used for human or animal consumption, or

(c) participation in a field trial.

(3) In sub-paragraph (2)(c) "field trial" means a competition (other than a hare coursing event within the meaning of section 5) in which dogs—

(a) flush animals out of cover or retrieve animals that have been shot (or both), and

(b) are assessed as to their likely usefulness in connection with shooting.

(4) The second condition is that the stalking or flushing out takes place on land—

(a) which belongs to the person doing the stalking or flushing out, or

(b) which he has been given permission to use for the purpose by the occupier or, in the case of unoccupied land, by a person to whom it belongs.

(5) The third condition is that the stalking or flushing out does not involve the use of more than two dogs.

(6) The fourth condition is that the stalking or flushing out does not involve the use of a dog below ground otherwise than in accordance with paragraph 2 below.

(7) The fifth condition is that—

(a) reasonable steps are taken for the purpose of ensuring that as soon as possible after being found or flushed out the wild mammal is shot dead by a competent person, and

(b) in particular, each dog used in the stalking or flushing out is kept under sufficiently close control to ensure that it does not prevent or obstruct achievement of the objective in paragraph (a).

Use of dogs below ground to protect birds for shooting

2. (1) The use of a dog below ground in the course of stalking or flushing out is in accordance with this paragraph if the conditions in this paragraph are satisfied.

(2) The first condition is that the stalking or flushing out is undertaken for the purpose of preventing or reducing serious damage to game birds or wild birds (within the meaning of section 27 of the Wildlife and Countryside Act 1981 (c. 69)) which a person is keeping or preserving for the purpose of their being shot.

(3) The second condition is that the person doing the stalking or flushing out—

(a) has with him written evidence—

(i)   that the land on which the stalking or flushing out takes place belongs to him, or

(ii) that he has been given permission to use that land for the purpose by the occupier or, in the case of unoccupied land, by a person to whom it belongs, and

(b) makes the evidence immediately available for inspection by a constable who asks to see it.

(4) The third condition is that the stalking or flushing out does not involve the use of more than one dog below ground at any one time.

(5) In so far as stalking or flushing out is undertaken with the use of a dog below ground in accordance with this paragraph, paragraph 1 shall have effect as if for the condition in paragraph 1(7) there were substituted the condition that—

(a) reasonable steps are taken for the purpose of ensuring that as soon as possible after being found the wild mammal is flushed out from below ground,

(b) reasonable steps are taken for the purpose of ensuring that as soon as possible after being flushed out from below ground the wild mammal is shot dead by a competent person,

(c) in particular, the dog is brought under sufficiently close control to ensure that it does not prevent or obstruct achievement of the objective in paragraph (b),

(d) reasonable steps are taken for the purpose of preventing injury to the dog, and

(e) the manner in which the dog is used complies with any code of practice which is issued or approved for the purpose of this paragraph by the Secretary of State.

Rats

3. The hunting of rats is exempt if it takes place on land—

(a) which belongs to the hunter, or

(b) which he has been given permission to use for the purpose by the occupier or, in the case of unoccupied land, by a person to whom it belongs.

Rabbits

4. The hunting of rabbits is exempt if it takes place on land—
   (a) which belongs to the hunter, or
   (b) which he has been given permission to use for the purpose by the occupier or, in the case of unoccupied land, by a person to whom it belongs.

Retrieval of hares

5. The hunting of a hare which has been shot is exempt if it takes place on land—
   (a) which belongs to the hunter, or
   (b) which he has been given permission to use for the purpose of hunting hares by the occupier or, in the case of unoccupied land, by a person to whom it belongs.

Falconry

6. Flushing a wild mammal from cover is exempt hunting if undertaken—
   (a) for the purpose of enabling a bird of prey to hunt the wild mammal, and
   (b) on land which belongs to the hunter or which he has been given permission to use for the purpose by the occupier or, in the case of unoccupied land, by a person to whom it belongs.

Recapture of wild mammal

7. (1) The hunting of a wild mammal which has escaped or been released from captivity or confinement is exempt if the conditions in this paragraph are satisfied.

   (2) The first condition is that the hunting takes place—
   (a) on land which belongs to the hunter,
   (b) on land which he has been given permission to use for the purpose by the occupier or, in the case of unoccupied land, by a person to whom it belongs, or
   (c) with the authority of a constable.

   (3) The second condition is that—
   (a) reasonable steps are taken for the purpose of ensuring that as soon as possible after being found the wild mammal is recaptured or shot dead by a competent person, and
   (b) in particular, each dog used in the hunt is kept under sufficiently close control to ensure that it does not prevent or obstruct achievement of the objective in paragraph (a).

   (4) The third condition is that the wild mammal—
   (a) was not released for the purpose of being hunted, and
   (b) was not, for that purpose, permitted to escape.

Rescue of wild mammal

8. (1) The hunting of a wild mammal is exempt if the conditions in this paragraph are satisfied.

   (2) The first condition is that the hunter reasonably believes that the wild mammal is or may be injured.

   (3) The second condition is that the hunting is undertaken for the purpose of relieving the wild mammal's suffering.

   (4) The third condition is that the hunting does not involve the use of more than two dogs.

   (5) The fourth condition is that the hunting does not involve the use of a dog below ground.

   (6) The fifth condition is that the hunting takes place—
   (a) on land which belongs to the hunter,
   (b) on land which he has been given permission to use for the purpose by the occupier or, in the case of unoccupied land, by a person to whom it belongs, or
   (c) with the authority of a constable.

   (7) The sixth condition is that—
   (a) reasonable steps are taken for the purpose of ensuring that as soon as possible after the wild mammal is found appropriate action (if any) is taken to relieve its suffering, and
   (b) in particular, each dog used in the hunt is kept under sufficiently close control to ensure that it does not prevent or obstruct achievement of the objective in paragraph (a).

   (8) The seventh condition is that the wild mammal was not harmed for the purpose of enabling it to be hunted in reliance upon this paragraph.

Research and observation

9. (1) The hunting of a wild mammal is exempt if the conditions in this paragraph are satisfied.

(2) The first condition is that the hunting is undertaken for the purpose of or in connection with the observation or study of the wild mammal.

(3) The second condition is that the hunting does not involve the use of more than two dogs.

(4) The third condition is that the hunting does not involve the use of a dog below ground.

(5) The fourth condition is that the hunting takes place on land—

    (a) which belongs to the hunter, or

    (b) which he has been given permission to use for the purpose by the occupier or, in the case of unoccupied land, by a person to whom it belongs.

(6) The fifth condition is that each dog used in the hunt is kept under sufficiently close control to ensure that it does not injure the wild mammal.

Gambling Act 2005

3 Gambling

In this Act "gambling" means—

    (a) gaming (within the meaning of section 6),

    (b) betting (within the meaning of section 9), and

    (c) participating in a lottery (within the meaning of section 14 and subject to section 15).

6 Gaming & game of chance

(1) In this Act "gaming" means playing a game of chance for a prize.

(2) In this Act "game of chance"—

    (a) includes—

        (i) a game that involves both an element of chance and an element of skill,

        (ii) a game that involves an element of chance that can be eliminated by superlative skill, and

        (iii) a game that is presented as involving an element of chance, but

    (b) does not include a sport.

(3) For the purposes of this Act a person plays a game of chance if he participates in a game of chance—

    (a) whether or not there are other participants in the game, and

    (b) whether or not a computer generates images or data taken to represent the actions of other participants in the game.

(4) For the purposes of this Act a person plays a game of chance for a prize—

    (a) if he plays a game of chance and thereby acquires a chance of winning a prize, and

    (b) whether or not he risks losing anything at the game.

(5) In this Act "prize" in relation to gaming (except in the context of a gaming machine)—

    (a) means money or money's worth, and

    (b) includes both a prize provided by a person organising gaming and winnings of money staked.

9 Betting: general

(1) In this Act "betting" means making or accepting a bet on—

    (a) the outcome of a race, competition or other event or process,

    (b) the likelihood of anything occurring or not occurring, or

    (c) whether anything is or is not true.

(2) A transaction that relates to the outcome of a race, competition or other event or process may be a bet within the meaning of subsection (1) despite the facts that—

    (a) the race, competition, event or process has already occurred or been completed, and

    (b) one party to the transaction knows the outcome.

(3) A transaction that relates to the likelihood of anything occurring or not occurring may be a bet within the meaning of subsection (1) despite the facts that—

(a) the thing has already occurred or failed to occur, and

(b) one party to the transaction knows that the thing has already occurred or failed to occur.

14 Lottery

(1) For the purposes of this Act an arrangement is a lottery, irrespective of how it is described, if it satisfies one of the descriptions of lottery in subsections (2) and (3).

(2) An arrangement is a simple lottery if—

(a) persons are required to pay in order to participate in the arrangement,

(b) in the course of the arrangement one or more prizes are allocated to one or more members of a class, and

(c) the prizes are allocated by a process which relies wholly on chance.

(3) An arrangement is a complex lottery if—

(a) persons are required to pay in order to participate in the arrangement,

(b) in the course of the arrangement one or more prizes are allocated to one or more members of a class,

(c) the prizes are allocated by a series of processes, and

(d) the first of those processes relies wholly on chance.

(4) In this Act "prize" in relation to lotteries includes any money, articles or services—

(a) whether or not described as a prize, and

(b) whether or not consisting wholly or partly of money paid, or articles or services provided, by the members of the class among whom the prize is allocated.

(5) A process which requires persons to exercise skill or judgment or to display knowledge shall be treated for the purposes of this section as relying wholly on chance if—

(a) the requirement cannot reasonably be expected to prevent a significant proportion of persons who participate in the arrangement of which the process forms part from receiving a prize, and

(b) the requirement cannot reasonably be expected to prevent a significant proportion of persons who wish to participate in that arrangement from doing so.

15 National Lottery

(2) Participating in a lottery which forms part of the National Lottery is gambling for the purposes of—

(a) section 42.

42 Cheating

(1) A person commits an offence if he—

(a) cheats at gambling, or

(b) does anything for the purpose of enabling or assisting another person to cheat at gambling. [E]

(2) For the purposes of subsection (1) it is immaterial whether a person who cheats—

(a) improves his chances of winning anything, or

(b) wins anything.

(3) Without prejudice to the generality of subsection (1) cheating at gambling may, in particular, consist of actual or attempted deception or interference in connection with—

(a) the process by which gambling is conducted, or

(b) a real or virtual game, race or other event or process to which gambling relates.

Mental Capacity Act 2005

2 People who lack capacity

(1) For the purposes of this Act, a person lacks capacity in relation to a matter if at the material time he is unable to make a decision for himself in relation to the matter because of an impairment of, or a disturbance in the functioning of, the mind or brain.

(2) It does not matter whether the impairment or disturbance is permanent or temporary.

(3) A lack of capacity cannot be established merely by reference to—

    (a) a person's age or appearance, or

    (b) a condition of his, or an aspect of his behaviour, which might lead others to make unjustified assumptions about his capacity.

(4) In proceedings under this Act or any other enactment, any question whether a person lacks capacity within the meaning of this Act must be decided on the balance of probabilities.

(5) No power which a person ("D") may exercise under this Act—

    (a) in relation to a person who lacks capacity, or

    (b) where D reasonably thinks that a person lacks capacity,

is exercisable in relation to a person under 16.

(6) Subsection (5) is subject to section 18(3).

3 Inability to make decisions

(1) For the purposes of section 2, a person is unable to make a decision for himself if he is unable—

    (a) to understand the information relevant to the decision,

    (b) to retain that information,

    (c) to use or weigh that information as part of the process of making the decision, or

    (d) to communicate his decision (whether by talking, using sign language or any other means).

(2) A person is not to be regarded as unable to understand the information relevant to a decision if he is able to understand an explanation of it given to him in a way that is appropriate to his circumstances (using simple language, visual aids or any other means).

(3) The fact that a person is able to retain the information relevant to a decision for a short period only does not prevent him from being regarded as able to make the decision.

(4) The information relevant to a decision includes information about the reasonably foreseeable consequences of—

    (a) deciding one way or another, or

    (b) failing to make the decision.

44 Ill-treatment or neglect

(1) Subsection (2) applies if a person ("D")—

    (a) has the care of a person ("P") who lacks, or whom D reasonably believes to lack, capacity,

    (b) is the donee of a lasting power of attorney, or an enduring power of attorney (within the meaning of Schedule 4), created by P, or

    (c) is a deputy appointed by the court for P.

(2) D is guilty of an offence if he ill-treats or wilfully neglects P. [E]

62 Scope of the Act

For the avoidance of doubt, it is hereby declared that nothing in this Act is to be taken to affect the law relating to murder or manslaughter or the operation of section 2 of the Suicide Act 1961 (assisting suicide).

Serious Organised Crime and Police Act 2005

128 Offence of trespassing on designated site

(1) A person commits an offence if he enters, or is on, any protected site in England and Wales or Northern Ireland as a trespasser. [S]

(1A) In this section "protected site" means—

    (a) a nuclear site; or

    (b) a designated site.

(1B) In this section "nuclear site" means—

    (a) so much of any premises in respect of which a nuclear site licence (within the meaning of the Nuclear Installations Act 1965) is for the time being in force as lies within the outer perimeter of the protection provided for those premises; and

(b) so much of any other premises of which premises falling within paragraph (a) form a part as lies within that outer perimeter.

(1C) For this purpose—

(a) the outer perimeter of the protection provided for any premises is the line of the outer-most fences, walls or other obstacles provided or relied on for protecting those premises from intruders; and

(b) that line shall be determined on the assumption that every gate, door or other barrier across a way through a fence, wall or other obstacle is closed.

(2) A "designated site" means a site—

(a) specified or described (in any way) in an order made by the Secretary of State, and

(b) designated for the purposes of this section by the order.

(3) The Secretary of State may only designate a site for the purposes of this section if—

(a) it is comprised in Crown land; or

(b) it is comprised in land belonging to Her Majesty in Her private capacity or to the immediate heir to the Throne in his private capacity; or

(c) it appears to the Secretary of State that it is appropriate to designate the site in the interests of national security.

(4) It is a defence for a person charged with an offence under this section to prove that he did not know, and had no reasonable cause to suspect, that the site in relation to which the offence is alleged to have been committed was a protected site.

(7) For the purposes of this section a person who is on any protected site as a trespasser does not cease to be a trespasser by virtue of being allowed time to leave the site.

(8) In this section—

(a) "site" means the whole or part of any building or buildings, or any land, or both;

(b) "Crown land" means land in which there is a Crown interest or a Duchy interest.

(9) For this purpose—

"Crown interest" means an interest belonging to Her Majesty in right of the Crown, and

"Duchy interest" means an interest belonging to Her Majesty in right of the Duchy of Lancaster or belonging to the Duchy of Cornwall.

145 Interference with contractual relationships so as to harm animal research organisation

(1) A person (A) commits an offence if, with the intention of harming an animal research organisation, he—

(a) does a relevant act, or

(b) threatens that he or somebody else will do a relevant act,

in circumstances in which that act or threat is intended or likely to cause a second person (B) to take any of the steps in subsection (2). [E]

(2) The steps are—

(a) not to perform any contractual obligation owed by B to a third person (C) (whether or not such non-performance amounts to a breach of contract);

(b) to terminate any contract B has with C;

(c) not to enter into a contract with C.

(3) For the purposes of this section, a "relevant act" is—

(a) an act amounting to a criminal offence, or

(b) a tortious act causing B to suffer loss or damage of any description;

but paragraph (b) does not include an act which is actionable on the ground only that it induces another person to break a contract with B.

(4) For the purposes of this section, "contract" includes any other arrangement (and "contractual" is to be read accordingly).

(5) For the purposes of this section, to "harm" an animal research organisation means—

(a) to cause the organisation to suffer loss or damage of any description, or

(b) to prevent or hinder the carrying out by the organisation of any of its activities.

(6) This section does not apply to any act done wholly or mainly in contemplation or furtherance of a trade dispute.

(7) In subsection (6) "trade dispute" has the same meaning as in Part 4 of the Trade Union and Labour Relations (Consolidation) Act 1992, except that section 218 of that Act shall be read as if—

    (a) it made provision corresponding to section 244(4) of that Act, and

    (b) in subsection (5), the definition of "worker" included any person falling within paragraph (b) of the definition of "worker" in section 244(5).

146   Intimidation of persons connected with animal research organisation

(1) A person (A) commits an offence if, with the intention of causing a second person (B) to abstain from doing something which B is entitled to do (or to do something which B is entitled to abstain from doing)—

    (a) A threatens B that A or somebody else will do a relevant act, and

    (b) A does so wholly or mainly because B is a person falling within subsection (2). [E]

(2) A person falls within this subsection if he is—

    (a) an employee or officer of an animal research organisation;

    (b) a student at an educational establishment that is an animal research organisation;

    (c) a lessor or licensor of any premises occupied by an animal research organisation;

    (d) a person with a financial interest in, or who provides financial assistance to, an animal research organisation;

    (e) a customer or supplier of an animal research organisation;

    (f) a person who is contemplating becoming someone within paragraph (c), (d) or (e);

    (g) a person who is, or is contemplating becoming, a customer or supplier of someone within paragraph (c), (d), (e) or (f);

    (h) an employee or officer of someone within paragraph (c), (d), (e), (f) or (g);

    (i) a person with a financial interest in, or who provides financial assistance to, someone within paragraph (c), (d), (e), (f) or (g);

    (j) a spouse, civil partner, friend or relative of, or a person who is known personally to, someone within any of paragraphs (a) to (i);

    (k) a person who is, or is contemplating becoming, a customer or supplier of someone within paragraph (a), (b), (h), (i) or (j); or

    (l) an employer of someone within paragraph (j).

(3) For the purposes of this section, an "officer" of an animal research organisation or a person includes—

    (a) where the organisation or person is a body corporate, a director, manager or secretary;

    (b) where the organisation or person is a charity, a charity trustee (within the meaning of the Charities Act 2011);

    (c) where the organisation or person is a partnership, a partner.

(4) For the purposes of this section—

    (a) a person is a customer or supplier of another person if he purchases goods, services or facilities from, or (as the case may be) supplies goods, services or facilities to, that other; and

    (b) "supplier" includes a person who supplies services in pursuance of any enactment that requires or authorises such services to be provided.

(5) For the purposes of this section, a "relevant act" is—

    (a) an act amounting to a criminal offence, or

    (b) a tortious act causing B or another person to suffer loss or damage of any description.

(6) The Secretary of State may by order amend this section so as to include within subsection (2) any description of persons framed by reference to their connection with—

    (a) an animal research organisation, or

    (b) any description of persons for the time being mentioned in that subsection.

(7) This section does not apply to any act done wholly or mainly in contemplation or furtherance of a trade dispute.

(8) In subsection (7) "trade dispute" has the meaning given by section 145(7).

148   Animal research organisations

(1) For the purposes of sections 145 and 146 "animal research organisation" means any person or organisation falling within subsection (1A), (2) or (3).

(1A) A person or organisation falls within this subsection if the person or organisation holds a licence granted under section 2C of the 1986 Act (licensing of undertakings involving the use of animals for scientific procedures).

(2) A person or organisation falls within this subsection if he or it is the owner, lessee or licensee of premises constituting or including a place specified in a licence granted under that section or under section 5 of the 1986 Act (licensing of projects involving the use of animals for scientific procedures).

(3) A person or organisation falls within this subsection if he or it employs, or engages under a contract for services, any of the following in his capacity as such—

(za) the holder of a licence granted under section 2C of the 1986 Act,

(zb) a person specified under section 2C(5) of that Act,

(a) the holder of a personal licence granted under section 4 of the 1986 Act, or

(b) the holder of a project licence granted under section 5 of that Act.

(4) The Secretary of State may by order amend this section so as to include a reference to any description of persons whom he considers to be involved in, or to have a direct connection with persons who are involved in, the application of regulated procedures.

(5) In this section—

"the 1986 Act" means the Animals (Scientific Procedures) Act 1986 (c. 14);

"organisation" includes any institution, trust, undertaking or association of persons;

"premises" includes any place within the meaning of the 1986 Act;

"regulated procedures" has the meaning given by section 2 of the 1986 Act.

149   Extension of sections 145 to 147

(1) The Secretary of State may by order provide for sections 145, 146 and 147 to apply in relation to persons or organisations of a description specified in the order as they apply in relation to animal research organisations.

(2) The Secretary of State may, however, only make an order under this section if satisfied that a series of acts has taken place and—

(a) that those acts were directed at persons or organisations of the description specified in the order or at persons having a connection with them, and

(b) that, if those persons or organisations had been animal research organisations, those acts would have constituted offences under section 145 or 146.

(3) In this section "organisation" and "animal research organisation" have the meanings given by section 148.

Animal Welfare Act 2006

1   Animals to which the Act applies

(1) In this Act, except subsections (4) and (5), "animal" means a vertebrate other than man.

(2) Nothing in this Act applies to an animal while it is in its foetal or embryonic form.

(3) The appropriate national authority may by regulations for all or any of the purposes of this Act—

(a) extend the definition of "animal" so as to include invertebrates of any description;

(b) make provision in lieu of subsection (2) as respects any invertebrates included in the definition of "animal";

(c) amend subsection (2) to extend the application of this Act to an animal from such earlier stage of its development as may be specified in the regulations.

(4) The power under subsection (3)(a) or (c) may only be exercised if the appropriate national authority is satisfied, on the basis of scientific evidence, that animals of the kind concerned are capable of experiencing pain or suffering.

(5) In this section, "vertebrate" means any animal of the Sub-phylum Vertebrata of the Phylum Chordata and "invertebrate" means any animal not of that Sub-phylum.

2 "Protected animal"

An animal is a "protected animal" for the purposes of this Act if—

> (a) it is of a kind which is commonly domesticated in the British Islands,
>
> (b) it is under the control of man whether on a permanent or temporary basis, or
>
> (c) it is not living in a wild state.

3 Responsibility for animals

(1) In this Act, references to a person responsible for an animal are to a person responsible for an animal whether on a permanent or temporary basis.

(2) In this Act, references to being responsible for an animal include being in charge of it.

(3) For the purposes of this Act, a person who owns an animal shall always be regarded as being a person who is responsible for it.

(4) For the purposes of this Act, a person shall be treated as responsible for any animal for which a person under the age of 16 years of whom he has actual care and control is responsible.

4 Unnecessary suffering

(1) A person commits an offence if—

> (a) an act of his, or a failure of his to act, causes an animal to suffer,
>
> (b) he knew, or ought reasonably to have known, that the act, or failure to act, would have that effect or be likely to do so,
>
> (c) the animal is a protected animal, and
>
> (d) the suffering is unnecessary. [E]

(2) A person commits an offence if—

> (a) he is responsible for an animal,
>
> (b) an act, or failure to act, of another person causes the animal to suffer,
>
> (c) he permitted that to happen or failed to take such steps (whether by way of supervising the other person or otherwise) as were reasonable in all the circumstances to prevent that happening, and
>
> (d) the suffering is unnecessary. [E]

(3) The considerations to which it is relevant to have regard when determining for the purposes of this section whether suffering is unnecessary include—

> (a) whether the suffering could reasonably have been avoided or reduced;
>
> (b) whether the conduct which caused the suffering was in compliance with any relevant enactment or any relevant provisions of a licence or code of practice issued under an enactment;
>
> (c) whether the conduct which caused the suffering was for a legitimate purpose, such as—
>
> > (i) the purpose of benefiting the animal, or
> >
> > (ii) the purpose of protecting a person, property or another animal;
>
> (d) whether the suffering was proportionate to the purpose of the conduct concerned;
>
> (e) whether the conduct concerned was in all the circumstances that of a reasonably competent and humane person.

(3A) In determining for the purposes of subsection (1) whether suffering is unnecessary in a case where it was caused by conduct for a purpose mentioned in subsection (3)(c)(ii), the fact that the conduct was for that purpose is to be disregarded if—

> (a) the animal was under the control of a relevant officer at the time of the conduct,
>
> (b) it was being used by that officer at that time, in the course of the officer's duties, in a way that was reasonable in all the circumstances, and
>
> (c) that officer is not the defendant.

(3B) In subsection (3A) "relevant officer" means—

  (a) a constable;

  (b) a person (other than a constable) who has the powers of a constable or is otherwise employed for police purposes or is engaged to provide services for police purposes;

  (c) a prisoner custody officer within the meaning of Part 4 of the Criminal Justice Act 1991.

(4) Nothing in this section applies to the destruction of an animal in an appropriate and humane manner.

5　Mutilation

(1) A person commits an offence if—

  (a) he carries out a prohibited procedure on a protected animal;

  (b) he causes such a procedure to be carried out on such an animal. [S]

(2) A person commits an offence if—

  (a) he is responsible for an animal,

  (b) another person carries out a prohibited procedure on the animal, and

  (c) he permitted that to happen or failed to take such steps (whether by way of supervising the other person or otherwise) as were reasonable in all the circumstances to prevent that happening. [S]

(3) References in this section to the carrying out of a prohibited procedure on an animal are to the carrying out of a procedure which involves interference with the sensitive tissues or bone structure of the animal, otherwise than for the purpose of its medical treatment.

(4) Subsections (1) and (2) do not apply in such circumstances as the appropriate national authority may specify by regulations.

(5) Before making regulations under subsection (4), the appropriate national authority shall consult such persons appearing to the authority to represent any interests concerned as the authority considers appropriate.

(6) Nothing in this section applies to the removal of the whole or any part of a dog's tail.

6　Docking of dogs' tails

(1) A person commits an offence if—

  (a) he removes the whole or any part of a dog's tail, otherwise than for the purpose of its medical treatment;

  (b) he causes the whole or any part of a dog's tail to be removed by another person, otherwise than for the purpose of its medical treatment. [S]

(2) A person commits an offence if—

  (a) he is responsible for a dog,

  (b) another person removes the whole or any part of the dog's tail, otherwise than for the purpose of its medical treatment, and

  (c) he permitted that to happen or failed to take such steps (whether by way of supervising the other person or otherwise) as were reasonable in all the circumstances to prevent that happening. [S]

(3) Subsections (1) and (2) do not apply if the dog is a certified working dog that is not more than 5 days old.

(4) For the purposes of subsection (3), a dog is a certified working dog if a veterinary surgeon has certified, in accordance with regulations made by the appropriate national authority, that the first and second conditions mentioned below are met.

(5) The first condition referred to in subsection (4) is that there has been produced to the veterinary surgeon such evidence as the appropriate national authority may by regulations require for the purpose of showing that the dog is likely to be used for work in connection with—

  (a) law enforcement,

  (b) activities of Her Majesty's armed forces,

  (c) emergency rescue,

  (d) lawful pest control, or

  (e) the lawful shooting of animals.

(6) The second condition referred to in subsection (4) is that the dog is of a type specified for the purposes of this subsection by regulations made by the appropriate national authority.

(7) It is a defence for a person accused of an offence under subsection (1) or (2) to show that he reasonably believed that the dog was one in relation to which subsection (3) applies.

(8) A person commits an offence if—
   (a) he owns a subsection (3) dog, and
   (b) fails to take reasonable steps to secure that, before the dog is 3 months old, it is identified as a subsection (3) dog in accordance with regulations made by the appropriate national authority.

(9) A person commits an offence if—
   (a) he shows a dog at an event to which members of the public are admitted on payment of a fee,
   (b) the dog's tail has been wholly or partly removed (in England and Wales or elsewhere), and
   (c) removal took place on or after the commencement day.

(10) Where a dog is shown only for the purpose of demonstrating its working ability, subsection (9) does not apply if the dog is a subsection (3) dog.

(11) It is a defence for a person accused of an offence under subsection (9) to show that he reasonably believed—
   (a) that the event was not one to which members of the public were admitted on payment of an entrance fee,
   (b) that the removal took place before the commencement day, or
   (c) that the dog was one in relation to which subsection (10) applies.

(12) A person commits an offence if he knowingly gives false information to a veterinary surgeon in connection with the giving of a certificate for the purposes of this section.

(16) In this section—

"commencement day" means the day on which this section comes into force;

"subsection (3) dog" means a dog whose tail has, on or after the commencement day, been wholly or partly removed without contravening subsection (1), because of the application of subsection (3).

7   Administration of poisons etc.

(1) A person commits an offence if, without lawful authority or reasonable excuse, he—
   (a) administers any poisonous or injurious drug or substance to a protected animal, knowing it to be poisonous or injurious, or
   (b) causes any poisonous or injurious drug or substance to be taken by a protected animal, knowing it to be poisonous or injurious. [S]

(2) A person commits an offence if—
   (a) he is responsible for an animal,
   (b) without lawful authority or reasonable excuse, another person administers a poisonous or injurious drug or substance to the animal or causes the animal to take such a drug or substance, and
   (c) he permitted that to happen or, knowing the drug or substance to be poisonous or injurious, he failed to take such steps (whether by way of supervising the other person or otherwise) as were reasonable in all the circumstances to prevent that happening. [S]

(3) In this section, references to a poisonous or injurious drug or substance include a drug or substance which, by virtue of the quantity or manner in which it is administered or taken, has the effect of a poisonous or injurious drug or substance.

8   Fighting etc.

(1) A person commits an offence if he—
   (a) causes an animal fight to take place, or attempts to do so;
   (b) knowingly receives money for admission to an animal fight;
   (c) knowingly publicises a proposed animal fight;
   (d) provides information about an animal fight to another with the intention of enabling or encouraging attendance at the fight;

(e) makes or accepts a bet on the outcome of an animal fight or on the likelihood of anything occurring or not occurring in the course of an animal fight;

(f) takes part in an animal fight;

(g) has in his possession anything designed or adapted for use in connection with an animal fight with the intention of its being so used;

(h) keeps or trains an animal for use for in connection with an animal fight;

(i) keeps any premises for use for an animal fight. [S]

(2) A person commits an offence if, without lawful authority or reasonable excuse, he is present at an animal fight. [S]

(3) A person commits an offence if, without lawful authority or reasonable excuse, he—

(a) knowingly supplies a video recording of an animal fight,

(b) knowingly publishes a video recording of an animal fight,

(c) knowingly shows a video recording of an animal fight to another, or

(d) possesses a video recording of an animal fight, knowing it to be such a recording, with the intention of supplying it. [S]

(4) Subsection (3) does not apply if the video recording is of an animal fight that took place—

(a) outside Great Britain, or

(b) before the commencement date.

(5) Subsection (3) does not apply—

(a) in the case of paragraph (a), to the supply of a video recording for inclusion in a programme service;

(b) in the case of paragraph (b) or (c), to the publication or showing of a video recording by means of its inclusion in a programme service;

(c) in the case of paragraph (d), by virtue of intention to supply for inclusion in a programme service.

(7) In this section—

"animal fight" means an occasion on which a protected animal is placed with an animal, or with a human, for the purpose of fighting, wrestling or baiting;

"commencement date" means the date on which subsection (3) comes into force;

"information society services" has the meaning given in Article 2(a) of Directive 2000/31/EC of the European Parliament and of the Council of 8 June 2000 on certain legal aspects of information society services, in particular electronic commerce in the Internal Market (Directive on electronic commerce);

"programme service" has the same meaning as in the Communications Act 2003;

"video recording" means a recording, in any form, from which a moving image may by any means be reproduced and includes data stored on a computer disc or by other electronic means which is capable of conversion into a moving image.

(8) In this section—

(a) references to supplying or publishing a video recording are to supplying or publishing a video recording in any manner, including, in relation to a video recording in the form of data stored electronically, by means of transmitting such data;

(b) references to showing a video recording are to showing a moving image reproduced from a video recording by any means.

9   Duty of person responsible for animal to ensure welfare

(1) A person commits an offence if he does not take such steps as are reasonable in all the circumstances to ensure that the needs of an animal for which he is responsible are met to the extent required by good practice.

(2) For the purposes of this Act, an animal's needs shall be taken to include—

(a) its need for a suitable environment,

(b) its need for a suitable diet,

(c) its need to be able to exhibit normal behaviour patterns,

(d) any need it has to be housed with, or apart from, other animals, and

(e) its need to be protected from pain, suffering, injury and disease.

(3) The circumstances to which it is relevant to have regard when applying subsection (1) include, in particular—

    (a) any lawful purpose for which the animal is kept, and

    (b) any lawful activity undertaken in relation to the animal.

(4) Nothing in this section applies to the destruction of an animal in an appropriate and humane manner.

11   Transfer of animals by way of sale or prize to persons under 16

(1) A person commits an offence if he sells an animal to a person whom he has reasonable cause to believe to be under the age of 16 years.

(2) For the purposes of subsection (1), selling an animal includes transferring, or agreeing to transfer, ownership of the animal in consideration of entry by the transferee into another transaction.

(3) Subject to subsections (4) to (6), a person commits an offence if—

    (a) he enters into an arrangement with a person whom he has reasonable cause to believe to be under the age of 16 years, and

    (b) the arrangement is one under which that person has the chance to win an animal as a prize.

(4) A person does not commit an offence under subsection (3) if—

    (a) he enters into the arrangement in the presence of the person with whom the arrangement is made, and

    (b) he has reasonable cause to believe that the person with whom the arrangement is made is accompanied by a person who is not under the age of 16 years.

(5) A person does not commit an offence under subsection (3) if—

    (a) he enters into the arrangement otherwise than in the presence of the person with whom the arrangement is made, and

    (b) he has reasonable cause to believe that a person who has actual care and control of the person with whom the arrangement is made has consented to the arrangement.

(6) A person does not commit an offence under subsection (3) if he enters into the arrangement in a family context.

57   Offences by bodies corporate

(1) Where an offence under this Act is committed by a body corporate and is proved to have been committed with the consent or connivance of or to be attributable to any neglect on the part of—

    (a) any director, manager, secretary or other similar officer of the body corporate, or

    (b) any person who was purporting to act in any such capacity,

he (as well as the body corporate) commits the offence and shall be liable to be proceeded against and punished accordingly.

(2) Where the affairs of a body corporate are managed by its members, subsection (1) applies in relation to the acts and defaults of a member in connection with his functions of management as if he were a director of the body corporate.

58   Scientific research

(1) Nothing in this Act applies to anything lawfully done under the Animals (Scientific Procedures) Act 1986.

(2) No power of entry, inspection or search conferred by or under this Act, except for any such power conferred by section 28, may be exercised in relation to a place which is specified in a licence granted under section 2C of the Animals (Scientific Procedures) Act 1986 (licensing of undertakings involving the use of animals for scientific procedures).

(3) Section 9 does not apply in relation to an animal which—

    (a) is being kept at a place specified in a licence granted under section 2C of the Animals (Scientific Procedures) Act 1986, and

(b) is being so kept for the purposes of, or in connection with, an activity mentioned in section 2B(2) of that Act that is pursued at that place in the course of carrying on the undertaking authorised by the licence.

59 Fishing

Nothing in this Act applies in relation to anything which occurs in the normal course of fishing.

Companies Act 2006

993 Punishment for fraudulent trading

(1) If any business of a company is carried on with intent to defraud creditors of the company or creditors of any other person, or for any fraudulent purpose, every person who was knowingly a party to the carrying on of the business in that manner commits an offence. [E]

(2) This applies whether or not the company has been, or is in the course of being, wound up. [E]

Education and Inspections Act 2006

90 Meaning of "disciplinary penalty"

(1) In this Chapter, "disciplinary penalty" means a penalty imposed on a pupil, by any school at which education is provided for him, where his conduct falls below the standard which could reasonably be expected of him (whether because he fails to follow a rule in force at any such school or an instruction given to him by a member of its staff or for any other reason).

(2) In subsection (1), the reference to conduct, in relation to a pupil, includes—

(a) conduct which occurs at a time when the pupil is not on the premises of a school and is not under the lawful control or charge of a member of the staff of a school, but only to the extent that it is reasonable for the school imposing the penalty to regulate the pupil's conduct at such a time, and

(b) conduct which consists of a failure by the pupil to comply with a penalty previously imposed on him.

91 Enforcement of disciplinary penalties: general

(1) This section applies in relation to a disciplinary penalty imposed on a pupil by any school at which education is provided for him, other than a penalty which consists of exclusion.

(2) The imposition of the disciplinary penalty is lawful if the following three conditions are satisfied.

(3) The first condition is that the imposition of the penalty on the pupil—

(a) is not in breach of any statutory requirement or prohibition, and

(b) is reasonable in all the circumstances.

(4) The second condition is that the decision to impose the penalty on the pupil was made—

(a) by any paid member of the staff of the school, except in circumstances where the head teacher has determined that the member of staff is not permitted to impose the penalty on the pupil, or

(b) by any other member of the staff of the school, in circumstances where the head teacher has authorised the member of the staff to impose the penalty on the pupil and it was reasonable for the head teacher to do so.

(5) The third condition is that the decision to impose the penalty was made, and any action taken on behalf of the school to implement the decision was taken—

(a) on the premises of the school, or

(b) elsewhere at a time when the pupil was under the lawful control or charge of a member of staff of the school.

(6) In determining for the purposes of subsection (3)(b) whether the imposition of the penalty is reasonable, the following matters must be taken into account—

    (a) whether the imposition of the penalty constitutes a proportionate punishment in the circumstances of the case, and

    (b) any special circumstances relevant to its imposition on the pupil which are known to the person imposing it (or of which he ought reasonably to be aware) including in particular—

        (i)   the pupil's age,

        (ii) any special educational needs he may have,

        (iii) any disability he may have, and

        (iv) any religious requirements affecting him.

(7) For the purposes of subsection (6)(b)(iii) a pupil has a disability if he has a disability for the purposes of the Equality Act 2010.

(8) A determination or authorisation by the head teacher for the purpose of subsection (4)(a) or (b) may be made—

    (a) in relation to a particular member of staff or members of staff of a particular description;

    (b) in relation to a particular disciplinary penalty or disciplinary penalties of a particular description;

    (c) in relation to a particular pupil or pupils of a particular description or generally in relation to pupils.

(9) Where the disciplinary penalty is detention outside school sessions, this section has effect subject to section 92.

(10) Nothing in this section authorises anything to be done in relation to a pupil which constitutes the giving of corporal punishment within the meaning of section 548 of the Education Act 1996.

(11) This section is not to be construed as restricting what may lawfully be done apart from this section.

(12) In this section, "paid member of the staff", in relation to a school, means any member of the staff who works at the school for payment, whether under a contract of employment or a contract for services; and, for this purpose, it is immaterial whether the contract of employment or contract for services is made with the governing body or proprietor of the school or with any other person.

92 Enforcement of disciplinary penalties: detention outside school sessions

(1) This section applies in relation to a disciplinary penalty which consists of the detention of a pupil outside school sessions.

(2) In relation to a disciplinary penalty to which this section applies, subsection (2) of section 91 has effect as if it required the following additional conditions to be satisfied, as well as the conditions set out in subsections (3) to (5) of that section.

(3) The additional conditions are—

    (a) that the pupil has not attained the age of 18,

    (b) that the head teacher of the school has previously determined, and has made generally known within the school and to parents of registered pupils at the school, that the detention of pupils outside school sessions is one of the measures that may be taken with a view to regulating the conduct of pupils,

    (c) that the detention is on a permitted day of detention, . . .

(4) The additional conditions set out in subsection (3)(a), (c) and (d) do not apply in the case of a detention during a break between school sessions on the same day.

(5) If arrangements have to be made for the pupil to travel to school for the purposes of the detention or to travel home after the detention, then in determining for the purposes of the condition in subsection (3) of section 91 whether the imposition of the detention is reasonable, subsection (6) of that section is to be read as if it also required the question whether suitable travelling arrangements can reasonably be made by his parent to be taken into account.

(6) Section 572 of the Education Act 1996, which provides for the methods by which notices may be served under that Act, does not preclude a notice under subsection (3)(d) from being given to the parent by any effective method.

(7) This section is not to be construed as restricting what may lawfully be done apart from this section.

(8) In this section, "permitted day of detention", in relation to a pupil, means any of the following days—

(a) a school day, other than a day on which the pupil has leave to be absent, and for this purpose "leave" means leave granted by a person authorised to do so by the governing body or proprietor of the school;

(b) a Saturday or Sunday during a school term, other than a Saturday or Sunday which falls during, or at a weekend immediately preceding or immediately following, a half-term break;

(c) a day (whether or not during a school term) which is set aside wholly or mainly for the performance of duties by members of the staff of the school other than teaching, other than such a day which is excluded by regulations made—

(i) in relation to England, by the Secretary of State.

93 Power of members of staff to use force

(1) A person to whom this section applies may use such force as is reasonable in the circumstances for the purpose of preventing a pupil from doing (or continuing to do) any of the following, namely—

(a) committing any offence,

(b) causing personal injury to, or damage to the property of, any person (including the pupil himself), or

(c) prejudicing the maintenance of good order and discipline at the school or among any pupils receiving education at the school, whether during a teaching session or otherwise.

(2) This section applies to a person who is, in relation to a pupil, a member of the staff of any school at which education is provided for the pupil.

(3) The power conferred by subsection (1) may be exercised only where—

(a) the member of the staff and the pupil are on the premises of the school in question, or

(b) they are elsewhere and the member of the staff has lawful control or charge of the pupil concerned.

(4) Subsection (1) does not authorise anything to be done in relation to a pupil which constitutes the giving of corporal punishment within the meaning of section 548 of the Education Act 1996.

(5) The powers conferred by subsection (1) are in addition to any powers exercisable apart from this section and are not to be construed as restricting what may lawfully be done apart from this section.

(6) In this section, "offence" includes anything that would be an offence but for the operation of any presumption that a person under a particular age is incapable of committing an offence.

Emergency Workers (Obstruction) Act 2006

1 Obstructing or hindering certain emergency workers responding to emergency circumstances

(1) A person who without reasonable excuse obstructs or hinders another while that other person is, in a capacity mentioned in subsection (2) below, responding to emergency circumstances, commits an offence. [S]

(2) The capacity referred to in subsection (1) above is—

(a) that of a person employed by a fire and rescue authority in England and Wales;

(aa) that of a Ministry of Defence fire-fighter (as defined in section 16 of the Armed Forces Act 2016);

(b) in relation to England and Wales, that of a person (other than a person falling within paragraph (a) or (aa)) whose duties as an employee or as a servant of the Crown involve—

    (i)   extinguishing fires; or
    (ii)   protecting life and property in the event of a fire;
  (c)   that of a person employed by a relevant NHS body in the provision of ambulance ser-
         vices (including air ambulance services), or of a person providing such services pur-
         suant to arrangements made by, or at the request of, a relevant NHS body;
  (d)   that of a person providing services for the transport of organs, blood, equipment or per-
         sonnel pursuant to arrangements made by, or at the request of, a relevant NHS body;
  (e)   that of a member of Her Majesty's Coastguard;
  (f)   that of a member of the crew of a vessel operated by—
         (i)   the Royal National Lifeboat Institution, or
         (ii)   any other person or organisation operating a vessel for the purpose of providing a
                rescue service,
or a person who musters the crew of such a vessel or attends to its launch or recovery.

(3) For the purposes of this section and section 2 of this Act, a person is responding to emergency circumstances if the person—
  (a)   is going anywhere for the purpose of dealing with emergency circumstances occurring
         there; or
  (b)   is dealing with emergency circumstances or preparing to do so.

(4) For the purposes of this Act, circumstances are "emergency" circumstances if they are present or imminent and—
  (a)   are causing or are likely to cause—
         (i)   serious injury to or the serious illness (including mental illness) of a person;
         (ii)   serious harm to the environment (including the life and health of plants and
                animals);
         (iii) serious harm to any building or other property; or
         (iv)   a worsening of any such injury, illness or harm; or
  (b)   are likely to cause the death of a person.

(5) In subsection (2) above "relevant NHS body" means—
  (a)   in relation to England and Wales, the Secretary of State in the exercise of public health
         functions, a local authority in the exercise of public health functions, the National
         Health Service Commissioning Board, a clinical commissioning group, an NHS foun-
         dation trust, National Health Service trust, Special Health Authority, or Local Health
         Board; ...

(6) In subsection (5)(a) above "public health functions"—
  (a)   in relation to the Secretary of State, has the same meaning as in section 1H(5)(a) of the
         National Health Service Act 2006;
  (b)   in relation to a local authority, has the same meaning as in section 1H(5)(b) of that Act.

2   Obstructing or hindering persons assisting emergency workers

(1) A person who without reasonable excuse obstructs or hinders another in the circumstances
described in subsection (2) below commits an offence. [S]

(2) Those circumstances are where the person being obstructed or hindered is assisting another while that other person is, in a capacity mentioned in section 1(2) of this Act, responding to
emergency circumstances.

3   Provisions supplementary to sections 1 and 2

(1) A person may be convicted of the offence under section 1 or 2 of this Act notwithstanding
that it is—
  (a)   effected by means other than physical means; or
  (b)   effected by action directed only at any vehicle, vessel, apparatus, equipment or other
         thing or any animal used or to be used by a person referred to in that section.

(2) For the purposes of sections 1 and 2 of this Act, circumstances to which a person is responding are to be taken to be emergency circumstances if the person believes and has reasonable grounds
for believing they are or may be emergency circumstances.

Fraud Act 2006

1 Fraud

(1) A person is guilty of fraud if he is in breach of any of the sections listed in subsection (2) (which provide for different ways of committing the offence). [E]

(2) The sections are—

(a) section 2 (fraud by false representation),

(b) section 3 (fraud by failing to disclose information), and

(c) section 4 (fraud by abuse of position).

2 Fraud by false representation

(1) A person is in breach of this section if he—

(a) dishonestly makes a false representation, and

(b) intends, by making the representation—

(i) to make a gain for himself or another, or

(ii) to cause loss to another or to expose another to a risk of loss.

(2) A representation is false if—

(a) it is untrue or misleading, and

(b) the person making it knows that it is, or might be, untrue or misleading.

(3) "Representation" means any representation as to fact or law, including a representation as to the state of mind of—

(a) the person making the representation, or

(b) any other person.

(4) A representation may be express or implied.

(5) For the purposes of this section a representation may be regarded as made if it (or anything implying it) is submitted in any form to any system or device designed to receive, convey or respond to communications (with or without human intervention).

3 Fraud by failing to disclose information

A person is in breach of this section if he—

(a) dishonestly fails to disclose to another person information which he is under a legal duty to disclose, and

(b) intends, by failing to disclose the information—

(i) to make a gain for himself or another, or

(ii) to cause loss to another or to expose another to a risk of loss.

4 Fraud by abuse of position

(1) A person is in breach of this section if he—

(a) occupies a position in which he is expected to safeguard, or not to act against, the financial interests of another person,

(b) dishonestly abuses that position, and

(c) intends, by means of the abuse of that position—

(i) to make a gain for himself or another, or

(ii) to cause loss to another or to expose another to a risk of loss.

(2) A person may be regarded as having abused his position even though his conduct consisted of an omission rather than an act.

5 "Gain" and "loss"

(1) The references to gain and loss in sections 2 to 4 are to be read in accordance with this section.

(2) "Gain" and "loss"—

(a) extend only to gain or loss in money or other property;

(b) include any such gain or loss whether temporary or permanent;

and "property" means any property whether real or personal (including things in action and other intangible property).

(3) "Gain" includes a gain by keeping what one has, as well as a gain by getting what one does not have.

(4) "Loss" includes a loss by not getting what one might get, as well as a loss by parting with what one has.

6 Possession etc. of articles for use in frauds

(1) A person is guilty of an offence if he has in his possession or under his control any article for use in the course of or in connection with any fraud. [E]

7 Making or supplying articles for use in frauds

(1) A person is guilty of an offence if he makes, adapts, supplies or offers to supply any article—

(a) knowing that it is designed or adapted for use in the course of or in connection with fraud, or

(b) intending it to be used to commit, or assist in the commission of, fraud. [E]

8 "Article"

(1) For the purposes of—

(a) sections 6 and 7, and

(b) the provisions listed in subsection (2), so far as they relate to articles for use in the course of or in connection with fraud,

"article" includes any program or data held in electronic form.

(2) The provisions are—

(a) section 1(7)(b) of the Police and Criminal Evidence Act 1984,

(b) section 2(8)(b) of the Armed Forces Act 2001, . . .

(meaning of "prohibited articles" for the purposes of stop and search powers).

9 Participating in fraudulent business carried on by sole trader etc.

(1) A person is guilty of an offence if he is knowingly a party to the carrying on of a business to which this section applies. [E]

(2) This section applies to a business which is carried on—

(a) by a person who is outside the reach of section 993 of the Companies Act 2006 (offence of fraudulent trading), and

(b) with intent to defraud creditors of any person or for any other fraudulent purpose.

(3) The following are within the reach of that section—

(a) a company (as defined in section 1(1) of the Companies Act 2006);

(b) a person to whom that section applies (with or without adaptations or modifications) as if the person were a company;

(c) a person exempted from the application of that section.

(5) "Fraudulent purpose" has the same meaning as in that section.

11 Obtaining services dishonestly

(1) A person is guilty of an offence under this section if he obtains services for himself or another—

(a) by a dishonest act, and

(b) in breach of subsection (2). [E]

(2) A person obtains services in breach of this subsection if—

(a) they are made available on the basis that payment has been, is being or will be made for or in respect of them,

(b) he obtains them without any payment having been made for or in respect of them or without payment having been made in full, and

(c) when he obtains them, he knows—

(i) that they are being made available on the basis described in paragraph (a), or

(ii) that they might be,

but intends that payment will not be made, or will not be made in full.

12 Liability of company officers for offences by company

(1) Subsection (2) applies if an offence under this Act is committed by a body corporate.

(2) If the offence is proved to have been committed with the consent or connivance of—

(a) a director, manager, secretary or other similar officer of the body corporate, or

(b) a person who was purporting to act in any such capacity,

he (as well as the body corporate) is guilty of the offence and liable to be proceeded against and punished accordingly.

(3) If the affairs of a body corporate are managed by its members, subsection (2) applies in relation to the acts and defaults of a member in connection with his functions of management as if he were a director of the body corporate.

Health Act 2006

7 Offence of smoking in smoke-free place

(1) In this section, a "smoke-free place" means any of the following—

(a) premises, so far as they are smoke-free under or by virtue of sections 2 and 3 (including premises which by virtue of regulations under section 3(5) are smoke-free except in relation to performers),

(b) a place, so far as it is smoke-free by virtue of section 4,

(c) a vehicle, so far as it is smoke-free by virtue of section 5.

(2) A person who smokes in a smoke-free place commits an offence. [S]

(3) But a person who smokes in premises which are not smoke-free in relation to performers by virtue of regulations under section 3(5) does not commit an offence if he is such a performer.

(4) It is a defence for a person charged with an offence under subsection (2) to show that he did not know, and could not reasonably have been expected to know, that it was a smoke-free place.

(5) If a person charged with an offence under this section relies on a defence in subsection (4), and evidence is adduced which is sufficient to raise an issue with respect to that defence, the court must assume that the defence is satisfied unless the prosecution proves beyond reasonable doubt that it is not.

8 Offence of failing to prevent smoking in smoke-free place

(1) It is the duty of any person who controls or is concerned in the management of smoke-free premises to cause a person smoking there to stop smoking.

(2) The reference in subsection (1) to a person smoking does not include a performer in relation to whom the premises are not smoke-free by virtue of regulations under section 3(5).

(3) Regulations made by the Secretary of State may provide for a duty corresponding to that mentioned in subsection (1) in relation to—

(a) places which are smoke-free by virtue of section 4,

(b) vehicles which are smoke-free by virtue of section 5.

The duty is to be imposed on persons, or on persons of a description, specified in the regulations.

(4) A person who fails to comply with the duty in subsection (1), or any corresponding duty in regulations under subsection (3), commits an offence. [S]

(5) It is a defence for a person charged with an offence under subsection (4) to show—

(a) that he took reasonable steps to cause the person in question to stop smoking, or

(b) that he did not know, and could not reasonably have been expected to know, that the person in question was smoking, or

(c) that on other grounds it was reasonable for him not to comply with the duty.

(6) If a person charged with an offence under this section relies on a defence in subsection (5), and evidence is adduced which is sufficient to raise an issue with respect to that defence, the court must assume that the defence is satisfied unless the prosecution proves beyond reasonable doubt that it is not.

(8) The references in this section, however expressed, to premises, places or vehicles which are smoke-free, are to those premises, places or vehicles so far as they are smoke-free under or by virtue of this Chapter (and references to smoke-free premises include premises which by virtue of regulations under section 3(5) are smoke-free except in relation to performers).

76   Offences by bodies corporate etc.

(1) If an offence committed by a body corporate is proved—

   (a) to have been committed with the consent or connivance of an officer, or

   (b) to be attributable to any neglect on his part,

the officer as well as the body corporate is guilty of the offence and liable to be proceeded against and punished accordingly.

(2) In subsection (1) "officer", in relation to the body corporate, means a director, manager, secretary or other similar officer of the body, or a person purporting to act in any such capacity.

(3) If the affairs of a body corporate are managed by its members, subsection (1) applies in relation to the acts and defaults of a member in connection with his functions of management as if he were a director of the body corporate.

(4) If an offence committed by a partnership is proved—

   (a) to have been committed with the consent or connivance of a partner, or

   (b) to be attributable to any neglect on his part,

the partner as well as the partnership is guilty of the offence and liable to be proceeded against and punished accordingly.

(5) In subsection (4) "partner" includes a person purporting to act as a partner.

(6) If an offence committed by an unincorporated association (other than a partnership) is proved—

   (a) to have been committed with the consent or connivance of an officer of the association or a member of its governing body, or

   (b) to be attributable to any neglect on the part of such an officer or member,

the officer or member as well as the association is guilty of the offence and liable to be proceeded against and punished accordingly.

(7) In this section and section 77 "offence" means an offence under any provision of this Act.

Immigration, Asylum and Nationality Act 2006

21   Employing unlawful immigrant

(1) A person commits an offence if he employs another ("the employee") knowing that the employee is disqualified from employment by reason of the employee's immigration status.

(1A) A person commits an offence if the person—

   (a) employs another person ("the employee") who is disqualified from employment by reason of the employee's immigration status, and

   (b) has reasonable cause to believe that the employee is disqualified from employment by reason of the employee's immigration status.

(1B) For the purposes of subsections (1) and (1A) a person is disqualified from employment by reason of the person's immigration status if the person is an adult subject to immigration control and—

   (a) the person has not been granted leave to enter or remain in the United Kingdom, or

   (b) the person's leave to enter or remain in the United Kingdom—

      (i)   is invalid,

      (ii) has ceased to have effect (whether by reason of curtailment, revocation, cancellation, passage of time or otherwise), or

      (iii) is subject to a condition preventing the person from accepting the employment.

22 Offence: bodies corporate, etc.

(1) For the purposes of section 21(1) a body (whether corporate or not) shall be treated as knowing a fact about an employee if a person who has responsibility within the body for an aspect of the employment knows the fact.

(1A) For the purposes of section 21(1A) a body (whether corporate or not) shall be treated as having reasonable cause to believe a fact about an employee if a person who has responsibility within the body for an aspect of the employment has reasonable cause to believe that fact.

(2) If an offence under section 21(1) or (1A) is committed by a body corporate with the consent or connivance of an officer of the body, the officer, as well as the body, shall be treated as having committed the offence.

(3) In subsection (2) a reference to an officer of a body includes a reference to—

(a) a director, manager or secretary,

(b) a person purporting to act as a director, manager or secretary, and

(c) if the affairs of the body are managed by its members, a member.

(4) Where an offence under section 21(1) or (1A) is committed by a partnership (whether or not a limited partnership) subsection (2) above shall have effect, but as if a reference to an officer of the body were a reference to—

(a) a partner, and

(b) a person purporting to act as a partner.

25 Interpretation

In sections 15 to 24—

(a) "adult" means a person who has attained the age of 16,

(b) a reference to employment is to employment under a contract of service or apprenticeship, whether express or implied and whether oral or written,

(c) a person is subject to immigration control if under the Immigration Act 1971 he requires leave to enter or remain in the United Kingdom, and

(d) "prescribed" means prescribed by order of the Secretary of State.

Terrorism Act 2006

PART 1   OFFENCES

1 Encouragement of terrorism

(1) This section applies to a statement that is likely to be understood by a reasonable person as a direct or indirect encouragement or other inducement, to some or all of the members of the public to whom it is published, to the commission, preparation or instigation of acts of terrorism or Convention offences.

(2) A person commits an offence if—

(a) he publishes a statement to which this section applies or causes another to publish such a statement; and

(b) at the time he publishes it or causes it to be published, he—

(i) intends members of the public to be directly or indirectly encouraged or otherwise induced by the statement to commit, prepare or instigate acts of terrorism or Convention offences; or

(ii) is reckless as to whether members of the public will be directly or indirectly encouraged or otherwise induced by the statement to commit, prepare or instigate such acts or offences. [E]

(3) For the purposes of this section, the statements that are likely to be understood by a reasonable person as indirectly encouraging the commission or preparation of acts of terrorism or Convention offences include every statement which—

(a) glorifies the commission or preparation (whether in the past, in the future or generally) of such acts or offences; and

(b) is a statement from which members of the public could reasonably be expected to infer that what is being glorified is being glorified as conduct that should be emulated by them in existing circumstances.

(4) For the purposes of this section the questions how a statement is likely to be understood and what members of the public could reasonably be expected to infer from it must be determined having regard both—

(a) to the contents of the statement as a whole; and

(b) to the circumstances and manner of its publication.

(5) It is irrelevant for the purposes of subsections (1) to (3)—

(a) whether anything mentioned in those subsections relates to the commission, preparation or instigation of one or more particular acts of terrorism or Convention offences, of acts of terrorism or Convention offences of a particular description or of acts of terrorism or Convention offences generally; and,

(b) whether any person is in fact encouraged or induced by the statement to commit, prepare or instigate any such act or offence.

(6) In proceedings for an offence under this section against a person in whose case it is not proved that he intended the statement directly or indirectly to encourage or otherwise induce the commission, preparation or instigation of acts of terrorism or Convention offences, it is a defence for him to show—

(a) that the statement neither expressed his views nor had his endorsement (whether by virtue of section 3 or otherwise); and

(b) that it was clear, in all the circumstances of the statement's publication, that it did not express his views and (apart from the possibility of his having been given and failed to comply with a notice under subsection (3) of that section) did not have his endorsement.

2 Dissemination of terrorist publications

(1) A person commits an offence if he engages in conduct falling within subsection (2) and, at the time he does so—

(a) he intends an effect of his conduct to be a direct or indirect encouragement or other inducement to the commission, preparation or instigation of acts of terrorism;

(b) he intends an effect of his conduct to be the provision of assistance in the commission or preparation of such acts; or

(c) he is reckless as to whether his conduct has an effect mentioned in paragraph (a) or (b). [E]

(2) For the purposes of this section a person engages in conduct falling within this subsection if he—

(a) distributes or circulates a terrorist publication;

(b) gives, sells or lends such a publication;

(c) offers such a publication for sale or loan;

(d) provides a service to others that enables them to obtain, read, listen to or look at such a publication, or to acquire it by means of a gift, sale or loan;

(e) transmits the contents of such a publication electronically; or

(f) has such a publication in his possession with a view to its becoming the subject of conduct falling within any of paragraphs (a) to (e).

(3) For the purposes of this section a publication is a terrorist publication, in relation to conduct falling within subsection (2), if matter contained in it is likely—

(a) to be understood, by a reasonable person as a direct or indirect encouragement or other inducement, to some or all of the persons to whom it is or may become available as a result of that conduct, to the commission, preparation or instigation of acts of terrorism; or

(b) to be useful in the commission or preparation of such acts and to be understood, by some or all of those persons, as contained in the publication, or made available to them, wholly or mainly for the purpose of being so useful to them.

(4) For the purposes of this section matter that is likely to be understood by a reasonable person as indirectly encouraging the commission or preparation of acts of terrorism includes any matter which—

(a) glorifies the commission or preparation (whether in the past, in the future or generally) of such acts; and

(b) is matter from which a person could reasonably be expected to infer that what is being glorified is being glorified as conduct that should be emulated by him in existing circumstances.

(5) For the purposes of this section the question whether a publication is a terrorist publication in relation to particular conduct must be determined—

(a) as at the time of that conduct; and

(b) having regard both to the contents of the publication as a whole and to the circumstances in which that conduct occurs.

(6) In subsection (1) references to the effect of a person's conduct in relation to a terrorist publication include references to an effect of the publication on one or more persons to whom it is or may become available as a consequence of that conduct.

(7) It is irrelevant for the purposes of this section whether anything mentioned in subsections (1) to (4) is in relation to the commission, preparation or instigation of one or more particular acts of terrorism, of acts of terrorism of a particular description or of acts of terrorism generally.

(8) For the purposes of this section it is also irrelevant, in relation to matter contained in any article whether any person—

(a) is in fact encouraged or induced by that matter to commit, prepare or instigate acts of terrorism; or

(b) in fact makes use of it in the commission or preparation of such acts.

(9) In proceedings for an offence under this section against a person in respect of conduct to which subsection (10) applies, it is a defence for him to show—

(a) that the matter by reference to which the publication in question was a terrorist publication neither expressed his views nor had his endorsement (whether by virtue of section 3 or otherwise); and

(b) that it was clear, in all the circumstances of the conduct, that that matter did not express his views and (apart from the possibility of his having been given and failed to comply with a notice under subsection (3) of that section) did not have his endorsement.

(10) This subsection applies to the conduct of a person to the extent that—

(a) the publication to which his conduct related contained matter by reference to which it was a terrorist publication by virtue of subsection (3)(a); and

(b) that person is not proved to have engaged in that conduct with the intention specified in subsection (1)(a).

(13) In this section—

"lend" includes let on hire, and "loan" is to be construed accordingly;

"publication" means an article or record of any description that contains any of the following, or any combination of them—

(a) matter to be read;

(b) matter to be listened to;

(c) matter to be looked at or watched.

3   Application of ss. 1 and 2 to internet activity etc.

(1) This section applies for the purposes of sections 1 and 2 in relation to cases where—

    (a) a statement is published or caused to be published in the course of, or in connection with, the provision or use of a service provided electronically; or

    (b) conduct falling within section 2(2) was in the course of, or in connection with, the provision or use of such a service.

(2) The cases in which the statement, or the article or record to which the conduct relates, is to be regarded as having the endorsement of a person ("the relevant person") at any time include a case in which—

    (a) a constable has given him a notice under subsection (3);

    (b) that time falls more than 2 working days after the day on which the notice was given; and

    (c) the relevant person has failed, without reasonable excuse, to comply with the notice.

(3) A notice under this subsection is a notice which—

    (a) declares that, in the opinion of the constable giving it, the statement or the article or record is unlawfully terrorism-related;

    (b) requires the relevant person to secure that the statement or the article or record, so far as it is so related, is not available to the public or is modified so as no longer to be so related;

    (c) warns the relevant person that a failure to comply with the notice within 2 working days will result in the statement, or the article or record, being regarded as having his endorsement; and

    (d) explains how, under subsection (4), he may become liable by virtue of the notice if the statement, or the article or record, becomes available to the public after he has complied with the notice.

(4) Where—

    (a) a notice under subsection (3) has been given to the relevant person in respect of a statement, or an article or record, and he has complied with it, but

    (b) he subsequently publishes or causes to be published a statement which is, or is for all practical purposes, the same or to the same effect as the statement to which the notice related, or to matter contained in the article or record to which it related, (a "repeat statement");

the requirements of subsection (2)(a) to (c) shall be regarded as satisfied in the case of the repeat statement in relation to the times of its subsequent publication by the relevant person.

(5) In proceedings against a person for an offence under section 1 or 2 the requirements of subsection (2)(a) to (c) are not, in his case, to be regarded as satisfied in relation to any time by virtue of subsection (4) if he shows that he—

    (a) has, before that time, taken every step he reasonably could to prevent a repeat statement from becoming available to the public and to ascertain whether it does; and

    (b) was, at that time, a person to whom subsection (6) applied.

(6) This subsection applies to a person at any time when he—

    (a) is not aware of the publication of the repeat statement; or

    (b) having become aware of its publication, has taken every step that he reasonably could to secure that it either ceased to be available to the public or was modified as mentioned in subsection (3)(b).

(7) For the purposes of this section a statement or an article or record is unlawfully terrorism-related if it constitutes, or if matter contained in the article or record constitutes—

    (a) something that is likely to be understood, by any one or more of the persons to whom it has or may become available, as a direct or indirect encouragement or other inducement to the commission, preparation or instigation of acts of terrorism or Convention offences; or

    (b) information which—

        (i) is likely to be useful to any one or more of those persons in the commission or preparation of such acts; and

        (ii) is in a form or context in which it is likely to be understood by any one or more of those persons as being wholly or mainly for the purpose of being so useful.

(8) The reference in subsection (7) to something that is likely to be understood as an indirect encouragement to the commission or preparation of acts of terrorism or Convention offences includes anything which is likely to be understood as—

    (a) the glorification of the commission or preparation (whether in the past, in the future or generally) of such acts or such offences; and

    (b) a suggestion that what is being glorified is being glorified as conduct that should be emulated in existing circumstances.

(9) In this section "working day" means any day other than—

    (a) a Saturday or a Sunday;

    (b) Christmas Day or Good Friday; or

    (c) a day which is a bank holiday under the Banking and Financial Dealings Act 1971 in any part of the United Kingdom.

5 Preparation of terrorist acts

(1) A person commits an offence if, with the intention of—

    (a) committing acts of terrorism, or

    (b) assisting another to commit such acts,

he engages in any conduct in preparation for giving effect to his intention. [I]

(2) It is irrelevant for the purposes of subsection (1) whether the intention and preparations relate to one or more particular acts of terrorism, acts of terrorism of a particular description or acts of terrorism generally.

6 Training for terrorism

(1) A person commits an offence if—

    (a) he provides instruction or training in any of the skills mentioned in subsection (3); and

    (b) at the time he provides the instruction or training, he knows that a person receiving it intends to use the skills in which he is being instructed or trained—

        (i)   for or in connection with the commission or preparation of acts of terrorism or Convention offences; or

        (ii) for assisting the commission or preparation by others of such acts or offences. [E]

(2) A person commits an offence if—

    (a) he receives instruction or training in any of the skills mentioned in subsection (3); and

    (b) at the time of the instruction or training, he intends to use the skills in which he is being instructed or trained—

        (i)   for or in connection with the commission or preparation of acts of terrorism or Convention offences; or

        (ii) for assisting the commission or preparation by others of such acts or offences. [E]

(3) The skills are—

    (a) the making, handling or use of a noxious substance, or of substances of a description of such substances;

    (b) the use of any method or technique for doing anything else that is capable of being done for the purposes of terrorism, in connection with the commission or preparation of an act of terrorism or Convention offence or in connection with assisting the commission or preparation by another of such an act or offence; and

    (c) the design or adaptation for the purposes of terrorism, or in connection with the commission or preparation of an act of terrorism or Convention offence, of any method or technique for doing anything.

(4) It is irrelevant for the purposes of subsections (1) and (2)—

    (a) whether any instruction or training that is provided is provided to one or more particular persons or generally;

    (b) whether the acts or offences in relation to which a person intends to use skills in which he is instructed or trained consist of one or more particular acts of terrorism or Convention offences, acts of terrorism or Convention offences of a particular description or acts of terrorism or Convention offences generally; and

    (c) whether assistance that a person intends to provide to others is intended to be provided to one or more particular persons or to one or more persons whose identities are not yet known.

(7) In this section—

"noxious substance" means—

    (a) a dangerous substance within the meaning of Part 7 of the Anti-terrorism, Crime and Security Act 2001 or

    (b) any other substance which is hazardous or noxious or which may be or become hazardous or noxious only in certain circumstances;

"substance" includes any natural or artificial substance (whatever its origin or method of production and whether in solid or liquid form or in the form of a gas or vapour) and any mixture of substances.

8 Attendance at a place used for terrorist training

(1) A person commits an offence if—

    (a) he attends at any place, whether in the United Kingdom or elsewhere;

    (b) while he is at that place, instruction or training of the type mentioned in section 6(1) of this Act or section 54(1) of the Terrorism Act 2000 (weapons training) is provided there;

    (c) that instruction or training is provided there wholly or partly for purposes connected with the commission or preparation of acts of terrorism or Convention offences; and

    (d) the requirements of subsection (2) are satisfied in relation to that person. [E]

(2) The requirements of this subsection are satisfied in relation to a person if—

    (a) he knows or believes that instruction or training is being provided there wholly or partly for purposes connected with the commission or preparation of acts of terrorism or Convention offences; or

    (b) a person attending at that place throughout the period of that person's attendance could not reasonably have failed to understand that instruction or training was being provided there wholly or partly for such purposes.

(3) It is immaterial for the purposes of this section—

    (a) whether the person concerned receives the instruction or training himself; and

    (b) whether the instruction or training is provided for purposes connected with one or more particular acts of terrorism or Convention offences, acts of terrorism or Convention offences of a particular description or acts of terrorism or Convention offences generally.

(6) References in this section to instruction or training being provided include references to its being made available.

9 Making and possession of devices or materials

(1) A person commits an offence if—

    (a) he makes or has in his possession a radioactive device, or

    (b) he has in his possession radioactive material,

with the intention of using the device or material in the course of or in connection with the commission or preparation of an act of terrorism or for the purposes of terrorism, or of making it available to be so used. [I]

(2) It is irrelevant for the purposes of subsection (1) whether the act of terrorism to which an intention relates is a particular act of terrorism, an act of terrorism of a particular description or an act of terrorism generally.

(4) In this section—

"radioactive device" means—

    (a) a nuclear weapon or other nuclear explosive device;

    (b) a radioactive material dispersal device;

    (c) a radiation-emitting device;

"radioactive material" means nuclear material or any other radioactive substance which—

    (a) contains nuclides that undergo spontaneous disintegration in a process accompanied by the emission of one or more types of ionising radiation, such as alpha radiation, beta radiation, neutron particles or gamma rays; and

    (b) is capable, owing to its radiological or fissile properties, of—

(i)   causing serious bodily injury to a person;

(ii)   causing serious damage to property;

(iii)   endangering a person's life; or

(iv)   creating a serious risk to the health or safety of the public.

(5)   In subsection (4)—

"device" includes any of the following, whether or not fixed to land, namely, machinery, equipment, appliances, tanks, containers, pipes and conduits;

"nuclear material" has the same meaning as in the Nuclear Material (Offences) Act 1983 (see section 6 of that Act).

10   Misuse of devices or material and misuse and damage of facilities

(1)   A person commits an offence if he uses—

(a)   a radioactive device, or

(b)   radioactive material,

in the course of or in connection with the commission of an act of terrorism or for the purposes of terrorism. [I]

(2)   A person commits an offence if, in the course of or in connection with the commission of an act of terrorism or for the purposes of terrorism, he uses or damages a nuclear facility in a manner which—

(a)   causes a release of radioactive material; or

(b)   creates or increases a risk that such material will be released. [I]

(4)   In this section—

"nuclear facility" means—

(a)   a nuclear reactor, including a reactor installed in or on any transportation device for use as an energy source in order to propel it or for any other purpose; or

(b)   a plant or conveyance being used for the production, storage, processing or transport of radioactive material;

"radioactive device" and "radioactive material" have the same meanings as in section 9.

(5)   In subsection (4)—

"nuclear reactor" has the same meaning as in the Nuclear Installations Act 1965 (see section 26 of that Act);

"transportation device" means any vehicle or any space object (within the meaning of the Outer Space Act 1986).

11   Terrorist threats relating to devices, materials or facilities

(1)   A person commits an offence if, in the course of or in connection with the commission of an act of terrorism or for the purposes of terrorism—

(a)   he makes a demand—

(i)   for the supply to himself or to another of a radioactive device or of radioactive material;

(ii)   for a nuclear facility to be made available to himself or to another; or

(iii)   for access to such a facility to be given to himself or to another;

(b)   he supports the demand with a threat that he or another will take action if the demand is not met; and

(c)   the circumstances and manner of the threat are such that it is reasonable for the person to whom it is made to assume that there is real risk that the threat will be carried out if the demand is not met. [I]

(2)   A person also commits an offence if—

(a)   he makes a threat falling within subsection (3) in the course of or in connection with the commission of an act of terrorism or for the purposes of terrorism; and

(b)   the circumstances and manner of the threat are such that it is reasonable for the person to whom it is made to assume that there is real risk that the threat will be carried out, or would be carried out if demands made in association with the threat are not met. [I]

(3)   A threat falls within this subsection if it is—

    (a) a threat to use radioactive material;

    (b) a threat to use a radioactive device; or

    (c) a threat to use or damage a nuclear facility in a manner that releases radioactive material or creates or increases a risk that such material will be released.

  (5) In this section—

"nuclear facility" has the same meaning as in section 10;

"radioactive device" and "radioactive material" have the same meanings as in section 9.

17 Commission of offences abroad

  (1) If—

    (a) a person does anything outside the United Kingdom, and

    (b) his action, if done in a part of the United Kingdom, would constitute an offence falling within subsection (2),

he shall be guilty in that part of the United Kingdom of the offence.

  (2) The offences falling within this subsection are—

    (a)   an offence under section 1 or 2 of this Act;

    (b)   an offence under section 5 or 6 or any of sections 8 to 11 of this Act;

    (c)   an offence under section 11(1) of the Terrorism Act 2000 (membership of proscribed organisations);

    (ca) an offence under section 12(1) or (1A) of that Act (inviting or expressing support for proscribed organisation);

    (cb) an offence under section 13 of that Act (uniform etc associated with proscribed organisation);

    (d)   an offence under section 54 of that Act (weapons training);

    (da) an offence under section 4 of the Explosive Substances Act 1883 (making or possessing explosives under suspicious circumstances) so far as committed for the purposes of an act of terrorism;

    (e)   conspiracy to commit an offence falling within this subsection;

    (f)   inciting a person to commit such an offence;

    (g)   attempting to commit such an offence;

    (h)   aiding, abetting, counselling or procuring the commission of such an offence.

  (3) Subsection (1) applies irrespective of whether the person is a British citizen, subject to subsection (3A) or, in the case of a company, a company incorporated in a part of the United Kingdom.

  (3A) Subsection (1) applies in the case of an offence falling within subsection (2)(ca) or (cb) only if at the time of committing the offence the person is a United Kingdom national or a United Kingdom resident.

  (3B) In subsection (3A)—

"United Kingdom national" means an individual who is—

    (a) a British citizen, a British overseas territories citizen, a British National (Overseas) or a British Overseas citizen,

    (b) a person who under the British Nationality Act 1981 is a British subject, or

    (c) a British protected person within the meaning of that Act;

"United Kingdom resident" means an individual who is resident in the United Kingdom.

18 Liability of company directors etc.

  (1) Where an offence under this Part is committed by a body corporate and is proved to have been committed with the consent or connivance of—

    (a) a director, manager, secretary or other similar officer of the body corporate, or

    (b) a person who was purporting to act in any such capacity,

he (as well as the body corporate) is guilty of that offence and shall be liable to be proceeded against and punished accordingly.

(3) In this section "director", in relation to a body corporate whose affairs are managed by its members, means a member of the body corporate.

20 Interpretation of Part 1

(1) Expressions used in this Part and in the Terrorism Act 2000 have the same meanings in this Part as in that Act.

(2) In this Part—

"act of terrorism" includes anything constituting an action taken for the purposes of terrorism, within the meaning of the Terrorism Act 2000 (see section 1(5) of that Act);

"article" includes anything for storing data;

"Convention offence" means an offence listed in Schedule 1 or an equivalent offence under the law of a country or territory outside the United Kingdom (and see subsection (2A));

"glorification" includes any form of praise or celebration, and cognate expressions are to be construed accordingly;

"public" is to be construed in accordance with subsection (3);

"publish" and cognate expressions are to be construed in accordance with subsection (4);

"record" means a record so far as not comprised in an article, including a temporary record created electronically and existing solely in the course of, and for the purposes of, the transmission of the whole or a part of its contents;

"statement" is to be construed in accordance with subsection (6).

(2A) Offences under any of the following paragraphs of Schedule 4 to the Space Industry Act 2018 are to be treated for the purposes of this Part as if they were Convention offences—

(a) paragraph 1 (hijacking of spacecraft);

(b) paragraph 2 (destroying, damaging or endangering safety of spacecraft);

(c) paragraph 3 (other acts endangering or likely to endanger safety of spacecraft);

(d) paragraph 4 (endangering safety at spaceports).

(3) In this Part references to the public—

(a) are references to the public of any part of the United Kingdom or of a country or territory outside the United Kingdom, or any section of the public; and

(b) except in section 9(4), also include references to a meeting or other group of persons which is open to the public (whether unconditionally or on the making of a payment or the satisfaction of other conditions).

(4) In this Part references to a person's publishing a statement are references to—

(a) his publishing it in any manner to the public;

(b) his providing electronically any service by means of which the public have access to the statement; or

(c) his using a service provided to him electronically by another so as to enable or to facilitate access by the public to the statement;

but this subsection does not apply to the references to a publication in section 2.

(5) In this Part references to providing a service include references to making a facility available; and references to a service provided to a person are to be construed accordingly.

(6) In this Part references to a statement are references to a communication of any description, including a communication without words consisting of sounds or images or both.

(7) In this Part references to conduct that should be emulated in existing circumstances include references to conduct that is illustrative of a type of conduct that should be so emulated.

(8) In this Part references to what is contained in an article or record include references—

(a) to anything that is embodied or stored in or on it; and

(b) to anything that may be reproduced from it using apparatus designed or adapted for the purpose.

Violent Crime Reduction Act 2006

28   Using someone to mind a weapon

(1) A person is guilty of an offence if—

    (a) he uses another to look after, hide or transport a dangerous weapon for him; and

    (b) he does so under arrangements or in circumstances that facilitate, or are intended to facilitate, the weapon's being available to him for an unlawful purpose. [I]

(2) For the purposes of this section the cases in which a dangerous weapon is to be regarded as available to a person for an unlawful purpose include any case where—

    (a) the weapon is available for him to take possession of it at a time and place; and

    (b) his possession of the weapon at that time and place would constitute, or be likely to involve or to lead to, the commission by him of an offence.

(3) In this section "dangerous weapon" means—

    (a) a firearm other than an air weapon or a component part of, or accessory to, an air weapon; or

    (b) a weapon to which section 141 or 141A of the Criminal Justice Act 1988 applies (specified offensive weapons, knives and bladed weapons).

32   Sales of air weapons by way of trade or business to be face to face

(1) This section applies where a person sells an air weapon by way of trade or business to an individual in Great Britain who is not registered as a firearms dealer.

(2) A person is guilty of an offence if, for the purposes of the sale, he transfers possession of the air weapon to the buyer otherwise than at a time when both—

    (a) the buyer, and

    (b) either the seller or a representative of his,

are present in person. [E]

(3) The reference in subsection (2) to a representative of the seller is a reference to—

    (a) a person who is employed by the seller in his business as a registered firearms dealer;

    (b) a registered firearms dealer who has been authorised by the seller to act on his behalf in relation to the sale; or

    (c) a person who is employed by a person falling within paragraph (b) in his business as a registered firearms dealer.

36   Manufacture, import and sale of realistic imitation firearms

(1) A person is guilty of an offence if—

    (a) he manufactures a realistic imitation firearm;

    (b) he modifies an imitation firearm so that it becomes a realistic imitation firearm;

    (c) he sells a realistic imitation firearm; or

    (d) he brings a realistic imitation firearm into Great Britain or causes one to be brought into Great Britain. [S]

(2) Subsection (1) has effect subject to the defences in section 37.

(11) In this section "realistic imitation firearm" has the meaning given by section 38.

37   Specific defences applying to the offence under s. 36

(1) It shall be a defence for a person charged with an offence under section 36 in respect of any conduct to show that the conduct was for the purpose only of making the imitation firearm in question available for one or more of the purposes specified in subsection (2).

(2) Those purposes are—

    (a) the purposes of a museum or gallery;

    (b) the purposes of theatrical performances and of rehearsals for such performances;

    (c) the production of films (within the meaning of Part 1 of the Copyright, Designs and Patents Act 1988—see section 5B of that Act);

    (d) the production of television programmes (within the meaning of the Communications Act 2003—see section 405(1) of that Act);

(e) the organisation and holding of historical re-enactments organised and held by persons specified or described for the purposes of this section by regulations made by the Secretary of State;

(f) the purposes of functions that a person has in his capacity as a person in the service of Her Majesty.

(3) It shall also be a defence for a person charged with an offence under section 36 in respect of conduct falling within subsection (1)(d) of that section to show that the conduct—

(a) was in the course of carrying on any trade or business; and

(b) was for the purpose of making the imitation firearm in question available to be modified in a way which would result in its ceasing to be a realistic imitation firearm.

(4) For the purposes of this section a person shall be taken to have shown a matter specified in subsection (1) or (3) if—

(a) sufficient evidence of that matter is adduced to raise an issue with respect to it; and

(b) the contrary is not proved beyond a reasonable doubt.

(7) In this section—

"historical re-enactment" means any presentation or other event held for the purpose of re-enacting an event from the past or of illustrating conduct from a particular time or period in the past;

"museum or gallery" includes any institution which—

(a) has as its purpose, or one of its purposes, the preservation, display and interpretation of material of historical, artistic or scientific interest; and

(b) gives the public access to it.

38 Meaning of "realistic imitation firearm"

(1) In sections 36 and 37 "realistic imitation firearm" means an imitation firearm which—

(a) has an appearance that is so realistic as to make it indistinguishable, for all practical purposes, from a real firearm; and

(b) is neither a de-activated firearm nor itself an antique.

(2) For the purposes of this section, an imitation firearm is not (except by virtue of subsection (3)(b)) to be regarded as distinguishable from a real firearm for any practical purpose if it could be so distinguished only—

(a) by an expert;

(b) on a close examination; or

(c) as a result of an attempt to load or to fire it.

(3) In determining for the purposes of this section whether an imitation firearm is distinguishable from a real firearm—

(a) the matters that must be taken into account include any differences between the size, shape and principal colour of the imitation firearm and the size, shape and colour in which the real firearm is manufactured; and

(b) the imitation is to be regarded as distinguishable if its size, shape or principal colour is unrealistic for a real firearm.

(7) In this section—

"colour" is to be construed in accordance with subsection (9);

"de-activated firearm" means an imitation firearm that consists in something which—

(a) was a firearm; but

(b) has been so rendered incapable of discharging a shot, bullet or other missile as no longer to be a firearm;

"real firearm" means—

(a) a firearm of an actual make or model of modern firearm (whether existing or discontinued); or

(b) something falling within a description which could be used for identifying, by reference to their appearance, the firearms falling within a category of actual modern firearms which, even though they include firearms of different makes or models (whether existing or discontinued) or both, all have the same or a similar appearance.

(8) In subsection (7) "modern firearm" means any firearm other than one the appearance of which would tend to identify it as having a design and mechanism of a sort first dating from before the year 1870.

(9) References in this section, in relation to an imitation firearm or a real firearm, to its colour include references to its being made of transparent material.

Wireless Telegraphy Act 2006

47 Misleading messages

(1) A person commits an offence if, by means of wireless telegraphy, he sends or attempts to send a message to which this section applies. [E]

(2) This section applies to a message which, to the person's knowledge—
- (a) is false or misleading; and
- (b) is likely to prejudice the efficiency of a safety of life service or to endanger the safety of a person or of a ship, aircraft or vehicle.

(3) This section applies in particular to a message which, to the person's knowledge, falsely suggests that a ship or aircraft—
- (a) is in distress or in need of assistance; or
- (b) is not in distress or not in need of assistance.

48 Interception and disclosure of messages

(1) A person commits an offence if, without lawful authority——
- (a) he uses wireless telegraphy apparatus with intent to obtain information as to the contents, sender or addressee of a message (whether sent by means of wireless telegraphy or not) of which neither he nor a person on whose behalf he is acting is an intended recipient, or
- (b) he discloses information as to the contents, sender or addressee of such a message. [S]

(2) A person commits an offence under this section consisting in the disclosure of information only if the information disclosed by him is information that would not have come to his knowledge but for the use of wireless telegraphy apparatus by him or by another person.

(3) A person does not commit an offence under this section consisting in the disclosure of information if he discloses the information in the course of legal proceedings or for the purpose of a report of legal proceedings.

(3A) A person does not commit an offence under this section consisting in any conduct if the conduct—
- (a) constitutes an offence under section 3(1) of the Investigatory Powers Act 2016 (offence of unlawful interception), or
- (b) would do so in the absence of any lawful authority (within the meaning of section 6 of that Act).

Corporate Manslaughter and Corporate Homicide Act 2007

1 The offence

(1) An organisation to which this section applies is guilty of an offence if the way in which its activities are managed or organised—
- (a) causes a person's death, and
- (b) amounts to a gross breach of a relevant duty of care owed by the organisation to the deceased. [I]

(2) The organisations to which this section applies are—
- (a) a corporation;
- (b) a department or other body listed in Schedule 1;
- (c) a police force;
- (d) a partnership, or a trade union or employers' association, that is an employer.

(3) An organisation is guilty of an offence under this section only if the way in which its activities are managed or organised by its senior management is a substantial element in the breach referred to in subsection (1).

(4) For the purposes of this Act—

    (a) "relevant duty of care" has the meaning given by section 2, read with sections 3 to 7;

    (b) a breach of a duty of care by an organisation is a "gross" breach if the conduct alleged to amount to a breach of that duty falls far below what can reasonably be expected of the organisation in the circumstances;

    (c) "senior management", in relation to an organisation, means the persons who play significant roles in—

        (i) the making of decisions about how the whole or a substantial part of its activities are to be managed or organised, or

        (ii) the actual managing or organising of the whole or a substantial part of those activities.

2   Meaning of "relevant duty of care"

(1) A "relevant duty of care", in relation to an organisation, means any of the following duties owed by it under the law of negligence—

    (a) a duty owed to its employees or to other persons working for the organisation or performing services for it;

    (b) a duty owed as occupier of premises;

    (c) a duty owed in connection with—

        (i) the supply by the organisation of goods or services (whether for consideration or not),

        (ii) the carrying on by the organisation of any construction or maintenance operations,

        (iii) the carrying on by the organisation of any other activity on a commercial basis, or

        (iv) the use or keeping by the organisation of any plant, vehicle or other thing;

    (d) a duty owed to a person who, by reason of being a person within subsection (2), is someone for whose safety the organisation is responsible.

(2) A person is within this subsection if—

    (a)   he is detained at a custodial institution or in a custody area at a court, a police station or customs premises;

    (aa) he is detained in service custody premises;

    (b)   he is detained at a removal centre, a short-term holding facility, or in pre-departure accommodation;

    (c)   he is being transported in a vehicle, or being held in any premises, in pursuance of prison escort arrangements or immigration escort arrangements;

    (d)   he is living in secure accommodation in which he has been placed;

    (e)   he is a detained patient.

(3) Subsection (1) is subject to sections 3 to 7.

(4) A reference in subsection (1) to a duty owed under the law of negligence includes a reference to a duty that would be owed under the law of negligence but for any statutory provision under which liability is imposed in place of liability under that law.

(5) For the purposes of this Act, whether a particular organisation owes a duty of care to a particular individual is a question of law. The judge must make any findings of fact necessary to decide that question.

(6) For the purposes of this Act there is to be disregarded—

    (a) any rule of the common law that has the effect of preventing a duty of care from being owed by one person to another by reason of the fact that they are jointly engaged in unlawful conduct;

    (b) any such rule that has the effect of preventing a duty of care from being owed to a person by reason of his acceptance of a risk of harm.

(7) In this section—

"construction or maintenance operations" means operations of any of the following descriptions—

    (a) construction, installation, alteration, extension, improvement, repair, maintenance, decoration, cleaning, demolition or dismantling of—

        (i) any building or structure,

      (ii) anything else that forms, or is to form, part of the land, or

      (iii) any plant, vehicle or other thing;

    (b) operations that form an integral part of, or are preparatory to, or are for rendering complete, any operations within paragraph (a);

"custodial institution" means a prison, a young offender institution, a secure training centre, a secure college, a young offenders institution, a young offenders centre, a juvenile justice centre or a remand centre;

"customs premises" means premises wholly or partly occupied by persons designated under section 3 (general customs officials) or 11 (customs revenue officials) of the Borders, Citizenship and Immigration Act 2009

"detained patient" means—

    (a) a person who is detained in any premises under—

      (i)   Part 2 or 3 of the Mental Health Act 1983 ("the 1983 Act"),

    (b) a person who (otherwise than by reason of being detained as mentioned in paragraph (a)) is deemed to be in legal custody by—

      (i)   section 137 of the 1983 Act,

"immigration escort arrangements" means arrangements made under section 156 of the Immigration and Asylum Act 1999;

"the law of negligence" includes—

    (a) in relation to England and Wales, the Occupiers' Liability Act 1957, the Defective Premises Act 1972 and the Occupiers' Liability Act 1984;

"prison escort arrangements" means arrangements made under section 80 of the Criminal Justice Act 1991 or under section 102 or 118 of the Criminal Justice and Public Order Act 1994;

"removal centre", "pre-departure accommodation", have the meaning given by section 147 of the Immigration and Asylum Act 1999;

"secure accommodation" means accommodation, not consisting of or forming part of a custodial institution, provided for the purpose of restricting the liberty of persons under the age of 18.

"service custody premises" has the meaning given by section 300(7) of the Armed Forces Act 2006.

3 Public policy decisions, exclusively public functions and statutory inspections

    (1) Any duty of care owed by a public authority in respect of a decision as to matters of public policy (including in particular the allocation of public resources or the weighing of competing public interests) is not a "relevant duty of care".

    (2) Any duty of care owed in respect of things done in the exercise of an exclusively public function is not a "relevant duty of care" unless it falls within section 2(1)(a), (b) or (d).

    (3) Any duty of care owed by a public authority in respect of inspections carried out in the exercise of a statutory function is not a "relevant duty of care" unless it falls within section 2(1)(a) or (b).

    (4) In this section—

"exclusively public function" means a function that falls within the prerogative of the Crown or is, by its nature, exercisable only with authority conferred—

    (a) by the exercise of that prerogative, or

    (b) by or under a statutory provision;

"statutory function" means a function conferred by or under a statutory provision.

4 Military activities

    (1) Any duty of care owed by the Ministry of Defence in respect of—

    (a) operations within subsection (2),

    (b) activities carried on in preparation for, or directly in support of, such operations, or

    (c) training of a hazardous nature, or training carried out in a hazardous way, which it is considered needs to be carried out, or carried out in that way, in order to improve or maintain the effectiveness of the armed forces with respect to such operations,

is not a "relevant duty of care".

(2) The operations within this subsection are operations, including peacekeeping operations and operations for dealing with terrorism, civil unrest or serious public disorder, in the course of which members of the armed forces come under attack or face the threat of attack or violent resistance.

(3) Any duty of care owed by the Ministry of Defence in respect of activities carried on by members of the special forces is not a "relevant duty of care".

(4) In this section "the special forces" means those units of the armed forces the maintenance of whose capabilities is the responsibility of the Director of Special Forces or which are for the time being subject to the operational command of that Director.

5 Policing and law enforcement

(1) Any duty of care owed by a public authority in respect of—

    (a) operations within subsection (2),

    (b) activities carried on in preparation for, or directly in support of, such operations, or

    (c) training of a hazardous nature, or training carried out in a hazardous way, which it is considered needs to be carried out, or carried out in that way, in order to improve or maintain the effectiveness of officers or employees of the public authority with respect to such operations,

is not a "relevant duty of care".

(2) Operations are within this subsection if—

    (a) they are operations for dealing with terrorism, civil unrest or serious disorder,

    (b) they involve the carrying on of policing or law-enforcement activities, and

    (c) officers or employees of the public authority in question come under attack, or face the threat of attack or violent resistance, in the course of the operations.

(3) Any duty of care owed by a public authority in respect of other policing or law-enforcement activities is not a "relevant duty of care" unless it falls within section 2(1)(a), (b) or (d).

(4) In this section "policing or law-enforcement activities" includes—

    (a) activities carried on in the exercise of functions that are—

        (i) functions of police forces, or

        (ii) functions of the same or a similar nature exercisable by public authorities other than police forces;

    (b) activities carried on in the exercise of functions of constables employed by a public authority;

    (c) activities carried on in the exercise of functions exercisable under Chapter 4 of Part 2 of the Serious Organised Crime and Police Act 2005 (protection of witnesses and other persons);

    (d) activities carried on to enforce any provision contained in or made under the Immigration Acts.

6 Emergencies

(1) Any duty of care owed by an organisation within subsection (2) in respect of the way in which it responds to emergency circumstances is not a "relevant duty of care" unless it falls within section 2(1)(a) or (b).

(2) The organisations within this subsection are—

    (a) a fire and rescue authority in England and Wales;

    (d) any other organisation providing a service of responding to emergency circumstances either—

        (i) in pursuance of arrangements made with an organisation within paragraph (a), (b) or (c) or

        (ii) (if not in pursuance of such arrangements) otherwise than on a commercial basis;

    (e) a relevant NHS body;

    (f) an organisation providing ambulance services in pursuance of arrangements—

        (i) made by, or at the request of, a relevant NHS body, or

        (ii) made with the Secretary of State or with the Welsh Ministers;

(g) an organisation providing services for the transport of organs, blood, equipment or personnel in pursuance of arrangements of the kind mentioned in paragraph (f);

(h) an organisation providing a rescue service;

(i) the armed forces.

(3) For the purposes of subsection (1), the way in which an organisation responds to emergency circumstances does not include the way in which—

(a) medical treatment is carried out, or

(b) decisions within subsection (4) are made.

(4) The decisions within this subsection are decisions as to the carrying out of medical treatment, other than decisions as to the order in which persons are to be given such treatment.

(5) Any duty of care owed in respect of the carrying out, or attempted carrying out, of a rescue operation at sea in emergency circumstances is not a "relevant duty of care" unless it falls within section 2(1)(a) or (b).

(6) Any duty of care owed in respect of action taken—

(a) in order to comply with a direction under Schedule 3A to the Merchant Shipping Act 1995 (safety directions), or

(b) by virtue of paragraph 4 of that Schedule (action in lieu of direction),

is not a "relevant duty of care" unless it falls within section 2(1)(a) or (b).

(7) In this section—

"emergency circumstances" means circumstances that are present or imminent and—

(a) are causing, or are likely to cause, serious harm or a worsening of such harm, or

(b) are likely to cause the death of a person;

"medical treatment" includes any treatment or procedure of a medical or similar nature;

"relevant NHS body" means—

(za) the National Health Service Commissioning Board;

(a) a clinical commissioning group, NHS trust, Special Health Authority or NHS foundation trust in England;

(b) a Local Health Board, NHS trust or Special Health Authority in Wales;

"serious harm" means—

(a) serious injury to or the serious illness (including mental illness) of a person;

(b) serious harm to the environment (including the life and health of plants and animals);

(c) serious harm to any building or other property.

(8) A reference in this section to emergency circumstances includes a reference to circumstances that are believed to be emergency circumstances.

7   Child-protection and probation functions

(1) A duty of care to which this section applies is not a "relevant duty of care" unless it falls within section 2(1)(a), (b) or (d).

(2) This section applies to any duty of care that a local authority or other public authority owes in respect of the exercise by it of functions conferred by or under—

(a) Parts 4 and 5 of the Children Act 1989, . . .

(3) This section also applies to any duty of care that a local probation board, a provider of probation services, or other public authority owes in respect of the exercise by it of functions conferred by or under—

(a) Chapter 1 of Part 1 of the Criminal Justice and Court Services Act 2000,

(aa) section 13 of the Offender Management Act 2007,

(4) This section also applies to any duty of care that a provider of probation services owes in respect of the carrying out by it of activities in pursuance of arrangements under section 3 of the Offender Management Act 2007.

8   Factors for jury

(1) This section applies where—

(a) it is established that an organisation owed a relevant duty of care to a person, and

(b) it falls to the jury to decide whether there was a gross breach of that duty.

(2) The jury must consider whether the evidence shows that the organisation failed to comply with any health and safety legislation that relates to the alleged breach, and if so—

(a) how serious that failure was;

(b) how much of a risk of death it posed.

(3) The jury may also—

(a) consider the extent to which the evidence shows that there were attitudes, policies, systems or accepted practices within the organisation that were likely to have encouraged any such failure as is mentioned in subsection (2), or to have produced tolerance of it;

(b) have regard to any health and safety guidance that relates to the alleged breach.

(4) This section does not prevent the jury from having regard to any other matters they consider relevant.

(5) In this section "health and safety guidance" means any code, guidance, manual or similar publication that is concerned with health and safety matters and is made or issued (under a statutory provision or otherwise) by an authority responsible for the enforcement of any health and safety legislation.

11 Application to Crown bodies

(1) An organisation that is a servant or agent of the Crown is not immune from prosecution under this Act for that reason.

(2) For the purposes of this Act—

(a) a department or other body listed in Schedule 1, or

(b) a corporation that is a servant or agent of the Crown,

is to be treated as owing whatever duties of care it would owe if it were a corporation that was not a servant or agent of the Crown.

(3) For the purposes of section 2—

(a) a person who is—

(i) employed by or under the Crown for the purposes of a department or other body listed in Schedule 1, or

(ii) employed by a person whose staff constitute a body listed in that Schedule,

is to be treated as employed by that department or body;

(b) any premises occupied for the purposes of—

(i) a department or other body listed in Schedule 1, or

(ii) a person whose staff constitute a body listed in that Schedule,

are to be treated as occupied by that department or body.

(4) For the purposes of sections 2 to 7 anything done purportedly by a department or other body listed in Schedule 1, although in law by the Crown or by the holder of a particular office, is to be treated as done by the department or other body itself.

12 Application to armed forces

(1) In this Act "the armed forces" means any of the naval, military or air forces of the Crown raised under the law of the United Kingdom.

(2) For the purposes of section 2 a person who is a member of the armed forces is to be treated as employed by the Ministry of Defence.

(3) A reference in this Act to members of the armed forces includes a reference to—

(a) members of the reserve forces (within the meaning given by section 1(2) of the Reserve Forces Act 1996) when in service or undertaking training or duties;

(b) persons serving on Her Majesty's vessels (within the meaning given by section 132(1) of the Naval Discipline Act 1957).

13 Application to police forces

(1) In this Act "police force" means—

(a) a police force within the meaning of—

(i) the Police Act 1996;

    (d) the British Transport Police Force;

    (e) the Civil Nuclear Constabulary;

    (f) the Ministry of Defence Police.

    (2) For the purposes of this Act a police force is to be treated as owing whatever duties of care it would owe if it were a body corporate.

    (3) For the purposes of section 2—

    (a) a member of a police force is to be treated as employed by that force;

    (b) a special constable appointed for a police area in England and Wales is to be treated as employed by the police force maintained by the local policing body for that area;

    (c) a special constable appointed for a police force mentioned in paragraph (d) or (f) of subsection (1) is to be treated as employed by that force;

    (d) a police cadet undergoing training with a view to becoming a member of a police force mentioned in paragraph (a), (aa) or (d) of subsection (1) is to be treated as employed by that force;

    (g) a member of a police force seconded to the National Crime Agency to serve as a National Crime Agency Officer is to be treated as employed by that Agency.

    (5) For the purposes of section 2 any premises occupied for the purposes of a police force are to be treated as occupied by that force.

    (6) For the purposes of sections 2 to 7 anything that would be regarded as done by a police force if the force were a body corporate is to be so regarded.

    (7) Where—

    (a) by virtue of subsection (3) a person is treated for the purposes of section 2 as employed by a police force, and

    (b) by virtue of any other statutory provision (whenever made) he is, or is treated as, employed by another organisation,

the person is to be treated for those purposes as employed by both the force and the other organisation.

14   Application to partnerships

    (1) For the purposes of this Act a partnership is to be treated as owing whatever duties of care it would owe if it were a body corporate.

    (4) This section does not apply to a partnership that is a legal person under the law by which it is governed.

18   No individual liability

    (1) An individual cannot be guilty of aiding, abetting, counselling or procuring the commission of an offence of corporate manslaughter.

    (1A) An individual cannot be guilty of an offence under Part 2 of the Serious Crime Act 2007 (encouraging or assisting crime) by reference to an offence of corporate manslaughter.

19   Convictions under this Act and under health and safety legislation

    (1) Where in the same proceedings there is—

    (a) a charge of corporate manslaughter or corporate homicide arising out of a particular set of circumstances, and

    (b) a charge against the same defendant of a health and safety offence arising out of some or all of those circumstances,

the jury may, if the interests of justice so require, be invited to return a verdict on each charge.

    (2) An organisation that has been convicted of corporate manslaughter or corporate homicide arising out of a particular set of circumstances may, if the interests of justice so require, be charged with a health and safety offence arising out of some or all of those circumstances.

    (3) In this section "health and safety offence" means an offence under any health and safety legislation.

20 Abolition of liability of corporations for manslaughter at common law

The common law offence of manslaughter by gross negligence is abolished in its application to cor-porations, and in any application it has to other organisations to which section 1 applies.

25 Interpretation

In this Act—

"armed forces" has the meaning given by section 12(1);

"corporation" does not include a corporation sole but includes any body corporate wherever incorporated;

"employee" means an individual who works under a contract of employment or apprenticeship (whether express or implied and, if express, whether oral or in writing), and related expressions are to be construed accordingly; see also sections 11(3)(a), 12(2) and 13(3) (which apply for the purposes of section 2);

"employers' association" has the meaning given by section 122 of the Trade Union and Labour Relations (Consolidation) Act 1992;

"enforcement authority" means an authority responsible for the enforcement of any health and safety legislation;

"health and safety legislation" means any statutory provision dealing with health and safety mat-ters, including in particular provision contained in the Health and Safety at Work etc. Act 1974 . . . and provision dealing with health and safety matters contained in Part 3 of the Energy Act 2013 (nuclear regulation);

"member", in relation to the armed forces, is to be read in accordance with section 12(3);

"partnership" means—

    (a) a partnership within the Partnership Act 1890, or

    (b) a limited partnership registered under the Limited Partnerships Act 1907,

or a firm or entity of a similar character formed under the law of a country or territory outside the United Kingdom;

"police force" has the meaning given by section 13(1);

"premises" includes land, buildings and moveable structures;

"public authority" has the same meaning as in section 6 of the Human Rights Act 1998 (disregard-ing subsections (3)(a) and (4) of that section);

"publicity order" means an order under section 10(1);

"remedial order" means an order under section 9(1);

"statutory provision", except in section 15, means provision contained in, or in an instrument made under, any Act;

"trade union" has the meaning given by section 1 of the Trade Union and Labour Relations (Consolidation) Act 1992 . . .

28 Extent and territorial application

    (3) Section 1 applies if the harm resulting in death is sustained in the United Kingdom or—

        (a) within the seaward limits of the territorial sea adjacent to the United Kingdom;

        (b) on a ship registered under Part 2 of the Merchant Shipping Act 1995;

        (c) on a British-controlled aircraft as defined in section 92 of the Civil Aviation Act 1982;

        (d) on a British-controlled hovercraft within the meaning of that section as applied in rela-tion to hovercraft by virtue of provision made under the Hovercraft Act 1968;

        (e) in any place to which an Order in Council under section 10(1) of the Petroleum Act 1998 applies (criminal jurisdiction in relation to offshore activities).

    (4) For the purposes of subsection (3)(b) to (d) harm sustained on a ship, aircraft or hovercraft includes harm sustained by a person who—

        (a) is then no longer on board the ship, aircraft or hovercraft in consequence of the wrecking of it or of some other mishap affecting it or occurring on it, and

        (b) sustains the harm in consequence of that event.

Serious Crime Act 2007

PART 2 ENCOURAGING OR ASSISTING CRIME

44   Intentionally encouraging or assisting an offence

(1) A person commits an offence if—

    (a) he does an act capable of encouraging or assisting the commission of an offence; and

    (b) he intends to encourage or assist its commission. [I] [E]

(2) But he is not to be taken to have intended to encourage or assist the commission of an offence merely because such encouragement or assistance was a foreseeable consequence of his act.

45   Encouraging or assisting an offence believing it will be committed

A person commits an offence if—

    (a) he does an act capable of encouraging or assisting the commission of an offence; and

    (b) he believes—

        (i)   that the offence will be committed; and

        (ii) that his act will encourage or assist its commission. [I] [E]

46   Encouraging or assisting offences believing one or more will be committed

(1) A person commits an offence if—

    (a) he does an act capable of encouraging or assisting the commission of one or more of a number of offences; and

    (b) he believes—

        (i)   that one or more of those offences will be committed (but has no belief as to which); and

        (ii) that his act will encourage or assist the commission of one or more of them. [I]

(2) It is immaterial for the purposes of subsection (1)(b)(ii) whether the person has any belief as to which offence will be encouraged or assisted.

(3) If a person is charged with an offence under subsection (1)—

    (a) the indictment must specify the offences alleged to be the "number of offences" mentioned in paragraph (a) of that subsection; but

    (b) nothing in paragraph (a) requires all the offences potentially comprised in that number to be specified.

(4) In relation to an offence under this section, reference in this Part to the offences specified in the indictment is to the offences specified by virtue of subsection (3)(a).

47   Proving an offence under this Part

(1) Sections 44, 45 and 46 are to be read in accordance with this section.

(2) If it is alleged under section 44(1)(b) that a person (D) intended to encourage or assist the commission of an offence, it is sufficient to prove that he intended to encourage or assist the doing of an act which would amount to the commission of that offence.

(3) If it is alleged under section 45(b) that a person (D) believed that an offence would be committed and that his act would encourage or assist its commission, it is sufficient to prove that he believed—

    (a) that an act would be done which would amount to the commission of that offence; and

    (b) that his act would encourage or assist the doing of that act.

(4) If it is alleged under section 46(1)(b) that a person (D) believed that one or more of a number of offences would be committed and that his act would encourage or assist the commission of one or more of them, it is sufficient to prove that he believed—

    (a) that one or more of a number of acts would be done which would amount to the commission of one or more of those offences; and

    (b) that his act would encourage or assist the doing of one or more of those acts.

(5) In proving for the purposes of this section whether an act is one which, if done, would amount to the commission of an offence—

    (a) if the offence is one requiring proof of fault, it must be proved that—

        (i) D believed that, were the act to be done, it would be done with that fault;

        (ii) D was reckless as to whether or not it would be done with that fault; or

        (iii) D's state of mind was such that, were he to do it, it would be done with that fault; and

    (b) if the offence is one requiring proof of particular circumstances or consequences (or both), it must be proved that—

        (i) D believed that, were the act to be done, it would be done in those circumstances or with those consequences; or

        (ii) D was reckless as to whether or not it would be done in those circumstances or with those consequences.

(6) For the purposes of subsection (5)(a)(iii), D is to be assumed to be able to do the act in question.

(7) In the case of an offence under section 44—

    (a) subsection (5)(b)(i) is to be read as if the reference to "D believed" were a reference to "D intended or believed"; but

    (b) D is not to be taken to have intended that an act would be done in particular circumstances or with particular consequences merely because its being done in those circumstances or with those consequences was a foreseeable consequence of his act of encouragement or assistance.

(8) Reference in this section to the doing of an act includes reference to—

    (a) a failure to act;

    (b) the continuation of an act that has already begun;

    (c) an attempt to do an act (except an act amounting to the commission of the offence of attempting to commit another offence).

(9) In the remaining provisions of this Part (unless otherwise provided) a reference to the anticipated offence is—

    (a) in relation to an offence under section 44, a reference to the offence mentioned in subsection (2); and

    (b) in relation to an offence under section 45, a reference to the offence mentioned in subsection (3).

48 Proving an offence under section 46

(1) This section makes further provision about the application of section 47 to an offence under section 46.

(2) It is sufficient to prove the matters mentioned in section 47(5) by reference to one offence only.

(3) The offence or offences by reference to which those matters are proved must be one of the offences specified in the indictment.

(4) Subsection (3) does not affect any enactment or rule of law under which a person charged with one offence may be convicted of another and is subject to section 57.

49 Supplemental provisions

(1) A person may commit an offence under this Part whether or not any offence capable of being encouraged or assisted by his act is committed.

(2) If a person's act is capable of encouraging or assisting the commission of a number of offences—

    (a) section 44 applies separately in relation to each offence that he intends to encourage or assist to be committed; and

    (b) section 45 applies separately in relation to each offence that he believes will be encouraged or assisted to be committed.

(3) A person may, in relation to the same act, commit an offence under more than one provision of this Part.

(4) In reckoning whether—

(a) for the purposes of section 45, an act is capable of encouraging or assisting the commission of an offence; or

(b) for the purposes of section 46, an act is capable of encouraging or assisting the commission of one or more of a number of offences;

offences under this Part and listed offences are to be disregarded.

(5) "Listed offence" means—

(a) in England and Wales, an offence listed in Part 1, 2 or 3 of Schedule 3;

(7) For the purposes of sections 45(b)(i) and 46(1)(b)(i) it is sufficient for the person concerned to believe that the offence (or one or more of the offences) will be committed if certain conditions are met.

50 Defence of acting reasonably

(1) A person is not guilty of an offence under this Part if he proves—

(a) that he knew certain circumstances existed; and

(b) that it was reasonable for him to act as he did in those circumstances.

(2) A person is not guilty of an offence under this Part if he proves—

(a) that he believed certain circumstances to exist;

(b) that his belief was reasonable; and

(c) that it was reasonable for him to act as he did in the circumstances as he believed them to be.

(3) Factors to be considered in determining whether it was reasonable for a person to act as he did include—

(a) the seriousness of the anticipated offence (or, in the case of an offence under section 46, the offences specified in the indictment);

(b) any purpose for which he claims to have been acting;

(c) any authority by which he claims to have been acting.

51 Protective offences: victims not liable

(1) In the case of protective offences, a person does not commit an offence under this Part by reference to such an offence if—

(a) he falls within the protected category; and

(b) he is the person in respect of whom the protective offence was committed or would have been if it had been committed.

(2) "Protective offence" means an offence that exists (wholly or in part) for the protection of a particular category of persons ("the protected category").

51A Exceptions to section 44 for encouraging or assisting suicide

Section 44 does not apply to an offence under section 2(1) of the Suicide Act 1961.

52 Jurisdiction over offences of assisting or encouraging an offence

(1) If a person (D) knows or believes that what he anticipates might take place wholly or partly in England or Wales, he may be guilty of an offence under section 44, 45 or 46 no matter where he was at any relevant time.

(2) If it is not proved that D knows or believes that what he anticipates might take place wholly or partly in England or Wales, he is not guilty of an offence under section 44, 45 or 46 unless paragraph 1, 2 or 3 of Schedule 4 applies.

(3) A reference in this section (and in any of those paragraphs) to what D anticipates is to be read as follows—

(a) in relation to an offence under section 44 or 45, it refers to the act which would amount to the commission of the anticipated offence;

(b) in relation to an offence under section 46, it refers to an act which would amount to the commission of any of the offences specified in the indictment.

55   Mode of trial

(1) An offence under section 44 or 45 is triable in the same way as the anticipated offence.

(2) An offence under section 46 is triable on indictment.

56   Persons who may be perpetrators or encouragers etc.

(1) In proceedings for an offence under this Part ("the inchoate offence") the defendant may be convicted if—

    (a) it is proved that he must have committed the inchoate offence or the anticipated offence; but

    (b) it is not proved which of those offences he committed.

(2) For the purposes of this section, a person is not to be treated as having committed the anticipated offence merely because he aided, abetted, counselled or procured its commission.

(3) In relation to an offence under section 46, a reference in this section to the anticipated offence is to be read as a reference to an offence specified in the indictment.

57   Alternative verdicts and guilty pleas

(1) If in proceedings on indictment for an offence under section 44 or 45 a person is not found guilty of that offence by reference to the specified offence, he may be found guilty of that offence by reference to an alternative offence.

(2) If in proceedings for an offence under section 46 a person is not found guilty of that offence by reference to any specified offence, he may be found guilty of that offence by reference to one or more alternative offences.

(3) If in proceedings for an offence under section 46 a person is found guilty of the offence by reference to one or more specified offences, he may also be found guilty of it by reference to one or more other alternative offences.

(4) For the purposes of this section, an offence is an alternative offence if—

    (a) it is an offence of which, on a trial on indictment for the specified offence, an accused may be found guilty; or

    (b) it is an indictable offence, or one to which section 40 of the Criminal Justice Act 1988 applies (power to include count for common assault etc. in indictment), and the condition in subsection (5) is satisfied.

(5) The condition is that the allegations in the indictment charging the person with the offence under this Part amount to or include (expressly or by implication) an allegation of that offence by reference to it.

(6) Subsection (4)(b) does not apply if the specified offence, or any of the specified offences, is murder or treason.

(7) In the application of subsection (5) to proceedings for an offence under section 44, the allegations in the indictment are to be taken to include an allegation of that offence by reference to the offence of attempting to commit the specified offence.

(8) Section 49(4) applies to an offence which is an alternative offence in relation to a specified offence as it applies to that specified offence.

(9) In this section—

    (a) in relation to a person charged with an offence under section 44 or 45, "the specified offence" means the offence specified in the indictment as the one alleged to be the anticipated offence;

    (b) in relation to a person charged with an offence under section 46, "specified offence" means an offence specified in the indictment (within the meaning of subsection (4) of that section), and related expressions are to be read accordingly.

(10) A person arraigned on an indictment for an offence under this Part may plead guilty to an offence of which he could be found guilty under this section on that indictment.

(11) This section applies to an indictment containing more than one count as if each count were a separate indictment.

(12) This section is without prejudice to—

    (a) section 6(1)(b) and (3) of the Criminal Law Act 1967.

59   Abolition of common law replaced by this Part

The common law offence of inciting the commission of another offence is abolished.

64   Encouraging or assisting the commission of an offence

A reference in this Part to encouraging or assisting the commission of an offence is to be read in accordance with section 47.

65   Being capable of encouraging or assisting

(1) A reference in this Part to a person's doing an act that is capable of encouraging the commission of an offence includes a reference to his doing so by threatening another person or otherwise putting pressure on another person to commit the offence.

(2) A reference in this Part to a person's doing an act that is capable of encouraging or assisting the commission of an offence includes a reference to his doing so by—

    (a) taking steps to reduce the possibility of criminal proceedings being brought in respect of that offence;

    (b) failing to take reasonable steps to discharge a duty.

(3) But a person is not to be regarded as doing an act that is capable of encouraging or assisting the commission of an offence merely because he fails to respond to a constable's request for assistance in preventing a breach of the peace.

66   Indirectly encouraging or assisting

If a person (D1) arranges for a person (D2) to do an act that is capable of encouraging or assisting the commission of an offence, and D2 does the act, D1 is also to be treated for the purposes of this Part as having done it.

67   Course of conduct

A reference in this Part to an act includes a reference to a course of conduct, and a reference to doing an act is to be read accordingly.

Criminal Justice and Immigration Act 2008

63   Possession of extreme pornographic images

(1) It is an offence for a person to be in possession of an extreme pornographic image. [E]

(2) An "extreme pornographic image" is an image which is both—

    (a) pornographic, and

    (b) an extreme image.

(3) An image is "pornographic" if it is of such a nature that it must reasonably be assumed to have been produced solely or principally for the purpose of sexual arousal.

(4) Where (as found in the person's possession) an image forms part of a series of images, the question whether the image is of such a nature as is mentioned in subsection (3) is to be determined by reference to—

    (a) the image itself, and

    (b) (if the series of images is such as to be capable of providing a context for the image) the context in which it occurs in the series of images.

(5) So, for example, where—

    (a) an image forms an integral part of a narrative constituted by a series of images, and

    (b) having regard to those images as a whole, they are not of such a nature that they must reasonably be assumed to have been produced solely or principally for the purpose of sexual arousal,

the image may, by virtue of being part of that narrative, be found not to be pornographic, even though it might have been found to be pornographic if taken by itself.

(5A) In relation to possession of an image in England and Wales, an "extreme image" is an image which—

    (a) falls within subsection (7) or (7A), and

    (b) is grossly offensive, disgusting or otherwise of an obscene character.

(7) An image falls within this subsection if it portrays, in an explicit and realistic way, any of the following—

    (a) an act which threatens a person's life,

    (b) an act which results, or is likely to result, in serious injury to a person's anus, breasts or genitals,

    (c) an act which involves sexual interference with a human corpse, or

    (d) a person performing an act of intercourse or oral sex with an animal (whether dead or alive),

and a reasonable person looking at the image would think that any such person or animal was real.

(7A) An image falls within this subsection if it portrays, in an explicit and realistic way, either of the following—

    (a) an act which involves the non-consensual penetration of a person's vagina, anus or mouth by another with the other person's penis, or

    (b) an act which involves the non-consensual sexual penetration of a person's vagina or anus by another with a part of the other person's body or anything else,

and a reasonable person looking at the image would think that the persons were real.

(7B) For the purposes of subsection (7A)—

    (a) penetration is a continuing act from entry to withdrawal;

    (b) "vagina" includes vulva.

(8) In this section "image" means—

    (a) a moving or still image (produced by any means); or

    (b) data (stored by any means) which is capable of conversion into an image within paragraph (a).

(9) In this section references to a part of the body include references to a part surgically constructed (in particular through gender reassignment surgery).

64 Exclusion of classified films etc.

(1) Section 63 does not apply to excluded images.

(2) An "excluded image" is an image which forms part of a series of images contained in a recording of the whole or part of a classified work.

(3) But such an image is not an "excluded image" if—

    (a) it is contained in a recording of an extract from a classified work, and

    (b) it is of such a nature that it must reasonably be assumed to have been extracted (whether with or without other images) solely or principally for the purpose of sexual arousal.

(4) Where an extracted image is one of a series of images contained in the recording, the question whether the image is of such a nature as is mentioned in subsection (3)(b) is to be determined by reference to—

    (a) the image itself, and

    (b) (if the series of images is such as to be capable of providing a context for the image) the context in which it occurs in the series of images;

and section 63(5) applies in connection with determining that question as it applies in connection with determining whether an image is pornographic.

(5) In determining for the purposes of this section whether a recording is a recording of the whole or part of a classified work, any alteration attributable to—

    (a) a defect caused for technical reasons or by inadvertence on the part of any person, or

    (b) the inclusion in the recording of any extraneous material (such as advertisements),

is to be disregarded.

(7) In this section—

"classified work" means (subject to subsection (8)) a video work in respect of which a classification certificate has been issued by a designated authority (whether before or after the commencement of this section);

"classification certificate" and "video work" have the same meanings as in the Video Recordings Act 1984;

"designated authority" means an authority which has been designated by the Secretary of State under section 4 of that Act;

"extract" includes an extract consisting of a single image;

"image" and "pornographic" have the same meanings as in section 63;

"recording" means any disc, tape or other device capable of storing data electronically and from which images may be produced (by any means).

(8) Section 22(3) of the Video Recordings Act 1984 (effect of alterations) applies for the purposes of this section as it applies for the purposes of that Act.

65   Defences: general

(1) Where a person is charged with an offence under section 63, it is a defence for the person to prove any of the matters mentioned in subsection (2).

(2) The matters are—

(a) that the person had a legitimate reason for being in possession of the image concerned;

(b) that the person had not seen the image concerned and did not know, nor had any cause to suspect, it to be an extreme pornographic image;

(c) that the person—

(i) was sent the image concerned without any prior request having been made by or on behalf of the person, and

(ii) did not keep it for an unreasonable time.

(3) In this section "extreme pornographic image" and "image" have the same meanings as in section 63.

66   Defence: participation in consensual acts

(A1) Subsection (A2) applies where in England and Wales—

(a) a person ("D") is charged with an offence under section 63, and

(b) the offence relates to an image that portrays an act or acts within subsection (7)(a) to (c) or (7A) of that section (but does not portray an act within subsection (7)(d) of that section).

(A2) It is a defence for D to prove—

(a) that D directly participated in the act or any of the acts portrayed, and

(b) that the act or acts did not involve the infliction of any non-consensual harm on any person, and

(c) if the image portrays an act within section 63(7)(c), that what is portrayed as a human corpse was not in fact a corpse, and

(d) if the image portrays an act within section 63(7A), that what is portrayed as non-consensual penetration was in fact consensual.

(3) For the purposes of this section harm inflicted on a person is "non-consensual" harm if—

(a) the harm is of such a nature that the person cannot, in law, consent to it being inflicted on himself or herself; or

(b) where the person can, in law, consent to it being so inflicted, the person does not in fact consent to it being so inflicted.

76   Reasonable force for purposes of self-defence etc.

(1) This section applies where in proceedings for an offence—

(a) an issue arises as to whether a person charged with the offence ("D") is entitled to rely on a defence within subsection (2), and

    (b) the question arises whether the degree of force used by D against a person ("V") was reasonable in the circumstances.

(2) The defences are—

    (a)   the common law defence of self-defence;

    (aa) the common law defence of property; and

    (b)   the defences provided by section 3(1) of the Criminal Law Act 1967 (use of force in prevention of crime or making arrest).

(3) The question whether the degree of force used by D was reasonable in the circumstances is to be decided by reference to the circumstances as D believed them to be, and subsections (4) to (8) also apply in connection with deciding that question.

(4) If D claims to have held a particular belief as regards the existence of any circumstances—

    (a) the reasonableness or otherwise of that belief is relevant to the question whether D genuinely held it; but

    (b) if it is determined that D did genuinely hold it, D is entitled to rely on it for the purposes of subsection (3), whether or not—

        (i)   it was mistaken, or

        (ii) (if it was mistaken) the mistake was a reasonable one to have made.

(5) But subsection (4)(b) does not enable D to rely on any mistaken belief attributable to intoxication that was voluntarily induced.

(5A) In a householder case, the degree of force used by D is not to be regarded as having been reasonable in the circumstances as D believed them to be if it was grossly disproportionate in those circumstances.

(6) In a case other than a householder case, the degree of force used by D is not to be regarded as having been reasonable in the circumstances as D believed them to be if it was disproportionate in those circumstances.

(6A) In deciding the question mentioned in subsection (3), a possibility that D could have retreated is to be considered (so far as relevant) as a factor to be taken into account, rather than as giving rise to a duty of retreat.

(7) In deciding the question mentioned in subsection (3) the following considerations are to be taken into account (so far as relevant in the circumstances of the case)—

    (a) that a person acting for a legitimate purpose may not be able to weigh to a nicety the exact measure of any necessary action; and

    (b) that evidence of a person's having only done what the person honestly and instinctively thought was necessary for a legitimate purpose constitutes strong evidence that only reasonable action was taken by that person for that purpose.

(8) Subsections (6A) and (7) are not to be read as preventing other matters from being taken into account where they are relevant to deciding the question mentioned in subsection (3).

(8A) For the purposes of this section "a householder case" is a case where—

    (a) the defence concerned is the common law defence of self-defence,

    (b) the force concerned is force used by D while in or partly in a building, or part of a building, that is a dwelling or is forces accommodation (or is both),

    (c) D is not a trespasser at the time the force is used, and

    (d) at that time D believed V to be in, or entering, the building or part as a trespasser.

(8B) Where—

    (a) a part of a building is a dwelling where D dwells,

    (b) another part of the building is a place of work for D or another person who dwells in the first part, and

    (c) that other part is internally accessible from the first part,

that other part, and any internal means of access between the two parts, are each treated for the purposes of subsection (8A) as a part of a building that is a dwelling.

(8C) Where—

> (a) a part of a building is forces accommodation that is living or sleeping accommodation for D,
> (b) another part of the building is a place of work for D or another person for whom the first part is living or sleeping accommodation, and
> (c) that other part is internally accessible from the first part,

that other part, and any internal means of access between the two parts, are each treated for the purposes of subsection (8A) as a part of a building that is forces accommodation.

(8D) Subsections (4) and (5) apply for the purposes of subsection (8A)(d) as they apply for the purposes of subsection (3).

(8E) The fact that a person derives title from a trespasser, or has the permission of a trespasser, does not prevent the person from being a trespasser for the purposes of subsection (8A).

(8F) In subsections (8A) to (8C)—

"building" includes a vehicle or vessel, and

"forces accommodation" means service living accommodation for the purposes of Part 3 of the Armed Forces Act 2006 by virtue of section 96(1)(a) or (b) of that Act.

(9) This section, except so far as making different provision for householder cases, is intended to clarify the operation of the existing defences mentioned in subsection (2).

(10) In this section—

> (a) "legitimate purpose" means—
> > (i) the purpose of self-defence under the common law,
> > (ia) the purpose of defence of property under the common law, or
> > (ii) the prevention of crime or effecting or assisting in the lawful arrest of persons mentioned in the provisions referred to in subsection (2)(b);
> (b) references to self-defence include acting in defence of another person; and
> (c) references to the degree of force used are to the type and amount of force used.

119 Offence of causing nuisance or disturbance on NHS premises

(1) A person commits an offence if—

> (a) the person causes, without reasonable excuse and while on NHS premises, a nuisance or disturbance to an NHS staff member who is working there or is otherwise there in connection with work,
> (b) the person refuses, without reasonable excuse, to leave the NHS premises when asked to do so by a constable or an NHS staff member, and
> (c) the person is not on the NHS premises for the purpose of obtaining medical advice, treatment or care for himself or herself. [S]

(3) For the purposes of this section—

> (a) a person ceases to be on NHS premises for the purpose of obtaining medical advice, treatment or care for himself or herself once the person has received the advice, treatment or care, and
> (b) a person is not on NHS premises for the purpose of obtaining medical advice, treatment or care for himself or herself if the person has been refused the advice, treatment or care during the last 8 hours.

Coroners and Justice Act 2009

54 Partial defence to murder: loss of control

(1) Where a person ("D") kills or is a party to the killing of another ("V"), D is not to be convicted of murder if—

> (a) D's acts and omissions in doing or being a party to the killing resulted from D's loss of self-control,

(b) the loss of self-control had a qualifying trigger, and

(c) a person of D's sex and age, with a normal degree of tolerance and self-restraint and in the circumstances of D, might have reacted in the same or in a similar way to D.

(2) For the purposes of subsection (1)(a), it does not matter whether or not the loss of control was sudden.

(3) In subsection (1)(c) the reference to "the circumstances of D" is a reference to all of D's circumstances other than those whose only relevance to D's conduct is that they bear on D's general capacity for tolerance or self-restraint.

(4) Subsection (1) does not apply if, in doing or being a party to the killing, D acted in a considered desire for revenge.

(5) On a charge of murder, if sufficient evidence is adduced to raise an issue with respect to the defence under subsection (1), the jury must assume that the defence is satisfied unless the prosecution proves beyond reasonable doubt that it is not.

(6) For the purposes of subsection (5), sufficient evidence is adduced to raise an issue with respect to the defence if evidence is adduced on which, in the opinion of the trial judge, a jury, properly directed, could reasonably conclude that the defence might apply.

(7) A person who, but for this section, would be liable to be convicted of murder is liable instead to be convicted of manslaughter.

(8) The fact that one party to a killing is by virtue of this section not liable to be convicted of murder does not affect the question whether the killing amounted to murder in the case of any other party to it.

55 Meaning of "qualifying trigger"

(1) This section applies for the purposes of section 54.

(2) A loss of self-control had a qualifying trigger if subsection (3), (4) or (5) applies.

(3) This subsection applies if D's loss of self-control was attributable to D's fear of serious violence from V against D or another identified person.

(4) This subsection applies if D's loss of self-control was attributable to a thing or things done or said (or both) which—

(a) constituted circumstances of an extremely grave character, and

(b) caused D to have a justifiable sense of being seriously wronged.

(5) This subsection applies if D's loss of self-control was attributable to a combination of the matters mentioned in subsections (3) and (4).

(6) In determining whether a loss of self-control had a qualifying trigger—

(a) D's fear of serious violence is to be disregarded to the extent that it was caused by a thing which D incited to be done or said for the purpose of providing an excuse to use violence;

(b) a sense of being seriously wronged by a thing done or said is not justifiable if D incited the thing to be done or said for the purpose of providing an excuse to use violence;

(c) the fact that a thing done or said constituted sexual infidelity is to be disregarded.

(7) In this section references to "D" and "V" are to be construed in accordance with section 54.

56 Abolition of common law defence of provocation

(1) The common law defence of provocation is abolished and replaced by sections 54 and 55.

62 Possession of prohibited images of children

(1) It is an offence for a person to be in possession of a prohibited image of a child. [E]

(2) A prohibited image is an image which—

(a) is pornographic,

(b) falls within subsection (6), and

(c) is grossly offensive, disgusting or otherwise of an obscene character.

(3) An image is "pornographic" if it is of such a nature that it must reasonably be assumed to have been produced solely or principally for the purpose of sexual arousal.

(4) Where (as found in the person's possession) an image forms part of a series of images, the question whether the image is of such a nature as is mentioned in subsection (3) is to be determined by reference to—

(a) the image itself, and

(b) (if the series of images is such as to be capable of providing a context for the image) the context in which it occurs in the series of images.

(5) So, for example, where—

(a) an image forms an integral part of a narrative constituted by a series of images, and

(b) having regard to those images as a whole, they are not of such a nature that they must reasonably be assumed to have been produced solely or principally for the purpose of sexual arousal,

the image may, by virtue of being part of that narrative, be found not to be pornographic, even though it might have been found to be pornographic if taken by itself.

(6) An image falls within this subsection if it—

(a) is an image which focuses solely or principally on a child's genitals or anal region, or

(b) portrays any of the acts mentioned in subsection (7).

(7) Those acts are—

(a) the performance by a person of an act of intercourse or oral sex with or in the presence of a child;

(b) an act of masturbation by, of, involving or in the presence of a child;

(c) an act which involves penetration of the vagina or anus of a child with a part of a person's body or with anything else;

(d) an act of penetration, in the presence of a child, of the vagina or anus of a person with a part of a person's body or with anything else;

(e) the performance by a child of an act of intercourse or oral sex with an animal (whether dead or alive or imaginary);

(f) the performance by a person of an act of intercourse or oral sex with an animal (whether dead or alive or imaginary) in the presence of a child.

(8) For the purposes of subsection (7), penetration is a continuing act from entry to withdrawal.

63 Exclusion of classified film etc.

(1) Section 62(1) does not apply to excluded images.

(2) An "excluded image" is an image which forms part of a series of images contained in a recording of the whole or part of a classified work.

(3) But such an image is not an "excluded image" if—

(a) it is contained in a recording of an extract from a classified work, and

(b) it is of such a nature that it must reasonably be assumed to have been extracted (whether with or without other images) solely or principally for the purpose of sexual arousal.

(4) Where an extracted image is one of a series of images contained in the recording, the question whether the image is of such a nature as is mentioned in subsection (3)(b) is to be determined by reference to—

(a) the image itself, and

(b) (if the series of images is such as to be capable of providing a context for the image) the context in which it occurs in the series of images;

and section 62(5) applies in connection with determining that question as it applies in connection with determining whether an image is pornographic.

(5) In determining for the purposes of this section whether a recording is a recording of the whole or part of a classified work, any alteration attributable to—

(a) a defect caused for technical reasons or by inadvertence on the part of any person, or

(b) the inclusion in the recording of any extraneous material (such as advertisements),

is to be disregarded.

(7) In this section—

"classified work" means (subject to subsection (8)) a video work in respect of which a classification certificate has been issued by a designated authority (whether before or after the commencement of this section);

"classification certificate" and "video work" have the same meaning as in the Video Recordings Act 1984;

"designated authority" means an authority which has been designated by the Secretary of State under section 4 of that Act;

"extract" includes an extract consisting of a single image;

"pornographic" has the same meaning as in section 62;

"recording" means any disc, tape or other device capable of storing data electronically and from which images may be produced (by any means).

(8) Section 22(3) of the Video Recordings Act 1984 (effect of alterations) applies for the purposes of this section as it applies for the purposes of that Act.

64 Defences

(1) Where a person is charged with an offence under section 62(1), it is a defence for the person to prove any of the following matters—

> (a) that the person had a legitimate reason for being in possession of the image concerned;
>
> (b) that the person had not seen the image concerned and did not know, nor had any cause to suspect, it to be a prohibited image of a child;
>
> (c) that the person—
>> (i) was sent the image concerned without any prior request having been made by or on behalf of the person, and
>>
>> (ii) did not keep it for an unreasonable time.

(2) In this section "prohibited image" has the same meaning as in section 62.

65 Meaning of "image" and "child"

(1) The following apply for the purposes of sections 62 to 64.

(2) "Image" includes—

> (a) a moving or still image (produced by any means), or
>
> (b) data (stored by any means) which is capable of conversion into an image within paragraph (a).

(3) "Image" does not include an indecent photograph, or indecent pseudo-photograph, of a child.

(4) In subsection (3) "indecent photograph" and "indecent pseudo-photograph" are to be construed—

> (a) in relation to England and Wales, in accordance with the Protection of Children Act 1978.

(5) "Child", subject to subsection (6), means a person under the age of 18.

(6) Where an image shows a person the image is to be treated as an image of a child if—

> (a) the impression conveyed by the image is that the person shown is a child, or
>
> (b) the predominant impression conveyed is that the person shown is a child despite the fact that some of the physical characteristics shown are not those of a child.

(7) References to an image of a person include references to an image of an imaginary person.

(8) References to an image of a child include references to an image of an imaginary child.

Policing and Crime Act 2009

30 Offence of persistently possessing alcohol in a public place

(1) A person under the age of 18 is guilty of an offence if, without reasonable excuse, the person is in possession of alcohol in any relevant place on 3 or more occasions within a period of 12 consecutive months. [S]

(2) "Relevant place", in relation to a person, means—

  (a) any public place, other than excluded premises, or

  (b) any place, other than a public place, to which the person has unlawfully gained access.

(4) For the purposes of subsection (2) a place is a public place if at the material time the public or any section of the public has access to it, on payment or otherwise, as of right or by virtue of express or implied permission.

(5) In subsection (2) "excluded premises"—

  (a) in relation to England and Wales, means—

    (i) premises which may by virtue of Part 3 or 5 of the Licensing Act 2003 (premises licence or permitted temporary activity) be used for the supply of alcohol,

    (ii) premises which may by virtue of Part 4 of that Act (club premises certificate) be used for the supply of alcohol to members or guests,

(6) In this section "alcohol"—

  (a) in relation to England and Wales, has the same meaning as in the Licensing Act 2003.

Bribery Act 2010

1 Offences of bribing another person

(1) A person ("P") is guilty of an offence if either of the following cases applies. [E]

(2) Case 1 is where—

  (a) P offers, promises or gives a financial or other advantage to another person, and

  (b) P intends the advantage—

    (i) to induce a person to perform improperly a relevant function or activity, or

    (ii) to reward a person for the improper performance of such a function or activity.

(3) Case 2 is where—

  (a) P offers, promises or gives a financial or other advantage to another person, and

  (b) P knows or believes that the acceptance of the advantage would itself constitute the improper performance of a relevant function or activity.

(4) In case 1 it does not matter whether the person to whom the advantage is offered, promised or given is the same person as the person who is to perform, or has performed, the function or activity concerned.

(5) In cases 1 and 2 it does not matter whether the advantage is offered, promised or given by P directly or through a third party.

2 Offences relating to being bribed

(1) A person ("R") is guilty of an offence if any of the following cases applies. [E]

(2) Case 3 is where R requests, agrees to receive or accepts a financial or other advantage intending that, in consequence, a relevant function or activity should be performed improperly (whether by R or another person).

(3) Case 4 is where—

  (a) R requests, agrees to receive or accepts a financial or other advantage, and

  (b) the request, agreement or acceptance itself constitutes the improper performance by R of a relevant function or activity.

(4) Case 5 is where R requests, agrees to receive or accepts a financial or other advantage as a reward for the improper performance (whether by R or another person) of a relevant function or activity.

(5) Case 6 is where, in anticipation of or in consequence of R requesting, agreeing to receive or accepting a financial or other advantage, a relevant function or activity is performed improperly—

(a) by R, or

(b) by another person at R's request or with R's assent or acquiescence.

(6) In cases 3 to 6 it does not matter—

(a) whether R requests, agrees to receive or accepts (or is to request, agree to receive or accept) the advantage directly or through a third party,

(b) whether the advantage is (or is to be) for the benefit of R or another person.

(7) In cases 4 to 6 it does not matter whether R knows or believes that the performance of the function or activity is improper.

(8) In case 6, where a person other than R is performing the function or activity, it also does not matter whether that person knows or believes that the performance of the function or activity is improper.

3   Function or activity to which bribe relates

(1) For the purposes of this Act a function or activity is a relevant function or activity if—

(a) it falls within subsection (2), and

(b) meets one or more of conditions A to C.

(2) The following functions and activities fall within this subsection—

(a) any function of a public nature,

(b) any activity connected with a business,

(c) any activity performed in the course of a person's employment,

(d) any activity performed by or on behalf of a body of persons (whether corporate or unincorporate).

(3) Condition A is that a person performing the function or activity is expected to perform it in good faith.

(4) Condition B is that a person performing the function or activity is expected to perform it impartially.

(5) Condition C is that a person performing the function or activity is in a position of trust by virtue of performing it.

(6) A function or activity is a relevant function or activity even if it—

(a) has no connection with the United Kingdom, and

(b) is performed in a country or territory outside the United Kingdom.

(7) In this section "business" includes trade or profession.

4   Improper performance to which bribe relates

(1) For the purposes of this Act a relevant function or activity—

(a) is performed improperly if it is performed in breach of a relevant expectation, and

(b) is to be treated as being performed improperly if there is a failure to perform the function or activity and that failure is itself a breach of a relevant expectation.

(2) In subsection (1) "relevant expectation"—

(a) in relation to a function or activity which meets condition A or B, means the expectation mentioned in the condition concerned, and

(b) in relation to a function or activity which meets condition C, means any expectation as to the manner in which, or the reasons for which, the function or activity will be performed that arises from the position of trust mentioned in that condition.

(3) Anything that a person does (or omits to do) arising from or in connection with that person's past performance of a relevant function or activity is to be treated for the purposes of this Act as being done (or omitted) by that person in the performance of that function or activity.

5   Expectation test

(1) For the purposes of sections 3 and 4, the test of what is expected is a test of what a reasonable person in the United Kingdom would expect in relation to the performance of the type of function or activity concerned.

(2) In deciding what such a person would expect in relation to the performance of a function or activity where the performance is not subject to the law of any part of the United Kingdom, any local custom or practice is to be disregarded unless it is permitted or required by the written law applicable to the country or territory concerned.

(3) In subsection (2) "written law" means law contained in—

    (a) any written constitution, or provision made by or under legislation, applicable to the country or territory concerned, or

    (b) any judicial decision which is so applicable and is evidenced in published written sources.

6 Bribery of foreign public officials

(1) A person ("P") who bribes a foreign public official ("F") is guilty of an offence if P's intention is to influence F in F's capacity as a foreign public official. [E]

(2) P must also intend to obtain or retain—

    (a) business, or

    (b) an advantage in the conduct of business.

(3) P bribes F if, and only if—

    (a) directly or through a third party, P offers, promises or gives any financial or other advantage—

        (i) to F, or

        (ii) to another person at F's request or with F's assent or acquiescence, and

    (b) F is neither permitted nor required by the written law applicable to F to be influenced in F's capacity as a foreign public official by the offer, promise or gift.

(4) References in this section to influencing F in F's capacity as a foreign public official mean influencing F in the performance of F's functions as such an official, which includes—

    (a) any omission to exercise those functions, and

    (b) any use of F's position as such an official, even if not within F's authority.

(5) "Foreign public official" means an individual who—

    (a) holds a legislative, administrative or judicial position of any kind, whether appointed or elected, of a country or territory outside the United Kingdom (or any subdivision of such a country or territory),

    (b) exercises a public function—

        (i) for or on behalf of a country or territory outside the United Kingdom (or any subdivision of such a country or territory), or

        (ii) for any public agency or public enterprise of that country or territory (or subdivision), or

    (c) is an official or agent of a public international organisation.

(6) "Public international organisation" means an organisation whose members are any of the following—

    (a) countries or territories,

    (b) governments of countries or territories,

    (c) other public international organisations,

    (d) a mixture of any of the above.

(7) For the purposes of subsection (3)(b), the written law applicable to F is—

    (a) where the performance of the functions of F which P intends to influence would be subject to the law of any part of the United Kingdom, the law of that part of the United Kingdom,

    (b) where paragraph (a) does not apply and F is an official or agent of a public international organisation, the applicable written rules of that organisation,

    (c) where paragraphs (a) and (b) do not apply, the law of the country or territory in relation to which F is a foreign public official so far as that law is contained in—

        (i) any written constitution, or provision made by or under legislation, applicable to the country or territory concerned, or

        (ii) any judicial decision which is so applicable and is evidenced in published written sources.

(8) For the purposes of this section, a trade or profession is a business.

7   Failure of commercial organisations to prevent bribery

(1) A relevant commercial organisation ("C") is guilty of an offence under this section if a person ("A") associated with C bribes another person intending—

(a) to obtain or retain business for C, or

(b) to obtain or retain an advantage in the conduct of business for C. [I]

(2) But it is a defence for C to prove that C had in place adequate procedures designed to prevent persons associated with C from undertaking such conduct.

(3) For the purposes of this section, A bribes another person if, and only if, A—

(a) is, or would be, guilty of an offence under section 1 or 6 (whether or not A has been prosecuted for such an offence), or

(b) would be guilty of such an offence if section 12(2)(c) and (4) were omitted.

(4) See section 8 for the meaning of a person associated with C and see section 9 for a duty on the Secretary of State to publish guidance.

(5) In this section—

"partnership" means—

(a) a partnership within the Partnership Act 1890, or

(b) a limited partnership registered under the Limited Partnerships Act 1907,

or a firm or entity of a similar character formed under the law of a country or territory outside the United Kingdom,

"relevant commercial organisation" means—

(a) a body which is incorporated under the law of any part of the United Kingdom and which carries on a business (whether there or elsewhere),

(b) any other body corporate (wherever incorporated) which carries on a business, or part of a business, in any part of the United Kingdom,

(c) a partnership which is formed under the law of any part of the United Kingdom and which carries on a business (whether there or elsewhere), or

(d) any other partnership (wherever formed) which carries on a business, or part of a business, in any part of the United Kingdom,

and, for the purposes of this section, a trade or profession is a business.

8   Meaning of associated person

(1) For the purposes of section 7, a person ("A") is associated with C if (disregarding any bribe under consideration) A is a person who performs services for or on behalf of C.

(2) The capacity in which A performs services for or on behalf of C does not matter.

(3) Accordingly A may (for example) be C's employee, agent or subsidiary.

(4) Whether or not A is a person who performs services for or on behalf of C is to be determined by reference to all the relevant circumstances and not merely by reference to the nature of the relationship between A and C.

(5) But if A is an employee of C, it is to be presumed unless the contrary is shown that A is a person who performs services for or on behalf of C.

12   Offences under this Act: territorial application

(1) An offence is committed under section 1, 2 or 6 in England and Wales, Scotland or Northern Ireland if any act or omission which forms part of the offence takes place in that part of the United Kingdom.

(2) Subsection (3) applies if—

(a) no act or omission which forms part of an offence under section 1, 2 or 6 takes place in the United Kingdom,

(b) a person's acts or omissions done or made outside the United Kingdom would form part of such an offence if done or made in the United Kingdom, and

(c) that person has a close connection with the United Kingdom.

(3) In such a case—

(a) the acts or omissions form part of the offence referred to in subsection (2)(a), and

(b) proceedings for the offence may be taken at any place in the United Kingdom.

(4) For the purposes of subsection (2)(c) a person has a close connection with the United Kingdom if, and only if, the person was one of the following at the time the acts or omissions concerned were done or made—

    (a) a British citizen,

    (b) a British overseas territories citizen,

    (c) a British National (Overseas),

    (d) a British Overseas citizen,

    (e) a person who under the British Nationality Act 1981 was a British subject,

    (f) a British protected person within the meaning of that Act,

    (g) an individual ordinarily resident in the United Kingdom,

    (h) a body incorporated under the law of any part of the United Kingdom,

    (i) a Scottish partnership.

(5) An offence is committed under section 7 irrespective of whether the acts or omissions which form part of the offence take place in the United Kingdom or elsewhere.

(6) Where no act or omission which forms part of an offence under section 7 takes place in the United Kingdom, proceedings for the offence may be taken at any place in the United Kingdom.

13   Defence for certain bribery offences etc.

(1) It is a defence for a person charged with a relevant bribery offence to prove that the person's conduct was necessary for—

    (a) the proper exercise of any function of an intelligence service, or

    (b) the proper exercise of any function of the armed forces when engaged on active service.

(2) The head of each intelligence service must ensure that the service has in place arrangements designed to ensure that any conduct of a member of the service which would otherwise be a relevant bribery offence is necessary for a purpose falling within subsection (1)(a).

(5) For the purposes of this section, the circumstances in which a person's conduct is necessary for a purpose falling within subsection (1)(a) or (b) are to be treated as including any circumstances in which the person's conduct—

    (a) would otherwise be an offence under section 2, and

    (b) involves conduct by another person which, but for subsection (1)(a) or (b), would be an offence under section 1.

(6) In this section—

"active service" means service in—

    (a) an action or operation against an enemy,

    (b) an operation outside the British Islands for the protection of life or property, or

    (c) the military occupation of a foreign country or territory,

"armed forces" means Her Majesty's forces (within the meaning of the Armed Forces Act 2006),

"civilian subject to service discipline" and "enemy" have the same meaning as in the Act of 2006,

"GCHQ" has the meaning given by section 3(3) of the Intelligence Services Act 1994,

"head" means—

    (a) in relation to the Security Service, the Director General of the Security Service,

    (b) in relation to the Secret Intelligence Service, the Chief of the Secret Intelligence Service, and

    (c) in relation to GCHQ, the Director of GCHQ,

"intelligence service" means the Security Service, the Secret Intelligence Service or GCHQ,

"relevant bribery offence" means—

    (a) an offence under section 1 which would not also be an offence under section 6,

    (b) an offence under section 2,

    (c) an offence committed by aiding, abetting, counselling or procuring the commission of an offence falling within paragraph (a) or (b),

    (d) an offence of attempting or conspiring to commit, or of inciting the commission of, an offence falling within paragraph (a) or (b), or

(e) an offence under Part 2 of the Serious Crime Act 2007 (encouraging or assisting crime) in relation to an offence falling within paragraph (a) or (b).

14 Offences under sections 1, 2 and 6 by bodies corporate etc.

(1) This section applies if an offence under section 1, 2 or 6 is committed by a body corporate or a Scottish partnership.

(2) If the offence is proved to have been committed with the consent or connivance of—

(a) a senior officer of the body corporate or Scottish partnership, or

(b) a person purporting to act in such a capacity,

the senior officer or person (as well as the body corporate or partnership) is guilty of the offence and liable to be proceeded against and punished accordingly.

(3) But subsection (2) does not apply, in the case of an offence which is committed under section 1, 2 or 6 by virtue of section 12(2) to (4), to a senior officer or person purporting to act in such a capacity unless the senior officer or person has a close connection with the United Kingdom (within the meaning given by section 12(4)).

(4) In this section—

"director", in relation to a body corporate whose affairs are managed by its members, means a member of the body corporate,

"senior officer" means—

(a) in relation to a body corporate, a director, manager, secretary or other similar officer of the body corporate, and

(b) in relation to a Scottish partnership, a partner in the partnership.

16 Application to Crown

This Act applies to individuals in the public service of the Crown as it applies to other individuals.

17 Consequential provision

(1) The following common law offences are abolished—

(a) the offences under the law of England and Wales and Northern Ireland of bribery and embracery.

Identity Documents Act 2010

4 Possession of false identity documents etc. with improper intention

(1) It is an offence for a person ("P") with an improper intention to have in P's possession or under P's control—

(a) an identity document that is false and that P knows or believes to be false,

(b) an identity document that was improperly obtained and that P knows or believes to have been improperly obtained, or

(c) an identity document that relates to someone else.

(2) Each of the following is an improper intention—

(a) the intention of using the document for establishing personal information about P;

(b) the intention of allowing or inducing another to use it for establishing, ascertaining or verifying personal information about P or anyone else.

(3) In subsection (2)(b) the reference to P or anyone else does not include, in the case of a document within subsection (1)(c), the individual to whom it relates. [I]

5 Apparatus designed or adapted for the making of false identity documents etc.

(1) It is an offence for a person ("P") with the prohibited intention to make or to have in P's possession or under P's control—

(a) any apparatus which, to P's knowledge, is or has been specially designed or adapted for the making of false identity documents, or

(b) any article or material which, to P's knowledge, is or has been specially designed or adapted to be used in the making of such documents.

(2) The prohibited intention is the intention—

(a) that P or another will make a false identity document, and

(b) that the document will be used by somebody for establishing, ascertaining or verifying personal information about a person. [I]

6   Possession of false identity documents etc. without reasonable excuse

(1) It is an offence for a person ("P"), without reasonable excuse, to have in P's possession or under P's control—

(a) an identity document that is false,

(b) an identity document that was improperly obtained,

(c) an identity document that relates to someone else,

(d) any apparatus which, to P's knowledge, is or has been specially designed or adapted for the making of false identity documents, or

(e) any article or material which, to P's knowledge, is or has been specially designed to be used in the making of such documents. [E]

7   Meaning of "identity document"

(1) For the purposes of sections 4 to 6 "identity document" means any document that is or purports to be—

(a) an immigration document,

(b) a United Kingdom passport (within the meaning of the Immigration Act 1971),

(c) a passport issued by or on behalf of the authorities of a country or territory outside the United Kingdom or by or on behalf of an international organisation,

(d) a document that can be used (in some or all circumstances) instead of a passport,

(e) a licence to drive a motor vehicle granted under Part 3 of the Road Traffic 1988 . . . , or

(f) a driving licence issued by or on behalf of the authorities of a country or territory outside the United Kingdom.

(2) In subsection (1)(a) "immigration document" means—

(a) a document used for confirming—

(i) the right of a person at a time before IP completion day under the EU Treaties in respect of entry or residence in the United Kingdom, or

(ii) the right of a person under the Immigration (European Economic Area) Regulations 2016 (as they continue to have effect by virtue of the Citizens' Rights (Application Deadline and Temporary Protection) (EU Exit) Regulations 2020) in respect of entry or residence in the United Kingdom,

(b) a document that is given in exercise of immigration functions and records information about leave granted to a person to enter or to remain in the United Kingdom, or

(c) a registration card (within the meaning of section 26A of the Immigration Act 1971).

(2A) In subsection 2(a)(i) "EU Treaties" includes a reference to those Treaties so far as applicable to and in the United Kingdom by virtue of Part 4 of the EU withdrawal agreement.

(3) In subsection (2)(b) "immigration functions" means functions under the Immigration Acts (within the meaning of the Asylum and Immigration (Treatment of Claimants, etc.) Act 2004).

(4) References in subsection (1) to the issue of a document include its renewal, replacement or re-issue (with or without modifications).

(5) In this section "document" includes a stamp or label.

8   Meaning of "personal information"

(1) For the purposes of sections 4 and 5 "personal information", in relation to an individual ("A"), means—

    (a) A's full name,

    (b) other names by which A is or has previously been known,

    (c) A's gender,

    (d) A's date and place of birth,

    (e) external characteristics of A that are capable of being used for identifying A,

    (f) the address of A's principal place of residence in the United Kingdom,

    (g) the address of every other place in the United Kingdom or elsewhere where A has a place of residence,

    (h) where in the United Kingdom and elsewhere A has previously been resident,

    (i) the times at which A was resident at different places in the United Kingdom or elsewhere,

    (j) A's current residential status,

    (k) residential statuses previously held by A, and

    (l) information about numbers allocated to A for identification purposes and about the documents (including stamps and labels) to which they relate.

  (2) In subsection (1) "residential status" means—

    (a) A's nationality,

    (b) A's entitlement to remain in the United Kingdom, and

    (c) if that entitlement derives from a grant of leave to enter or remain in the United Kingdom, the terms and conditions of that leave.

9 Other definitions

  (1) "Apparatus" includes any equipment, machinery or device and any wire or cable, together with any software used with it.

  (2) In relation to England and Wales and Northern Ireland, an identity document is "false" only if it is false within the meaning of Part 1 of the Forgery and Counterfeiting Act 1981 (see section 9(1)).

  (3) An identity document was "improperly obtained" if—

    (a) false information was provided in, or in connection with, the application for its issue to the person who issued it, or

    (b) false information was provided in, or in connection with, an application for its modification to a person entitled to modify it.

  (4) In subsection (3)—

    (a) "false" information includes information containing any inaccuracy or omission that results in a tendency to mislead,

    (b) "information" includes documents (including stamps and labels) and records, and

    (c) the "issue" of a document includes its renewal, replacement or re-issue (with or without modifications).

  (5) References to the making of false identity document include the modification of an identity document so that it becomes false.

  (6) This section applies for the purposes of sections 4 to 6.

Financial Services Act 2012

PART 7   OFFENCES RELATING TO FINANCIAL SERVICES

89 Misleading statements

  (1) Subsection (2) applies to a person ("P") who—

    (a) makes a statement which P knows to be false or misleading in a material respect,

    (b) makes a statement which is false or misleading in a material respect, being reckless as to whether it is, or

(c) dishonestly conceals any material facts whether in connection with a statement made by P or otherwise.

(2) P commits an offence if P makes the statement or conceals the facts with the intention of inducing, or is reckless as to whether making it or concealing them may induce, another person (whether or not the person to whom the statement is made)—

(a) to enter into or offer to enter into, or to refrain from entering or offering to enter into, a relevant agreement, or

(b) to exercise, or refrain from exercising, any rights conferred by a relevant investment. [E]

(3) In proceedings for an offence under subsection (2) brought against a person to whom that subsection applies as a result of paragraph (a) of subsection (1), it is a defence for the person charged ("D") to show that the statement was made in conformity with—

(a) price stabilising rules,

(b) control of information rules, or

(c) the relevant provisions of Article 5 (exemption for buy-back programmes and stabilisation) of the market abuse regulation.

(4) Subsections (1) and (2) do not apply unless—

(a) the statement is made in or from, or the facts are concealed in or from, the United Kingdom or arrangements are made in or from the United Kingdom for the statement to be made or the facts to be concealed,

(b) the person on whom the inducement is intended to or may have effect is in the United Kingdom, or

(c) the agreement is or would be entered into or the rights are or would be exercised in the United Kingdom.

90 Misleading impressions

(1) A person ("P") who does any act or engages in any course of conduct which creates a false or misleading impression as to the market in or the price or value of any relevant investments commits an offence if—

(a) P intends to create the impression, and

(b) the case falls within subsection (2) or (3) (or both). [E]

(2) The case falls within this subsection if P intends, by creating the impression, to induce another person to acquire, dispose of, subscribe for or underwrite the investments or to refrain from doing so or to exercise or refrain from exercising any rights conferred by the investments.

(3) The case falls within this subsection if—

(a) P knows that the impression is false or misleading or is reckless as to whether it is, and

(b) P intends by creating the impression to produce any of the results in subsection (4) or is aware that creating the impression is likely to produce any of the results in that subsection.

(4) Those results are—

(a) the making of a gain for P or another, or

(b) the causing of loss to another person or the exposing of another person to the risk of loss.

(5) References in subsection (4) to gain or loss are to be read in accordance with subsections (6) to (8).

(6) "Gain" and "loss"—

(a) extend only to gain or loss in money or other property of any kind;

(b) include such gain or loss whether temporary or permanent.

(7) "Gain" includes a gain by keeping what one has, as well as a gain by getting what one does not have.

(8) "Loss" includes a loss by not getting what one might get, as well as a loss by parting with what one has.

(9) In proceedings brought against any person ("D") for an offence under subsection (1) it is a defence for D to show—

  (a) to the extent that the offence results from subsection (2), that D reasonably believed that D's conduct would not create an impression that was false or misleading as to the matters mentioned in subsection (1),

  (b) that D acted or engaged in the conduct—

   (i) for the purpose of stabilising the price of investments, and

   (ii) in conformity with price stabilising rules,

  (c) that D acted or engaged in the conduct in conformity with control of information rules, or

  (d) that D acted or engaged in the conduct in conformity with the relevant provisions of Article 5 (exemption for buy-back programmes and stabilisation) of the market abuse regulation.

 (10) This section does not apply unless—

  (a) the act is done, or the course of conduct is engaged in, in the United Kingdom, or

  (b) the false or misleading impression is created there.

91 Misleading statements etc. in relation to benchmarks

 (1) A person ("A") who makes to another person ("B") a false or misleading statement commits an offence if—

  (a) A makes the statement in the course of arrangements for the setting of a relevant benchmark,

  (b) A intends that the statement should be used by B for the purpose of the setting of a relevant benchmark, and

  (c) A knows that the statement is false or misleading or is reckless as to whether it is. [E]

 (2) A person ("C") who does any act or engages in any course of conduct which creates a false or misleading impression as to the price or value of any investment or as to the interest rate appropriate to any transaction commits an offence if—

  (a) C intends to create the impression,

  (b) the impression may affect the setting of a relevant benchmark,

  (c) C knows that the impression is false or misleading or is reckless as to whether it is, and

  (d) C knows that the impression may affect the setting of a relevant benchmark. [E]

 (3) In proceedings for an offence under subsection (1), it is a defence for the person charged ("D") to show that the statement was made in conformity with—

  (b) control of information rules, or

  (c) the relevant provisions of Article 5 (exemption for buy-back programmes and stabilisation) of the market abuse regulation.

 (4) In proceedings brought against any person ("D") for an offence under subsection (2) it is a defence for D to show—

  (a) that D acted or engaged in the conduct—

   (i) for the purpose of stabilising the price of investments, and

   (ii) in conformity with price stabilising rules,

  (b) that D acted or engaged in the conduct in conformity with control of information rules, or

  (c) that D acted or engaged in the conduct in conformity with the relevant provisions of Article 5 (exemption for buy-back programmes and stabilisation) of the market abuse regulation.

 (5) Subsection (1) does not apply unless the statement is made in or from the United Kingdom or to a person in the United Kingdom.

 (6) Subsection (2) does not apply unless—

  (a) the act is done, or the course of conduct is engaged in, in the United Kingdom, or

  (b) the false or misleading impression is created there.

93 Interpretation of Part 7

 (1) This section has effect for the interpretation of this Part.

 (2) "Investment" includes any asset, right or interest.

(3) "Relevant agreement" means an agreement—

    (a) the entering into or performance of which by either party constitutes an activity of a kind specified in an order made by the Treasury, and

    (b) which relates to a relevant investment.

(4) "Relevant benchmark" means a benchmark of a kind specified in an order made by the Treasury.

(5) "Relevant investment" means an investment of a kind specified in an order made by the Treasury.

(8) "Price stabilising rules" and "control of information rules" have the same meaning as in the Financial Services and Markets Act 2000.

(8A) "Market abuse regulation" means Regulation (EU) No 596/2014 of the European Parliament and of the Council of 16 April 2014 on market abuse (market abuse regulation) and repealing Directive 2003/6/EC of the European Parliament and of the Council and Commission Directives 2003/124/EC, 2003/125/EC and 2004/72/EC.

(8B) References to Article 5 of the market abuse regulation include—

    (a) any directly applicable EU regulation originally made under that Article, which is retained direct EU legislation, and

    (b) any subordinate legislation (within the meaning of the Interpretation Act 1978) made under that Article on or after IP completion day.

(9) In this section "benchmark" has the meaning given in section 22(6) of the Financial Services and Markets Act 2000.

Legal Aid, Sentencing and Punishment of Offenders Act 2012

144   Offence of squatting in a residential building

(1) A person commits an offence if—

    (a) the person is in a residential building as a trespasser having entered it as a trespasser,

    (b) the person knows or ought to know that he or she is a trespasser, and

    (c) the person is living in the building or intends to live there for any period.

(2) The offence is not committed by a person holding over after the end of a lease or licence (even if the person leaves and re-enters the building).

(3) For the purposes of this section—

    (a) "building" includes any structure or part of a structure (including a temporary or moveable structure), and

    (b) a building is "residential" if it is designed or adapted, before the time of entry, for use as a place to live.

(4) For the purposes of this section the fact that a person derives title from a trespasser, or has the permission of a trespasser, does not prevent the person from being a trespasser.

(7) For the purposes of subsection (1)(a) it is irrelevant whether the person entered the building as a trespasser before or after the commencement of this section.

Protection of Freedoms Act 2012

54   Offence of immobilising etc. vehicles

(1) A person commits an offence who, without lawful authority—

    (a) immobilises a motor vehicle by the attachment to the vehicle, or a part of it, of an immobilising device, or

    (b) moves, or restricts the movement of, such a vehicle by any means,

intending to prevent or inhibit the removal of the vehicle by a person otherwise entitled to remove it. [E]

(2) The express or implied consent (whether or not legally binding) of a person otherwise entitled to remove the vehicle to the immobilisation, movement or restriction concerned is not lawful authority for the purposes of subsection (1).

(3) But, where the restriction of the movement of the vehicle is by means of a fixed barrier and the barrier was present (whether or not lowered into place or otherwise restricting movement) when the vehicle was parked, any express or implied consent (whether or not legally binding) of the driver of the vehicle to the restriction is, for the purposes of subsection (1), lawful authority for the restriction.

(4) A person who is entitled to remove a vehicle cannot commit an offence under this section in relation to that vehicle.

(6) In this section "motor vehicle" means a mechanically propelled vehicle or a vehicle designed or adapted for towing by a mechanically propelled vehicle.

Financial Services (Banking Reform) Act 2013

36 Offence relating to a decision causing a financial institution to fail
(1) A person ("S") commits an offence if—
    (a) at a time when S is a senior manager in relation to a financial institution ("F"), S—
        (i) takes, or agrees to the taking of, a decision by or on behalf of F as to the way in which the business of a group institution is to be carried on, or
        (ii) fails to take steps that S could take to prevent such a decision being taken,
    (b) at the time of the decision, S is aware of a risk that the implementation of the decision may cause the failure of the group institution,
    (c) in all the circumstances, S's conduct in relation to the taking of the decision falls far below what could reasonably be expected of a person in S's position, and
    (d) the implementation of the decision causes the failure of the group institution. [E]

(2) A "group institution", in relation to a financial institution ("F"), means F or any other financial institution that is a member of F's group for the purpose of Financial Services Management Act 2000 (FSMA 2000) (see section 421 of that Act).

(3) Subsections (1) and (2) are to be read with the interpretative provisions in section 37.

37 Section 36: interpretation
(1) This section has effect for the interpretation of section 36.
(2) "Financial institution" means a UK institution which—
    (a) meets condition A or B, and
    (b) is not an insurer or a credit union.

(3) Condition A is that it has permission under Part 4A of FSMA 2000 to carry on the regulated activity of accepting deposits.
(4) Condition B is that—
    (a) it is for the purposes of FSMA 2000 an investment firm (see section 424A of that Act),
    (b) it has permission under Part 4A of that Act to carry on the regulated activity of dealing in investments as principal, and
    (c) when carried on by it, that activity is a PRA-regulated activity.
(5) In subsection (2)—
    (a) "UK institution" means an institution which is incorporated in, or formed under the law of any part of, the United Kingdom;
    (b) "insurer" means an institution which is authorised under FSMA 2000 to carry on the regulated activity of effecting or carrying out contracts of insurance as principal;
    (c) "credit union" means a credit union as defined by section 31 of the Credit Unions Act 1979 . . .
(6) Subsections (3), (4) and (5)(b) are to be read in accordance with sections 22 and 22A of FSMA 2000, taken with Schedule 2 to that Act and any order under section 22.

(7) A person is a "senior manager" in relation to a financial institution if, under an arrangement entered into by the institution, or by a contractor of the institution, in relation to the carrying on by the institution of a regulated activity, the person performs a senior management function.

(8) "Senior management function" means—

(a) a function of a description specified in rules made by the FCA under section 59(3)(a) or (b) of FSMA 2000 which is designated as a senior management function by the FCA under section 59(6A) of that Act;

(b) a function of a description specified in rules made by the PRA under section 59(3)(a) of that Act.

(9) A financial institution ("F") is to be regarded as failing where—

(a) F enters insolvency,

(b) any of the stabilisation options in Part 1 of the Banking Act 2009 is achieved in relation to F, or

(c) F is taken for the purposes of the Financial Services Compensation Scheme to be unable, or likely to be unable, to satisfy claims against F.

(10) In subsection (9)(a) "insolvency" includes—

(a)   bankruptcy,

(b)   liquidation,

(c)   bank insolvency,

(ca) building society insolvency,

(cb) investment bank insolvency,

(d)   administration,

(e)   bank administration,

(ea) building society special administration,

(f)   receivership,

(g)   a composition between F and F's creditors, and

(h)   a scheme of arrangement of F's affairs.

(11) For the purposes of subsection (10)—

"bank administration" has the same meaning as in the Banking Act 2009 (see section 136 of that Act);

"bank insolvency" has the same meaning as in that Act (see section 90 of that Act);

"building society insolvency" and "building society special administration" have the same meaning as in the Building Societies Act 1986 (see section 119 of that Act);

"investment bank insolvency" means any procedure established by regulations under section 233 of the Banking Act 2009.

Prevention of Social Housing Fraud Act 2013

1   Unlawful sub-letting: secure tenancies

(1) A tenant of a dwelling-house in England let under a secure tenancy commits an offence if—

(a) in breach of an express or implied term of the tenancy, the tenant sublets or parts with possession of—

(i)   the whole of the dwelling-house, or

(ii) part of the dwelling-house without the landlord's written consent,

(b) the tenant ceases to occupy the dwelling-house as the tenant's only or principal home, and

(c) the tenant knows that the conduct described in paragraph (a) is a breach of a term of the tenancy. [S]

(2) A tenant of a dwelling-house in England let under a secure tenancy commits an offence if—

(a) dishonestly and in breach of an express or implied term of the tenancy, the tenant sub-lets or parts with possession of—

(i) the whole of the dwelling-house, or

(ii) part of the dwelling-house without the landlord's written consent, and

(b) the tenant ceases to occupy the dwelling-house as the tenant's only or principal home.
[E]

(3) The offence under subsection (1) is not committed where the tenant takes the action described in paragraphs (a) and (b) of that subsection because of violence or threats of violence by a person residing in, or in the locality of, the dwelling-house—

(a) towards the tenant, or

(b) towards a member of the family of the tenant who was residing with the tenant immediately before the tenant ceased to occupy the dwelling-house.

(4) The offence under subsection (1) is not committed if a person ("P") who occupies the dwelling-house as a result of the conduct described in subsection (1)(a) is—

(a) a person entitled to apply to the court for an order giving P a right to occupy the dwelling-house or to have the tenancy transferred to P, or

(b) a person in respect of whom an application may be made to have the tenancy transferred to P or to another person to be held for P's benefit.

2 Unlawful sub-letting: assured tenancies

(1) A tenant of a dwelling-house in England let under an assured tenancy to which this section applies commits an offence if—

(a) in breach of an express or implied term of the tenancy, the tenant sublets or parts with possession of the whole or part of the dwelling-house,

(b) the tenant ceases to occupy the dwelling-house as the tenant's only or principal home, and

(c) the tenant knows that the conduct described in paragraph (a) is a breach of a term of the tenancy. [S]

(2) A tenant of a dwelling-house let under an assured tenancy to which this section applies commits an offence if—

(a) dishonestly and in breach of an express or implied term of the tenancy, the tenant sub-lets or parts with possession of the whole or part of the dwelling-house, and

(b) the tenant ceases to occupy the dwelling-house as the tenant's only or principal home. [E]

(3) This section applies to an assured tenancy—

(a) under which the landlord is a private registered provider of social housing or a registered social landlord, and

(b) which is not a shared ownership lease.

(4) The offence under subsection (1) is not committed where the tenant takes the action described in paragraphs (a) and (b) of that subsection because of violence or threats of violence by a person residing in, or in the locality of, the dwelling-house—

(a) towards the tenant, or

(b) towards a member of the family of the tenant who was residing with the tenant immediately before the tenant ceased to occupy the dwelling-house.

(5) The offence under subsection (1) is not committed if a person ("P") who occupies the dwelling-house as a result of the conduct described in subsection (1)(a) is—

(a) a person entitled to apply to the court for an order giving P a right to occupy the dwelling-house or to have the tenancy transferred to P, or

(b) a person in respect of whom an application may be made to have the tenancy transferred to P or to another person to be held for P's benefit.

Scrap Metal Dealers Act 2013

12   Offence of buying scrap metal for cash etc.

(1) A scrap metal dealer must not pay for scrap metal except—

    (a) by a cheque which under section 81A of the Bills of Exchange Act 1882 is not transfer-able, or

    (b) by an electronic transfer of funds (authorised by credit or debit card or otherwise). [S]

(2) The Secretary of State may by order amend subsection (1) to permit other methods of payment.

(3) In this section paying includes paying in kind (with goods or services).

(4) If a scrap metal dealer pays for scrap metal in breach of subsection (1), each of the following is guilty of an offence—

    (a) the scrap metal dealer;

    (b) if the payment is made at a site, the site manager;

    (c) any person who makes the payment acting for the dealer.

(5) It is a defence for a person within subsection (4)(a) or (b) who is charged with an offence under this section to prove that the person—

    (a) made arrangements to ensure that the payment was not made in breach of subsection (1), and

    (b) took all reasonable steps to ensure that those arrangements were complied with.

Anti-social Behaviour, Crime and Policing Act 2014

PART 1   INJUNCTIONS

1   Power to grant injunctions

(1) A court may grant an injunction under this section against a person aged 10 or over ("the respondent") if two conditions are met.

(2) The first condition is that the court is satisfied, on the balance of probabilities, that the respondent has engaged or threatens to engage in anti-social behaviour.

(3) The second condition is that the court considers it just and convenient to grant the injunction for the purpose of preventing the respondent from engaging in anti-social behaviour.

(4) An injunction under this section may for the purpose of preventing the respondent from engaging in anti-social behaviour—

    (a) prohibit the respondent from doing anything described in the injunction;

    (b) require the respondent to do anything described in the injunction.

(5) Prohibitions and requirements in an injunction under this section must, so far as practicable, be such as to avoid—

    (a) any interference with the times, if any, at which the respondent normally works or attends school or any other educational establishment;

    (b) any conflict with the requirements of any other court order or injunction to which the respondent may be subject.

(6) An injunction under this section must—

    (a) specify the period for which it has effect, or

    (b) state that it has effect until further order.

In the case of an injunction granted before the respondent has reached the age of 18, a period must be specified and it must be no more than 12 months.

(7) An injunction under this section may specify periods for which particular prohibitions or requirements have effect.

(8) An application for an injunction under this section must be made to—

(a) a youth court, in the case of a respondent aged under 18;

(b) the High Court or the county court, in any other case.

Paragraph (b) is subject to any rules of court made under section 18(2).

2 Meaning of "anti-social behaviour"

(1) In this Part "anti-social behaviour" means—

(a) conduct that has caused, or is likely to cause, harassment, alarm or distress to any person,

(b) conduct capable of causing nuisance or annoyance to a person in relation to that person's occupation of residential premises, or

(c) conduct capable of causing housing-related nuisance or annoyance to any person.

(2) Subsection (1)(b) applies only where the injunction under section 1 is applied for by—

(a) a housing provider,

(b) a local authority, or

(c) a chief officer of police.

(3) In subsection (1)(c) "housing-related" means directly or indirectly relating to the housing management functions of—

(a) a housing provider, or

(b) a local authority.

(4) For the purposes of subsection (3) the housing management functions of a housing provider or a local authority include—

(a) functions conferred by or under an enactment;

(b) the powers and duties of the housing provider or local authority as the holder of an estate or interest in housing accommodation.

3 Requirements included in injunctions

(1) An injunction under section 1 that includes a requirement must specify the person who is to be responsible for supervising compliance with the requirement. The person may be an individual or an organisation.

(2) Before including a requirement, the court must receive evidence about its suitability and enforceability from—

(a) the individual to be specified under subsection (1), if an individual is to be specified;

(b) an individual representing the organisation to be specified under subsection (1), if an organisation is to be specified.

(3) Before including two or more requirements, the court must consider their compatibility with each other.

(4) It is the duty of a person specified under subsection (1)—

(a) to make any necessary arrangements in connection with the requirements for which the person has responsibility (the "relevant requirements");

(b) to promote the respondent's compliance with the relevant requirements;

(c) if the person considers that the respondent—

(i)   has complied with all the relevant requirements, or

(ii) has failed to comply with a relevant requirement,

to inform the person who applied for the injunction and the appropriate chief officer of police.

(5) In subsection (4)(c) "the appropriate chief officer of police" means—

(a) the chief officer of police for the police area in which it appears to the person specified under subsection (1) that the respondent lives, or

(b) if it appears to that person that the respondent lives in more than one police area, whichever of the relevant chief officers of police that person thinks it most appropriate to inform.

(6) A respondent subject to a requirement included in an injunction under section 1 must—

    (a) keep in touch with the person specified under subsection (1) in relation to that requirement, in accordance with any instructions given by that person from time to time;

    (b) notify the person of any change of address.

These obligations have effect as requirements of the injunction.

4 Power of arrest

(1) A court granting an injunction under section 1 may attach a power of arrest to a prohibition or requirement of the injunction if the court thinks that—

    (a) the anti-social behaviour in which the respondent has engaged or threatens to engage consists of or includes the use or threatened use of violence against other persons, or

    (b) there is a significant risk of harm to other persons from the respondent.

"Requirement" here does not include one that has the effect of requiring the respondent to participate in particular activities.

(2) If the court attaches a power of arrest, the injunction may specify a period for which the power is to have effect which is shorter than that of the prohibition or requirement to which it relates.

PART 3 DISPERSAL POWERS

35 Directions excluding a person from an area

(1) If the conditions in subsections (2) and (3) are met and an authorisation is in force under section 34, a constable in uniform may direct a person who is in a public place in the locality specified in the authorisation—

    (a) to leave the locality (or part of the locality), and

    (b) not to return to the locality (or part of the locality) for the period specified in the direction ("the exclusion period").

(2) The first condition is that the constable has reasonable grounds to suspect that the behaviour of the person in the locality has contributed or is likely to contribute to—

    (a) members of the public in the locality being harassed, alarmed or distressed, or

    (b) the occurrence in the locality of crime or disorder.

(3) The second condition is that the constable considers that giving a direction to the person is necessary for the purpose of removing or reducing the likelihood of the events mentioned in subsection (2)(a) or (b).

(4) The exclusion period may not exceed 48 hours.

The period may expire after (as long as it begins during) the period specified in the authorisation under section 34.

(5) A direction under this section—

    (a) must be given in writing, unless that is not reasonably practicable;

    (b) must specify the area to which it relates;

    (c) may impose requirements as to the time by which the person must leave the area and the manner in which the person must do so (including the route).

(6) The constable must (unless it is not reasonably practicable) tell the person to whom the direction is given that failing without reasonable excuse to comply with the direction is an offence.

(10) In this section "public place" means a place to which at the material time the public or a section of the public has access, on payment or otherwise, as of right or by virtue of express or implied permission.

(11) In this Part "exclusion period" has the meaning given by subsection (1)(b).

36 Restrictions

(1) A constable may not give a direction under section 35 to a person who appears to the constable to be under the age of 10.

(2) A constable may not give a direction under section 35 that prevents the person to whom it is given having access to a place where the person lives.

(3) A constable may not give a direction under section 35 that prevents the person to whom it is given attending at a place which the person is—

(a) required to attend for the purposes of the person's employment, or a contract of services to which the person is a party,

(b) required to attend by an obligation imposed by or under an enactment or by the order of a court or tribunal, or

(c) expected to attend for the purposes of education or training or for the purposes of receiving medical treatment,

at a time when the person is required or expected (as the case may be) to attend there.

(4) A constable may not give a direction to a person under section 35 if the person is one of a group of persons who are—

(a) engaged in conduct that is lawful under section 220 of the Trade Union and Labour Relations (Consolidation) Act 1992 (peaceful picketing), or

(b) taking part in a public procession of the kind mentioned in subsection (1) of section 11 of the Public Order Act 1986 in respect of which—

(i) written notice has been given in accordance with that section, or

(ii) written notice is not required to be given as provided by subsections (1) and (2) of that section.

(5) In deciding whether to give a direction under section 35 a constable must have particular regard to the rights of freedom of expression and freedom of assembly set out in articles 10 and 11 of the Convention.

"*Convention*" has the meaning given by section 21(1) of the Human Rights Act 1998.

39 Offences

(1) A person given a direction under section 35 who fails without reasonable excuse to comply with it commits an offence. [S]

PART 4   COMMUNITY PROTECTION

43 Power to issue community protection notices

(1) An authorised person may issue a community protection notice to an individual aged 16 or over, or a body, if satisfied on reasonable grounds that—

(a) the conduct of the individual or body is having a detrimental effect, of a persistent or continuing nature, on the quality of life of those in the locality, and

(b) the conduct is unreasonable.

(2) In subsection (1) "authorised person" means a person on whom section 53 (or an enactment amended by that section) confers power to issue community protection notices.

(3) A community protection notice is a notice that imposes any of the following requirements on the individual or body issued with it—

(a) a requirement to stop doing specified things;

(b) a requirement to do specified things;

(c) a requirement to take reasonable steps to achieve specified results.

(4) The only requirements that may be imposed are ones that are reasonable to impose in order—

(a) to prevent the detrimental effect referred to in subsection (1) from continuing or recurring, or

(b) to reduce that detrimental effect or to reduce the risk of its continuance or recurrence.

(5) A person (A) may issue a community protection notice to an individual or body (B) only if—

(a) B has been given a written warning that the notice will be issued unless B's conduct ceases to have the detrimental effect referred to in subsection (1), and

(b) A is satisfied that, despite B having had enough time to deal with the matter, B's conduct is still having that effect.

(6) A person issuing a community protection notice must before doing so inform any body or individual the person thinks appropriate.

(7) A community protection notice must—

(a) identify the conduct referred to in subsection (1);

(b) explain the effect of sections 46 to 51.

(8) A community protection notice may specify periods within which, or times by which, requirements within subsection (3)(b) or(c) are to be complied with.

44 Occupiers of premises etc.

(1) Conduct on, or affecting, premises (other than premises within subsection (2)) that a particular person—

(a) owns,

(b) leases,

(c) occupies,

(d) controls,

(e) operates, or

(f) maintains,

is treated for the purposes of section 43 as conduct of that person.

(2) Conduct on, or affecting, premises occupied for the purposes of a government department is treated for the purposes of section 43 as conduct of the Minister in charge of that department.

(3) This section does not treat an individual's conduct as that of another person if that person cannot reasonably be expected to control or affect it.

48 Offence of failing to comply with notice

(1) A person issued with a community protection notice who fails to comply with it commits an offence. [E]

(3) A person does not commit an offence under this section if—

(a) the person took all reasonable steps to comply with the notice, or

(b) there is some other reasonable excuse for the failure to comply with it.

59 Power to make orders

(1) A local authority may make a public spaces protection order if satisfied on reasonable grounds that two conditions are met.

(2) The first condition is that—

(a) activities carried on in a public place within the authority's area have had a detrimental effect on the quality of life of those in the locality, or

(b) it is likely that activities will be carried on in a public place within that area and that they will have such an effect.

(3) The second condition is that the effect, or likely effect, of the activities—

(a) is, or is likely to be, of a persistent or continuing nature,

(b) is, or is likely to be, such as to make the activities unreasonable, and

(c) justifies the restrictions imposed by the notice.

(4) A public spaces protection order is an order that identifies the public place referred to in subsection (2) ("the restricted area") and—

(a) prohibits specified things being done in the restricted area,

(b) requires specified things to be done by persons carrying on specified activities in that area, or

(c) does both of those things.

(5) The only prohibitions or requirements that may be imposed are ones that are reasonable to impose in order—

(a) to prevent the detrimental effect referred to in subsection (2) from continuing, occurring or recurring, or

(b) to reduce that detrimental effect or to reduce the risk of its continuance, occurrence or recurrence.

(6) A prohibition or requirement may be framed—

(a) so as to apply to all persons, or only to persons in specified categories, or to all persons except those in specified categories;

(b) so as to apply at all times, or only at specified times, or at all times except those specified;

(c) so as to apply in all circumstances, or only in specified circumstances, or in all circumstances except those specified.

(7) A public spaces protection order must—

(a) identify the activities referred to in subsection (2);

(b) explain the effect of section 63 (where it applies) and section 67;

(c) specify the period for which the order has effect.

(8) A public spaces protection order must be published in accordance with regulations made by the Secretary of State.

60 Duration of orders

(1) A public spaces protection order may not have effect for a period of more than 3 years, unless extended under this section.

(2) Before the time when a public spaces protection order is due to expire, the local authority that made the order may extend the period for which it has effect if satisfied on reasonable grounds that doing so is necessary to prevent—

(a) occurrence or recurrence after that time of the activities identified in the order, or

(b) an increase in the frequency or seriousness of those activities after that time.

(3) An extension under this section—

(a) may not be for a period of more than 3 years;

(b) must be published in accordance with regulations made by the Secretary of State.

(4) A public spaces protection order may be extended under this section more than once.

61 Variation and discharge of orders

(1) Where a public spaces protection order is in force, the local authority that made the order may vary it—

(a) by increasing or reducing the restricted area;

(b) by altering or removing a prohibition or requirement included in the order, or adding a new one.

(2) A local authority may make a variation under subsection (1)(a) that results in the order applying to an area to which it did not previously apply only if the conditions in section 59(2) and (3) are met as regards activities in that area.

(3) A local authority may make a variation under subsection (1)(b) that makes a prohibition or requirement more extensive, or adds a new one, only if the prohibitions and requirements imposed by the order as varied are ones that section 59(5) allows to be imposed.

(4) A public spaces protection order may be discharged by the local authority that made it.

(5) Where an order is varied, the order as varied must be published in accordance with regulations made by the Secretary of State.

(6) Where an order is discharged, a notice identifying the order and stating the date when it ceases to have effect must be published in accordance with regulations made by the Secretary of State.

62 Premises etc. to which alcohol prohibition does not apply

(1) A prohibition in a public spaces protection order on consuming alcohol does not apply to—

(a) premises (other than council-operated licensed premises) authorised by a premises licence to be used for the supply of alcohol;

(b) premises authorised by a club premises certificate to be used by the club for the supply of alcohol;

(c) a place within the curtilage of premises within paragraph (a) or (b);

(d) premises which by virtue of Part 5 of the Licensing Act 2003 may at the relevant time be used for the supply of alcohol or which, by virtue of that Part, could have been so used within the 30 minutes before that time;

(e) a place where facilities or activities relating to the sale or consumption of alcohol are at the relevant time permitted by virtue of a permission granted under section 115E of the Highways Act 1980 (highway-related uses).

(2) A prohibition in a public spaces protection order on consuming alcohol does not apply to council-operated licensed premises—

(a) when the premises are being used for the supply of alcohol, or

(b) within 30 minutes after the end of a period during which the premises have been used for the supply of alcohol.

(3) In this section—

"club premises certificate" has the meaning given by section 60 of the Licensing Act 2003;

"premises licence" has the meaning given by section 11 of that Act;

"supply of alcohol" has the meaning given by section 14 of that Act.

(4) For the purposes of this section, premises are "council-operated licensed premises" if they are authorised by a premises licence to be used for the supply of alcohol and—

(a) the licence is held by a local authority in whose area the premises (or part of the premises) are situated, or

(b) the licence is held by another person but the premises are occupied by a local authority or are managed by or on behalf of a local authority.

63   Consumption of alcohol in breach of prohibition in order

(1) This section applies where a constable or an authorised person reasonably believes that a person (P)—

(a) is or has been consuming alcohol in breach of a prohibition in a public spaces protection order, or

(b) intends to consume alcohol in circumstances in which doing so would be a breach of such a prohibition.

In this section "authorised person" means a person authorised for the purposes of this section by the local authority that made the public spaces protection order (or authorised by virtue of section 69(1)).

(2) The constable or authorised person may require P—

(a) not to consume, in breach of the order, alcohol or anything which the constable or authorised person reasonably believes to be alcohol;

(b) to surrender anything in P's possession which is, or which the constable or authorised person reasonably believes to be, alcohol or a container for alcohol.

(3) A constable or an authorised person who imposes a requirement under subsection (2) must tell P that failing without reasonable excuse to comply with the requirement is an offence.

(4) A requirement imposed by an authorised person under subsection (2) is not valid if the person—

(a) is asked by P to show evidence of his or her authorisation, and

(b) fails to do so.

(5) A constable or an authorised person may dispose of anything surrendered under subsection (2)(b) in whatever way he or she thinks appropriate.

Children and Families Act 2014

91   Purchase of tobacco, nicotine products etc. on behalf of persons under 18

(1) A person aged 18 or over who buys or attempts to buy tobacco, cigarette papers or a relevant nicotine product on behalf of an individual aged under 18 commits an offence. [S]

(2) Where a person is charged with an offence under this section it is a defence—

(a) that the person had no reason to suspect that the individual concerned was aged under 18, or

(b) in a case where the person has bought or attempted to buy cigarette papers, that the person had no reason to suspect that the individual concerned intended to use the papers for smoking.

(7) "Tobacco" has the same meaning in this section as in section 7 of the Children and Young Persons Act 1933 (offence of selling tobacco to children).

(8) In this section "relevant nicotine product" means a nicotine product within the meaning of section 92 the sale of which at the same time and in the same circumstances to the individual aged under 18 would be prohibited by regulations for the time being in force under subsection (1) of that section.

92   Prohibition of sale of nicotine products to persons under 18

(1) The Secretary of State may by regulations make provision prohibiting the sale of nicotine products to persons aged under 18.

(2) A person who breaches a prohibition in regulations under subsection (1) commits an offence. [S]

(3) Subsection (2) does not apply if—

(a) at the time of the sale, the person to whom the nicotine product is sold is employed by a manufacturer of nicotine products to which regulations under subsection (1) apply or by a dealer in such products (whether wholesale or retail), and

(b) the purchase of the product is for the purposes of the manufacturer's or dealer's business.

(4) Where a person is charged with an offence under this section it is a defence that the person took all reasonable precautions and exercised all due diligence to avoid committing the offence.

(9) For the purposes of this section "nicotine product" means—

(a) a device which is intended to enable nicotine to be consumed by an individual or otherwise to be delivered into the human body,

(b) an item which is intended to form part of a device within paragraph (a), or

(c) a substance or item which consists of or contains nicotine and which is intended for human consumption or otherwise to be delivered into the human body.

(10) It does not matter for the purposes of subsection (9)(a) whether the device is also intended to enable any other substance to be consumed by an individual or otherwise to be delivered into the human body.

(11) The following are not nicotine products for the purposes of this section—

(a) tobacco;

(b) cigarette papers;

(c) any device which is intended to be used for the consumption of lit tobacco.

(12) In this section—

"specified" means specified in regulations under this section;

"tobacco" has the same meaning as in section 7 of the Children and Young Persons Act 1933 (offence of selling tobacco to children).

Immigration Act 2014

33A   Offences: landlords

(1) The landlord under a residential tenancy agreement which relates to premises in England commits an offence if the first and second conditions are met.

(2) The first condition is that the premises are occupied by an adult who is disqualified as a result of their immigration status from occupying premises under a residential tenancy agreement.

(3) The second condition is that the landlord knows or has reasonable cause to believe that the premises are occupied by an adult who is disqualified as a result of their immigration status from occupying premises under a residential tenancy agreement.

(4) But unless subsection (5) applies the landlord does not commit an offence under subsection (1) if—

(a) the premises are located in an area in relation to which section 22 is in force,

(b) the adult mentioned in subsections (2) and (3) is a limited right occupier, and

(c) the eligibility period in relation to that occupier has not expired.

(5) This subsection applies if the Secretary of State has given a notice in writing to the landlord which—

    (a) identifies the adult mentioned in subsections (2) and (3), and

    (b) states that the adult is disqualified as a result of their immigration status from occupying premises under a residential tenancy agreement.

(6) It is a defence for a person charged with an offence under subsection (1) to prove that—

    (a) the person has taken reasonable steps to terminate the residential tenancy agreement, and

    (b) the person has taken such steps within a reasonable period beginning with the time when the person first knew or had reasonable cause to believe that the premises were occupied by the adult mentioned in subsections (2) and (3).

(7) In determining whether subsection (6)(a) or (b) applies to a person, the court must have regard to any guidance which, at the time in question, had been issued by the Secretary of State for the purposes of that subsection and was in force at that time.

(8) Guidance issued for the purposes of subsection (6)—

    (a) must be laid before Parliament in draft before being issued, and

    (b) comes into force in accordance with regulations made by the Secretary of State.

(9) Section 22(9) applies for the purposes of subsection (1) as it applies for the purposes of that section.

(10) A person commits an offence if—

    (a) there has been a post-grant contravention in relation to a residential tenancy agreement which relates to premises in England,

    (b) the person is the responsible landlord in relation to the post-grant contravention,

    (c) the person knows or has reasonable cause to believe that there has been a post-grant contravention in relation to the agreement, and

    (d) none of paragraphs (a), (b) and (c) of section 24(6) applies in relation to the post-grant contravention.

(11) Subsection (10) applies whether or not the landlord is given a notice under section 23 in respect of the contravention.

33B Offences: agents

(1) Subsection (2) applies to an agent who is responsible for a landlord's contravention of section 22 in relation to premises in England.

(2) The agent commits an offence if the agent—

    (a) knew or had reasonable cause to believe that the landlord would contravene section 22 by entering into the residential tenancy agreement in question,

    (b) had sufficient opportunity to notify the landlord of that fact before the landlord entered into the agreement, but

    (c) did not do so.

(3) Subsection (4) applies where—

    (a) a landlord contravenes section 22 in relation to a residential tenancy agreement relating to premises in England,

    (b) the contravention is a post-grant contravention, and

    (c) a person acting as the landlord's agent ("the agent") is responsible for the post-grant contravention.

(4) The agent commits an offence if—

    (a) the agent knows or has reasonable cause to believe that there has been a post-grant contravention in relation to the agreement, and

    (b) neither of paragraphs (a) and (b) of section 26(6) applies in relation to the post-grant contravention.

(5) Subsection (4) applies whether or not the agent is given a notice under section 25 in respect of the contravention.

Counter-Terrorism and Security Act 2015

1   Seizure of passports etc. from persons suspected of involvement in terrorism

(1) Schedule 1 makes provision for the seizure and temporary retention of travel documents where a person is suspected of intending to leave Great Britain or the United Kingdom in connection with terrorism-related activity.

2   Temporary exclusion orders

(1) A "temporary exclusion order" is an order which requires an individual not to return to the United Kingdom unless—

(a) the return is in accordance with a permit to return issued by the Secretary of State before the individual began the return, or

(b) the return is the result of the individual's deportation to the United Kingdom.

(2) The Secretary of State may impose a temporary exclusion order on an individual if conditions A to E are met.

(3) Condition A is that the Secretary of State reasonably suspects that the individual is, or has been, involved in terrorism-related activity outside the United Kingdom.

(4) Condition B is that the Secretary of State reasonably considers that it is necessary, for purposes connected with protecting members of the public in the United Kingdom from a risk of terrorism, for a temporary exclusion order to be imposed on the individual.

(5) Condition C is that the Secretary of State reasonably considers that the individual is outside the United Kingdom.

(6) Condition D is that the individual has the right of abode in the United Kingdom.

(7) Condition E is that—

(a) the court gives the Secretary of State permission under section 3, or

(b) the Secretary of State reasonably considers that the urgency of the case requires a temporary exclusion order to be imposed without obtaining such permission.

(8) During the period that a temporary exclusion order is in force, the Secretary of State must keep under review whether condition B is met.

3   Temporary exclusion orders: prior permission of the court

(1) This section applies if the Secretary of State—

(a) makes the relevant decisions in relation to an individual, and

(b) makes an application to the court for permission to impose a temporary exclusion order on the individual.

(2) The function of the court on the application is to determine whether the relevant decisions of the Secretary of State are obviously flawed.

(4) But that does not limit the matters about which rules of court may be made.

(5) In determining the application, the court must apply the principles applicable on an application for judicial review.

(6) In a case where the court determines that any of the relevant decisions of the Secretary of State is obviously flawed, the court may not give permission under this section.

(7) In any other case, the court must give permission under this section.

(8) Schedule 2 makes provision for references to the court etc. where temporary exclusion orders are imposed in cases of urgency.

4   Temporary exclusion orders: supplementary provision

(1) The Secretary of State must give notice of the imposition of a temporary exclusion order to the individual on whom it is imposed (the "excluded individual").

(2) Notice of the imposition of a temporary exclusion order must include an explanation of the procedure for making an application under section 6 for a permit to return.

(3) A temporary exclusion order—

(a) comes into force when notice of its imposition is given; and

(b) is in force for the period of two years (unless revoked or otherwise brought to an end earlier).

(4) The Secretary of State may revoke a temporary exclusion order at any time.

(5) The Secretary of State must give notice of the revocation of a temporary exclusion order to the excluded individual.

(6) If a temporary exclusion order is revoked, it ceases to be in force when notice of its revocation is given.

(7) The validity of a temporary exclusion order is not affected by the excluded individual—

(a) returning to the United Kingdom, or

(b) departing from the United Kingdom.

(8) The imposition of a temporary exclusion order does not prevent a further temporary exclusion order from being imposed on the excluded individual (including in a case where an order ceases to be in force at the expiry of its two year duration).

(9) At the time when a temporary exclusion order comes into force, any British passport held by the excluded individual is invalidated.

(10) During the period when a temporary exclusion order is in force, the issue of a British passport to the excluded individual while he or she is outside the United Kingdom is not valid.

(11) In this section "British passport" means a passport, or other document which enables or facilitates travel from one state to another (except a permit to return), that has been—

(a) issued by or for Her Majesty's Government in the United Kingdom, and

(b) issued in respect of a person's status as a British citizen.

5 Permit to return

(1) A "permit to return" is a document giving an individual (who is subject to a temporary exclusion order) permission to return to the United Kingdom.

(2) The permission may be made subject to a requirement that the individual comply with conditions specified in the permit to return.

(3) The individual's failure to comply with a specified condition has the effect of invalidating the permit to return.

(4) A permit to return must state—

(a) the time at which, or period of time during which, the individual is permitted to arrive on return to the United Kingdom;

(b) the manner in which the individual is permitted to return to the United Kingdom; and

(c) the place where the individual is permitted to arrive on return to the United Kingdom.

(5) Provision made under subsection (4)(a) or (c) may, in particular, be framed by reference to the arrival in the United Kingdom of a specific flight, sailing or other transport service.

(6) Provision made under subsection (4)(b) may, in particular, state—

(a) a route,

(b) a method of transport,

(c) an airline, shipping line or other passenger carrier, or

(d) a flight, sailing or other transport service,

which the individual is permitted to use to return to the United Kingdom.

(7) The Secretary of State may not issue a permit to return except in accordance with section 6 or 7.

(8) It is for the Secretary of State to decide the terms of a permit to return (but this is subject to section 6(3)).

6 Issue of permit to return: application by individual

(1) If an individual applies to the Secretary of State for a permit to return, the Secretary of State must issue a permit within a reasonable period after the application is made.

(2) But the Secretary of State may refuse to issue the permit if—

(a) the Secretary of State requires the individual to attend an interview with a constable or immigration officer at a time and a place specified by the Secretary of State, and

(b) the individual fails to attend the interview.

(3) Where a permit to return is issued under this section, the relevant return time must fall within a reasonable period after the application is made.

(4) An application is not valid unless it is made in accordance with the procedure for applications specified by the Secretary of State.

(5) In this section—

"application" means an application made by an individual to the Secretary of State for a permit to return to be issued;

"relevant return time" means—

(a) the time at which the individual is permitted to arrive on return to the United Kingdom (in a case where the permit to return states such a time), or

(b) the start of the period of time during which the individual is permitted to arrive on return to the United Kingdom (in a case where the permit to return states such a period).

7   Issue of permit to return: deportation or urgent situation

(1) The Secretary of State must issue a permit to return to an individual if the Secretary of State considers that the individual is to be deported to the United Kingdom.

(2) The Secretary of State may issue a permit to return to an individual if—

(a) the Secretary of State considers that, because of the urgency of the situation, it is expedient to issue a permit to return even though no application has been made under section 6, and

(b) there is no duty to issue a permit to return under subsection (1).

(3) Subsection (1) or (2) applies whether or not any request has been made to issue the permit to return under that provision.

9   Obligations after return to the United Kingdom

(1) The Secretary of State may, by notice, impose any or all of the permitted obligations on an individual who—

(a) is subject to a temporary exclusion order, and

(b) has returned to the United Kingdom.

(2) The "permitted obligations" are—

(a) any obligation of a kind that may be imposed (on an individual subject to a TPIM notice) under these provisions of Schedule 1 to the Terrorism Prevention and Investigation Measures Act 2011—

(i)   paragraph 10 (reporting to police station);

(ii) paragraph 10A (attendance at appointments etc.);

(b) an obligation to notify the police, in such manner as a notice under this section may require, of—

(i)   the individual's place (or places) of residence, and

(ii) any change in the individual's place (or places) of residence.

(3) A notice under this section—

(a) comes into force when given to the individual; and

(b) is in force until the temporary exclusion order ends (unless the notice is revoked or otherwise brought to an end earlier).

(4) The Secretary of State may, by notice, vary or revoke any notice given under this section.

(5) The variation or revocation of a notice under this section takes effect when the notice of variation or revocation is given to the individual.

(6) The validity of a notice under this section is not affected by the individual—

(a) departing from the United Kingdom, or

(b) returning to the United Kingdom.

(7) The giving of any notice to an individual under this section does not prevent any further notice under this section from being given to that individual.

10   Offences

(1) An individual subject to a temporary exclusion order is guilty of an offence if, without reasonable excuse, the individual returns to the United Kingdom in contravention of the restriction on return specified in the order.

(2) It is irrelevant for the purposes of subsection (1) whether or not the individual has a passport or other similar identity document.

(3) An individual subject to an obligation imposed under section 9 is guilty of an offence if, without reasonable excuse, the individual does not comply with the obligation. [E]

(7) In this section—

"relevant notice" means—

(a) notice of the imposition of a temporary exclusion order, or

(b) notice under section 9 imposing an obligation;

"restriction on return" means the requirement specified in a temporary exclusion order in accordance with section 2(1).

Criminal Justice and Courts Act 2015

20   Ill-treatment or wilful neglect: care worker offence

(1) It is an offence for an individual who has the care of another individual by virtue of being a care worker to ill-treat or wilfully to neglect that individual. [E]

(3) "Care worker" means an individual who, as paid work, provides—

(a) health care for an adult or child, other than excluded health care, or

(b) social care for an adult,

including an individual who, as paid work, supervises or manages individuals providing such care or is a director or similar officer of an organisation which provides such care.

(4) An individual does something as "paid work" if he or she receives or is entitled to payment for doing it other than—

(a) payment in respect of the individual's reasonable expenses,

(b) payment to which the individual is entitled as a foster parent,

(c) a benefit under social security legislation, or

(d) a payment made under arrangements under section 2 of the Employment and Training Act 1973 (arrangements to assist people to select, train for, obtain and retain employment).

(5) "Health care" includes—

(a) all forms of health care provided for individuals, including health care relating to physical health or mental health and health care provided for or in connection with the protection or improvement of public health, and

(b) procedures that are similar to forms of medical or surgical care but are not provided in connection with a medical condition,

and "excluded health care" has the meaning given in Schedule 4.

(6) "Social care" includes all forms of personal care and other practical assistance provided for individuals who are in need of such care or assistance by reason of age, illness, disability, pregnancy, childbirth, dependence on alcohol or drugs or any other similar circumstances.

(7) References in this section to a person providing health care or social care do not include a person whose provision of such care is merely incidental to the carrying out of other activities by the person.

(8) In this section—

"adult" means an individual aged 18 or over;

"child" means an individual aged under 18;

"foster parent" means—

(a) a local authority foster parent within the meaning of the Children Act 1989,

(b) a person with whom a child has been placed by a voluntary organisation under section 59(1)(a) of that Act, or

(c) a private foster parent within the meaning of section 53 of the Safeguarding Vulnerable Groups Act 2006.

21   Ill-treatment or wilful neglect: care provider offence

(1) A care provider commits an offence if—

  (a) an individual who has the care of another individual by virtue of being part of the care provider's arrangements ill-treats or wilfully neglects that individual,

  (b) the care provider's activities are managed or organised in a way which amounts to a gross breach of a relevant duty of care owed by the care provider to the individual who is ill-treated or neglected, and

  (c) in the absence of the breach, the ill-treatment or wilful neglect would not have occurred or would have been less likely to occur. [E]

(2) "Care provider" means—

  (a) a body corporate or unincorporated association which provides or arranges for the provision of—

    (i)   health care for an adult or child, other than excluded health care, or

    (ii) social care for an adult, or

  (b) an individual who provides such care and employs, or has otherwise made arrangements with, other persons to assist him or her in providing such care,

subject to section 22.

(3) An individual is "part of a care provider's arrangements" where the individual—

  (a) is not the care provider, but

  (b) provides health care or social care as part of health care or social care provided or arranged for by the care provider,

including where the individual is not the care provider but supervises or manages individuals providing health care or social care as described in paragraph (b) or is a director or similar officer of an organisation which provides health care or social care as described there.

(4) A "relevant duty of care" means—

  (a) a duty owed under the law of negligence, or

  (b) a duty that would be owed under the law of negligence but for a provision contained in an Act, or an instrument made under an Act, under which liability is imposed in place of liability under that law,

but only to the extent that the duty is owed in connection with providing, or arranging for the provision of, health care or social care.

(5) For the purposes of this section, there is to be disregarded any rule of the common law that has the effect of—

  (a) preventing a duty of care from being owed by one person to another by reason of the fact that they are jointly engaged in unlawful conduct, or

  (b) preventing a duty of care being owed to a person by reason of that person's acceptance of a risk of harm.

(6) A breach of a duty of care by a care provider is a "gross" breach if the conduct alleged to amount to the breach falls far below what can reasonably be expected of the care provider in the circumstances.

(7) In this section—

  (a) references to a person providing health care or social care do not include a person whose provision of such care is merely incidental to the carrying out of other activities by the person, and

  (b) references to a person arranging for the provision of such care do not include a person who makes arrangements under which the provision of such care is merely incidental to the carrying out of other activities.

(8) References in this section to providing or arranging for the provision of health care or social care do not include making payments under—

  (a) regulations under section 57 of the Health and Social Care Act 2001 (direct payments for community services and carers);

  (b) section 12A of the National Health Act 2006 (direct payments for health care);

  (c) section 31 or 32 of the Care Act 2014 (direct payments for care and support);

(9) In this section—
"adult", "child", "excluded health care", "health care" and "social care" have the same meaning as in section 20.

22   Care provider offence: excluded care providers

(1) A local authority in England is not a care provider for the purposes of section 21 to the extent that it carries out functions to which Chapter 4 of Part 8 of the Education and Inspections Act 2006 applies.

(2) A person is not a care provider for the purposes of section 21 to the extent that the person carries out a function of a local authority in England mentioned in subsection (1) in respect of which either of the following has effect—

  (a) a direction under section 15(6)(a) of the Local Government Act 1999 (power of Secretary of State to direct functions of a best value authority to be carried out by another person);
  (b) a direction under section 497A(4) or (4A) of the Education Act 1996 (power of Secretary of State to direct certain functions to be carried out by another person).

(3) Where a body corporate has entered into arrangements with a local authority in England under Part 1 of the Children and Young Persons Act 2008 (social work services for children and young persons), the body is not a care provider for the purposes of section 21 to the extent that it carries out relevant care functions of that authority (as defined in that Part of that Act) under those arrangements.

(6) A registered adoption society or registered adoption support agency is not a care provider for the purposes of section 21 to the extent that it provides adoption support services (as defined in section 2(6) of the Adoption and Children Act 2002).

(7) In this section, "local authority" means—

  (a) in England, a county council, a metropolitan district council, a non-metropolitan district council for an area for which there is no county council, a London borough council, the Council of the Isles of Scilly and (in its capacity as a local authority) the Common Council of the City of London, and

(8) In this section—
"child" has the same meaning as in section 20;
"registered adoption society" means an adoption society (as defined in section 2 of the Adoption and Children Act 2002) which is a voluntary organisation (as defined in that section) and in respect of which a person is registered under Part 2 of the Care Standards Act 2000;
"registered adoption support agency" means an adoption support agency (as defined in section 8 of the Adoption and Children Act 2002) in respect of which a person is registered under Part 2 of the Care Standards Act 2000.

24   Care provider offence: application to unincorporated associations

(1) For the purposes of sections 21 and 23, an unincorporated association is to be treated as owing whatever duties of care it would owe if it were a body corporate.

(2) Proceedings for an offence under those sections alleged to have been committed by an unincorporated association must be brought in the name of the association (and not in that of any of its members).

(5) A fine imposed on an unincorporated association on its conviction of an offence under section 21 or 23 is to be paid out of the funds of the association.

25   Care provider offence: liability for ancillary and other offences

(1) An individual cannot be guilty of—

  (a) aiding, abetting, counselling or procuring the commission of an offence under section 21, or
  (b) an offence under Part 2 of the Serious Crime Act 2007 (encouraging or assisting crime) by reference to an offence under section 21.

(2) Where, in the same proceedings, there is—

    (a) a charge under section 21 arising out of a particular set of circumstances, and

    (b) a charge against the same defendant of a relevant offence arising out of some or all of those circumstances,

the defendant may, if the interests of justice so require, be convicted of both offences.

(3) A person convicted of an offence under section 21 arising out of a particular set of circumstances may, if the interests of justice so require, be charged with a relevant offence arising out of some or all of those circumstances.

(4) "Relevant offence" means an offence under an Act, or an instrument made under an Act, dealing with—

    (a) health and safety matters, or

    (b) the provision of health care or social care.

(5) In this section—

"Act" includes an Act or Measure of the National Assembly for Wales;

"health care" and "social care" have the same meaning as in section 20.

26 Corrupt or other improper exercise of police powers and privileges

(1) A police constable listed in subsection (3) commits an offence if he or she—

    (a) exercises the powers and privileges of a constable improperly, and

    (b) knows or ought to know that the exercise is improper. [I]

(3) The police constables referred to in subsection (1) are—

    (a) a constable of a police force in England and Wales;

    (b) a special constable for a police area in England and Wales;

    (c) a constable or special constable of the British Transport Police Force;

    (d) a constable of the Civil Nuclear Constabulary;

    (e) a constable of the Ministry of Defence Police;

    (f) a National Crime Agency officer designated under section 9 or 10 of the Crime and Courts Act 2013 as having the powers and privileges of a constable.

(4) For the purposes of this section, a police constable exercises the powers and privileges of a constable improperly if—

    (a) he or she exercises a power or privilege of a constable for the purpose of achieving—

        (i)   a benefit for himself or herself, or

        (ii) a benefit or a detriment for another person, and

    (b) a reasonable person would not expect the power or privilege to be exercised for the purpose of achieving that benefit or detriment.

(5) For the purposes of this section, a police constable is to be treated as exercising the powers and privileges of a constable improperly in the cases described in subsections (6) and (7).

(6) The first case is where—

    (a) the police constable fails to exercise a power or privilege of a constable,

    (b) the purpose of the failure is to achieve a benefit or detriment described in subsection (4)(a), and

    (c) a reasonable person would not expect a constable to fail to exercise the power or privilege for the purpose of achieving that benefit or detriment.

(7) The second case is where—

    (a) the police constable threatens to exercise, or not to exercise, a power or privilege of a constable,

    (b) the threat is made for the purpose of achieving a benefit or detriment described in subsection (4)(a), and

    (c) a reasonable person would not expect a constable to threaten to exercise, or not to exercise, the power or privilege for the purpose of achieving that benefit or detriment.

(8) An offence is committed under this section if the act or omission in question takes place in the United Kingdom or in United Kingdom waters.

(9) In this section—

"benefit" and "detriment" mean any benefit or detriment, whether or not in money or other property and whether temporary or permanent;

"United Kingdom waters" means the sea and other waters within the seaward limits of the United Kingdom's territorial sea.

(10) References in this section to exercising, or not exercising, the powers and privileges of a constable include performing, or not performing, the duties of a constable.

(11) Nothing in this section affects what constitutes the offence of misconduct in public office at common law in England and Wales or Northern Ireland.

33 Disclosing, or threatening to disclose, private sexual photographs and films with intent to cause distress

(1) A person commits an offence if—

    (a) the person discloses, or threatens to disclose, a private sexual photograph or film in which another individual ("the relevant individual") appears,

    (b) by so doing, the person intends to cause distress to that individual, and

    (c) the disclosure is, or would be, made without the consent of that individual.

(2) But it is not an offence under this section for the person to disclose, or threaten to disclose, the photograph or film to the relevant individual.

(2A) Where a person is charged with an offence under this section of threatening to disclose a private sexual photograph or film, it is not necessary for the prosecution to prove—

    (a) that the photograph or film referred to in the threat exists, or

    (b) if it does exist, that it is in fact a private sexual photograph or film.

(3) It is a defence for a person charged with an offence under this section to prove that he or she reasonably believed that the disclosure was necessary for the purposes of preventing, detecting or investigating crime.

(4) It is a defence for a person charged with an offence under this section to show that—

    (a) the disclosure, or threat to disclose, was made in the course of, or with a view to, the publication of journalistic material, and

    (b) he or she reasonably believed that, in the particular circumstances, the publication of the journalistic material was, or would be, in the public interest.

(5) It is a defence for a person charged with an offence under this section to show that—

    (a) he or she reasonably believed that the photograph or film had previously been disclosed for reward, whether by the relevant individual or another person, and

    (b) he or she had no reason to believe that the previous disclosure for reward was made without the consent of the relevant individual.

(6) A person is taken to have shown the matters mentioned in subsection (4) or (5) if—

    (a) sufficient evidence of the matters is adduced to raise an issue with respect to it, and

    (b) the contrary is not proved beyond reasonable doubt.

(7) For the purposes of subsections (1) to (5)—

    (a) "consent" to a disclosure includes general consent covering the disclosure, as well as consent to the particular disclosure, and

    (b) "publication" of journalistic material means disclosure to the public at large or to a section of the public.

(8) A person charged with an offence under this section is not to be taken to have intended to cause distress by disclosing or threatening to disclose, a photograph or film merely because that was a natural and probable consequence of the disclosure or threat.

34 Meaning of "disclose" and "photograph or film"

(1) The following apply for the purposes of section 33, this section and section 35.

(2) A person "discloses" something to a person if, by any means, he or she gives or shows it to the person or makes it available to the person.

(3) Something that is given, shown or made available to a person is disclosed—

    (a) whether or not it is given, shown or made available for reward, and

    (b) whether or not it has previously been given, shown or made available to the person.

(4) "Photograph or film" means a still or moving image in any form that—

    (a) appears to consist of or include one or more photographed or filmed images, and

    (b) in fact consists of or includes one or more photographed or filmed images.

(5) The reference in subsection (4)(b) to photographed or filmed images includes photographed or filmed images that have been altered in any way.

(6) "Photographed or filmed image" means a still or moving image that—

    (a) was originally captured by photography or filming, or

    (b) is part of an image originally captured by photography or filming.

(7) "Filming" means making a recording, on any medium, from which a moving image may be produced by any means.

(8) References to a photograph or film include—

    (a) a negative version of an image described in subsection (4), and

    (b) data stored by any means which is capable of conversion into an image described in subsection (4).

35 Meaning of "private" and "sexual"

(1) The following apply for the purposes of section 33.

(2) A photograph or film is "private" if it shows something that is not of a kind ordinarily seen in public.

(3) A photograph or film is "sexual" if—

    (a) it shows all or part of an individual's exposed genitals or pubic area,

    (b) it shows something that a reasonable person would consider to be sexual because of its nature, or

    (c) its content, taken as a whole, is such that a reasonable person would consider it to be sexual.

(4) Subsection (5) applies in the case of—

    (a) a photograph or film that consists of or includes a photographed or filmed image that has been altered in any way,

    (b) a photograph or film that combines two or more photographed or filmed images, and

    (c) a photograph or film that combines a photographed or filmed image with something else.

(5) The photograph or film is not private and sexual if—

    (a) it does not consist of or include a photographed or filmed image that is itself private and sexual,

    (b) it is only private or sexual by virtue of the alteration or combination mentioned in subsection (4), or

    (c) it is only by virtue of the alteration or combination mentioned in subsection (4) that the relevant individual (within the meaning of section 33) is shown as part of, or with, whatever makes the photograph or film private and sexual.

Modern Slavery Act 2015

PART 1   OFFENCES

1 Slavery, servitude and forced or compulsory labour

(1) A person commits an offence if—

    (a) the person holds another person in slavery or servitude and the circumstances are such that the person knows or ought to know that the other person is held in slavery or servitude, or

    (b) the person requires another person to perform forced or compulsory labour and the circumstances are such that the person knows or ought to know that the other person is being required to perform forced or compulsory labour. [I]

(2) In subsection (1) the references to holding a person in slavery or servitude or requiring a person to perform forced or compulsory labour are to be construed in accordance with Article 4 of the Human Rights Convention.

(3) In determining whether a person is being held in slavery or servitude or required to perform forced or compulsory labour, regard may be had to all the circumstances.

(4) For example, regard may be had—

(a) to any of the person's personal circumstances (such as the person being a child, the person's family relationships, and any mental or physical illness) which may make the person more vulnerable than other persons;

(b) to any work or services provided by the person, including work or services provided in circumstances which constitute exploitation within section 3(3) to (6).

(5) The consent of a person (whether an adult or a child) to any of the acts alleged to constitute holding the person in slavery or servitude, or requiring the person to perform forced or compulsory labour, does not preclude a determination that the person is being held in slavery or servitude, or required to perform forced or compulsory labour.

2   Human trafficking

(1) A person commits an offence if the person arranges or facilitates the travel of another person ("V") with a view to V being exploited.

(2) It is irrelevant whether V consents to the travel (whether V is an adult or a child).

(3) A person may in particular arrange or facilitate V's travel by recruiting V, transporting or transferring V, harbouring or receiving V, or transferring or exchanging control over V.

(4) A person arranges or facilitates V's travel with a view to V being exploited only if—

(a) the person intends to exploit V (in any part of the world) during or after the travel, or

(b) the person knows or ought to know that another person is likely to exploit V (in any part of the world) during or after the travel.

(5) "Travel" means—

(a) arriving in, or entering, any country,

(b) departing from any country,

(c) travelling within any country.

(6) A person who is a UK national commits an offence under this section regardless of—

(a) where the arranging or facilitating takes place, or

(b) where the travel takes place.

(7) A person who is not a UK national commits an offence under this section if—

(a) any part of the arranging or facilitating takes place in the United Kingdom, or

(b) the travel consists of arrival in or entry into, departure from, or travel within, the United Kingdom.

3   Meaning of exploitation

(1) For the purposes of section 2 a person is exploited only if one or more of the following subsections apply in relation to the person.

Slavery, servitude and forced or compulsory labour

(2) The person is the victim of behaviour—

(a) which involves the commission of an offence under section 1, or

(b) which would involve the commission of an offence under that section if it took place in England and Wales.

Sexual exploitation

(3) Something is done to or in respect of the person—

(a) which involves the commission of an offence under—

(i) section 1(1)(a) of the Protection of Children Act 1978 (indecent photographs of children), or

(ii) Part 1 of the Sexual Offences Act 2003 (sexual offences), as it has effect in England and Wales, or

(b) which would involve the commission of such an offence if it were done in England and Wales.

Removal of organs etc.

(4) The person is encouraged, required or expected to do anything—

(a) which involves the commission, by him or her or another person, of an offence under section 32 or 33 of the Human Tissue Act 2004 (prohibition of commercial dealings in organs and restrictions on use of live donors) as it has effect in England and Wales, or

(b) which would involve the commission of such an offence, by him or her or another person, if it were done in England and Wales.

Securing services etc. by force, threats or deception

(5) The person is subjected to force, threats or deception designed to induce him or her—

(a) to provide services of any kind,

(b) to provide another person with benefits of any kind, or

(c) to enable another person to acquire benefits of any kind.

Securing services etc. from children and vulnerable persons

(6) Another person uses or attempts to use the person for a purpose within paragraph (a), (b) or (c) of subsection (5), having chosen him or her for that purpose on the grounds that—

(a) he or she is a child, is mentally or physically ill or disabled, or has a family relationship with a particular person, and

(b) an adult, or a person without the illness, disability, or family relationship, would be likely to refuse to be used for that purpose.

4   Committing offence with intent to commit offence under section 2

A person commits an offence under this section if the person commits any offence with the intention of committing an offence under section 2 (including an offence committed by aiding, abetting, counselling or procuring an offence under that section). [I]

13   Interpretation of Part 1

(1) In this Part—

"captain" means master (of a ship) or commander (of an aircraft);

"confiscation order" has the meaning given by section 8(8);

"the Human Rights Convention" means the Convention for the Protection of Human Rights and Fundamental Freedoms agreed by the Council of Europe at Rome on 4th November 1950;

"land vehicle" means any vehicle other than a ship or aircraft;

"ship" includes every description of vessel (including a hovercraft) used in navigation;

"slavery and trafficking reparation order" means an order made under section 8;

"UK national" means—

(a) a British citizen,

(b) a person who is a British subject by virtue of Part 4 of the British Nationality Act 1981 and who has a right of abode in the United Kingdom, or

(c) a person who is a British overseas territories citizen by virtue of a connection with Gibraltar.

PART 5   PROTECTION OF VICTIMS

45   Defence for slavery or trafficking victims who commit an offence*

(1) A person is not guilty of an offence if—

(a) the person is aged 18 or over when the person does the act which constitutes the offence,

(b) the person does that act because the person is compelled to do it,

(c) the compulsion is attributable to slavery or to relevant exploitation, and

* **Editor's note:** See Schedule 4 (not included) for the list of offences where this defence does not apply.

(d) a reasonable person in the same situation as the person and having the person's relevant characteristics would have no realistic alternative to doing that act.

(2) A person may be compelled to do something by another person or by the person's circumstances.

(3) Compulsion is attributable to slavery or to relevant exploitation only if—

(a) it is, or is part of, conduct which constitutes an offence under section 1 or conduct which constitutes relevant exploitation, or

(b) it is a direct consequence of a person being, or having been, a victim of slavery or a victim of relevant exploitation.

(4) A person is not guilty of an offence if—

(a) the person is under the age of 18 when the person does the act which constitutes the offence,

(b) the person does that act as a direct consequence of the person being, or having been, a victim of slavery or a victim of relevant exploitation, and

(c) a reasonable person in the same situation as the person and having the person's relevant characteristics would do that act.

(5) For the purposes of this section—

"relevant characteristics" means age, sex and any physical or mental illness or disability;

"relevant exploitation" is exploitation (within the meaning of section 3) that is attributable to the exploited person being, or having been, a victim of human trafficking.

(6) In this section references to an act include an omission.

(7) Subsections (1) and (4) do not apply to an offence listed in Schedule 4.

51   Presumption about age

(1) This section applies where—

(a) a public authority with functions under relevant arrangements has reasonable grounds to believe that a person may be a victim of human trafficking, and

(b) the authority is not certain of the person's age but has reasonable grounds to believe that the person may be under 18.

(2) Until an assessment of the person's age is carried out by a local authority or the person's age is otherwise determined, the public authority must assume for the purposes of its functions under relevant arrangements that the person is under 18.

(3) "Relevant arrangements" means arrangements for providing assistance and support to persons who are, or who there are reasonable grounds to believe may be, victims of human trafficking, as set out in—

(a) guidance issued under section 49(1)(b);

(b) any regulations made under section 50(1).

(4) "Local authority" has the same meaning as in the Children Act 1989 (see section 105 of that Act).

PART 7   MISCELLANEOUS AND GENERAL

56   Interpretation

(1) For the purposes of this Act a person is a victim of slavery if he or she is a victim of—

(a) conduct which constitutes an offence under section 1, or

(b) conduct which would have constituted an offence under that section if that section had been in force when the conduct occurred.

(2) For the purposes of this Act a person is a victim of human trafficking if he or she is the victim of—

(a) conduct which constitutes an offence under section 2, or would constitute an offence under that section if the person responsible for the conduct were a UK national, or

(b) conduct which would have been within paragraph (a) if section 2 had been in force when the conduct occurred.

(3) In this Act—

"child" means a person under the age of 18;

"country" includes territory or other part of the world;

"immigration officer" means a person appointed as an immigration officer under paragraph 1 of Schedule 2 to the Immigration Act 1971;

"public authority" means any public authority within the meaning of section 6 of the Human Rights Act 1998, other than a court or tribunal;

"UK national" has the meaning given by section 13.

Serious Crime Act 2015

45   Offence of participating in activities of organised crime group

(1) A person who participates in the criminal activities of an organised crime group commits an offence. [I]

(2) For this purpose, a person participates in the criminal activities of an organised crime group if the person takes part in any activities that the person knows or reasonably suspects—

    (a) are criminal activities of an organised crime group, or

    (b) will help an organised crime group to carry on criminal activities.

(3) "Criminal activities" are activities within subsection (4) or (5) that are carried on with a view to obtaining (directly or indirectly) any gain or benefit.

(4) Activities are within this subsection if—

    (a) they are carried on in England or Wales, and

    (b) they constitute an offence in England and Wales punishable on conviction on indictment with imprisonment for a term of 7 years or more.

(5) Activities are within this subsection if—

    (a) they are carried on outside England and Wales,

    (b) they constitute an offence under the law in force of the country where they are carried on, and

    (c) they would constitute an offence in England and Wales of the kind mentioned in subsection (4)(b) if the activities were carried on in England and Wales.

(6) "Organised crime group" means a group that—

    (a) has as its purpose, or as one of its purposes, the carrying on of criminal activities, and

    (b) consists of three or more persons who act, or agree to act, together to further that purpose.

(7) For a person to be guilty of an offence under this section it is not necessary—

    (a) for the person to know any of the persons who are members of the organised crime group,

    (b) for all of the acts or omissions comprising participation in the group's criminal activities to take place in England and Wales (so long as at least one of them does), or

    (c) for the gain or benefit referred to in subsection (3) to be financial in nature.

(8) It is a defence for a person charged with an offence under this section to prove that the person's participation was necessary for a purpose related to the prevention or detection of crime.

69   Possession of paedophile manual

(1) It is an offence to be in possession of any item that contains advice or guidance about abusing children sexually. [E]

(2) It is a defence for a person (D) charged with an offence under this section—

    (a) to prove that D had a legitimate reason for being in possession of the item;

    (b) to prove that—

        (i) D had not read, viewed or (as appropriate) listened to the item, and

        (ii) D did not know, and had no reason to suspect, that it contained advice or guidance about abusing children sexually; or

(c) to prove that—

    (i)   the item was sent to D without any request made by D or on D's behalf, and

    (ii) D did not keep it for an unreasonable time.

(8) In this section—

"abusing children sexually" means doing anything that constitutes—

(a) an offence under Part 1 of the Sexual Offences Act 2003, against a person under 16, or

(b) an offence under section 1 of the Protection of Children Act 1978, involving indecent photographs (but not pseudo-photographs), or

(c) an offence under section 2 of the Modern Slavery Act 2015 (human trafficking) committed with a view to exploitation that consists of or includes behaviour within section 3(3) of that Act (sexual exploitation),

or doing anything outside England and Wales or Northern Ireland that would constitute such an offence if done in England and Wales or Northern Ireland;

"item" includes anything in which information of any description is recorded;

"prohibited item" means an item within subsection (1).

76   Controlling or coercive behaviour in an intimate or family relationship

(1) A person (A) commits an offence if—

(a) A repeatedly or continuously engages in behaviour towards another person (B) that is controlling or coercive,

(b) at the time of the behaviour, A and B are personally connected (see subsection (6)),

(c) the behaviour has a serious effect on B, and

(d) A knows or ought to know that the behaviour will have a serious effect on B.

(2) A and B are "personally connected" if—

(a) A is in an intimate personal relationship with B, or

(b) A and B live together and—

    (i)   they are members of the same family, or

    (ii) they have previously been in an intimate personal relationship with each other.

(3) But A does not commit an offence under this section if at the time of the behaviour in question—

(a) A has responsibility for B, for the purposes of Part 1 of the Children and Young Persons Act 1933 (see section 17 of that Act), and

(b) B is under 16.

(4) A's behaviour has a "serious effect" on B if—

(a) it causes B to fear, on at least two occasions, that violence will be used against B, or

(b) it causes B serious alarm or distress which has a substantial adverse effect on B's usual day-to-day activities.

(5) For the purposes of subsection (1)(d) A "ought to know" that which a reasonable person in possession of the same information would know.

(6) For the purposes of subsection (2)(b)(i) A and B are members of the same family if—

(a) they are, or have been, married to each other;

(b) they are, or have been, civil partners of each other;

(c) they are relatives;

(d) they have agreed to marry one another (whether or not the agreement has been terminated);

(e) they have entered into a civil partnership agreement (whether or not the agreement has been terminated);

(f) they are both parents of the same child;

(g) they have, or have had, parental responsibility for the same child.

(7) In subsection (6)—

"civil partnership agreement" has the meaning given by section 73 of the Civil Partnership Act 2004;

"child" means a person under the age of 18 years;

"parental responsibility" has the same meaning as in the Children Act 1989;

"relative" has the meaning given by section 63(1) of the Family Law Act 1996.

(8) In proceedings for an offence under this section it is a defence for A to show that—

    (a) in engaging in the behaviour in question, A believed that he or she was acting in B's best interests, and

    (b) the behaviour was in all the circumstances reasonable.

(9) A is to be taken to have shown the facts mentioned in subsection (8) if—

    (a) sufficient evidence of the facts is adduced to raise an issue with respect to them, and

    (b) the contrary is not proved beyond reasonable doubt.

(10) The defence in subsection (8) is not available to A in relation to behaviour that causes B to fear that violence will be used against B.

76A   Offences under section 76 committed outside the United Kingdom

(1) If—

    (a) a person's behaviour consists of or includes behaviour in a country outside the United Kingdom,

    (b) the behaviour would constitute an offence under section 76 if it occurred in England and Wales, and

    (c) the person is a United Kingdom national or is habitually resident in England and Wales,

the person is guilty in England and Wales of that offence.

(2) In this section—

"country" includes territory;

"United Kingdom national" means an individual who is—

    (a) a British citizen, a British overseas territories citizen, a British National (Overseas) or a British Overseas citizen,

    (b) a person who under the British Nationality Act 1981 is a British subject, or

    (c) a British protected person within the meaning of that Act.

Investigatory Powers Act 2016

2   General duties in relation to privacy

(1) Subsection (2) applies where a public authority is deciding whether—

    (a) to issue, renew or cancel a warrant under Part 2 , 5, 6 or 7,

    (b) to modify such a warrant,

    (c) to approve a decision to issue, renew or modify such a warrant,

    (d) to grant, approve or cancel an authorisation under Part 3,

    (e) to give a notice in pursuance of such an authorisation or under Part 4 or section 252, 253 or 257,

    (f) to vary or revoke such a notice,

    (g) to approve a decision to give or vary a notice under Part 4 or section 252, 253 or 257,

    (h) to approve the use of criteria under section 153, 194 or 222,

    (i) to give an authorisation under section 219(3)(b),

    (j) to approve a decision to give such an authorisation, or

    (k) to apply for or otherwise seek any issue, grant, giving, modification, variation or renewal of a kind falling within paragraph (a), (b), (d), (e), (f) or (i).

(2) The public authority must have regard to—

    (a) whether what is sought to be achieved by the warrant, authorisation or notice could reasonably be achieved by other less intrusive means,

    (b) whether the level of protection to be applied in relation to any obtaining of information by virtue of the warrant, authorisation or notice is higher because of the particular sensitivity of that information,

    (c) the public interest in the integrity and security of telecommunication systems and postal services, and

    (d) any other aspects of the public interest in the protection of privacy.

(3) The duties under subsection (2)—

(a) apply so far as they are relevant in the particular context, and

(b) are subject to the need to have regard to other considerations that are also relevant in that context.

(4) The other considerations may, in particular, include—

(a) the interests of national security or of the economic well-being of the United Kingdom,

(b) the public interest in preventing or detecting serious crime,

(c) other considerations which are relevant to—

(i) whether the conduct authorised or required by the warrant, authorisation or notice is proportionate, or

(ii) whether it is necessary to act for a purpose provided for by this Act,

(d) the requirements of the Human Rights Act 1998, and

(e) other requirements of public law.

(5) For the purposes of subsection (2)(b), examples of sensitive information include—

(a) items subject to legal privilege,

(b) any information identifying or confirming a source of journalistic information, and

(c) relevant confidential information within the meaning given by paragraph 2(4) of Schedule 7 (certain information held in confidence and consisting of personal records, journalistic material or communications between Members of Parliament and their constituents).

3   Offence of unlawful interception

(1) A person commits an offence if—

(a) the person intentionally intercepts a communication in the course of its transmission by means of—

(i) a public telecommunication system,

(ii) a private telecommunication system, or

(iii) a public postal service,

(b) the interception is carried out in the United Kingdom, and

(c) the person does not have lawful authority to carry out the interception.

(2) But it is not an offence under subsection (1) for a person to intercept a communication in the course of its transmission by means of a private telecommunication system if the person—

(a) is a person with a right to control the operation or use of the system, or

(b) has the express or implied consent of such a person to carry out the interception.

(3) Sections 4 and 5 contain provision about—

(a) the meaning of "interception", and

(b) when interception is to be regarded as carried out in the United Kingdom.

(4) Section 6 contains provision about when a person has lawful authority to carry out an interception.

(5) For the meaning of the terms used in subsection (1)(a)(i) to (iii), see sections 261 and 262.

4   Definition of *"interception"* etc.

Interception in relation to telecommunication systems

(1) For the purposes of this Act, a person intercepts a communication in the course of its transmission by means of a telecommunication system if, and only if—

(a) the person does a relevant act in relation to the system, and

(b) the effect of the relevant act is to make any content of the communication available, at a relevant time, to a person who is not the sender or intended recipient of the communication.

For the meaning of "content" in relation to a communication, see section 261(6).

(2) In this section "relevant act", in relation to a telecommunication system, means—

(a) modifying, or interfering with, the system or its operation;

(b) monitoring transmissions made by means of the system;

(c) monitoring transmissions made by wireless telegraphy to or from apparatus that is part of the system.

(3) For the purposes of this section references to modifying a telecommunication system include references to attaching any apparatus to, or otherwise modifying or interfering with—

(a) any part of the system, or

(b) any wireless telegraphy apparatus used for making transmissions to or from apparatus that is part of the system.

(4) In this section "relevant time", in relation to a communication transmitted by means of a telecommunication system, means—

(a) any time while the communication is being transmitted, and

(b) any time when the communication is stored in or by the system (whether before or after its transmission).

(5) For the purposes of this section, the cases in which any content of a communication is to be taken to be made available to a person at a relevant time include any case in which any of the communication is diverted or recorded at a relevant time so as to make any content of the communication available to a person after that time.

(6) In this section "wireless telegraphy" and "wireless telegraphy apparatus" have the same meaning as in the Wireless Telegraphy Act 2006 (see sections 116 and 117 of that Act).

Interception in relation to postal services

(7) Section 125(3) of the Postal Services Act 2000 applies for the purposes of determining for the purposes of this Act whether a postal item is in the course of its transmission by means of a postal service as it applies for the purposes of determining for the purposes of that Act whether a postal packet is in course of transmission by post.

Interception carried out in the United Kingdom

(8) For the purposes of this Act the interception of a communication is carried out in the United Kingdom if, and only if—

(a) the relevant act or, in the case of a postal item, the interception is carried out by conduct within the United Kingdom, and

(b) the communication is intercepted—

(i)   in the course of its transmission by means of a public telecommunication system or a public postal service, or

(ii) in the course of its transmission by means of a private telecommunication system in a case where the sender or intended recipient of the communication is in the United Kingdom.

5 Conduct that is not interception

(1) References in this Act to the interception of a communication do not include references to the interception of any communication broadcast for general reception.

(2) References in this Act to the interception of a communication in the course of its transmission by means of a postal service do not include references to—

(a) any conduct that takes place in relation only to so much of the communication as consists of any postal data comprised in, included as part of, attached to, or logically associated with a communication (whether by the sender or otherwise) for the purposes of any postal service by means of which it is being or may be transmitted, or

(b) any conduct, in connection with conduct falling within paragraph (a), that gives a person who is neither the sender nor the intended recipient only so much access to a communication as is necessary for the purpose of identifying such postal data.

For the meaning of "postal data", see section 262.

6 Definition of "lawful authority"

(1) For the purposes of this Act, a person has lawful authority to carry out an interception if, and only if—

(a) the interception is carried out in accordance with—

(i)   a targeted interception warrant or mutual assistance warrant under Chapter 1 of Part 2, or

(ii) a bulk interception warrant under Chapter 1 of Part 6,

(b) the interception is authorised by any of sections 44 to 52, or

(c) in the case of a communication stored in or by a telecommunication system, the interception—

    (i) is carried out in accordance with a targeted equipment interference warrant under Part 5 or a bulk equipment interference warrant under Chapter 3 of Part 6,

    (ii) is in the exercise of any statutory power that is exercised for the purpose of obtaining information or taking possession of any document or other property, or

    (iii) is carried out in accordance with a court order made for that purpose.

(2) Conduct which has lawful authority for the purposes of this Act by virtue of subsection (1)(a) or (b) is to be treated as lawful for all other purposes.

(3) Any other conduct which—

    (a) is carried out in accordance with a warrant under Chapter 1 of Part 2 or a bulk interception warrant, or

    (b) is authorised by any of sections 44 to 52,

is to be treated as lawful for all purposes.

11   Offence of unlawfully obtaining communications data

(1) A relevant person who, without lawful authority, knowingly or recklessly obtains communications data from a telecommunications operator or a postal operator is guilty of an offence.

(2) In this section "relevant person" means a person who holds an office, rank or position with a relevant public authority (within the meaning of Part 3).

(3) Subsection (1) does not apply to a relevant person who shows that the person acted in the reasonable belief that the person had lawful authority to obtain the communications data.

Psychoactive Substances Act 2016

2   Meaning of "psychoactive substance" etc.

(1) In this Act "psychoactive substance" means any substance which—

    (a) is capable of producing a psychoactive effect in a person who consumes it, and

    (b) is not an exempted substance (see section 3).

(2) For the purposes of this Act a substance produces a psychoactive effect in a person if, by stimulating or depressing the person's central nervous system, it affects the person's mental functioning or emotional state; and references to a substance's psychoactive effects are to be read accordingly.

(3) For the purposes of this Act a person consumes a substance if the person causes or allows the substance, or fumes given off by the substance, to enter the person's body in any way.

3   Exempted substances

(1) In this Act "exempted substance" means a substance listed in Schedule 1.

(2) The Secretary of State may by regulations amend Schedule 1 in order to—

    (a) add or vary any description of substance;

    (b) remove any description of substance added under paragraph (a).

(3) Before making any regulations under this section the Secretary of State must consult—

    (a) the Advisory Council on the Misuse of Drugs, and

    (b) such other persons as the Secretary of State considers appropriate.

(4) The power to make regulations under this section is exercisable by statutory instrument.

(5) A statutory instrument containing regulations under this section may not be made unless a draft of the instrument has been laid before, and approved by a resolution of, each House of Parliament.

4   Producing a psychoactive substance

(1) A person commits an offence if—

    (a) the person intentionally produces a psychoactive substance,

    (b) the person knows or suspects that the substance is a psychoactive substance, and

    (c) the person—
        (i)   intends to consume the psychoactive substance for its psychoactive effects, or
        (ii) knows, or is reckless as to whether, the psychoactive substance is likely to be consumed by some other person for its psychoactive effects.
  (2) This section is subject to section 11 (exceptions to offences).

5 Supplying, or offering to supply, a psychoactive substance

  (1) A person commits an offence if—
    (a) the person intentionally supplies a substance to another person,
    (b) the substance is a psychoactive substance,
    (c) the person knows or suspects, or ought to know or suspect, that the substance is a psychoactive substance, and
    (d) the person knows, or is reckless as to whether, the psychoactive substance is likely to be consumed by the person to whom it is supplied, or by some other person, for its psychoactive effects.
  (2) A person ("P") commits an offence if—
    (a) P offers to supply a psychoactive substance to another person ("R"), and
    (b) P knows or is reckless as to whether R, or some other person, would, if P supplied a substance to R in accordance with the offer, be likely to consume the substance for its psychoactive effects.
  (3) For the purposes of subsection (2)(b), the reference to a substance's psychoactive effects includes a reference to the psychoactive effects which the substance would have if it were the substance which P had offered to supply to R.
  (4) This section is subject to section 11 (exceptions to offences).

6 Aggravation of offence under section 5

  (5) In this section—
"school premises" means land used for the purposes of a school, other than any land occupied solely as a dwelling by a person employed at the school;
"school" has the same meaning—
    (a) in England and Wales, as in section 4 of the Education Act 1996; . . .

7 Possession of psychoactive substance with intent to supply

  (1) A person commits an offence if—
    (a) the person is in possession of a psychoactive substance,
    (b) the person knows or suspects that the substance is a psychoactive substance, and
    (c) the person intends to supply the psychoactive substance to another person for its consumption, whether by any person to whom it is supplied or by some other person, for its psychoactive effects.
  (2) This section is subject to section 11 (exceptions to offences).

8 Importing or exporting a psychoactive substance

  (1) A person commits an offence if—
    (a) the person intentionally imports a substance,
    (b) the substance is a psychoactive substance,
    (c) the person knows or suspects, or ought to know or suspect, that the substance is a psychoactive substance, and
    (d) the person—
        (i)   intends to consume the psychoactive substance for its psychoactive effects, or
        (ii) knows, or is reckless as to whether, the psychoactive substance is likely to be consumed by some other person for its psychoactive effects.
  (2) A person commits an offence if—
    (a) the person intentionally exports a substance,
    (b) the substance is a psychoactive substance,

    (c) the person knows or suspects, or ought to know or suspect, that the substance is a psychoactive substance, and

    (d) the person—

        (i)   intends to consume the psychoactive substance for its psychoactive effects, or

        (ii) knows, or is reckless as to whether, the psychoactive substance is likely to be consumed by some other person for its psychoactive effects.

(3) In a case where a person imports or exports a controlled drug suspecting it to be a psychoactive substance, the person is to be treated for the purposes of this section as if the person had imported or exported a psychoactive substance suspecting it to be such a substance.

In this subsection "controlled drug" has the same meaning as in the Misuse of Drugs Act 1971.

(4) Section 5 of the Customs and Excise Management Act 1979 (time of importation, exportation, etc.) applies for the purposes of this section as it applies for the purposes of that Act.

(5) This section is subject to section 11 (exceptions to offences).

9 Possession of a psychoactive substance in a custodial institution

(1) A person commits an offence if—

    (a) the person is in possession of a psychoactive substance in a custodial institution,

    (b) the person knows or suspects that the substance is a psychoactive substance, and

    (c) the person intends to consume the psychoactive substance for its psychoactive effects.

(2) In this section "custodial institution" has the same meaning as in section 6.

(3) This section is subject to section 11 (exceptions to offences).

11 Exceptions to offences

(1) It is not an offence under this Act for a person to carry on any activity listed in subsection (3) if, in the circumstances in which it is carried on by that person, the activity is an exempted activity.

(2) In this section "exempted activity" means an activity listed in Schedule 2.

(3) The activities referred to in subsection (1) are—

    (a) producing a psychoactive substance;

    (b) supplying such a substance;

    (c) offering to supply such a substance;

    (d) possessing such a substance with intent to supply it;

    (e) importing or exporting such a substance;

    (f) possessing such a substance in a custodial institution (within the meaning of section 9).

(4) The Secretary of State may by regulations amend Schedule 2 in order to—

    (a) add or vary any description of activity;

    (b) remove any description of activity added under paragraph (a).

(5) Before making any regulations under this section the Secretary of State must consult—

    (a) the Advisory Council on the Misuse of Drugs, and

    (b) such other persons as the Secretary of State considers appropriate.

(6) The power to make regulations under this section is exercisable by statutory instrument.

(7) A statutory instrument containing regulations under this section may not be made unless a draft of the instrument has been laid before, and approved by a resolution of, each House of Parliament.

12 Meaning of "prohibited activity"

(1) In this Act "prohibited activity" means any of the following activities—

    (a) producing a psychoactive substance that is likely to be consumed by individuals for its psychoactive effects;

    (b) supplying such a substance;

    (c) offering to supply such a substance;

    (d) importing such a substance;

    (e) exporting such a substance;

    (f) assisting or encouraging the carrying on of a prohibited activity listed in any of paragraphs (a) to (e).

(2) The carrying on by a person of an activity listed in any of paragraphs (a) to (e) of subsection (1) is not the carrying on of a prohibited activity if the carrying on of the activity by that person would not be an offence under this Act by virtue of section 11.

56 Offences by directors, partners, etc

(1) Where an offence under this Act has been committed by a body corporate and it is proved that the offence—

    (a) has been committed with the consent or connivance of a person falling within subsection (2), or

    (b) is attributable to any neglect on the part of such a person,

that person (as well as the body corporate) is guilty of that offence and liable to be proceeded against and punished accordingly.

(2) The persons are—

    (a) a director, manager, secretary or similar officer of the body corporate;

    (b) any person who was purporting to act in such a capacity.

(3) Where the affairs of a body corporate are managed by its members, subsection (1) applies in relation to the acts and defaults of a member, in connection with that management, as if the member were a director of the body corporate.

(4) Where an offence under this Act has been committed by a Scottish firm and it is proved that the offence—

    (a) has been committed with the consent or connivance of a partner in the firm or a person purporting to act as such a partner, or

    (b) is attributable to any neglect on the part of such a person,

that person (as well as the firm) is guilty of that offence and liable to be proceeded against and punished accordingly.

SCHEDULE 1   EXEMPTED SUBSTANCES

Controlled drugs

1. Controlled drugs (within the meaning of the Misuse of Drugs Act 1971).

Medicinal products

2. Medicinal products.

In this paragraph "medicinal product" has the same meaning as in the Human Medicines Regulations 2012 (SI 2012/1916) (see regulation 2 of those Regulations).

Alcohol

3. Alcohol or alcoholic products.

In this paragraph—

"alcohol" means ethyl alcohol, and

"alcoholic product" means any product which—

    (a) contains alcohol, and

    (b) does not contain any psychoactive substance.

Nicotine and tobacco products

4. Nicotine.

Nicotine and tobacco products

5. Tobacco products.

In this paragraph "tobacco product" means—

    (a) anything which is a tobacco product within the meaning of the Tobacco Products Duty Act 1979 (see section 1 of that Act), and

    (b) any other product which—

(i)   contains nicotine, and

(ii) does not contain any psychoactive substance.

Caffeine

6. Caffeine or caffeine products.

In this paragraph "caffeine product" means any product which—

(a) contains caffeine, and

(b) does not contain any psychoactive substance.

Food

7. Any substance which—

(a) is ordinarily consumed as food, and

(b) does not contain a prohibited ingredient.

In this paragraph—

"enactment" includes—

(a) an enactment contained in subordinate legislation;

(b) an enactment contained in, or in an instrument made under, an Act of the Scottish Parliament;

(c) an enactment contained in, or in an instrument made under, a Measure or Act of the National Assembly for Wales;

(d) an enactment contained in, or in an instrument made under, Northern Ireland legislation;

"food" includes drink;

"prohibited ingredient", in relation to a substance, means any psychoactive substance—

(a) which is not naturally occurring in the substance, and

(b) the use of which in or on food is not authorised by an EU instrument.

SCHEDULE 2   EXEMPTED ACTIVITIES

Healthcare-related activities

1. Any activity carried on by a person who is a health care professional and is acting in the course of his or her profession.

In this paragraph "health care professional" has the same meaning as in the Human Medicines Regulations 2012 (SI 2012/1916) (see regulation 8 of those Regulations).

2. Any activity carried on for the purpose of, or in connection with—

(a) the supply to, or the consumption by, any person of a substance prescribed for that person by a health care professional acting in the course of his or her profession, or

(b) the supply to, or the consumption by, any person of a substance in accordance with the directions of a health care professional acting in the course of his or her profession.

In this paragraph "health care professional" has the same meaning as in the Human Medicines Regulations 2012 (see regulation 8 of those Regulations).

3. Any activity carried on in respect of an active substance by a person who—

(a) is registered in accordance with regulation 45N of the Human Medicines Regulations 2012, or

(b) is exempt from any requirement to be so registered by virtue of regulation 45M(2) or (3) of those Regulations.

In this paragraph "active substance" has the same meaning as in the Human Medicines Regulations 2012 (see regulation 8 of those Regulations).

Research

4. Any activity carried on in the course of, or in connection with, approved scientific research.

In this paragraph—

"approved scientific research" means scientific research carried out by a person who has approval from a relevant ethics review body to carry out that research;

"relevant ethics review body" means—

(a) a research ethics committee recognised or established by the Health Research Authority under Chapter 2 of Part 3 of the Care Act 2014, or

(b) a body appointed by any of the following for the purpose of assessing the ethics of research involving individuals—

(i) the Secretary of State;

(ii) a relevant NHS body;

(iii) United Kingdom Research and Innovation or a body that is a Research Council for the purposes of the Science and Technology Act 1965;

(iv) an institution that is a research institution for the purposes of Chapter 4A of Part 7 of the Income Tax (Earnings and Pensions) Act 2003 (see section 457 of that Act);

(v) a charity which has as its charitable purpose (or one of its charitable purposes) the advancement of health or the saving of lives;

"charity" means—

(a) a charity as defined by section 1(1) of the Charities Act 2011, . . .

"relevant NHS body" means—

(a) an NHS trust or NHS foundation trust in England, . . .

Criminal Finances Act 2017

45   Failure to prevent facilitation of UK tax evasion offences

(1) A relevant body (B) is guilty of an offence if a person commits a UK tax evasion facilitation offence when acting in the capacity of a person associated with B.

(2) It is a defence for B to prove that, when the UK tax evasion facilitation offence was committed—

(a) B had in place such prevention procedures as it was reasonable in all the circumstances to expect B to have in place, or

(b) it was not reasonable in all the circumstances to expect B to have any prevention procedures in place.

(3) In subsection (2) *"prevention procedures"* means procedures designed to prevent persons acting in the capacity of a person associated with B from committing UK tax evasion facilitation offences.

(4) In this Part *"UK tax evasion offence"* means—

(a) an offence of cheating the public revenue, or

(b) an offence under the law of any part of the United Kingdom consisting of being knowingly concerned in, or in taking steps with a view to, the fraudulent evasion of a tax.

(5) In this Part *"UK tax evasion facilitation offence"* means an offence under the law of any part of the United Kingdom consisting of—

(a) being knowingly concerned in, or in taking steps with a view to, the fraudulent evasion of a tax by another person,

(b) aiding, abetting, counselling or procuring the commission of a UK tax evasion offence, or

(c) being involved art and part in the commission of an offence consisting of being knowingly concerned in, or in taking steps with a view to, the fraudulent evasion of a tax.

(6) Conduct carried out with a view to the fraudulent evasion of tax by another person is not to be regarded as a UK tax evasion facilitation offence by virtue of subsection (5)(a) unless the other person has committed a UK tax evasion offence facilitated by that conduct.

(7) For the purposes of this section *"tax"* means a tax imposed under the law of any part of the United Kingdom, including national insurance contributions under—

(a) Part 1 of the Social Security Contributions and Benefits Act 1992, or

(b) Part 1 of the Social Security Contributions and Benefits (Northern Ireland) Act 1992.

46 Failure to prevent facilitation of foreign tax evasion offences

(1) A relevant body (B) is guilty of an offence if at any time—

    (a) a person commits a foreign tax evasion facilitation offence when acting in the capacity of a person associated with B, and

    (b) any of the conditions in subsection (2) is satisfied.

(2) The conditions are—

    (a) that B is a body incorporated, or a partnership formed, under the law of any part of the United Kingdom;

    (b) that B carries on business or part of a business in the United Kingdom;

    (c) that any conduct constituting part of the foreign tax evasion facilitation offence takes place in the United Kingdom;

and in paragraph (b) "*business*" includes an undertaking.

(3) It is a defence for B to prove that, when the foreign tax evasion facilitation offence was committed—

    (a) B had in place such prevention procedures as it was reasonable in all the circumstances to expect B to have in place, or

    (b) it was not reasonable in all the circumstances to expect B to have any prevention procedures in place.

(4) In subsection (3) "*prevention procedures*" means procedures designed to prevent persons acting in the capacity of a person associated with B from committing foreign tax evasion facilitation offences under the law of the foreign country concerned.

(5) In this Part "*foreign tax evasion offence*" means conduct which—

    (a) amounts to an offence under the law of a foreign country,

    (b) relates to a breach of a duty relating to a tax imposed under the law of that country, and

    (c) would be regarded by the courts of any part of the United Kingdom as amounting to being knowingly concerned in, or in taking steps with a view to, the fraudulent evasion of that tax.

(6) In this Part "*foreign tax evasion facilitation offence*" means conduct which—

    (a) amounts to an offence under the law of a foreign country,

    (b) relates to the commission by another person of a foreign tax evasion offence under that law, and

    (c) would, if the foreign tax evasion offence were a UK tax evasion offence, amount to a UK tax evasion facilitation offence (see section 45(5) and (6)).

Policing and Crime Act 2017

134 Possession of pyrotechnic articles at musical events

(1) It is an offence for a person to have a pyrotechnic article in his or her possession at any time when the person is—

    (a) at a place where a qualifying musical event is being held, or

    (b) at any other place that is being used by a person responsible for the organisation of a qualifying musical event for the purpose of—

        (i) regulating entry to, or departure from, the event, or

        (ii) providing sleeping or other facilities for those attending the event.

(2) Subsection (1) does not apply—

    (a) to a person who is responsible for the organisation of the event, or

    (b) to a person who has the article in his or her possession with the consent of a person responsible for the organisation of the event.

(4) In this section, "pyrotechnic article" means an article that contains explosive substances, or an explosive mixture of substances, designed to produce heat, light, sound, gas or smoke, or a combination of such effects, through selfsustained exothermic chemical reactions, other than—

    (a) a match, or

    (b) an article specified, or of a description specified, in regulations made by statutory instrument by the Secretary of State.

(5) In this section, "qualifying musical event" means an event at which one or more live musical performances take place and which is specified, or of a description specified, in regulations made by statutory instrument by the Secretary of State.

Data Protection Act 2018

83   Meaning of "controller" and "processor"

(1) In this Part, "controller" means the intelligence service which, alone or jointly with others—

    (a) determines the purposes and means of the processing of personal data, or

    (b) is the controller by virtue of subsection (2).

(2) Where personal data is processed only—

    (a) for purposes for which it is required by an enactment to be processed, and

    (b) by means by which it is required by an enactment to be processed,

the intelligence service on which the obligation to process the data is imposed by the enactment (or, if different, one of the enactments) is the controller.

(3) In this Part, "processor" means any person who processes personal data on behalf of the controller (other than a person who is an employee of the controller).

84   Other definitions

(1) This section defines other expressions used in this Part.

(2) "Consent", in relation to the processing of personal data relating to an individual, means a freely given, specific, informed and unambiguous indication of the individual's wishes by which the individual, by a statement or by a clear affirmative action, signifies agreement to the processing of the personal data.

(3) "Employee", in relation to any person, includes an individual who holds a position (whether paid or unpaid) under the direction and control of that person.

(4) "Personal data breach" means a breach of security leading to the accidental or unlawful destruction, loss, alteration, unauthorised disclosure of, or access to, personal data transmitted, stored or otherwise processed.

(5) "Recipient", in relation to any personal data, means any person to whom the data is disclosed, whether a third party or not, but it does not include a person to whom disclosure is or may be made in the framework of a particular inquiry in accordance with the law.

(6) "Restriction of processing" means the marking of stored personal data with the aim of limiting its processing for the future.

170   Unlawful obtaining etc of personal data

(1) It is an offence for a person knowingly or recklessly—

    (a) to obtain or disclose personal data without the consent of the controller,

    (b) to procure the disclosure of personal data to another person without the consent of the controller, or

    (c) after obtaining personal data, to retain it without the consent of the person who was the controller in relation to the personal data when it was obtained.

(2) It is a defence for a person charged with an offence under subsection (1) to prove that the obtaining, disclosing, procuring or retaining—

    (a) was necessary for the purposes of preventing or detecting crime,

(b) was required or authorised by an enactment, by a rule of law or by the order of a court or tribunal, or

(c) in the particular circumstances, was justified as being in the public interest.

(3) It is also a defence for a person charged with an offence under subsection (1) to prove that—

(a) the person acted in the reasonable belief that the person had a legal right to do the obtaining, disclosing, procuring or retaining,

(b) the person acted in the reasonable belief that the person would have had the consent of the controller if the controller had known about the obtaining, disclosing, procuring or retaining and the circumstances of it, or

(c) the person acted—

(i) for the special purposes,

(ii) with a view to the publication by a person of any journalistic, academic, artistic or literary material, and

(iii) in the reasonable belief that in the particular circumstances the obtaining, disclosing, procuring or retaining was justified as being in the public interest.

(4) It is an offence for a person to sell personal data if the person obtained the data in circumstances in which an offence under subsection (1) was committed.

(5) It is an offence for a person to offer to sell personal data if the person—

(a) has obtained the data in circumstances in which an offence under subsection (1) was committed, or

(b) subsequently obtains the data in such circumstances.

(6) For the purposes of subsection (5), an advertisement indicating that personal data is or may be for sale is an offer to sell the data.

(7) In this section—

(a) references to the consent of a controller do not include the consent of a person who is a controller by virtue of Article 28(10) of the UK GDPR or section 59(8) or 105(3) of this Act (processor to be treated as controller in certain circumstances);

(b) where there is more than one controller, such references are references to the consent of one or more of them.

171   Re-identification of de-identified personal data

(1) It is an offence for a person knowingly or recklessly to re-identify information that is de-identified personal data without the consent of the controller responsible for de-identifying the personal data.

(2) For the purposes of this section and section 172—

(a) personal data is "de-identified" if it has been processed in such a manner that it can no longer be attributed, without more, to a specific data subject;

(b) a person "re-identifies" information if the person takes steps which result in the information no longer being de-identified within the meaning of paragraph (a).

(3) It is a defence for a person charged with an offence under subsection (1) to prove that the re-identification—

(a) was necessary for the purposes of preventing or detecting crime,

(b) was required or authorised by an enactment, by a rule of law or by the order of a court or tribunal, or

(c) in the particular circumstances, was justified as being in the public interest.

(4) It is also a defence for a person charged with an offence under subsection (1) to prove that—

(a) the person acted in the reasonable belief that the person—

(i) is the data subject to whom the information relates,

(ii) had the consent of that data subject, or

(iii) would have had such consent if the data subject had known about the re-identification and the circumstances of it,

(b) the person acted in the reasonable belief that the person—

(i) is the controller responsible for de-identifying the personal data,

(ii) had the consent of that controller, or

      (iii) would have had such consent if that controller had known about the re-identification and the circumstances of it,

    (c) the person acted—

      (i) for the special purposes,

      (ii) with a view to the publication by a person of any journalistic, academic, artistic or literary material, and

      (iii) in the reasonable belief that in the particular circumstances the re-identification was justified as being in the public interest, or

    (d) the effectiveness testing conditions were met (see section 172).

(5) It is an offence for a person knowingly or recklessly to process personal data that is information that has been re-identified where the person does so—

    (a) without the consent of the controller responsible for de-identifying the personal data, and

    (b) in circumstances in which the re-identification was an offence under subsection (1).

(6) It is a defence for a person charged with an offence under subsection (5) to prove that the processing—

    (a) was necessary for the purposes of preventing or detecting crime,

    (b) was required or authorised by an enactment, by a rule of law or by the order of a court or tribunal, or

    (c) in the particular circumstances, was justified as being in the public interest.

(7) It is also a defence for a person charged with an offence under subsection (5) to prove that—

    (a) the person acted in the reasonable belief that the processing was lawful,

    (b) the person acted in the reasonable belief that the person—

      (i) had the consent of the controller responsible for de-identifying the personal data, or

      (ii) would have had such consent if that controller had known about the processing and the circumstances of it, or

    (c) the person acted—

      (i) for the special purposes,

      (ii) with a view to the publication by a person of any journalistic, academic, artistic or literary material, and

      (iii) in the reasonable belief that in the particular circumstances the processing was justified as being in the public interest.

(8) In this section—

    (a) references to the consent of a controller do not include the consent of a person who is a controller by virtue of Article 28(10) of the UK GDPR or section 59(8) or 105(3) of this Act (processor to be treated as controller in certain circumstances);

    (b) where there is more than one controller, such references are references to the consent of one or more of them.

172 Re-identification: effectiveness testing conditions

(1) For the purposes of section 171, in relation to a person who re-identifies information that is de-identified personal data, "the effectiveness testing conditions" means the conditions in subsections (2) and (3).

(2) The first condition is that the person acted—

    (a) with a view to testing the effectiveness of the de-identification of personal data,

    (b) without intending to cause, or threaten to cause, damage or distress to a person, and

    (c) in the reasonable belief that, in the particular circumstances, re-identifying the information was justified as being in the public interest.

(3) The second condition is that the person notified the Commissioner or the controller responsible for de-identifying the personal data about the re-identification—

    (a) without undue delay, and

    (b) where feasible, not later than 72 hours after becoming aware of it.

(4) Where there is more than one controller responsible for de-identifying personal data, the requirement in subsection (3) is satisfied if one or more of them is notified.

173 Alteration etc of personal data to prevent disclosure to data subject

(1) Subsection (3) applies where—

   (a) a request has been made in exercise of a data subject access right, and

   (b) the person making the request would have been entitled to receive information in response to that request.

(2) In this section, "data subject access right" means a right under—

   (a) Article 15 of the UK GDPR (right of access by the data subject);

   (b) Article 20 of the UK GDPR (right to data portability);

   (c) section 45 of this Act (law enforcement processing: right of access by the data subject);

   (d) section 94 of this Act (intelligence services processing: right of access by the data subject).

(3) It is an offence for a person listed in subsection (4) to alter, deface, block, erase, destroy or conceal information with the intention of preventing disclosure of all or part of the information that the person making the request would have been entitled to receive.

(4) Those persons are—

   (a) the controller, and

   (b) a person who is employed by the controller, an officer of the controller or subject to the direction of the controller.

(5) It is a defence for a person charged with an offence under subsection (3) to prove that—

   (a) the alteration, defacing, blocking, erasure, destruction or concealment of the information would have occurred in the absence of a request made in exercise of a data subject access right, or

   (b) the person acted in the reasonable belief that the person making the request was not entitled to receive the information in response to the request.

Laser Misuse (Vehicles) Act 2018

1 Offence of shining or directing a laser beam towards a vehicle

(1) A person commits an offence if—

   (a) the person shines or directs a laser beam towards a vehicle which is moving or ready to move, and

   (b) the laser beam dazzles or distracts, or is likely to dazzle or distract, a person with control of the vehicle.

(2) It is a defence to show—

   (a) that the person had a reasonable excuse for shining or directing the laser beam towards the vehicle, or

   (b) that the person—

      (i) did not intend to shine or direct the laser beam towards the vehicle, and

      (ii) exercised all due diligence and took all reasonable precautions to avoid doing so.

(3) A person is taken to have shown a fact mentioned in subsection (2) if—

   (a) sufficient evidence is adduced to raise an issue with respect to it, and

   (b) the contrary is not proved beyond reasonable doubt.

2 Offences relating to air traffic services

(1) A person commits an offence if

   (a) the person shines or directs a laser beam—

      (i) towards an air traffic facility, or

      (ii) towards a person providing air traffic services, and

   (b) the laser beam dazzles or distracts, or is likely to dazzle or distract, a person providing air traffic services.

(2) It is a defence to show—

    (a) that the person had a reasonable excuse for shining or directing the laser beam towards the facility or person, or

    (b) that the person—

        (i) did not intend to shine or direct the laser beam towards the facility or person, and

        (ii) exercised all due diligence and took all reasonable precautions to avoid doing so.

(3) A person is taken to have shown a fact mentioned in subsection (2) if—

    (a) sufficient evidence is adduced to raise an issue with respect to it, and

    (b) the contrary is not proved beyond reasonable doubt.

(6) In this section—

"air traffic facility" means any building, structure, vehicle or other place from which air traffic services are provided;

"air traffic services" has the meaning given by section 98(1) of the Transport Act 2000.

3 Interpretation

In this Act—

"aircraft" means any vehicle used for travel by air;

"laser beam" means a beam of coherent light produced by a device of any kind;

"vehicle" means any vehicle used for travel by land, water or air;

"vessel" has the meaning given by section 255(1) of the Merchant Shipping Act 1995.

Botulinum Toxin and Cosmetic Fillers (Children) Act 2021

1 Offence of administering certain substances to a child

(1) It is an offence for a person to administer, in England, to another person ("A")—

    (a) botulinum toxin, or

    (b) a subcutaneous, submucous or intradermal injection of a filler for a cosmetic purpose,

where A is under the age of 18.

(2) A "filler" is any substance used for dermal or mucous membrane filling (whether or not designed to be so used).

(3) For the purposes of subsection (1)(b), an injection of a filler is, in particular, to be taken to be for a cosmetic purpose if—

    (a) the filler is generally used for such a purpose, or

    (b) the likely effect of the injection is to alter the appearance of the person injected.

(4) It is a defence for a person charged with an offence under subsection (1) to show that at the time of the alleged offence—

    (a) the defendant was a registered medical practitioner,

    (b) the defendant was a regulated health professional who, in administering the botulinum toxin or the filler (as the case may be), was acting in accordance with the directions of a registered medical practitioner, or

    (c) the defendant—

        (i) had taken reasonable steps to establish A's age, and

        (ii) reasonably believed that A was aged 18 or over.

(5) A person is taken to have shown a matter mentioned in subsection (4) if—

    (a) sufficient evidence of the matter is adduced to raise an issue with respect to it, and

    (b) the contrary is not proved beyond reasonable doubt.

(7) In this section "regulated health professional" means—

    (a) a registered nurse;

    (b) a registered dentist within the meaning of the Dentists Act 1984 (see section 53 of that Act);

    (c) a registered pharmacist within the meaning of the Pharmacy Order 2010 (S.I. 2010/231) (see article 3 of that Order);

2 Offence by persons carrying on a business

(1) A person (a "business owner") commits an offence if in the course of the business owner's business—

    (a) a person other than an approved person administers, in England, to another person ("A")—

        (i) botulinum toxin, or

        (ii) a subcutaneous, submucous or intradermal injection of a filler for a cosmetic purpose,

      where A is under the age of 18;

    (b) arrangements are made, in England, by or on behalf of the business owner, for a person other than an approved person to administer, in England, to another person ("A")—

        (i) botulinum toxin, or

        (ii) a subcutaneous, submucous or intradermal injection of a filler for a cosmetic purpose,

      where A is under the age of 18.

(2) For the purposes of subsection (1), an injection of a filler is, in particular, to be taken to be for a cosmetic purpose if—

    (a) the filler injected, or arranged to be injected, is generally used for such a purpose, or

    (b) the likely effect of the injection is, or would be, to alter the appearance of the person injected.

(4) It is a defence for a business owner charged with an offence under subsection (1) to prove that the business owner took all reasonable precautions and exercised all due diligence to avoid committing it.

(5) In this section—

"approved person" means—

    (a) a registered medical practitioner;

    (b) a regulated health professional who, in administering the botulinum toxin or the filler (as the case may be), is or would be acting in accordance with the directions of a registered medical practitioner;

"filler" has the same meaning as in section 1;

"regulated health professional" has the same meaning as in section 1.

3 Offences by bodies corporate

(1) This section applies where an offence under section 2 is committed by a body corporate.

(2) If the offence is proved to have been committed with the consent or connivance of, or to be attributable to any neglect on the part of—

    (a) any director, manager or secretary of the body corporate, or

    (b) any person who was purporting to act in any such capacity,

that director, manager, secretary or person purporting to act as such (as well as the body corporate) commits the offence and is liable to be proceeded against and punished accordingly.

(3) The reference in subsection (2) to the director, manager or secretary of the body corporate includes a reference to any other similar officer of the body corporate.

Domestic Abuse Act 2021

71 Consent to serious harm for sexual gratification not a defence

(1) This section applies for the purposes of determining whether a person ("D") who inflicts serious harm on another person ("V") is guilty of a relevant offence.

(2) It is not a defence that V consented to the infliction of the serious harm for the purposes of obtaining sexual gratification (but see subsection (4)).

(3) In this section—

"relevant offence" means an offence under section 18, 20 or 47 of the Offences Against the Person Act 1861 ("the 1861 Act");

"serious harm" means—

    (a) grievous bodily harm, within the meaning of section 18 of the 1861 Act,

    (b) wounding, within the meaning of that section, or

    (c) actual bodily harm, within the meaning of section 47 of the 1861 Act.

(4) Subsection (2) does not apply in the case of an offence under section 20 or 47 of the 1861 Act where—

    (a) the serious harm consists of, or is a result of, the infection of V with a sexually transmitted infection in the course of sexual activity, and

    (b) V consented to the sexual activity in the knowledge or belief that D had the sexually transmitted infection.

(5) For the purposes of this section it does not matter whether the harm was inflicted for the purposes of obtaining sexual gratification for D, V or some other person.

(6) Nothing in this section affects any enactment or rule of law relating to other circumstances in which a person's consent to the infliction of serious harm may, or may not, be a defence to a relevant offence.

72 Offences against the person committed outside the UK: England and Wales

(1) If—

    (a) a person who is a United Kingdom national or is habitually resident in England and Wales does an act in a country outside the United Kingdom,

    (b) the act constitutes an offence under the law in force in that country, and

    (c) the act, if done in England and Wales, would constitute an offence to which this subsection applies,

the person is guilty in England and Wales of that offence.

(2) The offences to which subsection (1) applies are—

    (a) murder;

    (b) manslaughter;

    (c) an offence under section 18, 20 or 47 of the Offences Against the Person Act 1861 (offences relating to bodily harm or injury);

    (d) an offence under section 23 or 24 of that Act (administering poison);

    (e) an offence under section 1 of the Infant Life (Preservation) Act 1929 (child destruction).

(3) Subsection (1) does not apply where a person would, in the absence of that subsection, be guilty of an offence of murder or manslaughter under the law of England and Wales.

(4) An act punishable under the law in force in any country constitutes an offence under that law for the purposes of subsection (1)(b) however it is described in that law.

(5) The condition in subsection (1)(b) is to be taken to be met unless, not later than rules of court may provide, the defendant serves on the prosecution a notice—

    (a) stating that, on the facts as alleged with respect to the act in question, the condition is not in the defendant's opinion met,

    (b) showing the grounds for that opinion, and

    (c) requiring the prosecution to prove that it is met.

(6) But the court, if it thinks fit, may permit the defendant to require the prosecution to prove that the condition is met without service of a notice under subsection (5).

(7) In the Crown Court the question whether the condition is met is to be decided by the judge alone.

(8) In this section—

"act" includes a failure to act;

"country" includes territory;

"United Kingdom national" means an individual who is—

    (a) a British citizen, a British overseas territories citizen, a British National (Overseas) or a British Overseas citizen,

    (b) a person who under the British Nationality Act 1981 is a British subject, or

    (c) a British protected person within the meaning of that Act.

Finance Act 2021

77 Fraudulent evasion

(1) A person commits an offence if the person is knowingly concerned in, or in the taking of steps with a view to, the fraudulent evasion (by that person or another person) of plastic packaging tax.

(2) The reference in subsection (1) to the evasion of plastic packaging tax includes reference to obtaining, in circumstances where there is no entitlement to it—

    (a) a tax credit;

    (b) a repayment of plastic packaging tax.

78 Misstatements

(1) A person commits an offence if, for purposes connected with plastic packaging tax, the person—

    (a) produces or provides, causes to be produced or provided, or otherwise makes use of any document which is false in a material particular, and

    (b) does so intending to deceive any person or to secure that a machine will respond to the document as if it were a true document.

(2) A person commits an offence if, in providing any information under any provision made by or under this Part the person—

    (a) makes a statement which the person knows to be false in a material particular, or

    (b) recklessly makes a statement which is false in a material particular.

79 Conduct involving evasions or misstatements

(1) A person commits an offence if the person's conduct during any particular period must have involved the person committing one or more offences under section 77 or 78.

(2) For the purposes of any proceedings for an offence under this section it is immaterial whether the particulars of the offence or offences that must have been committed are known.

Overseas Operations (Service Personnel and Veterans) Act 2021

1 Prosecutorial decision regarding alleged conduct during overseas operations

(1) Where a relevant prosecutor makes a decision to which this section applies and the conditions in subsections (3) and (4) are met, the prosecutor must, in making the decision—

    (a) apply the principle set out in section 2, and

    (b) comply with section 3.

(2) This section applies to a decision of a relevant prosecutor as to—

    (a) whether or not proceedings should be brought against a person for a relevant offence, or

    (b) whether or not any proceedings against a person for a relevant offence should be continued,

(but does not apply to a prosecutor's decision so far as it relates to whether or not there is sufficient evidence to justify prosecution).

(3) The first condition is that the alleged conduct took place (outside the British Islands) at a time when the person was—

    (a) a member of the regular or reserve forces, or a member of a British overseas territory force to whom section 369(2) of the Armed Forces Act 2006 (persons subject to service law) applies, and

    (b) deployed on overseas operations.

(4) The second condition is that the period of 5 years beginning with the day on which the alleged conduct took place has expired.

(5) If the offence is alleged to have continued over a period of days, the 5 year period mentioned in subsection (4) is to be taken to begin with the last of those days.

(6) In this Part "overseas operations" means any operations outside the British Islands, including peacekeeping operations and operations for dealing with terrorism, civil unrest or serious public disorder, in the course of which members of Her Majesty's forces come under attack or face the threat of attack or violent resistance.

2 Presumption against prosecution

The principle referred to in section 1(1) is that it is to be exceptional for a relevant prosecutor making a decision to which that section applies to determine that proceedings should be brought against the person for the offence or, as the case may be, that the proceedings against the person for the offence should be continued.

3 Matters to be given particular weight

(1) In making a decision to which section 1 applies, a relevant prosecutor must give particular weight to the matters set out in subsection (2) (so far as they tend to reduce the person's culpability or otherwise tend against prosecution).

(2) Those matters are—

    (a) the adverse effect (or likely adverse effect) on the person of the conditions the person was exposed to during deployment on the operations mentioned in section 1(3)(b), including their experiences and responsibilities (for example, being exposed to unexpected or continuous threats, being in command of others who were so exposed, or being deployed alongside others who were killed or severely wounded in action);

    (b) in a case where there has been a relevant previous investigation and no compelling new evidence has become available, the public interest in finality (as regards how the person is to be dealt with) being achieved without undue delay.

(3) In considering the matter in subsection (2)(a), the prosecutor must have regard to the exceptional demands and stresses to which members of Her Majesty's forces are likely to be subject while deployed on overseas operations, regardless of their length of service, rank or personal resilience.

(4) In subsection (2)(a) "adverse effect", in relation to a person, means—

    (a) an adverse effect on their capacity to make sound judgements or exercise self control, or

    (b) any other adverse effect on their mental health,

and in this subsection "effect" means an effect at the time of the alleged conduct.

4 Section 3: Supplementary

(1) For the purposes of section 3(2)(b) and this section "relevant previous investigation" means an investigation into the alleged conduct which—

    (a) was carried out by an investigating authority,

    (b) has ceased to be active, and

    (c) either did not lead to any decision as to whether or not the person should be charged with an offence, or led to a decision that the person should not be charged with any offence.

(2) For the purposes of section 3(2)(b), where there has been at least one relevant previous investigation in relation to the alleged conduct, evidence—

(a) is not "new" if it has been taken into account in the relevant previous investigation (or in any of them);

(b) otherwise, is "new".

5   Requirement of consent to prosecute

(1) This section applies where—

(a) the condition in subsection (4) is met in relation to potential proceedings against a person for a relevant offence, and

(b) the period of 5 years beginning with the day on which the alleged conduct took place has expired.

(2) If the offence is a service offence, no proceedings may be instituted against the person for the offence under the Armed Forces Act 2006 except with the consent of the Attorney General.

(3) No proceedings may be instituted against the person for the offence—

(a) where the offence is punishable with a criminal penalty by the law of England and Wales, except with the consent of the Attorney General,

(4) The condition mentioned in subsection (1)(a) is that the alleged conduct took place (outside the British Islands) at a time when the person was—

(a) a member of the regular or reserve forces, or a member of a British overseas territory force to whom section 369(2) of the Armed Forces Act 2006 (persons subject to service law) applies, and

(b) deployed on overseas operations.

(5) If the offence is alleged to have continued over a period of days, the 5 year period mentioned in subsection (1)(b) is to be taken to begin with the last of those days.

6   Relevant offence

(1) "Relevant offence" means any of the following (but with the exceptions set out in subsections (2) to (5))—

(a) an offence under section 42 of the Armed Forces Act 2006 (criminal conduct) or any provision mentioned in paragraph 1(2)(a) to (c) of Schedule 1 (provisions superseded by that section), and

(b) an offence punishable with a criminal penalty by the law of any part of the United Kingdom.

(2) An offence is not a "relevant offence" if it is committed against an individual who at the time when the offence is committed is—

(a) a member of the regular or reserve forces,

(b) a member of a British overseas territory force,

(c) a Crown servant, or

(d) a defence contractor.

(3) A service offence is not a "relevant offence" if it is an excluded offence by virtue of Part 1 of Schedule 1.

(4) An offence punishable with a criminal penalty by the law of England and Wales, or of Northern Ireland, is not a "relevant offence" if it is an excluded offence in that part of the United Kingdom by virtue of Part 2 or 5 of Schedule 1.

(5) An offence punishable with a criminal penalty by the law of Scotland is not a "relevant offence" if it is an excluded offence in Scotland by virtue of Part 3 or 5 of Schedule 1.

(6) An offence is not a "relevant offence" if it is an excluded offence by virtue of Part 4 of Schedule 1.

7   General Interpretation

(1) Where—

(a) the offence mentioned in section 1(2) or 5(1)(a) is murder or any other offence one of the elements of which is causing a person's death, and

(b) the death occurred after the day on which the person sustained the injury that caused it, the day (or time) of the alleged conduct is not to be taken to be different from what it would have been if the death had occurred when the injury was sustained.

(2) In this Part references to the British Islands include the territorial sea adjacent to the United Kingdom and the territorial sea adjacent to any of the Channel Islands or the Isle of Man.

(3) The following are "relevant prosecutors" for the purposes of this Part—

    (a) the Director of Service Prosecutions and any person appointed under section 365 of the Armed Forces Act 2006 (prosecuting officers);

    (b) in England and Wales, the Director of Public Prosecutions, a Crown Prosecutor and any person to whom the institution or taking over of proceedings for the offence mentioned in section 1(2) has been assigned under section 5(1) of the Prosecution of Offences Act 1985;

(4) In this Part—

"alleged conduct", in relation to proceedings or potential proceedings for an offence, means the act or omission alleged to constitute the offence;

"British overseas territory force" means any of Her Majesty's forces that is raised under the law of a British overseas territory;

"Crown servant" means a person employed by or in the service of the Government of the United Kingdom;

"defence contractor" means a person engaged in providing goods or services for the purposes of any of Her Majesty's forces under contract (whether as, or on behalf of, a party to the contract);

"Her Majesty's forces" has the same meaning as in the Armed Forces Act 2006 (see section 374 of that Act);

"investigating authority" means—

    (a) a service police force,

    (b) a UK police force, or

    (c) an overseas police force;

"overseas operations" has the meaning given by section 1(6);

"overseas police force" has the same meaning as in the Armed Forces Act 2006 (see section 375 of that Act);

"the regular forces" has the same meaning as in the Armed Forces Act 2006 (see section 374 of that Act);

"relevant offence" has the meaning given by section 6;

"relevant previous investigation" has the meaning given by section 4;

"relevant prosecutor" has the meaning given by subsection (3);

"the reserve forces" has the same meaning as in the Armed Forces Act 2006 (see section 374 of that Act);

"service offence" has the same meaning as in the Armed Forces Act 2006 (see section 50(2) of that Act);

"service police force" has the same meaning as in the Armed Forces Act 2006 (see section 375 of that Act);

"UK police force" has the same meaning as in the Armed Forces Act 2006 (see section 375 of that Act).

(5) Subsections (2) and (3) of section 368 of the Armed Forces Act 2006 (references to members of the regular forces) apply for the purposes of this Part as they apply for the purposes of that Act.

UK Secondary Legislation

Consumer Protection from Unfair Trading Regulations 2008

2 Interpretation

(1) In these Regulations—

"average consumer" shall be construed in accordance with paragraphs (2) to (6);

"business" includes—

    (a) a trade, craft or profession, and

    (b) the activities of any government department or local or public authority;

"CMA" means the Competition and Markets Authority;

"code of conduct" means an agreement or set of rules (which is not imposed by legal or administrative requirements), which defines the behaviour of traders who undertake to be bound by it in relation to one or more commercial practices or business sectors;

"code owner" means a trader or a body responsible for—

    (a) the formulation and revision of a code of conduct; or

    (b) monitoring compliance with the code by those who have undertaken to be bound by it;

"commercial practice" means any act, omission, course of conduct, representation or commercial communication (including advertising and marketing) by a trader, which is directly connected with the promotion, sale or supply of a product to or from consumers, whether occurring before, during or after a commercial transaction (if any) in relation to a product;

"consumer" means an individual acting for purposes that are wholly or mainly outside that individual's business;

"DETINI" means the Department of Enterprise, Trade and Investment in Northern Ireland;

"digital content" means data which are produced and supplied in digital form;

"enforcement authority" means the CMA, every local weights and measures authority and DETINI;

"goods" means any tangible moveable items, but that includes water, gas and electricity if and only if they are put up for sale in a limited volume or set quantity;

"invitation to purchase" means a commercial communication which indicates characteristics of the product and the price in a way appropriate to the means of that commercial communication and thereby enables the consumer to make a purchase;

"local weights and measures authority" means a local weights and measures authority in Great Britain (within the meaning of section 69 of the Weights and Measures Act 1985);

"materially distort the economic behaviour" means in relation to an average consumer, appreciably to impair the average consumer's ability to make an informed decision thereby causing him to take a transactional decision that he would not have taken otherwise;

"premises" includes any place and any stall, vehicle, ship or aircraft;

"product" means—

    (a) goods,

    (b) a service,

    (c) digital content,

    (d) immoveable property,

(e) rights or obligations, or

(f) a product of the kind mentioned in paragraphs (1A) and (1B),

but the application of this definition to Part 4A is subject to regulations 27C and 27D;

"professional diligence" means the standard of special skill and care which a trader may reasonably be expected to exercise towards consumers which is commensurate with either—

(a) honest market practice in the trader's field of activity, or

(b) the general principle of good faith in the trader's field of activity;

"ship" includes any boat and any other description of vessel used in navigation;

"trader"—

(a) means a person acting for purposes relating to that person's business, whether acting personally or through another person acting in the trader's name or on the trader's behalf, and

(b) except in Part 4A, includes a person acting in the name of or on behalf of a trader;

"transactional decision" means any decision taken by a consumer, whether it is to act or to refrain from acting, concerning—

(a) whether, how and on what terms to purchase, make payment in whole or in part for, retain or dispose of a product; or

(b) whether, how and on what terms to exercise a contractual right in relation to a product; (but the application of this definition to regulations 5 and 7 as they apply for the purposes of Part 4A is subject to regulation 27B(2)).

(1A) A trader ("T") who demands payment from a consumer ("C") in full or partial settlement of C's liabilities or purported liabilities to T is to be treated for the purposes of these Regulations as offering to supply a product to C.

(1B) In such a case the product that T offers to supply comprises the full or partial settlement of those liabilities or purported liabilities.

(2) In determining the effect of a commercial practice on the average consumer where the practice reaches or is addressed to a consumer or consumers account shall be taken of the material characteristics of such an average consumer including his being reasonably well informed, reasonably observant and circumspect.

(3) Paragraphs (4) and (5) set out the circumstances in which a reference to the average consumer shall be read as in addition referring to the average member of a particular group of consumers.

(4) In determining the effect of a commercial practice on the average consumer where the practice is directed to a particular group of consumers, a reference to the average consumer shall be read as referring to the average member of that group.

(5) In determining the effect of a commercial practice on the average consumer—

(a) where a clearly identifiable group of consumers is particularly vulnerable to the practice or the underlying product because of their mental or physical infirmity, age or credulity in a way which the trader could reasonably be expected to foresee, and

(b) where the practice is likely to materially distort the economic behaviour only of that group,

a reference to the average consumer shall be read as referring to the average member of that group.

(6) Paragraph (5) is without prejudice to the common and legitimate advertising practice of making exaggerated statements which are not meant to be taken literally.

3 Prohibition of unfair commercial practices

(1) Unfair commercial practices are prohibited.

(2) Paragraphs (3) and (4) set out the circumstances when a commercial practice is unfair.

(3) A commercial practice is unfair if—

(a) it contravenes the requirements of professional diligence; and

(b) it materially distorts or is likely to materially distort the economic behaviour of the average consumer with regard to the product.

(4) A commercial practice is unfair if—
- (a) it is a misleading action under the provisions of regulation 5;
- (b) it is a misleading omission under the provisions of regulation 6;
- (c) it is aggressive under the provisions of regulation 7; or
- (d) it is listed in Schedule 1.

4 Prohibition of the promotion of unfair commercial practices

The promotion of any unfair commercial practice by a code owner in a code of conduct is prohibited.

5 Misleading actions

(1) A commercial practice is a misleading action if it satisfies the conditions in either paragraph (2) or paragraph (3).

(2) A commercial practice satisfies the conditions of this paragraph—
- (a) if it contains false information and is therefore untruthful in relation to any of the matters in paragraph (4) or if it or its overall presentation in any way deceives or is likely to deceive the average consumer in relation to any of the matters in that paragraph, even if the information is factually correct; and
- (b) it causes or is likely to cause the average consumer to take a transactional decision he would not have taken otherwise.

(3) A commercial practice satisfies the conditions of this paragraph if—
- (a) it concerns any marketing of a product (including comparative advertising) which creates confusion with any products, trade marks, trade names or other distinguishing marks of a competitor; or
- (b) it concerns any failure by a trader to comply with a commitment contained in a code of conduct which the trader has undertaken to comply with, if—
  - (i) the trader indicates in a commercial practice that he is bound by that code of conduct, and
  - (ii) the commitment is firm and capable of being verified and is not aspirational,

and it causes or is likely to cause the average consumer to take a transactional decision he would not have taken otherwise, taking account of its factual context and of all its features and circumstances.

(4) The matters referred to in paragraph (2)(a) are—
- (a) the existence or nature of the product;
- (b) the main characteristics of the product (as defined in paragraph 5);
- (c) the extent of the trader's commitments;
- (d) the motives for the commercial practice;
- (e) the nature of the sales process;
- (f) any statement or symbol relating to direct or indirect sponsorship or approval of the trader or the product;
- (g) the price or the manner in which the price is calculated;
- (h) the existence of a specific price advantage;
- (i) the need for a service, part, replacement or repair;
- (j) the nature, attributes and rights of the trader (as defined in paragraph 6);
- (k) the consumer's rights or the risks he may face.

(5) In paragraph (4)(b), the "main characteristics of the product" include—
- (a) availability of the product;
- (b) benefits of the product;
- (c) risks of the product;
- (d) execution of the product;
- (e) composition of the product;
- (f) accessories of the product;
- (g) after-sale customer assistance concerning the product;
- (h) the handling of complaints about the product;

(i)   the method and date of manufacture of the product;

(j)   the method and date of provision of the product;

(k)   delivery of the product;

(l)   fitness for purpose of the product;

(m) usage of the product;

(n)   quantity of the product;

(o)   specification of the product;

(p)   geographical or commercial origin of the product;

(q)   results to be expected from use of the product; and

(r)   results and material features of tests or checks carried out on the product.

(6) In paragraph (4)(j), the "nature, attributes and rights" as far as concern the trader include the trader's—

(a)   identity;

(b)   assets;

(c)   qualifications;

(d)   status;

(e)   approval;

(f)   affiliations or connections;

(g)   ownership of industrial, commercial or intellectual property rights; and

(h)   awards and distinctions.

(7) In paragraph (4)(k) "consumer's rights" include rights the consumer may have under sections 19 and 23 or 24 of the Consumer Rights Act 2015.

6   Misleading omissions

(1) A commercial practice is a misleading omission if, in its factual context, taking account of the matters in paragraph (2)—

(a)   the commercial practice omits material information,

(b)   the commercial practice hides material information,

(c)   the commercial practice provides material information in a manner which is unclear, unintelligible, ambiguous or untimely, or

(d)   the commercial practice fails to identify its commercial intent, unless this is already apparent from the context,

and as a result it causes or is likely to cause the average consumer to take a transactional decision he would not have taken otherwise.

(2) The matters referred to in paragraph (1) are—

(a)   all the features and circumstances of the commercial practice;

(b)   the limitations of the medium used to communicate the commercial practice (including limitations of space or time); and

(c)   where the medium used to communicate the commercial practice imposes limitations of space or time, any measures taken by the trader to make the information available to consumers by other means.

(3) In paragraph (1) "material information" means—

(a)   the information which the average consumer needs, according to the context, to take an informed transactional decision; and

(b)   any information requirement which applies in relation to a commercial communication as a result of an EU obligation.

(4) Where a commercial practice is an invitation to purchase, the following information will be material if not already apparent from the context in addition to any other information which is material information under paragraph (3)—

(a)   the main characteristics of the product, to the extent appropriate to the medium by which the invitation to purchase is communicated and the product;

(b) the identity of the trader, such as his trading name, and the identity of any other trader on whose behalf the trader is acting;

(c) the geographical address of the trader and the geographical address of any other trader on whose behalf the trader is acting;

(d) either—
    (i) the price, including any taxes; or
    (ii) where the nature of the product is such that the price cannot reasonably be calculated in advance, the manner in which the price is calculated;

(e) where appropriate, either—
    (i) all additional freight, delivery or postal charges; or
    (ii) where such charges cannot reasonably be calculated in advance, the fact that such charges may be payable;

(f) the following matters where they depart from the requirements of professional diligence—
    (i) arrangements for payment,
    (ii) arrangements for delivery,
    (iii) arrangements for performance,
    (iv) complaint handling policy;

(g) for products and transactions involving a right of withdrawal or cancellation, the existence of such a right.

7   Aggressive commercial practices

(1) A commercial practice is aggressive if, in its factual context, taking account of all of its features and circumstances—

(a) it significantly impairs or is likely significantly to impair the average consumer's freedom of choice or conduct in relation to the product concerned through the use of harassment, coercion or undue influence; and

(b) it thereby causes or is likely to cause him to take a transactional decision he would not have taken otherwise.

(2) In determining whether a commercial practice uses harassment, coercion or undue influence account shall be taken of—

(a) its timing, location, nature or persistence;

(b) the use of threatening or abusive language or behaviour;

(c) the exploitation by the trader of any specific misfortune or circumstance of such gravity as to impair the consumer's judgment, of which the trader is aware, to influence the consumer's decision with regard to the product;

(d) any onerous or disproportionate non-contractual barrier imposed by the trader where a consumer wishes to exercise rights under the contract, including rights to terminate a contract or to switch to another product or another trader; and

(e) any threat to take any action which cannot legally be taken.

(3) In this regulation—

(a) "coercion" includes the use of physical force; and

(b) "undue influence" means exploiting a position of power in relation to the consumer so as to apply pressure, even without using or threatening to use physical force, in a way which significantly limits the consumer's ability to make an informed decision.

8   Offences relating to unfair commercial practices

(1) A trader is guilty of an offence if—

(a) he knowingly or recklessly engages in a commercial practice which contravenes the requirements of professional diligence under regulation 3(3)(a); and

(b) the practice materially distorts or is likely to materially distort the economic behaviour of the average consumer with regard to the product under regulation 3(3)(b).

(2) For the purposes of paragraph (1)(a) a trader who engages in a commercial practice without regard to whether the practice contravenes the requirements of professional diligence shall be deemed recklessly to engage in the practice, whether or not the trader has reason for believing that the practice might contravene those requirements. [E]

9

A trader is guilty of an offence if he engages in a commercial practice which is a misleading action under regulation 5 otherwise than by reason of the commercial practice satisfying the condition in regulation 5(3)(b). [E]

10

A trader is guilty of an offence if he engages in a commercial practice which is a misleading omission under regulation 6. [E]

11

A trader is guilty of an offence if he engages in a commercial practice which is aggressive under regulation 7. [E]

12

A trader is guilty of an offence if he engages in a commercial practice set out in any of paragraphs 1 to 10, 12 to 27 and 29 to 31 of Schedule 1. [E]

SCHEDULE 1 COMMERCIAL PRACTICES WHICH ARE IN ALL CIRCUMSTANCES CONSIDERED UNFAIR

1. Claiming to be a signatory to a code of conduct when the trader is not.

2. Displaying a trust mark, quality mark or equivalent without having obtained the necessary authorisation.

3. Claiming that a code of conduct has an endorsement from a public or other body which it does not have.

4. Claiming that a trader (including his commercial practices) or a product has been approved, endorsed or authorised by a public or private body when the trader, the commercial practices or the product have not or making such a claim without complying with the terms of the approval, endorsement or authorisation.

5. Making an invitation to purchase products at a specified price without disclosing the existence of any reasonable grounds the trader may have for believing that he will not be able to offer for supply, or to procure another trader to supply, those products or equivalent products at that price for a period that is, and in quantities that are, reasonable having regard to the product, the scale of advertising of the product and the price offered (bait advertising).

6. Making an invitation to purchase products at a specified price and then—
    (a) refusing to show the advertised item to consumers,
    (b) refusing to take orders for it or deliver it within a reasonable time, or
    (c) demonstrating a defective sample of it,
with the intention of promoting a different product (bait and switch).

7. Falsely stating that a product will only be available for a very limited time, or that it will only be available on particular terms for a very limited time, in order to elicit an immediate decision and deprive consumers of sufficient opportunity or time to make an informed choice.

8. Undertaking to provide after-sales service to consumers with whom the trader has communicated prior to a transaction in a language which is not English (in the case of a trader located in the United Kingdom) or not an official language of the EEA State where the trader is located and then making such service available only in another language without clearly disclosing this to the consumer before the consumer is committed to the transaction.

9. Stating or otherwise creating the impression that a product can legally be sold when it cannot.

10. Presenting rights given to consumers in law as a distinctive feature of the trader's offer.

11. Using editorial content in the media to promote a product where a trader has paid for the promotion without making that clear in the content or by images or sounds clearly identifiable by the consumer (advertorial).

12. Making a materially inaccurate claim concerning the nature and extent of the risk to the personal security of the consumer or his family if the consumer does not purchase the product.

13. Promoting a product similar to a product made by a particular manufacturer in such a manner as deliberately to mislead the consumer into believing that the product is made by that same manufacturer when it is not.

14. Establishing, operating or promoting a pyramid promotional scheme where a consumer gives consideration for the opportunity to receive compensation that is derived primarily from the introduction of other consumers into the scheme rather than from the sale or consumption of products.

15. Claiming that the trader is about to cease trading or move premises when he is not.

16. Claiming that products are able to facilitate winning in games of chance.

17. Falsely claiming that a product is able to cure illnesses, dysfunction or malformations.

18. Passing on materially inaccurate information on market conditions or on the possibility of finding the product with the intention of inducing the consumer to acquire the product at conditions less favourable than normal market conditions.

19. Claiming in a commercial practice to offer a competition or prize promotion without awarding the prizes described or a reasonable equivalent.

20. Describing a product as "gratis", "free", "without charge" or similar if the consumer has to pay anything other than the unavoidable cost of responding to the commercial practice and collecting or paying for delivery of the item.

21. Including in marketing material an invoice or similar document seeking payment which gives the consumer the impression that he has already ordered the marketed product when he has not.

22. Falsely claiming or creating the impression that the trader is not acting for purposes relating to his trade, business, craft or profession, or falsely representing oneself as a consumer.

23. Creating the false impression that after-sales service in relation to a product is available in the United Kingdom (if the product is sold there) or in an EEA State other than the one in which the product is sold.

24. Creating the impression that the consumer cannot leave the premises until a contract is formed.

25. Conducting personal visits to the consumer's home ignoring the consumer's request to leave or not to return, except in circumstances and to the extent justified to enforce a contractual obligation.

26. Making persistent and unwanted solicitations by telephone, fax, e-mail or other remote media except in circumstances and to the extent justified to enforce a contractual obligation.

27. Requiring a consumer who wishes to claim on an insurance policy to produce documents which could not reasonably be considered relevant as to whether the claim was valid, or failing systematically to respond to pertinent correspondence, in order to dissuade a consumer from exercising his contractual rights.

28. Including in an advertisement a direct exhortation to children to buy advertised products or persuade their parents or other adults to buy advertised products for them.

29. Demanding immediate or deferred payment for or the return or safekeeping of products supplied by the trader, but not solicited by the consumer.

30. Explicitly informing a consumer that if he does not buy the product or service, the trader's job or livelihood will be in jeopardy.

31. Creating the false impression that the consumer has already won, will win, or will on doing a particular act win, a prize or other equivalent benefit, when in fact either—

    (a) there is no prize or other equivalent benefit, or

    (b) taking any action in relation to claiming the prize or other equivalent benefit is subject to the consumer paying money or incurring a cost.

EU Materials

Regulation (EC) No 178/2002 of the European Parliament and of the Council of 28 January 2002 laying down the general principles and requirements of food law, establishing the European Food Safety Authority and laying down procedures in matters of food safety

Article 2   Definition of "food"

For the purposes of this Regulation, "food" (or "foodstuff") means any substance or product, whether processed, partially processed or unprocessed, intended to be, or reasonably expected to be ingested by humans.

"Food" includes drink, chewing gum and any substance, including water, intentionally incorporated into the food during its manufacture, preparation or treatment. It includes water after the point of compliance as defined in Article 6 of Directive 98/83/EC and without prejudice to the requirements of Directives 80/778/EEC and 98/83/EC.

"Food" shall not include:

(a) feed;

(b) live animals unless they are prepared for placing on the market for human consumption;

(c) plants prior to harvesting;

(d) medicinal products within the meaning of Council Directives 65/65/EEC and 92/73/EEC;

(e) cosmetics within the meaning of Council Directive 76/768/EEC;

(f) tobacco and tobacco products within the meaning of Council Directive 89/622/EEC;

(g) narcotic or psychotropic substances within the meaning of the United Nations Single Convention on Narcotic Drugs, 1961, and the United Nations Convention on Psychotropic Substances, 1971;

(h) residues and contaminants.

(i) medical devices within the meaning of Regulation (EU) 2017/745 of the European Parliament and of the Council.

Article 14   Food safety requirements

1. Food shall not be placed on the market if it is unsafe.

2. Food shall be deemed to be unsafe if it is considered to be:

(a) injurious to health;

(b) unfit for human consumption.

3. In determining whether any food is unsafe, regard shall be had:

(a) to the normal conditions of use of the food by the consumer and at each stage of production, processing and distribution, and

(b) to the information provided to the consumer, including information on the label, or other information generally available to the consumer concerning the avoidance of specific adverse health effects from a particular food or category of foods.

4. In determining whether any food is injurious to health, regard shall be had:

    (a) not only to the probable immediate and/or short-term and/or long-term effects of that food on the health of a person consuming it, but also on subsequent generations;

    (b) to the probable cumulative toxic effects;

    (c) to the particular health sensitivities of a specific category of consumers where the food is intended for that category of consumers.

5. In determining whether any food is unfit for human consumption, regard shall be had to whether the food is unacceptable for human consumption according to its intended use, for reasons of contamination, whether by extraneous matter or otherwise, or through putrefaction, deterioration or decay.

6. Where any food which is unsafe is part of a batch, lot or consignment of food of the same class or description, it shall be presumed that all the food in that batch, lot or consignment is also unsafe, unless following a detailed assessment there is no evidence that the rest of the batch, lot or consignment is unsafe.

7. Food that complies with specific legislation in force in the relevant constituent territory of Great Britain governing food safety shall be deemed to be safe insofar as the aspects covered by the specific provisions are concerned.

8. Conformity of a food with specific provisions applicable to that food shall not bar the competent authorities from taking appropriate measures to impose restrictions on it being placed on the market or to require its withdrawal from the market where there are reasons to suspect that, despite such conformity, the food is unsafe.

Directive 2002/87/EC of the European Parliament and of the Council of 16 December 2002 on the supplementary supervision of credit institutions, insurance undertakings and investment firms in a financial conglomerate

Article 2   Definitions

. . .

12. "group" means a group of undertakings, which consists of a parent undertaking, its subsidiaries and the entities in which the parent undertaking or its subsidiaries hold a participation, or undertakings linked to each other by a relationship within the meaning of Article 12(1) of Directive 83/349/EEC, including any subgroup thereof;

Appendix 1

Criminal Law [Draft] Bill 1993

(Report No. 218)

PART II GENERAL DEFENCES AND OTHER PROVISIONS

24 Application of this Part

The provisions of this Part apply in relation to all offences under the law of England and Wales, . . .

Duress

25 Duress by threats

(1) No act of a person constitutes an offence if the act is done under duress by threats.

(2) A person does an act under duress by threats if he does it because he knows or believes—

    (a) that a threat has been made to cause death or serious injury to himself or another if the act is not done, and

    (b) that the threat will be carried out immediately if he does not do the act or, if not immediately, before he or that other can obtain effective official protection, and

    (c) that there is no other way of preventing the threat being carried out, and the threat is one which in all the circumstances (including any of his personal characteristics that affect its gravity) he cannot reasonably be expected to resist.

It is for the defendant to show that the reason for his act was such knowledge or belief as is mentioned in paragraphs (a) to (c).

(3) This section applies in relation to omissions as it applies in relation to acts.

(4) This section does not apply to a person who knowingly and without reasonable excuse exposed himself to the risk of the threat made or believed to have been made.

If the question arises whether a person knowingly and without reasonable excuse exposed himself to such a risk, it is for him to show that he did not.

26 Duress of circumstances

(1) No act of a person constitutes an offence if the act is done under duress of circumstances.

(2) A person does an act under duress of circumstances if—

    (a) he does it because he knows or believes that it is immediately necessary to avoid death or serious injury to himself or another, and

    (b) the danger that he knows or believes to exist is such that in all the circumstances (including any of his personal characteristics that affect its gravity) he cannot reasonably be expected to act otherwise.

It is for the defendant to show that the reason for his act was such knowledge or belief as is mentioned in paragraph (a).

(3) This section applies in relation to omissions as it applies in relation to acts.

(4) This section does not apply to a person who knowingly and without reasonable excuse exposed himself to the danger known or believed to exist.

If the question arises whether a person knowingly and without reasonable excuse exposed himself to that danger, it is for him to show that he did not.

(5) This section does not apply to—

    (a) an act done in the knowledge or belief that a threat has been made to cause death or serious injury to himself or another (see section 25), or

    (b) the use of force within the meaning of section 27 or 28, or an act immediately preparatory to the use of force, for the purposes mentioned in section 27(1) or 28(1).

Self-defence, prevention of crime, etc.

27 Justifiable use of force: protection of person or property, prevention of crime, etc.

(1) The use of force by a person for any of the following purposes, if only such as is reasonable in the circumstances as he believes them to be, does not constitute an offence—

    (a) to protect himself or another from injury, assault or detention caused by a criminal act;

    (b) to protect himself or (with the authority of that other) another from trespass to the person;

    (c) to protect his property from appropriation, destruction or damage caused by a criminal act or from trespass or infringement;

    (d) to protect property belonging to another from appropriation, destruction or damage caused by a criminal act or (with the authority of the other) from trespass or infringement; or

    (e) to prevent crime or a breach of the peace.

(2) The expressions "use of force" and "property" in subsection (1) are defined and extended by sections 29 and 30 respectively.

(3) For the purposes of this section an act involves a "crime" or is "criminal" although the person committing it, if charged with an offence in respect of it, would be acquitted on the ground that—

    (a) he was under ten years of age, or

    (b) he acted under duress, whether by threats or of circumstances, or

    (c) his act was involuntary, or

    (d) he was in a state of intoxication, or

    (e) he was insane, so as not to be responsible, according to law, for the act.

(4) The references in subsection (1) to protecting a person or property from anything include protecting him or it from its continuing; and the reference to preventing crime or a breach of the peace shall be similarly construed.

(5) For the purposes of this section the question whether the act against which force is used is of a kind mentioned in any of paragraphs (a) to (e) of subsection (1) shall be determined according to the circumstances as the person using the force ("D") believes them to be.

In the following provisions of this section references to unlawful or lawful acts are to acts which are or are not of such a kind.

(6) Where an act is lawful by reason only of a belief or suspicion which is mistaken, the defence provided by this section applies as in the case of an unlawful act, unless—

    (a) D knows or believes that the force is used against a constable or a person assisting a constable, and

    (b) the constable is acting in the execution of his duty,

in which case the defence applies only if D believes the force to be immediately necessary to prevent injury to himself or another.

(7) The defence provided by this section does not apply to a person who causes conduct or a state of affairs with a view to using force to resist or terminate it.

But the defence may apply although the occasion for the use of force arises only because he does something he may lawfully do, knowing that such an occasion may arise.

28 Justifiable use of force: effecting or assisting arrest

(1) The use of force by a person in effecting or assisting in a lawful arrest, if only such as is reasonable in the circumstances as he believes them to be, does not constitute an offence.

(2) The expression "use of force" in subsection (1) is defined and extended by section 29.

(3) For the purposes of this section the question whether the arrest is lawful shall be determined according to the circumstances as the person using the force believed them to be.

29 Meaning of "use of force" and related provisions

(1) For the purposes of sections 27 and 28—

(a) a person uses force in relation to another person or property not only where he applies force to, but also where he causes an impact on, the body of that person or that property;

(b) a person shall be treated as using force in relation to another person if—

(i) he threatens him with its use, or

(ii) he detains him without actually using it; and

(c) a person shall be treated as using force in relation to property if he threatens a person with its use in relation to property.

(2) Those sections apply in relation to acts immediately preparatory to the use of force as they apply in relation to acts in which force is used.

(3) A threat of force may be reasonable although the actual use of force would not be.

(4) The fact that a person had an opportunity to retreat before using force shall be taken into account, in conjunction with other relevant evidence, in determining whether the use of force was reasonable.

30 Meaning of "property" and related provisions

(1) For the purposes of section 27(1)(c) and (d) (justifiable use of force: protection of property) the expression "property" means property of a tangible nature, whether real or personal, or any right, interest or privilege in or over any such property, whether created by grant, licence or otherwise.

The expression also includes—

(a) money,

(b) wild creatures which have been tamed or are ordinarily kept in captivity, and

(c) any other wild creatures or their carcasses if, but only if, they have been reduced into possession which has not been lost or abandoned or are in the course of being reduced into possession,

but not mushrooms growing wild on any land or flowers, fruit or foliage of a plant growing wild on any land.

For this purpose "mushroom" includes any fungus and "plant" includes any shrub or tree.

(2) Property shall be treated for the purposes of section 27(1)(c) and (d) as belonging to any person—

(a) having the custody or control of it,

(b) having in it any proprietary right or interest (not being an equitable interest arising only from an agreement to transfer or grant an interest), or

(c) having a charge on it;

and where a property is subject to a trust, the persons to whom it belongs shall be treated as including any person having a right to enforce the trust.

Property of a corporation sole shall be treated as belonging to the corporation notwithstanding a vacancy in the corporation.

34 Interpretation of Part II

In this Part—

"fault", in relation to an offence, means an element of the offence consisting of either or both of the following—

(a) a state of mind with which a person acts, or

(b) a failure to comply with a standard of conduct, and references to a person being at fault shall be construed accordingly; and

"injury" means—

(a) physical injury, including pain, unconsciousness, or any other impairment of a person's physical condition, or

(b) impairment of a person's mental health.

Appendix 2

Prosecuting Policy

Code for Crown Prosecutors (2018)

Introduction

1.1 The Code for Crown Prosecutors (the Code) is issued by the Director of Public Prosecutions (DPP) under section 10 of the Prosecution of Offences Act 1985. This is the eighth edition of the Code and replaces all earlier versions.

1.2 The DPP is the head of the Crown Prosecution Service (CPS), which is the principal public prosecution service for England and Wales. The DPP operates independently, under the superintendence of the Attorney General who is accountable to Parliament for the work of the CPS.

1.3 The Code gives guidance to prosecutors on the general principles to be applied when making decisions about prosecutions. The Code is issued primarily for prosecutors in the CPS, but other prosecutors follow the Code, either through convention or because they are required to do so by law.

1.4 In this Code:

- "suspect" is used to describe a person who is under consideration as the subject of formal criminal proceedings;
- "defendant" is used to describe a person who has been charged or summonsed;
- "offender" is used to describe a person who has admitted guilt as to the commission of an offence, or who has been found guilty in a court of law;
- "victim" is used to describe a person against whom an offence has been committed, or the complainant in a case being considered or prosecuted by the CPS.

General Principles

2.1 The independence of the prosecutor is central to the criminal justice system of a democratic society. Prosecutors are independent from persons or agencies that are not part of the prosecution decision-making process. CPS prosecutors are also independent from the police and other investigators. Prosecutors must be free to carry out their professional duties without political interference and must not be affected by improper or undue pressure or influence from any source.

2.2 It is not the function of the CPS to decide whether a person is guilty of a criminal offence, but to make assessments about whether it is appropriate to present charges for the criminal court to consider. The CPS assessment of any case is not in any sense a finding of, or implication of, any guilt or criminal conduct. A finding of guilt can only be made by a court.

2.3 Similarly, a decision not to bring criminal charges does not necessarily mean that an individual has not been a victim of crime. It is not the role of the CPS to make such determinations.

2.4 The decision to prosecute or to recommend an out-of-court disposal is a serious step that affects suspects, victims, witnesses and the public at large and must be undertaken with the utmost care.

2.5 It is the duty of prosecutors to make sure that the right person is prosecuted for the right offence and to bring offenders to justice wherever possible. Casework decisions taken fairly, impartially and with integrity help to secure justice for victims, witnesses, defendants and the public.

Prosecutors must ensure that the law is properly applied, that relevant evidence is put before the court, and that obligations of disclosure are complied with.

2.6 Although each case must be considered on its own facts and on its own merits, there are general principles that apply in every case.

2.7 When making decisions, prosecutors must be fair and objective. They must not let any personal views about the ethnic or national origin, gender, disability, age, religion or belief, sexual orientation, or gender identity of the suspect, defendant, victim or any witness influence their decisions. Neither must they be motivated by political considerations. Prosecutors must always act in the interests of justice and not solely for the purpose of obtaining a conviction.

2.8 Prosecutors must be even-handed in their approach to every case, and have a duty to protect the rights of suspects and defendants, while providing the best possible service to victims.

2.9 The CPS is a public authority for the purposes of current, relevant equality legislation. Prosecutors are bound by the duties set out in this legislation.

2.10 Prosecutors must apply the principles of the European Convention on Human Rights, in accordance with the Human Rights Act 1998, at each stage of a case. They must comply with any guidelines issued by the Attorney General and with the policies and guidance of the CPS issued on behalf of the DPP, unless it is determined that there are exceptional circumstances. CPS guidance contains further evidential and public interest factors for specific offences and offenders and is available for the public to view on the CPS website. Prosecutors must also comply with the Criminal Procedure Rules and Criminal Practice Directions, and have regard to the Sentencing Council Guidelines and the obligations arising from international conventions.

2.11 The CPS prosecutes on behalf of some other Government departments. In such cases, prosecutors should have regard to any relevant enforcement policies of those departments.

2.12 Some offences may be prosecuted by either the CPS or by other prosecutors in England and Wales. When making decisions in these cases, CPS prosecutors may, where they think it appropriate, have regard to any relevant enforcement or prosecution policy or code of the other prosecutor.

2.13 Where the law differs in England and Wales prosecutors must apply the Code and have regard to any relevant policy, guidance or charging standard.

The Decision Whether to Prosecute

3.1 In more serious or complex cases, prosecutors decide whether a person should be charged with a criminal offence and, if so, what that offence should be. Prosecutors may also advise on or authorise out-of-court disposals as an alternative to prosecution. They make their decisions in accordance with this Code, the DPP's Guidance on Charging and any relevant legal guidance or policy. The police apply the same principles in deciding whether to start criminal proceedings against a person in those cases for which they are responsible.

3.2 The police and other investigators are responsible for conducting inquiries into any alleged crime and for deciding how to deploy their resources. This includes decisions to start or continue an investigation and on the scope of the investigation. Prosecutors should advise the police and other investigators about possible reasonable lines of inquiry, evidential requirements, pre-charge procedures, disclosure management and the overall investigation strategy. This can include decisions to refine or narrow the scope of the criminal conduct and the number of suspects under investigation. Such advice assists the police and other investigators to complete the investigation within a reasonable period of time and to build the most effective prosecution case.

3.3 Prosecutors cannot direct the police or other investigators. However, prosecutors must have regard to the impact of any failure to pursue an advised reasonable line of inquiry or to comply with a request for information, when deciding whether the application of the Full Code Test should be deferred or whether the test can be met at all.

3.4 Prosecutors should identify and, where possible, seek to rectify evidential weaknesses but, subject to the Threshold Test (see section 5), they should quickly stop cases which do not meet the evidential stage of the Full Code Test (see section 4) and which cannot be strengthened by further investigation, or where the public interest clearly does not require a prosecution (see section 4).

Although prosecutors primarily consider the evidence and information supplied by the police and other investigators, the suspect or those acting on his or her behalf may also submit evidence or information to the prosecutor, before or after charge, to help inform the prosecutor's decision. In appropriate cases, the prosecutor may invite the suspect or their representative to do so.

3.5 Prosecutors should not start or continue a prosecution where their view is that it is highly likely that a court will rule that a prosecution is an abuse of its process, and stay the proceedings.

3.6 Prosecutors review every case they receive from the police or other investigators. Review is a continuing process and prosecutors must take account of any change in circumstances that occurs as the case develops. This includes what becomes known of the defence case, any further reasonable lines of inquiry that should be pursued, and receipt of any unused material that may undermine the prosecution case or assist the defence case, to the extent that charges should be altered or discontinued or the prosecution should not proceed. If a case is to be stopped, care should be taken when choosing the method of termination, as this can affect the victim's position under the Victims' Right to Review scheme. Wherever possible, prosecutors should consult the investigator when considering changing the charges or stopping the case. Prosecutors and investigators work closely together, but the final responsibility for the decision whether or not a case should go ahead rests with the CPS.

3.7 Parliament has decided that a limited number of offences should only be taken to court with the agreement of the DPP. These are called consent cases. In such cases the DPP, or a prosecutor acting on their behalf, applies the Code in deciding whether to give consent to a prosecution.

3.8 There are also certain offences that can only be taken to court with the consent of the Attorney General. Prosecutors must follow current guidance when referring any such cases to the Attorney General. Some offences require the consent of a Secretary of State before a prosecution is started. Prosecutors must obtain such consent prior to charge and apply any relevant guidance in these cases. Additionally, the Attorney General will be kept informed of certain cases as part of his or her superintendence of the CPS and accountability to Parliament for its actions.

The Full Code Test

4.1 Prosecutors must only start or continue a prosecution when the case has passed both stages of the Full Code Test. The exception is when the Threshold Test may be applied (see section 5).

4.2 The Full Code Test has two stages: (i) the evidential stage; followed by (ii) the public interest stage.

4.3 The Full Code Test should be applied: a) when all outstanding reasonable lines of inquiry have been pursued; or b) prior to the investigation being completed, if the prosecutor is satisfied that any further evidence or material is unlikely to affect the application of the Full Code Test, whether in favour of or against a prosecution.

4.4 In most cases, prosecutors should only consider whether a prosecution is in the public interest after considering whether there is sufficient evidence to prosecute. However there will be cases where it is clear, prior to the collection and consideration of all the likely evidence, that the public interest does not require a prosecution. In these instances, prosecutors may decide that the case should not proceed further.

4.5 Prosecutors should only take such a decision when they are satisfied that the broad extent of the criminality has been determined and that they are able to make a fully informed assessment of the public interest. If prosecutors do not have sufficient information to take such a decision, the investigation should continue and a decision taken later in accordance with the Full Code Test set out in this section.

The Evidential Stage

4.6 Prosecutors must be satisfied that there is sufficient evidence to provide a realistic prospect of conviction against each suspect on each charge*. They must consider what the defence case may be, and how it is likely to affect the prospects of conviction. A case which does not pass the evidential stage must not proceed, no matter how serious or sensitive it may be.

---

* For the purposes of the Code for Crown Prosecutors, "conviction" includes a finding that "the person did the act or made the omission" in circumstances where the person is likely to be found not guilty on the grounds of insanity.

4.7 The finding that there is a realistic prospect of conviction is based on the prosecutor's objective assessment of the evidence, including the impact of any defence and any other information that the suspect has put forward or on which they might rely. It means that an objective, impartial and reasonable jury or bench of magistrates or judge hearing a case alone, properly directed and acting in accordance with the law, is more likely than not to convict the defendant of the charge alleged. This is a different test from the one that the criminal courts themselves must apply. A court may only convict if it is sure that the defendant is guilty.

4.8 When deciding whether there is sufficient evidence to prosecute, prosecutors should ask themselves the following:

Can the evidence be used in court?

Prosecutors should consider whether there is any question over the admissibility of certain evidence. In doing so, prosecutors should assess:

- the likelihood of that evidence being held as inadmissible by the court; and
- the importance of that evidence in relation to the evidence as a whole.

Is the evidence reliable?

Prosecutors should consider whether there are any reasons to question the reliability of the evidence, including its accuracy or integrity.

Is the evidence credible?

Prosecutors should consider whether there are any reasons to doubt the credibility of the evidence.

Is there any other material that might affect the sufficiency of evidence?

Prosecutors must consider at this stage and throughout the case whether there is any material that may affect the assessment of the sufficiency of evidence, including examined and unexamined material in the possession of the police, and material that may be obtained through further reasonable lines of inquiry.

The Public Interest Stage

4.9 In every case where there is sufficient evidence to justify a prosecution, or to offer an out-of-court disposal, prosecutors must go on to consider whether a prosecution is required in the public interest.

4.10 It has never been the rule that a prosecution will automatically take place once the evidential stage is met. A prosecution will usually take place unless the prosecutor is satisfied that there are public interest factors tending against prosecution which outweigh those tending in favour. In some cases the prosecutor may be satisfied that the public interest can be properly served by offering the offender the opportunity to have the matter dealt with by an out-of-court disposal rather than bringing a prosecution.

4.11 When deciding the public interest, prosecutors should consider each of the questions set out below in paragraphs 4.14 a) to g) so as to identify and determine the relevant public interest factors tending for and against prosecution. These factors, together with any public interest factors set out in relevant guidance or policy issued by the DPP, should enable prosecutors to form an overall assessment of the public interest.

4.12 The explanatory text below each question in paragraphs 4.14 a) to g) provides guidance to prosecutors when addressing each particular question and determining whether it identifies public interest factors for or against prosecution. The questions identified are not exhaustive, and not all the questions may be relevant in every case. The weight to be attached to each of the questions, and the factors identified, will also vary according to the facts and merits of each case.

4.13 It is quite possible that one public interest factor alone may outweigh a number of other factors which tend in the opposite direction. Although there may be public interest factors tending against prosecution in a particular case, prosecutors should consider whether nonetheless a prosecution should go ahead and those factors put to the court for consideration when sentence is passed.

4.14 Prosecutors should consider each of the following questions:

a) How serious is the offence committed?

- The more serious the offence, the more likely it is that a prosecution is required.

- When deciding the seriousness of an offence, prosecutors should include in their consideration the suspect's culpability and the harm caused, by asking themselves the questions at b) and c).

b) What is the level of culpability of the suspect?

- The greater the suspect's level of culpability, the more likely it is that a prosecution is required.

- Culpability is likely to be determined by:

  i.   the suspect's level of involvement;

  ii.   the extent to which the offending was premeditated and/or planned;

  iii. the extent to which the suspect has benefitted from criminal conduct;

  iv.   whether the suspect has previous criminal convictions and/or out-of-court disposals and any offending whilst on bail or whilst subject to a court order;

  v.   whether the offending was or is likely to be continued, repeated or escalated; and

  vi.   the suspect's age or maturity (see paragraph d below).

- A suspect is likely to have a much lower level of culpability if the suspect has been compelled, coerced or exploited, particularly if they are the victim of a crime that is linked to their offending.

- Prosecutors should also have regard to whether the suspect is, or was at the time of the offence, affected by any significant mental or physical ill health or disability as in some circumstances this may mean that it is less likely that a prosecution is required. However, prosecutors will also need to consider how serious the offence was, whether the suspect is likely to re-offend and the need to safeguard the public or those providing care to such persons.

c) What are the circumstances of and the harm caused to the victim?

- The circumstances of the victim are highly relevant. The more vulnerable the victim's situation, or the greater the perceived vulnerability of the victim, the more likely it is that a prosecution is required.

- This includes where a position of trust or authority exists between the suspect and victim.

- A prosecution is also more likely if the offence has been committed against a victim who was at the time a person serving the public.

- It is more likely that prosecution is required if the offence was motivated by any form of prejudice against the victim's actual or presumed ethnic or national origin, gender, disability, age, religion or belief, sexual orientation or gender identity; or if the suspect targeted or exploited the victim, or demonstrated hostility towards the victim, based on any of those characteristics.

- Prosecutors also need to consider if a prosecution is likely to have an adverse effect on the victim's physical or mental health, always bearing in mind the seriousness of the offence, the availability of special measures and the possibility of a prosecution without the participation of the victim.

- Prosecutors should take into account the views expressed by the victim about the impact that the offence has had. In appropriate cases, this may also include the views of the victim's family.

- However, the CPS does not act for victims or their families in the same way as solicitors act for their clients, and prosecutors must form an overall view of the public interest.

d) Was the suspect under the age of 18 at the time of the offence?

- The criminal justice system treats children and young people differently from adults and significant weight must be attached to the age of the suspect if they are a child or young person under 18.

- The best interests and welfare of the child or young person must be considered, including whether a prosecution is likely to have an adverse impact on their future prospects that is disproportionate to the seriousness of the offending.

- Prosecutors must have regard to the principal aim of the youth justice system, which is to prevent offending by children and young people. Prosecutors must also have regard to the obligations arising under the United Nations 1989 Convention on the Rights of the Child.

- Prosecutors should consider the suspect's maturity, as well as their chronological age, as young adults will continue to mature into their mid-twenties.

- As a starting point, the younger the suspect, the less likely it is that a prosecution is required.

- However, there may be circumstances which mean that, notwithstanding the fact that the suspect is under 18 or lacks maturity, a prosecution is in the public interest. These include where:

  i.   the offence committed is serious;

  ii. the suspect's past record suggests that there are no suitable alternatives to prosecution; and

  iii. the absence of an admission means that out-of-court disposals that might have addressed the offending behaviour are not available.

e) *What is the impact on the community?*

- The greater the impact of the offending on the community, the more likely it is that a prosecution is required.

- The prevalence of an offence in a community may cause particular harm to that community, increasing the seriousness of the offending.

- Community is not restricted to communities defined by location and may relate to a group of people who share certain characteristics, experiences or backgrounds, including an occupational group.

- Evidence of impact on a community may be obtained by way of a Community Impact Statement.

f) *Is prosecution a proportionate response?*

- In considering whether prosecution is proportionate to the likely outcome, the following may be relevant:

  i   The cost to the CPS and the wider criminal justice system, especially where it could be regarded as excessive when weighed against any likely penalty. Prosecutors should not decide the public interest on the basis of this factor alone. It is essential that regard is also given to the public interest factors identified when considering the other questions in paragraphs 4.14 a) to g), but cost can be a relevant factor when making an overall assessment of the public interest.

  ii Cases should be prosecuted in accordance with principles of effective case management. For example, in a case involving multiple suspects, prosecution might be reserved for the main participants in order to avoid excessively long and complex proceedings.

g) *Do sources of information require protecting?*

- In cases where public interest immunity does not apply, special care should be taken when proceeding with a prosecution where details may need to be made public that could harm sources of information, ongoing investigations, international relations or national security. It is essential that such cases are kept under continuing review.

The Threshold Test

5.1 In limited circumstances, where the Full Code Test is not met, the Threshold Test may be applied to charge a suspect. The seriousness or circumstances of the case must justify the making of an immediate charging decision, and there must be substantial grounds to object to bail.

5.2 There must be a rigorous examination of the five conditions of the Threshold Test, to ensure that it is only applied when necessary and that cases are not charged prematurely. All five conditions must be met before the Threshold Test can be applied. Where any of the conditions are not met, there is no need to consider any of the other conditions, as the Threshold Test cannot be applied and the suspect cannot be charged.

First condition—There are reasonable grounds to suspect that the person to be charged has committed the offence

5.3 Prosecutors must be satisfied, on an objective assessment of the evidence, that there are reasonable grounds to suspect that the person to be charged has committed the offence. The assessment must consider the impact of any defence or information that the suspect has put forward or on which they might rely.

5.4 In determining whether there are reasonable grounds to suspect, prosecutors must consider all of the material or information available, whether in evidential format or otherwise. Prosecutors must be satisfied that the material to be relied on at this stage is capable of being:

- put into an admissible format for presentation in court;
- reliable; and
- credible.

Second condition—Further evidence can be obtained to provide a realistic prospect of conviction

5.5 Prosecutors must be satisfied that there are reasonable grounds to believe that the continuing investigation will provide further evidence, within a reasonable period of time, so that when all the evidence is considered together, including material which may point away from as well as towards a particular suspect, it is capable of establishing a realistic prospect of conviction in accordance with the Full Code Test.

5.6 The likely further evidence must be identifiable and not merely speculative.

5.7 In reaching this decision prosecutors must consider:
- the nature, extent and admissibility of any likely further evidence and the impact it will have on the case;
- the charges that all the evidence will support;
- the reasons why the evidence is not already available;
- the time required to obtain the further evidence, including whether it could be obtained within any available detention period; and
- whether the delay in applying the Full Code Test is reasonable in all the circumstances.

Third condition—The seriousness or the circumstances of the case justifies the making of an immediate charging decision

5.8 The seriousness and the circumstances of the case should be assessed in relation to the alleged offending and should be linked to the level of risk created by granting bail.

Fourth condition—There are continuing substantial grounds to object to bail in accordance with the Bail Act 1976 and in all the circumstances of the case it is proper to do so

5.9 This determination must be based on a proper risk assessment, which reveals that the suspect is not suitable to be bailed, even with substantial conditions. For example, a dangerous suspect who poses a serious risk of harm to a particular person or the public, or a suspect who poses a serious risk of absconding or interfering with witnesses. Prosecutors should not accept, without careful enquiry, any unjustified or unsupported assertions about risk if release on bail were to take place.

Fifth condition—It is in the public interest to charge the suspect

5.10 Prosecutors must apply the public interest stage of the Full Code Test based on the information available at that time.

Reviewing the Threshold Test

5.11 A decision to charge under the Threshold Test must be kept under review. The prosecutor should be proactive to secure from the police the identified outstanding evidence or other material in accordance with an agreed timetable. The evidence must be regularly assessed to ensure that the charge is still appropriate and that continued objection to bail is justified. The Full Code Test must be applied as soon as the anticipated further evidence is received and, in any event, in Crown Court cases, usually before the formal service of the prosecution case.

Selection of Charges

6.1 Prosecutors should select charges which:
- reflect the seriousness and extent of the offending;
- give the court adequate powers to sentence and impose appropriate post-conviction orders;
- allow a confiscation order to be made in appropriate cases, where a defendant has benefitted from criminal conduct; and
- enable the case to be presented in a clear and simple way.

6.2 This means that prosecutors may not always choose or continue with the most serious charge where there is a choice and the interests of justice are met by selecting the lesser charge.

6.3 Prosecutors should never go ahead with more charges than are necessary just to encourage a defendant to plead guilty to a few. In the same way, they should never go ahead with a more serious charge just to encourage a defendant to plead guilty to a less serious one.

6.4 Prosecutors should not change the charge simply because of the decision made by the court or the defendant about where the case will be heard.

6.5 Prosecutors must take account of any relevant change in circumstances as the case progresses after charge.

Out-of-Court Disposals

7.1 An out-of-court disposal may take the place of a prosecution if it is an appropriate response to the offender and/or the seriousness and consequences of the offending.

7.2 Prosecutors must follow any relevant guidance when asked to advise on or authorise an out-of-court disposal, including any appropriate regulatory proceedings, a punitive or civil penalty, or other disposal. They should ensure that the appropriate evidential standard for the specific out-of-court disposal is met including, where required, a clear admission of guilt, and that the public interest would be properly served by such a disposal.

Court Venue

8.1 Prosecutors must have regard to the current guidelines on sentencing and allocation when making submissions to the magistrates' court about where the defendant should be tried.

8.2 Speed must never be the only reason for asking for a case to stay in the magistrates' court. But prosecutors should consider the effect of any likely delay if a case is sent to the Crown Court, including the possible effect on any victim or witness.

Venue for trial in cases involving youths

8.3 Prosecutors must bear in mind that children and young people (under 18s) should be tried in the youth court wherever possible. It is the court which is best designed to meet their specific needs. A trial of a child or young person in the Crown Court should be reserved for the most serious cases or where the interests of justice require a child to be jointly tried with an adult.

Accepting Guilty Pleas

9.1 Defendants may want to plead guilty to some, but not all, of the charges. Alternatively, they may want to plead guilty to a different, possibly less serious, charge because they are admitting only part of the crime.

9.2 Prosecutors should only accept the defendant's plea if:
- the court is able to pass a sentence that matches the seriousness of the offending, particularly where there are aggravating features;

- it enables the court to make a confiscation order in appropriate cases, where a defendant has benefitted from criminal conduct; and
- it provides the court with adequate powers to impose other ancillary orders, bearing in mind that these can be made with some offences but not with others.

9.3 Particular care must be taken when considering pleas which would enable the defendant to avoid the imposition of a mandatory minimum sentence.

9.4 Prosecutors must never accept a guilty plea just because it is convenient.

9.5 In considering whether the pleas offered are acceptable, prosecutors should ensure that the interests and, where possible, the views of the victim, or in appropriate cases the views of the victim's family, are taken into account when deciding whether it is in the public interest to accept the plea. However, the decision rests with the prosecutor.

9.6 It must be made clear to the court on what basis any plea is advanced and accepted. In cases where a defendant pleads guilty to the charges but on the basis of facts that are different from the prosecution case, and where this may significantly affect sentence, the court should be invited to hear evidence to determine what happened, and then sentence on that basis.

9.7 Where a defendant has previously indicated that they will ask the court to take an offence into consideration when sentencing, but then declines to admit that offence at court, prosecutors will consider whether a prosecution is required for that offence. Prosecutors should explain to the defence advocate and the court that the prosecution of that offence may be subject to further review, in consultation with the police or other investigators wherever possible.

Reconsidering a Prosecution Decision

10.1 People should be able to rely on decisions taken by the CPS. Normally, if the CPS tells a suspect or defendant that there will not be a prosecution, or that the prosecution has been stopped, the case will not start again. But occasionally there are reasons why the CPS will overturn a decision not to prosecute or to deal with the case by way of an out-of-court disposal or when it will restart the prosecution, particularly if the case is serious.

10.2 These cases include:

a) cases where a further review of the original decision shows that it was wrong and, in order to maintain confidence in the criminal justice system, a prosecution should be brought despite the earlier decision;

b) cases which are stopped so that further anticipated evidence which is likely to become available in the fairly near future, can be collected and prepared. In these cases, the prosecutor will tell the defendant that the prosecution may well start again;

c) cases which are not prosecuted or are stopped because of a lack of evidence but where more significant evidence is discovered later; and

d) cases involving a death in which a review following the findings of an inquest concludes that a prosecution should be brought, notwithstanding any earlier decision not to prosecute.

Policy for Cases of Encouraging or Assisting Suicide (2010; updated 2014)

37 ... Where there is sufficient evidence to justify a prosecution, prosecutors must go on to consider whether a prosecution is required in the public interest.

38 In cases of encouraging or assisting suicide, prosecutors must apply the public interest factors set out in the Code for Crown Prosecutors and the factors set out in this policy in making their decision. A prosecution will usually take place unless the prosecutor is sure that there are public interest factors tending against prosecution which outweigh those tending in favour.

39 Assessing the public interest is not simply a matter of adding up the number of factors on each side and seeing which side has the greatest number. Each case must be considered on its own facts and on its own merits. Prosecutors must decide the importance of each public interest factor in the circumstances of each case and go on to make an overall assessment. It is quite possible that one factor may outweigh a number of other factors which tend in the opposite direction. Although there may be public interest factors tending against prosecution in a particular case, prosecutors should consider whether nonetheless a prosecution should go ahead and for those factors to be put to the court for consideration when sentence is passed.

40 The absence of a factor does not necessarily mean that it should be taken as a factor tending in the opposite direction. For example, just because the victim was not "under 18 years of age" does not transform the "factor tending in favour of prosecution" into a "factor tending against prosecution".

41 It may sometimes be the case that the only source of information about the circumstances of the suicide and the state of mind of the victim is the suspect. Prosecutors and investigators should make sure that they pursue all reasonable lines of further enquiry in order to obtain, wherever possible, independent verification of the suspect's account.

42 Once all reasonable enquiries are completed, if the reviewing prosecutor is doubtful about the suspect's account of the circumstances of the suicide or the state of mind of the victim which may be relevant to any factor set out below, he or she should conclude that there is insufficient information to support that factor.

Public interest factors tending in favour of prosecution

43 A prosecution is more likely to be required if:

(1) the victim was under 18 years of age;

(2) the victim did not have the capacity (as defined by the Mental Capacity Act 2005) to reach an informed decision to commit suicide;

(3) the victim had not reached a voluntary, clear, settled and informed decision to commit suicide;

(4) the victim had not clearly and unequivocally communicated his or her decision to commit suicide to the suspect;

(5) the victim did not seek the encouragement or assistance of the suspect personally or on his or her own initiative;

(6) the suspect was not wholly motivated by compassion; for example, the suspect was motivated by the prospect that he or she or a person closely connected to him or her stood to gain in some way from the death of the victim;

(7) the suspect pressured the victim to commit suicide;

(8) the suspect did not take reasonable steps to ensure that any other person had not pressured the victim to commit suicide;

(9) the suspect had a history of violence or abuse against the victim;

(10) the victim was physically able to undertake the act that constituted the assistance him or herself;

(11) the suspect was unknown to the victim and encouraged or assisted the victim to commit or attempt to commit suicide by providing specific information via, for example, a website or publication;

(12) the suspect gave encouragement or assistance to more than one victim who were not known to each other;

(13) the suspect was paid by the victim or those close to the victim for his or her encouragement or assistance;

(14) the suspect was acting in his or her capacity as a medical doctor, nurse, other healthcare professional, a professional carer [whether for payment or not], or as a person in authority, such as a prison officer, and the victim was in his or her care[1];

(15)   the suspect was aware that the victim intended to commit suicide in a public place where it was reasonable to think that members of the public may be present;

(16)   the suspect was acting in his or her capacity as a person involved in the management or as an employee (whether for payment or not) of an organisation or group, a purpose of which is to provide a physical environment (whether for payment or not) in which to allow another to commit suicide.

Note [1]: For the avoidance of doubt the words "and the victim was in his or her care" qualify all of the preceding parts of this paragraph. This factor does not apply merely because someone was acting in a capacity described within it: it applies only where there was, in addition, a relationship of care between the suspect and the victims such that it will be necessary to consider whether the suspect may have exerted some influence on the victim.

44 On the question of whether a person stood to gain, (paragraph 43(6) see above), the police and the reviewing prosecutor should adopt a common sense approach. It is possible that the suspect may gain some benefit—financial or otherwise—from the resultant suicide of the victim after his or her act of encouragement or assistance. The critical element is the motive behind the suspect's act. If it is shown that compassion was the only driving force behind his or her actions, the fact that the suspect may have gained some benefit will not usually be treated as a factor tending in favour of prosecution. However, each case must be considered on its own merits and on its own facts.

Public interest factors tending against prosecution

45 A prosecution is less likely to be required if:

(1)   the victim had reached a voluntary, clear, settled and informed decision to commit suicide;

(2)   the suspect was wholly motivated by compassion;

(3)   the actions of the suspect, although sufficient to come within the definition of the offence, were of only minor encouragement or assistance;

(4)   the suspect had sought to dissuade the victim from taking the course of action which resulted in his or her suicide;

(5)   the actions of the suspect may be characterised as reluctant encouragement or assistance in the face of a determined wish on the part of the victim to commit suicide;

(6)   the suspect reported the victim's suicide to the police and fully assisted them in their enquiries into the circumstances of the suicide or the attempt and his or her part in providing encouragement or assistance.

46 The evidence to support these factors must be sufficiently close in time to the encouragement or assistance to allow the prosecutor reasonably to infer that the factors remained operative at that time. This is particularly important at the start of the specific chain of events that immediately led to the suicide or attempt.

47 These lists of public interest factors are not exhaustive and each case must be considered on its own merits.

48 If the course of conduct goes beyond encouraging or assisting suicide, for example, because the suspect goes on to take or attempt or take the life of the victim, the public interest factors tending in favour of or against prosecution may have to be evaluated differently in the light of the overall criminal conduct.

Index